YOUR
INTUITIVE
MOON

YOUR INTUITIVE MOON

*Using Lunar Signs and
Cycles to Enhance
Your Intuition*

Trish MacGregor

NEW AMERICAN LIBRARY

NAL Books
Published by New American Library, a division of
Penguin Putnam Inc., 375 Hudson Street, New York, New York 10014, U.S.A.
Penguin Books Ltd, 27 Wrights Lane, London W8 5TZ, England
Penguin Books Australia Ltd, Ringwood, Victoria, Australia
Penguin Books Canada Ltd, 10 Alcorn Avenue, Toronto, Ontario, Canada M4V 3B2
Penguin Books (N.Z.) Ltd, 182–190 Wairau Road, Auckland 10, New Zealand

Penguin Books Ltd, Registered Offices: Harmondsworth, Middlesex, England

First published by New American Library, a division of Penguin Putnam Inc.

First New American Library Printing, December 2000
10 9 8 7 6 5 4 3 2 1

 REGISTERED TRADEMARK—MARCA REGISTRADA

LIBRARY OF CONGRESS CATALOGING-IN-PUBLICATION DATA:
MacGregor, T. J.
Your intuitive moon : using lunar signs and cycles to enhance your intuition /
Trish MacGregor.
p.   cm.
ISBN 0-451-20201-5 (alk. paper)
1. Astrology.   2. Moon—Miscellanea.
3. Intuition (Psychology)—Miscellanea.   I. Title.
BF1723 M34 2000
113.5'32—dc21   00-56081

Printed in the United States of America
Set in Goudy and Post Antiqua
Designed by Eve L. Kirch

In memory of Richard "the Fids" Demien,
fellow Gemini and seeker: 6/5/48–8/1/99;
to Megan and Rob, my anchors;
and to Mom and Dad

Thanks, as always, to Al Zuckerman,
and to Laura Anne Gilman.

CONTENTS

Part Two. Your Lunar Neighborhood

Part Three. Lunar Cycles

Introduction

When I was a kid, one of my greatest pleasures was watching the full moon rise over the mountains that surrounded the city where I lived, Caracas, Venezuela. There was—and still is, as far as I know—a hotel on top of the highest peak that could be reached on foot or by cable car. As moonlight spilled into the valley, the hotel stood darkly against all the light, a sentinel at a gate between worlds.

Bit by bit, the entire slope of the mountain was revealed in a way that I simply couldn't see by daylight. The network of the cable car system seemed intricate and mysterious. The hundreds of ranchitos or shacks that dotted the hillside were no longer an eyesore; they formed an intricate and complex city. As the moonlight flooded the valley, I saw Caracas in a completely new way. And in my memories, it's the nighttime version that remains most vivid because it's softer, mysterious, and mystical, and speaks to a deeper part of me.

In astrology, that's what the moon is about—the deeper parts of us that others don't see. It's yin, receptive. It symbolizes our experience of Mom or her equivalent, our relationships with women, the way we nurture and are nurtured. It reveals how we react when we're hurt. The moon symbolizes our connection to our roots and, deeper still, to the collective sea that unites us all. It is our common ancient heritage, that distant past when life unfolded in synchronization with the lunar cycle. And through that connection, the moon also represents our intuition.

What is intuition? It's the feeling you get about the guy your mother thinks you should go out with. He's bright and personable, but something about him puts you off. It's a hunch, a gut feeling, and you can't explain it. It's the unease you feel about getting on a particular flight, or a sense of urgency that seizes you for no logical reason that your child is in trouble.

Intuition is the sense that allows us to come to conclusions that have little or nothing to do with our reasoning minds.

This kind of pure, swift knowing differs for each of us. The moon in our birth charts holds the blueprint of our intuition—the area of our lives where it's strongest or weakest, and how we experience it. It represents our right-brain self, the self that perceives the whole picture *in here* and seeks to manifest its deepest desires and needs *out there*. It's how we seek to fulfill ourselves, to live to our highest potential.

These components—phase, sign, house placement, nodes, aspects, eclipses, the whole lunar package—describe our intuitive capacities and the best expression of our intuition. They explain how we can use our intuition to enhance and change our lives, improve our health, and alter our reality.

When I was younger, intuition was something that other people had. The carnival gypsy who read palms, the tea-leaf reader who lived alone in the big house on the hill, the medium who communed with dead grandmothers. In the world I inhabited, these intuitives lived on the fringe.

In the last twenty-five years, our concept of intuition has changed dramatically. It's no longer seen as something *out there*, or as a talent that only certain people possess. We've all got it. And the more we use it, the stronger it gets.

Intuition manifests differently for each of us. You might sense it in your body, in a dream, as a creative breakthrough, or even as one of those *aha!* moments when pieces of some puzzle snap into place. However you experience it, your natal horoscope holds vital clues about your intuitive capacity and how you can develop it. And that's what this book is really about.

Intuition allows us to integrate our right-brained lunar selves with our left-brained solar selves, and come up with a self we can live with.

But Is It Practical?

"If intuition is such a practical tool, then how come I haven't won the lottery?" Or found the right man or woman? Or the right job? Or the right house?

I've heard this question, in various forms, frequently over the years and have certainly asked it myself. The truth is that there's no easy answer.

Theoretically, you should be able to use your intuition for anything. But first, you have to recognize an intuitive impression when you get one, and second, you have to trust your impression. It seems to me that most of us, at least in the western world, have a tough time mastering the trust part of this equation.

How can we be sure that a hunch, a vision, or simply an impression that we get about something is, well, *true*? Maybe it's just wishful thinking or fear. Maybe it's something we read or saw in a movie. Maybe this, maybe that.

Part of the problem in trusting an intuitive impression may be due to acculturation. Even though intuition isn't regarded as the dark stepchild that it was in the past, logic and left-brained skills are still considered to be more desirable.

When we allow our intuition to flourish, however, and listen to what it says, it becomes easier to "live in the flow," to follow our natural rhythms and inclinations, and to trust ourselves. And if that isn't practical, then what is?

In the Flow

One evening on the island of Cedar Key, on Florida's Gulf coast, my daughter, husband, and I were walking along the pier when a pod of wild dolphins appeared. We'd seen dolphins before, but never like this, close enough so that we could feel their joy and spontaneity. Their clicks echoed in the summer air as they surfaced and dived again and again. It was then I fully understood what it means to live *in the flow*.

When we live in the flow, our intuition works smoothly and effortlessly. If you have any doubt what this means, then hang out with some young kids for a few hours. They make caves out of sheets, play with imaginary friends, hunt big game in their back yards, and create worlds out of nothing more than their imaginations. When they're hurt or angry, they verbalize it. When they're scared or sad, they let you know. Since they haven't learned to censor their emotions or impulses, they live in the *intuitive flow*.

This flow is what we, as adults, seek to recapture when we're old enough to realize its value.

Using This Book

You don't need your natal chart to use this book. The tables in Appendix 1 list the date and time the moon enters a sign between the years of 1945 to 2005. Simply follow the directions to locate your moon sign.

The moon is the most rapidly moving body in the sky, traveling from one sign to another in two and a half days and circling the zodiac in twenty-eight days. If the moon changed signs on the day you were born, going from Virgo to Libra, for instance, then read the sections for both Virgo and Libra.

Most people know their sun signs. But since there are references to them throughout the book, I've included a table in Appendix 2 that provides the beginning and end dates for each sun sign.

Part One

WALKING ON THE MOON

". . . three giant steps for mankind . . ."
—Neil Armstrong

1

The Face of the Moon

Concepts of the Moon

Throughout the millennia, the moon has been the stuff of myths and fairy tales, poetry and legends. It has been worshiped and cursed and endowed with magical and curative powers. Religions have grown up around it. Sacrifices have been made to it.

In the early fifties, the moon was a favorite theme in science fiction books and movies, and the story lines rarely varied: the aliens came from the moon, we colonized the moon, or the moon fell out of orbit . . . you get the general picture.

But then, in 1969, Neil Armstrong took three giant steps for mankind, and our concept of the moon was forever changed. We now had some idea what it really looked like and the news was far from good. Dust, dust, and more dust. A black vacuum. Unimaginable cold. Nothingness. In memory, I can still see the dust that flew up around those giant steps of Armstrong's and I can see the brilliant points of light impaled against the black sky overhead. What's most vivid in my mind, though, is how the Earth looked from the moon—a swirling turquoise gem, a blue pearl turning in space. Our planet literally looked alive.

This was the year when the Vietnam War was in full swing. Americans arrived home in body bags, riots swept across college campuses, LSD was the drug of choice. People were tuning in and dropping out faster than the pictures of the moon were beamed back to earth.

This was the year that half a million people converged on the tiny town of Woodstock, New York, to hear Hendrix, The Who, Crosby, Stills and Nash, and all the other musicians who had captured the emotional reality of war and chaos. Women threw off their shackles. Carlos Castaneda and Aldous Huxley hurled open the doors to other realities. Camelot was dead, Martin Luther King was dead, but we had walked on the moon.

In many ways, those steps of Armstrong's signaled that we were finally ready to confront our unconscious selves, our feminine, intuitive selves.

Fast-forward to the summer of 1997, July 4 to be exact. In the opening scenes of the movie *Independence Day*, a mammoth shadow falls across the surface of the moon. What ensues is pure Hollywood, with Will Smith holding the record for aliens annihilated. But *Independence Day*, like Armstrong's three giant steps, is part of our contemporary, collective perceptions of the moon, its essential beauty and sublime mysteries.

Despite Hollywood and NASA, each of us has some personal concept about the moon. After all, we drop our heads back on any given night and there it is. It speaks to us. We speak to it. Romance, madness, werewolves, witches, pagans, Druids, ocean tides and blood tides, or a sharp rise in murder and mayhem: it's all fair game where the moon is concerned. Every notion that we hold about the moon is true *for us* and that subjective texture is certainly in keeping with the nature of the moon in astrology.

If the sun is Apollo in your corner of the universe, then the moon is your personal oracle. If the sun represents your life force, then the moon represents the internal landscape that supports and maintains the life force. In astrology, lunar energy is embodied in that mythological moment when Luke Skywalker recognizes that Darth Vader is his father or when, in *ET*, the alien is getting drunk and the boy is trying to dissect a frog at school and their psyches mesh.

Lunar energy is the MO in *Thelma and Louise*, in *Jacob's Ladder*, and in *What Dreams May Come*. It's the psychic visions the young boy has in *The Shining* or the visions another young boy has in *The*

Sixth Sense. It's the mother's anguish in *The Deep End of the Ocean*, and it's Oprah being Oprah on weekday afternoons. Without lunar energy, we would be empty shells, automatons, the burn-the-books society of *Farenheit 451*, powerless puppets who accept everything at face value.

Lunar Facts and Oddities

Most of us learn facts about the moon in grade school science class. Today's kids have a distinct advantage over their parents, of course, because information is so readily accessible through the Internet. When I entered the word *moon* in a search engine, I came up with 277,000 hits, providing information on every facet of the moon you could possibly want to know about.

One particular site, moon-watch.com is for "moon enthusiasts." It has a wealth of information on current research and includes regular updates on the discoveries by NASA's Lunar Prospector spacecraft. The spacecraft entered the lunar orbit on January 11, 1998, and has conducted its mapping missions from fifteen to sixty-three miles above the moon's surface.

This mapping by the Lunar Prospector has added credence to a long-held theory that the bulk of the moon was ripped away from the Earth when an object the size of Mars collided with it four to five million years ago. A March 16, 1999, press release from NASA read: "Similarities in the mineral composition of the Earth and Moon indicate that they share a common origin."

The moon is our only satellite and its average distance from Earth is 238,857 miles. Its revolution around the Earth takes twenty-seven days, seven hours, and forty-three minutes. Even though it's only a quarter the size of Earth, its gravitational pull is the main cause of our ocean tides.

Since our bodies are primarily water, the moon's gravitational pull on the tides also affects our bodily fluids, metabolic rates, and, of course, our emotions. The link, for instance, between the full moon and violent aggression has been noted for years by police officers, hospital workers, and employees at mental institutions.

In the 1970s, a Miami psychiatrist, Arnold Lieber, decided to conduct a scientific study to find out if these observations were true. As a med student at Jackson Memorial Hospital in Miami, he'd noticed recurring periods when patients on the psychiatric ward were more disturbed than usual. These periods would last for several days, then the patients would resume their normal behavior. He became curious about the phenomenon and finally conducted a scientific study. His findings, later backed by four other independent studies, confirmed that during the full moon and, to a lesser extent, during the new moon, there are increases in all violent crimes—homicide, rape, assault. There's also an increase in lesser crimes—burglary, auto theft, larceny, and drunken and disorderly behavior.

Is it any coincidence, then, that the word *lunatic* is derived from the word *lunar*?

Hospital workers and maternity ward nurses have long noticed that more babies are born at the full and new moons than at any other time of the month. These births may be due to the fact that the gravitational pull is strongest when the moon, sun, and Earth are aligned, as they are during the new and full moons. These observations have been backed by scientific studies. Interestingly enough, the lunar calendar is still the basis for calculating a pregnancy. The nine months are synodic months (the length of time it takes the moon to orbit earth).

Since the moon has no atmosphere, it has nothing to protect it from meteor strikes, which is why its surface is pocked with impact craters. Since it has no tectonic or volcanic activity, its surface is immune to the erosive effects of atmospheric weathering, tectonic shifts, and volcanic upheavals that reshape the surface of our planet. On the moon, even the footprints left by the Apollo astronauts will be intact for millions of years unless a meteor strike obliterates them.

The moon's gravity is about a sixth of ours; that's why the Apollo astronauts looked like they were jumping rope up there. Despite appearances to the contrary, the moon has no light of its own. That gorgeous full moon you see each month is the reflected light of our sun.

In ancient cultures, the passage of time was marked according to the lunation—or cycle—of the moon. A *month* was the time between one new moon and the next and, in a typical year, there were thirteen lunar cycles. This way of marking time still exists among some pagan sects today and may be closer to the natural rhythms of human life than our present solar calendar.

Astrological Lunar Facts

The moon in your horoscope is every bit as important as your sun sign. In fact, Eastern astrologers give the moon greater emphasis than the sun sign. The moon rules the sign of Cancer and the fourth house in the horoscope. She represents Mom or whoever plays that role for you, and also symbolizes other women in your life. The moon is feminine, yin, our intuitive selves.

In the physical body, her territory pertains primarily to women— breasts, ovaries, womb. In both genders, she rules internal fluids and the stomach, and, of course, she's our emotional barometer, the gauge of our inner health. Not surprisingly, the moon rules conception.

A Czech physician theorized that every woman has a fertility cycle that depends on the phase of the moon under which she is born. Eugene Jones developed a fertilization calendar based on his theory, which allegedly showed a 98 percent success rate. He charged an astronomical fee for his calendar, but people who were desperate to have children paid it.

Jones claimed that if a woman used his methods, she could choose the gender of her child. His technique was based on the rules of classical astrology, which he'd studied, and boils down to using the gender of moon signs. If conception took place on a Leo day, the child would be male, because Leo is a male sign. On a Taurus day, the child would be a girl.

The medical establishment went berserk over his claims. But when a panel of gynecologists challenged him to predict the genders of babies based only on their conception dates, Jones's accuracy rate was 87 percent.

The moon is exalted in the sign of Taurus, in her fall in Scorpio, and in detriment in Capricorn. But what, exactly, do these terms mean? If your moon is in Scorpio or Capricorn, are you cursed for life? The terms are just jargon. The thing to remember about *exalted, fall*, and *detriment* is that they simply describe how lunar energies mesh with the energy of particular signs.

I was about eighteen when I read my first description of my Capricorn moon. It was hardly a rave review. Adjectives like *ruthless* and *power-hungry* and comparisons to Hitler sent me back to the astrologer who had erected my chart. "This isn't me. There must be some mistake."

Nope, no mistake.

In the years since then, I've come to appreciate my Capricorn moon. It grounds me and keeps me focused. When my Gemini sun is scattered in the wind, the energy of my Capricorn moon brings me back to where I should be. When my external world is disordered and chaotic, my Capricorn moon is my emotional fortress. But when I got fed up teaching Spanish to hormonal seventh graders and entertained the idea of becoming a fulltime writer, my Capricorn moon balked—*too much uncertainty, no regular income, no health insurance*. Then, once it got all those objections out of the way without my deviating from the notion, it shouted, *Go for it*.

Those descriptions I read way back when made me more conscious of the characteristics inherent in a Capricorn moon, so I tried harder to channel the negative traits into more constructive channels. "Integration of lunar energy" may sound like pseudo psychobabble, but it's a key factor in summoning and using your intuition.

Astrologer Robert Hand, in his excellent book *Horoscope Symbols*, writes: "At a certain level, the lunar parts of the mind are in touch with everything, everywhere. The Moon, then, becomes one of the indicators of psychic ability, a mode of perception in which everything is in some way connected."

In a sense, your natal moon allows you to perceive the big picture, the forest, and its myriad connections to the matrix of life. Not bad for a satellite, right?

The Signs and Elements

Moon signs have the same names as sun signs—Aries, Taurus, Gemini, and so on around the zodiac. And, like sun signs, they have two broad groupings—by element and by mode. These categories reveal a great deal about the nature of the signs and make it easier to place your natal moon into a simple context.

The elements are what you learned about in grade school science class: fire, earth, air, and water. Three signs go with each element. Aries, Leo, and Sagittarius are fire; Taurus, Virgo, and Capricorn are earth; Gemini, Libra, and Aquarius are air; and Cancer, Scorpio, and Pisces are water. Simple enough. But what's it *mean* in real life?

It means that if you're a Libra sun married to a Taurus sun, two signs that aren't particularly compatible, and have been married successfully for twenty-five years, then chances are your moon signs get along famously. Maybe your moon is in Virgo and your spouse's moon is in Pisces, earth and water respectively. Or perhaps your partner's sun sign is the same as your moon sign, which gives you an instinctive, emotional understanding of each other. It may also indicate a karmic connection between you, something that originated in other lives.

Compatibility in terms of elements is just common sense. Air feeds fire, water nurtures earth. Other combinations can work, of course, but may not be quite as compatible. An Aries sun sign may feel that his Scorpio mate is always trying to "dampen his fire." A Libra may resent the way her Capricorn mate tries to smother her with practicality. You get the general idea here.

Swiss psychologist Carl Jung studied the charts of 483 married couples to see if there was something particular in their charts that made their marriages work. He found three common factors: a conjunction (union) between one partner's moon and the other partner's sun (same sign and close in degree); the same moon signs in both charts; and one partner's moon on the other partner's ascendant. His findings make perfect astrological sense.

The first combination (sun and moon in same sign) gives you and your partner an instinctive understanding of each other's needs. The second combination (same moon) gives you similar emotional needs and responses. The third combination (moon and ascendant in same sign) means that one partner's emotional needs mesh with the self the other person presents to the world.

Fire

The nature of fire is to burn. But fire exists in many forms: candlelight, fireworks, brush fires, solar flares, explosions, forest fires, fire from a match, in a fireplace. We use fire for light, to cook our food, to stay warm. It's all the same energy and whether it's constructive or destructive depends on the way we use it.

In astrology, the fire signs as a group—Aries, Leo, and Sagittarius—are energetic, passionate, enthusiastic, impulsive and impetuous, filled with vitality. They're the Indiana Jones of the zodiac, action-oriented. They're great at starting things, at getting projects off the ground. They're innovators, paradigm-busters. They can also be emotionally explosive, sharp-tongued, and consumed by their own energies.

As a fire sign moon, your intuitive insights are likely to come to you in abrupt flashes, with an explosive force that seizes your attention. This could be the *aha!* that grabs you in the middle of the night or the answer that slams into you when you're doing sixty on the freeway. The insight is usually sudden and unexpected, but it concerns something you've been working on or mulling over for a while.

You would think that fire signs, moon or sun, should get along best with other fire signs. But I've seen too many explosive combinations, between fire signs. It's as if all that action and vitality is just too much under a single roof. In general, fire gets along best with air signs.

Earth

The earth signs—Taurus, Virgo, and Capricorn—are definitely calmer than their fire cousins. These folks are practical, efficient, and pay attention to details. They're grounded. It's unlikely that an earth sign would head off to Tahiti on the spur of the moment. But a Sagittarian would do it in a heartbeat, with nothing more than a backpack and his ATM card.

Earth signs often enjoy gardening, sports, camping, being outdoors. They tend to be athletic and usually like cooking and gourmet foods. They can be security-conscious, ambitious individuals, but always move at their own leisurely pace, which can drive everyone around them crazy.

As an earth sign moon, your intuitive insights are felt mostly in the physical body. You talk about "gut feelings." You're acutely aware of the energy that other people radiate. A sprained muscle, a cold, even a headache: this is the voice of your intuition. The trick is figuring out what the symptom is saying. If you work in the health field, then one of the skills you develop is being able to interpret other people's symptoms. By this, I mean you're able to pinpoint the emotional cause of the symptom. The paragon of this ability is the medical intuitive, but all earth signs have it to some degree.

It's interesting to look at families where everyone has an earth moon. Regardless of what their sun signs say about how they get along as a unit, the common earth moon gives the family unit a practical, efficient focus.

Air

In many ways, the air signs—Gemini, Libra, and Aquarius—are the most ephemeral of the zodiac, the hardest to pin down. We can see fire, earth, and water, but not air. However, we perceive the effects of air—a sea breeze, wind blowing through trees, hurricanes, tornadoes, La Niña, El Niño, smog, and fog. Then, of course, there's the simple fact that if we don't breathe, we die.

The mind is the air sign's domain and it's through the mind that you explore your emotions, the realm of the moon. This may seem contradictory, since we usually don't think of emotions as a mental process. But for an air sign moon, it isn't enough to just feel something; you have to *understand* it, and that's the job of the mind. You're good with language, communication, and abstract thought. You go to sleep with your mind buzzing away and wake up with that same buzz in your head.

As an air sign moon, your intuitive flashes come to you through your intellect. You might get vivid mental images, mind pictures.

You might tune in to your intuition through writing, art, or speaking. Clairvoyance may be your vehicle.

Air signs generally do great with other air signs. Part of it may be that they always have something to talk about. They also get along well with fire signs.

Water

We drink it, swim in it, bathe in it. It feeds our lawns, our flowers, our slice of earth. It covers most of our planet and constitutes 80 percent of our bodies. It molds itself to whatever vessel contains it. Like air, we can't live without it.

Cancer, Scorpio, and Pisces. This trio hits us where we are the most vulnerable: our homes, our sexuality, our karma. This trio is entirely about emotion. They *feel* their way through life. All too often, the water signs can be so intense that you want to strangle them. But always, there's a sense that they're connected to something larger, that they know stuff that eludes the rest of us. And, quite often, they do. They are the natural psychics of the zodiac, deeply compassionate.

These people usually aren't as objective as air or fire signs and tend to see everything through a subjective lens. This makes them well-suited for the medical and health fields, artistic pursuits of all kinds, teaching, metaphysics, and counseling.

As a water moon, your intuitive insights come to you through dreams, visions, meditation, fantasy, and when you're involved in something creative. Your sense of touch may be so acute that you can pick up intuitive impressions when you touch people or objects. Precognition may be something that comes to you naturally.

In a family where everyone has a water moon, you can always feel the fluidity of emotions eddying around them. Chances are they live close to water, too, or wish they did. Water regenerates their spirits.

Modes of Being

Some people fall so obviously into categories that they become our prototypes for certain kinds of people: the prom queen, the jock, the cheerleader, the computer nerd, the missionary, the scatter-brain, the social butterfly. They are prototypes for certain characteristics that usually fall into three broad groupings: focused, resolute, and adaptable.

These words can describe not only characteristics, but ways of us-ing energy. In astrology, there are three such groupings, or triplici-ties: *cardinal* (focused), *fixed* (resolute), and *mutable* (adaptable). Each grouping holds one sign of each element. In other words, a Virgo—earth—and a Gemini—air—may not seem to have much in common on the surface. Yet, because both are mutable signs, they are oddly compatible. They use energy in the same way, through adapting to people and circumstances and being flexible.

With moon signs, triplicities are particularly revealing because the energy is primarily emotional and intuitive. This explains why two people whose sun signs are at complete odds get along incredi-bly well. A Taurus and a Gemini sun, for example, are the typical tortoise and hare couple. The Taurus is Ferdinand the bull, content to snooze in the sun and smell the flowers. The Gemini, meanwhile, is zipping around, stirring up the field and trampling the flowers. But if both of them have moons in the same triplicity—Libra and Capri-corn, for instance, or Aquarius and Leo—then they use emotional and intuitive energy in the same way. They have an instinctive un-derstanding of each other's deeper needs.

If you're a *cardinal moon* sign (Aries, Cancer, Libra, Capricorn), then you move primarily in one direction, along a single focused path. You're able to draw on emotional reserves you probably don't even know you have. You're not a quitter unless you lose interest, then you walk away without resentment or guilt because you simply don't care anymore. Intuitively, you're at your best when your goal is utterly clear in your own heart.

If you're a *fixed moon* sign (Taurus, Leo, Scorpio, Aquarius), then you're in for the long haul. Your emotions tend to cluster around a particular area in your life and you don't change your opinion or convictions just because someone you know believes something else. Your intuition is immediate, all-encompassing, and expresses itself through the element of your moon sign.

If you've got a *mutable moon* (Gemini, Virgo, Sagittarius, Pisces), you're an emotionally flexible person. You adapt to whatever suits you, can fit your emotions to someone else's, and can easily put yourself in the other guy's shoes. Intuitively, you're quick, the kind of person who can assess the mood of a group as soon as you walk into it. It's as if you adapt yourself to the other person's mood.

Table 1 outlines the elements and mode of each moon sign. In Table 2, brief descriptions are provided for each sign.

Table 1: Elements and Modes

Moon Sign	Symbol	Element	Mode
Aries	♈	fire	cardinal
Taurus	♉	earth	fixed
Gemini	♊	air	mutable
Cancer	♋	water	cardinal
Leo	♌	fire	fixed
Virgo	♍	earth	mutable
Libra	♎	air	cardinal
Scorpio	♏	water	fixed
Sagittarius	♐	fire	mutable
Capricorn	♑	earth	cardinal
Aquarius	♒	air	fixed
Pisces	♓	water	mutable

Table 2: Key Words for Moon Signs

Moon Sign	Key Words
Aries, cardinal fire	Primal energy, self-starter, impatient and impetuous. Focused as long as interest holds. Can be emotionally explosive. Emphasis on self. Sudden insights.
Taurus, fixed earth	Stubborn, persistent, slow to change opinion. Great endurance. Security-conscious. Appreciation for the finer things in life. Intuition is tactile. Gets "gut feelings."
Gemini, mutable air	Communicator, versatile, adaptable, emotionally flexible. Quick changes in mood, erratic temperament. Mentally intuitive, gets clairvoyant impressions.

Moon Sign	Key Words
Cancer, cardinal water	Sensitive, nurturing, home-oriented. Emotionally elusive, needs deep roots, introspective. Intuition works best through emotions and dreams.
Leo, fixed fire	Bold, dramatic emotions played on public stage. Enjoys attention. Emotionally volatile, particularly when involving kids or creativity or some strong belief. Intuition is quick, hot, immediate, an aha!
Virgo, mutable earth	Emotionally detached, a perfectionist, practical. Mentally intuitive. Intuition is tactile. Also works through health and the body.
Libra, cardinal air	Seeks balance emotionally. Inner need for harmony. Mentally intuitive. Clear impressions come through dreams, visions, and in relationships with others.
Scorpio, fixed water	Powerful and intense. Emotionally intuitive, a swift, immediate *knowing*. Intuition may also work through sexuality, dreams, any connection to deeper layers of life.
Sagittarius, mutable fire	Think of the New Hampshire motto: live free or die. Emotionally adaptable, but only to a point. Intuition usually future-oriented, involving the larger picture. Simply "knows" things.
Capricorn, cardinal earth	Emotions are compartmentalized. Has emotional reservoirs that can be tapped during times of stress or crisis. Intuition works primarily through the body and can be particularly strong through touch and hearing.
Aquarius, fixed air	Future-oriented, visionary. Mentally intuitive, like Gemini, but intuition can manifest through dreams and visions, similar to fixed Scorpio.
Pisces, mutable water	Emotionally ambivalent, yet adaptable. Very compassionate. Intuition naturally strong. Gets "gut feelings," may have precognitive dreams and visions. Mystical.

2

Who We Were, Who We Are: Your Nodal Axis

The Moon and Past Lives

Even if you don't believe in past lives, your astrologer probably does. Most western astrologers, in fact, have certain things they look for in a natal chart that relates to past lives. Saturn and the aspects or angles it makes to other planets, Pluto and its aspects, and the moon and the moon's nodes are some of the preferred.

Regardless of what planet or aspect an astrologer uses, it won't yield details of your past lives unless the astrologer is also psychic. Past lives, in fact, have less to do with who we *were* than with *who we are*, and with the patterns of behavior, needs, beliefs, and desires we brought into *this* life. The moon's nodes are excellent indicators about past life patterns that may be operating in our lives now.

The Nodes

It's one thing to talk about a planetary body that we can see. But it's something else to talk about points that have no physical reality. Specifically, the moon's nodes are points formed by the moon's orbit around the earth as it intersects the ecliptic—the earth's orbit around the sun.

Every planet has a north and south node, but when astrologers use the term, they usually mean the moon's nodes. The north node (Ω), called the dragon's head, and the south node (☋), the dragon's tail, are always opposite each other and form a "nodal axis." This is a kind of fulcrum, a seesaw that can be as precarious as a tightrope act or as easy as walking across the street, depending on how well we integrate the opposing energies into who we are.

The south node represents talents, abilities, and behavioral patterns that are deeply embedded in our psyches. Since these patterns have prevailed in past lives, they are familiar and comfortable to us, but when we get stuck in them, our lives don't work quite right. The south node represents the past that we have to move beyond and the north node points the way. To evolve as spiritual beings, we need to embrace the essence of the north node, which represents the future and our spiritual evolvement.

The signs of the nodes represent the shift that must take place for us to make the successful transition from past to future *in this life*. The houses in which the nodes fall explain the kinds of experiences that allow us to make that transition. The sign and house placement of the moon and the aspects it makes to other planets describe the ways in which our intuition can help us to make that transition.

Chris, a forty-two-year-old single mother, has a north node in Scorpio and a south node in Taurus. During her fifteen-year marriage, she felt progressively stifled. She and her husband seemed to move farther and farther apart until their daughter was all they had in common. She felt used up, her self-respect at an all-time low, but she hung in there for another two years, hoping things would change. Things didn't change. She ended up in the hospital with a gall bladder problem and in the deepest parts of herself, she knew it was over. So she filed for divorce.

Now she and her daughter live alone, with a menagerie of pets. Her home is considerably smaller, she works harder than she ever has to make ends meet, but she's happier. She learned that her need for security (Taurus south node) wasn't worth the sacrifice of her self-worth and sexuality (Scorpio north node). She learned that she hungered for intense experiences and deeper understanding of herself and her life (Scorpio north node), and when the pressure and the need to evolve became too much, she overthrew the tenacity of that south node and struck out on her own.

Interestingly enough, her moon is also in Taurus. This suggests that by allowing her intuitive voice to be heard, by being tenacious in developing and trusting her intuition and by putting it to practical use, she will attract and embrace the deeper understanding she hungers for.

The nodal axis is key to understanding how to balance old patterns of the south node with the needed challenges and growth indicated by the north node.

The Nodal Axis

The twelve zodiac signs can be viewed as pairs of six that encompass opposite qualities but use energy in the same way. In each pair, the elements are always different, but the modes are the same. For example, Aries, a fire sign, emphasizes the self, while Libra, an air sign, emphasizes relationships with others. Yet, both are cardinal signs.

In practical terms, this means that if your north node is in Aries and your south node is in Libra, then your growth potential is greatest if you rely on yourself, form your own values, and follow your own initiative. If your north node is in Libra and the south node falls in Aries, you would work best with strong leadership or mentoring.

Every astrologer has an opinion about the nodal axis, and the opinion depends on what kind of astrology is practiced. Karmic astrologers view the south node as karma, deeply embedded patterns acquired over successive lives that must be overcome through the north node sign and placement. Humanistic astrologers focus on the south node as biases set down in early childhood, unconscious patterns that must be released through the sign and position of the north node. Astrologer and author Robert Hand views the nodes as "connections to other people; that is, they are an axis of relationship. In this context, the north node has a joining quality and the south node has a separating quality."

Even if we remove reincarnation from the equation, the nodal axis is about living consciously. Once you realize that your north node represents the path to your greatest fulfillment, it's nearly impossible to go back to the snooze control of the south node, no matter how familiar it is or how safe it feels.

Use Appendix 3 to determine your nodes.

The Axis in Action

Aries north node, Libra south node: Trust your impulses and hunches even when they run contrary to what others think. You gravitate toward independent, self-reliant individuals who exude the qualities you are attempting to develop. And yet, you tend to want to please everyone and to avoid conflict at any cost, patterns you used in the past. But this time around, suppressing your own needs only leads to major conflicts later. Speak your mind. Don't be afraid to lead. When in doubt about the difference one lone voice can make, rent *Braveheart*.

Libra north node, Aries south node: Your natural urge is to seek independence at any cost. This is part of the pattern you should strive to leave behind. This time around, you gain from using your abilities to support and empower other people. You must learn consideration for others and how to remain nonjudgmental. Intimate relationships are one of your challenges, and are the area in which your intuition shines.

Taurus north node, Scorpio south node: Part of what you need to leave behind is your absolute intensity about everything. You're here this time to learn patience and tolerance and to develop your own values. Financial responsibility may be one of the most difficult lessons you learn. You're one of the "master builders," but you need to learn to build without first destroying. Your intuition is your most loyal guide in this journey. Allow it to speak and it won't fail you.

Scorpio north node, Taurus south node: You may not like it, but part of what you're here to learn is how to accept help from others. Don't be afraid to take risks, even if it means releasing everything that is familiar and known. In fact, once you realize that you can enjoy without owning, you're on your way toward the fulfillment of your potential. The movie *Resurrection* is a great depiction of this axis. Ellen Burstyn is the Scorpio north node; her boyfriend is the Taurus south node.

Gemini north node, Sagittarius south node: *Oops, there's been a mistake*, joked one individual with these nodes. *It was supposed to be the other way around. What happened?* What happened was that self-righteousness just doesn't cut it this time around. You need to listen to other people, to try to understand their beliefs and opinions, and realize that what's right for you may not be right for someone else. You already know *your* truth; this is the life to be open to other people's truths. Embrace the unknown.

Sagittarius north node, Gemini south node: Get out there and be adventurous. Take risks. Be spontaneous. Trust yourself. Forget logic—that's the past. This time around, you're here to tune in to the larger world. Read anything by Joseph Campbell, and then go out and find your personal myth. What do you *really* believe?

Cancer north node, Capricorn south node: Here's the deal. You hurt. But you're afraid that if you express it, you'll look too vulnerable, too weak, too . . . well, too something that will make you look bad. The lesson here is *so what*. Part of what you're here to learn is the validity of your own emotions and to treat others the way you yourself want to be treated. Your innate intuition is your greatest ally.

Capricorn north node, Cancer south node: You tend to nurture everything and everyone in your immediate environment and, somehow, never get on to the business of your own life independent from others. This is the past. This time around, you need to develop self-sufficiency; define your goals, and go after them. Nostalgia sometimes prompts you to hang onto a relationship or situation even though it clearly isn't working. Instead, take charge by expressing what you feel, and then get on with your life.

Leo north node, Aquarius south node: You tend to worry a lot about the opinion of the group and often do things out of peer pressure. That's the past. This is the life in which you're to express yourself and realize your creative potential. Be dramatic. Take center stage in your own life. The secret to doing this lies in living in the moment and in following your intuitive impulses and hunches instead of thinking something to death.

Aquarius north node, Leo south node: Your natural inclination for center stage is fine as long as you use it toward humanitarian causes. If you pursue something only for the ego glory, you lose. You're not afraid of taking risks and that's admirable; but before you leap into something, weigh the consequences to other people. Part of what you're here to learn this time around is how to share your unconventional viewpoints and beliefs, even when they don't fit other people's image of you. Your motives for doing things in this life must be in keeping with your highest wisdom, and that wisdom often comes to you through your intuition.

Virgo north node, Pisces south node: Yes, you're sensitive. But sometimes your sensitivity clouds the reality of a situation so deeply that you feel your only recourse is to withdraw or give up completely. When this happens, step back from the situation or relationship and try to look at it objectively. Victim consciousness is part of what you're here to release and you can do it through self-analysis and attention to detail. Your deeply intuitive nature and spiritual perceptions are strong and clear, built over numerous lifetimes. This time around, use your intuitive talents to live more fully in the moment, paying attention to the fine details.

Pisces north node, Virgo south node: Your quest for perfection is a hangover from the past and won't get you where you want to go any faster. Riding tandem with this quest is a nitpicky, critical streak. The sooner you learn to trust that your life is unfolding as it should, the more at peace you'll be. Your challenge is to realize it's okay to make mistakes and to be less than perfect. Compassion is your intuitive vehicle to fulfilling your potential.

3

Phases of the Moon

There's something about the sight of a full moon that creates poetry in our hearts and stirs the ancient part of our souls. At the same time, it brings to mind legends of werewolves, witches, and things that go bump in the night. It's *mysterious* and *mythical*, that ubiquitous eye suspended up there in the black sky, casting enough light on earth that we can see our shadows at midnight.

The full moon is hard to miss. But most of us probably don't even notice the phases before and after the full moon. Blame the modern world. Blame electricity, TVs, movies, CDs, and all the rest of it. The moon simply isn't as *necessary* to our lives as it was in ancient times. On a deeper level, this is a comment about our estrangement from our unconscious, intuitive selves.

Each month, the moon goes through eight distinct phases, a lunation cycle. At the beginning of the cycle, the sun and the moon are conjunct—in the same sign and degree. This is known as a new moon and it covers the first three and a half days of the lunation cycle. The moon then "waxes," or grows, into a crescent (days 3½ to 7), a first quarter (days 7 to 10½), a gibbous (days 10½ to 14), and finally the full moon. At this point, the sun and moon are exactly opposite each other. The full moon usually occurs between fourteen and seventeen and a half days into the cycle. From this point, the moon begins to wane, to shrink into the disseminating phase (days

17½ to 21), the last quarter (days 21 to 24½), and the balsamic or "dark" moon (days 24½ to 28 or 29).

In a birth chart, each phase represents a psychological type, a particular approach to life, an archetype, and describes how we handle conflict. An individual born under a new moon, for instance, tends to be an innovator, restless and impulsive, the solar equivalent of an Aries. A person born under the balsamic moon often has an awareness of the forces that direct and shape his or her life, a sense of destiny.

Since the moon phases are directly related to the moon's position relative to the position of the sun, your moon phase describes how the solar and lunar energies in your particular horoscope work together. Do the energies support each other? Are they always locked in combat? Do they blend with or oppose each other?

Since New Moon types usually have the sun and the moon in the same sign, the energy flow between their emotions and their outer selves is facilitated. In contrast, for Full Moon types, the sun and moon are opposite or nearly opposite each other, usually in opposing signs, which means their emotions are at war with their outer selves. The bottom line, though, is how all this translates into your daily life.

Use Table 3 to determine the phase of your natal moon.

Table 3: The Phase of Your Natal Moon

Locate your sun sign in the vertical column and your moon sign in the horizontal column. The place where they meet is the phase of your moon. The abbreviations are for the first two letters of the sign's name. AR is Aries, TA is Taurus, and so on, except for Capricorn, which is Cap.

Due to the degrees of the various types (0–45 for a new moon, for instance) and the fact that each sign has 30 degrees, there are some overlaps in the phases. If you were born at the end of March, in the early part of Aries, and have a moon in Taurus, then your moon may be new or crescent, so read both descriptions.

	WAXING				*WANING*			
	New	*Crescent*	*1st Q*	*Gibbous*	*Full*	*Dis.*	*3rd Q*	*Dark*
AR	AR-TA	GE-CA	CA-LE	LE-VI	LI-SC	SC-CA	CAP-AQ	PI-AR
TA	TA-GE	CA-LE	LE-VI	VI-LI	SC-SA	SA-CAP	AQ-PI	AR-TA
GE	GE-CA	LE-VI	VI-LI	LI-SC	SA-CAP	CAP-AQ	PI-AR	TA-GE
CA	CA-LE	VI-LI	LI-SC	SC-SA	CAP-AQ	AQ-PI	AR-TA	GE-CA

	New	Crescent	1st Q	Gibbous	Full	Dis.	3rd Q	Dark
LE	LE-VI	LI-SC	SC-SA	SA-CAP	AQ-PI	PI-AR	TA-GE	CA-LE
VI	VI-LI	SC-SA	SA-CAP	CAP-AQ	PI-AR	AR-TA	GE-CA	LEO-VI
LI	LI-SC	SA-CAP	CAP-AQ	AQ-PI	AR-TA	TA-GE	CA-LE	VI-LI
SC	SC-SA	CAP-AQ	AQ-PI	PI-AR	TA-GE	GE-CA	LE-VI	LI-SC
SA	SA-CAP	AQ-PI	PI-AR	AR-TA	GE-CA	CA-LE	VI-LI	SC-SA
CAP	CAP-AQ	PI-AR	AR-TA	TA-GE	CA-LE	LE-VI	LI-SC	SA-CAP
AQ	AQ-PI	AR-TA	TA-GE	GE-CA	LE-VI	VI-LI	SC-SA	CAP-AQ
PI	PI-AR	TA-GE	GE-CA	CA-LE	VI-LI	LI-SC	SA-CAP	AQ-PI

New Moon
(0 to 45 degrees ahead of sun)
Innovation, new seeds

If you're a New Moon type, you were born at the new moon or during the three and a half days afterward. As corny as it might sound, the *Star Trek* motto fits you; you're one of those people who "boldly goes where no one has gone before." Well, maybe people have been there before, but they didn't take the route you're taking. You act and react instinctively, boldly, without fear. Like an Aries, you may be somewhat self-involved, but you need that egocentrism to leave your personal stamp on the world.

You can be brash, impulsive, and blunt. One of your challenges is to realize when it's okay to be like that, and when you should keep your opinions to yourself. You may have trouble defining boundaries between yourself and your mother. In fact, the closer the conjunction between sun and moon, the hazier the boundaries.

You're an innovator with an uncanny perception. You're able to spot the next trend and if you trust your intuition, you can use this to your advantage. Your intuitive impressions come to you rather suddenly at times—an impulse to do something, a dream fragment that addresses a concern that you have, even through what another person says or does. Once you develop the ability to recognize and act on these intuitive impressions, your path becomes much clearer.

You can be very emotional at times, and your perception is definitely subjective. But this explains why your intuition runs through you like a river. When you're aware of it, you can dip into it at your leisure; when you're not aware, it spills its banks, flooding your unconscious until you pay attention.

My daughter is a New Moon type and fits the mold perfectly. Impatience characterizes her and always has. When she was a toddler, she was so eager to begin walking that she bypassed the crawling stage entirely. She spoke her first word at seven months—*kitty*—then didn't utter another intelligible word until she was nearly two. She was an early reader, insatiably curious about her immediate environment (read: into everything), and not a good sleeper. Once she understood the concept of friend, she never displayed a shred of shyness. She's blunt, quick, and the first on the block to try something new. In short, she's a New Moon through and through.

New Moon in a fire sign: All the New Moon characteristics are intensified. You're a regular powerhouse of energy and ideas, with terrific forward thrust in life. You experience many sudden insights and aha! moments in your life.

New Moon in an air sign: Energy is channeled into mental and intellectual pursuits. Your intuition works best when making connections between ideas or concepts. Intuitively quick. Perceptive.

New Moon in an earth sign: The energy of the new moon is expressed through structure and what is tangible. You probably won't find many individuals in this category who are out there bungee jumping on weekends. Instead, they'll be building cities, establishing organizations, or writing books. They apply their intuition to obtain tangible results.

New Moon in a water sign: The energy of the new moon is expressed emotionally and psychically. This New Moon type is probably the most naturally psychic, able to tap deep reservoirs of imagination, creativity, and knowledge.

Waxing Crescent Moon
(45 to 90 degrees ahead of sun)
Expansion

In this phase, the sun and moon are one or two signs apart. Growth and a search for new horizons are what you're about. Your ideas and approach to life are fresh, vital, and infectious. People gravitate toward you because of the strength and clarity you emit.

One of your challenges lies in overcoming a certain inertia that may plague you from time to time. You usually feel it most when you're trying to move forward in your life and situations, events, and people seem to conspire to prevent you from doing that. These "obstacles" are what astrologer Dane Rudhyar (*The Lunation Cycle*) calls "ghosts of the past." These deeply unconscious patterns and habits are vestiges of past lives that must be overcome before you can embrace the growth that comes with this cycle.

For some Crescent Moon types, these restrictions are apparent in their family structures or in some other facet of their lives. Martin Luther King, for instance, had to overcome prejudice against his race. Elvis Presley had to overcome extreme poverty.

As a result of these struggles and obstacles, you're at your intuitive best when you follow your impulses and hunches in delving into the past and applying what you learn to creating the kind of future you want. You may feel your intuition as a nervous excitement in the pit of your stomach.

Since this moon time exemplifies a cycle of growth, it has produced a number of leaders, entertainers, and celebrities: for example, George Lucas, Elvis Presley, Jacques Cousteau, Alfred Hitchcock, James Caan, and Bette Davis.

Crescent Moon in a fire sign: Your emotional and inner growth happen in spurts and surges, through your taking action. Anger can be an effective tool in breaking through unconscious patterns, as long as your anger isn't directed to other people, or inward toward yourself. Your intuition shines when you're focused on a particular goal or path.

Crescent Moon in an air sign: Your emotional and inner growth happen through the intellectual connections that you make about ideas and belief systems. Information is vital to your understanding of yourself and your world. Once you've gathered all the pieces, your intuition puts them together for you.

Crescent Moon in an earth sign: Your emotional and inner growth unfold at the pace that you set, according to guidelines and conditions that you select. The selection process, however, is largely instinctive—that is, you don't think much about it. You're interested in concrete results and work tirelessly toward that end.

Crescent Moon in a water sign: Your emotional and inner growth unfold on very deep levels—in dreams and unconscious realms. The challenge for you is to bring that intuitive knowledge forward into your conscious mind.

First Quarter Moon
(90 to 135 degrees ahead of the sun)
Crisis in action

The moon is half-full now, forming a ninety-degree angle to the sun; this position is known as a square. It creates friction.

Rudhyar called this phase "crisis in action," an apt description for your life. Circumstances often force you to make decisions, and some of those decisions go against the status quo in your own life and against societal norms. You chafe at any restrictions people try to impose on you, and feel an incessant itch to move beyond the world that's familiar to you. This can make you something of a renegade who thwarts established thinking.

You're also a risk-taker. The rest of us may think you're doing it for the thrill, but there is usually a deeper significance, even though you may not be sure what it is. Part of your challenge is to integrate what you know with what you sense intuitively.

This moon phase has its share of notable people: Lillian Hellman, Ellen Burstyn, Sylvester Stallone, Joan of Arc, and Queen Elizabeth.

First Quarter Moon in a fire sign: Pity the fool who makes you mad. You don't mince words when you're angry, but once you've said your piece, you generally don't hold grudges, either. You bring tremendous action and determination to everything you take on. Intuitively, you're at your best in times of crisis.

First Quarter Moon in an air sign: Your emotional conflicts can make you argumentative until you realize you're only arguing with yourself. When you bring your powerful intellect to bear against obstacles, your intuition guides you to people and situations that enable you to realize your goals.

First Quarter Moon in an earth sign: You tackle obstacles in a practical way, moving at your own pace, and keeping your own counsel. Your efficiency allows you to focus on whatever it is you're doing. The more intent your focus, the deeper your intuition.

First Quarter Moon in a water sign: Your strongest ally is your intuition. It runs through you like blood. When you allow your inner voice to help you navigate the maze of your emotions, you get where you're going much more quickly and smoothly.

Gibbous Moon
(135 to 180 degrees ahead of the sun)
Analyze and perfect

The sun and moon are now four or five signs apart. At four signs apart, they are at a harmonious angle called a trine and are usually in the same element. At five signs apart, the compatibility is unraveling because the moon is moving toward its opposition to the sun—the full moon.

You tend to scrutinize your personal development and, in some way, relate it to the larger society and world. Growth is paramount for you, just as it is for the Crescent Moon types, but you constantly monitor your growth to be sure you're making progress.

Introspection is key to your personality and usually runs to very deep levels. You dig around in your own psyche, ferreting out what's hidden and unknown until all the unconscious *stuff* is laid bare. This is exactly the kind of focus you bring to whatever you're trying to achieve in your personal and professional life, and is precisely what proves key to your later success.

Notable Gibbous Moon folks: Shirley MacLaine, Liza Minelli, Sai Baba, Peter Bogdanovich, James Brolin, and Ernest Hemingway.

Gibbous Moon in a fire sign: You're a powerhouse of drive and ambition, able to take on the work of two people and pull it off with grace. If Aries figures into your Gibbous Moon equation, you're either a pioneer or a crusader.

Gibbous Moon in an air sign: You're a charmer with the gift of gab, a smooth talker who culls information the way other people cull power. Books, language, and research are one venue for your growth. With a Gibbous Moon in Libra, you're a natural mediator; in Gemini, you're quick and loquacious; in Aquarius, you're a revolutionary thinker and doer.

Gibbous Moon in an earth sign: You're eminently practical, with an excellent business sense. You use that practicality to nurture your own growth, and to attract the experiences that best answer your myriad questions.

Gibbous Moon in a water sign: You're here to feel and experience a full spectrum of emotions, which you will in turn relate to the larger world. If that sounds like a tall order, don't worry about it. Just live it.

Full Moon
(opposite or 135 degrees behind the sun)
Harvest, fulfill, illuminate

This is the first phase of the waxing cycle, when the perceptions become objective instead of subjective. Awareness and acting consciously is key to growth in this phase.

The good news is that you don't change into a werewolf or wander the moors in search of your next victim. But at times you may feel that way. There's a constant tug of war with this moon phase because the moon and the sun are nearly or directly opposite each other. This polarization prompts you to seek your life purpose *consciously*, through clearly defined goals that you attain by following intuitive leads. This may sound like a contradiction to other people, but makes perfect sense to you.

Relationships are important to you. Many Full Moon types seek the perfect partner, the elusive soulmate, in the hopes that the other person will give their lives meaning. But the bottom line is that there are no perfect partners. We're all human and you're asking for trouble by elevating a partner to a pedestal. Part of what you're here to learn as a Full Moon type is how your actions and decisions affect others. Think before you act. Try to understand the ramifications of your decisions before you decide.

The way you integrate your emotional polarization can go one of several ways. You can try to escape and avoid the emotional turmoil, the tug of war. Judy Garland sought escape through drugs and alcohol. You can channel it into something creative, as author Michael Crichton has done through his novels. Other notable Full Mooners: Buddha, Janis Joplin, Goldie Hawn, Robert De Niro, and Faye Dunaway.

Full Moon in a fire sign: You're a paragon of contradictory urges and needs, with a deep restlessness that demands to be sated. How you resolve these emotional issues depends on the sign of the moon. An Aries Full Moon may become a crusader against social ills. A Sagittarius Full Moon looks for truth. A Leo Full Moon seeks resolution through dramatic confrontations and gestures.

Full Moon in an air sign: You deal with emotional issues through your intellect, and your interactions with other people. Your success in this endeavor depends on the level of your conscious awareness and how you apply that awareness in your daily life.

Full Moon in an earth sign: Make it practical. Make it useful. Bring it into daily life. That's your motto. And it's exactly what you seek to do when you live consciously, aware of your dichotomies and attempting to weave them into something meaningful.

Full Moon in a water sign: Yes, it's okay to be honest about what you feel. It's okay to put those feelings into songs or poetry or to weave them into whatever form suits you. Once you begin living your emotions consciously, it will begin to make sense.

Disseminating Moon
(moon 135 to 190 degrees behind sun)
Spreading the word

This phase starts about three and a half days after the full moon. It looks exactly like a gibbous moon, except the part of the moon that is lopped off is on the opposite side because the moon is waning. When the moon is four signs behind the sun, their energies blend well and work smoothly together. When they're five signs apart, the residual tension of the full moon makes them work less smoothly. This is why it's beneficial to know the position of your moon relative to the sun's.

Your main thrust in life is to spread the word. Yes, "the word" may differ for each Disseminating type. But for everyone born under this phase, it will evolve around the truth you've discovered through the other five phases. *Your truth*. The conflict, of course, at least in Western culture, is that we're taught to doubt "our truth" and to buy into society's version of truth. You need to stick to your truth, and trust that eventually you'll attract other people who believe as you do.

As you move through your life, you meet many people who hold opposing or different views from your own. Your job is to synthesize these views by comparing and contrasting them with your own, then integrating them into who you are and disseminating them to others. Quite often, the "others" can become the public at large. This moon phase produces teachers, writers, and people who are generally an inspiration to others. Albert Einstein, and Helen Keller are notable examples. The danger with this moon phase is that you can become fanatical about your beliefs, as Hitler did. This negative manifestation of the Disseminating Moon doesn't understand why other people don't see things the same way.

Disseminating Moon in a fire sign: Your restlessness and impatience can thwart your goals if you're not careful. Be sure about your values and beliefs before disseminating them to others. Your tremendous energy is part of your charisma, and once you find the appropriate vehicle for sharing, nothing stops you from achieving what you desire.

Disseminating Moon in an air sign: Writing, speaking, networking, and the entertainment field in general are good vehicles for you. You're nonjudgmental about other people's beliefs, and have such a charming way of presenting your own take on things that other people listen.

Disseminating Moon in an earth sign: Practicality is your hallmark. It may take you longer than a fire moon to define your belief system, but once you do, you systematically proceed to communicate what you've discovered. Your focus is on practical beliefs and values that can be implemented into daily life.

Disseminating Moon in a water sign: Your emotions and intuition are the vehicles through which you uncover and define your values and beliefs. Your piercing insights are powerful and persuasive and, regardless of the venue you use for communicating them, your ability to influence others is profound.

Last Quarter Moon
(45 to 90 degrees behind the sun)
Reorientation

Your search for meaning and purpose is a major focus in your inner life, and this is reflected in your outer life as rebellion against established thinking. Initially, your rebellion may not be obvious to others. You tend to be secretive about yourself and what you believe.

You may act in a way that is consistent with how other people perceive you. But when you say or do something that isn't consistent, the shock to the people around you proves to be considerable.

Rudhyar calls this moon phase "crisis in consciousness," as opposed to the "crisis in action" of the First Quarter type. With the First Quarter moon, the crisis is turned outward; with this type, the crisis is turned inward. As you release the structure of your old beliefs, certain things and people will fall out of your life, as if to make room for the new relationships and situations that your emerging new beliefs will attract. The danger lies in the between stage, when you've discarded the old, but the new isn't entirely in place yet.

Carl Jung turned his inward crisis to the study of myth and how it relates to the human psyche—and discovered the collective unconscious. James Dean's inner crisis galvanized an entire generation of youth, but ended tragically for him. Diarist Anaïs Nin chronicled her inner crisis from a very young age and left behind a legacy.

Last Quarter Moon in a fire sign: Your nature is emotionally volatile. All this energy propels you out of your familiar circumstances and belief systems into a vast unknown. The tricky thing with this moon is balance. Be sure that when you make a decision, it doesn't undermine a previous decision. Your intuition speaks to you most loudly through impulses, but you must understand them as well as act upon them.

Last Quarter Moon in an air sign: Information, networking, and education are the vehicles you use to illuminate your internal conflicts. You're the type of person who can walk into a bookstore not knowing exactly what you're looking for, and the book you need will fall off the shelf at your feet. Intuitively, you connect ideas and ideologies that allow you to break free of your past structures.

Last Quarter Moon in an earth sign: You tackle your internal conflicts the way you do everything else in your life—methodically, with attention to detail. You want to get it right. Just be careful that you don't spend so much time trying to perfect the transformative process that you lose sight of the process itself.

Last Quarter Moon in a water sign: This one can be tough simply because water moons are so naturally intuitive. Emotional conflict isn't normal for you. When you're feeling deeply conflicted, the internal pressure is almost too intense to bear. But this pressure is exactly what you need to break through to new belief systems.

Balsamic or Dark Moon
(0 to 45 degrees behind sun)
Release

This phase occurs within three and a half days of the new moon and is the last of the eight lunar phases. In terms of past lives, some astrologers consider this phase to be the last of eight incarnations, in which the individual is preparing himself or herself for a new incarnation cycle.

In fact, from the time you were very young, you may have felt that you have a special destiny. You may be prophetic and you definitely are future-oriented, though at times you may feel chained to the past. You have many intense encounters with other people. These encounters aren't necessarily romantic, but they are usually karmic.

Astrologer Demeter George, born under a balsamic moon, believes these individuals are the true visionaries of the zodiac. In *Finding Our Way Through the Dark*, she writes: "When Balsamic people realize that it is this prophetic visionary quality that sets them apart from others, they can begin to release much of the shame that has built up from trying to conceal the ways in which they are different in order to prevent being ridiculed or rejected."

But what about people born under this phase who don't feel any sense of destiny, or mystical yearnings to plant seeds for future generations? What about Balsamic Moon types who just want to have their families and live happy, fruitful lives? We can't all be Abraham Lincoln or Elizabeth Kübler-Ross, Karl Marx or Beethoven.

This lunar phase intrigues me because my mother was born under a balsamic moon and doesn't seem to fit the general descriptions. As far as I know, she has never felt any sense of destiny. She has never been interested in metaphysical thought, and considers astrology to be rather silly.

Yet in her daily life, she has exhibited profound loyalty to people and beliefs that are of importance to her. She is kind and nurturing, extending both qualities to strangers. Animals and children hold a special place in her heart. But she never seemed to feel the angst of this lunar phase—or perhaps she simply blocked it out, stuck it away somewhere.

Now my mother is eighty-two years old, and in an Alzheimer's unit. I feel sure there's a spiritual component to her disease, but because we're not a culture that puts much stock in the connection between spirit and disease, information on this aspect of Alzheimer's is almost nonexistent. In the course of her disease, however, I've noticed that in many ways she is more intuitively receptive now. It's as if now that her focus is concentrated elsewhere, her intuitive self is burgeoning.

If the path of the Balsamic Moon person isn't lived consciously throughout life, with awareness, then particular types of illnesses are one possible outcome. As medical intuitive Carolyn Myss writes, "When an illness is part of your spiritual journey, no medical intervention can heal you until your spirit has begun to make the changes that the illness was designed to inspire."

4

Intuitive Reality Check #1: Your Intuitive Profile

When I was in middle school, I went through a period where I could feel my teeth growing. They seemed to be expanding sideways in my mouth, as if the enamel were flexible, like rubber or soft plastic. I initially found this sensation to be somewhat frightening, simply because it felt so incredibly weird.

I mentioned it to my parents and ended up at the doctor's office. He couldn't find any physical explanation for it and implied that it was all my imagination. I quickly learned not to talk about it. The sensations happened off and on for several months and I began to notice a pattern. Whenever friends asked me a question about some future event or situation, my teeth would feel like they were growing.

The questions were the kind you expect for that age. *Do you think Tom is going to invite me to the prom? Am I going to ace math this quarter?*

As soon as I felt the sensation, I would feel an urge to answer yes or no to the question. Pretty soon, kids I didn't know were asking me questions. I had no context into which I could place the sensation or the answers I got. We were living in an American community in a foreign country, and the kind of information I needed wasn't available. Eventually, the sensations stopped.

In retrospect, I realize this was intuition in action. I would experience a physical sensation that seemed to signal the shift in consciousness, then the answer would come. I believe the sensations ceased because I didn't know what was happening, had no framework into which I could put it, and it scared me. So I turned my intuition off—at least in that sense—and went on with my life as a kid.

In college, I rediscovered my intuition, but through an external source—the *I Ching* and the works of Carl Jung. From this, I ventured out into astrology, the tarot, and, gradually, into the gamut of metaphysical thoughts and beliefs. My *intuition found acceptable frameworks through which it could function.* These external devices or triggers brought me fully back into the flow.

Fortunately, intuition isn't the black sheep these days that it used to be. It's no longer viewed like a vestigial organ, a spiritual appendix. Now we're beginning to realize that intuition is as essential as the ability to think concisely and clearly and to act on our decisions.

As we begin the twenty-first century, there's a resurgence of the feminine, the *yin*; what Carl Jung called the anima. It's socially acceptable now to be *intuitive.* In casual conversation, people refer as frequently to how they *feel* as they do to what they *think.* It's now okay to admit that you have "hunches" or "gut feelings," or that you "sense" something. It's so socially acceptable now to be intuitive that "intuitives" have hit prime time.

There are medical intuitives, animal intuitives, therapeutic intuitives. There are business and professional workshops to teach you how to release your intuition. There are seminars on how to use your intuition to make money. Intuition has become a cottage industry. But at the heart of it all, workshops, seminars, and books merely offer insight into what we already possess.

Synchronicity

As you develop your intuition, you'll suddenly find your life riddled with strange occurences. At first, it happens simply. Perhaps you're thinking about someone you haven't seen for a while and five minutes later, the phone rings and it's that person. Or a letter or an e-mail arrives from the individual you've been thinking about. These types of experiences happen to all of us throughout the course of our lives and we usually dismiss them as interesting "coincidences"—i.e., without significance.

But as you continue to flex your intuitive muscles, these "coincidences" may become increasingly more complex. They may become metaphorical, like dreams, and the metaphors will beg for interpretation. You'll begin to view these experiences in a different light, as events with definite significance.

Swiss psychologist Carl Jung called these "meaningful coincidences" *synchronicities*. In his introduction to Richard Wilhelm's translation of the *I Ching*, one of the most widely known and respected divination systems, Jung wrote: ". . . synchronicity takes the coincidence of events in space and time as meaning something more than mere chance, namely a peculiar interdependence of objective events among themselves as well as with the subjective (psychic) states of the observer. . . ." In other words, outer events reflect inner conditions.

Jung contended that synchronicity explains why the *I Ching* works, why the *pattern* created by the toss of coins is significant and personally insightful. Synchronicity is at the heart of all oracles, all divination systems, and all intuitive work. It's the language of intuition, its mythology, its deeper truth.

A forty-five-year-old man, while actively trying to deepen his intuition, noticed that shortly before something momentous happened to him or his spouse, the shelves in their closet would collapse. Over a period of three or four months, it happened half a dozen times, despite repeated repairing of the shelves. Within twenty-four to forty-eight hours of the shelves collapsing, the event would occur. These events included a death and illness in the family, winning a prize, an unexpected trip, and a new and lucrative client account. If the event happened to him, the shelves on his side of the closet would collapse. If the event happened to his wife, her shelves would collapse.

Consensus reality would dismiss these incidents as "bizarre coincidences." Jung would call it synchronicity. Regardless of what *we* call it, we should sit up and take notice when a phenomenon repeats itself. This man's Virgo moon in the fifth house of creativity—a detail-oriented moon—prompted him to look beyond consensus reality. By delving into the nature of the experience itself, he gained a deeper understanding of how his intuition functioned—and became a shelf handyman as well!

The whole notion of "meaningful coincidences" doesn't fit with the mechanistic view of the universe that has prevailed for centuries. In that view, the universe is like a giant machine with separate and independent parts that follow predictable movements. Anything can be predicted because nature's laws are inviolate.

But physicist David Bohm and neurophysiologist Karl Pribram, working independently of each other, changed all that. They theorized that the whole is greater than the sum of its parts, that there's a deeper, hidden level of reality, an *implicate* or enfolded order. Its opposite, Bohm said, is our level of reality, the *explicate* or unfolded order.

In this view, the universe resembles a huge hologram rather than a machine, and everything in it is interconnected. Each of us isn't just connected to the whole; we contain it. This notion of the universe as a hologram, a pattern of unbroken wholeness, is why synchronicity works. The explicate or unfolded order—our ordinary, daily lives—is a reflection of the implicate or enfolded order. Or, to put it another way, our deepest beliefs create our reality, which in turn reflects our beliefs.

A synchronicity unfolds from the hidden order of our lives and can involve virtually anything—names, animals, people, times, places. One of the most interesting examples happened to author and mythologist Joseph Campbell. At the time, he was in his fourteenth-floor apartment in Manhattan, researching Bushman mythology, specifically a story in which the praying mantis plays the part of the hero. He was sitting at a window that faced Sixth Avenue and suddenly felt an urge to open the window. He glanced right and saw a praying mantis walking up the side of the building to the rim of his window. The creature's face, Campbell said, looked like that of a Bushman.

This synchronicity is similar to what Carl Jung experienced when a patient was recounting a dream she'd had of a scarab. At that moment, something struck the window of the room where they were sitting and when Jung opened it, he saw a beetle.

A synchronicity can be dramatic, amusing, even irritating, as in the shelves example. But it always grabs our attention and forces us to pay attention to whatever is going on in our lives. Synchronicities often occur in clusters, over a period of days, weeks, or months, like the repeating incident with the closet shelves. They can also occur as singular experiences that bring some underlying emotion into greater clarity, or warn us of an impending event. Synchronicities often occur around landmarks in our lives—births, marriage, divorce, death.

Author Nancy Pickard told me about a fascinating synchronicity that occurred in conjunction with her father's death. He passed away after eleven months and eleven days in a nursing home, at eleven minutes past the eleventh hour. This was obviously a synchronicity involving numbers, but neither of us had a clue what it meant. Then one day several months later, it hit me. Nancy studies the *I Ching* and I was certain the elevens related to the eleventh hexagram—*Peace*. When I told Nancy about it, she agreed. Her father, after a long illness, had died in peace.

As you develop intuitively, synchronicities will proliferate in your life; expect it, embrace it. It means you're tapping into the depths of your lunar energy.

Three Questions

One afternoon at a book signing for my suspense novel, *The Seventh Sense*, I decided to try something a little different with the audience. I gave a synopsis of the book and explained that the "seventh sense" is the big picture, which we can access through our sixth sense—intuition. I then told the audience that they were going to do an intuitive reading for themselves. I asked them to write down a single question and place it aside. The question was to be simple but specific, with a time frame of no more than six months from now.

We then went on to some other intuitive exercises to bolster self-confidence in their own impressions. At the end of the hour, we did the final exercise. When they were finished with it, I told them they had just answered the question they'd written down at the beginning of the hour. Since they hadn't known the purpose of the exercise, their left-brain censor couldn't have intervened. *Their intuition had kicked in.*

You're going to do something similar here. In the activity chart that follows, list three questions. Make each question *simple* and *specific*. Instead of asking, for example, whether your relationship with so and so will work out, ask if the commitment will deepen over a specific period of time, or if you're going to get married. By the end of this book, the three questions you list will have been answered—by using your intuition.

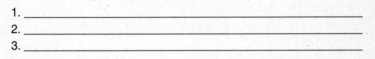

YOUR QUESTIONS

1. _____
2. _____
3. _____

Your Intuitive Profile: Senders and Receivers

Are you telepathically receptive? When the phone rings, do you know who's calling? Do you pick up the thoughts and feelings of the people around you? Or are you more of a sender, the kind of person whose emotions are so intense that they seem to radiate from you like light?

Most of us tend to fall into one category or another. My daughter is definitely a stronger receiver than a sender. Since she was old enough to understand the concept of color, we have played a game in which one of us would mentally send the other a color. We change roles, of course, and sometimes I pick up the color she's sending me, but invariably, she remains strongest at receiving and I'm strongest at sending.

Circumstances, of course, have a lot to do with it. In a crisis, all bets are off; we all can be equally good at receiving and sending. But most of the time, our daily lives aren't in crisis. And that's what the following activity addresses: how you are most of the time.

YOUR INTUITIVE PROFILE

Complete parts A and B of this activity by answering yes or no to the statements. If you honestly don't know an answer, leave it blank.

A.

1. I like bold, vivid colors—reds, bright oranges, vibrant blues. _____
2. I can't turn my head off when I get in bed at night._____
3. I have at least one interest about which I'm passionate._____
4. I have a hot temper._____
5. I'm not shy about saying what I feel at a given moment._____
6. I don't have many close friends, but the ones I have are very close; they are friends for the long haul._____
7. I consider myself monogamous in relationships._____
8. I have clear, distinct goals._____
9. I'm able to disguise my true emotions in most situations._____
10. I am very focused._____

B.

1. I can change my opinions easily._____
2. It takes a lot for me to get upset or lose my temper._____
3. My feelings are easily hurt._____
4. I can usually see both sides of a dispute._____
5. I have many types of friends, from many walks of life._____
6. I prefer pastels—tropical blues, pale yellows, quiet pinks._____
7. I'm adaptable; toss me into an unfamiliar situation and I'll make it work to my advantage._____
8. My emotions are right out front; essentially, what you see is what you get._____
9. I had an imaginary playmate when I was a kid._____
10. I am very close to animals; they gravitate toward me._____

If most of your yes answers fell into the A section, then you're strongest as a sender; if the B section got the most yes answers, then your strength is as a receiver. Neither is better than the other. They are merely different.

At certain times in your life, you may find that you're better at sending than receiving or vice versa. Crisis circumstances tend to give you strength in the area where you have been weakest. Also, when you're intimately involved with someone, when all your emotions are engaged, you flip back and forth between the two.

I used to think of women as strong receivers, perhaps because their yin energy is usually so dominant. But those easy categories and divisions seem to be changing and I've concluded that nothing, especially gender, is so cut and dried.

In general, I've found that people with water and earth moons are primarily receptive; people with air and fire moons are best as transmitters. But don't take my word for it. Experiment on your own, with a partner. In Appendix 1, find the moon sign for your partner—your significant other, a friend, a co-worker. The element of that person's moon sign should be different than yours, and in one of the opposing elements. If you've got an air or fire sign moon, then select someone whose moon is in earth or water; if you're earth or water, choose someone who is air or fire.

The person whose moon sign falls into the transmitter group should, at some unexpected point in the course of a day, "send" something to the receiver. Keep it simple at first. Make sure the other person agrees to the experiment. Keep notes on what happens.

Usually, the receiver expresses whatever the transmitter has "sent" in a relatively short period of time. In crisis situations, this can happen almost instantaneously; under ordinary circumstances, it can take from a few minutes to as long as thirty. If it doesn't work the first time, try it again and increase your *intent*. Whatever the transmitter sends to the receiver will be expressed in a way that is in keeping with the receiver's personality and intuitive capacity. It might be words, a visual image, an idea. You'll recognize it.

Your Intuitive Moon

The next twelve chapters describe the moon signs. They are described in terms of "the journey," the child, the "hidden" or shadow side of the particular moon sign, and the intuitive part of the sign. Activities are included with each sign that are designed to trigger the intuition. Have fun with them. Approach them with a sense of playfulness. And watch how your intuition deepens. Now turn to *your* moon sign.

5

Aries Moon

Cardinal, Fire
Ruler: Mars

The Journey

No doubt about it—you're a fearless pioneer, a dynamo whose emotions are the fuel that moves you from point A to point B in half the time it takes someone else to travel the same distance. When your passions are aroused, you have almost no equal in getting the job done. The challenge for you lies in sustaining that passion when your interest begins to wane.

Since the moon also represents your experience of your mother, your mom is undoubtedly a whirlwind of energy who encouraged your independence from a very young age. She wasn't the type to coddle and baby you. If you came inside crying from a skinned knee, she tended to it and sent you back outside to play. But if you ever got into serious difficulties, she was your fiercest defender.

You have a quick temper, but rarely hold grudges. When your anger is channeled in constructive ways, it enables you to break through restrictive beliefs and obstacles. Anger, in fact, is the one emotion that you express most consistently. You avoid other emotions through constant activity, forever looking outward, then surprise yourself and others when you explode suddenly and seemingly without provocation.

You aren't the world's most patient person. This is readily apparent when other people *just don't get it*. In this case, "it" is whatever seems obvious to you but not to others. In this same vein of impatience, any kind of waiting is anathema to you. Traffic, lines in stores, airport delays: it's enough to drive you nuts. Even if you're a *Star Wars* fan, you probably weren't camped out in front of any theater for *your* tickets. You would be more inclined to send a patient friend or significant other in your place.

You pride yourself on your self-sufficiency, and why shouldn't you? You've spent time and energy developing that part of yourself. You may have invested so much energy in self-sufficiency, however, that it's difficult for you to depend on others when it would certainly lighten your own load. You also don't like to feel vulnerable, which makes it tough for you to lower your guard and defenses—even if you're in need of comforting and hugs from the people who love you most.

Aries really isn't a comfortable placement for the moon. This cardinal fire sign requires so much action, busyness, and activity that you don't have time for reflection. But you should strive to make time; otherwise, events and situations may force you to do so. You're an emotionally complex person and benefit enormously from unraveling the labyrinth of your emotions.

In relation to other people you like to be the leader, and this trait was probably apparent from the time you were a youngster. You're not interested in power for the sake of power; you just like calling the shots and having the freedom to do what you want to do, when you want to do it.

The sign of Aries rules the head and face, the upper teeth, surgical procedures, headaches and colds, fevers and inflammations, burns and skin eruptions. If your emotions (moon) are blocked, your health can be affected in the areas that Aries rules.

The Aries Moon Child

This child may make you gray before your time, but every gray hair will be worth it. She's the neighborhood pioneer, completely fearless and into everything, a leader before she hits the ripe old age of two. Her impatience and zeal demand constant stimulation and her energy level never seems to wane. Forget naps for this kid, unless she's totally worn out or sick.

She can be an early reader when encouraged, especially if Mom or Dad are doing the reading. She needs that kind of parental closeness. Quiet time is important to this child's emotional balance and instills an appreciation for the art of reflection.

You can expect strays of every type and shape to grace your doorstep throughout her childhood. She has a natural affinity with animals, and learns compassion through her interactions with them. Compassion is an important lesson for the Aries moon child; it helps temper her impatience and know-it-all attitude.

Her sense of security in life lies in *doing.* The sooner you, as her parent, understand this, the smoother your relationship will be. It's as if her prime directive is to *experience* the entire smorgasbord of physical life. Her nemesis, though, may be her tendency to experience everything *now, this instant.* If you encourage her at a young age to talk about what she feels, then later in life her emotions won't seem as foreign to her as they might be otherwise.

The Aries moon child is usually very intuitive and may enjoy the exercises at the end of this chapter, particularly if you do them with her. The practice helps to cultivate the intuitive and reflective part of her nature.

If your Aries moon child was born under a new moon in which both sun and moon are in Aries, then the Aries characteristics are enhanced. If she's born under a full moon (sun in Libra, moon in Aries), then relationships are going to be a major focus in her life.

Hidden Aries

Your bravado and constant activity make the core of who you are invisible to most people. In fact, that core may be invisible to you as well. To really understand your fundamental nature, your very roots, go back to basic mythology.

Remember Mars, the Roman god of war? He rules Aries. In fact, the Greeks referred to Mars as *Ares.* He was the son of Jupiter (the Greek Zeus) and Juno (the Greeks called her Hera). By most accounts, he loved battle and thought nothing of taking what he wanted, even if that something belonged to someone else. He favored dragons, vultures, and dogs. He hardly sounds like the type you'd take home to meet Mom.

On the other hand, Mars got things done. He was *focused*, courageous, aggressive, a defender and a fighter. He never took "no" for an answer. He was a leader who acted independently of the consensus of opinion. Sound familiar?

If Mars had turned some of his enormous energy toward reflection and introspection, he might not have been so eager to rush into war. He might have tempered his physical aggression, admitted that he really didn't know everything, and that his way wasn't always the best way. This would have damaged the Roman pantheon, but made Mars much more pleasant to be around.

With an Aries moon, you should use the strengths of Mars to excavate your own unconscious and make the invisible visible and the unknown known. This doesn't mean you have to meditate an hour a day, or go through therapy. Just apply some of the Aries energy to understanding yourself, through whatever means is comfortable for you.

Instead of fuming when you're stuck in traffic, explore why you feel so impatient and irritable. Is it because you're running late or because you feel things at work (or at home or wherever) will fall apart unless you're there? If it's the latter, why do you feel your presence is so essential to the success of any endeavor? This sort of emotional probing will probably annoy you at first. It'll go against your grain. But if you keep at it, you'll begin to recognize and understand your emotional patterns.

If you enjoy the outdoors, you may find that your best times for reflection happen while swimming, hiking, or even puttering in your yard. This type of reflection doesn't require any rigid schedule or anything other than a willingness to reflect. If physical activity isn't your thing, you might try keeping a journal and writing about what you feel. Again, this practice doesn't have to follow any set schedule. The point is to allow your emotions to move through you and to explore them consciously.

What are the broad patterns? How do they influence events and relationships in your life now—and in the past? How can you best utilize your emotions and willpower to create your future? To reach goals? To find the right house? To meet the love of your life?

Intuitive Aries

A young man writes a medical thriller while still in med school and it's published under a pseudonym because he doesn't want any of the other students to know he has written a novel. By the time he has graduated, he has written another novel, this one with a definite science fiction edge, which he also sells, this time under his real name. It is also made into a movie.

The young man never does get around to the practice of medicine. He's too busy writing bestselling novels in which he creates and *pioneers* new worlds: *The Andromeda Strain*, *West World*, *Sphere*, *Terminal Man*, *Jurassic Park*, *The Lost World*. Michael Crichton also wrote a nonfiction book called *Travels*, an intimate look at his spiritual and intuitive quest. It spans the continents that Crichton traveled in search of answers. He doesn't really divulge the central question, but maybe he didn't know what the question was. Maybe the question mattered less than the journey itself.

When you read *Travels*, you're really in the company of someone with an Aries moon. He's pioneering, uncovering, discovering, and you can taste what he tastes, hear what he hears, doubt and believe as he does. His quest somehow becomes yours.

During a live chat on the Internet shortly before the release of *Jurassic Park*, Crichton said that the idea for the book had occurred to him years earlier. But twenty years ago, the technology didn't exist to extract DNA from insects fossilized in amber, so he had to wait until the technology caught up with his idea. By then, computerized special effects also had evolved to the point where realistic dinosaurs could be created for the big screen. True to his Aries (full) moon, Crichton pioneered a unique concept which became a publishing and film phenomenon.

As a cardinal fire sign, your Aries moon naturally seeks to pioneer, to seed, to forge ahead, and often does so in a spontaneous yet focused manner. Your intuition works in the same way, spontaneously, in sudden flashes of "knowing," and as impulses to do something you haven't consciously considered or which may seem uncharacteristic of you.

Many of us have been taught to distrust our impulses, as though they might drive us to do something terrible if we indulge them. While this sort of restriction may have been necessary when we were toddlers and felt like running out into the middle of a road, there's no reason to carry the pattern into adulthood. An impulse is an urge toward creative growth. By squashing or ignoring an impulse, you cut off this potential for growth. It's like that Robert Frost poem about the fork in the path. If you don't follow the impulse, you'll always wonder about the road not taken.

Rita, a young woman with an Aries (crescent) moon, was going through a divorce and needed to find a place to live for herself, her two kids, and their assorted pets. Every house she looked at was either too expensive or didn't allow animals. Then, one afternoon when she left work, she had an impulse to take a long way home, through a neighborhood that had always seemed way out of her league. She hesitated about doing it because she was tired and just wanted to get home, but the impulse won.

On a shaded street she'd never noticed before, she found a house for rent that had a fenced yard. Instead of just jotting down the phone number, she went up to the front door and rang the bell. The result? She and the owner hit it off and a month later, Rita, her kids, and their pets were in their new home.

For Rita, intuition worked through an impulse. For Jim, a New Moon Aries, intuition rarely informs him of something he *should* do, only what he *shouldn't* do. "It most often stirs when I'm meeting someone new. Even if the first impression seems to be positive, I can feel it in my gut that it's negative. To me, my instinct is the first, very first, response that pops into my head. Many times I think *no* and say *yes*. I don't listen. I shrug it off."

You, like Rita and Jim and so many of us, may have a natural inclination to shrug off impulses and intuitive impressions. It's most likely a habitual response, endemic to a society where logic and reason are given more credence than intuition. When your intuition is working, your left brain is acting like a petty dictator, tossing out objections and arguments, ordering you not to listen.

Before you can take full advantage of your intuition, you have to shut off the voice of the petty dictator, that irrepressible censor. The best way to do this is to ignore the internal ruckus that immediately follows an impulse or impression. But "best" may not necessarily be easy or simple, at least not in the beginning.

Creating a Sacred Space

When I want to get away from the activity around the house for a while, I retreat with a book to a spot near a mango tree in my yard. Here, the sun warms my feet, birds twitter and fuss, butterflies cast fleeting shadows against my lap. I can hear laughter and splashing from the pool across the street, music from a passing car, and the whisper of the breeze through the branches. Usually, one of my cats or the dog join me outside, content to laze by my side. No one bothers me here, the phone, fax, and computer are all out of reach.

I've come to think of this spot as my sacred place. It grounds and refreshes me. I have gone there in many different moods, at many different times of the day and night. The details are vivid to me—the smell and texture of the grass, the sweet scent of mangos ripening on the trees, the rich blue curves of sky, the tiny wildlife humming and buzzing in the blades of grass.

When I need mental space, it's this physical place that I conjure up, that I recreate in my mind. Over the years, I've found that I can create this mental space regardless of where I am physically—on a plane, in the car, at a mall, at a party, it doesn't matter. When I want to listen to my intuition, I "go" to this sacred place and pull its calm into myself. If I'm centered, the censor's voice has a tougher time making itself heard. My intuition flows more freely. My cardinal moon, like yours, needs to be redirected at times and this little mental exercise is a great way of doing it. Shutting up the censor is an added bonus.

This mental place that you create can be anything or anywhere. It was helpful for me to mold it after a real place because it made the details more vivid. But it can be an imaginary place, or somewhere in another era. It can even be a place that you sketch or that you create on paper. Wherever it is, the point is that you should feel comfortable there. Make it as real as possible, adding textural details, colors, shading, smells, tastes. Engage all of your senses.

If you're in the middle of a mall or driving your car, it isn't too smart to shut your eyes and conjure your sacred place. It's helpful to have some sort of signal that allows the shift in consciousness to take place naturally. You may want to roll your eyes quickly upward, toward the hairline between your eyes. Or maybe a double tap of your right or left foot or a certain phrase repeated to yourself will do the trick.

Once you feel the place taking shape around you, let its calmness and serenity suffuse your senses. Then listen to your intuition and your impulses without the voice of your censor confusing things.

During Crichton's Internet chat, he said that when he starts a book, he gets up very early in the morning, writes for several hours, breaks for lunch, then goes back to writing. As the book progresses, he gets up earlier and earlier until he isn't sleeping at all. In this way, he finishes the actual writing in about a month. This sure sounds like an Aries moon—plunge ahead until the job is either done or you've lost interest. Perhaps Crichton's sacred place is his sleeplessness—an intense, focused marathon to the finish line. It may not be calm the way the rest of us figure calm should be, but you go with whatever works.

Testing Your Intuition

In the exploration chart that follows, write out a single question. Keep it simple and focused. It should be something that can be answered in a relatively short period of time—several days to a week—so that you, the most impatient of moon signs, don't lose interest. Then create your sacred space in your mind, pose the question silently, and let your intuition answer it.

Go with your first impression and jot down as much detail about it as you can. Remind yourself that what's at work here is synchronicity, a kind of collision between the inner and outer you. Remember that the answer may be symbolic. If you ask a simple yes or no question, you may feel the answer somewhere in your body. Date the question and the answer. When the event or situation happens, make note of this, too.

If you want confirmation of the answer you get, try a dictionary reading. This is a simple predictive technique in which you pose your question, open a dictionary, and point at a word or phrase. When you do this with a sincere intention, the results can be astonishingly accurate, and flesh out your own intuitive impressions.

The point of using an external confirmation is to develop trust in your own abilities so that you can eventually do away with tools. The ideal is that in the very near future, you'll be able to signal your intuition in whatever way you've chosen to do so, pose your question, and get an answer.

ARIES EXPLORATION

Date: _____

Question: _____

_____

_____

Answer: _____

_____

_____

_____

_____

What actually happened: _____

_____

_____

Engaging Your Senses

Our senses are constantly at work, conveying information to us about our immediate environment. We can tell by the smell of the air if rain is on the way. A shadow in our peripheral vision alerts us to someone else's presence. The taste of food tells us whether or not it's fresh. Our senses alert us to danger and to exercise caution and they also alert us to the other extreme, pleasurable situations and people, and to everything in between.

Our senses are often our most immediate and direct connection with our intuition. But in the hustle and bustle of daily life, we sometimes don't pay attention to what they tell us. We're all guilty of it. Since your Aries moon makes you emotionally rash and impulsive, you often ignore what your senses are telling you. The following activity is intended to engage all of your senses.

YOUR SENSES

Describe a place in as much detail as possible. It can be anywhere—the place where you are right this second, a location you've visited, a city, town, park, river, hotel, museum. Use all of your senses when describing this place. *Be fully there.*

_____

_____

_____

_____

_____

_____

You've just answered a question without knowing what the question is. Your intuition knew, though, and through this sensory exercise answered the question.

Now turn to Intuitive Reality Check #2, Chapter 17, to see what question you've answered in this activity.

6

Taurus Moon

Fixed, Earth
Ruler: Venus

The Journey

The moon loves Taurus nearly as much as it loves Cancer, the sign that it rules. In Taurus, the lunar energies work smoothly, effortlessly, and that makes your intuition easier to develop and use.

Many astrologers draw analogies between Taurus and Ferdinand the bull. The author probably wasn't thinking about Taurus when he created the character, but Ferdinand is the perfect archetype for Taurus. Ferdinand enjoyed peaceful surroundings and so do you. In fact, peacefulness and harmony are vital to your emotional well-being. You need these qualities the way a Gemini moon needs books or education or communication with other people. It usually takes a lot to anger you, but repeated provocation can trigger your "bull's rush" fury, the human equivalent of Ferdinand's reaction to the bee-sting. Some of the things that can set you off are: incessant nagging by someone who wants you to do something you don't want to do; insistence that you act in a particular way; unreasonable demands or actions by anyone.

This isn't to say that all of these things will send you ballistic. Generally, though, you and your Taurus sun brother don't tolerate violation of your private space, whatever that space happens to be. If someone stumbles into your private zone, they not only discover your bull's rush, but they find out just how stubborn the bull can be. This moon sign is the most stubborn in the zodiac. And when you dig in your heels, nothing can force you to move—no threat, no enticement, no promised seduction.

As a fixed moon sign, you are slow to change your opinions—and your feelings. This is a "prove it to me" moon. *You love me? You want to be with me? Prove it to me. Intuition is natural? Prove it to me.* The fixed nature of Taurus makes you somewhat conservative, especially when it comes to finances and your personal possessions.

The moon represents your experience of *the person who nurtured you.* For many of us, that's Mom, but for some it's Dad, or a grandparent, an aunt, etc. Your experience as a child was about as good as it gets. Your mother, or primary nurturer, was always there for you with soothing words, a lap to crawl into, cookies after school. She made you feel secure and loved.

I know a number of Taurus moon women whose primary nurturers were their fathers. Edie, a massage therapist, is still closer to her father than she is to her mother. His profession as an alternative healer deeply influenced her own choice of profession and molded her compassion and empathy for others.

Although physical appearance usually is connected with your ascendant (or the sign that was rising at your birth), many Taurus moon people have the thick neck and broad shoulders that mark the sign. They may also have a tendency to gain weight, since Taurus in general often turns to comfort foods when stressed or upset.

Taurus rules the neck, throat, and cervical vertebrae. When you're emotionally blocked or upset, you're likely to feel the tension in these areas of your body.

The Taurus Moon Child

That adage about still waters running deep definitely fits this child. Under that mellow exterior lies a mystic in the making, a rich, curious mind that seeks to make connections between inner and outer experiences. The child, like the adult he becomes, explores his inner life through vivid dreams, books, nature, and some form of art or music. This is a creative moon sign and even from a young age, that creativity needs an outlet.

As a parent, the major obstacle you'll come up against with your

Taurus moon child is his stubbornness. You can't force or cajole him to do something he finds objectionable. And forget time out. It won't phase him. He'll simply outwait you. If he does something you don't like, it's best to explain to him the whats and whys of your feelings.

Your Taurus moon child is naturally introspective. If you want to know what's going on inside him, you'll have to ask, to draw him out, to encourage him to express his feelings, concerns, and curiosities. He loves being outdoors and some of your closest times together happen when you're canoeing, camping, hiking, or just sitting together under a splendid night sky.

When this child is young, expose him to the vast smorgasbord of the arts—music, drawing, theater, writing. The more he's exposed to, the greater his opportunities for finding the right creative outlet.

Hidden Taurus

Back to mythology. Venus, as the ruler of Taurus, holds the key to understanding the invisible side of your personality. Venus, known as Aphrodite among the ancient Greeks, was the babe of the Roman pantheon. Born to Jupiter and Diane, she was the goddess of beauty and had the power to grant beauty to other people. She was honored in the poetry of Chaucer and Shakespeare. Along with her son, Cupid, she presided over the affairs of lovers. As the ruler of Taurus, she confers deep sensuality that extends to all physical experiences in life.

Your senses are highly developed and serve you well as the vehicle through which you explore and learn about your world. For you, sex isn't just a physical experience, but is often transformative. If you cook, the food you prepare isn't simply food; it's art. When you dress, you're aware of how the fabric feels against your skin. When you're involved in outdoor activities, you're acutely aware of the scent of the air and the grass, the stretching of muscles in your body, the brilliance of the sky. In other words, none of your sensory impressions escape you.

At the extreme, a Taurus moon can produce a hedonist—Mick Jagger, for instance. But at the other end, it also produces people with incredible artistic or musical talents—Dionne Warwick and Katharine Hepburn are prime examples.

While the Aries moon needs to tone down the hustle and bustle in life, you simply need to learn to trust your initial impressions. The quickest way to do that is to dispense with the prove-it-to-me stuff and to shove aside your resistance to change. Okay, so that may not be any easier for you to do than it is for an Aries moon to slow down and look within. But you have such natural intuitive talent that a little effort on your part will go a very long way.

So where do you start?

Intuitive Taurus

As a fixed earth sign, your body registers not only tensions, but your intuitive impressions as well. The spot in your body where you feel the impression is often as revealing as the impression itself.

Let's say, for instance, that you've agreed to meet a business associate for dinner, but have to cancel because several hours before you suddenly develop a painful stiff neck, the weakest part of the Taurus anatomy. Before you run to your massage therapist or chiropractor, before you start applying cold packs, ask yourself if the individual you were supposed to meet for dinner is "a pain in the neck." Be honest about it. No one has to know this except you. If you decide that yes, this individual is a pain in the neck, then take steps to limit your association with the person, if at all possible. If you decide the person isn't a pain in the neck, then take stock of your immediate environment and figure out who or what is. Or ask yourself if you're being "stiff" or rigid about something.

Any kind of body symptom is your intuition trying to seize your attention. Some symptoms, like the stiff neck, are easy to figure out, although the cause may take some honest probing. Other symptoms may be as complex as whatever caused them. For Chris, an Aquarian with a Taurus moon, gall bladder problems several years ago put her in the hospital. I looked at transits (daily movement of the planets) to her birth chart, but didn't see any health problems that would result in hospitalization. Since the gall bladder is involved in digestion of fats, I suspected she was having trouble "digesting" something in her life.

As it turned out, she was trying to "digest" the fact (fats?) that her marriage was ending and that she would have to confront it and deal with it. But because Taurus is a fixed sign and tends to be very loyal, she hung in there for another two years. During that time, she developed an acid reflex in her esophagus. The esophagus is part of the fifth energy center or chakra, which has to do with communication. My take on this was that Chris wasn't expressing her anger and disappointment about the demise of her marriage and that she hadn't informed her husband that she wanted a divorce.

Now that she's divorced, her health problems have cleared up.

Any time I see these kinds of intuitive metaphors involved in health and the body, particularly among fixed signs, I recommend three books: Louise Hay's *You Can Heal Your Life* (Hay House, 1987), Carolyn Myss's *Anatomy of the Spirit* (Random House, 1997), and Mona Lisa Schultz's *Awakening Intuition* (Three Rivers Press, 1999). Each of these women is a medical intuitive and each has her own particular take on the role of intuition in the maintenance of physical, emotional, and spiritual health.

Your intuition may also speak to you through "gut feelings," hunches, dreams, and any sort of creative work. In 1898, author Morgan Robertson published a novel called *The Wreck of the Titan* about the maiden voyage of a transatlantic ship called *Titan* that hit an iceberg and sank. Fourteen years later, the *Titanic* hit an iceberg and sank. The similarities between the fictional *Titan* and the *Titanic* were eerie. In both instances, the wreck occurred in April. In the novel, three thousand people lost their lives; in the real world, over twenty-two hundred people were killed. The number of lifeboats differed by only four. Both ships had three propellers. The length of the fictional and the real ship differed by a mere eighty-two feet. Robertson's intuition flowed through his writing.

Right about now you're probably saying, *Yeah, fine—but prove it to me.*

Proving It: How Your Inner Oracle Works

I can't prove it to you; you have to prove it to yourself. So let's have some fun. In the Taurus exploration section, jot down one question that you really want or need an answer to. It can be a simple yes/no question or something more complex. Below the question, write: *The next voice I hear will answer my question or provide additional information about it.* Then turn on the radio or the TV.

I suggest writing the above phrase, because the act of writing often makes your intent that much clearer to your unconscious mind. Eventually, you won't have to write the above phrase; you'll merely think it with sincere intent and that will be enough. If you already know how to do this, then either play along or skip the exercise.

Some years ago, my husband was waiting for a call from an editor about a project. I was out running errands and on my way home wondered if the editor had called Rob while I was gone. I was feeling pretty tense and irritable about the whole thing because there had been repeated delays and I knew he was fed up with waiting. Within sixty seconds, I saw a white truck headed toward me, coming from my neighborhood. As it passed, I read the sign on the side and exploded with laughter. The name of the company was the editor's last name. I knew Rob had gotten his call and the project.

Your answer can come from virtually anywhere—the radio, the TV, the Net, a person, a book, or the side of a truck. Again, it's synchronicity in action. *An external event confirms or answers a concern that you have.*

In certain spiritual traditions, intent is vital. It's the key. It's everything. By "intent" I mean the motive, passion, and need behind your question. In life, your intent often makes the difference between wishing and obtaining, between hope and tangible results.

Now have fun with the exploration!

TAURUS EXPLORATION

Date: _____

My question: _____

My intent: _____

My answer came through: _____

My interpretation:_____

_____

_____

This type of exercise should boost your trust quotient in your own abilities. Your challenge, after all, isn't like that of the Aries moon, who has to learn to slow down and listen. You listen constantly to your intuition. But most of the time, you mull over what it says and argue with yourself about whether or not to believe it. You're the prototype of the doubting Thomas, the skeptic who really wants to believe but has to overcome a hundred self-imposed hurdles to do it.

Other Tricks

In her book *The Artists' Way*, author Julia Cameron explores the connection between intuition and creativity. To awaken the inner muse, she advises writing morning pages—three handwritten pages that express what you're feeling, why you're feeling it, or any other thing you want to write about. The act of writing first thing in the morning provides a bridge to the inner self, that secret self that feels and thinks things it shares with no one else.

There is a certain sensuality in this which will appeal to one side of you, even while the other side insists you should be doing something more productive. If that other side starts to win, think of this. Diarist Anaïs Nin chronicled most of her adult life in pages like Cameron's "morning pages." To read even a single volume of her work is to understand what it means when we say, "a rich inner life."

In writing, Nin ordered her life. She imposed a structure on it. She attached meaning to who she was. She lived closer to the core of her intuition. In writing, she transcended who she was and became something larger. *She connected with her intuition and it transformed her life.*

If the morning pages don't interest you, then at the very least keep a small notebook with you—in a pocket, your car, your brief-case, wherever it's convenient. Here, you can jot down whatever you're feeling, positive or negative, as well as any intuitive insights you have, then explore them later at your leisure. The point is to keep a record, which serves to confirm your intuitive impressions.

Engaging Your Senses

Your Taurus moon is well-suited to sensory information. And because you tend to mull things over, you usually pay attention to what that sensory information is telling you. So for you, the following exercise is merely to flex your sensory muscles.

YOUR SENSES

Describe a place in as much detail as possible. It can be anywhere—the place where you are right this second, a location you've visited, a city, town, park, river, hotel, museum. Use all your senses when describing this place. *Be fully there.*

You've just answered a question without knowing what the question is. Your intuition knew, though, and through this sensory exercise answered the question.

Now turn to Intuitive Reality Check #2, Chapter 17, to see what question you've answered.

7

Gemini Moon

Mutable, Air
Ruler: Mercury

The Journey

Your nemesis is boredom. If you were put in a bare room without windows, books, TV, radio, computer, paper or pen, phone, fax, or anything else, you would freak within the hour. This may be true of the other air sign moons as well, but for the Gemini moon, it's a sure thing. Your emotional well-being needs mental stimulation and the means to communicate with others.

Gemini is a dual sign, symbolized by the twins. The only other sign that is represented by two of anything is Pisces—the two fish. The standing joke about Geminis—sun, moon, or rising—is that you're never sure which one comes down to breakfast in the morning. Is it the upbeat, witty twin? Or the sullen twin? Sometimes, you're not even sure yourself which twin is dominant on a given day.

One thing is for sure, though—your wit and mental quickness are among your strongest assets. You can talk to virtually anyone, anywhere, any time, and you can talk about almost anything. You have an excellent memory for trivia and when the trivia is backed by strong emotion, your memory is nothing short of incredible. You're adept at stringing together seemingly disparate bits of information and putting them together in new ways.

The general consensus about this moon sign is that it produces shallow people who are capable of rationalizing virtually anything they do—or don't do. But generalities like this rarely give the full picture and don't do justice to the sign. You feel with your mind. This may sound like an oxymoron to a Scorpio or Cancer moon, but it's business as usual for you.

When your emotions shift into overdrive, you cope by trying to figure out what you're feeling and why. Since you don't react to emotional situations the way other moon signs do, you are sometimes perceived as being cold or distant. But if you try to change to suit other people's expectations, if you try to become something you're not, you'll end up feeling miserable.

As the quintessential mutable sign, Gemini dislikes confronting obstacles head on. In terms of the moon, this means you tend to move around emotional obstacles rather than plow your way through them. If the emotional heat becomes too strong, you simply change what you feel or adapt to the situation. Your adaptability, humor, and innate curiosity are all part of your survival package.

Your moon sign governs your experience with your mother—or whoever was your primary nurturer. It's likely that your mother is one of those people who is always on the move. When you were a kid, she nurtured your intellect with books, lots of talk and ideas, and encouraged you to express what you felt. Your childhood home may have been chaotic, with people coming and going all the time, and lots of intellectual discussions.

Education is a primary force in your life and one of your security blankets. It feeds your thirst for facts and nurtures your emotional security. In fact, your greatest security lies in understanding something thoroughly enough to be able to explain it to others. The urge for communication is so strong with this moon sign that it usually makes for excellent teachers, writers, comedians, and public relations people.

Gemini rules the parts of the upper body that come in pairs— lungs, arms, shoulders, and hands. When you're emotionally blocked or upset, these are the areas where you're most likely to feel it.

The Gemini Moon Child

She's there, then—oops—she's gone. That's how quick this kid is. She's quick mentally, too. You rarely have to explain something more than once to this child. Her little mind is quite literally a sponge that soaks up every random bit of information and seeks to connect it to other random bits.

The main challenge with this child is her impatience. She wants everything yesterday. The world just doesn't move quickly enough for her. Impatience and curiosity combine in a way that produces endless questions. Why is the sky blue? What is God? How did I get here? And, of course, the traveling question: *Are we there yet?*

When she's very young, she enjoys being read to. This seems to trigger her passion for books, so this child is often an early reader. She loves stories in any medium, though, and may be particularly fond of movies. As she gets older, her own storytelling ability starts to shine. As a natural tangent, she's usually good at word games, too.

The Gemini moon child can be quite prescient, especially if her intuition is encouraged and nurtured at a young age. If she's raised to believe in her own intuitive abilities, then she moves through life with her intuition as her greatest and most loyal ally.

Hidden Gemini

The winged messenger: in Roman mythology, he was known as Mercury. The Greeks called him Hermes. In both cultures, he was the guardian of travelers, the god of oratory. He was always symbolized as a youthful person who had a hat with small wings that allowed him to become invisible, and he wore winged sandals that permitted him to move very fast. All of these characteristics are folded into the sign of Gemini—mental and physical quickness and agility, the gift of gab, the freedom-loving traveler. But beneath all this, remains the essential enigma. Did anyone *really* know Mercury? Does anyone *really* know you? Do you really know yourself?

The hidden Gemini is the twin who lives beneath the rush and flurry of your normal days, the one who goes along for the ride as long as she's in the mood, then jumps ship for some solitude. She's the one who has to digest what the other twin has learned. Her job is assimilation. And the way she assimilates most efficiently is through her intuition.

For you, intuition can seem haphazard because it comes to you in a variety of ways: through touch, a hunch, an intense certainty about something, dreams, clairvoyance, clairaudience. But your best venue for intuition may be communication. When you write, talk, draw, dance, play music, act, or *do something that conveys ideas or beliefs* to other people, then you're *plugged in* to something larger than yourself. You're *emotionally involved* and your intuition comes through loud and clear.

Janice is a fifty-two-year-old high school teacher, a skier, a runner, mother of two. Two years ago, while she and her husband were out jogging, Tom suddenly clutched his chest, keeled over, and died of a massive heart attack before he hit the ground. In about ten seconds, Janice's entire life turned inside out.

In the aftermath, Janice grappled with grief and depression that her doctor tried to fix by prescribing an antidepressant. With her Gemini moon, the moon that really doesn't want to plunge into the unpleasant morass of emotions, she should have loved the happy pill. She could have stayed on that happy pill for the rest of her life.

Instead, she quickly realized the happy pills blocked the very emotions that she needed to reconcile if she was ever to heal from her husband's sudden death. So she stopped taking them and tried to work through her feelings in a journal. This led to poetry, an artistic expression of what she felt, a structure for emotional healing.

GOING THE DISTANCE

How far is it?
One mile to a date?
Two miles to a kiss?
Three miles to intimacy?
Four miles to long term love?
10K to commitment?
Marathon to marriage?
Run away from the rock.
Run till your heart bursts
Or you are alone
Whichever comes first.
Run toward the light,
But it eludes you

Becoming dark as you approach.
Run till you both see It.
Before you hit the Wall.
Run till your rhythm is his rhythm
And vice-versa.
Run till your hearts beat together
And cannot be separated.
Run till you no longer ask,
"How far is it to the Finish?"
Because you know the Finish won't be the End.
And you still must go the Distance.

—Janice Cutbush, October 28, 1998, 4:00 A.M.
Ballston Spa, NY

When she chose to explore her emotions and committed to whatever that journey entailed, she chose life.

Intuitive Gemini

Okay, here's the nitty gritty. Go buy a journal. Or open a journal directory on your computer. Then get busy keeping track of what you feel and why you feel it. You may surprise yourself and come up with insights in your journal that might have escaped you otherwise.

Once you get into the rhythm of keeping a journal, you may want to experiment with your insights and intuitions. One woman with a Gemini moon wanted to develop her precognitive ability, so she experimented by trying to tune in on tomorrow's headlines. She practiced visualizing the front page of a newspaper with tomorrow's date and headlines. Then she would check her impressions against the actual headlines the next day. With practice, she became pretty good at this. But the most important part of the exercise was that it gave her intuitive self permission to flex its muscles, to stretch, to expand.

If keeping a journal isn't your thing, then try recalling and recording your dreams. There are numerous books on working with your dreams, but the basics don't change from system to system:

1. State your intent. This is best done as you're falling asleep and should be kept as simple as possible. *I'd like some intuitive guidance on my relationship with* . . . Or: *Which job should I accept?* If you're looking for intuitive information about the future, rather than guidance, then state your question in a way that makes it clear. *What's going to happen with so and so or such and such in the next week?*

2. Request that you recall the dream. Be specific when you make this request. Since your subconscious mind takes your requests literally, don't ask that you wake up after every dream! It's wiser to request that you wake up after the dream that answers your need or question.

3. Record the dream. You can either keep a notebook under your pillow or a tape recorder next to your bed. I've done both and find the notebook easier.

4. Decipher the symbols. The problem with dream dictionaries is that the definitions of the symbols aren't specific to you. As you work with your dreams, certain symbols will begin to leap out at you, personal symbols. Other symbols will be archetypal—the wise old man or woman; the innocent child; the spooky house.

5. Put it all together. The meaning of some dreams will be completely obvious once you read over what you've written. But other dreams will seem obtuse, mystifying, maybe even incomprehensible, until the day that certain images from the dream replay themselves in your life.

Since Gemini moons are as social as Gemini suns, you may want to join a group that is exploring your intuitive interests. Thanks to the Internet, you don't even have to leave home to do this now.

Before You Commit

Before you run out and invest in a journal, tape recorder, or an online service, be sure it's what you want to do. You, like Aries, need to be convinced that something is worth your time and interest before you fully commit to it. For the Aries moon, this happens after the initial, passionate plunge. But for you, the need for commitment and convincing may happen on your second or third pass through the neighborhood.

In other words, maybe this intuition stuff interested you twenty years ago but then you got sidetracked. Twelve years ago, it might have seized your interest again, but you got distracted. Now here you are again. So let's test your current intuitive level and let you decide whether you're up to this particular journey.

In this activity, you're going to use a divination tool to deepen your intuition. In the preliminary stage of your intuitive development, tools like this can be immensely helpful, and bolster your confidence in your intuitive abilities. The tool you'll be using is color. This type of tool, like any divination device, works because of synchronicity; the colors you select *create a pattern that depicts an inner condition.*

Think of a simple question that is important to you, and jot it down. Under the question, list five colors as they come immediately to mind. Choose your colors without thinking about and analyzing it. This exercise is designed to bolster your self-confidence. Have fun with it, let loose!

GEMINI EXPLORATION

My question: _____

_____

My five colors:

1. _____   4. _____

2. _____   5. _____

3. _____

This activity is adapted from *The Rainbow Oracle,* by Rob Mac-Gregor and Tony Grosso (Ballantine Books, 1988), a system of color divination. The book comes with a set of colored cubes that are tossed as a question is asked. The meanings of the five color positions are: (1) the issue, your question; (2) the challenge or obstacle; (3) what is emerging; (4) what's visible, the now, the moment; (5) the resolution. Refer to table 4, chapter 17, to determine your answers.

For an example of how to interpret your color choices to arrive at your answer, see the Rainbow Oracle reading in Chapter 17. If you've chosen a color that isn't listed in table 5, then you'll have to interpolate. Let's say you chose tan in the second place, the challenge or obstacle. Tan is a mixture of brown and white, so it would mean that you need to develop an intuitive understanding of your security needs. What do you need for a solid foundation?

Convinced Yet?

If you're now convinced that you want to commit to journaling or dream work, then by all means buy your journal, tape recorder, or whatever tools you need. If you're not convinced, then work through the exercises in the Intuitive Reality Check sections. There's enough diversity in them to keep your restless spirit busy.

Engaging Your Senses

You're usually in such a hurry, rushing around and into so many things, that you may overlook the information that your senses convey. This can be simple information about the temperature of the air or more complex stuff, like the mood that predominates in a room when you walk into it. Your senses are your most immediate and direct approach to your intuitive self. In the following exercise, you're going to really flex your sensory muscles.

YOUR SENSES

Describe a place in as much detail as possible. It can be anywhere—the place where you are right this second, a location you've visited, a city, town, park, river, hotel, museum. Use all your senses when describing this place. *Be fully there.*

_____

_____

_____

_____

_____

_____

You've just answered a question without knowing what the question is. Your intuition knew, though, and through this sensory exercise answered the question.

Now turn to Intuitive Reality Check #2, Chapter 17, to see what question you've answered.

8

Cancer Moon

Cardinal, Water
Ruler: Moon

The Journey

When you are recalling something from the past, you're able to conjure up sights, smells, tastes, sounds and textures with vivid detail. The event you're recalling may have happened thirty years ago, but in your memory it's just as fresh and detailed as the day it happened. Thank your Cancer moon for that.

The Moon rules Cancer, so it's at home in this sign. This is where its energies express themselves most smoothly. With this moon, you're an emotional person who is easily hurt by others. Quite often, this hurt isn't intended. But your acute sensitivity makes you feel vulnerable, and it isn't easy for you to step back and view a situation or relationship dispassionately.

Family, home, and roots are important to you and are the elements around which your life revolves. This doesn't necessarily mean that your "family" exists in the traditional sense of the word; a family can be any group of people with whom you share a deep bond. It may be a spiritual practice that bonds you, or the fact that you all work in the same office, or something else altogether.

You have deep attachments to the past and this makes it difficult for you to ever toss out anything. Your closets are a collector's paradise, with small treasures tucked away in every nook and cranny. But they may be the stuff of nightmares for your significant other.

At times, you can talk at great length about your life, mentioning people and places that don't mean anything to someone else. You simply assume that other people know who these characters are and are as fascinated by them as you are. People who know you well love your storytelling, but strangers may not be quite as enthused. Don't take offense. How's that saying go? Different strokes and so on? Well, your strokes are different, for sure, and it's those very differences that make you interesting to other people.

Cancer—whether it's sun, moon, or rising—is the most nurturing sign in the zodiac. When your kids or loved ones hurt, you hurt. Your home is literally your castle and you make it comfortable and welcome to strangers and friends alike. Your kitchen probably holds the faint aroma of apple pie and spice, and if it doesn't, then your mother's kitchen did. And that brings us to the next aspect of the Cancer moon—your experience with your mother, or whoever nurtured you.

Mom or her equivalent was the archetypal mother, the dependable soul in your early childhood. She was there when you got up in the morning, there when you got home from school in the afternoon, there when you were hurt, sad, or ecstatic. She was the best mom on the block, in other words, and that made it easier for you to overlook her occasional histrionics and crying jags, her odd little quirks, her sometimes clingy behavior.

If you've ever watched reruns of *The Wonder Years* on Nickelodeon's "Nick at Night," the mother on the show fits the Cancer Moon like the proverbial shoe. She's sweet and understanding, she works occasionally, maybe she goes shopping or takes an art class now and then. She gets weirdly emotional at times and does things no one else understands. But basically, she's a homebody. With her family is where she wants most to be.

Cancer moon people usually have a soft spot in their hearts for animals. But these animals aren't regarded as pets or any lower in the evolutionary scale—they're *family*. We aren't just talking about dogs and cats, either. To the true animals lovers of this sign, the extended family includes wildlife—the goose that flies in every morning, the bluejays in the trees, the opossum that sneaks into the garage when it rains.

Not every Cancer moon sign, of course, craves home and family. The deeper craving is for roots. For one Cancer moon, that might mean returning to the ancestral home; for another, it might mean buying an RV so home can move around the country. Family may mean a houseful of kids or a yard filled with animals.

Editor Kate Duffy, with Kensington Books, has a Cancer moon. She has no children and, at the moment, no animals. But she has nurtured hundreds of books from their birth as ideas to their growing pains as manuscripts to the finished product. This is also a manifestation of the Cancer moon—the nurturing of creative projects.

Roots for a Cancer Moon satisfies one burning question: *Who am I and where do I fit in the scheme of things?*

The Cancer Moon Child

This kid is your heart's delight. Most of the time, he's fun, witty, a real conversationalist. You may not be sure half the time what he's talking about, but that's okay. It's his conviction that you like, the fluidity of his emotions, and the fact that he wants to talk to you, to confide in you.

His moodiness, though, can put a damper on all that. Sometimes, it's like a black cloud that drifts in through the open windows in your house and clamps down over the very air that you breathe. When you ask him what's wrong, he either shrugs and doesn't reply or he tells you something that you know isn't the real thing at all. Like the crab, he's evasive. He avoids the true emotional issue.

But then the mood passes. He's his usual self again, bringing home strays, eager to play with his friends, but not particularly keen on spending the night away from home. Camp? Okay, but not if it's sleep-away. You get the idea.

Your Cancer kid isn't like other kids. His quirks aside, he's a psychic sponge that soaks up every emotion around him. In this way, he's like his brother water signs, but different, too. His feelings are easily hurt. You never have to yell at him and, if you do, prepare to feel like the world's worst heel. He loves you blindly, but as he matures, you may irritate the hell out of him.

What you learn from him is probably more important than what he learns from you. The challenge is to figure out what that means.

Hidden Cancer

Your emotional evasiveness perplexes other people nearly as much as it perplexes you. Most of the time, you don't even realize you're being evasive; that's how deeply embedded the response is. Since your intuition works most smoothly through your emotions, it's to your advantage to confront and deal with what you feel head on.

Cancer's symbol is the crab. Its shell protects it from predators and the elements. It evades capture by darting sideways through the sand or remaining perfectly still, as if playing dead. When it is forced to fight, its claws latch on and cling tenaciously. Your shell is the wall you build between yourself and other people. The "capture" you evade is being pinned down to express what you feel and why you feel it. When you're up against a wall, you cling to what is familiar, judging the present and the future by what has happened in the past.

This "clingy" part of Cancer shows up in a variety of ways. The house guest who doesn't know when to leave. The smothering mother who makes the kids feel guilty when they're ready to leave the nest. The school teacher who considers her students her children. The neighbor who calls four times a day because she wants to be a friend. At the heart of all this clinging, however, is a deep loneliness that gets worse every time these people withhold their feelings from the people they love.

This kind of withholding can create emotional blocks which, if not dissolved, may eventually manifest in your physical body. Cancer rules the digestive system, breasts, and stomach, so physical problems are likely to show up in these areas.

Where Gemini lives so much in her mind that she's out of touch with what she feels, you're awash in emotion but are afraid to share what you feel. As long as this fear persists, you block the full power of your intuition.

One Cancer moon man I knew years ago had a very tough time expressing emotion, much less talking about what he felt. But the minute he was around an animal, he opened up and all that emotion came pouring out. Animals can be therapeutic for any moon sign, but for the Cancer moon person who is deeply blocked emotionally, animals literally open up the world.

Intuitive Cancer

You're most intuitive when it comes to your family—or people who are like family—and other people you love. Those impressions tend to come suddenly and unexpectedly, out of the blue. When it comes to getting intuitive information for yourself, your emotions often get in the way. The challenge, then, is to glean intuitive information when you need it, and about whatever concerns you at the time. Then use your emotions and your reasoning mind to confirm the impressions you receive.

As a cardinal sign, your energy tends to work in a single, focused direction, a definite intuitive asset. The only possible drawback is that you may fail to recognize peripheral cues that hold intuitive information. So, pay attention to everything you sense and feel. Don't allow your past experiences to influence or block the impressions you pick up.

There are several ways to facilitate the process. Your attitude should be open and receptive. Your intuition may flow more easily if you're near water—the beach, a lake, a river, even a pond. In the absence of all those, set a bowl of fresh water nearby. Give yourself five to ten minutes when you won't be interrupted by kids, phones, or anything else. If you're a night person, you may want to try the exercise at night. If you're a morning person, the very early morning hours may work best for you. Have paper and pen or a recorder nearby.

If you don't pick up anything at first, jot that down and sit awhile longer, allowing yourself to remain calm and centered. It's likely that impressions will begin to well up after a few minutes. Trust the process. Engage all your senses. Let loose. Don't allow your reasoning mind to censor. Once your impressions begin to flow, try the Cancer exploration.

Testing Your Intuition

In the Cancer exploration chart below, write out a single question which you will then try to answer intuitively. Keep your question simple and focused. If, for instance, you want to know if you and the current love of your life are going to get married, be more specific and ask for a time frame.

The question should be something that can be answered in a relatively short period of time—several hours or a day to a week—so that you will get feedback on your intuition fairly quickly. There's a similar exploration in the Aries moon section (you're both cardinal signs), but it has one important difference. Aries, due to the restless pace at which he lives, needs to create a sacred space in which to do the exercise. All you have to do is find the spot that feels right for you and keep the kids away for five or ten minutes.

After you pose your question, jot down your first impressions in as much detail as possible. If your impressions are influenced by external factors—outside sounds, the heat of the sun against your head, the smell of the grass or of fresh coffee—that's okay. These are peripheral cues that may represent some facet of your question.

If you ask a simple yes or no question, note how you feel the answer. Do you feel it in your body? As heat or cold? Do you perceive it in visual symbols? Do you get numbers? A time frame? Write down everything, no matter how silly it may seem. Date the question and the answer. When the event or situation happens, date it and make note of how accurate you were.

Even Cancer moon people, who have so much natural intuitive ability, may feel uncertain in the beginning about the impressions they get. This is when a divination tool like tarot cards or the *I Ching* can be helpful because it can confirm your own impressions, which builds confidence. Eventually, you won't feel the need for an external confirmation. But at the onset of your intuitive development, don't hesitate to use them if you feel the need.

As part of the exploration exercise, once you've jotted down your impressions, confirm what you've gotten with a dictionary reading. This is a simple predictive technique in which you ask a question, open a dictionary at random, and point at a word or phrase without looking at it first. When you do this with sincere intention, the results can be astonishingly accurate and flesh out your own intuitive impressions. With a dictionary reading, like any intuitive technique, you need to interpret the symbols through association.

Let's say you ask if you and the person you're seeing will get married by November of this year. Your intuitive impressions say yes. The word you point at in the dictionary is *couple*. This would suggest that your intuitive impression is accurate. If, instead, you pointed at the word *partition*, it would suggest that something might come between you two before November to delay the marriage.

CANCER EXPLORATION

Date: _____

Question: _____

_____

_____

Your intuitive impression: _____

_____

Dictionary word or phrase: _____

Date/what actually happened: _____

_____

Engaging Your Senses

Our senses are constantly relaying information to us about our environment. The aroma of fresh coffee in the morning means that your roommate or significant other is already up and about. The sound of rain signals that traffic may be bad, so you should leave the house a little early. On a deeper, more complex level, our senses alert us to danger or to potentially advantageous situations, and lead us to the right people at the right time. Our senses are also our most immediate connection to our intuition.

You're particularly good at gauging other people's moods. You're able to feel what they feel. Sometimes, you're able to see what they see, hear what they hear, taste what they taste, almost as if you're zipped up inside the other person's skin. The evolved expression of this ability is what medical intuitives use when doing health readings for people. In the movie *Resurrection*, Ellen Burstyn's profound empathy for other people allowed her to take on their symptoms and then transmute them through her own body.

The following activity is designed to allow you to flex your sensory muscles. Again, engage all your senses. Have fun!

YOUR SENSES

Describe a place in as much detail as possible. It can be anywhere—the place where you are right this second, a location you've visited, a city, town, park, river, hotel, museum. Use all your senses when describing this place. *Be fully there.*

_____

_____

_____

_____

_____

_____

You've just answered a question without knowing what the question is. Your intuition knew, though, and through this sensory exercise answered the question.

Now turn to Intuitive Reality Check #2, Chapter 17, to see what question you've answered.

9

Leo Moon

Fixed, Fire
Ruler: Sun

The Journey

Lights! Curtain! It's showtime! When you enter a room, people notice you. And if for some reason they don't, then you make sure that they do. This isn't just an ego thing. Applause and being noticed are vital to your well-being even if your only audience is your family. *You need to be recognized as someone special.*

Okay, so now that we got that part over with, let's get down to the fundamentals of your Leo moon. You love kids and animals, and are the kind of person who gets down on the rug and rolls around with a three-year-old without thinking twice about it. Pop psychologists call this being in touch with your inner child, but whatever you call it, it's part of who you are and you aren't going to change.

You have a real dramatic flair that usually serves you well, unless you fail to get the recognition you crave, then all that drama can get really obnoxious. You cry, you rant and rave, you kick doors, *you act out.* People who know you either walk away rolling their eyes or they endure your tirade and pay attention to you.

Even though the moon generally doesn't govern physical appearance, there are exceptions. People with a Leo sun, moon, or rising usually have a lion's mane of hair. It may be short and curly or long and straight, or any combination of the two, but it's always thick and somehow distinctive.

Leo moons generally don't have any fear about public speaking, so it's not surprising that a number of celebrities have this moon sign. Faye Dunaway, Jacques Cousteau, author William Golding, and Rita Hayworth are some of the notables in this lineup. Dale Carnegie, the man who started the Dale Carnegie courses of public speaking, also had a Leo moon.

We're not all celebrities, of course, and not all Leo moons go around kicking chairs and acting out. But one way or another, the drama and flamboyance of the Leo moon play out in your family, community, work scene, or social groups. Phyllis, my co-author for the book *Power Tarot*, plays out her dramatic flair within her family. We joke about what her "next drama" will be.

With this moon, your experience of Mom or her equivalent (your primary nurturer) was rarely boring but frequently exasperating. She was the queen, her family was her court, and she never took a backseat to anyone. She could be explosive, but once she exploded, that was it. She wasn't the type to hold grudges and neither are you. Despite Mom's flamboyance, she was very protective of you. Any artistic interest you had as a child was nurtured because Mom understood the importance of passion. The extreme of this type of mother can be the stage mom, who lives through her child and takes credit for all his or her accomplishments.

You appear to be self-confident and assured and because of it can attract a significant other who is either equally independent or who is the exact opposite, an insecure type drawn to your inner strength. As long as this person appreciates you and feeds your need for adulation, the relationship functions smoothly. Problems crop up when the other person tries to control or dominate you or restrict your freedom in some way.

Thanks to the generally upbeat disposition of this moon sign, your outlook is usually optimistic. You're one of those people who refers to a cup as being "half-full" rather than half-empty. And it's this optimism that gets you through most of the challenges in your life.

You're loyal to the people you love and always extend yourself to a friend in need. You can't stand to see any human or animal suffer and do what you can to alleviate suffering when you see it. One Leo Moon woman, for example, heard that a friend of a friend had fallen on hard times and was living on the streets of New York. She sent him money without any thought or expectation of recompense. This is the true generosity of the Leo moon.

The Leo Moon Child

He's king of the jungle and he does everything he can to make sure you and everyone else remembers that. He's also warm and generous, often to a fault, and is one of the most affectionate kids in the zodiac.

At times, his need to be the center of attention can make him difficult to live with. When he's younger, this can be particularly trying for parents. He's better off as an only child, so that he has his parents' exclusive attention. If he comes from a large family, then he establishes early on that he is at the top of the kid pecking order.

When he doesn't get the attention he craves so deeply, he creates situations and "dramas" that garnish the attention. As a young child, this could mean temper tantrums, racing away from you on his bike, or showing off in a way that puts him at risk. As he gets older, these little ploys take more subtle and often insidious forms—a chronic health problem, a history of bumpy and failed relationships, thwarted ambitions.

When this kid is encouraged to believe in himself and his talents, there's nothing he can't accomplish. His passions are strong and determined. He takes his cues from Mom. If she lives on an emotional roller coaster, so does he. If she conducts herself with dignity, so does he. This talent to mimic is part of what makes Leo moon children terrific actors.

Like the adult Leo moon, this child can be so generous he gives away his entire allowance to a friend in need. He has a soft spot for animals of any type, but may favor cats. Just watch him at a zoo, drawn irresistibly toward the lions who symbolize his sign.

Hidden Leo

For a Leo moon, the word *hidden* may seem like an oxymoron. But hidden parts of you are what create the flamboyance for which you're known. At the heart of all that flamboyance lies an odd insecurity about being the front seat driver. Although you always want to be in charge, you often torture yourself with doubts about whether you're qualified for the job. One way to overcome this lack of trust in yourself and your abilities is to let your natural passion and energy do the job in spite of your doubts, and to allow your intuitive nature to shine.

Phyllis lived in the same neighborhood with her daughters and grandchildren. They all wanted to move because the noise in the neighborhood had gotten out of hand. They put their townhouses up for sale and started searching for the ideal neighborhood.

They found two homes they liked in a quiet, upscale neighborhood. The problem was that a pending contract on one of the townhouses had fallen through and Phyllis didn't want to stretch herself too thin financially by buying a home before at least one of the townhouses had sold. She dipped into her savings to put a deposit on one of the houses and then all her doubts crept in. Had she made the right decision? Would the townhouses ever sell? Would they be better off staying where they were and just making the best of it?

Things came to a virtual standstill while Phyllis struggled against her doubts, arguing the pros and cons with herself. Then her oldest daughter was robbed at knifepoint while walking in their neighborhood one night. That was the turning point for Phyllis. One of her kids had been threatened and all that Leo moon protectiveness surged.

She focused her intuition and will on finding a speedy resolution and, backed with her passion, need, and intent, one of the townhouses sold within several weeks and she bought one of the homes that they wanted. A month later, everyone moved into the new house and two months later, Phyllis sold the other townhouse and bought her own new home.

It took a threat to one of her kids for her passion and intuition to squash her doubt, break through the obstacle, and make things happen. By using the intuitive energy of her fixed, fire sign moon in a focused, directed way, *she altered her reality*. The challenge is to be able to do that on demand.

Other Leo moons go through their bouts of insecurity and doubt, then wake up one morning knowing exactly what they should do and how they should do it. It's as if something internal shifted during the night and now nothing stops them from getting to where they want to go.

This is the fixed, fire nature of the sign in action. Once you get over the humps, your stubborn strength takes you the distance.

Intuitive Leo

Okay, there's the doubt. But that doesn't make you any different from anyone else. Your fixed brother, Taurus, has his skepticism, Gemini doesn't have the time, and Aries is too consumed with his pioneering. In each instance, these various traits can be launchpads for intuitive explorations.

Thanks to your buddy, Doubt, you may believe you need external tools to be intuitive. Cards, dice, dictionaries, the *I Ching*, sticks and stones: there's nothing inherently wrong with any of them. In the beginning, oracular tools will build your confidence in your intuitive ability so that your doubt loses its hold over you.

External tools are also excellent venues for developing your intuition and for learning how it works best. You may find out, for instance, that it's easy for you to garner intuitive information about relationships, but more difficult when it comes to your professional life or vice versa. Eventually, when you feel more comfortable with your intuitive process, try to dispense with the tools.

Millie, a psychic from West Virginia, uses a deck of playing cards when she does readings. One night she laid out her cards for me and proceeded to talk. Ace of hearts, five of clubs, eight of diamonds: to me, these were just numbers and colors, but everything she said resonated. "You'll be going to New York shortly," she said.

I interrupted. "Hold on. The two of diamonds told you that? I'm going to New York?"

She started laughing and tapped her temple. "This told me. I just lay out the cards to give my hands something to do."

Millie doesn't have a Leo moon, but her story illustrates the point. Intuition supplies the information. The cards have significance only when a meaning is attached to them. Handling the cards keeps her censor quiet so that she can hear her intuition. Simple, isn't it?

Your body often acts as an intuitive vessel. Aches and pains may be unexpressed emotions or emotional blockages. One Leo moon woman was going through a tough time in her marriage and over a period of several weeks, wrenched her knee, her wrist, and developed tennis elbow. I referred her to the list of ailments at the back of Louise Hay's book *You Can Heal Your Life*.

According to Hay, joints "represent changes in direction in life and the ease of these movements." The knees represent "stubborn ego and pride, fear, inflexibility, won't give in." Wrists represent movement. Elbows represent "changing directions and accepting new experiences." This woman admitted that all the entries fit her situation—she needed to file for divorce and hadn't done it yet. She ended up having surgery on her knee, getting a couple of cortisone shots for her elbow, and then tackled the real problem by filing for divorce.

Leo rules the heart, back, and spinal cord. Major emotional blockages may show up in these areas, but other warning signs usually show up long before the problem affects those areas.

Leo Exploration

Remember that scene in *Rain Man* where Tom Cruise knocks a box of toothpicks to the floor and Dustin Hoffman, the autistic brother, glances at them and announces the exact number on the floor? He didn't count them; *he perceived a pattern*. That's exactly what your intuition does.

With Hoffman, his intuition focused on the spilled toothpicks and came up with the correct number. You're also going to use a box of toothpicks to trigger your intuition, but in a slightly different way.

Dump at least half a box of toothpicks on a surface in front of you and proceed to arrange the toothpicks into whatever shapes you want. Have fun with it. Pretend. Get into it. If you have kids, do it with them. Notice what thoughts, if any, go through your mind as you're doing it. After a few minutes, stop and glance at the pattern you've made. Does it remind you of anything? What's it look like?

Are the geometric angles precise or is the whole thing more of a free flow?

My impressions:_____

_____

_____

_____

_____

Before you interpret what you've written, ask yourself if anything in particular strikes you. Does the pattern remind you of anything? Make associations. This is a right-brain activity, where you're looking for "the big picture."

My interpretation:_____

_____

By doing this activity, you free up your intuitive self to make associations from the *patterns* the toothpicks form. The patterns and associations pertain to inner conditions. By writing your interpretation, the proof that your intuition works is right in front of you.

One man with a Leo moon was house hunting when he did the toothpick activity. His toothpicks fell into a pattern that resembled a two-story house. He interpreted this to mean that he should make an offer on one of the two-story houses that he had looked at.

The question you've just answered in this exercise is at the end of the chapter.

Engaging Your Senses

Every second, even when we're sleeping, our senses convey information to us about our environment and about ourselves. They are tireless workers, these senses of ours, gathering data that ranges from the mundane to the esoteric so that we may navigate our lives with more ease. Our senses are also our most immediate connection to our intuition; this activity is designed to flex your sensory muscles.

YOUR SENSES

Describe a place in as much detail as possible. It can be anywhere—the place where you are right this second, a location you've visited, a city, town, park, river, hotel, museum. Use all your senses when describing this place. *Be fully there.*

_____

_____

_____

_____

_____

_____

You've just answered a question without knowing what the question is. Your intuition knew, though, and through this sensory activity answered the question.

Now turn to Intuitive Reality Check #2, Chapter 17, to see what question you've answered.

NOTE: The question you answered in the Leo exploration activity is: How can my intuition serve me best at this moment in my life?

10

Virgo Moon

Mutable, Earth
Ruler: Mercury

The Journey

You're trying to sketch a tree. But your tree has funny leaves or too many branches or the trunk lacks texture. So you crumple up the drawing, tear a fresh sheet from your sketchpad, and start over again. This quest for perfection typifies your inner journey.

This facet of the sign used to bother me whenever I was around someone with a Virgo moon. I felt that I—or my home, my den, my clothes, my hair, my speech, take your pick—was under constant scrutiny. I could almost hear the person thinking: *Too much clutter.* Or: *How's she find anything in here?* Or even: *Hello, forget the jeans for a day and wear a dress.*

I avoided people with Virgo moons. I avoided Virgos, period. Then I married a man with a Virgo moon, got published, and found myself with Virgo editors, close Virgo friends, a Virgo agent, and a daughter with a sun and moon in Virgo. Once I became an astrologer, this whole Virgo thing became a lot clearer.

In my natal chart, I have no planets in Virgo. But my Vertex—a sensitive point in a chart that involves fateful or "destined" encounters—is in Virgo in my eleventh house of wishes and dreams and group associations. Virgo and my Vertex are intercepted or completely contained within that house. What this means is that instead of having each sign, from Aries to Pisces, on the cusp or border between houses, my eleventh house has Leo on the cusp with Virgo swallowed inside of it. This means they're roommates, they share the same tube of toothpaste.

Sometimes, an intercepted sign simply means that you've integrated the qualities and energy of that sign into who you are. But in my case, it apparently means that I have stuff to learn from Virgos and people who have that sign prominent in their charts. These individuals are instrumental in teaching, showing, or enabling me to reach for and attain my dreams.

It's taken me a long time not to get defensive when my husband critiques something I've written and finds it lacking. Now I try to detach emotionally and consider what he says in light of what I've written. Or when my daughter accuses me of breaking a promise—and then goes on to cite chapter and verse of every broken promise—I listen. Or when my friend Nancy explains an obscure changing line in an *I Ching* hexagram, a light goes on in my head. When my agent, Al, says my proposal needs work and then details exactly what that work entails, I hunker down and do the work.

In each instance, I am struck by the clarity, perception, and practicality of Virgo, by its cool detachment and attention to detail and perfection. *Be the best that you can be:* that's the Virgo message.

With all this in mind, is it any surprise that you thrive on order and perfection? Not perfection just for the sake of perfection, but perfection as an ideal, a state of mind, a state of being. For some Virgo moons, this can show up as concern for external order—no clutter, furniture arranged just right, books alphabetized by author or subject or, at the extreme, by the Dewey decimal system. More likely for a Virgo moon, however, is a need for emotional order. If your emotions are cluttered, you feel out of sorts. You need to understand what's out of sorts and take steps to rectify it.

If you ignore whatever isn't working, then the emotional confusion may find an outlet through criticism of others or self-criticism. Once you're aware of this tendency, you'll realize that the people and situations you criticize (even yourself) reflect some facet of your emotional life that needs attention. Before you dismiss this notion as too facile to have merit, try it out. Pay close attention to what and who you criticize and then apply it to your emotional life.

Virgo is the natural ruler of the sixth house in the horoscope and rules the intestines, abdomen, and female reproductive system.

When you're upset or nervous, it can show up first as indigestion or an upset stomach. Allergies are also common with this moon sign. In an infant with this moon sign, colic may be prominent.

Many people with a Virgo sun, moon, or rising are health-conscious. With some types, it's obvious—they work out, they run, they're vegetarians, they practice moderation. With other people, the focus turns inward. They meditate, practice a spiritual discipline, and seek to balance their emotional, spiritual, and physical selves. With both types, awareness is the common denominator and in all of them, intuition is focused and detail-oriented. You're the type that sees the dots that connect a pattern.

Your experience with your mother, or primary nurturer, is governed by the Virgo moon. The first type of experience is that of a workaholic who either works outside the home or runs her own home-based business. She's efficient and organized in everything she does, which includes mothering. A skinned knee when you were little probably meant a quick hug, a Band-Aid, and then she sent you off again.

The second type is the detail-oriented mom. She's the type for whom everything has to match—rugs with draperies, draperies with furnishings; handbag with shoes, shoes with outfit. Dinner is punctual and includes the major food groups. When you were a kid, she made sure you hadn't outgrown your clothes and used Clorox on the T-shirts that had stains on them. *Detail and perfection, those are her things*.

The third type of Virgo mother is probably the most difficult to live with and move beyond. She's the super-critical perfectionist who insists that you live up to her standards. This type of mother may haunt you well into adulthood.

Since your moon sign also symbolizes how you nurture and mother other people, you may recognize yourself in one of the three types or as a blend of the three.

Virgo, as ruler of the sixth house, is considered a service-oriented sign. In classical astrological texts, this service orientation was often described in terms that would make any person with a Virgo moon want to climb back into the womb and be born under some other moon. But in the contemporary world, in everyday life, this moon sign is about doing things for other people without any thought of what that person might do for you. You do it because you want to do it, because you enjoy helping.

Your neighbor has surgery and you bake a casserole and take it over. Your friend's car breaks down, she needs a ride home from the garage, and you gladly accommodate her. You witness a car accident and leap out of your car and run over to see how you can help. These are the kinds of "services" that are common to daily life for your moon sign.

Due to Virgo's connection to health and your innate compassion for others, many people with the sign prominent in their charts enter the medical/health professions, or have an abiding interest in the field. You may also be interested in alternative health, particularly in the mind/body connection.

You are, in your own way, a deeply spiritual and mystical person. In the romance department, you're seeking someone who complements that part of you and can also nurture and appreciate your curious and restless intellect.

The Virgo Moon Child

He's usually a sweetheart of a kid, even-tempered and fun to be with, eager to help and to do his share in the family. Like the adult he will become, he's great at details. Ask him to make a list of what you need for the family camping trip and he'll spend hours compiling the list, laboring over it with all the concentration of a sculptor with a piece of clay.

The order part of the Virgo moon equation is often quirky with kids. My daughter the double Virgo doesn't mind if her room is an obstacle course of clutter. But she's absolutely adamant that the pillows on her bed are perfectly aligned when she goes to sleep at night. Or that her container of yogurt doesn't have liquid floating on the top. These quirks tend to show up early on and if you attempt to change them, you'll only meet with stringent resistance.

Some Virgo moon children are fussy eaters; others eat whatever is in front of them. The fussier eaters are more likely to have colic as infants and allergies of some kind as they get older unless they develop more wholesome eating habits.

Your Virgo moon child has a deep compassion for other people who are less fortunate. This trait usually shows up early on in the child's life and may be expressed first about animals. He brings home neighborhood strays, puts out food for them, and eventually succeeds in moving the strays into the house. As he gets older, this compassion extends to other kids and even to adults.

After our family decided to put my mother into an Alzheimer's unit, an astrologer friend asked if my daughter went with me when I visited. I told her that Megan enjoys visiting the facility and knows most of the residents on my mother's wing by name. We sometimes take one or two of her friends with us and they put on spontaneous shows—dancing, singing, whatever strikes their fancy. The astrologer listened to all this, then chuckled. "Of course. She's a double Virgo!"

There are deep creative wells in this child. If nurtured, these wells don't dry up as your child gets older. One of the ways a Virgo child may work through emotional and growing dilemmas is through art, dance, writing, and poetry. This is probably true of most kids, but for the Virgo child, who often keeps her emotions hidden, these artistic pursuits provide helpful outlets and are often insightful for parents.

During a week at a horseback riding camp, where horses and riding were the complete focus of each day, Megan wrote several poems that expressed her feelings about a difficult day when she was riding a horse she hadn't ridden before. Until we read the poem, neither my husband nor I had any idea that she'd had a rough day with the horse.

SILENT TIME

You believe—
Sail, sing
silly play
go behind, through this
darkest dream
that really does bring
winter.

—Megan MacGregor, July 1999

Hidden Virgo

Who are you in the silence of your own heart? What thoughts run through your head when you're alone? Busy thoughts? Deep thoughts? Constant analysis?

Virgo, like Gemini, is ruled by Mercury, the planet that concerns communication, cognitive skills, and common sense. What it means for you is that there's a constant conversation going on in your mind—inner dialogues, replays of your conversations with other people, what you're going to do tomorrow, your vacation next month, your relationship issues, details details details. This may be true of all of us to a certain extent, but for the Virgo moon, the chatter is constant.

It can be exhausting even when you're not consciously aware of it. The challenge is to pay attention to what goes on in your head—don't analyze it or pick it apart, just become aware of these internal dialogues. If you find that many of your thoughts are negative, then seek the deeper cause. Are you clinging to a past hurt? A relationship that no longer works? A job you merely tolerate? Find the root of the negative thought or emotion and work through it until you understand it. Once you understand it, it loses power and dissolves. It's like a monster in a nightmare. Confront it and it flees.

The hidden Virgo lies in these internal dialogues, which hold information about your "mind stuff," the core of who you are. Once you become aware of the chatter in your head, your deepest beliefs are more obvious and it's easier to change the beliefs that may be holding you back. As a mutable earth sign, your greatest strengths are your adaptability and your practical efficiency. By bringing these strengths to bear against any negative "core belief" that you discover in yourself, you quickly learn how to alter your beliefs—and your life.

Although Mercury is the traditional ruler of Virgo, its rulership has come under doubt by some astrologers. Part of this is due to the discovery of asteroids and planets that have muddled the ancient picture. But technology is also to blame. With the advent of computers and astrology software, research is easier and the results come in much faster. And since astrology is a living, breathing system, it is expanding and reinventing itself for the world of the twenty-first century. Certain associations that existed when earth was still believed to be flat are going to vanish like last summer's tan.

Astrologers Eleanor Bach and Robert Hand have suggested that the four major asteroids—Ceres, Pallas Athene, Juno, and Vesta—rule Virgo. This theory lends new meaning to the confusion factor already inherent in astrology. And yet, if you go back to mythology, to the significance these goddesses held, it makes sense.

The issue of rulership aside, your Virgo moon allows you to access deep reservoirs of intuitive wisdom. You may not think of it like that, but as you begin to notice the thoughts that run through your head, the voice of your intuition is likely to get much stronger.

Intuitive Virgo

A number of years ago, I read a travel book by a celebrity. I was appalled at myself for buying the book at all because celebrity books don't usually interest me. But from the opening chapters, this book really grabbed me. Even now, decades later, I can recall the vivid description of how Masai tribesmen in Africa milk cows for their blood, which the tribe later drinks. Some years later, I read another book by this celebrity about her spiritual awakening and certain descriptions of her adventures in Peru are still vivid in my mind.

As a writer, I've come to realize that what fascinated me about these books, what held my attention, wasn't the celebrity—it was the magnificence of details. When I read the description of the blood-letting, *I was there*, in Africa, with the cows, with the tribesmen. When she described Machu Pichu, I was moving through the ancient ruins with her. The writing seduced my senses. The author, Shirley MacLaine, has a Virgo moon.

It's through details that your intuition functions most efficiently. A nuance, a bit of seemingly random information, something glimpsed as you're driving—all this is fodder that your intuition uses to create the larger picture. Virgo moon individuals are generally good at recognizing a synchronicity, perhaps because synchronicities usually involve a series of details.

Like your mutable Gemini cousin, writing is an easy and natural way for you to get in touch with your intuitive self. In Julia Cameron's book *The Artists' Way*, she recommends writing "morning pages" to get in touch with your creativity. The morning pages are where you pour whatever is in your head, without censorship or editing. This same technique should help you facilitate your connection with your intuition. Cameron recommends writing these pages in longhand, but if that seems cumbersome, then do whatever is comfortable for you. The point is to write without censoring yourself.

As you become accustomed to doing your morning pages, you'll discover answers to questions you probably haven't even realized you've asked. You may find certain repetitive themes or images. Explore these, because they probably come from your intuitive self.

Some people freeze up initially when faced with a blank page. If that happens to you, just take a couple of deep breaths and tell your internal censor to head south for a while. Then write down one word. Then the next word. And the next. One friend of mine who tried this exercise got hung up in punctuation and grammar. *It doesn't sound right,* she said. *The syntax is wrong.* This isn't an English lesson; it's supposed to free up your intuition.

Virgo Exploration

Think of a movie or book you've liked. It can be any kind of movie or book, old or contemporary, that has stuck in your mind. Now pick a vivid scene from that movie or book and write about it. Be detailed (of course!) and describe colors, characters, emotions, the place, what was going on, everything you liked about the scene and how it fit into or fleshed out the larger picture.

Write until the words dry up. There's no right or wrong way of doing this. What you're doing here is allowing your intuition to answer a question that's listed at the end of this chapter. Even though you don't consciously know the question, your intuition already knows it and is going to answer it through this activity.

The movie/book: _____

The scene: _____

_____

_____

_____

_____

   Take a look at the end of the chapter, where you'll find the question you've just answered. If you had known the question before you described this movie scene, your description might not have been as spontaneous. Your inner censor would have been butting in, urging you to slant the description in a particular way.

   Now that you know the question, interpret your description in light of your life right now. Project the issue a month into the future. How does it fit? Does it resonate for you? Does it feel right?

My interpretation: _____

_____

_____

_____

_____

Engaging Your Senses

   Our senses are our most immediate and direct connection to our intuition. Through touch, taste, sight, hearing, and smell, we glean enormous amounts of information about our immediate environment and make dozens of decisions based on that information. But much of this happens at an unconscious level. In the following activity, you're going to become conscious of your sensory universe, the first step in intuitive development.

YOUR SENSES

   Describe a place in as much detail as possible. It can be anywhere—the place where you are right this second, a location you've visited, a city, town, park, river, hotel, museum. Use all your senses when describing this place. *Be fully there.*

_____

_____

_____

_____

_____

You've just answered a question without knowing what the question is. Your intuition knew, though, and through this sensory exercise answered the question.

Now turn to Intuitive Reality Check #2, Chapter 17, to see what question you've answered.

*NOTE: The question you answered in the Virgo exploration activity is: In what area of my life will my intuition be most useful to me in the next four weeks?

11

Libra Moon

Cardinal, Air
Ruler: Venus

The Journey

Among astrologers, certain moon signs stir the soul for the sheer beauty of what they represent. The Libra moon is one of these.

At the heart of it, you're a lover, a true romantic. Moonlit beaches, bouquets of roses, books of poetry, going to the opera, a summer rain: this is the language your soul really speaks. You specialize in relationships in all their varied and myriad forms. That's what you're here for. *To be involved.* To learn cooperation and balance within relationships.

In a group, you're the mediator, the one who can see both sides of an issue with such clarity that you often end up quelling arguments and disagreements. Due to your amiable personality, some people think you're a pushover. These are the same people who fail to realize that you use diplomacy and intelligence to get what you want from them.

Your need for harmony prompts you to keep the peace in any given situation and sometimes, this is peace at any cost. As a result, you may resort to secrecy now and then. You might, for instance, not tell your spouse that your daughter got a C on a math test because you know he or she will overreact. So you and your daughter keep the secret to yourselves and you work with her on math for the next few weeks, until she aces the next exam. In this way, you avoid a confrontation and maintain peace.

Another example with this moon involves duplicity in relationships. He or she is married, things aren't going well in the marriage, it all starts innocently, one friend to another, then quickly escalates to something else entirely. Or maybe you're married and things aren't going well. The romance between the two of you has fizzled. Your attention begins to stray and suddenly you're involved with someone else. In relationships, your life shifts into high gear. You live and feel more intensely.

In this scenario, the "other" relationship has to be kept secret so that no one gets hurt. But sooner or later, someone or everyone gets hurt. One of your challenges this time around is to realize the grass is rarely greener elsewhere.

The whole issue of duplicity actually revolves around your need to be liked. You're afraid that if you say no to someone, that person won't like you. Or you're afraid your response will create too much disharmony. So you keep saying *yes, yes, yes* until your life and your emotions are so muddled they're nearly incomprehensible to you. The remedy requires you to be honest with yourself about what you really feel and believe, separate from the emotions and beliefs of the people you're involved with at the moment.

One of the ways this honesty happens for you is through the arts. People with a prominent Libra in their charts are usually aesthetically inclined in some way and are involved in the arts—dance, music, poetry, writing, sculpture, painting, drawing, acting. If you grew up in a household where you weren't discouraged from showing your talent, then you probably have a lot of artistic talent yourself. Even if you don't recognize your own talents, you recognize artistic talents in others, perhaps in your children, and help nurture those talents.

Which brings us to the mother or primary nurturer represented by the Libra moon—or, rather, your experience of her. She comes in two distinct types—the one who is aware of her artistic and intuitives gifts and the one who isn't. The first type teaches you an appreciation of the arts through the expression of her own creative gifts. She might collect art or love music or have a wonderful eye for color and design. Or she herself might be an artist. She's there for you, but you won't ever hear her raise her voice or directly confront someone on your behalf. Instead, she charms the pants off them.

The second type of mother has the same loves as the first, but she projects them all onto you. Through you, she lives vicariously in the arts. She's a true balancing act, this mom. She carpools, she does the PTA, she urges you to reach for your dreams. She's also married or involved and holds down a full-time job. But if you're an adult with a Libra moon, then you probably have figured this out long ago. Since the moon also represents how you nurture others, what do these descriptions tell you about yourself?

Libra rules the lower back and diaphragm. When you are "stuck" emotionally, it may show up in those two areas.

The Libra Moon Child

Never forget: this child is social. She needs other people to define who she is, and this begins nearly as soon as she opens her eyes.

In her early pre-school years, her parents are initially the focus of her attention. She unconsciously studies their relationship by observing them, how they interact, how they're the same or different. By the time she enters kindergarten, she has many friends and the friendships are, well, somewhat fickle. If one friend can't play today, then she's on the phone calling another friend. The point is the interaction and it doesn't much matter who is on the other end, as long as someone is there.

Now: apply this to the adult version of the child and you begin to understand how an early childhood pattern can carry forward into adulthood. As a sign, Libra in a birth chart is important because it reveals what types of social interactions will be most important for your child. A Libra sun child has all the qualities of the Libra moon, but the energy is directed outward, into the larger world. A Libra rising seeks to balance her inner needs with her outer life and is usually perceived by others as a diplomat, a mediator.

The Libra moon child benefits from exposure to all the arts, so that she has some basis for comparison later on. Books and reading open up worlds to this child, so expose her early to books and don't restrict her choices. If she selects a book three grade levels above her own reading level, let her have it. She needs to flex her mental muscles. The beauty of this moon child is that, given the chance, she understands her own strengths and weaknesses. Don't nag her, don't breathe down her neck, simply guide her.

Hidden Libra

Remember those secrets mentioned earlier? Well, such secrets constitute the hidden Libra moon. There's an entire world within you that no one else sees or knows about. There are times when you would like very much to share that world, but then you start projecting with *what if* . . .

What if the other person didn't like you once you'd shared that world? *What if* the sharing itself creates problems or, worse, an outright confrontation? Nope, best to keep that world under wraps, hidden, private. The secret to unraveling this hidden part of yourself lies in the planet that governs your sign.

Venus also rules Taurus, but brings very different traits to each sign. In Taurus, Venus is more earthy, lusty, and in need of beautiful physical surroundings. In Libra, Venus is all about affairs of the heart, about *romance*. And this is the area where your hidden self must become visible. The surest way to do this is by being honest about what you feel. First, you must be honest with yourself. *Okay, fine*, you reply. *I love both of them*. Or all three of them. But if you're honest with yourself, you realize that the quality of your love differs with each of them and that the bottom line has to do more with who *you* are than who *they* are. What parts of you does each relationship complement? What parts of you does each relationship repress or bring out?

Once you begin asking yourself these types of questions, it becomes easier to be more honest and forthright in your relationships with others, even if it means a confrontation or disharmony in your life. Balance, Libra moon, that's the key that unlocks everything, even your fundamental honesty.

While you're great at helping other people find balance, you find it difficult to do the same for yourself. Like your cardinal cousin, Aries, you're too busy doing and experiencing to analyze and reflect. But if you don't reflect willingly, then circumstances will intervene in such a way that you are *forced* to reflect and, yes, that's going to hurt. Instead of boxing yourself into a corner, let your intuition flow through you. Listen to it.

Usually when you begin to listen to your intuition, you experience a period of anger. Repressed anger. Stuff you haven't allowed yourself to express for fear it would alienate someone. Well, guess what? It's time to vent. Time to come clean. When your significant other squeezes the toothpaste tube so hard in the middle that it looks like an anorexic wearing a girdle, then don't suffer in silence. Don't just roll up the bottom and be done with it.

Say something. Say it nicely, say it firmly, say it matter of factly. But *say it.* What you don't say may later show up in your body as a physical ailment. Libra rules the lower back and the diaphragm, so emotional blockages are likely to show up first in those areas.

Intuitive Libra

Libra moon people usually make excellent clairvoyants once they learn to stay focused and to decipher the language of their intuitive impressions. In fact, like your cardinal cousin, Aries, your intuition comes to you in sudden flashes or in impulses. Like your other cardinal cousin, Cancer, your intuitive impressions generally center around other people. The challenge for you, then, is twofold: to focus on these intuitive impressions when they happen and to encourage their appearance when you need answers and information for yourself.

Right about now, you're balking. *What? Intuition on demand?* But isn't that the point? We taste and see, hear and feel and touch on demand, so why should our sixth sense be any different?

The best way to get started is to set aside five minutes when you won't be interrupted by phones or people. It can be anywhere—your home, your office, a park, your yard, the beach, wherever you feel comfortable. If you want, light a candle or a stick of incense or put on your favorite music. This acts as a signal to your conscious mind that you're about to do something different and personally important.

Relax. Ground yourself with gentle breathing. Let go of daily concerns. Once you're in the right state of mind, shut your eyes, pose a silent question to yourself, and wait for intuitive impressions to bubble up. When your intuitive journey is just beginning, it's a good idea to have a notebook handy and write out your question and what you experience as you experience it. The notebook is useful because it gives you some sense of continuity, provides a record of your progress, and boosts your self-confidence.

Be clear about your questions. Keep them simple and, at least in the beginning, make the time frame short enough so you can get feedback rather quickly. Tomorrow. Next week. As soon as you get home.

Libra Exploration

Try this exercise. In a notebook, write a succinct question in the middle of the page and draw a circle around it. Then take several deep breaths to center yourself and, moving around the circle, jot down the words and phrases that come immediately to mind. Don't force it, don't think about it, and stop when the words dry up on their own.

Now look over your words for common themes and images. Make associations. What do the words tell you about your question?

This is how the exploration looked for one Libra moon woman, who was contemplating a move to be with the man she had been dating. She had conflicting feelings about the move and, on a deeper level, about the relationship, which is reflected in her exploration.

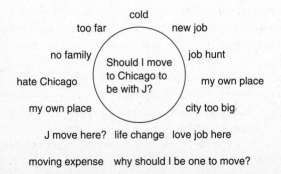

The common theme here seems to be resistance to the move. The woman was aware of her resistance before she did this exploration, but kept shoving it aside, trying to bury it. By doing the exploration in this way, her left-brain censor couldn't interfere with the honesty of her feelings.

As you work with your intuition, you'll get to the point where you don't need to draw pictures or use external tools to access it. You'll simply be able to sit back, shut your eyes, and focus on your question.

Engaging Your Senses

Our senses allow us immediate and direct contact with our intuition. Through taste, touch, sight, hearing, and smell, we cull vast amounts of intuitive information about our immediate environment and makes dozens of decisions every day. But a lot of this happens at an unconscious level. The point is to bring this information into your conscious awareness, which the next activity does by allowing you to flex your sensory muscles.

YOUR SENSES

Describe a place in as much detail as possible. It can be anywhere— the place where you are right this second, a location you've visited, a city, town, park, river, hotel, museum. Use all your senses when describing this place. *Be fully there.*

_____

_____

_____

_____

_____

_____

_____

_____

You've just answered a question without knowing what the question is. Your intuition knew, though, and through this sensory exercise answered the question. Now turn to Intuitive Reality Check #2, Chapter 17, to find out what question you've answered.

12

Scorpio Moon

Fixed, Water
Ruler: Pluto

The Journey

This moon is one of the most fascinating of the zodiac and one of the most difficult to understand. But that's probably not news to you, who have been living with the energy of this moon since you drew your first breath.

There are plenty of times when your lunar journey feels pretty lonely. People either don't have a clue what you're about, or they think they know and they've got it all wrong. Actually, you're not all that sure sometimes who you are.

Your emotions are intense and, at times, so sweepingly powerful, that it's as if you're seized by a force beyond your control. Despite how it feels, this sense of outside forces is just an illusion. Your emotions are your most powerful allies. They provide you with a direct, immediate connection to the deepest parts of your intuitive self and are capable of instantly transforming your reality.

This transformation happens when you bring your considerable will, intent, and desire to bear against whatever it is that you want to change. When the energy of this moon is focused and backed with passion, this change occurs at the quantum level and can result in the remission of illness or disease, sudden rise in wealth and fame, an explosion of psychic ability . . . well, you get the general idea.

Scorpio is also about power—the power we wield over others and the power others wield over us. All too often, this lunar energy is misused or abused when it concerns power issues; then its tremendous capacity for positive transformation becomes negative. The difference seems to be self-awareness.

This moon often acts like a psychic sponge, so that you absorb the moods and feelings of the people around you. For this reason, it's important that you associate with positive, upbeat people. If you find yourself in circumstances where you can't do this, then it's to your advantage to "protect" yourself by imagining a white light around you. In a psychic sense, this cocoon of light acts like a kind of mirror that deflects the negativity. This may sound like a flaky idea, but don't dismiss the suggestion until you've tried it.

The abundance of raw psychic talent that comes with this moon sign can produce a closet mystic, the neighborhood tea-leaf reader, or an outright clairvoyant. With some people, the ability shows up at a young age. With other people, it's a talent they grow into. In either case, though, you may have a natural attraction for "Scorpio things": mystical books and philosophies, near-death research and affairs of the dead, sex and sexual issues. Your investigative abilities in these areas can be astonishing.

The moon represents your experience of your mother or primary nurturer. With a Scorpio moon, your experience of your mother as you were growing up was undoubtedly intense. At times, you may have felt smothered by her good intentions. She worried too much about where you were and who you were with and what you were doing. If you sensed resentment in her toward you, it was probably because you distracted her from the intense richness of her own emotions, her eternal personal puzzle. Mom undoubtedly loved you deeply, but she may have come up a bit short in the nurturing department.

She probably wasn't the sort of mom you could have crazy fun with—forget impulsive trips to the local water park, an evening at the carnival, or a concert featuring teenage bands. One extreme of this mother type, in fact, might take you to a séance; the other type might take you on a picnic that actually has a larger agenda—to counsel you about something or to find out what was really bothering you. Mom's personal agenda was often as much a secret as the rest of her life. In retrospect, as an adult, can you say with any certainty that you really know her?

You, like your mother, have a sharp edge that comes out when you or your own kids are threatened in some way. It can show up in your speech, as a biting sarcasm, or as a deep penchant for secrecy. Sometimes, this sharp edge shows up in sexual issues, another area particularly pertinent to this moon sign.

Scorpio is the natural ruler of the eighth house in the horoscope and rules the sexual organs, rectum, and reproductive system. As a water sign, its domain is emotion. Emotions that you internalize can accrue in your body over a period of time and may create health problems. It's vital that you have some way of releasing or expressing what you feel. A physical exercise regimen would be a good place to start, even if it's only a twenty-minute walk a day. One man I know with a Scorpio moon keeps a punching bag in his garage. What began as a way to release tension has become his physical exercise.

I've found that people with a Scorpio moon often have deep compassion for others and are able to empathize to such a degree that they can make terrific healers, psychologists, and counselors. The key to developing these talents lies in self-awareness.

As a fixed sign, your Scorpio moon can be nearly as stubborn as a Taurus moon where emotions are concerned. Quite often, these fixed emotional patterns stem from early childhood responses or from past life experiences. To evolve and grow, it may be necessary for you to change these emotional patterns. The path to that change lies in using your intuition.

There's another facet to this moon that's worth mentioning: it never forgets a slight. In unaware people, this can result in vindictiveness, a need to get even at any cost.

The Scorpio Moon Child

Still waters run deep: the adage fits this moon child to a T. Beneath all that stillness lies a rich inner life that you—as her parent—may or may not be privy to. This child has incredible insight into other people, into what motivates and moves them. Her perspicacity is innate and, if it's nurtured, burgeons into heightened intuition.

As a youngster, her greatest challenges come from herself, from her rich and layered inner life. Quite often, her own emotions confuse and puzzle her, and she needs someone with whom she can discuss what she feels. She may be hesitant to trust a friend unless that friend has proven her loyalty. You won't ever change this hesitation on her part, but you can encourage her to talk about her feelings, and act as her confidante when she needs one.

This kid is going to ask many tough questions in her life and the questions start almost as soon as she learns to talk. *What's God? What happens when we die? Where did I come from?* Glib answers just won't satisfy her. She wants depth, complexity, honesty. She has a deep inner need to order her world around big issues, and won't settle for superficialities.

Most people with Scorpio moons—adults and kids alike—have a biting sarcasm that comes out when they are hurt or feel threatened. It's a defense mechanism, but when you're on the receiving end of that sting, you don't care what prompts it; you simply want to get away from it. As a parent, you can teach your little Scorpio moon when sarcasm is inappropriate, but it's unlikely that you'll ever eradicate it from her personality. It's as much a part of her as the color of her eyes.

One of the things you won't escape with this child is honesty about sex. Intense sexual experiences and feelings ride tandem with this moon sign. If you're open and honest about sexuality and sexual issues and create a loving environment in childhood, then a lot of the adolescent perils can be alleviated.

Although this child has the capacity for profound transformation and healing of herself and others, she may have obsessive edges to her personality. This can show up as a need to control and manipulate others or a need to get even with people who have hurt her. The symbol for Scorpio, after all, is the scorpion. But if you're aware of this tendency, you can confront and deal with it when she's still young.

Hidden Scorpio

Your secrecy is probably legendary among your family and friends. It's not that you intentionally try to keep things from the people you love, only that you keep your private thoughts private and that's how it's always been. It's one of those fixed emotional patterns inherent in this moon sign.

This is right in keeping with Pluto, the planet that rules Scorpio. In mythology, Pluto ruled the underworld, the place where souls went after death. He was secretive, enigmatic, often ruthless, and used his enormous power to manipulate lesser gods. That pretty much sums up the negative qualities of the Scorpio moon.

On the positive side, however, lies unrecognized or undeveloped artistic and psychic talents, piercing insight, and an emotional intelligence that has almost no equal in the zodiac. But to draw on all that positive energy may require that you delve into the secretive side of your nature and understand its source. Once you commit to this kind of self-exploration, the transformation is likely to be profound and far-reaching.

The best place to start is by noticing the kinds of secrets you keep. Do they concern money? Emotions? Relationships? Certain types of experiences? One Scorpio moon woman realized that the secrets she kept from her significant other involved her spiritual interests. She knew that he wouldn't approve of her deepest beliefs, so she kept them to herself. But as she continued to live more consciously, she met other people who shared her beliefs and it became increasingly difficult to keep her secret. The relationship eventually fell apart and the woman ended up meeting a man who shared her beliefs.

A commitment to this path doesn't necessarily mean relationships will end or that your personal life will be turned inside out. It all depends on what purpose your secrets serve in your life, and whether a relationship is restricting you or holding you back in some way. The whole point of self-awareness is to evolve and grow so that you can fulfill your potential.

You may want to start a journal for this discovery process. The very act of writing about your secrets creates an awareness about their function in your life. These journal entries don't have to be long and drawn out. A few paragraphs daily, for whatever length of time feels comfortable to you, should do the trick. Eventually, your awareness will become second nature and you won't need the journal anymore.

As you establish a rhythm with your journal writing, your intuition will deepen considerably and will become an invaluable companion on your inner journey.

Intuitive Scorpio

You probably are well acquainted with the voice of your intuition. Even if you call it by some other name—hunch, gut feeling, impulse—your intuition has been a part of your life as long as you can remember. Maybe your intuition is particularly strong when you're dreaming. Or perhaps it's such a natural part of your life that you don't think about it very much; you simply act on it.

Each of the fixed signs experiences intuition in a different way. For Taurus, body sensations are particularly strong; for Aquarius, the intellect is the strongest intuitive vehicle; for Leo, intuition works best through action; and for the Scorpio moon, intuition is strongest in the emotional realm. A sudden, inexplicable fluctuation in your emotions is often the first signal that your intuition is trying to seize your attention.

Think back to a time when you felt an urge or impulse to do something you hadn't consciously decided on doing. How did you feel emotionally? Were you sad? Happy? Uneasy? Frustrated? Exhilarated? Did you feel anything in your body—heartburn, tightness in the chest, butterflies in the stomach? How did you feel after you followed your hunch? Record the experience and your emotions.

This kind of entry is a useful prototype for your journal. It not only signals your conscious mind that you've committed to an intuitive journey, but also provides a record for feedback.

Intuition is often a symbolic language, so some of your intuitive impressions may come to you through symbolism. Take note of any such symbols. Over time, you'll compile your own symbolic "dictionary," an entire encoded language unique to *you*.

Scorpio Exploration

Pick out a novel that you love and describe a particularly moving scene that has stuck in your mind. Conjure up as much detail as you can. Where did the scene take place? Who was involved? What was going on? Why do you remember the scene? Was it frightening? Romantic? Thought-provoking? Describe colors, sensations, emotions. Write until the words dry up naturally.

What you're doing in this activity is allowing your intuition to answer a question that your conscious mind isn't aware of. While your conscious mind is busy doing the activity, your intuition flows through the writing itself. This type of activity also provides you with an ongoing record of your "hits" and "misses"—when you're right, when you're wrong—an important step in intuitive development.

The novel:_____

The scene:_____

_____

_____

_____

_____

The question you've just answered is at the end of the chapter. If you'd known the question before you described the scene, your description might not have been spontaneous. Your inner censor would have intruded.

Now that you know the question, interpret your description in light of your life *at this moment*. Project the issue a month into the future. Does it feel right? Does it *resonate*?

My interpretation: _____

_____

_____

_____

_____

_____

Engaging Your Senses

An astonishing amount of information comes to us through our senses. In any given moment, we know how something looks, feels, tastes, and smells. If it makes sounds, we hear them. Our senses tell us whether that something is hot, cold, or in between. We constantly make decisions based on that information. Our senses, though, are also our most direct and immediate connection with our intuition. By developing an awareness of our sensory universe, our intuition has an easier time expressing itself.

YOUR SENSES

Describe a place in as much detail as possible. It can be anywhere—the place where you are right this second, a location you've visited, a city, town, park, river, hotel, museum. Use all your senses when describing this place. *Be fully there.*

_____

_____

_____

_____

Now turn to Intuitive Reality Check #2, Chapter 17, to see what question you've answered.

NOTE: The question you answered in the Scorpio exploration activity is: In what area of my life will my intuition be most useful to me in the next four weeks?

13

Sagittarius Moon

Mutable, Fire
Ruler: Jupiter

The Journey

Oh, baby, let the good times roll! For a Sagittarian moon, those good times mean music, deep talk, exotic travel, esoteric ideas. At heart, you're an explorer and the expression of that eagerness depends entirely on your free will.

Astrologers often refer to the Sagittarius moon as the Oprah Winfrey moon because she illustrates so well what the moon is about. But other notable people also illustrate facets of this complex moon: Neil Armstrong, Yoko Ono, Al Pacino.

In one form or another, the search for a higher truth is what you're about. Even though you may go for years without being able to identify the inner itch that propels you from one experience to another, at some point you're able to identify the source of that itch. That moment of illumination may be triggered by an external event, a relationship, or some inner experience that literally transforms you.

The Sagittarian moon, like the Sag sun, is often blunt when dealing with others, particularly when the other guy just doesn't get what seems so obvious to you. Patience and nuance aren't your strong points. The exception to this occurs when you're pursuing something about which you feel passionate; then you have the patience of Mother Theresa and are as detail-oriented as a Virgo.

You're an animal lover and this love spans the gamut from the very small to the very large. With some Sagittarians, this love of animals filters down through every facet of life, resulting in a vegetarian, an animal rights activist, or an environmentalist. You have a sense of animals that often approaches the uncanny and have an innate conviction that they are every bit as self-aware as we are.

In the nurturing department, your Sagittarius moon indicates that your experience of your mother when you were younger was of a woman who valued integrity, education, and spirituality. She was probably a teacher in the truest sense of the word, ever mindful that you not only did your homework but that you understood whatever it entailed. She used every experience you had as a lesson about life.

If she was a traveler, then you were probably exposed to many diverse cultures from a young age. If she wasn't a traveler, then you were exposed to a vast array of ideologies and spiritual beliefs that still influence you as an adult. Or maybe you were lucky enough to get both. At any rate, Mom was definitely one of those people who listened to a different drummer, and while her song may not be yours, you're grateful for everything that she imparted to you.

Like your fire cousin, Aries, your thing is action. You would rather do than think about doing. As a mutable sign, you're emotionally adaptable. You have opinions about virtually everything and aren't the least bit hesitant in expressing these opinions. This becomes a problem if you're dogmatic or bombastic about what you believe and try to convert others to your way of thinking.

You're great at grasping the *big picture*. The challenge is to see the trees as clearly as you do the forest and to relate it to your daily life. With practice, your intuition can provide the essential details of that larger picture. For author Carol Bowman, a Libra with a Sagittarian moon, intuition proved crucial in what eventually became her life's work. When her four-year-old son developed a deep fear of loud noises at a fourth of July celebration, she didn't just dismiss it as something that would pass. She explored it, seeking the deeper reason behind his fear, and her research subsequently became a book, *Children's Past Lives*, and completely changed her life and that of her family.

This is the Sagittarian archetype in action, a journey that begins for a very personal reason and ends up as something much larger that benefits everyone.

Sometimes, a Sagittarian moon indicates that you, your mother, or one of her parents, was born in a foreign country, lived abroad, or married someone from a foreign country. More on this can be derived from the moon's placement in the horoscope houses, which is discussed in Part Two.

Recently at a literary conference, I struck up a conversation with a woman in her seventies who started telling me about her life. She had been born and raised in Kenya, a child of big game hunters, and had seen and experienced extraordinary things before she even hit her teens. Then her life underwent a vast change when she was in her early twenties. She left Kenya and ended up in Paris, dancing at the Moulin Rouge. At this point in her story, I asked if she was a Sagittarian.

"How'd you know?" she asked.

Because the life she described fit the archetypal Sagittarius. Sun, moon, or rising, this sign is easy to spot in others if you listen and observe.

Sagittarius rules the hips, thighs, liver and hepatic system. When you're blocked emotionally, health problems are likely to show up first in one of these areas in the body. This is when mind/body books may prove beneficial to you—*Anatomy of the Spirit* (Carolyn Myss), *Awakening Intuition* (Mona-Lisa Schultz), *The Intuitive Healer* (Marcia Emery), and Louise Hay's seminal work, *You Can Heal Your Life*. If reading isn't a direct enough experience for you, then attend mind/body workshops and seminars. In either case, put your intuition to work for you.

The Sagittarian Moon Child

Your little Sag rarely wastes time on the fine points. He jumps straight to the chase. His need to understand the bigger picture usually shows up as soon as he can get around on his own. Think of the Rugrats, exploring the world in their back yards with the eager innocence of Magellan or Marco Polo, and you'll have a fairly accurate picture of this child's motivating force.

This child asks the same kinds of piercing questions that a Scorpio moon child does, but for different reasons. Scorpio seeks the underlying power; Sagittarius seeks the underlying truth. It's important that your little Sag understands whatever he asks about; otherwise, his frustration overwhelms him and makes life difficult for you.

Given the opportunity, he can be an early reader. Books open worlds to him and help him to order his inner life. But even books can't be a substitute for direct experience. Like Aries and Leo, vicarious living isn't his preference.

The greatest gift you can give this child is exposure to a smorgasbord of cultures, belief systems, and experiences. This richness allows him to move through his adult life with a solid foundation of wisdom that only such experiences can build.

The wit associated with this moon sign shows up early. This is a child who understands jokes that even adults don't get and who has his own humorous take on events. You, as his parent, may not find the events very funny, but you'll appreciate his grasp of concepts.

Hidden Sagittarius

Even to the people who know you best, there doesn't seem to be much about you that is hidden. You're not a keeper of secrets, like Scorpio. Your head isn't buzzing with details, like Virgo. You tend to be very up front—sometimes too much so—about who you are and what you want. The hidden part of you actually has more to do with your life's direction than anything else. Blame Jupiter, your ruling planet.

Jupiter is about expansion, luck, serendipity. As ruler of Sagittarius, he brings luck and expansion into your life, often when you least expect it. In Greek mythology, Jupiter was called Zeus. Among the Romans, he was known as Jove. When the gods divided up the world, he was given Mount Olympus, from which he ruled the world of gods and men. Heady stuff. You can see why some Sagittarians often think their way is the only way, their beliefs are the only right beliefs. For the mere mortals ruled by Jupiter, the challenge lies in finding your single most burning passion, then making it your life's direction.

If you already know what your passion is and make your living at it, then don't read the rest of this section. It won't tell you anything you don't already know. If you know what your passion is and would like to make it your livelihood, then you may find the next part of this chapter helpful. In fact, as you become more intuitive, you may shortly find yourself in exactly the right place at the right time, talking to exactly the right person who will facilitate your dreams and ambitions.

The beauty of this moon is that once an awareness is awakened to synchronistic patterns, the concept is immediately grasped and incorporated into that bigger picture, then used at a practical level.

Intuitive Sagittarius

Flashes of intuition aren't new to you. An impulse, a hunch, a certain feeling: these things may be such an ordinary part of your life that you don't give them much thought. The next time it happens, take note of how you feel. Is there a sensation in the pit of your stomach? Does your head ache? Do you feel anxious or relaxed? What were you doing just before the flash hit you? What were you thinking? Had you been concerned with a particular issue or problem for which you were seeking a solution? In other words, was there a discernible *pattern*?

One woman with a Sagittarius moon usually feels lightheaded right before "a piece of the big picture slides into place." Sometimes, her fingertips tingle. Another young man feels butterflies in his stomach. If you don't feel anything physical, then you may sense a distinct shift in your consciousness. However it happens for you, recognizing the pattern is vital to understanding how your intuition works and how you can access it when you need it.

As you begin to take notice of the process, synchronicities will proliferate in your life. Consider them to be signposts that you're on the right track. Pay attention to what they're telling you about your passions, needs, and desires. Are you working in a dead-end job just to pay for health insurance? Is a close relationship draining your energy? Would you like to sell everything you own and buy an RV? Would you like to quit your job and go back to school? Whatever your desires and needs, synchronicities and your intuition help you recognize them. And once you've recognized them, it's easier to act on them.

You may want to keep some sort of record of the synchronicities you experience during this period because, as a cluster, they will contain signs and symbols unique to you and your intuitive discovery. Select whatever medium best suits you. One young man carried a journal in his pocket, a tape recorder in his car, and kept a computer file on his home PC. He began keeping track of his hunches as well, so that he had a running record of hits and misses. This helped him to build confidence in his intuition and to recognize the pattern that preceded an intuitive flash.

If this system or some permutation of it doesn't work for you, then devise a system that does. You don't have to use it forever, just long enough so that you can recognize the patterns that operate in your own life. Once you recognize those patterns, your intuition becomes more readily accessible to you.

In the next section, you're going to put your intuition to work in a new way. Don't worry about the process or the question, just be fully centered in the moment. It's really that easy!

Sagittarius Exploration

Think of a particularly vivid and emotional experience from your life. Maybe it happened in your childhood. Maybe it happened last week. The *when* is less important than the vividness of the experience. Describe that experience in the activity chart below.

This activity is designed to trigger your intuition, which will answer a question at the end of the chapter. Don't look at the question until you're finished with the exercise. *Trust* that your intuition already knows the question—and the answer.

My experience: _____

_____

_____

_____

_____

Now look at the question at the end of the chapter. If you'd known the question before you wrote about this experience, you might have slanted what you wrote in a particular way. Your inner censor might have interfered.

Now that you know the question, interpret your description in light of your life *right now*. Does it seem to fit? Does it *resonate*?

My interpretation: _____

_____

_____

_____

_____

The interpretation allows you to make associations between the patterns in what you wrote and your own life. Remember: all of this depicts an inner condition. Your intuition works to make the inner condition conscious.

Engaging Your Senses

Our senses are beautifully equipped for helping us live in the physical world. Through sight, taste, touch, smell, and hearing, we cull vast amounts of information about our physical environment and make hundreds of decisions daily based on that information. Much of this happens at an unconscious level. We do it by rote; it's part of our routine. But our senses are also our most direct link to our intuition; that's why it's called the "sixth sense."

In the activity that follows, you're going to become more acutely aware of your sensory universe and observe how your intuition often works through your senses.

YOUR SENSES

Describe a place in as much detail as possible. It can be anywhere—the place where you are right now, a location you've visited, a city, town, park, river, hotel, museum. Use all of your senses when describing this place. *Be fully there.*

_____

_____

_____

_____

_____

_____

Now turn to Intuitive Reality Check #2, Chapter 17, to see what question you've answered.

NOTE: The question you answered in the Sagittarius exploration section is: How can my intuition help me find a way to make my living at what I love doing?

14

Capricorn Moon

Cardinal, Earth
Ruler: Uranus

The Journey

Okay, the bad news first: the moon isn't comfortable here. It chafes at all the restrictions and rules that Capricorn seeks to impose and dislikes all that earthy grounding. Even worse, this was Hitler's moon.

The good news? The Dalai Lama also has a Capricorn moon.

These two extremes symbolize the essential puzzle of this moon and the way that free will influences the blueprint of a birth chart. So despite the fact that astrologers consider the Capricorn moon to be in detriment—i.e., that lunar energy doesn't work as smoothly in this sign—it's your moon and you need to understand its highest energy so that you can use it to your advantage.

One of the ways that astrologers define the qualities of planets in signs and houses as well as the aspects planets make to each other is by examining the birth charts of historical figures and celebrities. Unless you know these people, of course, it's impossible to know precisely what they felt or feel or what kind of inner lives they lived. But the *archetypal pattern* is apparent. With this in mind, a vast diversity lies between the two extremes of Hitler and the Dalai Lama.

Take George Washington. How did his Capricorn moon come into play? *Through structure.* How about Norman Rockwell? Structure certainly came into play through his art, but the focus was on *nostalgia for bygone days.* What about Lucille Ball? At first glance, she seems about as far from a Capricorn moon as you can get, particularly if you recall some of those slapstick episodes. But if you scratch beneath the surface, there it is: *a sound business sense*. She was one of the richest women in Hollywood.

What about J. D. Salinger? The man is known for basically a single work—*Catcher in the Rye*, which has become a classic. It has *staying power*. The man is a recluse, has published nothing in more than three decades, and we wonder, *who is this guy?* Several years ago, Joyce Maynard wrote about her brief affair with Salinger and suddenly some of that Capricorn moon influence snapped into clarity—*power and control over others through emotional detachment that borders on cruelty*, the shadow side of this moon sign.

Then there's Rod Steiger. No matter what movie he's in, his presence adds *quality* and *dignity*.

In each example, part of the sign's archetype is expressed and captured in a particular way. There is holding power with this moon sign, a kind of relentless persistence that endures despite whatever challenges and obstacles are encountered. No wonder the sign is symbolized by the goat, that most benign of creatures, capable of scaling a rocky incline with graceful endurance. It may take the goat his entire life to climb the summit, but he eventually makes it.

You set long-term goals and have the vision to maintain those goals while you're trying to achieve them. Sometimes, it seems like such a struggle that you question what you're doing and the path you're taking to get there. But usually, your tenacity is stronger than your doubt. And when it isn't, then you reassess your goals and either fine-tune them or find new ones. If the goal is built around a childhood dream, however, all bets are off. The dream is rooted so deeply in your psyche that nothing shakes you from it.

The problem with this kind of goal is that it can consume you to the point of obsession. Once you're obsessed, your judgment is skewed and it's too easy to compromise your integrity to achieve what you desire. Control becomes the primary issue. In essence, you set yourself up for a monumental fall. Richard Nixon is a prime example.

Capricorn loves structure, rules, and regulations. As a result, you may be locked into a rigid belief system that blocks you in some area of your life. It would be to your advantage to scrutinize your deepest beliefs and question whether they work well in your life. Maybe you're trapped in a dead-end marriage but can't bring yourself to get out because of the kids or because your religious beliefs forbid it. Maybe you believe that all doctors are god or that conventional thinking is always right. Regardless of how this rigidness shows up in your life, question the beliefs behind it. The mere act of questioning often triggers your intuition to reach out and find the answers you're seeking.

You may have a number of friendships or relationships with people who are older than you, or maybe you're involved with the elderly in some way. This peculiarity of the Capricorn moon is due to the influence of Saturn, which rules the sign. You may have nostalgia for "the good old days" or may value old things—antiques, for instance, or old photos. Or maybe you're a collector, the sort of person whose attic is jammed with *stuff*.

I've noticed many variations on this aspect of the Capricorn archetype. You may hit the garage sales and flea markets on weekends, looking for old costume jewelry. Or maybe you collect old postcards. Maybe you're not a collector in the conventional sense; maybe you, like me and my Capricorn moon, don't have any particular fondness for old things or even nostalgia for bygone days, but in some area of your life, you accumulate things, so many things that the mere thought of moving is overwhelming.

I collect books—not old books, not first editions, not even autographed books. Just books. I love to read, to browse, to page through books in a bookstore. My idea of a good time is to go to a bookstore and sip cappuccino as I browse the aisles of *books*. I rarely leave a bookstore without a book or, at the very least, a magazine. I'm a bookseller's dream. I even have a box of books next to my desk that I think of as my "emergency books," the ones I will take with me if I ever evacuate my house because of a hurricane. These are books I would take with me to that proverbial desert island. I can't live without them.

Maybe you have some collection like that. The point is that Capricorn moon defines itself to one extent or another through its possessions. And those possessions—whether it's beliefs or conventions or, well, books—may stifle your intuitive nature.

Capricorn rules the knees, skin, and bones, and is the natural ruler of the tenth house of the horoscope. When you're blocked emotionally, it may show up first in one of these areas, particularly if you're dealing with issues that relate to changing direction in your personal or professional life.

The Capricorn Moon Child

Wear your bike helmet. Don't cross the street on a red light. Say your prayers at night. Rules: this child knows them by heart, and lives by them. He's conscientious, a tireless worker, and even from a young age has a sound business sense. He's the kid who doesn't just set up a Saturday morning lemonade stand in front of the house; he sells franchises to his friends!

If you work with him in setting goals when he's young, you lay down the roots of a valuable lesson. In practice, this could entail earning and saving money for something expensive that he wants to buy. One father of a Capricorn moon child agreed to pay his son $5 a week for cleaning his room and giving the dog a bath. He also agreed to pay him a certain amount for every A he got on his report card. The boy saved every dime he made, his grades shot up, and within six months, he was able to buy the CD player that he wanted.

One of the most important lessons you can teach this child is how to relax, *really relax*, to kick back and enjoy the moment. This is incredibly hard for him to do. Even if he's camping or at the beach, for instance, he's *doing something*—collecting shells, hauling wood for the fire, setting up the tent. It's part of the task-oriented nature of the sign. It will be to his advantage—and yours, as his parent—if he develops a particular interest at a young age—books, a sport, animals. This will occupy his busy mind during down times and, in the long run, will benefit him spiritually, emotionally, and physically.

At some point, probably during his teens, your Capricorn moon child will overthrow all those rules and try to redefine himself. It may not be a pleasant time for you as a parent, but the process is necessary to your child's development as an individual. During this period, your greatest gift to him will be patience and understanding.

In the darker moments, however, repeat to yourself, "This, too, shall pass."

Hidden Capricorn

Under that tough, independent exterior lies an inner world often riddled with emotional insecurities. No telling why or when it originated, but it shadows you like some faithful pet and rears up to bite you when you least expect it. Saturn, the planet that rules Capricorn, is to blame for that.

In Roman mythology, he was known as Cronus and, not to put too fine a spin on it, he was one nasty dude. He castrated his father, Uranus, with a jagged sickle and devoured all of his own children. No wonder, then, that for years, astrologers considered Saturn a "malefic," a genuine bad guy.

Even though he still isn't the preferred planet in the zodiac, his role has been somewhat redefined in contemporary times. Without structure and rules, after all, we would have anarchy. Without goals, we would drift aimlessly through life. Without conscience, we would be a society of misfits and renegades. The problems start when we place too much emphasis on these qualities. If there's too much Saturn in a society, it becomes a police state, the world of *Farenheit 451*. If there's too much Saturn in our personal lives, we become workaholics, drones wearing blinders. Our creativity and spontaneity wither and eventually atrophy. If ambition and power overtake our lives, they become our reason for being and our hearts turn to stone.

Intuitive Capricorn

Thanks to Saturn's heavy-handed way of doing things, you probably are quite adept at categorizing your emotions. You push them into some convenient slot "until you can get to them." Your emotions are often like bothersome neighbors you seek to avoid until it's convenient for you to deal with them. If you do this long enough, you lose touch with what you feel. And once that happens, your intuition goes into hibernation.

The solution is obvious. Keep your finger on your heart's pulse. Pay attention to what you feel during the course of a day. Pay attention to where your thoughts take you. Is there a vast gulf between the two? Are your heart and mind in sync?

Keeping a record of your impressions is helpful; that recommendation is included with nearly every moon sign in this book. Use whatever feels most comfortable to you—a notebook, a tape recorder, a file on your computer. Seeing your "hits"—when your intuition is on target—builds confidence in your intuition. But if you're not a journal sort of person, then strive to be more aware of your feelings, to deal with each emotion as you feel it, rather than pushing it aside to deal with later. This will lead you directly into your intuitive self.

Once you get past your inner censor, you can be exceptionally intuitive, particularly when you're in need of information. Then, it's as if your censor simply steps aside and lets the intuitive flow rush in.

But the proof is in the doing, right?

As a cardinal earth sign, you're great at moving in a singular, practical direction in your life. You have a routine that grounds you, fixes you in time and space. You may not be crazy about abrupt change. But for just a few moments, imagine your life as it might be *if it were ideal*. Get wild and crazy. Where would you live? What kind of work would you do? What are your passions in this other life? Are you married or single? What colors are the rooms in which you live? Where do you work? Do you have kids? Animals?

Now, in the space below, write about this ideal life until the images and words dry up on their own. The point here is to let your creative, intuitive self flow out and, in doing so, answer a question you haven't seen which is noted at the end of the chapter. Trust that your intuition knows the question and the answer.

Read over what you've written and look for recurring themes, colors, ideas, anything you mention more than once. These repetitive words or phrases may be patterns that are emerging around the question listed at the end of the chapter. Now take a look at the question and interpret what you've written in light of the question. By writing out your interpretation, you become more aware of the language of your intuition.

CAPRICORN EXPLORATION

My ideal life: _____

_____

_____

_____

_____

_____

_____

_____

My interpretation: _____

_____

_____

_____

_____

Your Power Object

While browsing in a bookstore one day, I came across a book so small and slender it was almost lost in the stacks. It was called *little stone*. Its author, James Wanless, is the creator of the splendid Voyager Tarot, a deck well-known to people who collect tarot decks or who read tarot cards. Curious, and secretly hoping it was the companion of a new deck Wanless had created, I snatched it off the shelf and started reading.

There's no tarot in this book, but there's plenty of magic. It's about how to find and use a stone as a personal power object. Power objects are used in many Native American spiritual traditions and Carl Jung, in his autobiography, *Memories, Dreams, and Reflections*, writes movingly of a stone he found as a child. He kept it in a matchbox and carried it around with him. He told his secrets to this stone. He communicated with it. This stone was his friend, his companion, and in many ways it also became his mentor.

"In little stone, what you are seeking is a friend, a friend for life," Wanless writes. What you're seeking is an immediate, direct connection with your intuition and a stone might be just the ticket. It appeals to the earthy side of you.

Where you look is as vital to your search as the frame of mind that goes with you. The day my daughter and I went searching, it was drizzling. Our dog was with us and she kept distracting us. We found ugly rocks—little chunks of concrete or limestone hidden under hedges. We decided collecting shells at the beach was more fun and gave up looking for stones. But the idea of the little stone stayed with me. I couldn't shake the notion that both of us might find stones that are conduits to our intuition. So we've decided that on our vacation north this summer, we'll look along riverbanks for flat, smooth stones.

Look for your own personal power object. It doesn't have to be a stone, but it should be something connected to the earth, that speaks to *you*. It should also be small enough to carry with you. Once you've found your power object, spend a few minutes imbuing it with your own energy through touching it, meditating with it, or merely sitting quietly with it between your fingers or in the palm of your hand. Then, while holding your object, shut your eyes, focus on what you would like to know, and relax.

You probably will feel a shift in your awareness and may start to get impressions about your question. If nothing happens, try again later. Once you get into the habit of using your power object in this way, it becomes an automatic signal to your subconscious that you're seeking intuitive information. Your inner censor steps out of the way.

Engaging Your Senses

Which of your five senses is the sharpest? Sight? Tastebuds? Touch? Do you have an acute sense of hearing or smell? An enormous amount of information comes to us through our senses and we make decisions daily based on that information. But do we really engage our senses to the fullest? It's important that we do because our senses are our most immediate link to our intuition.

In the activity that follows, you're going to call fully on your sensory universe to answer a question. You don't consciously know what question you'll be answering, but trust that your intuition not only knows the question but the answer as well.

Describe a place in as much detail as possible and use all of your senses. The place can be anywhere—a location or city you've visited, the place where you live, a town, park, river, forest, hotel, museum. *Be fully there.*

_____

_____

_____

_____

_____

Turn to Intuitive Reality Check #2, Chapter 17, to see what question you've just answered.

NOTE: The question you answered in the Capricorn exploration exercise is: What changes can I make in my life in the next four months that will enable me to achieve my goals?

15

Aquarius Moon

Fixed, Air
Ruler: Uranus

The Journey

The adage about marching to a different drummer fits you. In fact, at times you hear its music in your very cells, and feel compelled to decipher the message and act on it. This is the sign, after all, that ushers in new paradigms by refusing to go along with the status quo.

The visionary component to this moon sign gives you an edge on new trends. You spot the next wave long before anyone else does. The trick is acting on it and putting it to work for you in your personal and professional life. All too often your rational mind gets in the way, arguing and putting up blocks, trying to keep you within the confining box of consensus reality. Or someone close to you—a parent, close friend, significant other—inadvertently plays that role and you suddenly find yourself on the defensive.

This doesn't mean that you're always in a defensive position. It does mean, however, that until you incorporate the visionary component into your daily life, you may feel considerable emotional discomfort. The area of your life where you're most likely to feel this depends on the house in which your moon falls in your natal horoscope. Is it in one-to-one relationships where you feel this discomfort most? Then it's likely that your moon is in the seventh house—or forms significant aspects or angles (see Part Three) to your seventh house.

You gravitate toward groups of people who share some of your beliefs and interests. This is true to some extent for all of us, but for you it's particularly important. The groups often encompass humanitarian ideals, a particular spiritual belief system, or some unique interest that you have. The people in this group may not be your closest friends, but the thread that binds you is strong.

One writer with an Aquarian moon meets every Friday with her writers' group. They discuss ideas, critique each other's work, and generally provide support for each other. They appreciate the individuality that each person brings to the group and emphasize that individuality in their critiques of each other's work and ideas.

This focus on individuality is another facet of the Aquarian moon. Despite your involvement with group activities, you recognize that each of us is unique. You're very tolerant of people who think and believe differently than you do and yet, you can't abide social injustices of any sort. This is where your humanitarian bent and your radical ideas may show up most strongly.

Since the moon also symbolizes your experience of your childhood caregiver, it's likely that you perceived Mom as a bright, capable woman, although somewhat emotionally detached. This detachment may have baffled you when you were a kid. Instead of the hug you hoped for when you skinned your knee, you got, "It's fine, hon. Now go on out and play." You didn't see Mom as a cuddler; she wasn't the type to tickle your back as you went to sleep at night. If she read you bedtime stories, then the stories were ones that *she* wanted to read, not the kind you necessarily wanted to hear.

But when it came to your mind and your spirit, she was the best. She nurtured your curiosity about the world in whatever way she could—books, museums, movies, music, *experiences*. She included you in her various pet projects and passions—funding drives for the homeless, the local literacy program, a museum restoration project. She acknowledged your creative potential and you, in turn, will do the same for the people you nurture.

Your will is particularly strong and you understand intuitively how to focus it to achieve what you desire. The challenge is to understand consciously how your will and your intent create your reality, and then apply what you know to create the kind of life that you want. It really is as simple or as difficult as *you* make it.

Aquarius rules the ankles, shins, and circulatory system.

The Aquarian Moon Child

This kid is a paradigm buster before he's out of diapers. He doesn't follow any agenda except his own, so you might as well toss out all those books about baby and toddler milestones, because he won't fit the norm.

If you're not convinced of this when he's an infant, you're sure to change your mind when he's old enough to have friends. He gravitates toward kids who are unusual or eccentric in some way and, bottom line, you may not like all these kids. But as long as they aren't mean or hurtful to your child in any way, you're better off not interfering. In fact, one of the reasons you have an Aquarian moon child is to shake up your perceptions about what is "normal" or "ordinary." So when your child brings home the unusual or the strange—human, animal or otherwise—pay attention. There's something here for you to learn as well.

Given the opportunity, this child is an early reader. Books help him to define and understand his world. He needs concepts to work with, ideas that he can mull over, analyze, dissect, and apply to his own life. As he gets older, these concepts can become large, sweeping canvases against which he builds his own life. Remember: this moon is an air sign. It's mental. Without intellectual stimulation, this child's energy withers and his potential remains only that— *potential.*

This child may besiege you with questions, just as his Gemini moon cousin does. But where the Gemini sometimes asks just to hear himself asking, the Aquarian moon child asks with a profundity that may sound like a Zen koan. *Hey, Dad, what's the sound of one hand clapping?*

If there's any rule to follow with this child, it's this: expect the unexpected. And then you, as his parent, must embrace it.

Hidden Aquarius

One of the best descriptions of the Aquarius moon comes from astrologer Edmond H. Wollmann, in his book *The Integrated Astro-*

logical Guide to Self-Empowerment (Altair, 1998). "The moon in Aquarius needs to be recognized for its uniqueness."

The same thing might be said about your fixed cousin, the Leo moon, but with one important difference. The Leo moon pounds his fists against his chest and screams, "Hey, recognize me, I'm here!" The Aquarius moon gains recognition through acting on his convictions.

So you hear the drummer, the beat, your spiritual call of the wild, but you can't follow it because you don't trust what you hear, or because you believe the tide of your life is moving against it.

Maybe you detest your day job but you can't bring yourself to leave it to pursue your real passion, photography. Maybe you believe that: (a) you need the health insurance and benefits; (b) no photographer makes a living snapping the shutter or: (c) you haven't mastered your craft. Whatever reason your rational mind has provided, there's only one thing you need to ask yourself. Can you live for the next ten or twenty years knowing that you may never attain what you really desire because you stuck to the safe route?

The hidden part of you hungers for deeper knowledge, deeper experiences, the bigger picture. And you probably aren't going to get much of that on the safe route. But no one can tell you any of this. You have to discover it for yourself, and it's likely that you discover it through an individual or a group of individuals who seem to embody some belief or ideal that you hold. As you seek to discover that deeper knowledge, your intuition becomes a major voice in your life.

Uranus rules Aquarius and there is no planet that is more unpredictable, erratic, or individualistic. In astrological terms, I think of this planet as a dramatic display of lightning, that kind of lightning you see during the hottest parts of the summer, jagged bolts that shatter the perfection of a navy-blue sky.

In the movie *Virus*, an electrical energy is "transmitted" from the Russian space station through the satellite dishes on a Russian research vessel in the South Pacific. In typical Hollywood fashion, the energy is the enemy. But in astrological terms, this energy is alive, it's a life form, it's *Uranian*. It's immensely powerful, erratic, intelligent. And when this kind of energy pierces your intuition, you are changed. Irrevocably. Forever.

A number of years ago, writer and Aquarian moon Nancy Pickard bought Louse Hay's classic, *How to Heal Your Life*. She'd suffered for years from chronic neck pain and, every night, took a Tylenol to relieve her discomfort. After she read Hay's book, she bought Hay's audio tapes and worked with them in an attempt to get rid of the neck pain once and for all. Within thirty days, she had done exactly that.

This marked the beginning of a paradigm shift for her. Now that she had proven to herself that her will was an exceptionally powerful tool for creating her reality, Nancy proceeded to apply it to all areas of her life. Her intuition burgeoned. Eight years later, she felt confident enough in her beliefs about "living in a safe universe" to drop her health insurance. If and when she gets sick, she seeks the underlying reason and works with it; she doesn't look for the quick fix of drugs and doctors. At the most fundamental levels, she believes that she creates her own reality, that her intuition is the most vital force in her life, and she's now living that belief.

This story represents Uranian energy at its pinnacle—heightened intuition, beliefs that others might consider eccentric or, at the least, highly unusual, a profound paradigm shift, and, finally, a leap into the void, the unknown. It illustrates the hidden power of the visionary Aquarian moon.

But this path isn't for everyone with an Aquarian moon. It requires total commitment and an honest scrutiny of your deepest core beliefs, keen observation of how these beliefs are reflected in your daily life, and a desire to change the beliefs that no longer work. Unless you're willing to do the belief work, however, I don't recommend that you or anyone else cancel health insurance or ignore doctors and medicine.

If you're ready to do the work, though, you'll find hundreds of resources on the Internet.

Intuitive Aquarius

Let's play a game. In the spaces below, jot down seven words or phrases that come immediately to mind. Don't think too much about this; a few seconds per word is sufficient. What you're doing in this activity is allowing your intuition to answer a question that your conscious mind isn't aware of.

1. _____
2. _____
3. _____
4. _____
5. _____
6. _____
7. _____

Are there any immediate associations among these words that strike you? Do they have a common theme, such as color or shape? Do they concern emotions? Places? People? Sounds? Impressions? Music?

Some lists, like the one below that was made by a young man with an Aquarian moon, have obvious themes:

1. hunger
2. taste of ginger
3. smell of salt water
4. a slight discomfort in my temple
5. my chair is too hard
6. relaxing by the ocean
7. Mississippi River

The two primary themes are water and physical sensations. Your themes may be something entirely different. If no particular theme leaps out at you, then look for a connection between the words themselves. Quite often, some emotion or memory will be the connecting thread. Remember: this is synchronicity in action, the language of your intuition.

The question you've answered with this list is: *How can I develop my intuition most fully right now?* For the young man in the above example, the answer seems to be that his body is his most direct link with his intuition and that proximity to water may figure into that development in some way. This young man admits that he has a lot of gut feelings and hunches. Sometimes, he gets a hot or burning sensation in his solar plexus when he "just knows" information he has no logical way of knowing.

What conclusion do you draw from your own list?

One of the quickest ways to develop and expand your intuition is to seize your fears and confront them. Most of us fear the unknown, but what you're looking for is the specific fears that keep you awake at night, the ones that make your throat go tight and hot, and that prevent you from doing something you need or want to do. When you try to overcome a fear—any fear—you put yourself in an unfamiliar situation. Your senses suddenly sharpen and you're more attuned intuitively. The challenge is to listen to your intuition and act on what it tells you.

In the beginning, your inner censor, your left brain, is going to argue stridently about why you should or shouldn't do something. Eventually, if you keep to your path, it becomes easier to trust your intuition so that, ultimately, your intuitive and logical minds work together. That's the ideal.

Testing Your Intuition

As a fixed sign, your beliefs and opinions build slowly over the course of your life and once they're in place, you hold on to them fiercely. This can be a problem when you're trying to release old beliefs that no longer serve your best interests.

So now you're going to do an exercise that will help you identify broad patterns that are operating in your life, the first step to recognizing which beliefs no longer work for you. A similar version of this exercise appears in the Leo moon section, another fixed sign that is reluctant to shed what no longer works.

Get a box of toothpicks and dump the contents on a smooth, hard surface—a table or floor work best. Don't rearrange them or mess with them in any way. Stand up and step back a foot or so and look at them. Think of the scene in *Rain Man* where Tom Cruise knocks a box of toothpicks to the floor and his autistic brother, Dustin Hoffman, glances at them and announces the exact number scattered at his feet. He didn't count them. *He perceived a pattern.* That's what you're trying to do.

What shapes do the toothpicks form? Is there a discernible pattern? Be playful, let your imagination fill in the blanks and connect the dots. Jot your impressions in the space below. Be detailed. If some of the toothpicks seem to suggest a tree, then imagine what the tree looks like. Is it a summer tree, green and full? Or is it a winter tree, stripped to the bone? Once you've recorded your impressions, interpret them, creating a kind of story from them related to your own life. What you're doing in this activity is allowing your intuition to answer a question posed at the end of this chapter. The point is to bring home the fact that your intuition already knows the question and the answer, even though you don't know it consciously.

AQUARIUS EXPLORATION

My impressions: _____

_____

_____

_____

_____

My interpretation: _____

_____

_____

_____

_____

_____

Turn to the end of the chapter to see what question you've just answered.

Engaging Your Senses

Human beings are beautifully equipped for physical life. Our senses are finely tuned instruments that gather and disseminate information that allows us to live in our environment. Daily, we make dozens of decisions based on what our senses tell us. But how many of us really think about our senses?

Our senses are our most intimate and direct link to our intuition. By becoming more aware of our sensory universe, we encourage our intuition to express itself. That's what you're doing in this activity.

YOUR SENSES

Describe a place in as much detail as possible. It can be anywhere—your home, a garden, museum, plaza, church, even someplace imaginary. Use all your senses when you describe this place. *Be fully there.*

_____

_____

_____

_____

Now turn to Intuitive Reality Check #2, Chapter 17, to see what question you've answered.

NOTE: In the toothpick exercise, you answered the question: What belief or fear is holding me back?

16

Pisces Moon

Mutable, Water
Ruler: Neptune

The Journey

Okay, do you want the bottom line first? No, probably not. Maybe a middle line or a diagonal line, but please, not the bottom line. Not today. Maybe next week you'll be in a better frame of mind to deal with The Bottom Line. Or maybe not. In fact, it's likely that you may never want to hear the bottom line, that your life is much happier without Bottom Lines. If that's the case, then skip the next few paragraphs. But if you think you're ready for The Bottom Line, then keep reading.

You're the archetypal dreamer, your feet never really firmly rooted on the earth. *Flaky* or *mushhead* may be adjectives you heard as a kid, but the people who called you that didn't have a clue about who you really were or are. This moon sign is the most compassionate of the zodiac, the true bleeding heart.

You can't pass a homeless person on the street without giving him money, and you definitely can't resist the soulful gaze of a stray pup or kitten. Injustices of any sort fill you with such sadness that quite often you feel overcome and depressed by what you see around you. Your challenge is to detach emotionally from situations and people who cause you this kind of anguish.

Part of the problem is that you're a psychic sponge who soaks up the emotions and moods of the people around you. This alone makes it vital that you associate with upbeat, positive people and situations that boost your energy rather than sap it. In this way, you're like the Cancer and Scorpio moons, except for you it's worse, much worse.

Women with this moon sign tend to be deeply intuitive, if not outright psychic, and often walk a fine line between devotion to their loved ones and families and martyrdom. Men with this moon sign are often torn between what their minds demand and what their hearts whisper. As a result, they have trouble with commitment. They either commit and then vanish or they go overboard like the Duke of Windsor, who gave up the throne to marry the divorcée he loved.

At the core, though, both men and women with Pisces moons are misty-eyed romantics who are forever seeking some idealized version of the opposite sex. When the person doesn't measure up, the relationship usually falls apart, so they become their own worst enemies where relationships are concerned.

As a mutable water sign, you have the adaptability of Gemini and Sagittarius and the emotional intelligence of Cancer and Scorpio. Pisces is the only other sign besides Gemini that's symbolized by two of something—in this case, two fish swimming in opposite directions. Duality is inherent in both signs, but with Gemini, it's a mental duality and with Pisces, it's emotional. The negative manifestation of this emotional duality is that you often have a tough time making decisions. *Should I stay in the marriage or get out?* For some Pisces moon people, this indecisiveness extends to even the smallest decisions. *Should I have cereal or cantaloupe for breakfast?* There's no easy way to combat indecisiveness like this except to make a decision and then stick with it.

At the heart of this indecisiveness lies a lack of trust in yourself, in your own worth as a unique individual. Perhaps this lack of self-confidence is one of the reasons that Pisces moon people have a general tendency to play the role of victim. Since lack of confidence and feelings of worthlessness usually have their roots in early childhood, it's important to take a look at what the Pisces moon says about your experience of your mother.

Pisces moon people have three broad types of experiences with their mothers. The first type of experience is that of a dependent woman who is frequently an emotional basket case in some area of her life—relationships, jobs, health, and money are several that I've run across repeatedly. She is more of a friend than a mother and considers her child to be one of her closest confidantes. Quite often, she has substance abuse problems, notably alcohol. Her dependency can sometimes turn toward you, her child, so that you may end up caring for her when she's ill or putting her to bed when she's too drunk to stand. You grow up fast with this kind of mother.

The second type of mother is the perennial bleeding heart. She nurtures the lost, the weary, the bereaved, the substance abuser, the mentally ill. You name it, she takes care of it and, as a result, neglects her own loved ones. She, of course, wouldn't see it that way. After all, she loves her children, provides for them, tends to them. And yet . . . why do her kids spend more time at the homes of their friends than they do in their own home?

The third type is tougher to pin down. She lives in a dream world, or a Cinderella land, or a Middle Earth where magic still reigns. She is deeply spiritual, mystical, perhaps even clairvoyant, and always sees things you wish that she didn't. She may also be a martyr to a cause—and you may be that cause. You may be her mission. This type of mother usually has a deep understanding of the mysterious connections in life, the odd synchronicities, the weird and the strange topics that no other mother will acknowledge, much less discuss. Life with her is rarely boring.

Pisces rules the feet and the lymphatic system. When you're blocked emotionally, the blockage is likely to show up in one of these areas first. The wonderful thing about you, however, is that you live so close to the heart of your emotions that you know almost instantly when something is out of whack. Even if you can't pinpoint the exact cause, you *feel* the imbalance. Your challenge is to trust that feeling.

The Pisces Moon Child

Those huge dreamy eyes. That heart as big as the outdoors. That quick, often mischievous smile. This kid wins you over as soon as you look at her. Even from her earlier years, she isn't like other kids.

She perceives things that others don't, may have imaginary play-mates, and is often fascinated by the weird and the strange. As she gets older, she may exhibit a clairvoyance that can be unsettling to a parent who isn't prepared for it.

During a camping trip to northern Florida, my ten-year-old daughter, Megan, and her buddy, Samantha, had been experiment-ing with psychometry—the ability to read objects through the sense of touch. They had a wonderful opportunity to try out what they'd learned when we visited an old fort that been used to imprison Seminole Indians during the 1800s. In one room, I suggested they put their hands against the cold, moist walls, shut their eyes, and see what impressions they could pick up. Megan (Pisces rising) and Sam (Pisces moon), had no idea what had taken place in this room in the distant past. But both reported they heard people crying and moaning and felt a deep and terrible sadness. Both also said they sensed these people had been horribly thirsty and hungry.

Common sense says that of course prisoners in the 1800s would be hungry, thirsty, and sad in such a place. But this particular room wasn't in the area where prisoners had been held. We later asked a tour guide what the room had been used for and were told that pris-oners had been brought here for punishment. In this room, they were deprived of food and water.

This was a prime example of Piscean clairvoyance in action.

This same Piscean energy, however, can drive you nuts when your child has to make a decision about something and changes her mind half a dozen times in as many minutes. Quite often, *you* end up making the decision for her. Even more maddening is the Pisces moon kid who, when asked what she wants to do, shrugs and says, *I don't know,* or *I don't care.*

If you handle this by always making the decision for your child, then she may become a co-dependent adult who expects other peo-ple to make decisions for her. If you handle it by waiting for her to make up her mind (which can take a *very* long time), then she may become the sort of adult who uses ambivalence and indecisiveness as a way of controlling and manipulating situations and other people.

The answer? Suggest she rely on her intuition. What does she *feel* about the situation? Does it make her uncomfortable? Happy?

What? Once you begin to speak this child's language, life becomes easier for both of you.

And in the meantime, well, there are plenty of ways to redirect her attention. Books, music, dancing, art. She has a reservoir of artistic talent begging to be tapped. She also loves animals; they speak each other's language.

She's different, this one, and while she's on loan to you, your life is deeply enriched.

Hidden Pisces

Here's the deal. Whether you believe it was accident, destiny, or choice, you have the ability to tap into universes and you do it best when you're relaxed, at the edge of sleep, or dreaming. These are the times when the barrier between your physical world and other worlds becomes translucent—and, with practice, transparent.

In the movie *The Sixth Sense*, a young boy sees the dead. He doesn't see them occasionally; he sees them all of the time. This ability terrorizes him and causes him unimagined anguish. When the boy finally confides his "secret" to child psychologist Bruce Willis, Willis thinks the kid will have to be institutionalized. Willis, of course, gradually realizes the boy really can see the dead. But the journey that both boy and man take to arrive at this point is riveting and pure Piscean. You have a gift; don't be afraid to use it.

Millie Gemondo, a West Virginia intuitive, is a Sagittarian with a Pisces moon. She is uncannily accurate about picking up when someone the client knows is going to "pass over." For some of her other clients, she has brought messages from the dead that she had no way of knowing, the kind of messages that resonate so strongly the client breaks down in tears. Millie doesn't particularly like this aspect of her work. She prefers good news. But she has successfully integrated her intuition into the rest of her life and says what she sees.

This isn't to say that all Pisces moon people are psychics who commune with the dead. But most Pisces moons are deeply intuitive, and the sooner you let this part of yourself out of the closet, the happier you will be.

Intuitive Pisces

As with your water siblings, Cancer and Scorpio, emotions are the lens through which you perceive the world and are the vehicle through which you connect to your intuition. But Cancer's intuitive focus is often on family and loved ones, and Scorpio's focus revolves around power issues. Your intuition differs from the other two in that it's deeper and broader. With little conscious effort, you're able to tap into psychic reservoirs for information in virtually any area of your life.

Yeah, sure, you're probably saying. *How do I do that?*

The irony is that you probably do it all of the time without even thinking about it. The difference is that now you're going to develop a conscious awareness of how your intuition works. The following activity is designed to do exactly that.

Pick a spot where you won't be interrupted for five or ten minutes, and have paper and pen handy. Center yourself with some deep breathing. You might want to try alternate nostril breathing, which brings both halves of the brain into alignment. Pinch your right nostril shut, inhale through the left, hold to the count of ten, then exhale through the right nostril. Then pinch your left nostril shut, inhale and hold to the count of ten, and exhale through the left nostril. Repeat this several times.

Now you're going to try to tune in on tomorrow and "see" a headline from tomorrow's newspaper. If it comes to you in symbols, in much the same way that dreams often do, then record the symbols and don't try to interpret them until later. You may get an impression, a bodily sensation, or just a feeling. However it comes to you, jot it down in the space below.

TOMORROW'S HEADLINE

Date: _____

My impression: _____

_____

_____

_____

My interpretation:_____

_____

_____

_____

Check the headlines the day after you do this activity. Were you correct? Then you've got a "hit." If you were wrong, it's a "miss."

With practice, your accuracy and confidence in your own intuitive ability should increase dramatically. Eventually, you won't have to use the breathing technique at all; you'll simply pose a question to yourself and focus.

One Pisces moon woman found that when she gave her intuition a signal, her answers came more quickly. She shuts her eyes and rolls them upward until she feels a tension in the middle of her forehead. Experiment and find your own signal.

Testing Your Intuition

Let's have some fun. In the next activity, you're going to recall a scene from a movie that stuck in your mind. In the space below, write about the scene and use as many details as you can. Where and when did the scene occur? Who were the characters and why do you feel what you do about them? What were the characters wearing and doing? What was going on in this particular scene? Write until you have nothing left to say.

This activity will prove to you just how accurate your intuition is. What you are doing is answering a question that is noted at the end of the chapter. Your intuition already knows the question you're answering, even though you don't know consciously what it is.

PISCES EXPLORATION

The movie: _____

The scene: _____

_____

_____

_____

Now look up the question at the end of the chapter. If you had known the question before you described the scene, your inner censor might have interfered.

Now that you know the question, interpret your description in light of your life *at this moment*.

My interpretation: _____

_____

_____

_____

Does this resonate? Does it feel right?

Engaging Your Senses

Our senses act as our conduits in the physical world. They cull information about our immediate environment that allows us to make decisions. Our senses are also our most intimate and immediate connection to our intuition. The next activity is going to make you aware of your sensory universe and how your intuition works through your senses.

YOUR SENSES

Describe a place in as much detail as possible. It can be anywhere—the place where you are right this second, a location you've visited, a city, town, park, river. Use all of your senses when describing this place. *Be fully there.*

_____

_____

_____

_____

_____

_____

Now turn to Intuitive Reality Check #2, Chapter 17, to see what question you've just answered.

NOTE: The question you answered in the Pisces exploration area is: What can I expect in my personal relationships (significant other) in the next four weeks?

17

Intuitive Reality Check #2: Oracles and Intuition

Getting Started

Some people who seek intuitive development do it on a whim, an impulse, to satisfy an itch they don't understand. Other people seek it consciously, and they usually are the ones who begin with some type of oracle.

When you enter the word *oracle* on Amazon.com's search engine, more than a hundred hits come up. These oracles range from African and angel oracles to Druids and goddess oracles to runes, the tarot, and the *I Ching*. Although astrologers don't like to think of astrology as an oracle, it's exactly that.

All oracles have certain attributes in common: a unique language, special rules, a particular tool—astrological symbols, cards, runes, coins. In each instance, the tool creates a *pattern* that relates to an inner condition *as it exists in this moment*. The pattern is an expression of that inner condition; it's the internal made manifest. In physicist David Bohm's terms, the pattern is the explicate order and it has unfolded out of the implicate or hidden order. The pattern is the synchronicity and the synchronicity is the language of intuition.

Oracles of any type provide an excellent means for discovering, developing, and learning to use your intuition. As you become able to make full use of your own lunar energies, you gradually dispense with the external oracle and become your own oracle by interpreting the hidden signals in your life. Until you get to that point, let's take a look at some of the commonly used oracles you can employ to access your intuition.

Cards

One popular type of oracle is divination, or fortunetelling cards. You can use either a regular deck of playing cards or specialized cards such as the tarot. Whichever you choose, you have to learn the meanings of the cards before you can use them. With the tarot, that means learning seventy-eight cards, and if you read reversed positions, that figure doubles. In addition to learning the meanings, you need to know a layout or spread for the cards, where each position means something—present-past-future, for instance, is the simplest type of spread. Then it's necessary to learn how to string the meanings of the cards together to form a story. Your intuition kicks in when you interpret that story.

Some excellent tarot books are *Power Tarot* by myself and Phyllis Vega (Simon & Schuster), any tarot book by Mary Greer, and *The Voyager Tarot* by James Wanless.

If tarot cards don't speak to you, try using a regular deck of playing cards. Again, you'll have to learn the individual meanings of the fifty-two cards, and how to use them in layouts and string together a story. As with the tarot cards, what you're looking for is a pattern, a singular theme, a plot thread that runs throughout the pattern. Books on regular playing cards as oracles aren't as numerous as books on the tarot. But check the New Age section of your local bookstore.

If you have a water moon, either type of deck will do because you have the innate intuitive ability to perceive patterns in anything. Air and earth moons gravitate toward the tarot because of the artwork on the decks. Fire moons like whichever is easier to learn and use.

There are more than three hundred different tarot decks presently on the market, and the artwork on many of them is exquisite. There's even a Salvadore Dali deck, which retails for about $100. In most instances, tarot decks are fashioned after the traditional Rider-Waite deck, which is recommended for beginners. Once you learn the meanings of the cards and feel comfortable using them, you may want to sample other decks. Different artwork speaks differently to your intuition and provides new kinds of interpretations. You may find that one deck will work better for personal questions and another deck for professional questions. Air and earth moon signs are the most likely ones to collect decks.

As you become proficient with cards, you may find that you use them only for confirmation of what your intuition is telling you. Or you may use them in conjunction with some other oracle, for a different perspective on the same question or issue.

The I Ching

The *I Ching*, or *Book of Changes*, is an ancient Chinese book of wisdom and prophecy. This Chinese oracle has more than five thousand years of history behind it. Richard Wilhelm began his translation of the book in 1913, while living in China, and completed it in 1923. The book didn't reach a wider readership until 1950, when the Wilhelm edition was published by the Bollingen Foundation with Carl Jung's now-famous forward that introduced the concept of synchronicity.

The *I Ching* contains sixty-four hexagrams and accompanying commentary. The easiest way to use the *I Ching* is to toss coins. Use three coins, each side assigned a numerical value. To determine your hexagram, you toss the coins six times, once for each line. Most editions of the *I Ching* contain instructions for how this works. If the first hexagram contains at least one "changing line," you will get a second hexagram. Traditionally, the first hexagram is the situation as it exists now; the second hexagram is the evolvement of the situation. The second unfolds from the first.

The language of the *I Ching* is couched in terms of Chinese thought and culture, which can make it difficult for the Western mind to understand. It's filled with metaphors and symbolism that must be interpreted in light of your particular question. It's not for everyone. But it has one distinct advantage over cards and some other types of oracles because, as one friend of mine puts it, "the *Ching* is chatty." It talks to you in words, as opposed to visual symbols.

I first discovered the *I Ching* in 1968 and have used it off and on ever since. I still find it difficult to understand, but there are times when its answers are so specific and immediate to my question that there's no room for misinterpretation. Other times, it seems to be addressing issues other than what I asked about and I don't get anything out of it. You'll have to decide on your own. Experiment with it.

People with earth sign moons seem to have the endurance to study and use the *I Ching*. Fire sign moons usually lack the patience the *I Ching* requires. Air sign moons tackle it, wrestle with it, and may eventually master it intellectually. Water sign moons respond emotionally to the *I Ching*, feeling their way through the material.

While the *I Ching* is an excellent intuitive device and really provides a picture of how synchronicity works, you may want to start with a book that interprets the hexagrams with the Western reader in mind. One of the best is Carolyn Anthony's *A Guide to the I Ching* (Anthony Publishing).

Runes

Runes are characters used for inscriptions by early Germanic and Scandinavian peoples. Ralph Blum's *The Book of Runes* (St. Martin's, 1997) remains the seminal work on runic oracles. His book comes with a bag of runes imprinted on ceramic tiles. The interpretations are easy to read, succinct, and intuitive. Other editions of runic oracles come with the symbols imprinted on gemstones.

The runes themselves allegedly date back to the time of the Vikings. As with the tarot, you first have to learn the meanings of the symbols, then string them together to form a coherent story or picture of your question. Although I've used the runes, I've never responded to them intuitively. But I know many people who swear by them and carry their little bag of runes with them wherever they go.

One of the easiest interpretations of runes is found in R. T. Kaser's *Runes in 10 Minutes*, part of a series on oracles that's published by Avon.

Books as Oracles

This is one of the simplest types of oracles. You can do it any-where, any time, as long as you have a book with you. Just pose your question, open the book at random, and, with your eyes closed, point at the page. Like other oracles, this one operates on the prin-ciple of synchronicity; your intuition guides you to the right page and the right word or phrase to answer your question.

In the Cancer Moon chapter, there's an exercise involving a dic-tionary reading. You can actually use any type of book, but dictio-naries are excellent for these types of readings because they cover such a vast spectrum of ideas. Your intuition is immediately engaged in connecting the word or phrase with your question, and you'll usu-ally feel a resonance that signals whether or not it fits your question.

Water moons usually enjoy this kind of oracle. Their intuition works in such a fluid way that they immediately bridge the gap be-tween the word and their question. This one is good for fire moons, too, because it's quick and easy. Earth moons can go either way. Air moons might find it most useful as a supplement to some other ora-cle or as a confirmation of their own intuition.

Color: The Rainbow Oracle

Unless we're color-blind, we live in a world where the sky and ocean are blue and the grass is green. We talk about "feeling blue" or being so angry we literally "see red." In our homes, we use colors that express how we feel and who we are. We assess other people, in part, by the color of the clothes they wear, the color of the cars they drive, even the color of their eyes.

In the late eighties, author and entrepreneur Carole Jackson wrote *Color Me Beautiful*, a system of selecting the right colors for your hair and skin tone, and then sold Color Me Beautiful fran-chises countrywide. She was obviously onto something.

No surprise, then, that scientific research has proven what many of us already sensed: colors influence our moods (pink is calming), our appetites (think red and Chinese restaurants), even the way we think and perceive (we associate green with money and growth).

Each of the seven chakras or energy systems in the body is related to a color. Intuitives who read the energy or auric field around an individual see colors that are related to the physical condition of that person's body. A lot of red in an auric field, for instance, can indicate intense energy. If the red is a very deep hue, it indicates anger or even rage. The energy field colors, beginning at the base of the spine and moving upward through the body, range from red, at the base or root chakra, to violet, at the crown chakra. A lot of violet in an auric field would indicate a deeply spiritual individual.

Colors permeate our lives, and if you pay close attention, you can glean an enormous amount of intuitive information on nothing more than that. Some years ago, my husband and I interviewed director Michael Mann for a book we were writing called *The Making of Miami Vice*. The interview took place in his office in Hollywood.

I guess I was expecting pastels in his office, an Art Deco revival. This was the guy, after all, whose TV show had recreated Miami Beach and turned it into the Art Deco capital of the U.S.: hotels that are bubble-gum pink, neon signs a soda-pop blue, exquisite pale yellow sunrises and sunsets. I guess I was expecting pizzazz, tropical flamboyance. Instead, Rob and I were ushered into an office as black as a cave.

Black. Not dark, not almost dark, but black. Black walls. Black ceiling. And Michael Mann dressed in black and sitting behind a massive desk. It unsettled me. Throughout the interview, I was never quite able to get a grasp on Mann the man. He remained Mann the enigma. In retrospect, of course, it makes sense. Black is the absolute absence of color. We can project whatever we want onto it. It's the perfect shade to wear or to surround yourself with when you don't want anyone to know who you really are.

Look around you. What colors are dominant in your environment? What color is the clothing you wore today? Why did you select that particular outfit? Did it have anything to do with your mood? What do the colors around you tell you about yourself?

ACTIVITY: COLOR

In the activity below, list five colors off the top of your head. Don't think about them, just write down whatever comes into your head. You're going to do a Rainbow Oracle reading for yourself. Don't cheat by looking ahead!

1. _____
2. _____
3. _____
4. _____
5. _____

Essentially, what you're doing in this activity is using color as an oracle, as an intuitive device. The meanings of the colors listed in table 4 are taken from a book called *The Rainbow Oracle* that my husband co-authored with psychic Tony Grosso. The book came with a set of color cubes that are tossed as a question is asked. The cubes included regular colors and intensified colors, represented by a slash through the center. The intensified colors are the equivalent of reversed cards in the tarot: negative. Since you just listed the colors, intensified hues would be any deep hue—magenta instead of red, for instance, or deep purple instead of violet. The meaning of a deeper or intensified color is the reverse of its lighter counterpart. Rainbow, black, and white are the only colors that aren't also intensified.

Before you look at the table, read through the Rainbow Oracle reading below. This will give you a better idea about how to interpret your reading.

Example of a Rainbow Oracle Reading

At the time that I was writing the Gemini moon chapter, which includes a Rainbow Oracle reading, my daughter saw the colored cubes on my desk and asked what they were. As soon as I explained, she was eager to try them out. Her question was: *How will fifth grade be for me?*

The colors she threw were: purple, pink, green, white, and red. No intensified colors were selected.

The meanings of the five color positions are: (1) the question or the issue; (2) the challenge or the obstacle; (3) what's emerging; (4) what's visible now; (5) the resolution.

With purple in the first position, I knew that the real question here was how she would do in a structured environment after all the freedom of summer. It meant restrictions, rules, and the imposition of a schedule. The challenge, with pink in the second position, would be to work with the structure rather than against it, to go with the flow and love it. What was emerging with green in the third position was a lot of change and growth. This would be fifth grade, the tenth year, a step away from middle school and an increased interest in *boys*. In the fourth position, white indicated that she already intuited what was coming up and that she understood it would be a year of change and growth. Red, as the resolution, meant a lot of energy would go into school this year, and that her emotions would be intense and powerful.

This reading resonated with both of us.

Your Own Rainbow Oracle Reading

Now you're ready to do your own Rainbow Oracle reading. Find your colors in table 4 and interpret them according to their positions in your list.

Table 4 provides the keyword definitions for the colors. Perhaps because color is so universal, divination systems using color seem to appeal to moon signs of every element. Even impatient fire sign moons like it.

Table 4. Color Key Words

Red	energy, passion, intensity, high emotions
Orange	harmony, balance between the mind and emotions
Yellow	happiness, contracts, learning, logic, legal documents
Green	change, growth, healing, money, renewal, birth, new ideas
Blue	tranquility, calm, serenity, devotion, private
Purple	rules and regulations, tradition, the past
Pink	tenderness, gentle love, sensitivity, maintenance of health
Brown	solid foundations, security, stability, a fertile time

Peach	mellowness, happiness, joy
Violet	the highest order of anything, wisdom, spirituality, idealism
Gold	success, creative thought, attainment of goals, positive thinking
Gray	confusion, fear, misunderstanding, muddled thinking
White	insight, intuition, realization, protection, understanding reached through clear and positive thinking
Black	something that's hidden or isn't being revealed
Rainbow	free will, adaptability, a lucky streak

If you selected colors that aren't included in table 4, then you'll have to interpolate the meanings. Lime green, for instance, would be green with a bit of yellow and white in it. Therefore, change and growth (green) would come about through learning (yellow) and understanding (white).

Rainbow Oracle Interpretation: _____

_____

_____

_____

_____

_____

_____

Your Three Questions

In the sensory activity at the end of each of the moon chapters, you're asked to describe a place. You may want to turn back to your moon section to see what you wrote.

This is the answer to the third question you asked in the first reality check, chapter 4. Does it *feel* right to you? Does it *resonate*?

Let's move on into your lunar neighborhood.

Part Two

YOUR LUNAR NEIGHBORHOOD

"Each individual must examine his or her individual beliefs, or begin with feelings which will inevitably lead to them."

—Seth, *The Nature of Personal Reality*

18

Horoscope Houses

Where You Live

Your lunar neighborhood is the terrain of your inner, intuitive life. It's the realm of dreams and the personal unconscious and is linked to your conscious life and awareness through hunches and synchronicities. In your birth chart, your lunar neighborhood is the house into which your moon falls.

A horoscope is divided into twelve wedge-shaped slices, like a pizza or a pie, and each slice or house represents an area of your life. The houses vary in size, depending on the degrees on their cusps or the borders between them. The sign that was rising at your birth—known as the Ascendant—determines the layout of the houses. If, for instance, you have a sun in Aries and were born at 5:30 a.m. in the U.S., then it's probable that your rising sign is Aries. That means Aries rules your first house, Taurus rules the second, and so on around the zodiac. If your moon is in Taurus, then your moon probably falls in the second house.

A simple way of finding your rising sign is illustrated in table 5. This is only going to give you an estimated rising sign—only a computerized chart will give you an exact one—but it will enable you to tell which house your moon falls into. You do need your accurate time of birth, however, to use the table.

Locate your sun sign in the left vertical column, follow it across to your time of birth, then up to the rising sign across the top of the table. These times are for U.S. standard time. If you were born during Daylight Saving Time or War Time, you have to subtract an hour from your birth time before using the table. If you were born in the first two weeks of a sun sign, use the rising sign for the previous sun sign for the appropriate time. If you were born in the last two weeks of a sign, use the next rising sign for the next sun sign period.

Let's say you were born August 31, at 8:10 p.m. Virgo begins on August 23, so it falls within the first two weeks of the sun sign. It also falls during Daylight Saving Time. That means you subtract an hour from the birth time, making it 7:10 p.m., and use Leo as your sun sign. That gives you a rising sign in Pisces.

If you were born close to the cusp of two signs—on August 23, for instance—then read the rising for both Leo and Virgo.

In a normal horoscope, each sign follows the next on the cusp of each house. But some charts have the same sign on several house cusps, which means two signs won't appear on any cusp, but are contained within a house. So if the description of your moon's house placement doesn't seem quite right, it may be because you have an interception somewhere in your chart.

Table 5: Your Rising Sign

Rising sign:	♈	♉	♊	♋	♌	♍	♎	♏	♐	♑	♒	♓
Sun sign:												
♈ **Aries**	5am	7am	9am	11am	1pm	3pm	5pm	7pm	9pm	11pm	1am	3am
	7am	9am	11am	1pm	3pm	5pm	7pm	9pm	11pm	1am	3am	5am
♉ **Taurus**	3am	5am	7am	9am	11am	1pm	3pm	5pm	7pm	9pm	11pm	1am
	5am	7am	9am	11am	1pm	3pm	5pm	7pm	9pm	11pm	1am	3am
♊ **Gemini**	1am	3am	5am	7am	9am	11am	1pm	3pm	5pm	7pm	9pm	11pm
	3am	5am	7am	9am	11am	1pm	3pm	5pm	7pm	9pm	11pm	1am
♋ **Cancer**	11pm	1am	3am	5am	7am	9am	11am	1pm	3pm	5pm	7pm	9pm
	1am	3am	5am	7am	9am	11am	1pm	3pm	5pm	7pm	9pm	11pm
♌ **Leo**	9pm	11pm	1am	3am	5am	7am	9am	11am	1pm	3pm	5pm	7pm
	11pm	1am	3am	5am	7am	9am	11am	1pm	3pm	5pm	7pm	9pm
♍ **Virgo**	7pm	9pm	11pm	1am	3am	5am	7am	9am	11am	1pm	3pm	5pm
	9pm	11pm	1am	3am	5am	7am	9am	11am	1pm	3pm	5pm	7pm

Rising sign:	♈	♉	♊	♋	♌	♍	♎	♏	♐	♑	♒	♓
Sun sign:												
♎ Libra	5pm	7pm	9pm	11pm	1am	3am	5am	7am	9am	11am	1pm	3pm
	7pm	9pm	11pm	1am	3am	5am	7am	9am	11am	1pm	3pm	5pm
♏ Scorpio	3pm	5pm	7pm	9pm	11pm	1am	3am	5am	7 am	9am	11am	1pm
	5pm	7pm	9pm	11pm	1am	3am	5am	7am	9am	11am	1pm	3pm
♐ Sag.	1pm	3pm	5pm	7pm	9pm	11pm	1am	3am	5am	7am	9am	11am
	3pm	5pm	7pm	9pm	11pm	1am	3am	5am	7am	9am	11am	1pm
♑ Cap.	11am	1pm	3pm	5pm	7pm	9pm	11pm	1am	3am	5am	7am	9am
	1pm	3pm	5pm	7pm	9pm	11pm	1am	3am	5am	7am	9am	11am
♒ Aqua.	9am	11am	1pm	3pm	5pm	7pm	9pm	11pm	1am	3am	5am	7am
	11am	1pm	3pm	5pm	7pm	9pm	11pm	1 am	3am	5am	7am	9am
♓ Pisces	7am	9am	11am	1pm	3pm	5pm	7pm	9pm	11 pm	1am	3am	5am
	9am	11am	1pm	3pm	5pm	7pm	9pm	11pm	1am	3am	5am	7am

Once you've determined your rising sign, use one of the blank charts in Appendix 4 to set up your horoscope. Then place your moon and sun in the appropriate houses. Your rising sign, incidentally, symbolizes the self you present to the world.

What a Chart Looks Like

In Appendix 4, locate Chart 1, the natal chart for author Jane Roberts, who channeled a number of books from an "energy essence" who called himself Seth. Roberts also published a number of nonchanneled nonfiction books and several works of fiction.

She was born May 8, 1929, at 11:31 p.m., EDT. Her rising, the sign that was rising at her birth, found smack in the middle of the left-hand side of the chart, is 01°♑46′ or one degree and forty-six minutes of Capricorn. The cusp of her second house is 11°♒57′, and on around the chart, each sign following in sequence. In her fourth house are three planets—the sun, moon, and Jupiter—and the north node (☉☽♃☊).

Her Taurus moon lies at sixteen degrees and twenty-eight minutes. Notice how close it is to her Taurus sun (18° ♉01′). Whenever you see the sun and moon this close together in a chart, the phase of the moon is either balsamic or new. If the moon is behind the sun—or in fewer degrees, like Jane's—then it's a balsamic moon. If the moon is even with or up to sixty degrees ahead of the sun, it's a new moon.

Immediately, we know that Jane was here this time around to tie up loose ends. That double whammy of Taurus sun and moon means she was incredibly stubborn and fixed in her opinions and beliefs. In keeping with her moon, she was also a private individual who never sought the spotlight. In most ways, she was a reluctant prophet.

The moon in the fourth house is an intuitive placement. It can indicate many changes of residence and strong memories of childhood (either good or bad). The nurturing parent is represented by this house, and that parent exerts a strong influence over the individual. Again, that influence can be either good or bad; it depends on the angles other planets make to the moon.

Jane's mother was certainly a major influence in her life—predominately a negative influence. When Jane was quite young, her mother became disabled from rheumatoid arthritis, the same disease from which Jane later suffered and which ultimately killed her. Her mother had trouble caring for Jane and herself, they went on welfare, and the church (Catholic) stepped in to help. As her mother's health got worse, Jane became a ward of the state. Her childhood memories, by her own admission, remained strong throughout her life, but weren't particularly good. All of this fits in with her fourth house moon in Taurus. This doesn't mean, however, that every fourth house placement of the moon indicates negative memories or experiences of your mother. But that's what it meant for Roberts.

In Table 6, the house meanings are defined and include key words that make them easy to remember.

Table 6: Key Words for the Houses

1st House: personality; your beginnings, early life, physical health and appearance; an angular house

2nd House: finances; what you value; your money, assets, and earning capacity; your attitudes about money; your expenditures; security issues

3rd House: communication; your "daily" mind; short journeys; siblings, neighbors, and relatives

4th House: home; your personal environment, family life, and domestic affairs; the nurturing parent; your roots and native land; real estate; the end of your life; an angular house

5th House: creativity; children (the firstborn); creative passions; pleasures of all sorts; gambling and speculative ventures; love affairs; small pets

6th House: health and work; working conditions and environment, competence and skill, general health; service

7th House: partnerships; marriage, any one-on-one partnership, open enemies, and conflicts; lawsuits; another angular house

8th House: transformation; other people's money; resources you share with others; death; inheritance; metaphysics

9th House: higher mind; religion and philosophy; the law; higher education; consciousness expansion; long journeys

10th House: profession; your career, social status, and public reputation; the authoritarian parent; people who have power over you; the last of the angular houses

11th House: shared ideals; organizations you belong to; aspirations and hopes you share with a group

12th House: disowned power; your unconscious mind; power/energy you disown throughout your life; secret/hidden enemies; institutions; "Karma"

The Houses in Depth

ASCENDANT AND FIRST HOUSE
Natural home for Aries
Ruler: Mars

When you enter someone's house for the first time, you form an immediate impression about the person based strictly on what you see. The rooms might be cluttered but warm and friendly; the walls may be white and the furnishings a tropical paradise. Maybe dust balls lounge in corners; maybe the place is so tidy and clean you can literally eat off the floors. These details leap out at you and leave a permanent imprint.

In much the same way, your rising sign or ascendant is the doorway to your life, the first thing other people see when they meet you. It's the face you present to others, the projection of what you allow them to see. It governs your physical appearance and health, your personality, and some of the psychological defenses you use to protect yourself. It also has quite a bit to say about the conditions of your early childhood that helped mold you into the adult you are.

Your rising sign offers powerful clues about your intuitive abilities, too, and how that sign's ruling planet plays into the overall intuitive scheme of things. The ascendant is one of the four critical or most important angles in a chart. The others are the cusp of the fourth house (I.C.), of the seventh house (descendant), and the tenth house (M.C.). Any planet found on or near one of these angles is especially significant.

The planet that rules the ascendant is said to rule the chart, a vital link in the horoscope interpretation. If your rising sign is Pisces, for example, then Pisces rules your first house and any planet in Pisces that falls within the degree of the first and second house cusps goes there. Pisces is ruled by Neptune, which would be the ruler of your chart.

The first house is an angular house, just like the fourth, seventh, and tenth houses. Any planets in these houses, just like planets on their cusps, are given extra weight.

Table 7, at the end of this chapter, lists the signs, the planets that rule them, and provides a thumbnail sketch of the planet itself.

Look at Jane Roberts's chart. Her first house is empty, indicating that she has no planets in Capricorn, her rising sign. Saturn (♄) rules Capricorn, so that planet is particularly significant in her chart.

In addition to the traits and characteristics already mentioned for the rising sign, the first house is about self-expression. It governs the head, face, and skin.

SECOND HOUSE
Natural home for Taurus
Ruler: Venus

Look around you. What do you see? What would be immediately obvious to a stranger about what you value?

I have a writer friend who lives in Key West with his wife and two dogs in an absolutely wonderful house. As you come through the gate, the grounds are lushly and perfectly landscaped. Off to the right, a stone trail leads through all the green. On the other side, the grounds open up to a long, narrow pool and an open deck area that personifies life in the tropics. You can almost picture Bogie and Bacall in the moonlight, playing out a scene from *Key Largo*.

Inside, the immediate sensation is one of space and comfort, the gracious lifestyle of two uniquely talented people. The concrete floors are custom designed. Original artwork decorates the walls and upon closer inspection, you discover that some of it is actually literary memorabilia.

In the guest bathroom, for instance, is a framed party invitation signed by Tennessee Williams. Writers, many of them as famous as Williams, play a prominent role in *what this couple values*. They have lived in Key West for years and know just about every writer who calls the city home for even part of the year. They also value their home and, in fact, tend to buy houses, redo them completely while living there, then sell them for handsome profits and move on to the next place.

The second house, then, symbolizes the value we place on money and possessions, stuff that eventually becomes extensions of ourselves, even if we aren't always aware of it. Moveable property falls in this house—jewelry, art, collections of any sort. Here, too, you find your attitudes about your possessions and what you value.

THIRD HOUSE
Natural home for Gemini
Ruler: Mercury

How do your neighbors feel about you? Do they love you so much that they call you for lunch, for advice, for a short-term loan? Do they gossip about you? Your experience of neighbors falls into this house. So do your brothers and sisters and just about everyone else except your parents.

The third house symbolizes a hodgepodge of restless activity. Here you find your communication skills, how you communicate in your daily world, and all the activities that compose your daily life.

Are you a soccer parent who drives to every game? Look to your third house. I have one friend who is definitely a soccer mom. One weekend, she's driving her son and four friends to Colorado; the next weekend, it might be a game in the next town. Regardless, she's always there. Yet, she doesn't have any planets in the third house. However, her son's sun sign—Sagittarius—is on the cusp of the third house, one of those odd synchronicities you find all the time in astrology.

The third house represents that part of your mind that runs on automatic, the way you think when you're running around, trying to negotiate traffic on your way to work or the grocery store. This house doesn't include quantum leaps in your intuitive or unconscious understanding; that's the ninth house.

FOURTH HOUSE AND IC
Natural home for Cancer
Ruler: the moon

The first cellar I ever went into was in my aunt's home in Tulsa, Oklahoma, when I was about eight years old. We were visiting her from Venezuela, where we lived at the time. There were no cellars in Caracas. I had nothing to compare this to. But even now, decades later, I can still recall the smells, the sights, the details. Even now, I can hear the creak of the cellar door as it shut behind me. I can hear the creak of the old wooden steps.

The fourth house is a lot like that. You don't forget anything associated with this house. The memory is cellular; it follows you into this life and shadows you throughout your life. This house symbolizes your roots, your personal history, and your personal life in its most intimate ramifications. It symbolizes what makes you feel secure, that warm, fuzzy feeling we all seek when we're scared or uncertain.

It's your family—both childhood and adult—and your experience of your mother or father, whoever is most nurturing. Here, too, is your psychological connection to the collective unconscious, which links us with everyone, everywhere, all the time.

As the basement of the chart, the fourth house also represents your personal slice of earth, your home and the land it sits on. Here, too, is found the end of life, usually the last twenty years or so.

In doing family charts, it's not unusual to find one of the parent's sun or moon signs on the cusp of the fourth. This sometimes works for several generations, too, and is one of the confirmations I use when rectifying a chart if the person doesn't have the exact birth time. In my own chart, for instance, I have Capricorn on the cusp of the fourth house; my mother is a Capricorn. My daughter has Gemini on the cusp; I'm a Gemini.

Take another look at Jane Roberts's chart. She has three planets in the fourth—the sun, moon, and Jupiter, as well as the north node, all in Taurus. This is indicative of a very private and intuitive individual whose primary perception is subjective. The fact that her sun and moon are in the same sign means that her inner and outer energies worked smoothly together, which perhaps help to explain how she was able to channel so clearly. The fourth house planets also confirm Jane's "spiritual pragmatism," which may explain why the Seth books are so infinitely readable and practical.

FIFTH HOUSE
Natural home for Leo
Ruler: the sun

Our creative urges, that's what this house is really about. Such urges can find expression in any number of ways—through the "children" we create in music, art, writing, or acting; through actual physical children; or through the pleasures and amusements we seek.

In Jane Roberts's chart, Mercury in Gemini (☿ 08 ♊ 19) in the fifth house is a clear indication that Jane's creative urges focused on writing. Mercury is the ruler of Gemini, which rules all forms of communication. She has Taurus (21 ♉ 59) on the cusp of the fifth, indicating that she worked out of her home and was quite stubborn about doing things her way.

This house also includes all forms of speculative ventures—gambling, investments, stocks. Love affairs go in here, too, primarily as a form of creative expression.

Traditional astrology puts pets in the sixth house, along with servants and other chattel. But this sort of thinking smacks of the nineteenth century and the placements have always bothered me. I consider my pets and other small animals as part of the family, "the furry kids," as my daughter once said, the little guys who bring us enormous pleasure. So I always look to this house for a person's experience of pets.

SIXTH HOUSE
Natural home for Virgo
Ruler: Mercury

In ancient times, this house was called "the house of slavery." That's probably how servants and chattel ended up associated with the sixth. But how many of us in today's world have servants or chattel? Even the key word definition I use for this house—health and work—raises certain questions. Does the health part refer to health as it relates to work? Yes, in the sense that if your work isn't gratifying or seemingly has no purpose, then illness may be one of the end results. But the sixth, which also includes nutrition and your general concerns about your health, isn't the only house related to health. The eighth symbolizes life-threatening illnesses and the general health falls into the first. The core meaning of this house lies much deeper.

Most of us know someone who does things for other people without expecting any sort of compensation. You know the kind of person I mean—the friend who drives thirty miles in the middle of the night to rescue you and your car from the interstate where it broke down; the art teacher who works after hours with your daughter, helping her put together a portfolio she can submit for admission into art school; or the neighbor who brings home baked bread when you're laid up with the flu.

There's also another type of service implied in this house—people who work in "service" professions. This would include any type of profession within an institution—hospital, prison, nursing home. In the last few years, my own experience with sixth house professions and the people who work in them has been refined somewhat because my mother has been in an Alzheimer's unit. On her unit, there are at least three caregivers—the people who are most intimately involved with the residents—and an LPN who exemplify sixth house energies. They all go the extra mile to ensure that their charges are comfortable, safe, and well cared for.

One more note on the work front for the sixth house: look here for the daily minutia you perform on the job and your relationship with your employer and other employees.

Glance at Jane Roberts's natal chart again. When I first saw it, the empty sixth house surprised me. She died of complications from rheumatoid arthritis when she was fifty-five years old, after more than five hundred days in the hospital. She struggled against the "symptoms" of the disease during the twenty years that she channeled the Seth material. I expected to see *something* in this house. Then I looked at crowded fourth, with three planets and the north node all in Taurus and her illness suddenly made sense.

In most of the Seth books, there are references to Jane's "symptoms," her "stubbornness," and her early childhood conditioning. With the Taurus planets and the north node in the fourth, it seems that her illness had its roots in her early childhood, as a result of her relationship with her mother, who became crippled with rheumatoid arthritis. Despite twenty years of the Seth material, despite all the work she undertook to change her deepest beliefs, the very stubbornness that made her such a clear and excellent channel also proved to be her undoing.

SEVENTH HOUSE AND DESCENDANT
Natural home for Libra
Ruler: Venus

Partnerships: that's it in a nutshell. But as usual, it's not quite that succinct or simple. After all, what do we mean by partnerships? Our spouses? Business associates? Significant others? Our shrink? Our attorney?

Actually, all of the above fit into this house. So do open conflicts and open enemies. Even with our opponents and our enemies we are involved in a kind of partnership.

Usually, the seventh house describes our experiences with our partners rather than the partners themselves. But I've seen a number of instances where the sign on the cusp of the seventh house is the actual sun sign of the partner. This is the same thing that can happen with kids and their parents and the sign on the cusp of the fourth or the tenth. Usually, the seventh house synchronicity means that the couple has opposing rising signs. In other words, if you have Taurus rising, then you have Scorpio on the cusp of the seventh.

At each stage of life, of course, the meanings of the houses apply to our lives in different ways. For younger kids, the seventh indicates their experiences of their close friendships. For a professional adult, the seventh includes business partnerships.

In Jane Roberts's chart, Cancer (♋) lies on the cusp of the seventh house. This indicates that she nurtured her relationship with her husband, who was also her creative and business partner.

EIGHTH HOUSE
Natural home for Scorpio
Ruler: Pluto

I think of the eighth as the Woody Allen house because so many of the cosmic biggies are jammed in here: death and resurrection, taxes, sex, inheritances, transformation, shared resources, and psychic matters.

It governs most of the things that people in the Western world don't like to discuss, much less think about. It's why the emotions associated with this house are so profound and powerful and why the events linked to the eighth house often feel fated.

The meaning of the eighth becomes easier to understand if you think of it in the transformative sense. Death is one type of transformation, sex is another, and psychic experiences are another. All eighth-house experiences lead us, in some way, toward growth and expansion.

In Jane Roberts's chart, Leo (♌) lies on the cusp of her eighth house. She has one planet in there—Neptune (♆), indicating that she had the ability to tap deep psychic reservoirs when dealing with eighth-house matters, which she did for the last twenty years of her life.

NINTH HOUSE
Natural home for Sagittarius
Ruler: Jupiter

Here's where you look for the big picture in your life, where you see the entire forest rather than just the trees. The ninth house is about mind expansion, the burgeoning of consciousness, and that's why it includes issues like religion, philosophy, law, higher education, and your deepest beliefs.

Even though the ninth is considered a social house in that it involves other people, these people aren't individuals with whom you have close relationships. They contribute to your understanding of how the small fits into the large, or how the trees are integrated into the forest. When I do a natal chart on someone with strong spiritual beliefs or beliefs that most people would find eccentric, I look to the ninth.

This is also the house of "long journeys" and foreign countries, cultures, people, and beliefs. If you've lived in a foreign country for part of your life and that experience had an appreciable influence on who you are, then you probably have planets or aspects to this house. I was born in a foreign country and lived there for nearly seventeen years; I have Mercury in Cancer in the ninth house, an indication that I felt at home there (Cancer), that I can communicate comfortably with foreigners, and that the experience influenced the way I think (Mercury).

When we're in unfamiliar territory, just as when we're abroad, our senses are often heightened. Sights, tastes, smells—everything seems acute. Our intuition is also heightened. We see trouble coming before it arrives; we often end up in the right place at the right time; synchronicities abound. This is also ninth-house stuff.

TENTH HOUSE AND MC
Natural home for Capricorn
Ruler: Saturn

This is the house where you interact with the larger world, the place where you test what you are. While the fourth house is our most private and personal world, the tenth is our most public. It symbolizes our experiences of employers, authoritarian figures, and one of our parents.

As kids, our parents are the people who prepare us to interact with the larger world, so this house also represents the authoritarian parent. Even in traditional astrology, there is doubt about whether the tenth belongs to the father and the fourth to the mother or vice versa. In the contemporary world, with nearly as many women as men in the workforce, the answer has become even less clear.

For some of us, the fourth is clearly Mom; for others, it's Dad. Another sticky point is that the nurturing and authoritarian roles that parents play change as children grow and mature. My best advice is to remain flexible about which parent goes where.

Astrologer Robert Hand brings out another intriguing facet of the tenth house. In *Horoscope Symbols*, he writes: "The tenth house can be the key to understanding one's self-transcendence: that is, in what direction one must evolve until one is living out the symbolism of one's horoscope at the highest, most conscious level, with all the various energies within the self integrated with each other to the highest possible degree. . . . The tenth can be a calling beyond the mere calling of how we make a living."

ELEVENTH HOUSE
Natural home for Aquarius
Ruler: Uranus

The heart of this house is group associations, how that group supports your aspirations and dreams, and how that support helps you to achieve them. It's the local theater group you belong to, the bridge club, the writers' organization, your church organization. You share the ideals of the group.

This house naturally brings its opposite—the fifth—also into focus. Whereas the fifth is creative self-expression that we tend to do by ourselves, the eleventh is how we express ourselves through groups. When you're a kid, this house symbolizes your experiences with the people you hang out with—the soccer team, the chess club, Girl Scouts, the neighborhood clutch.

As you mature, the eleventh can be any professional or volunteer organization you're associated with. In the elderly, the eleventh can represent everything from a retiree club to a condo or volunteer organization to a nursing home.

This house always seemed vague to me until my daughter was born. I have Virgo on the cusp of the eleventh, with no planets in that house. But I do have a point called a Vertex that is associated with destined or fated encounters with other people. My daughter's

Virgo sun makes a direct conjunction to my Vertex in Virgo, indicating the "destined" encounter. Through her, I have been drawn into various types of groups that share my interests and aspirations.

Jane Roberts's eleventh house is empty. For a period of several years, though, she and her husband held ESP classes in her home, in which Seth was one of the major players. This type of *transformative group experience* is right in keeping with Scorpio (♏) on the cusp of the eleventh. Some of these class members have gone on to become authors and researchers into the nature of reality and consciousness.

TWELFTH HOUSE
Natural home of Pisces
Ruler: Neptune

Karma, hidden enemies, institutions, self-sacrifice, imprisonment: this is hardly the stuff to write home about.

In the contemporary world, the twelfth house also represents the power we disown to keep the peace, to be liked and loved, to attain what we desire. It's what we repress in the course of our lives, the psychic garbage we don't want or are unable to deal with. If we continually push the garbage underground, it eventually finds expression as a physical illness or as festering sores in our personal unconscious.

As for the karma traditionally associated with this house, well, what does that mean exactly? If you believe that everything that happens to you is fated, that you have no power whatsoever to change that destiny, then your twelfth house reality will reflect that. If you believe that you create your reality from your deepest beliefs, attracting what and who you need to evolve to your highest potential, then the energy of the twelfth house is one of your greatest allies.

Jane Roberts had Sagittarius (♐) on the cusp of her twelfth house. It demanded that she use her intuitive abilities to discover her truth, her particular version of the big picture, and then teach it. She had only one planet in that house—Saturn (♄)—sitting almost smack on her ascendant. When Saturn is this close to the ascendant, one of its meanings is hardship in early childhood and heavy responsibility at a young age. Saturn was her impetus to transcend that early childhood conditioning by using her intuitive abilities to reclaim the power she had disowned.

Sign Rulers

Every sign is ruled by a planet, which colors the expression of that sign. Aries, for instance, is ruled by Mars, so if you have Aries rising, then Mars is said to rule your chart and assumes special significance in the chart.

In terms of moon signs, the expression of your intuitive lunar energies is colored by the planet that rules the sign. An Aries moon person expresses Mars-like attributes in his or her intuitive interests and approaches. A Gemini moon—ruled by Mercury—expresses Mercury-like traits in his or her intuitive interests and approaches. Table 7 lists the signs and the planets that rule them and provides a thumbnail sketch of the ruling planet's qualities.

Table 7: Signs and Ruling Planets

Sign	Planet	Description of Planet
Aries ♈	Mars ♂	Energy, action, sexual drive, courage, restlessness, aggression, stamina, achievement, anger, athletic talent, competitive spirit. Fight or flight syndrome.
Taurus ♉	Venus ♀	Your aesthetics, beauty, romance, artistic instinct, social contacts, love life, earning capacity, extravagance, laziness, love of mother for her children. Luck.
Gemini ♊	Mercury ☿	Your intellect, communication skills, the left brain, how you think, brothers and sisters, neighbors. Rules writing, teaching, speaking, short-distance travel. When retrograde, don't sign contracts, and always reconfirm travel plans.
Cancer ♋	Moon ☽	Your intuition, emotions, inner life, the feminine, mother or nurturing parent, a man's wife, yin energy.

Sign	Planet	Description of Planet
Leo ♌	Sun ☉	Essence and energy of life, your ego, father, a woman's husband, authority and power, rules the heart, back, spine, and spinal cord.
Virgo ♍	Mercury ☿	See Gemini.
Libra ♎	Venus ♀	See Taurus.
Scorpio ♏	Pluto ♀	Transcendence, redemption, power, transformation, breakdown of ordinary reality, evolutionary power, sexual magnetism, profound change.
Sagittarius ♐	Jupiter ♃	Expansion, luck, higher mind, philosophy, law, religion and spiritual beliefs, abstract mind, foreign countries and cultures. Rules publishing, organized religion, travel professions, universities and higher education. Luck.
Capricorn ♑	Saturn ♄	Responsibility, discipline, limitations and restrictions, building foundations, structure, the rules of the game in physical reality, "karma." Governs bones, joints, skin, teeth.
Aquarius ♒	Uranus ♅	Your individuality, sudden and unexpected disruptions, genius, eccentricity, break down of old paradigms, originality. Rules astrology, higher mind, computers, humanity.
Pisces ♓	Neptune ♆	Your visionary self, your illusions, psychic and spiritual insight, dreams, flashes of insight, artistic inspiration, mystical tendencies, synchronistic connections, all forms of escapism.

19

Moon in the Houses

Hemispheres

A horoscope is divided into hemispheres, just like a globe. The horizon in a chart is the ascendant or rising sign and astrologers often refer to it as the ascendant/descendant or the horizontal axis. Planets either fall above or below this axis.

Remember: your rising sign symbolizes the mask you wear, the self you present to others. It describes your physical appearance as well. Your descendant or the sign on the cusp of your seventh house describes your general approach to partnerships—business or romantic. In a normal chart, one in which each sign appears on the cusp of the houses as you move counterclockwise around the horoscope, the sign on the ascendant is always the opposite of the one on the descendant. In other words, if you have Aries rising, you'll have Libra on the descendant or cusp of your seventh house. In Jane Roberts's chart in Appendix 4, Capricorn is rising and Cancer, its opposite, is found on the cusp of the seventh house.

There's also another division in a chart: the line that runs vertically through the middle, the MC/IC or vertical axis, and planets fall either to the right or left of it. The MC or Midheaven is the cusp of the tenth house and describes the broad strokes of your career and profession. The IC is the cusp of the fourth house and it describes the big picture about your home and family, your immediate personal environment. It also describes your experience of your primary caretaker.

These two lines form the four critical or most important angles in a horoscope.

In a balanced chart, planets are evenly divided among the four quarters. If you have most of the planets above the horizon, then you're probably outgoing, friendly, and more generally sociable. Your perceptions are largely subjective. If you have the majority of the planets under the horizon, you're a somewhat private individual whose perceptions are primarily subjective. Of the two, the chart with the most planets under the horizon tends to be most intuitive. The location of planets in relation to the horizontal axis has to do with the way you approach and assimilate experience.

If you have the majority of planets to the left of the MC/IC axis (called the East, where the planets are rising), then you tend to be self-determined. You act on your choices. If the majority of your planets are to the right or West of the vertical axis, you consider your choices before acting.

Your Moon's House Placement

To figure out what house your moon is in, you need to know the sign of your moon (Appendix 1) and your rising sign (Table 5, in Chapter 18). Then look at Table 8. Locate your rising sign across the top, then go down the moon sign column and across to find the house number. Then read the description of your moon's house placement in the sections that follow. Keep in mind, though, that these are only approximations, so it's a good idea to read the house descriptions before and after the house number listed in the table as well.

Table 8: Your Moon's House Placement

Moon	♈	♉	♊	♋	♌	♍	♎	♏	♐	♑	♒	♓
♈	1	12	11	10	9	8	7	6	5	4	3	2
♉	2	1	12	11	10	9	8	7	6	5	4	3
♊	3	2	1	12	11	10	9	8	7	6	5	4
♋	4	3	2	1	12	11	10	9	8	7	6	5
♌	5	4	3	2	1	12	11	10	9	8	7	6
♍	6	5	4	3	2	1	12	11	10	9	8	7
♎	7	6	5	4	3	2	1	12	11	10	9	8
♏	8	7	6	5	4	3	2	1	2	3	4	5
♐	9	8	7	6	5	4	3	2	1	12	11	10
♑	10	9	8	7	6	5	4	3	2	1	12	11
♒	11	10	9	8	7	6	5	4	3	2	1	12
♓	12	11	10	9	8	7	6	5	4	3	2	1

(Rising Sign across the top)

Moon in the 1st House: Your Personality

You're moody, emotional, and deeply intuitive. Your hunches and gut feelings about yourself, and other people, and the events in your life are quite powerful, even when you try to ignore that power or attribute it to something or someone else.

You have exceptionally vivid dreams and excellent recall of the dreams with barely any effort at all. With this placement, it's not uncommon to recall several dreams a night in the most minute detail.

Your memory is exceptional, especially when the memories are deeply connected to your emotions. If your mother was wearing a red dress on the day you first hopped on a bike and rode off down the road, you remember that. Your inner senses took a snapshot of the moment and you can call it up at any time. These memories are one of the ways in which you nurture yourself. Your roots are important to you.

In early childhood, your mother had a profound influence on you. As a kid, you may have felt that she smothered you, but she was always there for you, ready to do whatever was required to facilitate your life. The bond between you has always been especially strong and psychic. Now that you're an adult, your roles may be reversed, with *you* nurturing *her*. Maybe you look after her finances, run errands for her, whatever is required.

When the moon has company in this house, its basic nature is colored somewhat by that of the other planets and vice versa. Saturn in here, for instance, would create a rather somber emotional nature and can indicate restrictions of some kind in childhood. If you toss Mars in with the moon, then the person has abundant energy and may have had a childhood riddled with tensions and arguments. Or perhaps the energy showed up as an athletic household, everyone into baseball, soccer, and other sports.

Due to your fluctuating emotions and natural intuitive abilities, you may feel at times that you're coming unhinged. The best thing to do then is to get off by yourself or with a close friend (the undemanding kind of friend) and do something you enjoy.

Your emotions are right at the surface, lying there like cream on milk. Despite efforts to hide what you feel, you're not very good at it unless you've trained yourself to be good at it. The same is true of your intuition. If your moon is in a water sign, this trait is even more pronounced. But why worry about it or try to change it? Accept it, integrate these qualities into who you are, and put your moon to work for you.

Begin by turning back to your moon sign chapter. In the sensory activity at the end, you're asked to describe a place and employ all your senses. Now you're going to do this activity somewhat differently. Instead of describing a place you remember, describe a place you would most like to be. It can be an internal place or a real place, but it's got to be somewhere you've never been before and would like to visit. As with the previous activities, your intuition already knows the question and what you describe here will (synchronicity again) answer it. Then flip to the end of this chapter to look up the question you've just answered.

_____

_____

_____

_____

Moon in the 2nd House: Your Finances

For you, financial security equals peace of mind. As a kid, you were the type who saved your allowance, did extra chores to earn more money, and you probably had some sort of job as soon as you were old enough to work. As an adult, these habits have carried over. But you may have periods of wild extravagance, binge spending in which you rebel against the restrictions you've placed on yourself.

Your intuition is strong when it comes to your security issues and to earning money. You're in the right place at the right time. You buy and sell stocks based on your own feelings about what's hot and what's not, and may be on the cutting edge of the next fashionable trend in the world of finances. You're a risk taker, but only when your gut says the risk will pay off.

Despite all this, your finances sometimes go through phases, like the moon—up one month, down the next. From one year to the next, your income may fluctuate wildly and it's enough to drive you nuts. When you start experiencing these extremes, try to step back and detach yourself emotionally. Attempt to see which patterns in your own beliefs and actions have helped bring about such extremes. Once you identify such patterns, work to change them.

The skeptic's argument against such facile solutions boils down to this: if we *do* create our reality from the substance of our deepest beliefs, then how come we're not all millionaires with perfect health and perfect lives? If I had a dollar for every time I've asked myself that question, I would be a multimillionaire. That said, though, the solution isn't really as facile as it appears.

As kids, most of us adapted the beliefs of our parents, our churches, our schools, and some of those beliefs are so deeply embedded in who we are that they influence our lives without our even knowing it. But when we begin to question what we truly believe—as opposed to the beliefs we were taught—then change comes about. Sometimes the change is gradual, sometimes it literally happens overnight.

For anyone doing this kind of belief work, I recommend a book called *Beyond the Winning Streak* (Woodbridge Group, 1993) by Lynda Dahl. Her story of how she created a million bucks isn't just compelling, it's useful. And part of the secret centers around intuition—nurturing it, listening to it, following your impulses and hunches.

Now turn to the sensory activity at the end of your moon sign chapter. There, you described a place you had been; here, you're going to describe a place—a state of mind sort of place or real—where you would most like to be but have never been before. Once again, this activity illustrates how easily your intuition works when you give it a chance. Your description will answer a question noted at the end of this chapter.

———————————————————————————

———————————————————————————

———————————————————————————

———————————————————————————

Moon in 3rd House: Communication

You work through your feelings by talking or writing about them. Or by teaching other people how to communicate what they feel. This is an excellent position, in fact, for orators, writers, teachers, anyone involved in the communication field.

Your mother is probably big on communication, too. She may have made up stories for you when you were a kid, tall tales that you still remember which influenced your own ability with language. Your memories are connected intimately with language and with communication. You may not be able to recall the red dress your mother was wearing the day you rode a bike for the first time, but you undoubtedly recall her shouting, *"Go for it!"*

Some people pick up intuitive visual impressions; your strength lies in your internal hearing; you have *clairaudient* abilities. In the movie *The Sixth Sense*, the little boy saw "people who are dead." That's clairvoyance. But he also carried on conversations with them; that's clairaudience.

At times, you're going to fight the intuitive part of this moon placement. You're going to bring the full power of your rational mind against all this weird stuff and try to rationalize it away. And for a while, that ploy may work. But eventually, the bottom line comes back to that inner voice.

You give comfort to others by talking to them, communicating with them, finding common emotional points that bond you, however briefly. You, in turn, are also comforted by these exchanges. You're close to your brothers, sisters, and other relatives. Some of your neighbors may also be close friends.

You manage to rejuvenate yourself through short vacations, a long weekend here, a long weekend there. Even the endless movement of your daily life is somehow emotionally satisfying simply because it gets you out and about, among people and the rest of the world.

Now put your moon to work for you by turning back to the chapter on your moon sign. In the sensory activity at the end of that chapter, you're asked to describe a place that you remember. In the space below, describe a place you've never been that you would like to visit. It can be a state of mind kind of place or a real location. Then turn to the end of this chapter to see what question you've answered in your description.

_____

_____

_____

_____

Moon in the 4th House: Your Home

Remember: the fourth is an angular house; the moon here holds special significance. It's a very intuitive placement.

Some of what they say about you may not be true *for you*. It depends on aspects other planets make to your moon and on the sign of the moon. Supposedly, this moon is deeply into traditions, rituals, the past. I haven't found this to be necessarily true of all moons in the fourth. What *does* seem to apply, however, is an attachment to your home, family, and your roots.

With the moon in the fourth, you may move frequently throughout your life, but you retain good memories of your childhood home and may feel a certain nostalgia for the early part of your life. Your recall of your childhood is excellent. Even thirty years after you've left your old neighborhood, you may be able to recall streets, the placement of houses, your friends' backyards.

Your sense of security revolves around your home and family. When things aren't going well at home, every other part of your life is affected, too. At such times, it's best to step back and ask yourself: What's the worst that can happen? This helps put everything into perspective and you usually realize the situation isn't as dire as it appears to be.

Since the fourth house is Cancer's natural home and the moon rules Cancer, the moon here is accidentally dignified. That basically means that the moon's energies work well here. It also indicates that the latter part of your life is apt to be more stable than the early part.

The moon in the fourth often indicates a preference for living near water or, at the very least, having access to a body of water. It's as if your proximity to water feeds your intuition and calms your soul.

To put your moon to work for you, turn back to the sensory activity at the end of your moon sign chapter. There, you were asked to describe a place you remember. Now you're going to describe a place you would like to visit. It can be an internal place or a real location, as long as you've never been there. Then turn to the end of this chapter to see what question you've answered in your description.

This activity is designed to illustrate how smoothly your intuition works when you give it a chance.

_____

_____

_____

_____

Moon in the 5th House: Your Creativity

Your artistic nature allows you to perceive life much differently than your contemporaries. The difference is often subtle, but always profound. You nurture your artistic side in the same way that you nurture your kids, with deep love and compassion, and tend to be very generous to all of your children, whether creative or physical.

There's a pleasure-seeking element to the moon in the fifth, pleasure for the sake of pleasure. This trait seems to dominate in the teens and twenties, when hormones are running wild and you're trying to find your way in the world. You may have periods of great extravagance, when you go on buying sprees of one kind or another. It's not really the *things* that comfort you; it's the buying itself. You may also go on sexual "sprees." Again, it's not the person you're with who is important; it's the act of sex itself.

Your intuition shines whenever your kids or your creative endeavors are concerned. The sign and element of the moon are important factors in how your intuition is applied and how it expresses itself. An air sign moon is more likely to have an intellectual flash of creative inspiration or insight, whereas a water moon will experience it emotionally.

Traditional astrology places domestic pets in the sixth house, under the heading of chattel, but I associate pets and small animals with the fifth because they bring us pleasure. With the moon here, you're likely to have pets. Maybe even a lot of pets.

At times, the moon in this house lends itself to gambling and speculative ventures. It doesn't have to be financial gambling and speculating, either. I've seen fifth house moon people gambling on creative ventures—writing a book or doing a painting or sculpture that breaks all the rules but works. Or they gamble on a marriage, a relationship, a job. The gambles pay off when the individuals have followed their intuitive voice; when they've acted contrary to that voice, the gambles can have long-range consequences, not all of them pleasant.

One woman I know with a Leo moon in the fifth house married a man while on rebound from another. Their eighteen years together produced three kids, a beautiful home in the suburbs, a life which on the surface looked so good it approached the modern version of Beaver Cleaver. But beneath that surface lurked all kinds of shadows—the husband's alcoholism and greed, religious fundamentalism used as a weapon against the woman, to keep her "in line," and a gross materialism. Now the woman and her spouse are in the midst of a divorce, their beautiful home is for sale, and the dispute over who gets custody is likely to be bitter.

So why did she marry him? He appealed to the vanity of that Leo moon in the fifth. He sold her a bill of goods, a facade that appealed to whatever she perceived as security at the time, and she swallowed it whole. She did this despite her friends, who gave the marriage five years at the most; did it despite her family, who disliked the man from the beginning; did it despite her own *misgivings*. Now she's pushing fifty and her entire life is in tumult.

This is the kind of long-range consequence that happens to the moon in this house when gambles go against the intuitive voice.

For the next activity turn back to the sensory activity at the end of your moon sign chapter. There, you were asked to describe a place you remember. In the space below, describe a place you've never been that you would like to visit. It can be an internal place or a real location. Then turn to the end of this chapter to see what question you've answered in your description.

_____

_____

_____

_____

Moon in the 6th House: Health and Work

Your health is directly linked to your emotions. Yes, the same can be said for all of us, but for the moon in the sixth, the link is utterly obvious. A child with this moon position might get sick within forty-eight hours of hearing his parents argue. An infant with this moon position might develop colic. Anyone with the moon here may have allergies.

When my daughter was in second grade, she used to get red, inflamed eyes. The school nurse called it pink eye and sent her home. Her ophthalmologist blamed it on pollen or some other external source. Desperate for an answer, I finally turned to Louise Hay's classic *You Can Heal Your Life*.

The book has a list of ailments and their probable emotional source which is invaluable. Under eyes, Hay says the emotional cause has to do with something we don't want to see. The next time that Megan was sent home with pink eye, I asked if she'd had a problem with someone at school. It turned out that she'd argued with a girl who was her close friend at the time. Over the course of the next few weeks, every time she was sent home with pink eye, she'd had a disagreement with this particular girl.

I mentioned the link to Megan and sensed that she absorbed everything I said and filed it away for future reference. She was seven then; now she's ten. She still has an occasional flare-up with her eyes, but nothing like when she was in second grade. And that's the other point of the sixth house moon. Once you're *conscious* of the deeper reason behind any health problem, the problem usually clears up.

The link between emotions and work with this moon location is equally obvious. When things aren't going well for you at work, it's reflected in your personal life and in your health. Your intuition can be immensely helpful in this regard, guiding you toward whatever you need.

Since the sixth house is associated with Virgo, it's likely that you're very good with details. You're an expert at connecting the dots, at fitting this detail with that detail, linking information in ways that other people don't see. This is a terrific moon position for a researcher or a private detective, anyone whose job requires not only detail work, but a certain perfectionism.

You have a natural affinity for animals, and your relationship with them nurtures you emotionally. They may also serve as an intuitive conduit for you and it's possible that you may work professionally in some capacity with animals.

The biggest challenge with this moon position is to learn to balance your work with the rest of your life. So try the next activity with that in mind.

Turn back to your moon sign chapter. In the sensory activity at the end of the chapter you were asked to describe a place you remember. Now you're going to describe a place you've never been but would like to visit. It can be an internal place or a real location. Then turn to the end of this chapter to see what question you've answered in your description.

_____

_____

_____

Moon in the 7th House: Partnerships

"When the moon is in the seventh house and Jupiter aligns with Mars ..." That line comes from the Broadway musical *Hair* and refers to the dawning of the age of Aquarius. There's a special flavor about this location for the moon (which isn't related to Aquarius) because it's the first of the social houses, those above the horizon, and it's another angular house.

This house is closely allied with Libra, which means that a significant relationship is of prime importance for you. When you were a kid, you liked having at least one very close friend whom you could pal around with at school, after school, on weekends. When this friend hurt your feelings, you were totally crushed. When things went well with this friend, you were on top of the world. As a teenager, this emotional need went from a special friend to a boyfriend or girlfriend. As an adult, the need was transferred to a significant other.

You're happiest when you're involved in a committed relationship. You need that closeness. You crave it. It suits the texture of your emotions. And when you're committed, everything in your life works more smoothly.

A moon in the seventh generally indicates an unusual closeness to your mother. If you're a man, this can mean that you delay marriage or true commitment until your mother has passed away. If you're a woman, it can mean that your mother interferes somehow with your committed relationships.

Your intuition is especially clear when it involves people you love. If you learn to listen to that intuitive voice when you're young, your intimate relationships will evolve much more smoothly. Otherwise, you're in for a world of heartache because you consistently get involved with people who aren't right for you.

The moon's location in any of the houses is colored by other planets which also occupy that house. But for the moon in the seventh, there are some notable combinations that hold strong clues to your experiences of intimate relationships. If Mars, for instance, is also here, a lot of your energy goes into intimate relationships and they may be marred by arguments and disharmony. With Venus here, the chance of a happy marriage is indicated. With Jupiter, you benefit in every respect from your partner. With Saturn, your partner may be significantly older than you are.

The challenge with this location of the moon is figuring out how to detach from your emotions when it comes to relationships and to allow your intuition its say even when it's not what you want to hear.

Now turn back to the sensory activity at the end of your moon sign chapter. There, you were asked to describe a place you remember. Now, in the space below, describe a place you've never been but would like to visit. It can be an internal place or a real location. Then turn to the end of this chapter to see what question you've answered in your description.

_____

_____

_____

_____

Moon in the 8th House: Transformation

Even though it's not an angular house, the moon in the eighth is always important. It's the place where our lives are transformed at the deepest levels.

Your mother is emotionally intense. She has deep beliefs and opinions, particularly if your moon is in a fixed sign. She may have come from a wealthy family and her emotions are tied up somehow with money issues and shared resources. Some of her beliefs rubbed off on you, so that at some point in your life you'll have to come to terms with your own attitudes about shared resources. In fact, your joint finances are likely to go through many fluctuations until you do come to terms with your issues in this area.

On the positive side, it's likely that you'll inherit money, probably from your mother's side of the family, or will benefit somehow through women. You gain in general through the affairs of the dead. You have a piercing insight into other people's motives, secrets, and hidden fears.

This house location is similar in nature to the Scorpio moon. You have an inherent ability to transform your life at the core, through dealing with life and death issues, occult matters, and all things related to this house. When other planets join the moon here, their energies blend in with that of the moon. Jupiter here, for instance, indicates that you benefit enormously through marriage and partnerships. Saturn might indicate the need for structure and discipline related to the affairs of this house.

One seventeen-year-old boy with this moon position is an ardent, enormously talented musician. His entire life revolves around his music and he maintains a clear focus about where he's going. He and another musician friend are about to cut a demo for a record producer and there's little doubt among the people who know him that he's going to succeed in music. True to the nature of the house position, his mother came from a wealthy family.

The challenge with a moon here really boils down to maintaining a sense of inner peace despite the heavy issues that you confront throughout your life. A creative outlet, regular meditation, yoga, and/or an artistic interest all help you keep your perspective when things get tough. But none of these things work as well as they can if you use your innate intuition to navigate the often tumultuous waters of this house. To begin doing that, glance back at the sensory activity at the end of your moon sign chapter. There, you were asked to describe a place you remember. Now, in the space below, you're going to describe a place you would like to visit. It can be an internal place or a real location, as long as you've never been there. Then turn to the end of this chapter to see what question you've answered in your description.

Moon in the 9th House: Higher Mind

Some people who travel to foreign countries discover edges in themselves that are probably better left alone. Travel brings out the worst in them. Fortunately, you're the exact opposite. Travel opens your conscious mind in ways you never anticipated. You're hungry for the new experiences, the foreign culture and belief systems, and come home rejuvenated by the experience. Travel helps you to create your own philosophy and outlook about life.

You're rarely content with your life the way it is. Your hunger for new experiences propels you forward and allows you to sample many different philosophies and spiritual beliefs. This is a great moon location for teachers, especially when the subject they're teaching fascinates them.

Your inner life is inordinately rich. As a kid, you may have had an imaginary playmate and excellent recall of dreams. As an adult, your recall of dreams is still good and if you keep track of your dreams, you may find that many of them are of a psychic nature. Precognitive dreams aren't unusual, particularly if your moon is in a water sign. You're the type who can request a dream on a concern you have or some issue about which you need information and wake up the next morning with the remembrance of a dream that contains whatever you asked for.

The association of the ninth house with the sign of Sagittarius means that you're always on the lookout for The Big Picture, The Ultimate Truth, The Final Answer. Your beliefs go through many phases—some good, some bad. All of it gets tossed into the higher mind pot and you take a little from here and a little from there and eventually come up with a belief system that works for you most of the time.

Your intuition is an invaluable guide in this restless journey you've undertaken. But if you don't pay attention to it, you may stray into spiritual or religious views that are so unorthodox they cause you nothing but trouble. This doesn't mean that you should stick to organized religious thought or, at the other extreme, that you should hook up with the next guru who comes around the bend. It just means that your search this time around is exactly that—*your* search.

You may live part of your life in a country other than your birthplace. This becomes even more likely if your moon is in Sagittarius.

Since the ninth house rules publishing and education, it isn't uncommon to find people with this moon location working in the publishing industry or in universities.

The challenge with this moon location is to integrate everything you learn into your life rather than allowing it to fragment your life. By allowing your intuition to do *its* work, the challenge becomes much easier. Test your intuition now by looking back at your moon sign chapter. In the sensory activity at the end of that chapter you were asked to describe a place you remember. Now, in the space below, you're going to describe a place you've never been that you would like to visit. It can be an internal place or a real location. Then turn to the end of this chapter to see what question you've answered in your description.

_____

_____

_____

_____

Moon in the 10th House: Profession

Look at it this way: you and George Lucas have something in common, the moon in the tenth.

This house location for the moon gives you the ability and opportunity to read the tide of public opinion and to influence mass thinking. Your intuition is so finely honed that most of the time you act on it without even thinking about it. When you strive to make the intuitive process more conscious, so that you're acutely aware of what's happening in the deeper levels of yourself, then you begin to make monumental strides in achieving your goals. Until that point, you experience many changes and fluctuations in your career.

The tenth house is angular, with its cusp—the MC or Midheaven—as another critical angle in a horoscope. If your moon lies at the exact degree of the MC, so that it's the highest point in the chart, its significance is magnified.

Since the tenth house also represents your experience with authority and authority figures, the moon here can imply a fluctuating relationship with one of your parents. Your attitude toward authority (as in bureaucratic authority or, more immediately, your boss) goes through similar phases—good one day, bad the next. Your charm is one of your greatest assets and enables you to get out of even the stickiest situations without offending anyone. So the next time you get stopped for speeding, just look the cop in the eye and turn on the charm.

The challenge here is to become aware of the lunar energies that ride tandem with this house position so that you can call on your intuition when you need it, on demand. Many of the exercises in this book are designed to help you do exactly that.

Take a look at the sensory activity at the end of the chapter on your moon sign. There, you were asked to describe a place you had been. Now, in the space below, describe a place you've never been but would like to be. It can be an internal place or a real location. Once again, use all your senses. Then turn to the end of this chapter to see what question you've answered in your description.

_____

_____

_____

_____

Moon in the 11ᵗʰ House: Shared Ideals

Your network of acquaintances is large and varied and reflects your interests and passions. Some of these acquaintances are people you've met over the Internet in chat rooms or on bulletin boards. You also network in person through groups and organizations to which you belong. If you're an aspiring writer, for instance, then you may belong to a writers' group that meets regularly to talk about writing and critique each other's work.

One chart I did for a woman I'd never met had five planets crowded into the eleventh house; it turned out that she was active in a local theater group. My mother has three planets and the North Node in the eleventh house; her social world revolved around her bridge groups and volunteer organizations. The common thread that unites your group activities is *support of your interests and passions*.

Many of your acquaintances are female and may be celebrities or public figures. If your eleventh house moon is in a water sign or in Aquarius, your intuition is very highly developed and helps you make the types of connections that you need at any given time in your life.

The nature of this house is Aquarian, which brings unusual and creative people into your life who have eccentric interests and beliefs. You all have a shared vision and there's a great deal of nurturing and compassion among you. You come together as a *support group* and that means that when one in the group achieves a personal goal, the group cheers her on.

The eleventh house moon naturally highlights its opposite, the fifth. The two form an axis, just like all the opposing houses do, and whether the fifth is occupied by other planets or completely vacant, your creative expression is somehow involved in your group associations and in achieving what you desire.

The challenge with this moon position is that you become so enmeshed in the group that you lose sight of your own dreams. Usually, this happens because your intuition is urging you to do or undertake something that you feel you're not ready for. If you belong to a writers' group, for example, you may hesitate to write your own novel because you feel you aren't a good enough writer yet or that your ideas aren't marketable. It's easier to sit around talking about writing and critiquing other people's work than it is to write yourself.

Fear like this can paralyze you and kill your creativity. After Sue Grafton's novel *A is for Alibi* was published, she had writer's block for four years and finally had to go through hypnosis to break through it. Writer's block is caused primarily by fear—fear that you aren't a good enough writer, that your next book won't be as good as your last, that reviewers will pan what you write, that no editor will buy it, etc. The list is limited only by your imagination.

The point is that your intuitive self only has your best interests at heart, and if you've got an impulse to move in a particular direction in your life, then go with the flow and worry about it later. In the meantime, go back to the chapter about your moon sign and read through the sensory activity at the end. There, you were asked to describe a place you had been. Now, describe a place you've never been but would like to be. It can be a place in your mind or a real location. Once again, use all your senses. Then turn to the end of this chapter to see what question you've answered in your description.

_____

_____

_____

_____

Moon in the 12ᵗʰ House: Disowned Power

Through your inherent psychic and intuitive ability, you're able to reach out to other people in a way that eludes you emotionally. This doesn't mean that you're incapable of feeling for other people;

you actually feel deeply and are a compassionate person. But you don't know how to express it openly.

Traditional astrology lays the blame for that on one of your parents, usually your mother. But I've seen plenty of instances where the moon symbolizes the father, so you may be blaming him, too. The difficulties in childhood with this parent may have stemmed from the parent's own emotional problems.

The traditional explanation bothers me. It's too easy to blame our parents and our childhoods for things that go wrong in our adult lives. We create the fabric of our lives from our deepest beliefs; our reality is a reflection of those beliefs. So if you're experiencing the negative side of this moon placement—escapism through addictions to alcohol, food, drugs, sex—then use your intuition to change your beliefs instead of passing the buck to Mom and Dad.

You're able to work out many of your emotional dilemmas through dreams, meditation, and spiritual pursuits. Your compassion for others is part of what makes you such a good friend to a friend in need. You're a good listener and able to offer advice and counsel that comforts the other person. This moon position, in fact, is excellent for counselors, psychologists, fiction writers, and other behind-the-scenes professions where insight into human personality and motives is needed.

The karma associated with this house may well be the unfinished business we bring in from other lives. But what's more important is how the moon in the twelfth relates to power we've disowned in *this* life. As a kid, you quickly learned that certain types of emotions weren't rewarded or acknowledged, so you pushed those emotions underground and there they stayed, rumbling, stewing, and festering until you were old enough to deal with them. If you don't confront and resolve them, then addictive behaviors or other emotional problems may enter the picture.

The resolution of "twelfth house stuff," is a challenge and the way to confront and deal with it is through the development and use of your intuition. Allow yourself to follow your impulses. Allow yourself the luxury of time alone so that you can delve into whatever you have buried. Go through therapy. Attend intuitive workshops. If you continue to ignore the issues, the situation only gets worse.

Put the power of your moon to work for you now by going back to the chapter about your moon sign and read through the sensory activity at the end. There, you were asked to describe a place you had been. Now, in the space below, describe a place you've never been but would like to be. It can be an internal place or a real location. Once again, use all your senses. Then turn to the end of this chapter to see what question you've answered in your description.

_____

_____

_____

_____

NOTE: You just answered the second question that you listed in Chapter 4.

20

Intuitive Reality Check #3:
Navigation

Another Visit to Synchronicities

Now that you realize how important synchronicities are in the development of your intuition and that they form the heart of all divination systems, let's take a deeper look at how synchronicities can act as your personal oracle.

In our family, frogs symbolize good luck. Baby tree frogs seem to appear whenever we have something good on the way. The area of the house in which the frogs appear also seems to be significant. A frog in the family room would indicate something that will affect *the family*. So when we returned from a long weekend and found a dead baby frog and a broken ceramic frog on the floor of the family room, I told myself it didn't mean anything. But my daughter pointed at it and exclaimed, "This is bad. This is very bad."

Two days later, my husband got a call from his mother that his father had had a stroke while driving the car. Rob left for Minneapolis the next day and his father died the following night without regaining consciousness. The dead and broken frogs didn't tell us the specifics of the event that transpired several days later, but it did reveal *a pattern—death in the family*.

To people who are unfamiliar with "meaningful coincidences," these kinds of stories sound like episodes from *The Twilight Zone*. But once you start paying attention to the *patterns* in these kinds of experiences, they hold important clues about your life. In essence, these synchronicities allow you to become your own oracle.

Inventory

Over the years, I've developed a sort of mental inventory that I refer to periodically. Even though the inventory changes frequently, a quick glance on a given day gives me a pretty good idea about what's really going on in my life. I've used this inventory in intuitive workshops and people are usually astonished at how their answers reflect inner conditions in their personal lives.

The answers you give to the questions that follow may need to be interpreted in the same way that you would interpret a metaphor in a dream. Look for underlying themes and emotions, for links that connect one answer with another.

YOUR INVENTORY

Answer honestly. There's no right or wrong answer. The point is to become aware of what's going on in your life, so that your life becomes your personal oracle. All the questions pertain to *now* (within the last week to ten days). Be specific.

1. What kind of shape is your car in? Has it been repaired recently?

_____

_____

_____

_____

2. Have you had house repairs recently? If so, what kind of repairs? Roof? Walls? Cellar? Plumbing? Appliances? Garage door?

_____

_____

_____

_____

3. Describe any confrontation you've had with an authority figure in the last week to ten days.

_____

_____

_____

_____

4. If you have indoor plants, what kind are they? Are they healthy? Or are the leaves brown and shriveled? Describe.

_____

_____

_____

_____

5. What does your yard look like? Is it healthy?

_____

_____

_____

_____

6. Describe the best view through a window in your home.

_____

_____

_____

_____

7. Describe the worst view.

_____

_____

_____

_____

8. Have you made any insurance claims recently? If so, for what?

_____

_____

_____

_____

9. Describe the best thing that has happened to you in the last week or ten days: people, places, emotions, everything.

_____

_____

_____

_____

10. Describe the worst thing.

_____

_____

_____

_____

11. How's your love life?

_____

_____

_____

_____

12. Have any unexpected events happened to you in the last week? What were they? Were they pleasant or unpleasant?

_____

_____

_____

_____

13. If you have pets, are they healthy? If not, what has ailed them recently?

_____

_____

_____

_____

14. If you have kids, how are they doing right now? Are they healthy? Happy? Doing well in school?

_____

_____

_____

_____

15. How is your health?

_____

_____

_____

_____

16. Are you happy at your job? In your career? Has anything unexpected happened in that area recently? If so, was it good or bad?

_____

_____

_____

_____

17. Has your life in general gone through any recent upheavals? If so, what were they?

_____

_____

_____

_____

18. Describe one unusual event that happened to you recently.

_____

_____

_____

_____

19. If you could change your life today, what changes would you make?

_____

_____

_____

_____

Before you interpret what you've written, read Rita's answers. She's a forty-four-year-old school teacher, married, with two teenagers, a boy and a girl. She was born under a full moon in Taurus.

RITA'S INVENTORY

My car, a Toyota 4-Runner, is in pretty good shape. Four days ago, though, I got into my car after a really bad day at school and the battery was dead. I had to call AAA and they came out and gave me a jump start so I could get to the garage.

Right now, my house is okay. But over the past month, we've had all sorts of appliances break down: the TV, the refrigerator, the garage door. One of the toilets sprang a leak, too.

No confrontation with authority figures.

Indoors plants are flourishing.

Bob, my husband, takes care of the yard and it's really looking good now, a veritable jungle with a pond, a stone path, and plenty of spots for the cats to snooze in the sun. I think the best view in our house is from the windows that overlook the yard. It's peaceful. On cooler days, I like to sit out there and read.

The worst view? I can't think of any "worst" view.

No insurance claims.

The best thing that happened to me in the last week concerns my daughter: she got into an art program at a magnet high school.

The worst thing that happened to me recently was an unpleasant confrontation with two other teachers, nasty confrontations, actually.

My love life: no complaints at all!

The only unexpected event I can think of was my dead car battery. Definitely unpleasant.

We have two cats and a dog. The dog recently had an ear infection, but other than that, they're all okay.

Kids. My son has been having trouble with his social studies teacher, but other than that, everything seems to be okay.

My health is fine, except that I don't sleep well at night. I lie awake and worry about money, about retirement, about my kids, everything. Ridiculous, since there's really nothing to worry about in all those areas, nothing big, anyway.

My job is okay, but I've been doing this for twenty years and am ready for a change. I'd like to be able to do something at home, so I could spend more time with my kids. My brother has the ideal situation: he's a writer who works at home!

The only unexpected thing in this area is the confrontation I mentioned earlier with the two teachers.

No big upheavals in the last week to ten days.

An unusual event involved a weird little coincidence with my brother. I was trying to call him, got a busy signal, and then a beep, indicating another call was coming through. When I hung up on one line and picked up the incoming call, it was my brother!

The most obvious theme in Rita's inventory revolves around her job. By her own admission, she would like to be doing something different and working out of her home. Notice that she says there are *no bad views* from her house. She already had a confrontation with two *teachers*, her son is having trouble with one of his *teachers*, and she herself is a *teacher*. Her battery died (depleted energy?) after a trying day at *school*.

The house repairs within the last month are revealing. The TV represents information and entertainment; the fridge is certainly about food (sustenance) and convenience; the garage door could represent what she allows to enter and leave her life. A leaky toilet might represent energy that's escaping or, if the leak is due to a blockage somewhere, to a block in her own creative energy. Her only health problem is insomnia, but this hints at an underlying dissatisfaction with certain elements of her life. To top it off, the synchronicity occurred with her brother, who has the "ideal situation."

Your Life as Oracle

Now interpret what you've written. What does it tell you about the fundamentals in your life? Are changes due? Are you living your dream life?

_____

_____

_____

_____

_____

_____

_____

_____

_____

_____

When you bring the intuitive ability of your natal moon to bear against any condition in your life, and then enter the intuitive flow, the conditions change. The inventory is just a step to nudge you in the direction you really want to go.

Part Three

LUNAR CYCLES

"Every day, it gets harder for me to believe my thoughts are separate from my reality."

—Scott Adams, creator of the *Dilbert* comic strip

21

The Transiting Moon

Daily Movements

The moon, as the fastest moving celestial body, enters a new sign every two and a half days, then speeds through a particular house in our horoscopes. That sign colors our feelings and intuitive awareness and stimulates the affairs of the house that it transits.

As I'm working on this chapter, for instance, the moon is in Aquarius, cruising through my fourth house. Family affairs are stimulated and contacts with unusual or eccentric women are indicated. Sure enough, my aunt, sister, and nephews are arriving for a family reunion and my daughter's tenth birthday is coming up. While everyone is visiting, the moon will move into Pisces, which is contained or intercepted in my fifth house of creativity and children, and by the time they leave, it will be in Taurus, which rules my seventh house of partnerships.

In addition to the family stimulus, the transiting moon paints a picture of deepened intuition regarding my creative endeavors and my relationship with kids, some sort of new project or perhaps new ideas related to work and health, and some fluctuation in my partnerships.

While the moon is moving through the signs, it's also moving through its various phases, all of which add another layer of meaning. The moon in Pisces tomorrow night, for instance, will be full in my fifth house, indicating pleasurable pursuits and recreation with family and relatives. But because it's opposite the eleventh house, there will be a tug of war between my creativity (also part of the fifth) and group activities.

The phases of the moon, as well as its waxing and waning, have played a vital role throughout history in the planting and harvesting of crops, the tending of gardens, the rituals of some ancient religions, in conception and childbirth, and in certain magical rites. Wiccans, for instance, have certain rituals that are practiced only when the moon is new or full. In voodoo and Santeria, a Cuban mystery religion, some magical spells supposedly work best when performed at particular lunar intervals. Among some magical practitioners, the quality of particular herbs and what they're used for change according to the phase of moon in which they are planted and harvested.

Most newspapers list the phase of the moon, but not the moon's sign. Astrological calendars are valuable in this respect, cost about $10, and cover lunar aspects for each day of the year. If you have access to the Internet, however, the sign of the transiting moon is easy to find. Search engines usually allow you to personalize your homepage to include virtually anything you want—a daily horoscope, the phase of the moon, even the time of high and low tide. *The Farmer's Almanac* also has useful information about the moon's phases.

Table 9 provides an overview of meanings for the transiting moon by sign and house. This table is by no means complete. Entire books have been written about these subjects. The table is just to get you started. If you discover that you're especially sensitive to lunar transits (water signs seem to be), you may want to keep a notebook about what you experience as the moon passes through each of the signs and each of the phases.

Use one of the blank charts in the back of this book for keeping track of which houses the transiting moon hits. Remember: the sign describes the kinds of things you might experience and the house tells you which areas of your life are highlighted. I've combined them in the table for easier reference. The house description applies to a moon in any sign transiting that house.

Table 9: Transits of the Moon Through the Signs and Houses

Sign/House	Meaning
Aries ♈	Pioneering spirit prevails. Launch new projects. Intuitive flashes about new ideas. Emotional insecurity. Temper may flare up. A deep restlessness. Anything launched now may not be sustained if your interest and passion wane. And by all means relax when you can. This is a busy-two plus days.
1st house	Treat yourself to new clothes, a new haircut, a new look. Buy that new laptop you've had your eye on; you can't beat the discount. Do whatever it takes to feel good about how you present yourself. Follow your impulses.
Taurus ♉	Stability. Calmness. Money and security issues may crop up. Endurance. Increased stamina and strength. Good time to reassess what you value. Outdoor activities like gardening can be beneficial. Artistic talents are heightened. Intuition seeks practical solutions.
2nd house	Clean up your financial affairs. Balance the books. Make sure you know where your money is going. Intuition is helpful in security issues, personal values, and new money-making opportunities. Take time to be sensuous with whomever you love.
Gemini ♊	Communication and relatives are highlighted. Abundant energy. Restlessness. Writing, books, education and travel are emphasized in some way. Curiosity is stimulated. Intuition seeks new ideas.
3rd house	Good time to run errands, catch up on e-mail, attend workshops and conferences, and tie up loose ends. Visits with neighbors and relatives are likely. Intuition brings clarity to communication and ideas.
Cancer ♋	Old memories and their accompanying emotions surface. One parent is prominent or parental issues are highlighted. Excellent time to putter in garden. Intuition focuses on family.
4th house	Home is highlighted. Complete projects, have friends and relatives over for dinner, take your mother shopping or do something that she enjoys. If you're a parent, then do something fun with your kids. Also take time for yourself.

Sign/House	**Meaning**
Leo ♌	Need for attention. Public self highlighted in some way. Children play important role. Prima donna behavior. Intuition revolves around self.
5th house	Enjoy yourself these next few days. This is a fun, pleasurable, and creative time. Let loose, relax, enjoy your kids, start that book or painting that has been on the back burner, finish paneling your darkroom.
Virgo ♍	You may be more critical of yourself and others right now. Intuition brings details into greater clarity. Work and health are highlighted. You may need to find a balance between the two.
6th house	You're working long hours and may feel burned out. Boost your immune system with vitamins and herbs, exercise, and more nutritious meals. Your intuition will guide you toward exactly what you need if you listen to it. Try not to get bogged down in so many details that you lose sight of where you're going.
Libra ♎	Relationships snap to the forefront. Your attempts to keep the peace may be done at your own emotional expense unless you're aware of what's really happening. Artistic endeavors are important now. Don't avoid an issue to keep from hurting someone you love; people are stronger than you think. Your intuition is very strong in the relationship area.
7th house	Pay attention to your significant other and let romance suffuse the air. Be alert for new partnership opportunities in business. If you have enemies, they come out into the open now. Smother them with kindness.
Scorpio ♏	Passionate sexuality. Transcendent sex. Issues surrounding joint finances. Secrets may surface—either yours or those of someone close to you. A good time for regenerating your own energy. If you feel like getting even with someone, squash the urge. An urge to brood over past injuries.
8th house	In debt? Now is the time to handle the problem. Set up a budget. If the debt is held jointly, reach an agreement with your partner about how to pay it off. Your emotions, sexuality, and intuition are especially heightened during this transit.
Sagittarius ♐	Expansive, upbeat feelings. An itch to travel, to get out and about with people of like mind. Take a work-

Sign/House	*Meaning*
	shop, attend a seminar, look for the bigger picture in whatever you encounter and experience. Your intuition is especially busy and eager now.
9th house	Get in your car and start driving. Do it without any plan in mind; trust in your intuition to guide you. Issues about truth surface now and so do concerns about what you believe. Are your beliefs really yours, or did they actually come from someone else?
Capricorn ♑	Lay out or take stock of your career strategy. What are your goals? How hard are you willing to work to reach those goals? You're in a serious mood and instead of letting it depress you, use it to your advantage. Start an exercise regime that calls for self-discipline. Take up yoga. Converse with your intuition about which direction is best for you.
10th house	A professional wakeup call. You're ready to take action and are willing to do whatever it takes to achieve your goals. Run-ins with authority are possible—parents, bosses, the cruising cop looking to tie up his month's quota of speeding tickets. Your intuition is focused on practical application.
Aquarius ♒	Get together with friends of like mind and share ideas, dreams, hopes for the future. Get involved in your community, whether it's where you live or where you hang out online. Your radical ideas and beliefs need an outlet. Let your intuition whip you along in the right direction.
11th house	Renew friendships and contacts. Hook up with your network of buddies. Join a group of people who think and believe as you do. Offer support to a friend in need. Let your highest dreams, whatever they are, come through.
Pisces ♓	An emotional time. Your compassion spills over into every area of your life. You take in strays—animal, human, even plants. Your feelings get hurt easily now. Instead of crawling off to wallow and feel sorry for yourself, go to the beach. Laze by a river. Do something kind for someone else. Intuition is very strong now. Listen closely to its voice.
12th house	Dream recall is excellent. Good time for any spiritual pursuit. Find a place to kick back by yourself and just let your dreamy mood unroll.

Lunation: The Waxing and Waning of the Moon

From one new moon to the next, the moon waxes or increases in size as it moves away from the sun, then wanes or shrinks in size as it moves back toward the sun again. Each cycle lasts about two weeks. If you know where the month's new moon and full moon fall in your chart, you have a valuable timing device at your fingertips.

Waxing Cycle

In lunar time, the month begins at the new moon, when the moon and the sun are in the same sign. This is also the beginning of the waxing phase of the moon, a time of rising energy and expanding lunar light. This period lasts fourteen or fifteen days, until the full moon, when the moon is exactly opposite the sun. The cycle breaks down into distinct periods.

New Moon

The new moon period lasts three and a half days. The natural impulse during this time is toward growth. That impulse finds expression in any number of ways, from initiating new ideas and projects to freeing yourself from old and restrictive behavior patterns. The new moon, for instance, would be a great time to begin your intuitive development.

During this period, you might start a new job or launch a new business. Your ideas may come so quickly at times that it's a good idea to carry a notebook or tape recorder with you so that nothing gets away from you. Your dreams at the new moon can be especially vivid, offering fresh perspectives and creative ideas related to the dominant issues in your life. Dreams during this three and a half day period can offer insight about the tone of the entire lunar month.

Intuitive impressions during the new moon usually relate to the affairs of the house where the new moon is occurring. If you know where a new moon falls in your chart—which house it hits—then it's wise to take on something pertaining to that house and to follow any intuitive impressions you get.

In his book *The Lunation Cycle* (Aurora Press, 1986), astrologer Dane Rudhyar points out that the beginning of this new cycle is "surrounded by ghosts"—the loose ends of the previous cycle that have to be overcome or folded into the new cycle. In other words, if you buy a new house under a new moon, you still have to attend to unfinished details concerning the move—bus schedules for your kids and their new school, getting your mortgage coupon book from the lender, having your mail forwarded, and so on.

Crescent Moon

Think expansion for this phase. It occurs three and a half days into the lunar cycle and lasts until the seventh day. It's the time when you break fully from your habitual way of doing things and seek to develop the seeds you planted when the moon was new. You're beginning to look at what you started in terms of its pragmatism and efficiency.

If, for instance, you started your intuitive development under a new moon, then by the crescent phase, you should be expanding your foundation. This might entail establishing a daily routine for your intuitive development, ten or fifteen minutes devoted exclusively to inner work. Or it might involve reading books on intuitive development or signing up for a workshop.

In the move example, you may now find little things wrong with the house you bought, inconveniences that you failed to notice during the final walk-through at the closing. You may even feel that you made a mistake. If you decide to stay, this is the time when you paint the house, arrange and rearrange your furniture, buy new carpet, get tile laid, and have the phones hooked up. You're making your home habitable and personalizing it.

First Quarter Moon

"Crisis in action" is the term that astrologer Dane Rudhyar tagged onto this phase, and it certainly fits. You're committed now to what you initiated under the new moon and you throw yourself into making it all work. This is an intense, productive period where your commitment is tested. You're confronted with important decisions about the direction you've taken.

The first quarter moon begins on the seventh day of the lunar cycle and ends ten and a half days into it. During this part of the cycle, your intuitive voice may be quite strong, urging you in particular directions or to make certain choices. Maybe you have a chance to go away the same weekend of your workshop and have to decide if you're committed enough to attend the workshop.

In the move example, the first quarter phase is when you're galvanized to take action about glitches in your new house. Maybe the plumbing is defective or the roof has a leak or some of the floor tiles are broken. Whatever it is, you have to deal with the glitches, which deepens your commitment to the house. Or perhaps your commitment is what spurs you to action. In either case, though, you're in for the long haul.

Gibbous Moon

Rudhyar refers to this part of the cycle as "overcoming." You're compelled to tidy up details, to fine-tune whatever you've undertaken, and even if you feel at times that you would like to forget the whole thing, you don't.

This phase occurs from ten and a half days into the lunar cycle to the fourteenth day. You realize now that you have to live with the decisions you've made. The easiest way to navigate this period is by remaining flexible and rolling with the punches. Your intuition is also a valuable resource now, and if you've learned to muster it on demand, you're able to overcome whatever obstacles and challenges you encounter.

In the new home example, this might be when you discover your home needs a new roof or a new air-conditioning compressor—expensive items that may force you to dig into your savings or take out a home equity loan. You go through with the repair because you've committed to doing so.

Full Moon

Under this phase, things seem to happen in one of two directions—fulfillment and illumination or separation and release. The sun and moon are opposed to each other now and nothing is hidden; you can clearly see the consequences of your decisions.

This phase starts two weeks into the lunar cycle and ends three and a half days later. The struggle between your head and your heart or your left and right brain may be intense during this period. You want to listen to your intuition, but you fight it all the way. If you know which house in your natal chart is hit by a transiting full moon, you can prepare yourself ahead of time by reflecting on the last two weeks and inviting your intuitive voice to guide you in the direction that is best for you.

Maybe you've attended your intuitive workshop and didn't like it. This has forced you to reconsider your approach to intuitive development. Now you either have to release your chosen method and find a new approach or you explore why you didn't like the workshop and give your method another chance.

When I'm writing fiction and the full moon hits me in the fifth house, I experience a tight, inner tension about the story, about whether it's unfolding the way it should. If I adjust my story intuitively, the inner tension eases and I go on my way. If I tackle it analytically, the tension remains, I get frustrated, and suddenly I have other obligations that force me away from the writing. I've learned that the key to using the inner tension of the full moon is to allow my intuition to guide me.

Disseminating Moon

Rudhyar refers to this phase as "demonstration." You take whatever you've realized at the full moon and try to integrate it into whatever you started at the new moon. In the house example, you realize the place isn't perfect, but you attempt to work with those imperfections and use them rather than fight against them. In the intuitive development example, this phase would be when you start talking about what you're learning with other people.

This is a good time to publicize whatever you started at the new moon. Teach a seminar, send out résumés, submit your novel or screenplay, seek funding for your business.

Look for this phase seventeen and a half days into the lunar cycle. On the twentieth day, the moon shifts into the last quarter.

Last Quarter Moon

Okay, you've done everything you can possibly do with whatever you initiated at the new moon. What hasn't been assimilated gets tossed out, cut away. You're in a reorientation stage, where things you've set in motion either work or don't work. Rudhyar refers to this phase as a "crisis in consciousness," rather than action, because the process concerns ideologies.

So how does this apply to the house you just bought? Well, you've got a new roof, a new AC compressor, and your plumbing problems have been fixed. You've done everything you can to make the place comfortable. It's not the perfect house, but it's a long shot from the worst place you ever lived. For now, in fact, it's just fine.

Balsamic or Dark Moon

Release, release, release. This phase can feel uncomfortable if you haven't integrated each step of the lunation cycle into the total picture. The whole point now is to reflect on what has and hasn't worked in whatever you undertook at the new moon, and crystallize it. You're setting the stage now for the next new moon.

Meditation or solitary periods are beneficial during these three days. Your inner life—intuition, dreams, visionary periods—is richer. If the balsamic moon coincides with a weekend, then get away by yourself or with someone who doesn't make demands on you—then kick back and relax.

In the house example, this is the time when you enjoy your home and all the features that attracted you in the first place. Even while you're enjoying it, though, your intuition is casting around for the next home improvement.

In the intuitive development example, this phase of the moon might be when you commit fully to the path, but not to the method you employed earlier. Maybe you realize you're happier working on your own than with strangers in a workshop.

Your Lunar Month

The best way to become aware of how the lunation cycle works in your own life is to observe it. Few of us have the time to regularly keep track of where the moon falls in our natal chart every three and a half days and how its location impacts our daily lives. But if you try it for just one month, you'll clearly see the effects.

Use the space below to jot quick notes to yourself during each phase, or make separate entries in a notebook or on your computer. Include the sign of the moon, too, so you can observe how the various signs color your experiences. Also note how your intuition functions during each phase. At the end of the month, read back what you've written. You'll probably find a common theme or emotion to each of the entries.

MY LUNAR CYCLE

New Moon, Days 0–3.5

_____

_____

_____

_____

Crescent Moon, Days 3.5–7

_____

_____

_____

_____

First Quarter Moon, Days 7–10.5

_____

_____

_____

_____

Gibbous Moon, Days 10.5–14

_____

_____

_____

_____

Full Moon, Days 14–17.5

_____

_____

_____

_____

Disseminating Moon, Days 17.5–21

_____

_____

_____

_____

Last Quarter Moon, Days 21–24.5

_____

_____

_____

_____

Balsamic or Dark Moon, Days 24.5–29.5

_____

_____

_____

_____

22

Eclipses

Preliminaries

Most of us learn about eclipses in elementary school science and by the time we're adults, we can't remember exactly what happens during a solar or lunar eclipse. So, just to refresh your memory, let's look quickly at the basics.

A solar eclipse takes place when the moon comes between the earth and the sun. This can happen only at a new moon, when the sun and moon are conjunct. To us here on earth, the day goes from bright to twilight to partial or full darkness, depending on whether it's a partial or total eclipse. If it's total, the black disk you see when you look up is actually the moon. The aura of light around it—the corona—is light from the sun.

A lunar eclipse occurs when the earth moves between the sun and the moon, cutting off the sun's light to the moon. In most years, the two solar and two lunar eclipses happen when the sun reaches the sign of the north or south node. Generally, a lunar eclipse happens first, with a solar eclipse two weeks later. Eclipses run in cycles and series—called Saros series—and can be quite useful in predictive astrology.

Astrologically, solar eclipses are usually the most powerful of the two types and the degree of power is determined by the amount of light that is cut off. A total eclipse, then, is far more powerful than a partial eclipse. A total lunar eclipse, however, can be as powerful as a partial solar eclipse.

A solar eclipse tends to bring some conscious concern and external events into focus. If it falls in the tenth house, for instance, then something related to career, the public, authority, or a father figure is highlighted. This, in turn, also impacts the opposite house, which in this example is the fourth house. In any eclipse, the opposite house must also be considered.

In a lunar eclipse, inner needs are triggered—our emotional and instinctive feelings and reactions. Unresolved conflicts and fears may surface, problems with one of our parents, whatever we haven't been able to integrate into the rest of our lives.

Astrologers have various ways of using eclipses for predictive purposes. They note the houses of a natal chart that are affected, the angles the eclipse makes to other planets, and when the eclipse point may be triggered later by a transiting planet in the same degree as the eclipse. Astrologers differ about how long an eclipse's effects endure. Some feel the effects of the combined solar and lunar eclipse series lasts until the next sequence of eclipses; others contend that the effects may be felt initially in the month preceding the eclipse.

Astrologer Charles Jayne who, along with Edward Johndro did extensive research into eclipses, felt that the influence of a solar eclipse could be felt ninety days before and up to a year after the eclipse. The effects of a lunar eclipse, according to these two astrologers, can be felt up to six weeks on either side of the eclipse. Both men believed that transits over the eclipse degrees could be felt before and after.

In using eclipses for predictive purposes, I've found that each chart is unique in the way it responds to eclipses. Some people are influenced several months before and after; other people may feel the effects of a particular eclipse years later, when a planet transits the degree of the eclipse.

If you're born during or very close to an eclipse, you may be particularly sensitive to eclipses in general. The house in your chart where a lunar eclipse occurs tends to trigger your intuition in the area of your life represented by that house. A lunar eclipse that hits you in the fifth house, for instance, will heighten your intuition regarding kids, creative projects, and pleasurable pursuits in general.

Even a rudimentary understanding of how solar and lunar eclipses hit your natal chart can be helpful. If you know the house placements of your sun and moon, you can easily track the impact of eclipses on your life. Eclipses are usually listed in newspapers, astrological calendars, and *The Farmer's Almanac*, as well as on the Internet.

A Personal Perspective

My daughter was born one day after a solar eclipse at 8 degrees Virgo and two weeks after a lunar eclipse at 24 degrees Aquarius. Virgo rules her sixth house, Aquarius rules her twelfth.

In the fall of 1997, she entered a gifted elementary school program that entailed changing schools. She'd spent her first three years at a school within walking distance of our house and the new school, though only a few miles away, was a complete change of environment and children.

On September 1, 1997, a few days after the school year started, there was a solar eclipse at 10 degrees Virgo, a two-degree conjunction with her natal sun in her sixth house of health and work. Two weeks later, on September 16, 1997, there was a lunar eclipse at 24 degrees Pisces, a close conjunction with her Pisces ascendant. The lunar eclipse not only highlighted the ascendant/first house, but also affected its polar opposite, the descendant or the cusp of the seventh house. So this series of eclipses affected her first and seventh houses, and her sixth and twelfth houses—self, partnerships, health and work, and disowned power.

At first, she seemed content at her new school. She made new friends easily (seventh house), found the work (sixth house) challenging and interesting, and her self-esteem (first house) surged. But she wasn't crazy about her teacher (seventh house), who piled on the homework and ruled the classroom like a petty dictator.

During October, as the transiting moon approached the degree of the lunar eclipse, her emotional turmoil expressed itself in her health (sixth house). She developed sinus headaches and allergies and, over the next several months, missed about two weeks of school. Her pediatrician insisted the cause was stress and a persistent sinus infection. But by February, with a total solar eclipse at 8 degrees Pisces, exactly opposite September's eclipse, things got so bad that my husband and I talked about putting her in another school. The February eclipse hit her twelfth house and all sorts of negative feelings were triggered—feelings of inadequacy, of not being smart enough—and we thought if we removed her from the situation, things would improve for her. But she chose to stay.

During those months, we referred to her allergies as "sensitivities" so that the concept of *allergy* wouldn't become ingrained in her frame of reference. When she came home with a sinus headache, we talked about the emotions that had triggered it. She began to recognize *a pattern*. Her intuition related to herself was heightened. Her perceptions expanded.

At this same time, Pluto (transformation) in Sagittarius was transiting her Midheaven. One of the expressions of this transit is power issues with authorities. In a child's life, authority usually translates as parents, teachers, and older relatives. In Megan's case, the authority was definitely the teacher.

With the lunar eclipse that followed in March of 1998 at 22 degrees Virgo, the pressure the first and second solar eclipses had put on her sun now eased and the headaches became less frequent. By summer, they were gone. One could argue, of course, that the arrival of summer was the cure, but the deeper issues can't be explained away that easily. Megan learned important lessons that year about herself, about her self-criticism (Virgo moon), and how that impacts her health.

I realized most of this in retrospect, which is a rather pathetic confession for an astrologer to make. As a result, I now pay very close attention to how eclipses impact a natal chart and, closer to home, how eclipses affect myself and my immediate family.

Eclipses and Death

No astrologer in her right mind would predict anyone's death. But whenever a celebrity dies suddenly, astrologers get right down to the business of looking for the pattern that might indicate a sudden death. It's not that we're morbid. It's just that we're always on the lookout for patterns that add to the existing body of knowledge.

Within hours of Princess Diana's death on August 31, 1997, the astrology areas on the Web literally hummed with speculation. One of the possible culprits was the eclipse of September 1, 1997—the one that affected my daughter so strongly.

According to astrologer Celeste Teal, an eclipse may also have played an important role in the death of Jim Morrison, lead musician of The Doors. But in Morrison's case, the important eclipse had happened five years before he died and was triggered by a transit of Saturn in the degree of the eclipse that happened shortly before he died.

Obviously, this is an area that needs a lot more research, and yet I'm not sure what good can ultimately come of it. If an astrologer had warned Princess Di to be particularly cautious around the time of the eclipse on September 1, 1997, would it have made a difference?

If we have free will and it extends as far as we can imagine, to the point where our higher selves choose our parents, the circumstances into which we're born, even the time of our birth and death, then probably not. Any natal chart, as a blueprint of possibilities, undoubtedly has numerous points where death *might* occur. If it doesn't happen at one point, then maybe other, dormant elements in the natal chart are activated and develop until the next possible juncture with death and so on until the Self decides it's time.

After the fact, it's not very difficult to see death in a chart. Eclipses sometimes play a role, but so do other signs that astrologers use. The problem is that any of these "signs" can express themselves in ways other than death. That's free will. And in the end, the ways in which we assert our will is what really matters.

An interviewer once asked Isaac Asimov what he would do if he knew he were to die tomorrow. "Write faster," he said. If we knew when we would die, perhaps we would writer faster, live faster, love faster. Maybe we would cut to the chase and perhaps lose something valuable in the process.

Eclipses and World Events

In July and August of 1999, the last lunar and solar eclipses of the millennium occurred. The lunar eclipse on July 28 was in 5 degrees Aquarius; the solar eclipse on August 11 was in 18 degrees Leo. The eclipse shadowed a huge area of the globe, with the darkest path covering the east coast of India, the Middle East, Europe, and parts of the Atlantic. The eclipse formed a grand cross in fixed signs (Taurus, Leo, Scorpio, and Aquarius), which indicated heightened tension that would seek release. For months, astrologers had been making all sorts of predictions concerning the repercussions of this sequence of eclipses.

Astrologer Bill Meridian, writing in *Dell Horoscope's 1999 Yearbook*, predicted: "Relations with foreign countries are strained to the point of conflict. The President will likely have to send troops somewhere on the globe, and it will probably be the Mideast. Fires, explosions, and industrial accidents are also in the cards. . . . The USA and the Islamic world are likely to clash." He also predicted that old border disputes would be triggered in the Mideast, possibly between Turkey and Iraq.

Two days before the eclipse, astrologer Renie Wiley and I were talking about what the repercussions might be. "Within eighteen months following the eclipse," she said, "there will be massive land movements in some of the areas that were in the path of totality."

"What do you mean by land movements?" I asked. "Volcanos? Earthquakes? Refugees?"

"Any of the above," she replied.

Several days later, there was a 7.4 earthquake in Turkey. By the end of the week, three powerful hurricanes spun in the Atlantic, there had been an explosion near the Kremlin, and the death toll in Turkey had risen to ten thousand. Every day when I went on the Web to check the news, everything I read seemed to be bad and getting worse. I started checking the Global Earthquake Report on the Web, which lists every earthquake and tremor anywhere in the world. On the day after the earthquake, more than twenty earthquakes of varying magnitudes had occurred worldwide. On September 1, several weeks after the earthquake, the list was still long.

Now that I was disaster-conscious, I started daily checks of the Web for worldwide natural disasters—volcanic rumblings and eruptions, floods, droughts, tornadoes. You name it, I looked for it. Then one morning I woke up and decided I wouldn't check any of the disaster pages that day. All it did was depress me and make me anxious. And maybe that's the point about dire predictions surrounding eclipses and prophecies of any sort: your consciousness is flooded with negativity and over time, it can begin to erode whatever optimism you have.

So now I look for more cheerful news on the Web and in the news. Just tonight, for instance, Iraq announced that it was giving Turkey $10 million in oil, its response to the $9 million relief the U.S. has pledged. The jaded part of me says it's a ploy, but the part of me seeking more upbeat news is encouraged.

Prenatal Eclipses

One of the other fascinating areas that Charles Jayne and Edward Johndro researched was prenatal eclipses. They conducted their research in the late thirties, long before personal computers and astrological software made it so easy to erect charts. These prenatal eclipses—solar and lunar—are believed to be important in the overall scheme of your life. In a sense, they add color and texture to your natal chart, influence your intuitive abilities, and exert influence throughout your life.

The nature of this influence depends on the astrologer's perspective about eclipses. Astrologers Jan Spiller and Karen McCoy, in their intriguing book *Spiritual Astrology* (Fireside, 1988), say that the sign of your prenatal solar eclipse "determines what your responsibility is to the collective whole, the energy you have promised to share with your fellow beings." The sign of your prenatal lunar eclipse represents "the lesson that the soul wants to integrate into its evolutionary pattern." The house placements of the eclipses indicate the areas of your life where you're learning to share what you know (solar) and the areas into which you're learning to integrate what you learn (lunar).

Jane Roberts was born under a solar eclipse at 18 degrees Taurus.

In other words, that *is* her solar prenatal eclipse. If you glance at her natal chart, you'll see that the solar eclipse hits her fourth house. The lunar eclipse closest to her date of birth was at 4 degrees Gemini, which hits her fifth house.

According to Spiller and McCoy, then, she was supposed to share and teach what she learned about prosperity consciousness and having strong spiritual values (Taurus), and to do so while maintaining a sense of her own values. She did this in a very personal way (through intuitive work, channeling, and working out of her home), communicating her lessons (Gemini) in a creative way (fifth house). This is a truncated version of the picture, but should give you some idea of how to interpret your own prenatal eclipses.

Roberts died on September 3, 1984. When I checked my eclipse tables to see if either a solar or lunar eclipse occurred around that time in the degree or sign of her prenatal solar and lunar eclipses, I discovered that there was a lunar eclipse on November 8, 1984, at 16 degrees Taurus, the degree of her natal moon. This in itself wouldn't necessarily indicate death, but is one of the *patterns* I look for when I'm advising other people about possible trouble spots that are coming up in their lives.

The best recent example of this type of pattern occurred with a friend. Richard was born on June 5, 1948. His prenatal solar eclipse was (coincidentally?) the same as Jane Roberts's—18 degrees Taurus. His prenatal lunar eclipse was 3 degrees Scorpio. If you look at his natal chart in Appendix 3 (chart 2), you'll see that the prenatal solar eclipse falls in his fourth house and the prenatal lunar eclipse falls less than one degree short of his Midheaven.

Richard, like Jane Roberts, had a Taurus moon in the fourth house. Like Roberts, he was also very psychic and spiritually aware. Like Roberts, he had an immune disorder—chronic fatigue syndrome. Like Roberts, he was stubborn and fixed in his opinions.

Some time on August 1, 1999, during a terrible heat wave in Manhattan, he died suddenly and unexpectedly. My husband and I had seen him only two weeks earlier in New York, when he'd asked me to take a look at his chart. I still hadn't done so when we heard about his death. When I studied his chart, I realized he'd died eleven days short of the August 11, 1999, solar eclipse at 18 degrees Leo, a perfect square (tension) to the degree of his prenatal solar eclipse. The cusp of his eighth house, which is often involved with death patterns, is 18 degrees and 59 minutes of Leo.

Leo rules the heart. Although the final results of his autopsy aren't in yet, my guess is that he died of a heart attack. The lunar nodes are also involved at times in death patterns, so I looked at where they were transiting on the day he died. The north node on August 1, 1999, was at 12 degrees and 56 minutes in Leo, an exact conjunction with his natal Pluto at 12 degrees and 57 minutes, square his natal north node in the fourth house at 12 degrees and 30 minutes Taurus, and square his south node in the tenth house at 12 degrees and 30 minutes of Scorpio. The transits created a T-square (a stress aspect) to his first house of self.

What all this jargon means is that a definite pattern had emerged. And yet, if I had looked at his chart before he'd died and seen all the details of this pattern, I certainly wouldn't have told him he might die sometime near the eclipse. I might have cautioned him to take better care of himself, to be careful during the early days of August, to get out of the city and into a cooler place. I would definitely have advised him to pay attention to any intuitive impressions about himself that emerged. The pattern could be expressed in many ways and death was just one of the possibilities, but the one that his soul chose.

So there you have it again, free will versus the blueprint of the natal chart. Possibilities, probabilities, patterns: that's what astrologers look for.

Eclipse Tables

It's beyond the scope of this book to provide eclipse tables. *Predicting Events With Astrology* (Llewellyn Publications, 1999) by Celeste Teal and *The Eagle and the Lark* (Samuel Weiser, 1992) by Bernadette Brady provide eclipse tables that cover the twentieth century and part of the twenty-first century. Brady's book also includes the series to which each eclipse belongs and a brief explanation about each series.

23

Aspects

A Bit of Geometry

The angles that planets make to each other are called aspects. They are analogous to the people who live in your neighborhood—friendly or hostile, difficult or easy to get along with, mysterious or open. Some aspects, like some people, create enormous inner tension and friction; others create ease and a smooth flow of energy.

There are dozens of aspects that astrologers can use when interpreting charts. But there are only five to seven major aspects, and these are classified according to how easy or difficult they are. Major aspects are considered more powerful than minor aspects, but minor aspects often add flavor and texture to a birth chart. Tables 11 and 12 provide a list of major aspects and the most commonly used minor aspects, with key word definitions that are easy to remember.

In the tables, the aspects are listed according to their exactness. A conjunction, for example, is two planets in the same sign and degree, or 0 degrees of separation. A square is formed when two planets are separated by 90 degrees. Astrologers, however, differ about how many degrees of *orb* an aspect can vary and still be effective. In other words, if two planets are separated by 93 degrees instead of 90, are they square to each other? Absolutely. Some astrologers allow a 10-degree orb when a major aspect involves the sun or moon and an orb of half that when a major aspect involves another planet or point. I prefer smaller orbs, of 3 to 5 degrees, unless a chart doesn't have many aspects.

At any rate, the issue of orbs tends to be an individual matter. As Robert Hand writes in *Horoscope Symbols* (Whitford Press, 1981): "What the question boils down to is not how far out of orb an aspect can be and still have an effect, but rather how subtle a linkage one will accept as significant."

In Jane Roberts's chart, Jupiter (♃) and the north node of the moon (☊) are exactly conjunct at 21 degrees Taurus in the fourth house. Her sun (☉) at 18 degrees Taurus and her moon (☽) at 16 degrees Taurus are separated by only two degrees. Those two degrees definitely qualify as a conjunction. Even though her Jupiter and moon are separated by nearly five degrees, they also qualify as conjunctions. Her Saturn in the twelfth house (♄ 29 ♐ 50) at 29 degrees Sagittarius is also considered to be a conjunction with her ascendant (01 ♑ 46) because they're separated by less than two degrees.

Conjunctions are the easiest aspects to spot in a chart because they cluster in the same area. Squares are a bit more difficult, but at a glance, look for planets and cusps in the same degree. In Roberts's chart, her Mars in the seventh house (♂ 27 ♋ 51) and her Midheaven at 27 ♎ 26 obviously form some sort of aspect because they share the same degree. Cancer is three signs—or 90 degrees—away from Libra, so you have a square.

Fortunately, astrology software provides an aspectarian that makes it easy to identify aspects in a chart. It's found in the lower left hand corner of Roberts's chart.

Table 10: Major Aspects

Aspect	Distance	Orb	Key Words
Conjunction ♂	0°	5°	Unity, strength. Can be disruptive if the conjunct planets aren't harmonious.
Sextile ✳	60°	3–5°	Beneficial. Easy flow. Opportunities.
Square ▢	90°	3–5°	Friction. Challenge. Dynamic, forceful energy.

Aspect	Distance	Orb	Key Words
Trine △	120°	3–5°	Harmonious energies. Buffer against turmoil. Too many trines can result in passivity.
Opposition ☍	180°	3–5°	Forces change through conflict. Involves polarities. Projection onto others.

Astrologer Charles Jayne popularized the use of two other major aspects—the parallel and contraparallel. They are measured by declination—that is, the number of degrees by which a planet is north or south of the equator. Two planets that are parallel to each other are usually, but not always, in conjunction. Two planets that are contraparallel to each other are usually, but not always, in opposition.

Jayne contended that parallels and contraparallels often explain the primary theme in a chart that can't be explained by other aspects. For our purposes, consider the parallel similar in strength to a conjunction; it confers power and emphasis. A contraparallel is similar to an opposition, creating a tug of war within the person.

Table 11: Minor Aspects

Aspect	Distance	Orb	Key Words
Novile ⑨	40°	1°	Spiritual rebirth, re-evaluation of past life attitudes, restrictions.
Semisquare ∠	45°	30′–1°	Resistant to change.
Septile ⑦	51°26′	0°	Karmic in nature, predisposition to occult, how we receive inspiration.
Quintile Q	72°	30′	Creative ability, a talent, extended perception, occult knowledge.
Sesquiquadrate ⊡	135°	30′	Excessive reaction to minor conflicts.
Quincunx ⊼	150°	1°	Adjustments, incongruity.

To Use or Not to Use

I always look at the minor aspects in a chart to see if they repeat a common theme and use them for interpretation when a horoscope lacks a lot of major aspects. But the problem with trying to interpret ever smaller pieces of a horoscope is that your intuitive voice gets lost. *Don't overdo it!*

The descriptions that follow pertain only to aspects formed between the moon and other planets. For those readers who have erected their horoscopes using the blank charts at the back of the book, then read just the aspects formed between the moon and the sun, the moon and the rising, the moon and the Midheaven, and the moon and each of the nodes.

For readers who have complete natal charts, read all of the aspects.

Conjunction, 0°

Conjunctions of the moon intensify the emotions, unconscious mind, and intuitive perceptions. It colors our instinctive and intuitive reactions to events and to people—notably to women.

Moon conjunct Sun: Your will and ego work smoothly together, enabling you to attain what you want. Your strong creative urges originate at instinctive and intuitive levels. You have deep ties to your family, parents, spouse, and home.

You tend to be very impulsive. If you learn to differentiate between impulses that rise from frustration and those that rise from intuition, you'll be able to use the intuitive impulses to your advantage. Your high energy can make you impatient with others.

Moon conjunct Mercury: Your thoughts are colored by your emotions and your intuitive perceptions. You enjoy variety and change and dislike being restricted by emotional demands that others make on you. Your memory is excellent. Your relationships with brother and sisters go through fluctuating phases, but you generally get along with them. You may be interested in books, writing, the communication field.

Moon conjunct Venus: You have a charming, outgoing personality that matches your physical beauty, especially if you're a woman. Your artistic talents are most impressive and can be easily enhanced through conscious use of your intuition. You may be shy, but other people usually don't know it. In a man's chart, this combination means favors from women and a good relationship generally with women.

Moon conjunct Mars: Magnetism. Powerful, intense emotions. Your intuition is a driving, instinctive force in your life. You're mentally quick, with a storehouse of memories that possess a strong, emotional content. This aspect, especially if combined with Venus, brings musical and artistic talent. It also indicates fortunate financial affairs. In a woman's chart, it suggests a drive to achieve recognition commensurate with a man's.

Moon conjunct Jupiter: A generous and sympathetic nature. You enjoy people of diverse cultures and backgrounds, you gain from and through women. You have sympathy and compassion for people less fortunate than yourself and these feelings may expand and deepen as you get older, resulting in a "social conscience." You enjoy all sorts of travel, especially to foreign countries, where your perceptions are broadened.

Moon conjunct Saturn: Okay, so you're a bit more serious than many people you know. Part of the problem is that the moon and Saturn are uneasy neighbors, not very compatible, really, when you get right down to it. But since the aspect is yours, make the best of it. Congratulate yourself for not being a quitter, for being someone who other people can depend on to get the job done. You're somewhat introverted and your emotions and intuition may be repressed. Once you're aware of this tendency, though, you can take steps to remedy it.

Moon conjunct Uranus: This aspect lends itself to unusual emotional and intuitive responses to circumstances and people. The moon seeks traditions and Uranus seeks the new, the unusual, the eccentric: that's the basic conflict. The challenge is to integrate the dual needs in a way that allows your life to be stimulating and exciting without sacrificing your inner needs. Once you do that, the rewards are great.

Moon conjunct Neptune: Finely tuned intuition. At times, you're so attuned to other people's emotions that you act as a psychic sponge, soaking up every bit of negative and positive energy around you. Once you learn how to use your psychic ability to help others heal themselves, you're functioning at the highest level of this conjunction. Your attraction to the arts and music probably won't win you any brownie points with your parents or other authority figures and neither will your lack of pragmatism. On the other hand, your intuition allows you to pierce mysteries that others don't even know exist.

Moon conjunct Pluto: The truth? This one can be tough to deal with. Your intense emotions can erupt without warning and may lead to drastic breaks with your family. On the other hand, once you commit to someone or something, you're loyal to the end. Power issues and struggles may be a theme in your intimate relationships, with family members, and with close friends. The challenge is to learn to channel your powerful emotions in a constructive manner, perhaps through some creative outlet. If you listen to your intuition, the power issues won't be such an issue.

Moon conjunct north node: Your intuition nudges you in new and unfamiliar directions. If you go with the flow, you discover that your finger is on the public pulse and that you can use this to your advantage. Women play important roles in your life and are beneficial to you in some way.

Moon conjunct south node: You attract people with whom you have past life connections and some sort of karmic debt to repay. This aspect also pertains to timing that isn't quite in sync and, as a result, opportunities are missed. If you learn to discipline your efforts, you succeed against the odds.

Moon conjunct ascendant: Early childhood is still with you, buried somewhere deep in your psyche, and it colors your emotional responses as an adult. You have deep ties to your family and roots and, in part, your empathy for others stems from those ties. Other people see you as more intuitive than you see yourself.

Moon conjunct Midheaven: At least a portion of your life will be lived in the public eye. This is an excellent position for influencing mass thought and is often found in the charts of public figures, actors, and other prominent individuals. Women and one of your parents help you to achieve your goals. Your intuition revolves around your career and profession.

Squares, 90°

Moon squares indicate unconscious blocks, prejudices, and deeply rooted habits that hinder emotional expression. In a woman's chart, health can be impacted if emotions aren't expressed. Although intuition remains strong, it may go unheeded.

Moon square sun: Blame it on your childhood or your mother, blame it on whatever or whomever you want. But the battle between your willpower—your conscious mind—and your emotions continues until you bring up the old stuff and try to integrate it into your life. Your intuition can be a valuable ally in this process, so in tackling old behavioral patterns, you may want to start with nurturing your intuition.

Moon square Mercury: The challenge is to keep your innermost thoughts to yourself. Strangers don't want to listen to what you discuss with your therapist. If you're nervous and feel the urge to chatter, take a couple of deep breaths and turn your attention to the other person. Focus on him or her and not on yourself.

Moon square Venus: If you act as though you're worthy of other people's attention, love, and respect, then eventually you'll begin to believe it. And once you believe it, some of your compensating habits will vanish. You won't feel the need anymore to overspend, won't allow others to take advantage of you, and will act on the courage of your convictions. Learn to trust your intuition. It won't ever fail you.

Moon square Mars: Lighten up. Don't take everything so personally. Your emotions are volatile, which isn't necessarily bad unless you turn it on others. When you were younger, your emotions probably ran amok, creating havoc in your relationship with your parents. The friction and inner tension you feel can be released through some type of regular exercise program. Astrologer Grant Lewi said this aspect frequently manifests as precociousness in childhood.

Moon square Jupiter: You're generous to a fault and it may have something to do with ego and pride. That's fine, as long as you're aware of it. On the other hand, your generosity may simply be a nearly overwhelming compassion for other people's tragedies. In either case, you go to extremes with people you love, showering them with the same excesses that you shower on yourself. The challenge is to curb your appetites and extravagances, but to do it without losing your belief in an abundant universe.

Moon square Saturn: Saturn has a bad rep. It's the heavy in the astrological universe, the task master, the sadist with the whip who shouts, *Work harder, move faster!* So conventional wisdom would deem its combination with the moon as bad. Not so. Astrologer Grant Lewi wrote, "This is perhaps the most powerful single aspect you can have in a horoscope. It gives both ambition and the ability to concentrate on it." While Lewi acknowledged that moodiness and depression might be health factors with this aspect, it nonetheless produces success in some line of work. Intuitive development definitely helps deal with the challenge of this square.

Moon square Uranus: The moon isn't too crazy about keeping company in this way with Uranus. You feel a constant war within yourself for personal freedom and yet, the past and all your roots keep pulling you back. In your restless thrust for freedom, you search for the ultimate. The problem is that you may not have defined yet what *the ultimate* is. Until you do, your exceptional talents and individualism carry you exactly as far as you wish to go. Just be sure that you live close to your spiritual bone, whatever that may be for you, because if you don't, something big may wake you up—a sudden illness, a natural disaster, something disruptive and unexpected.

Moon square Neptune: You're a dreamer, no way around it. You would excel at writing fantasy novels that take place in some far-flung universe on the other side of the rainbow. The challenge is that you're not quite sure how to make your incredible ideas concrete. Where should you start? How are you supposed to get from point A to point B? The answer should be obvious: let your intuition take you there.

Moon square Pluto: Chill. Take half a dozen deep breaths, shut your eyes, and imagine stepping into a cool mountain stream. This will serve you far better than your usual intense and emotional reaction. Any time Pluto keeps company with the moon, deeply rooted power issues are part of the challenge. Pluto, though, gives as well as takes; your intuitive ability is often piercing and can take you much farther than you imagine.

Moon square nodes: Ouch. This aspect forms a T-square, a pattern of intense internal pressure. If your moon is in Leo, then your nodes are square when they fall in either Taurus or Scorpio, within a three-to-five-degree orb. The key to relieving this pressure lies in the house toward which the T-square points. In other words, let's say your Leo moon is in the seventh house, with the nodes in houses four and seven. This would put the remedy in the first house, which represents the self. It means you overcome emotional or unconscious biases by your own efforts.

Moon square ascendant: Other people see you as emotionally reticent. They rarely hear you express what you feel. They perceive you as an observer of human nature, rather than a participator. Yes, it might go back to childhood and an accumulation of unconscious perceptions. But so what? Once you become conscious of what you're doing and why, you begin to discover your niche in life and then your passion frees you.

Moon square Midheaven (and IC): You allow domestic responsibilities to interfere with your professional ambitions. You really don't have to do everything, you know. Despite what you learned as a kid, delegating work and responsibility is okay. But you have to believe it's okay before it feels comfortable to you. Once you do, people will respond to it just fine.

Moon Oppositions

If I were arranging the discussion of aspects in the traditional way, by degrees of separation, moon sextiles would follow conjunctions and trines would come before oppositions. This means that the end of the aspect section would leave a sour taste in your mouth. I dislike ending anything on a negative note, so I've saved the best to the last and put the worst here in the middle. And that's what oppositions are: the toughest aspects to work with.

Most astrologers agree that conjunctions and oppositions are the most dynamic and powerful aspects. Other adjectives that fit are: *demanding, tough, challenging, emotionally painful.*

The enormous inner tension and conflict they create are usually projected outward onto people in your life, who then become a mirror of your own worst characteristics. Your intuition can help you integrate the energies into the rest of your life.

Moon opposed sun: This is a relentless struggle between ego and intuition, between left-brained and right, between the scientist and the mystic. This is tension in the most obvious ways, a spiritual discomfort that can plunge you into a depressing abyss or propel you to dizzying heights. Extremes, that's what we're talking about here.

Your relationships with the opposite sex leave a lot to be desired. And if you don't resolve the central conflict, your health may suffer, especially in a woman's horoscope. The bottom line is that you really don't have to choose between self and other; you just think that you do.

Moon opposed Mercury: The dichotomy itself is pretty simple. Privacy versus openness, emotions versus logic. You have to learn to balance the two. Until you do, your relationships are often filled with friction and disruption. You're indecisiveness causes you to go first one way, then another, which creates confusion for yourself and others. Think before you speak and consider how what you say may affect others.

Moon opposed Venus: You feel socially inept and uneasy in the company of others. This deeply rooted pattern goes back to your childhood, when you felt unloved or unappreciated by your parents, especially your mother. The emotional walls you erect to protect yourself actually isolate you, and the people you love have a difficult time breaking through them. To compensate, you sometimes over-spend and indulge in extravagances that easy your unease. Aware-ness of the pattern and developing your intuition go a long way toward mitigating it.

Moon opposed Mars: You're an emotional powerhouse, impul-sive, restless, impatient, and volatile. At the very negative end of this scale, you may dislike women; in men, this aspect can indicate abusiveness toward women. The tension of the opposition comes out in relationships, which always seem to be marked by arguments and dissension. Once again, part of the problem stems from child-hood and Mom gets the bulk of the blame. Her emotional distance left a deep imprint on you. As a result, you go for excitement and variety in relationships and prefer to avoid the deeper stuff. Your in-tuition, often buried within impulses you don't understand, can be a valuable aid if you heed it. It provides insight and clarity you need to recognize and deal with this deeply embedded pattern.

Moon opposed Jupiter: A part of you wants to be swept away into new vistas that will expand your spiritual and philosophical views and your general perspective on life. But another part of you clings to certain emotional patterns that work against you. You worry too much about insignificant things and may be somewhat rigid in your religious views, still believing the tenets you learned in childhood. Your generosity is sincere and well intended, but may be misplaced because you want to believe only good things about other people. If you can detach somewhat from your emotions and allow your intuition equal say, much of the above is mitigated.

Moon opposed Saturn: You may feel restricted somewhat emotionally, due (again) to childhood conditions and/or early responsibilities you assumed. You may withdraw emotionally in social situations, which makes it more difficult for other people to get to know you. You're adept at shoving unpleasant emotions into a shuttered closet in your heart to deal with later. These emotions need to be released and, quite often, a creative passion helps to do that. This opposition gives you drive, ambition, and the focus to succeed at whatever you take on. You may have problems with authority figures and employers, so it's best to become self-employed.

Moon opposed Uranus: Your inner life is often a battleground of opposing needs. Part of you craves freedom and the constant stimulation of new experiences. Another part of you clings to what is familiar and feels secure. As a result, your moods seem to be in a continual state of flux and change. Your erratic personality makes intimate relationships difficult. As a parent, you're likely to feel restricted and bored by your responsibilities. As a marriage partner, you may feel the grass is always greener elsewhere. If you intuitively grasp the bigger picture of your particular patterns, however, you have the talent and ability to change your life and to attract significant others who understand your needs. It's a tall order, so get busy.

Moon opposed Neptune: This very psychic placement often feels like you're being flooded with impressions and feelings you don't understand. And actually, that's exactly what's happening. Like the moon square Neptune aspect, the opposition makes you a psychic sponge, soaking up every dreg and bit of psychic residue from the people around you. It creates a lot of problems in your relationships because you project your confusion onto other people. If you learn to channel your psychic energy constructively, it becomes easier for you to set goals and stick to them.

Moon opposed Pluto: Power issues. Pluto is always about power issues, and in this instance, the power has to do with emotions. You control your own very tightly, which leads to emotional explosions that damage your intimate relationships. You often seek to control other people, too, and this only feeds into the vicious power circle.

Your intuition is highly developed, but you may not listen to it except under extreme circumstances. Disputes with your family about finances and inheritances are likely. Your best bet for navigating this difficult aspect is to allow the people you love equal say and to realize that your way isn't always the right way for everyone else.

Moon opposed north node: Your beliefs can literally change your life, and with this aspect, your beliefs may be impeding your progress in every facet of your existence. The house that holds the north node will give you some idea of the direction you should be headed. Change your beliefs and watch the miracles unfold.

Moon opposed south node: You're here this time around to release deeply embedded psychological patterns so that you can progress in new directions. Let your intuition guide you in the process of unfoldment.

Moon opposed ascendant: Your emotional responses to other people can be explosive, hurtful to you, and deepen your frustration. Think before you blurt out what you're feeling. Your insight into other people can be piercing and, when coupled with your intuition, should help you to understand their motives—and your own. Be careful that you don't become emotionally dependent on others.

Moon opposed Midheaven: Your closeness to your parents and your fond memories of childhood never leave you. If you still cling to the spiritual beliefs of your childhood, however, this can create problems because you may have outgrown those beliefs. You enjoy your home and your family and don't like leaving them for any length of time, which can cause conflicts in your career responsibilities.

Moon Sextiles and Trines

I've combined these two because their effects are similar. Sextiles concern opportunities that come to us through little effort of our own; trines are points of ease and the smooth flow of energy. People who have a lot of these easy aspects in their charts and few squares or oppositions, may not have sufficient friction to impel them to action.

Moon sextile or trine sun: You have a gift with people and are successful in working with the public. The smooth flow of energy between your will and your intuition enhances your psychic and creative abilities. You attempt to create the kind of harmony in your own home that you knew in childhood. At times, your life is so pleasant and happy that you don't see any point in asserting yourself.

Moon sextile or trine Mercury: Your remarkable memory can muster the scent of roses in a garden thirty years ago or recall a conversation you had with your grandmother. Your emotions, intuition, and intellect function harmoniously. A great aspect for writers or anyone in the communication field. The trine is good for people who work with their hands in some capacity. If you're self-employed, you may work out of your home.

Moon sextile or trine Venus: Your intuition is strongest in the arena of relationships, which are usually harmonious for you. You're a charmer and your generous nature attracts the right people and opportunities at the right time. Your artistic and creative abilities spring from deeply intuitive sources, and if you're willing to take the necessary risks, you can earn your living doing what you love best. The trine is a lucky aspect that favors financial prosperity.

Moon sextile or trine Mars: No two ways about it. You're known as the person who gets things done. Your energy, self-confidence, and ease with the public helps you to achieve your ambitions. Your intuition is especially good at urging you in particular career directions. Your temper flares up occasionally, but you aren't the type to hold grudges and, besides, who's got the time to mull over past injuries? You're too busy living each moment as it arrives.

Moon sextile or trine Jupiter: It doesn't get much better than this. Your intuitive feelings about situations and people are usually accurate and, with a bit of practice, can get even more so. Your generous nature allows you to see the good in people and you are, in fact, the kind of person for whom a day is always partly sunny rather than partly cloudy. Your memory is terrific; little that makes an impression on you ever escapes you. You enjoy foreign travel, but it's even better if it's travel with a purpose—a dig at an ancient site, your own past-life connections with other parts of the world, even a vision quest. The trine usually indicates a happy home life and financial prosperity.

Moon sextile or trine Saturn: Your business sense is remarkable. It's as if you were born knowing how to play a hunch and how to make it work in your favor. You have excellent insight into the inner workings of personal relationships, and that may be part of what makes you such a loyal friend and partner. You see through the camouflage. You're able to structure your creative talents and impulses into practical projects.

Moon sextile or trine Uranus: Magnetism—that's you. And it's this magnetism that attracts stimulating people and situations into your life. You're a progressive thinker with impeccable timing, and your intuition allows you to quickly grasp the inner workings of any situation. Your interests lie more with the future than the past and this is faithfully reflected in your passions and activities. The trine aspect indicates an interest in astrology.

Moon sextile or trine Neptune: Your artistic and creative abilities are forces every bit as powerful in your life as your intuitive ability. One feeds the other. The creative part of you may be at home in any of the arts, from dance to theater, to writing and music. Your imagination alone would make you an excellent fiction writer. Your memory is excellent, due in part to the deep imprints that your psychic impressions leave on you. You're essentially a gentle, compassionate person.

Moon sextile or trine Pluto: Your penetrating insight into other people allows you to expand your vistas and to understand what really lies at the heart of any matter. You're adept at using your imagination to visualize what you want—and thus, to attract that very situation or person. You're deeply sensitive to other people's needs and issues and often feel an obligation to right the social wrongs of the world. You may work with children or animals in some capacity, since your humanity recognizes no limits in terms of color, race, or species. These aspects are very powerful and sometimes suggest a sense of destiny.

Moon sextile or trine nodes: Your instincts are sound and when they urge you to embrace the future, you do it without resistance. This adage applies to you: when the student is ready, the teacher appears. Are you the student or the teacher? Remain open to both possibilities.

Moon sextile or trine ascendant: Little is hidden about you. Your emotions are right out front and so are your passions and interests. You need people around you and enjoy the company of your tightly knit family. You're sensitive to criticism and remember who has criticized you for what, but you don't hold grudges. Your own sensitivity toward other people enables you to get along with virtually anyone.

Moon sextile or trine Midheaven: Women are helpful to you professionally. Synchronicities play an important part in both your professional and personal life. If you study their underlying patterns, the knowledge you glean will tell you a great deal about your professional goals and ambitions. Your intuition is a major force in helping you achieve your professional goals.

Unaspected Moon

When the moon doesn't form angles to any other planets, it is *unaspected*. It means the moon is a loner, isolated in the chart, unable to interact with other planets. It doesn't function to its full potential and makes the individual feel emotionally vulnerable, frequently unstable, and isolated.

24

Intuitive Reality Check #4: In the Shadow of the Moon

Your Hidden Agenda

The dark side of the moon represents the deepest, most unconscious beliefs we hold. Most of these beliefs are invisible to our conscious minds. We've accepted them throughout our lives from our parents, schools, religions, and the society in which we live. They are the basis from which we function in the world.

Even though these beliefs are invisible to our conscious minds, they are evident in our lives in what we experience and through the people we attract. If we learn to interpret the experiences, our lives become our oracles.

When I was pregnant with my daughter, my husband and I were living in a townhouse in Fort Lauderdale. It was one of those walled communities so common in South Florida. Behind the walls, life was fine. But outside the walls, just two blocks south, was the worst crack neighborhood in the city.

One evening we had pulled into a gas station on the corner to vacuum the inside of the car. While Rob was vacuuming under the seats, I was feeding quarters into the machine. My car door was open, my purse resting on the floor. A car pulled up just in front of us, two men inside. The guy in the passenger seat got out and strode my way. I thought he was going to ask if we were nearly finished with the vacuum. Instead, he shoved me to one side, grabbed my purse, and ran for the car, which sped out of the lot.

This happened so fast that I literally had no time to react. I remember glancing at Rob, who was still vacuuming and hadn't seen a thing. The vacuum went off, we got back into the car, and only then did I say, "Someone just stole my purse."

He looked at me like I was crazy. "What? When?"

Once I told him the story, he asked, as anyone would, why I hadn't screamed or said anything until we'd gotten back into the car. I didn't have an answer. Looking back, I guess I was just stunned into disbelief that it had actually happened. I called the police when we got home and reported what had happened.

As we were talking, a report came in that the men had been caught, but they didn't have the purse. I didn't have much money in my wallet, but it contained my credit cards and driver's license and now I would have to report everything stolen and go through the tedious process of obtaining another license.

The next afternoon, a woman who lived a mile away called me and said she had my wallet. The two men had run through her backyard the night before and tossed the purse. The cash was gone, but everything else was still inside.

I had lived in that townhouse for ten years and had never been robbed, assaulted, shot at, or anything else. So what had it all really been about? *What was the deeper meaning?*

Two days after this incident, Rob and I started looking at homes farther north. I still hadn't figured out what the incident had really been about, but I was absolutely certain now that I wasn't going to bring up a child two blocks from the worst crack neighborhood in Lauderdale. When Megan was six weeks old, we moved into our house forty miles north, in a neighborhood with kids and trees.

I realize now that a *core belief* attracted that experience. The belief was this: *a pregnant woman is vulnerable because pregnancy is like an illness. It weakens you.* I'm not sure where this belief came from or when it originated. I was never sick during my pregnancy—no morning sickness, no complications, nothing unusual except a long labor at the end. Yet, from the very beginning, I was treated like a sick woman by the medical establishment. I *did* feel vulnerable.

Rob and I had talked about moving, but not seriously. The sheer enormity of moving—looking for a house, packing up, the hassle and expense . . . We had a lot of good arguments. But once my purse was stolen, we got the hint and took action, something we might not have done until much later.

So, in an odd sort of way, I now see the thieves as nothing more than personifications of my beliefs at the time, the internal made manifest. I wasn't hurt, my credit cards weren't stolen, and I didn't have to spend five hours in line at the driver's license bureau. In short, I didn't have to experience any of those things to get the message. It was time to move—out of Lauderdale and into the future.

Until the incident happened, though, I didn't realize that I held this core belief about pregnancy. It's not enough that our experiences push us in one direction or another; we need to understand why and our intuition makes the search for meaning easier than it might be otherwise. If we can identify the core belief that attracts or creates our experiences, then our understanding is accelerated, the core belief is dissolved, and our lives change.

Core beliefs *are* the hidden agenda.

Identifying Core Beliefs

Our core beliefs emerge in the most casual of conversations. If you listen to yourself sometime, really listen, you're bound to hear a core belief within a few minutes. Some of the most common I've heard over the years are:

All politicians are corrupt
We never have enough money
The teen years are the pits
Cars fall apart after 75,000 miles
I'm not a lucky person
My health isn't good
It's a dog-eat-dog world
I'll never get a raise

These statements are *not* reality; they're just beliefs about reality. Change the beliefs and your reality changes.

Scott Adams, in his book *The Dilbert Future* (HarperCollins, 1997), tells some intriguing stories about how his comic strip, *Dilbert*, became so successful. His secret? Affirmations. This is what you repeat, like a mantra or a prayer, over and over again until your unconscious mind believes it to be true. The odds, Dilbert says, of becoming a syndicated cartoonist are about 10,000 to 1. Even though he knew the odds, he figured the odds didn't apply to him. "When I submitted samples by mail to the major cartoon syndicates, I had a feeling of being exactly where I needed to be and doing exactly what I needed to do. I never once doubted it would work out the way it did."

He didn't doubt because he had proven it to himself before and a number of synchronicities and experiences had confirmed this new belief. One such experience involved his score on the GMAT test, the equivalent of SAT scores for an MBA program. He had taken the test several years before and had gotten a 77, not high enough to qualify for Berkeley, where he wanted to go. He knew his score had to be over the ninetieth percentile for him to get in to Berkeley. So he chose the ninety-forth percentile as his "specific outlandish target."

He didn't let it rest there. He bought study books, took the practice tests, and kept doing his visualizations of that ninety-forth percentile on his GMAT results form. He took the test and continued the visualization and affirmations as he waited for the results. On the day the results arrived, he removed the letter from the mailbox and hesitated before opening it. "When I think back to my GMAT results, I believe the contents of the envelope were variable until the moment I perceived what was inside," he wrote.

This sounds a lot like quantum physics, in which the world outside of us is an ocean of wave probabilities. The waves collapse into particles as soon as they are observed or *as soon as consciousness enters the equation.*

Adams opened the envelope and there, in that same spot he'd visualized it, was a 94. "I know now that I have a better outlook on life when I think of reality in terms of infinite universes."

To make it short and sweet: you get what you believe. If there's even a remote possibility that affirmations and visualizations can help, then why not use them? If there's even a remote possibility that your intuition can make life easier, then why not develop and use it?

So let's start with what you believe. Write true or false to the statements below. The more honest you are, the more insight you'll have.

1. It seems like I can't get ahead financially. _____
2. My intimate relationships don't work. _____
3. A job pays the bills, that's it. Nothing more, nothing less. _____
4. If it comes too easily, it can't be any good. _____
5. Money doesn't grow on trees. _____
6. After the age of 40 (or 50 or 60) it's all downhill. _____
7. Parenting is hard work. _____
8. Being creative is hard work. _____
9. Women don't make as much money as men. _____
10. Men aren't as intuitive as women. _____
11. I need breast or prostrate exams every year. _____
12. Everyone needs health insurance. _____
13. A woman alone is vulnerable. _____
14. A single man isn't as happy as a married man. _____
15. Big dogs bite. _____
16. It's tough to be self-employed. _____
17. As we age, our health gets worse. _____
18. A married man isn't as happy as a single man. _____
19. Money is the root of all evil. _____
20. I'll never lose weight. _____
21. I'm always in debt. _____
22. My life is in chaos. _____

You may not hold any of these beliefs and may, in fact, hold others that are equally limiting. This list represents the most common limited beliefs I've heard.

We hold many root beliefs similar to these. If we make these beliefs conscious, then we can change the ones that work against us through affirmations, visualizations, and any other method that works. We can become *conscious creators* of our realities.

Changing Core Beliefs

Since core beliefs can be difficult to identify (that in itself may be one of my core beliefs), you may want to start with a condition in your life that you don't like and create a positive affirmation to counteract the condition.

Suppose you're having money problems. A positive affirmation might be: *I am prosperous.* Or: *I'm open to the infinite abundance of the universe.* When you're doing visualizations, write or type the affirmation and post it where you'll see it frequently—next to the computer, on the refrigerator, on a bathroom mirror. As you start doing your affirmations, you'll experience more synchronicities and your intuition will become sharper and easier to use.

Some years ago, I tried an affirmation related to one of my novels. I wrote out the ideal review of the book and posted it next to my computer. I read it several dozen times a day for several months. Although the book wasn't reviewed in a lot of places, one of the reviews duplicated what I had written almost verbatim.

A friend of mine, who was single and tired of running into men who weren't exactly what she was looking for, listed qualities that she hoped to find in a man. Several months after she made the list, she met a man who met nearly every criterion she'd listed. The problem was that they had few mutual interests, something she had neglected to include in her list. So be sure to be specific in your affirmations, and yet, not so specific that you limit yourself.

Louise Hay emphasizes the cultivation of gratitude regardless of what you're trying to create in your life. If you're trying to increase your income, for instance, and find a five-dollar bill in the parking lot, don't just stick it in your pocket and forget about it. *Be grateful.* The five-dollar bill is a definite sign that your affirmations are starting to work. Hay also advocates making symbolic gestures that are in line with what you're trying to create. If it's more income that you're attempting to generate, then each week spend something on yourself that supports your belief in universal abundance. And don't waste energy envying what other people have. As Hay says, "We don't want someone else's good. We want to have our *own* good."

Think of an area of your life you want to change. How do you want this area to change? What are you willing to do to bring this change about? What time frame do you want to work with? Two weeks? Three months? Six months? Be specific.

My goal: _____

My time frame: _____

What I want to change: _____

_____

_____

_____

My new core belief: _____

_____

_____

What I'm willing to do to bring this about:

_____

_____

_____

_____

_____

_____

Affirmations for Moon Signs

Aries: I have all the time I need to accomplish what I desire.

Taurus: I am safe and secure.

Gemini: I love and accept all parts of myself.

Cancer: I trust the flow of life.

Leo: I am at peace.

Virgo: I live in harmony with myself.

Libra: All my relationships are loving and harmonious.

Scorpio: I release the past and embrace the future.

Sagittarius: I surround myself with the fullness of life.

Capricorn: Everything I desire comes to me at the right time, in the right way.

Aquarius: I am centered in my life.

Pisces: I attract the right opportunities at the right time.

One Final Game to Play

Write a paragraph that describes where you are right now, your physical location, as you're reading this. What color are the walls? What room are you in? Is it tidy or messy? What do you smell or hear in this room?

_____

_____

_____

_____

_____

_____

You've just answered the second question you asked in the first Reality Check, Chapter 4. Once again, you may have to interpret what you've written, looking for the dominant theme. Does it feel right to you? Does it *resonate*?

Parting Thoughts

Your Intuitive Moon offers a place for you to begin your intuitive development. Now it's up to you to put your moon to work for you in nurturing and deepening your intuition. Perhaps an adage applies here: "Use it or lose it."

By using your intuition, you enrich your life. How can that possibly be anything but good?

Feel free to contact the author at: trmacgregor@worldnet.att.net.

APPENDIX 1
Moon Tables, 1945–2005

To use the moon tables, it's best if you know your exact time of birth. If you don't know the exact time, then you'll have to work with an approximation.

The tables list the date and time that the moon entered a new sign, under Eastern Standard Time. Look at the first two entries under January 1945:

1-2-1945, Mo cnj Vi, 11:50 a.m.
1-4-1945, Mo cnj Li, 11:45 p.m.

Translated, this means that on January 2, 1945, the moon conjuncted (entered) Virgo at 11:50 a.m., Eastern Standard Time. On January 4, 1945, the moon entered Libra at 11:45 p.m., EST. The signs are abbreviated to the first two letters of the word—Ar for Aries, Ta for Taurus, and so on around the zodiac.

Let's say you were born at noon in Los Angeles on January 4, 1945. You would subtract three hours from your birth time to compensate for the difference between Pacific Standard Time and Eastern Standard Time. That would put your birth time at 8:00 a.m. on January 4, so you would have a Virgo moon.

If you were born outside the U.S., figure out the difference between that time zone and Eastern Standard Time and subtract from your birth time. If you were born during Daylight Saving Time, sub-tract one hour from your birth time to compensate.

There are some notable exceptions to the above rules. From Feb-ruary 9, 1942, to September 30, 1945, the U.S. was on War Time. Some states, like Indiana and Illinois, had complicated time changes in the mid part of the twentieth century. If you're unsure about the area where you were born, check the definitive book on time—*The American Atlas* by Neil F. Michelsen (ACS Publications, 1978).

These tables and all the astrological charts used in this book were generated by the Winstar Plus, version 2, astrology program.

January 1945
01-02-1945,Mo Cnj Vi,11:50 am
01-04-1945,Mo Cnj Li,11:45 pm
01-07-1945,Mo Cnj Sc,12:14 pm
01-09-1945,Mo Cnj Sa,10:56 pm
01-12-1945,Mo Cnj Ca,06:28 am
01-14-1945,Mo Cnj Aq,10:57 am
01-16-1945,Mo Cnj Pi,01:27 pm
01-18-1945,Mo Cnj Ar,03:21 pm
01-20-1945,Mo Cnj Ta,05:48 pm
01-22-1945,Mo Cnj Ge,09:35 pm
01-25-1945,Mo Cnj Ca,03:06 am
01-27-1945,Mo Cnj Le,10:33 am
01-29-1945,Mo Cnj Vi,08:09 pm

February 1945
02-01-1945,Mo Cnj Li,07:46 am
02-03-1945,Mo Cnj Sc,08:23 pm
02-06-1945,Mo Cnj Sa,07:57 am
02-08-1945,Mo Cnj Ca,04:29 pm
02-10-1945,Mo Cnj Aq,09:12 pm
02-12-1945,Mo Cnj Pi,10:53 pm
02-14-1945,Mo Cnj Ar,11:13 pm
02-17-1945,Mo Cnj Ta,00:06 am
02-19-1945,Mo Cnj Ge,03:02 am
02-21-1945,Mo Cnj Ca,08:43 am
02-23-1945,Mo Cnj Le,04:59 pm
02-26-1945,Mo Cnj Vi,03:14 am
02-28-1945,Mo Cnj Li,02:57 pm

March 1945
03-03-1945,Mo Cnj Sc,03:32 am
03-05-1945,Mo Cnj Sa,03:45 pm
03-08-1945,Mo Cnj Ca,01:38 am
03-10-1945,Mo Cnj Aq,07:41 am
03-12-1945,Mo Cnj Pi,09:51 am
03-14-1945,Mo Cnj Ar,09:33 am
03-16-1945,Mo Cnj Ta,08:55 am
03-18-1945,Mo Cnj Ge,10:05 am
03-20-1945,Mo Cnj Ca,02:32 pm
03-22-1945,Mo Cnj Le,10:32 pm
03-25-1945,Mo Cnj Vi,09:11 am
03-27-1945,Mo Cnj Li,09:15 pm
03-30-1945,Mo Cnj Sc,09:50 am

April 1945
04-01-1945,Mo Cnj Sa,10:08 pm
04-04-1945,Mo Cnj Ca,08:52 am

04-06-1945,Mo Cnj Aq,04:29 pm
04-08-1945,Mo Cnj Pi,08:11 pm
04-10-1945,Mo Cnj Ar,08:38 pm
04-12-1945,Mo Cnj Ta,07:40 pm
04-14-1945,Mo Cnj Ge,07:31 pm
04-16-1945,Mo Cnj Ca,10:14 pm
04-19-1945,Mo Cnj Le,04:52 am
04-21-1945,Mo Cnj Vi,03:03 pm
04-24-1945,Mo Cnj Li,03:15 am
04-26-1945,Mo Cnj Sc,03:53 pm
04-29-1945,Mo Cnj Sa,03:57 am

May 1945
05-01-1945,Mo Cnj Ca,02:41 pm
05-03-1945,Mo Cnj Aq,11:06 pm
05-06-1945,Mo Cnj Pi,04:21 am
05-08-1945,Mo Cnj Ar,06:25 am
05-10-1945,Mo Cnj Ta,06:24 am
05-12-1945,Mo Cnj Ge,06:12 am
05-14-1945,Mo Cnj Ca,07:51 am
05-16-1945,Mo Cnj Le,12:57 pm
05-18-1945,Mo Cnj Vi,09:57 pm
05-21-1945,Mo Cnj Li,09:44 am
05-23-1945,Mo Cnj Sc,10:21 pm
05-26-1945,Mo Cnj Sa,10:12 am
05-28-1945,Mo Cnj Ca,08:24 pm
05-31-1945,Mo Cnj Aq,04:35 am

June 1945
06-02-1945,Mo Cnj Pi,10:25 am
06-04-1945,Mo Cnj Ar,01:51 pm
06-06-1945,Mo Cnj Ta,03:23 pm
06-08-1945,Mo Cnj Ge,04:15 pm
06-10-1945,Mo Cnj Ca,06:02 pm
06-12-1945,Mo Cnj Le,10:21 pm
06-15-1945,Mo Cnj Vi,06:08 am
06-17-1945,Mo Cnj Li,05:07 pm
06-20-1945,Mo Cnj Sc,05:36 am
06-22-1945,Mo Cnj Sa,05:27 pm
06-25-1945,Mo Cnj Ca,03:14 am
06-27-1945,Mo Cnj Aq,10:36 am
06-29-1945,Mo Cnj Pi,03:51 pm

July 1945
07-01-1945,Mo Cnj Ar,07:30 pm
07-03-1945,Mo Cnj Ta,10:05 pm
07-06-1945,Mo Cnj Ge,00:20 am

07-08-1945,Mo Cnj Ca,03:11 am
07-10-1945,Mo Cnj Le,07:44 am
07-12-1945,Mo Cnj Vi,02:58 pm
07-15-1945,Mo Cnj Li,01:12 am
07-17-1945,Mo Cnj Sc,01:29 pm
07-20-1945,Mo Cnj Sa,01:36 am
07-22-1945,Mo Cnj Ca,11:29 am
07-24-1945,Mo Cnj Aq,06:17 pm
07-26-1945,Mo Cnj Pi,10:27 pm
07-29-1945,Mo Cnj Ar,01:08 am
07-31-1945,Mo Cnj Ta,03:29 am

August 1945
08-02-1945,Mo Cnj Ge,06:23 am
08-04-1945,Mo Cnj Ca,10:23 am
08-06-1945,Mo Cnj Le,03:52 pm
08-08-1945,Mo Cnj Vi,11:24 pm
08-11-1945,Mo Cnj Li,09:21 am
08-13-1945,Mo Cnj Sc,09:25 pm
08-16-1945,Mo Cnj Sa,09:56 am
08-18-1945,Mo Cnj Ca,08:31 pm
08-21-1945,Mo Cnj Aq,03:33 am
08-23-1945,Mo Cnj Pi,07:06 am
08-25-1945,Mo Cnj Ar,08:30 am
08-27-1945,Mo Cnj Ta,09:34 am
08-29-1945,Mo Cnj Ge,11:47 am
08-31-1945,Mo Cnj Ca,03:59 pm

September 1945
09-02-1945,Mo Cnj Le,10:19 pm
09-05-1945,Mo Cnj Vi,06:36 am
09-07-1945,Mo Cnj Li,04:49 pm
09-10-1945,Mo Cnj Sc,04:48 am
09-12-1945,Mo Cnj Sa,05:38 pm
09-15-1945,Mo Cnj Ca,05:12 am
09-17-1945,Mo Cnj Aq,01:20 pm
09-19-1945,Mo Cnj Pi,05:19 pm
09-21-1945,Mo Cnj Ar,06:11 pm
09-23-1945,Mo Cnj Ta,05:53 pm
09-25-1945,Mo Cnj Ge,06:31 pm
09-27-1945,Mo Cnj Ca,09:38 pm
09-30-1945,Mo Cnj Le,03:47 am

October 1945
10-02-1945,Mo Cnj Vi,12:34 pm
10-04-1945,Mo Cnj Li,11:17 pm
10-07-1945,Mo Cnj Sc,11:24 am

10-10-1945,Mo Cnj Sa,00:18 am
10-12-1945,Mo Cnj Ca,12:33 pm
10-14-1945,Mo Cnj Aq,10:06 am
10-17-1945,Mo Cnj Pi,03:34 am
10-19-1945,Mo Cnj Ar,05:09 am
10-21-1945,Mo Cnj Ta,04:30 am
10-23-1945,Mo Cnj Ge,03:50 am
10-25-1945,Mo Cnj Ca,05:11 am
10-27-1945,Mo Cnj Le,09:56 am
10-29-1945,Mo Cnj Vi,06:13 pm

November 1945
11-01-1945,Mo Cnj Li,05:08 am
11-03-1945,Mo Cnj Sc,05:29 pm
11-06-1945,Mo Cnj Sa,06:18 am
11-08-1945,Mo Cnj Ca,06:35 pm
11-11-1945,Mo Cnj Aq,04:59 am
11-13-1945,Mo Cnj Pi,12:05 pm
11-15-1945,Mo Cnj Ar,03:25 pm
11-17-1945,Mo Cnj Ta,03:48 pm
11-19-1945,Mo Cnj Ge,03:03 pm
11-21-1945,Mo Cnj Ca,03:14 pm
11-23-1945,Mo Cnj Le,06:12 pm
11-26-1945,Mo Cnj Vi,00:59 am
11-28-1945,Mo Cnj Li,11:18 am
11-30-1945,Mo Cnj Sc,11:43 pm

December 1945
12-03-1945,Mo Cnj Sa,12:30 pm
12-06-1945,Mo Cnj Ca,00:24 am
12-08-1945,Mo Cnj Aq,10:35 am
12-10-1945,Mo Cnj Pi,06:21 pm
12-12-1945,Mo Cnj Ar,11:16 pm
12-15-1945,Mo Cnj Ta,01:30 am
12-17-1945,Mo Cnj Ge,02:03 am
12-19-1945,Mo Cnj Ca,02:27 am
12-21-1945,Mo Cnj Le,04:30 am
12-23-1945,Mo Cnj Vi,09:43 am
12-25-1945,Mo Cnj Li,06:45 pm
12-28-1945,Mo Cnj Sc,06:43 am
12-30-1945,Mo Cnj Sa,07:33 pm

January 1946
01-02-1946,Mo Cnj Ca,07:12 am
01-04-1946,Mo Cnj Aq,04:39 pm
01-06-1946,Mo Cnj Pi,11:48 pm
01-09-1946,Mo Cnj Ar,04:56 am

01-11-1946,Mo Cnj Ta,08:25 am
01-13-1946,Mo Cnj Ge,10:42 am
01-15-1946,Mo Cnj Ca,12:32 pm
01-17-1946,Mo Cnj Le,03:03 pm
01-19-1946,Mo Cnj Vi,07:40 pm
01-22-1946,Mo Cnj Li,03:32 am
01-24-1946,Mo Cnj Sc,02:41 pm
01-27-1946,Mo Cnj Sa,03:28 am
01-29-1946,Mo Cnj Ca,03:19 pm

February 1946
02-01-1946,Mo Cnj Aq,00:24 am
02-03-1946,Mo Cnj Pi,06:33 am
02-05-1946,Mo Cnj Ar,10:38 am
02-07-1946,Mo Cnj Ta,01:47 pm
02-09-1946,Mo Cnj Ge,04:45 pm
02-11-1946,Mo Cnj Ca,07:59 pm
02-13-1946,Mo Cnj Le,11:51 pm
02-16-1946,Mo Cnj Vi,05:03 am
02-18-1946,Mo Cnj Li,12:37 pm
02-20-1946,Mo Cnj Sc,11:06 pm
02-23-1946,Mo Cnj Sa,11:42 am
02-26-1946,Mo Cnj Ca,00:02 am
02-28-1946,Mo Cnj Aq,09:34 am

March 1946
03-02-1946,Mo Cnj Pi,03:25 pm
03-04-1946,Mo Cnj Ar,06:23 pm
03-06-1946,Mo Cnj Ta,08:08 pm
03-08-1946,Mo Cnj Ge,10:12 pm
03-11-1946,Mo Cnj Ca,01:29 am
03-13-1946,Mo Cnj Le,06:15 am
03-15-1946,Mo Cnj Vi,12:33 pm
03-17-1946,Mo Cnj Li,08:41 pm
03-20-1946,Mo Cnj Sc,07:05 am
03-22-1946,Mo Cnj Sa,07:31 pm
03-25-1946,Mo Cnj Ca,08:18 am
03-27-1946,Mo Cnj Aq,06:51 am
03-30-1946,Mo Cnj Pi,01:26 am

April 1946
04-01-1946,Mo Cnj Ar,04:17 am
04-03-1946,Mo Cnj Ta,04:57 am
04-05-1946,Mo Cnj Ge,05:26 am
04-07-1946,Mo Cnj Ca,07:22 am
04-09-1946,Mo Cnj Le,11:38 am

04-11-1946,Mo Cnj Vi,06:20 pm
04-14-1946,Mo Cnj Li,03:13 am
04-16-1946,Mo Cnj Sc,02:03 pm
04-19-1946,Mo Cnj Sa,02:30 am
04-21-1946,Mo Cnj Ca,03:29 pm
04-24-1946,Mo Cnj Aq,02:57 am
04-26-1946,Mo Cnj Pi,10:55 am
04-28-1946,Mo Cnj Ar,02:46 pm
04-30-1946,Mo Cnj Ta,03:32 pm

May 1946
05-02-1946,Mo Cnj Ge,03:04 pm
05-04-1946,Mo Cnj Ca,03:23 pm
05-06-1946,Mo Cnj Le,06:05 pm
05-08-1946,Mo Cnj Vi,11:57 pm
05-11-1946,Mo Cnj Li,08:53 am
05-13-1946,Mo Cnj Sc,08:09 pm
05-16-1946,Mo Cnj Sa,08:46 am
05-18-1946,Mo Cnj Ca,09:43 pm
05-21-1946,Mo Cnj Aq,09:32 am
05-23-1946,Mo Cnj Pi,06:39 pm
05-26-1946,Mo Cnj Ar,00:05 am
05-28-1946,Mo Cnj Ta,02:04 am
05-30-1946,Mo Cnj Ge,01:55 am

June 1946
06-01-1946,Mo Cnj Ca,01:29 am
06-03-1946,Mo Cnj Le,02:39 am
06-05-1946,Mo Cnj Vi,06:57 am
06-07-1946,Mo Cnj Li,02:57 pm
06-10-1946,Mo Cnj Sc,02:05 am
06-12-1946,Mo Cnj Sa,02:51 pm
06-15-1946,Mo Cnj Ca,03:40 am
06-17-1946,Mo Cnj Aq,03:16 pm
06-20-1946,Mo Cnj Pi,00:43 am
06-22-1946,Mo Cnj Ar,07:20 am
06-24-1946,Mo Cnj Ta,10:56 am
06-26-1946,Mo Cnj Ge,12:07 pm
06-28-1946,Mo Cnj Ca,12:10 pm
06-30-1946,Mo Cnj Le,12:48 pm

July 1946
07-02-1946,Mo Cnj Vi,03:45 pm
07-04-1946,Mo Cnj Li,10:21 pm
07-07-1946,Mo Cnj Sc,08:42 am
07-09-1946,Mo Cnj Sa,09:21 pm
07-12-1946,Mo Cnj Ca,10:06 am

07-14-1946,Mo Cnj Aq,09:17 pm
07-17-1946,Mo Cnj Pi,06:15 am
07-19-1946,Mo Cnj Ar,12:59 pm
07-21-1946,Mo Cnj Ta,05:35 pm
07-23-1946,Mo Cnj Ge,08:19 pm
07-25-1946,Mo Cnj Ca,09:44 pm
07-27-1946,Mo Cnj Le,10:58 pm
07-30-1946,Mo Cnj Vi,01:33 am

August 1946
08-01-1946,Mo Cnj Li,07:05 am
08-03-1946,Mo Cnj Sc,04:23 pm
08-06-1946,Mo Cnj Sa,04:36 am
08-08-1946,Mo Cnj Ca,05:23 pm
08-11-1946,Mo Cnj Aq,04:24 am
08-13-1946,Mo Cnj Pi,12:41 pm
08-15-1946,Mo Cnj Ar,06:37 pm
08-17-1946,Mo Cnj Ta,11:00 pm
08-20-1946,Mo Cnj Ge,02:23 am
08-22-1946,Mo Cnj Ca,05:07 am
08-24-1946,Mo Cnj Le,07:38 am
08-26-1946,Mo Cnj Vi,10:54 am
08-28-1946,Mo Cnj Li,04:15 pm
08-31-1946,Mo Cnj Sc,00:49 am

September 1946
09-02-1946,Mo Cnj Sa,12:31 pm
09-05-1946,Mo Cnj Ca,01:24 am
09-07-1946,Mo Cnj Aq,12:42 pm
09-09-1946,Mo Cnj Pi,08:46 pm
09-12-1946,Mo Cnj Ar,01:49 am
09-14-1946,Mo Cnj Ta,05:04 am
09-16-1946,Mo Cnj Ge,07:46 am
09-18-1946,Mo Cnj Ca,10:42 am
09-20-1946,Mo Cnj Le,02:13 pm
09-22-1946,Mo Cnj Vi,06:38 pm
09-25-1946,Mo Cnj Li,00:40 am
09-27-1946,Mo Cnj Sc,09:12 am
09-29-1946,Mo Cnj Sa,08:33 pm

October 1946
10-02-1946,Mo Cnj Ca,09:30 am
10-04-1946,Mo Cnj Aq,09:28 pm
10-07-1946,Mo Cnj Pi,06:10 am
10-09-1946,Mo Cnj Ar,11:05 am
10-11-1946,Mo Cnj Ta,01:21 pm
10-13-1946,Mo Cnj Ge,02:36 pm

10-15-1946,Mo Cnj Ca,04:23 pm
10-17-1946,Mo Cnj Le,07:35 pm
10-20-1946,Mo Cnj Vi,00:35 am
10-22-1946,Mo Cnj Li,07:33 am
10-24-1946,Mo Cnj Sc,04:41 pm
10-27-1946,Mo Cnj Sa,04:04 am
10-29-1946,Mo Cnj Ca,05:00 pm

November 1946
11-01-1946,Mo Cnj Aq,05:37 am
11-03-1946,Mo Cnj Pi,03:32 pm
11-05-1946,Mo Cnj Ar,09:28 pm
11-07-1946,Mo Cnj Ta,11:49 pm
11-10-1946,Mo Cnj Ge,00:07 am
11-12-1946,Mo Cnj Ca,00:15 am
11-14-1946,Mo Cnj Le,01:53 am
11-16-1946,Mo Cnj Vi,06:05 am
11-18-1946,Mo Cnj Li,01:13 pm
11-20-1946,Mo Cnj Sc,10:59 pm
11-23-1946,Mo Cnj Sa,10:44 am
11-25-1946,Mo Cnj Ca,11:40 pm
11-28-1946,Mo Cnj Aq,12:30 pm
11-30-1946,Mo Cnj Pi,11:29 pm

December 1946
12-03-1946,Mo Cnj Ar,07:05 am
12-05-1946,Mo Cnj Ta,10:49 am
12-07-1946,Mo Cnj Ge,11:30 am
12-09-1946,Mo Cnj Ca,10:50 am
12-11-1946,Mo Cnj Le,10:47 am
12-13-1946,Mo Cnj Vi,01:09 pm
12-15-1946,Mo Cnj Li,07:08 pm
12-18-1946,Mo Cnj Sc,04:44 am
12-20-1946,Mo Cnj Sa,04:49 pm
12-23-1946,Mo Cnj Ca,05:50 am
12-25-1946,Mo Cnj Aq,06:29 pm
12-28-1946,Mo Cnj Pi,05:43 am
12-30-1946,Mo Cnj Ar,02:31 pm

January 1947
01-01-1947,Mo Cnj Ta,08:07 pm
01-03-1947,Mo Cnj Ge,10:27 pm
01-05-1947,Mo Cnj Ca,10:28 pm
01-07-1947,Mo Cnj Le,09:54 pm
01-09-1947,Mo Cnj Vi,10:45 pm
01-12-1947,Mo Cnj Li,02:54 am
01-14-1947,Mo Cnj Sc,11:15 am

01-16-1947,Mo Cnj Sa,11:03 pm
01-19-1947,Mo Cnj Ca,12:11 pm
01-22-1947,Mo Cnj Aq,00:38 am
01-24-1947,Mo Cnj Pi,11:24 am
01-26-1947,Mo Cnj Ar,08:11 pm
01-29-1947,Mo Cnj Ta,02:46 am
01-31-1947,Mo Cnj Ge,06:53 am

February 1947
02-02-1947,Mo Cnj Ca,08:39 am
02-04-1947,Mo Cnj Le,09:01 am
02-06-1947,Mo Cnj Vi,09:42 am
02-08-1947,Mo Cnj Li,12:39 pm
02-10-1947,Mo Cnj Sc,07:28 pm
02-13-1947,Mo Cnj Sa,06:16 am
02-15-1947,Mo Cnj Ca,07:13 pm
02-18-1947,Mo Cnj Aq,07:39 am
02-20-1947,Mo Cnj Pi,05:58 pm
02-23-1947,Mo Cnj Ar,01:58 am
02-25-1947,Mo Cnj Ta,08:08 am
02-27-1947,Mo Cnj Ge,12:47 pm

March 1947
03-01-1947,Mo Cnj Ca,03:59 pm
03-03-1947,Mo Cnj Le,06:00 pm
03-05-1947,Mo Cnj Vi,07:47 pm
03-07-1947,Mo Cnj Li,10:51 pm
03-10-1947,Mo Cnj Sc,04:51 am
03-12-1947,Mo Cnj Sa,02:35 pm
03-15-1947,Mo Cnj Ca,03:01 am
03-17-1947,Mo Cnj Aq,03:36 pm
03-20-1947,Mo Cnj Pi,01:58 am
03-22-1947,Mo Cnj Ar,09:23 am
03-24-1947,Mo Cnj Ta,02:29 am
03-26-1947,Mo Cnj Ge,06:16 pm
03-28-1947,Mo Cnj Ca,09:26 pm
03-31-1947,Mo Cnj Le,00:22 am

April 1947
04-02-1947,Mo Cnj Vi,03:31 am
04-04-1947,Mo Cnj Li,07:40 am
04-06-1947,Mo Cnj Sc,01:57 pm
04-08-1947,Mo Cnj Sa,11:13 pm
04-11-1947,Mo Cnj Ca,11:09 am
04-13-1947,Mo Cnj Aq,11:51 pm
04-16-1947,Mo Cnj Pi,10:47 am
04-18-1947,Mo Cnj Ar,06:25 pm

04-20-1947,Mo Cnj Ta,10:56 pm
04-23-1947,Mo Cnj Ge,01:28 am
04-25-1947,Mo Cnj Ca,03:23 am
04-27-1947,Mo Cnj Le,05:45 am
04-29-1947,Mo Cnj Vi,09:16 am

May 1947
05-01-1947,Mo Cnj Li,02:24 pm
05-03-1947,Mo Cnj Sc,09:36 pm
05-06-1947,Mo Cnj Sa,07:09 am
05-08-1947,Mo Cnj Ca,06:55 pm
05-11-1947,Mo Cnj Aq,07:41 am
05-13-1947,Mo Cnj Pi,07:20 pm
05-16-1947,Mo Cnj Ar,03:57 am
05-18-1947,Mo Cnj Ta,08:52 am
05-20-1947,Mo Cnj Ge,10:52 am
05-22-1947,Mo Cnj Ca,11:27 am
05-24-1947,Mo Cnj Le,12:19 pm
05-26-1947,Mo Cnj Vi,02:50 pm
05-28-1947,Mo Cnj Li,07:54 pm
05-31-1947,Mo Cnj Sc,03:42 am

June 1947
06-02-1947,Mo Cnj Sa,01:54 pm
06-05-1947,Mo Cnj Ca,01:52 am
06-07-1947,Mo Cnj Aq,02:38 pm
06-10-1947,Mo Cnj Pi,02:48 am
06-12-1947,Mo Cnj Ar,12:35 pm
06-14-1947,Mo Cnj Ta,06:46 pm
06-16-1947,Mo Cnj Ge,09:22 pm
06-18-1947,Mo Cnj Ca,09:33 pm
06-20-1947,Mo Cnj Le,09:07 pm
06-22-1947,Mo Cnj Vi,10:01 pm
06-25-1947,Mo Cnj Li,01:51 am
06-27-1947,Mo Cnj Sc,09:17 am
06-29-1947,Mo Cnj Sa,07:46 pm

July 1947
07-02-1947,Mo Cnj Ca,08:03 am
07-04-1947,Mo Cnj Aq,08:50 pm
07-07-1947,Mo Cnj Pi,09:04 am
07-09-1947,Mo Cnj Ar,07:35 pm
07-12-1947,Mo Cnj Ta,03:12 am
07-14-1947,Mo Cnj Ge,07:17 am
07-16-1947,Mo Cnj Ca,08:14 am
07-18-1947,Mo Cnj Le,07:34 am
07-20-1947,Mo Cnj Vi,07:19 am

07-22-1947,Mo Cnj Li,09:33 am
07-24-1947,Mo Cnj Sc,03:41 pm
07-27-1947,Mo Cnj Sa,01:41 am
07-29-1947,Mo Cnj Ca,02:02 pm

August 1947
08-01-1947,Mo Cnj Aq,02:50 am
08-03-1947,Mo Cnj Pi,02:49 pm
08-06-1947,Mo Cnj Ar,01:20 am
08-08-1947,Mo Cnj Ta,09:43 am
08-10-1947,Mo Cnj Ge,03:17 pm
08-12-1947,Mo Cnj Ca,05:50 pm
08-14-1947,Mo Cnj Le,06:06 pm
08-16-1947,Mo Cnj Vi,05:49 pm
08-18-1947,Mo Cnj Li,07:05 pm
08-20-1947,Mo Cnj Sc,11:45 pm
08-23-1947,Mo Cnj Sa,08:35 am
08-25-1947,Mo Cnj Ca,08:31 pm
08-28-1947,Mo Cnj Aq,09:18 am
08-30-1947,Mo Cnj Pi,09:03 pm

September 1947
09-02-1947,Mo Cnj Ar,07:02 am
09-04-1947,Mo Cnj Ta,03:10 pm
09-06-1947,Mo Cnj Ge,09:18 pm
09-09-1947,Mo Cnj Ca,01:13 am
09-11-1947,Mo Cnj Le,03:04 am
09-13-1947,Mo Cnj Vi,03:51 am
09-15-1947,Mo Cnj Li,05:17 am
09-17-1947,Mo Cnj Sc,09:11 am
09-19-1947,Mo Cnj Sa,04:50 pm
09-22-1947,Mo Cnj Ca,03:58 am
09-24-1947,Mo Cnj Aq,04:37 pm
09-27-1947,Mo Cnj Pi,04:25 am
09-29-1947,Mo Cnj Ar,01:58 pm

October 1947
10-01-1947,Mo Cnj Ta,09:16 pm
10-04-1947,Mo Cnj Ge,02:44 am
10-06-1947,Mo Cnj Ca,06:48 am
10-08-1947,Mo Cnj Le,09:42 am
10-10-1947,Mo Cnj Vi,11:57 am
10-12-1947,Mo Cnj Li,02:32 pm
10-14-1947,Mo Cnj Sc,06:46 pm
10-17-1947,Mo Cnj Sa,01:53 am
10-19-1947,Mo Cnj Ca,12:14 pm
10-22-1947,Mo Cnj Aq,00:39 am

10-24-1947,Mo Cnj Pi,12:46 pm
10-26-1947,Mo Cnj Ar,10:32 pm
10-29-1947,Mo Cnj Ta,05:17 am
10-31-1947,Mo Cnj Ge,09:36 am

November 1947
11-02-1947,Mo Cnj Ca,12:32 pm
11-04-1947,Mo Cnj Le,03:04 pm
11-06-1947,Mo Cnj Vi,05:55 pm
11-08-1947,Mo Cnj Li,09:42 pm
11-11-1947,Mo Cnj Sc,03:02 am
11-13-1947,Mo Cnj Sa,10:34 am
11-15-1947,Mo Cnj Ca,08:38 pm
11-18-1947,Mo Cnj Aq,08:46 am
11-20-1947,Mo Cnj Pi,09:17 pm
11-23-1947,Mo Cnj Ar,07:54 am
11-25-1947,Mo Cnj Ta,03:06 pm
11-27-1947,Mo Cnj Ge,06:55 pm
11-29-1947,Mo Cnj Ca,08:31 pm

December 1947
12-01-1947,Mo Cnj Le,09:30 pm
12-03-1947,Mo Cnj Vi,11:24 pm
12-06-1947,Mo Cnj Li,03:14 am
12-08-1947,Mo Cnj Sc,09:25 am
12-10-1947,Mo Cnj Sa,05:50 pm
12-13-1947,Mo Cnj Ca,04:15 am
12-15-1947,Mo Cnj Aq,04:16 pm
12-18-1947,Mo Cnj Pi,04:59 am
12-20-1947,Mo Cnj Ar,04:37 pm
12-23-1947,Mo Cnj Ta,01:11 am
12-25-1947,Mo Cnj Ge,05:47 am
12-27-1947,Mo Cnj Ca,07:03 am
12-29-1947,Mo Cnj Le,06:42 am
12-31-1947,Mo Cnj Vi,06:47 am

January 1948
01-02-1948,Mo Cnj Li,09:10 am
01-04-1948,Mo Cnj Sc,02:52 pm
01-06-1948,Mo Cnj Sa,11:41 pm
01-09-1948,Mo Cnj Ca,10:42 am
01-11-1948,Mo Cnj Aq,10:54 pm
01-14-1948,Mo Cnj Pi,11:35 am
01-16-1948,Mo Cnj Ar,11:44 pm
01-19-1948,Mo Cnj Ta,09:42 am
01-21-1948,Mo Cnj Ge,04:02 pm
01-23-1948,Mo Cnj Ca,06:24 pm

01-25-1948,Mo Cnj Le,06:00 pm
01-27-1948,Mo Cnj Vi,04:57 pm
01-29-1948,Mo Cnj Li,05:30 pm
01-31-1948,Mo Cnj Sc,09:28 pm

February 1948
02-03-1948,Mo Cnj Sa,05:26 am
02-05-1948,Mo Cnj Ca,04:30 pm
02-08-1948,Mo Cnj Aq,04:59 am
02-10-1948,Mo Cnj Pi,05:37 pm
02-13-1948,Mo Cnj Ar,05:38 am
02-15-1948,Mo Cnj Ta,04:08 pm
02-17-1948,Mo Cnj Ge,11:57 pm
02-20-1948,Mo Cnj Ca,04:10 am
02-22-1948,Mo Cnj Le,05:07 am
02-24-1948,Mo Cnj Vi,04:22 am
02-26-1948,Mo Cnj Li,04:05 am
02-28-1948,Mo Cnj Sc,06:24 am

March 1948
03-01-1948,Mo Cnj Sa,12:41 pm
03-03-1948,Mo Cnj Ca,10:51 pm
03-06-1948,Mo Cnj Aq,11:14 am
03-08-1948,Mo Cnj Pi,11:54 pm
03-11-1948,Mo Cnj Ar,11:34 am
03-13-1948,Mo Cnj Ta,09:41 pm
03-16-1948,Mo Cnj Ge,05:46 am
03-18-1948,Mo Cnj Ca,11:14 am
03-20-1948,Mo Cnj Le,01:58 pm
03-22-1948,Mo Cnj Vi,02:42 pm
03-24-1948,Mo Cnj Li,03:01 pm
03-26-1948,Mo Cnj Sc,04:49 pm
03-28-1948,Mo Cnj Sa,09:47 pm
03-31-1948,Mo Cnj Ca,06:34 am

April 1948
04-02-1948,Mo Cnj Aq,06:19 pm
04-05-1948,Mo Cnj Pi,06:57 am
04-07-1948,Mo Cnj Ar,06:29 pm
04-10-1948,Mo Cnj Ta,03:59 am
04-12-1948,Mo Cnj Ge,11:20 am
04-14-1948,Mo Cnj Ca,04:41 pm
04-16-1948,Mo Cnj Le,08:16 pm
04-18-1948,Mo Cnj Vi,10:30 pm
04-21-1948,Mo Cnj Li,00:16 am
04-23-1948,Mo Cnj Sc,02:50 am
04-25-1948,Mo Cnj Sa,07:32 am

04-27-1948,Mo Cnj Ca,03:22 pm
04-30-1948,Mo Cnj Aq,02:17 am

May 1948
05-02-1948,Mo Cnj Pi,02:44 pm
05-05-1948,Mo Cnj Ar,02:28 am
05-07-1948,Mo Cnj Ta,11:48 am
05-09-1948,Mo Cnj Ge,06:20 pm
05-11-1948,Mo Cnj Ca,10:38 pm
05-14-1948,Mo Cnj Le,01:39 am
05-16-1948,Mo Cnj Vi,04:15 am
05-18-1948,Mo Cnj Li,07:08 am
05-20-1948,Mo Cnj Sc,10:56 am
05-22-1948,Mo Cnj Sa,04:23 pm
05-25-1948,Mo Cnj Ca,00:08 am
05-27-1948,Mo Cnj Aq,10:31 am
05-29-1948,Mo Cnj Pi,10:46 pm

June 1948
06-01-1948,Mo Cnj Ar,10:55 am
06-03-1948,Mo Cnj Ta,08:43 pm
06-06-1948,Mo Cnj Ge,03:06 am
06-08-1948,Mo Cnj Ca,06:29 am
06-10-1948,Mo Cnj Le,08:12 am
06-12-1948,Mo Cnj Vi,09:49 am
06-14-1948,Mo Cnj Li,12:34 pm
06-16-1948,Mo Cnj Sc,05:04 pm
06-18-1948,Mo Cnj Sa,11:29 pm
06-21-1948,Mo Cnj Ca,07:51 am
06-23-1948,Mo Cnj Aq,06:15 pm
06-26-1948,Mo Cnj Pi,06:23 am
06-28-1948,Mo Cnj Ar,06:56 pm

July 1948
07-01-1948,Mo Cnj Ta,05:40 am
07-03-1948,Mo Cnj Ge,12:48 pm
07-05-1948,Mo Cnj Ca,04:07 pm
07-07-1948,Mo Cnj Le,04:54 pm
07-09-1948,Mo Cnj Vi,05:04 pm
07-11-1948,Mo Cnj Li,06:31 pm
07-13-1948,Mo Cnj Sc,10:28 pm
07-16-1948,Mo Cnj Sa,05:11 am
07-18-1948,Mo Cnj Ca,02:13 pm
07-21-1948,Mo Cnj Aq,01:02 am
07-23-1948,Mo Cnj Pi,01:13 pm
07-26-1948,Mo Cnj Ar,01:58 am

07-28-1948,Mo Cnj Ta,01:35 pm
07-30-1948,Mo Cnj Ge,10:02 pm

August 1948
08-02-1948,Mo Cnj Ca,02:21 am
08-04-1948,Mo Cnj Le,03:13 am
08-06-1948,Mo Cnj Vi,02:32 am
08-08-1948,Mo Cnj Li,02:29 am
08-10-1948,Mo Cnj Sc,04:56 am
08-12-1948,Mo Cnj Sa,10:49 am
08-14-1948,Mo Cnj Ca,07:52 pm
08-17-1948,Mo Cnj Aq,07:03 am
08-19-1948,Mo Cnj Pi,07:24 pm
08-22-1948,Mo Cnj Ar,08:06 am
08-24-1948,Mo Cnj Ta,08:04 pm
08-27-1948,Mo Cnj Ge,05:40 am
08-29-1948,Mo Cnj Ca,11:34 am
08-31-1948,Mo Cnj Le,01:41 pm

September 1948
09-02-1948,Mo Cnj Vi,01:20 pm
09-04-1948,Mo Cnj Li,12:35 pm
09-06-1948,Mo Cnj Sc,01:34 pm
09-08-1948,Mo Cnj Sa,05:52 pm
09-11-1948,Mo Cnj Ca,01:57 am
09-13-1948,Mo Cnj Aq,12:59 pm
09-16-1948,Mo Cnj Pi,01:27 am
09-18-1948,Mo Cnj Ar,02:02 pm
09-21-1948,Mo Cnj Ta,01:45 am
09-23-1948,Mo Cnj Ge,11:40 am
09-25-1948,Mo Cnj Ca,06:46 pm
09-27-1948,Mo Cnj Le,10:35 pm
09-29-1948,Mo Cnj Vi,11:41 pm

October 1948
10-01-1948,Mo Cnj Li,11:30 pm
10-03-1948,Mo Cnj Sc,11:59 pm
10-06-1948,Mo Cnj Sa,02:56 am
10-08-1948,Mo Cnj Ca,09:32 am
10-10-1948,Mo Cnj Aq,07:42 pm
10-13-1948,Mo Cnj Pi,08:03 am
10-15-1948,Mo Cnj Ar,08:36 pm
10-18-1948,Mo Cnj Ta,07:54 am
10-20-1948,Mo Cnj Ge,05:15 pm
10-23-1948,Mo Cnj Ca,00:22 am
10-25-1948,Mo Cnj Le,05:10 am
10-27-1948,Mo Cnj Vi,07:54 am

10-29-1948,Mo Cnj Li,09:16 am
10-31-1948,Mo Cnj Sc,10:32 am

November 1948
11-02-1948,Mo Cnj Sa,01:11 pm
11-04-1948,Mo Cnj Ca,06:40 pm
11-07-1948,Mo Cnj Aq,03:41 am
11-09-1948,Mo Cnj Pi,03:33 pm
11-12-1948,Mo Cnj Ar,04:12 am
11-14-1948,Mo Cnj Ta,03:25 pm
11-17-1948,Mo Cnj Ge,00:03 am
11-19-1948,Mo Cnj Ca,06:12 am
11-21-1948,Mo Cnj Le,10:33 am
11-23-1948,Mo Cnj Vi,01:49 pm
11-25-1948,Mo Cnj Li,04:33 pm
11-27-1948,Mo Cnj Sc,07:19 pm
11-29-1948,Mo Cnj Sa,10:52 pm

December 1948
12-02-1948,Mo Cnj Ca,04:16 am
12-04-1948,Mo Cnj Aq,12:32 pm
12-06-1948,Mo Cnj Pi,11:46 pm
12-09-1948,Mo Cnj Ar,12:30 pm
12-12-1948,Mo Cnj Ta,00:09 am
12-14-1948,Mo Cnj Ge,08:45 am
12-16-1948,Mo Cnj Ca,02:01 am
12-18-1948,Mo Cnj Le,05:03 am
12-20-1948,Mo Cnj Vi,07:19 pm
12-22-1948,Mo Cnj Li,09:59 pm
12-25-1948,Mo Cnj Sc,01:38 am
12-27-1948,Mo Cnj Sa,06:29 am
12-29-1948,Mo Cnj Ca,12:47 pm
12-31-1948,Mo Cnj Aq,09:08 pm

January 1949
01-03-1949,Mo Cnj Pi,07:59 am
01-05-1949,Mo Cnj Ar,08:41 pm
01-08-1949,Mo Cnj Ta,09:03 am
01-10-1949,Mo Cnj Ge,06:31 pm
01-12-1949,Mo Cnj Ca,11:57 pm
01-15-1949,Mo Cnj Le,02:07 am
01-17-1949,Mo Cnj Vi,02:52 am
01-19-1949,Mo Cnj Li,04:03 am
01-21-1949,Mo Cnj Sc,07:00 am
01-23-1949,Mo Cnj Sa,12:09 pm
01-25-1949,Mo Cnj Ca,07:22 pm

01-28-1949,Mo Cnj Aq,04:27 am
01-30-1949,Mo Cnj Pi,03:27 pm

February 1949
02-02-1949,Mo Cnj Ar,04:04 am
02-04-1949,Mo Cnj Ta,04:57 pm
02-07-1949,Mo Cnj Ge,03:40 am
02-09-1949,Mo Cnj Ca,10:22 am
02-11-1949,Mo Cnj Le,01:01 pm
02-13-1949,Mo Cnj Vi,01:06 pm
02-15-1949,Mo Cnj Li,12:44 pm
02-17-1949,Mo Cnj Sc,01:53 pm
02-19-1949,Mo Cnj Sa,05:50 pm
02-22-1949,Mo Cnj Ca,00:51 am
02-24-1949,Mo Cnj Aq,10:26 am
02-26-1949,Mo Cnj Pi,09:54 pm

March 1949
03-01-1949,Mo Cnj Ar,10:35 am
03-03-1949,Mo Cnj Ta,11:33 pm
03-06-1949,Mo Cnj Ge,11:05 am
03-08-1949,Mo Cnj Ca,07:22 pm
03-10-1949,Mo Cnj Le,11:34 pm
03-13-1949,Mo Cnj Vi,00:24 am
03-14-1949,Mo Cnj Li,11:40 pm
03-16-1949,Mo Cnj Sc,11:26 pm
03-19-1949,Mo Cnj Sa,01:31 am
03-21-1949,Mo Cnj Ca,07:05 am
03-23-1949,Mo Cnj Aq,04:10 am
03-26-1949,Mo Cnj Pi,03:50 am
03-28-1949,Mo Cnj Ar,04:41 pm
03-31-1949,Mo Cnj Ta,05:30 am

April 1949
04-02-1949,Mo Cnj Ge,05:03 pm
04-05-1949,Mo Cnj Ca,02:11 am
04-07-1949,Mo Cnj Le,08:00 am
04-09-1949,Mo Cnj Vi,10:32 am
04-11-1949,Mo Cnj Li,10:48 am
04-13-1949,Mo Cnj Sc,10:27 am
04-15-1949,Mo Cnj Sa,11:23 am
04-17-1949,Mo Cnj Ca,03:16 pm
04-19-1949,Mo Cnj Aq,10:59 pm
04-22-1949,Mo Cnj Pi,10:08 am
04-24-1949,Mo Cnj Ar,11:01 pm
04-27-1949,Mo Cnj Ta,11:42 am
04-29-1949,Mo Cnj Ge,10:49 pm

May 1949
05-02-1949,Mo Cnj Ca,07:44 am
05-04-1949,Mo Cnj Le,02:11 pm
05-06-1949,Mo Cnj Vi,06:11 pm
05-08-1949,Mo Cnj Li,08:07 pm
05-10-1949,Mo Cnj Sc,08:54 pm
05-12-1949,Mo Cnj Sa,09:57 pm
05-15-1949,Mo Cnj Ca,00:57 am
05-17-1949,Mo Cnj Aq,07:19 am
05-19-1949,Mo Cnj Pi,05:27 pm
05-22-1949,Mo Cnj Ar,06:03 am
05-24-1949,Mo Cnj Ta,06:42 pm
05-27-1949,Mo Cnj Ge,05:27 am
05-29-1949,Mo Cnj Ca,01:39 pm
05-31-1949,Mo Cnj Le,07:36 pm

June 1949
06-02-1949,Mo Cnj Vi,11:53 pm
06-05-1949,Mo Cnj Li,02:58 am
06-07-1949,Mo Cnj Sc,05:14 am
06-09-1949,Mo Cnj Sa,07:24 am
06-11-1949,Mo Cnj Ca,10:40 am
06-13-1949,Mo Cnj Aq,04:27 pm
06-16-1949,Mo Cnj Pi,01:39 am
06-18-1949,Mo Cnj Ar,01:45 pm
06-21-1949,Mo Cnj Ta,02:30 am
06-23-1949,Mo Cnj Ge,01:20 pm
06-25-1949,Mo Cnj Ca,09:01 pm
06-28-1949,Mo Cnj Le,02:01 am
06-30-1949,Mo Cnj Vi,05:27 am

July 1949
07-02-1949,Mo Cnj Li,08:23 am
07-04-1949,Mo Cnj Sc,11:22 am
07-06-1949,Mo Cnj Sa,02:46 pm
07-08-1949,Mo Cnj Ca,07:03 pm
07-11-1949,Mo Cnj Aq,01:09 am
07-13-1949,Mo Cnj Pi,10:01 am
07-15-1949,Mo Cnj Ar,09:43 pm
07-18-1949,Mo Cnj Ta,10:36 am
07-20-1949,Mo Cnj Ge,09:57 pm
07-23-1949,Mo Cnj Ca,05:52 am
07-25-1949,Mo Cnj Le,10:19 am
07-27-1949,Mo Cnj Vi,12:36 pm
07-29-1949,Mo Cnj Li,02:20 pm
07-31-1949,Mo Cnj Sc,04:44 pm

August 1949

08-02-1949,Mo Cnj Sa,08:25 pm
08-05-1949,Mo Cnj Ca,01:36 am
08-07-1949,Mo Cnj Aq,08:34 am
08-09-1949,Mo Cnj Pi,05:46 pm
08-12-1949,Mo Cnj Ar,05:20 am
08-14-1949,Mo Cnj Ta,06:18 pm
08-17-1949,Mo Cnj Ge,06:23 am
08-19-1949,Mo Cnj Ca,03:16 pm
08-21-1949,Mo Cnj Le,08:08 pm
08-23-1949,Mo Cnj Vi,09:56 pm
08-25-1949,Mo Cnj Li,10:24 pm
08-27-1949,Mo Cnj Sc,11:20 pm
08-30-1949,Mo Cnj Sa,02:00 am

September 1949

09-01-1949,Mo Cnj Ca,07:05 am
09-03-1949,Mo Cnj Aq,02:37 pm
09-06-1949,Mo Cnj Pi,00:26 am
09-08-1949,Mo Cnj Ar,12:14 pm
09-11-1949,Mo Cnj Ta,01:13 am
09-13-1949,Mo Cnj Ge,01:47 pm
09-15-1949,Mo Cnj Ca,11:52 pm
09-18-1949,Mo Cnj Le,06:05 am
09-20-1949,Mo Cnj Vi,08:34 am
09-22-1949,Mo Cnj Li,08:41 am
09-24-1949,Mo Cnj Sc,08:20 am
09-26-1949,Mo Cnj Sa,09:21 am
09-28-1949,Mo Cnj Ca,01:07 pm
09-30-1949,Mo Cnj Aq,08:14 pm

October 1949

10-03-1949,Mo Cnj Pi,06:20 am
10-05-1949,Mo Cnj Ar,06:28 pm
10-08-1949,Mo Cnj Ta,07:27 am
10-10-1949,Mo Cnj Ge,08:03 pm
10-13-1949,Mo Cnj Ca,06:51 am
10-15-1949,Mo Cnj Le,02:35 pm
10-17-1949,Mo Cnj Vi,06:42 pm
10-19-1949,Mo Cnj Li,07:48 pm
10-21-1949,Mo Cnj Sc,07:19 pm
10-23-1949,Mo Cnj Sa,07:08 pm
10-25-1949,Mo Cnj Ca,09:11 pm
10-28-1949,Mo Cnj Aq,02:51 am
10-30-1949,Mo Cnj Pi,12:22 pm

November 1949

11-02-1949,Mo Cnj Ar,00:35 am
11-04-1949,Mo Cnj Ta,01:37 pm
11-07-1949,Mo Cnj Ge,01:55 am
11-09-1949,Mo Cnj Ca,12:35 pm
11-11-1949,Mo Cnj Le,09:01 pm
11-14-1949,Mo Cnj Vi,02:43 am
11-16-1949,Mo Cnj Li,05:36 am
11-18-1949,Mo Cnj Sc,06:19 am
11-20-1949,Mo Cnj Sa,06:16 am
11-22-1949,Mo Cnj Ca,07:20 am
11-24-1949,Mo Cnj Aq,11:25 am
11-26-1949,Mo Cnj Pi,07:35 pm
11-29-1949,Mo Cnj Ar,07:18 am

December 1949

12-01-1949,Mo Cnj Ta,08:22 pm
12-04-1949,Mo Cnj Ge,08:29 am
12-06-1949,Mo Cnj Ca,06:32 pm
12-09-1949,Mo Cnj Le,02:28 am
12-11-1949,Mo Cnj Vi,08:32 am
12-13-1949,Mo Cnj Li,12:46 pm
12-15-1949,Mo Cnj Sc,03:14 pm
12-17-1949,Mo Cnj Sa,04:32 pm
12-19-1949,Mo Cnj Ca,06:00 pm
12-21-1949,Mo Cnj Aq,09:24 pm
12-24-1949,Mo Cnj Pi,04:20 am
12-26-1949,Mo Cnj Ar,03:05 pm
12-29-1949,Mo Cnj Ta,03:58 am

January 1950

01-03-1950,Mo Cnj Ca,01:57 am
01-05-1950,Mo Cnj Le,08:58 am
01-07-1950,Mo Cnj Vi,02:06 pm
01-09-1950,Mo Cnj Li,06:09 pm
01-11-1950,Mo Cnj Sc,09:28 pm
01-14-1950,Mo Cnj Sa,00:16 am
01-16-1950,Mo Cnj Ca,03:06 am
01-18-1950,Mo Cnj Aq,07:07 am
01-20-1950,Mo Cnj Pi,01:41 pm
01-22-1950,Mo Cnj Ar,11:38 pm
01-25-1950,Mo Cnj Ta,12:09 pm
01-28-1950,Mo Cnj Ge,00:44 am
01-30-1950,Mo Cnj Ca,10:51 am

February 1950

02-01-1950,Mo Cnj Le,05:34 pm
02-03-1950,Mo Cnj Vi,09:36 pm

02-06-1950,Mo Cnj Li,00:19 am
02-08-1950,Mo Cnj Sc,02:50 am
02-10-1950,Mo Cnj Sa,05:51 am
02-12-1950,Mo Cnj Ca,09:45 am
02-14-1950,Mo Cnj Aq,02:58 pm
02-16-1950,Mo Cnj Pi,10:11 pm
02-19-1950,Mo Cnj Ar,08:01 am
02-21-1950,Mo Cnj Ta,08:12 pm
02-24-1950,Mo Cnj Ge,09:03 am
02-26-1950,Mo Cnj Ca,08:03 pm

March 1950
03-01-1950,Mo Cnj Le,03:30 am
03-03-1950,Mo Cnj Vi,07:24 am
03-05-1950,Mo Cnj Li,09:00 am
03-07-1950,Mo Cnj Sc,09:55 am
03-09-1950,Mo Cnj Sa,11:38 am
03-11-1950,Mo Cnj Ca,03:07 pm
03-13-1950,Mo Cnj Aq,08:53 pm
03-16-1950,Mo Cnj Pi,05:00 am
03-18-1950,Mo Cnj Ar,03:21 pm
03-21-1950,Mo Cnj Ta,03:32 am
03-23-1950,Mo Cnj Ge,04:28 pm
03-26-1950,Mo Cnj Ca,04:17 am
03-28-1950,Mo Cnj Le,01:04 pm
03-30-1950,Mo Cnj Vi,06:01 pm

April 1950
04-01-1950,Mo Cnj Li,07:41 pm
04-03-1950,Mo Cnj Sc,07:36 pm
04-05-1950,Mo Cnj Sa,07:38 pm
04-07-1950,Mo Cnj Ca,09:30 pm
04-10-1950,Mo Cnj Aq,02:25 am
04-12-1950,Mo Cnj Pi,10:38 am
04-14-1950,Mo Cnj Ar,09:31 pm
04-17-1950,Mo Cnj Ta,09:59 am
04-19-1950,Mo Cnj Ge,10:54 pm
04-22-1950,Mo Cnj Ca,11:02 am
04-24-1950,Mo Cnj Le,08:58 pm
04-27-1950,Mo Cnj Vi,03:31 am
04-29-1950,Mo Cnj Li,06:26 am

May 1950
05-01-1950,Mo Cnj Sc,06:38 am
05-03-1950,Mo Cnj Sa,05:51 am
05-05-1950,Mo Cnj Ca,06:08 am
05-07-1950,Mo Cnj Aq,09:22 am

05-09-1950,Mo Cnj Pi,04:34 pm
05-12-1950,Mo Cnj Ar,03:18 am
05-14-1950,Mo Cnj Ta,03:59 pm
05-17-1950,Mo Cnj Ge,04:53 am
05-19-1950,Mo Cnj Ca,04:51 pm
05-22-1950,Mo Cnj Le,03:07 am
05-24-1950,Mo Cnj Vi,10:51 am
05-26-1950,Mo Cnj Li,03:26 pm
05-28-1950,Mo Cnj Sc,05:01 pm
05-30-1950,Mo Cnj Sa,04:43 pm

June 1950
06-01-1950,Mo Cnj Ca,04:27 pm
06-03-1950,Mo Cnj Aq,06:18 pm
06-05-1950,Mo Cnj Pi,11:57 pm
06-08-1950,Mo Cnj Ar,09:44 am
06-10-1950,Mo Cnj Ta,10:13 pm
06-13-1950,Mo Cnj Ge,11:06 am
06-15-1950,Mo Cnj Ca,10:46 pm
06-18-1950,Mo Cnj Le,08:38 am
06-20-1950,Mo Cnj Vi,04:32 pm
06-22-1950,Mo Cnj Li,10:09 pm
06-25-1950,Mo Cnj Sc,01:19 am
06-27-1950,Mo Cnj Sa,02:26 am
06-29-1950,Mo Cnj Ca,02:48 am

July 1950
07-01-1950,Mo Cnj Aq,04:20 am
07-03-1950,Mo Cnj Pi,08:52 am
07-05-1950,Mo Cnj Ar,05:25 pm
07-08-1950,Mo Cnj Ta,05:14 am
07-10-1950,Mo Cnj Ge,06:02 pm
07-13-1950,Mo Cnj Ca,05:34 am
07-15-1950,Mo Cnj Le,02:52 pm
07-17-1950,Mo Cnj Vi,10:05 pm
07-20-1950,Mo Cnj Li,03:34 am
07-22-1950,Mo Cnj Sc,07:27 am
07-24-1950,Mo Cnj Sa,09:56 am
07-26-1950,Mo Cnj Ca,11:40 am
07-28-1950,Mo Cnj Aq,01:56 pm
07-30-1950,Mo Cnj Pi,06:19 pm

August 1950
08-02-1950,Mo Cnj Ar,02:03 am
08-04-1950,Mo Cnj Ta,01:06 pm
08-07-1950,Mo Cnj Ge,01:44 am
08-09-1950,Mo Cnj Ca,01:27 pm

08-11-1950,Mo Cnj Le,10:36 pm
08-14-1950,Mo Cnj Vi,05:03 am
08-16-1950,Mo Cnj Li,09:31 am
08-18-1950,Mo Cnj Sc,12:50 pm
08-20-1950,Mo Cnj Sa,03:36 pm
08-22-1950,Mo Cnj Ca,06:24 pm
08-24-1950,Mo Cnj Aq,09:53 pm
08-27-1950,Mo Cnj Pi,03:02 am
08-29-1950,Mo Cnj Ar,10:45 am
08-31-1950,Mo Cnj Ta,09:19 pm

September 1950
09-03-1950,Mo Cnj Ge,09:45 am
09-05-1950,Mo Cnj Ca,09:54 pm
09-08-1950,Mo Cnj Le,07:35 am
09-10-1950,Mo Cnj Vi,01:55 pm
09-12-1950,Mo Cnj Li,05:28 pm
09-14-1950,Mo Cnj Sc,07:27 pm
09-16-1950,Mo Cnj Sa,09:13 pm
09-18-1950,Mo Cnj Ca,11:49 pm
09-21-1950,Mo Cnj Aq,04:00 am
09-23-1950,Mo Cnj Pi,10:09 am
09-25-1950,Mo Cnj Ar,06:32 pm
09-28-1950,Mo Cnj Ta,05:08 am
09-30-1950,Mo Cnj Ge,05:27 pm

October 1950
10-03-1950,Mo Cnj Ca,06:00 am
10-05-1950,Mo Cnj Le,04:41 pm
10-07-1950,Mo Cnj Vi,11:54 pm
10-10-1950,Mo Cnj Li,03:29 am
10-12-1950,Mo Cnj Sc,04:31 am
10-14-1950,Mo Cnj Sa,04:44 am
10-16-1950,Mo Cnj Ca,05:55 am
10-18-1950,Mo Cnj Aq,09:27 am
10-20-1950,Mo Cnj Pi,03:53 pm
10-23-1950,Mo Cnj Ar,00:59 am
10-25-1950,Mo Cnj Ta,12:03 pm
10-28-1950,Mo Cnj Ge,00:23 am
10-30-1950,Mo Cnj Ca,01:04 pm

November 1950
11-02-1950,Mo Cnj Le,00:38 am
11-04-1950,Mo Cnj Vi,09:21 am
11-06-1950,Mo Cnj Li,02:10 pm
11-08-1950,Mo Cnj Sc,03:29 pm
11-10-1950,Mo Cnj Sa,02:51 pm

11-12-1950,Mo Cnj Ca,02:25 pm
11-14-1950,Mo Cnj Aq,04:15 pm
11-16-1950,Mo Cnj Pi,09:39 pm
11-19-1950,Mo Cnj Ar,06:40 am
11-21-1950,Mo Cnj Ta,06:08 pm
11-24-1950,Mo Cnj Ge,06:39 am
11-26-1950,Mo Cnj Ca,07:13 pm
11-29-1950,Mo Cnj Le,07:02 am

December 1950
12-01-1950,Mo Cnj Vi,04:53 pm
12-03-1950,Mo Cnj Li,11:29 pm
12-06-1950,Mo Cnj Sc,02:20 am
12-08-1950,Mo Cnj Sa,02:17 am
12-10-1950,Mo Cnj Ca,01:17 am
12-12-1950,Mo Cnj Aq,01:35 am
12-14-1950,Mo Cnj Pi,05:11 am
12-16-1950,Mo Cnj Ar,12:59 pm
12-19-1950,Mo Cnj Ta,00:10 am
12-21-1950,Mo Cnj Ge,12:49 pm
12-24-1950,Mo Cnj Ca,01:18 am
12-26-1950,Mo Cnj Le,12:45 pm
12-28-1950,Mo Cnj Vi,10:41 pm
12-31-1950,Mo Cnj Li,06:21 am

January 1951
01-02-1951,Mo Cnj Sc,10:59 am
01-04-1951,Mo Cnj Sa,12:39 pm
01-06-1951,Mo Cnj Ca,12:32 pm
01-08-1951,Mo Cnj Aq,12:36 pm
01-10-1951,Mo Cnj Pi,02:56 pm
01-12-1951,Mo Cnj Ar,09:05 pm
01-15-1951,Mo Cnj Ta,07:10 am
01-17-1951,Mo Cnj Ge,07:36 pm
01-20-1951,Mo Cnj Ca,08:06 am
01-22-1951,Mo Cnj Le,07:12 am
01-25-1951,Mo Cnj Vi,04:27 am
01-27-1951,Mo Cnj Li,11:47 am
01-29-1951,Mo Cnj Sc,05:04 pm
01-31-1951,Mo Cnj Sa,08:17 pm

February 1951
02-02-1951,Mo Cnj Ca,09:53 pm
02-04-1951,Mo Cnj Aq,11:04 pm
02-07-1951,Mo Cnj Pi,01:29 am
02-09-1951,Mo Cnj Ar,06:43 am
02-11-1951,Mo Cnj Ta,03:33 pm

02-14-1951,Mo Cnj Ge,03:18 am
02-16-1951,Mo Cnj Ca,03:52 pm
02-19-1951,Mo Cnj Le,03:02 am
02-21-1951,Mo Cnj Vi,11:43 am
02-23-1951,Mo Cnj Li,06:01 pm
02-25-1951,Mo Cnj Sc,10:31 pm
02-28-1951,Mo Cnj Sa,01:49 am

March 1951
03-02-1951,Mo Cnj Ca,04:29 am
03-04-1951,Mo Cnj Aq,07:11 am
03-06-1951,Mo Cnj Pi,10:46 am
03-08-1951,Mo Cnj Ar,04:16 pm
03-11-1951,Mo Cnj Ta,00:33 am
03-13-1951,Mo Cnj Ge,11:37 am
03-16-1951,Mo Cnj Ca,00:07 am
03-18-1951,Mo Cnj Le,11:45 am
03-20-1951,Mo Cnj Vi,08:39 pm
03-23-1951,Mo Cnj Li,02:21 am
03-25-1951,Mo Cnj Sc,05:35 am
03-27-1951,Mo Cnj Sa,07:40 am
03-29-1951,Mo Cnj Ca,09:51 am
03-31-1951,Mo Cnj Aq,01:02 pm

April 1951
04-02-1951,Mo Cnj Pi,05:45 pm
04-05-1951,Mo Cnj Ar,00:16 am
04-07-1951,Mo Cnj Ta,08:53 am
04-09-1951,Mo Cnj Ge,07:41 pm
04-12-1951,Mo Cnj Ca,08:05 am
04-14-1951,Mo Cnj Le,08:18 am
04-17-1951,Mo Cnj Vi,06:07 am
04-19-1951,Mo Cnj Li,12:13 pm
04-21-1951,Mo Cnj Sc,02:55 pm
04-23-1951,Mo Cnj Sa,03:40 pm
04-25-1951,Mo Cnj Ca,04:20 pm
04-27-1951,Mo Cnj Aq,06:33 pm
04-29-1951,Mo Cnj Pi,11:14 pm

May 1951
05-02-1951,Mo Cnj Ar,06:27 am
05-04-1951,Mo Cnj Ta,03:47 pm
05-07-1951,Mo Cnj Ge,02:51 pm
05-09-1951,Mo Cnj Ca,03:13 pm
05-12-1951,Mo Cnj Le,03:49 am
05-14-1951,Mo Cnj Vi,02:44 pm
05-16-1951,Mo Cnj Li,10:05 pm

05-19-1951,Mo Cnj Sc,01:24 am
05-21-1951,Mo Cnj Sa,01:44 am
05-23-1951,Mo Cnj Ca,01:08 am
05-25-1951,Mo Cnj Aq,01:42 am
05-27-1951,Mo Cnj Pi,05:05 am
05-29-1951,Mo Cnj Ar,11:53 am
05-31-1951,Mo Cnj Ta,09:33 pm

June 1951
06-03-1951,Mo Cnj Ge,09:03 am
06-05-1951,Mo Cnj Ca,09:31 pm
06-08-1951,Mo Cnj Le,10:12 am
06-10-1951,Mo Cnj Vi,09:47 pm
06-13-1951,Mo Cnj Li,06:31 am
06-15-1951,Mo Cnj Sc,11:17 am
06-17-1951,Mo Cnj Sa,12:26 pm
06-19-1951,Mo Cnj Ca,11:38 am
06-21-1951,Mo Cnj Aq,11:04 am
06-23-1951,Mo Cnj Pi,12:49 pm
06-25-1951,Mo Cnj Ar,06:13 pm
06-28-1951,Mo Cnj Ta,03:17 am
06-30-1951,Mo Cnj Ge,02:52 pm

July 1951
07-03-1951,Mo Cnj Ca,03:28 am
07-05-1951,Mo Cnj Le,04:01 pm
07-08-1951,Mo Cnj Vi,03:37 am
07-10-1951,Mo Cnj Li,01:05 pm
07-12-1951,Mo Cnj Sc,07:19 pm
07-14-1951,Mo Cnj Sa,10:03 pm
07-16-1951,Mo Cnj Ca,10:14 pm
07-18-1951,Mo Cnj Aq,09:41 pm
07-20-1951,Mo Cnj Pi,10:29 pm
07-23-1951,Mo Cnj Ar,02:22 am
07-25-1951,Mo Cnj Ta,10:07 am
07-27-1951,Mo Cnj Ge,09:08 pm
07-30-1951,Mo Cnj Ca,09:43 am

August 1951
08-01-1951,Mo Cnj Le,10:08 pm
08-04-1951,Mo Cnj Vi,09:18 am
08-06-1951,Mo Cnj Li,06:34 pm
08-09-1951,Mo Cnj Sc,01:24 am
08-11-1951,Mo Cnj Sa,05:31 am
08-13-1951,Mo Cnj Ca,07:18 am
08-15-1951,Mo Cnj Aq,07:53 am
08-17-1951,Mo Cnj Pi,08:53 am

08-19-1951,Mo Cnj Ar,11:59 am
08-21-1951,Mo Cnj Ta,06:27 pm
08-24-1951,Mo Cnj Ge,04:28 am
08-26-1951,Mo Cnj Ca,04:44 pm
08-29-1951,Mo Cnj Le,05:10 am
08-31-1951,Mo Cnj Vi,04:00 pm

September 1951
09-03-1951,Mo Cnj Li,00:32 am
09-05-1951,Mo Cnj Sc,06:49 am
09-07-1951,Mo Cnj Sa,11:11 am
09-09-1951,Mo Cnj Ca,02:07 pm
09-11-1951,Mo Cnj Aq,04:12 pm
09-13-1951,Mo Cnj Pi,06:22 pm
09-15-1951,Mo Cnj Ar,09:48 pm
09-18-1951,Mo Cnj Ta,03:42 am
09-20-1951,Mo Cnj Ge,12:47 pm
09-23-1951,Mo Cnj Ca,00:34 am
09-25-1951,Mo Cnj Le,01:07 pm
09-28-1951,Mo Cnj Vi,00:06 am
09-30-1951,Mo Cnj Li,08:09 am

October 1951
10-02-1951,Mo Cnj Sc,01:24 pm
10-04-1951,Mo Cnj Sa,04:49 pm
10-06-1951,Mo Cnj Ca,07:31 pm
10-08-1951,Mo Cnj Aq,10:20 pm
10-11-1951,Mo Cnj Pi,01:47 am
10-13-1951,Mo Cnj Ar,06:20 am
10-15-1951,Mo Cnj Ta,12:37 pm
10-17-1951,Mo Cnj Ge,09:22 pm
10-20-1951,Mo Cnj Ca,08:43 am
10-22-1951,Mo Cnj Le,09:25 pm
10-25-1951,Mo Cnj Vi,09:02 am
10-27-1951,Mo Cnj Li,05:26 pm
10-29-1951,Mo Cnj Sc,10:10 pm

November 1951
11-01-1951,Mo Cnj Sa,00:20 am
11-03-1951,Mo Cnj Ca,01:40 am
11-05-1951,Mo Cnj Aq,03:43 am
11-07-1951,Mo Cnj Pi,07:23 am
11-09-1951,Mo Cnj Ar,12:53 pm
11-11-1951,Mo Cnj Ta,08:07 pm
11-14-1951,Mo Cnj Ge,05:15 am
11-16-1951,Mo Cnj Ca,04:28 pm
11-19-1951,Mo Cnj Le,05:13 pm

11-21-1951,Mo Cnj Vi,05:36 pm
11-24-1951,Mo Cnj Li,03:09 am
11-26-1951,Mo Cnj Sc,08:32 am
11-28-1951,Mo Cnj Sa,10:20 am
11-30-1951,Mo Cnj Ca,10:22 am

December 1951
12-02-1951,Mo Cnj Aq,10:45 am
12-04-1951,Mo Cnj Pi,01:08 pm
12-06-1951,Mo Cnj Ar,06:18 pm
12-09-1951,Mo Cnj Ta,02:05 am
12-11-1951,Mo Cnj Ge,11:55 am
12-13-1951,Mo Cnj Ca,11:23 pm
12-16-1951,Mo Cnj Le,12:05 pm
12-19-1951,Mo Cnj Vi,00:52 am
12-21-1951,Mo Cnj Li,11:41 am
12-23-1951,Mo Cnj Sc,06:39 pm
12-25-1951,Mo Cnj Sa,09:27 pm
12-27-1951,Mo Cnj Ca,09:24 pm
12-29-1951,Mo Cnj Aq,08:36 pm
12-31-1951,Mo Cnj Pi,09:10 pm

January 1952
01-03-1952,Mo Cnj Ar,00:42 am
01-05-1952,Mo Cnj Ta,07:44 am
01-07-1952,Mo Cnj Ge,05:43 pm
01-10-1952,Mo Cnj Ca,05:34 am
01-12-1952,Mo Cnj Le,06:19 pm
01-15-1952,Mo Cnj Vi,07:00 am
01-17-1952,Mo Cnj Li,06:19 pm
01-20-1952,Mo Cnj Sc,02:44 am
01-22-1952,Mo Cnj Sa,07:22 am
01-24-1952,Mo Cnj Ca,08:39 am
01-26-1952,Mo Cnj Aq,08:07 am
01-28-1952,Mo Cnj Pi,07:46 am
01-30-1952,Mo Cnj Ar,09:33 am

February 1952
02-01-1952,Mo Cnj Ta,02:51 pm
02-03-1952,Mo Cnj Ge,11:55 pm
02-06-1952,Mo Cnj Ca,11:44 am
02-09-1952,Mo Cnj Le,00:36 am
02-11-1952,Mo Cnj Vi,01:02 pm
02-14-1952,Mo Cnj Li,00:00 am
02-16-1952,Mo Cnj Sc,08:45 am
02-18-1952,Mo Cnj Sa,02:43 pm
02-20-1952,Mo Cnj Ca,05:50 pm

02-22-1952,Mo Cnj Aq,06:49 pm
02-24-1952,Mo Cnj Pi,07:01 pm
02-26-1952,Mo Cnj Ar,08:12 pm
02-29-1952,Mo Cnj Ta,00:01 am

March 1952
03-02-1952,Mo Cnj Ge,07:36 am
03-04-1952,Mo Cnj Ca,06:40 pm
03-07-1952,Mo Cnj Le,07:30 am
03-09-1952,Mo Cnj Vi,07:52 pm
03-12-1952,Mo Cnj Li,06:17 am
03-14-1952,Mo Cnj Sc,02:21 pm
03-16-1952,Mo Cnj Sa,08:16 pm
03-19-1952,Mo Cnj Ca,00:19 am
03-21-1952,Mo Cnj Aq,02:55 am
03-23-1952,Mo Cnj Pi,04:39 am
03-25-1952,Mo Cnj Ar,06:34 am
03-27-1952,Mo Cnj Ta,10:05 am
03-29-1952,Mo Cnj Ge,04:36 pm

April 1952
04-01-1952,Mo Cnj Ca,02:39 am
04-03-1952,Mo Cnj Le,03:11 pm
04-06-1952,Mo Cnj Vi,03:41 am
04-08-1952,Mo Cnj Li,01:56 pm
04-10-1952,Mo Cnj Sc,09:13 pm
04-13-1952,Mo Cnj Sa,02:08 am
04-15-1952,Mo Cnj Ca,05:41 am
04-17-1952,Mo Cnj Aq,08:43 am
04-19-1952,Mo Cnj Pi,11:40 am
04-21-1952,Mo Cnj Ar,02:57 pm
04-23-1952,Mo Cnj Ta,07:15 pm
04-26-1952,Mo Cnj Ge,01:41 am
04-28-1952,Mo Cnj Ca,11:06 am
04-30-1952,Mo Cnj Le,11:13 pm

May 1952
05-03-1952,Mo Cnj Vi,11:58 am
05-05-1952,Mo Cnj Li,10:39 pm
05-08-1952,Mo Cnj Sc,05:49 am
05-10-1952,Mo Cnj Sa,09:50 am
05-12-1952,Mo Cnj Ca,12:09 pm
05-14-1952,Mo Cnj Aq,02:14 pm
05-16-1952,Mo Cnj Pi,05:06 pm
05-18-1952,Mo Cnj Ar,09:08 pm
05-21-1952,Mo Cnj Ta,02:30 am
05-23-1952,Mo Cnj Ge,09:38 am

05-25-1952,Mo Cnj Ca,07:06 pm
05-28-1952,Mo Cnj Le,06:59 am
05-30-1952,Mo Cnj Vi,07:57 pm

June 1952
06-02-1952,Mo Cnj Li,07:26 am
06-04-1952,Mo Cnj Sc,03:19 pm
06-06-1952,Mo Cnj Sa,07:21 pm
06-08-1952,Mo Cnj Ca,08:47 pm
06-10-1952,Mo Cnj Aq,09:27 pm
06-12-1952,Mo Cnj Pi,11:01 pm
06-15-1952,Mo Cnj Ar,02:29 am
06-17-1952,Mo Cnj Ta,08:11 am
06-19-1952,Mo Cnj Ge,04:03 pm
06-22-1952,Mo Cnj Ca,02:04 am
06-24-1952,Mo Cnj Le,02:02 pm
06-27-1952,Mo Cnj Vi,03:06 am
06-29-1952,Mo Cnj Li,03:18 pm

July 1952
07-02-1952,Mo Cnj Sc,00:26 am
07-04-1952,Mo Cnj Sa,05:28 am
07-06-1952,Mo Cnj Ca,07:03 am
07-08-1952,Mo Cnj Aq,06:55 am
07-10-1952,Mo Cnj Pi,07:00 am
07-12-1952,Mo Cnj Ar,08:56 am
07-14-1952,Mo Cnj Ta,01:45 pm
07-16-1952,Mo Cnj Ge,09:37 pm
07-19-1952,Mo Cnj Ca,08:05 am
07-21-1952,Mo Cnj Le,08:20 pm
07-24-1952,Mo Cnj Vi,09:25 am
07-26-1952,Mo Cnj Li,09:55 pm
07-29-1952,Mo Cnj Sc,08:05 am
07-31-1952,Mo Cnj Sa,02:38 pm

August 1952
08-02-1952,Mo Cnj Ca,05:28 pm
08-04-1952,Mo Cnj Aq,05:41 pm
08-06-1952,Mo Cnj Pi,05:05 pm
08-08-1952,Mo Cnj Ar,05:33 pm
08-10-1952,Mo Cnj Ta,08:46 pm
08-13-1952,Mo Cnj Ge,03:37 am
08-15-1952,Mo Cnj Ca,01:53 pm
08-18-1952,Mo Cnj Le,02:20 am
08-20-1952,Mo Cnj Vi,03:23 pm
08-23-1952,Mo Cnj Li,03:42 am
08-25-1952,Mo Cnj Sc,02:10 pm

08-27-1952,Mo Cnj Sa,09:53 pm
08-30-1952,Mo Cnj Ca,02:24 am

September 1952
09-01-1952,Mo Cnj Aq,04:03 am
09-03-1952,Mo Cnj Pi,04:00 am
09-05-1952,Mo Cnj Ar,03:57 am
09-07-1952,Mo Cnj Ta,05:48 am
09-09-1952,Mo Cnj Ge,11:07 am
09-11-1952,Mo Cnj Ca,08:25 pm
09-14-1952,Mo Cnj Le,08:39 am
09-16-1952,Mo Cnj Vi,09:42 pm
09-19-1952,Mo Cnj Li,09:41 am
09-21-1952,Mo Cnj Sc,07:43 pm
09-24-1952,Mo Cnj Sa,03:33 am
09-26-1952,Mo Cnj Ca,09:06 am
09-28-1952,Mo Cnj Aq,12:25 pm
09-30-1952,Mo Cnj Pi,01:53 pm

October 1952
10-02-1952,Mo Cnj Ar,02:35 pm
10-04-1952,Mo Cnj Ta,04:06 pm
10-06-1952,Mo Cnj Ge,08:16 pm
10-09-1952,Mo Cnj Ca,04:16 am
10-11-1952,Mo Cnj Le,03:50 pm
10-14-1952,Mo Cnj Vi,04:51 am
10-16-1952,Mo Cnj Li,04:44 pm
10-19-1952,Mo Cnj Sc,02:10 am
10-21-1952,Mo Cnj Sa,09:12 am
10-23-1952,Mo Cnj Ca,02:29 pm
10-25-1952,Mo Cnj Aq,06:29 pm
10-27-1952,Mo Cnj Pi,09:24 pm
10-29-1952,Mo Cnj Ar,11:35 pm

November 1952
11-01-1952,Mo Cnj Ta,01:59 am
11-03-1952,Mo Cnj Ge,06:02 am
11-05-1952,Mo Cnj Ca,01:12 pm
11-07-1952,Mo Cnj Le,11:56 pm
11-10-1952,Mo Cnj Vi,12:47 pm
11-13-1952,Mo Cnj Li,00:57 am
11-15-1952,Mo Cnj Sc,10:19 am
11-17-1952,Mo Cnj Sa,04:34 pm
11-19-1952,Mo Cnj Ca,08:41 pm
11-21-1952,Mo Cnj Aq,11:52 pm
11-24-1952,Mo Cnj Pi,02:55 am
11-26-1952,Mo Cnj Ar,06:09 am

11-28-1952,Mo Cnj Ta,09:54 am
11-30-1952,Mo Cnj Ge,02:53 pm

December 1952
12-02-1952,Mo Cnj Ca,10:09 pm
12-05-1952,Mo Cnj Le,08:23 am
12-07-1952,Mo Cnj Vi,08:58 pm
12-10-1952,Mo Cnj Li,09:36 am
12-12-1952,Mo Cnj Sc,07:40 pm
12-15-1952,Mo Cnj Sa,02:00 am
12-17-1952,Mo Cnj Ca,05:17 am
12-19-1952,Mo Cnj Aq,07:02 am
12-21-1952,Mo Cnj Pi,08:46 am
12-23-1952,Mo Cnj Ar,11:30 am
12-25-1952,Mo Cnj Ta,03:46 pm
12-27-1952,Mo Cnj Ge,09:48 pm
12-30-1952,Mo Cnj Ca,05:54 am

January 1953
01-01-1953, Mo Cnj Le,04:18 pm
01-04-1953,Mo Cnj Vi,04:42 am
01-06-1953,Mo Cnj Li,05:37 pm
01-09-1953,Mo Cnj Sc,04:44 am
01-11-1953,Mo Cnj Sa,12:14 pm
01-13-1953,Mo Cnj Ca,03:55 pm
01-15-1953,Mo Cnj Aq,04:57 pm
01-17-1953,Mo Cnj Pi,05:07 pm
01-19-1953,Mo Cnj Ar,06:09 pm
01-21-1953,Mo Cnj Ta,09:21 pm
01-24-1953,Mo Cnj Ge,03:22 am
01-26-1953,Mo Cnj Ca,12:07 pm
01-28-1953,Mo Cnj Le,11:07 pm
01-31-1953,Mo Cnj Vi,11:36 am

February 1953
02-03-1953,Mo Cnj Li,00:32 am
02-05-1953,Mo Cnj Sc,12:21 pm
02-07-1953,Mo Cnj Sa,09:20 pm
02-10-1953,Mo Cnj Ca,02:32 am
02-12-1953,Mo Cnj Aq,04:17 am
02-14-1953,Mo Cnj Pi,03:58 am
02-16-1953,Mo Cnj Ar,03:31 am
02-18-1953,Mo Cnj Ta,04:51 am
02-20-1953,Mo Cnj Ge,09:28 am
02-22-1953,Mo Cnj Ca,05:48 pm
02-25-1953,Mo Cnj Le,05:06 am
02-27-1953,Mo Cnj Vi,05:51 pm

March 1953

03-02-1953,Mo Cnj Li,06:41 am
03-04-1953,Mo Cnj Sc,06:31 pm
03-07-1953,Mo Cnj Sa,04:20 am
03-09-1953,Mo Cnj Ca,11:11 am
03-11-1953,Mo Cnj Aq,02:38 pm
03-13-1953,Mo Cnj Pi,03:18 pm
03-15-1953,Mo Cnj Ar,02:39 pm
03-17-1953,Mo Cnj Ta,02:45 pm
03-19-1953,Mo Cnj Ge,05:35 pm
03-22-1953,Mo Cnj Ca,00:29 am
03-24-1953,Mo Cnj Le,11:14 am
03-27-1953,Mo Cnj Vi,00:04 am
03-29-1953,Mo Cnj Li,12:52 pm

April 1953

04-01-1953,Mo Cnj Sc,00:20 am
04-03-1953,Mo Cnj Sa,09:59 am
04-05-1953,Mo Cnj Ca,05:30 pm
04-07-1953,Mo Cnj Aq,10:28 pm
04-10-1953,Mo Cnj Pi,00:50 am
04-12-1953,Mo Cnj Ar,01:19 am
04-14-1953,Mo Cnj Ta,01:31 am
04-16-1953,Mo Cnj Ge,03:27 am
04-18-1953,Mo Cnj Ca,08:53 am
04-20-1953,Mo Cnj Le,06:27 pm
04-23-1953,Mo Cnj Vi,06:53 am
04-25-1953,Mo Cnj Li,07:41 pm
04-28-1953,Mo Cnj Sc,06:53 am
04-30-1953,Mo Cnj Sa,03:53 pm

May 1953

05-02-1953,Mo Cnj Ca,10:55 pm
05-05-1953,Mo Cnj Aq,04:13 am
05-07-1953,Mo Cnj Pi,07:47 am
05-09-1953,Mo Cnj Ar,09:49 am
05-11-1953,Mo Cnj Ta,11:12 am
05-13-1953,Mo Cnj Ge,01:27 pm
05-15-1953,Mo Cnj Ca,06:17 pm
05-18-1953,Mo Cnj Le,02:48 am
05-20-1953,Mo Cnj Vi,02:32 pm
05-23-1953,Mo Cnj Li,03:17 am
05-25-1953,Mo Cnj Sc,02:33 pm
05-27-1953,Mo Cnj Sa,11:08 pm
05-30-1953,Mo Cnj Ca,05:17 am

June 1953

06-01-1953,Mo Cnj Aq,09:45 am
06-03-1953,Mo Cnj Pi,01:12 pm
06-05-1953,Mo Cnj Ar,04:01 pm
06-07-1953,Mo Cnj Ta,06:42 pm
06-09-1953,Mo Cnj Ge,10:03 pm
06-12-1953,Mo Cnj Ca,03:18 am
06-14-1953,Mo Cnj Le,11:28 am
06-16-1953,Mo Cnj Vi,10:37 pm
06-19-1953,Mo Cnj Li,11:17 am
06-21-1953,Mo Cnj Sc,10:58 pm
06-24-1953,Mo Cnj Sa,07:48 am
06-26-1953,Mo Cnj Ca,01:29 pm
06-28-1953,Mo Cnj Aq,04:52 pm
06-30-1953,Mo Cnj Pi,07:09 pm

July 1953

07-02-1953,Mo Cnj Ar,09:24 pm
07-05-1953,Mo Cnj Ta,00:24 am
07-07-1953,Mo Cnj Ge,04:43 am
07-09-1953,Mo Cnj Ca,10:54 am
07-11-1953,Mo Cnj Le,07:28 pm
07-14-1953,Mo Cnj Vi,06:28 am
07-16-1953,Mo Cnj Li,07:03 pm
07-19-1953,Mo Cnj Sc,07:17 am
07-21-1953,Mo Cnj Sa,04:59 pm
07-23-1953,Mo Cnj Ca,11:07 pm
07-26-1953,Mo Cnj Aq,02:03 am
07-28-1953,Mo Cnj Pi,03:08 am
07-30-1953,Mo Cnj Ar,03:56 am

August 1953

08-01-1953,Mo Cnj Ta,05:57 am
08-03-1953,Mo Cnj Ge,10:11 am
08-05-1953,Mo Cnj Ca,04:59 pm
08-08-1953,Mo Cnj Le,02:15 am
08-10-1953,Mo Cnj Vi,01:33 pm
08-13-1953,Mo Cnj Li,02:08 am
08-15-1953,Mo Cnj Sc,02:44 pm
08-18-1953,Mo Cnj Sa,01:31 am
08-20-1953,Mo Cnj Ca,08:54 am
08-22-1953,Mo Cnj Aq,12:29 pm
08-24-1953,Mo Cnj Pi,01:12 pm
08-26-1953,Mo Cnj Ar,12:46 pm
08-28-1953,Mo Cnj Ta,01:10 pm
08-30-1953,Mo Cnj Ge,04:06 pm

September 1953
09-01-1953,Mo Cnj Ca,10:30 pm
09-04-1953,Mo Cnj Le,08:05 am
09-06-1953,Mo Cnj Vi,07:47 pm
09-09-1953,Mo Cnj Li,08:28 am
09-11-1953,Mo Cnj Sc,09:06 pm
09-14-1953,Mo Cnj Sa,08:32 am
09-16-1953,Mo Cnj Ca,05:21 pm
09-18-1953,Mo Cnj Aq,10:30 pm
09-21-1953,Mo Cnj Pi,00:06 am
09-22-1953,Mo Cnj Ar,11:30 pm
09-24-1953,Mo Cnj Ta,10:45 pm
09-27-1953,Mo Cnj Ge,00:01 am
09-29-1953,Mo Cnj Ca,04:57 am

October 1953
10-01-1953,Mo Cnj Le,01:54 pm
10-04-1953,Mo Cnj Vi,01:41 am
10-06-1953,Mo Cnj Li,02:29 pm
10-09-1953,Mo Cnj Sc,02:56 am
10-11-1953,Mo Cnj Sa,02:19 pm
10-13-1953,Mo Cnj Ca,11:51 pm
10-16-1953,Mo Cnj Aq,06:34 am
10-18-1953,Mo Cnj Pi,09:55 am
10-20-1953,Mo Cnj Ar,10:27 am
10-22-1953,Mo Cnj Ta,09:47 am
10-24-1953,Mo Cnj Ge,10:05 am
10-26-1953,Mo Cnj Ca,01:24 pm
10-28-1953,Mo Cnj Le,08:56 pm
10-31-1953,Mo Cnj Vi,08:05 am

November 1953
11-02-1953,Mo Cnj Li,08:51 pm
11-05-1953,Mo Cnj Sc,09:12 am
11-07-1953,Mo Cnj Sa,08:06 pm
11-10-1953,Mo Cnj Ca,05:18 am
11-12-1953,Mo Cnj Aq,12:31 pm
11-14-1953,Mo Cnj Pi,05:18 pm
11-16-1953,Mo Cnj Ar,07:36 pm
11-18-1953,Mo Cnj Ta,08:16 pm
11-20-1953,Mo Cnj Ge,08:55 pm
11-22-1953,Mo Cnj Ca,11:32 pm
11-25-1953,Mo Cnj Le,05:41 am
11-27-1953,Mo Cnj Vi,03:41 pm
11-30-1953,Mo Cnj Li,04:05 am

December 1953
12-02-1953,Mo Cnj Sc,04:30 pm
12-05-1953,Mo Cnj Sa,03:09 am
12-07-1953,Mo Cnj Ca,11:33 am
12-09-1953,Mo Cnj Aq,06:00 pm
12-11-1953,Mo Cnj Pi,10:47 pm
12-14-1953,Mo Cnj Ar,02:07 am
12-16-1953,Mo Cnj Ta,04:23 am
12-18-1953,Mo Cnj Ge,06:28 am
12-20-1953,Mo Cnj Ca,09:40 am
12-22-1953,Mo Cnj Le,03:23 pm
12-25-1953,Mo Cnj Vi,00:24 am
12-27-1953,Mo Cnj Li,12:11 pm
12-30-1953,Mo Cnj Sc,00:43 am

January 1954
01-01-1954,Mo Cnj Sa,11:40 am
01-03-1954,Mo Cnj Ca,07:46 pm
01-06-1954,Mo Cnj Aq,01:10 am
01-08-1954,Mo Cnj Pi,04:44 am
01-10-1954,Mo Cnj Ar,07:27 am
01-12-1954,Mo Cnj Ta,10:10 am
01-14-1954,Mo Cnj Ge,01:29 pm
01-16-1954,Mo Cnj Ca,06:01 pm
01-19-1954,Mo Cnj Le,00:24 am
01-21-1954,Mo Cnj Vi,09:14 am
01-23-1954,Mo Cnj Li,08:31 pm
01-26-1954,Mo Cnj Sc,09:04 am
01-28-1954,Mo Cnj Sa,08:43 pm
01-31-1954,Mo Cnj Ca,05:27 am

February 1954
02-02-1954,Mo Cnj Aq,10:38 am
02-04-1954,Mo Cnj Pi,01:03 pm
02-06-1954,Mo Cnj Ar,02:14 pm
02-08-1954,Mo Cnj Ta,03:47 pm
02-10-1954,Mo Cnj Ge,06:54 pm
02-13-1954,Mo Cnj Ca,00:10 am
02-15-1954,Mo Cnj Le,07:36 am
02-17-1954,Mo Cnj Vi,05:01 pm
02-20-1954,Mo Cnj Li,04:15 am
02-22-1954,Mo Cnj Sc,04:44 pm
02-25-1954,Mo Cnj Sa,05:00 am
02-27-1954,Mo Cnj Ca,02:58 pm

March 1954
03-01-1954,Mo Cnj Aq,09:07 pm
03-03-1954,Mo Cnj Pi,11:32 pm
03-05-1954,Mo Cnj Ar,11:40 pm
03-07-1954,Mo Cnj Ta,11:33 pm
03-10-1954,Mo Cnj Ge,01:07 am
03-12-1954,Mo Cnj Ca,05:38 am
03-14-1954,Mo Cnj Le,01:18 pm
03-16-1954,Mo Cnj Vi,11:22 pm
03-19-1954,Mo Cnj Li,10:58 am
03-21-1954,Mo Cnj Sc,11:26 pm
03-24-1954,Mo Cnj Sa,11:56 am
03-26-1954,Mo Cnj Ca,10:55 pm
03-29-1954,Mo Cnj Aq,06:38 am
03-31-1954,Mo Cnj Pi,10:17 am

April 1954
04-02-1954,Mo Cnj Ar,10:41 am
04-04-1954,Mo Cnj Ta,09:44 am
04-06-1954,Mo Cnj Ge,09:41 am
04-08-1954,Mo Cnj Ca,12:29 pm
04-10-1954,Mo Cnj Le,07:06 pm
04-13-1954,Mo Cnj Vi,05:03 am
04-15-1954,Mo Cnj Li,04:58 pm
04-18-1954,Mo Cnj Sc,05:32 am
04-20-1954,Mo Cnj Sa,05:55 pm
04-23-1954,Mo Cnj Ca,05:12 am
04-25-1954,Mo Cnj Aq,02:03 pm
04-27-1954,Mo Cnj Pi,07:22 pm
04-29-1954,Mo Cnj Ar,09:09 pm

May 1954
05-01-1954,Mo Cnj Ta,08:43 pm
05-03-1954,Mo Cnj Ge,08:07 pm
05-05-1954,Mo Cnj Ca,09:30 pm
05-08-1954,Mo Cnj Le,02:29 am
05-10-1954,Mo Cnj Vi,11:23 am
05-12-1954,Mo Cnj Li,11:04 pm
05-15-1954,Mo Cnj Sc,11:42 am
05-17-1954,Mo Cnj Sa,11:54 pm
05-20-1954,Mo Cnj Ca,10:50 am
05-22-1954,Mo Cnj Aq,07:49 pm
05-25-1954,Mo Cnj Pi,02:09 am
05-27-1954,Mo Cnj Ar,05:32 am
05-29-1954,Mo Cnj Ta,06:34 am
05-31-1954,Mo Cnj Ge,06:41 am

June 1954
06-02-1954,Mo Cnj Ca,07:46 am
06-04-1954,Mo Cnj Le,11:34 am
06-06-1954,Mo Cnj Vi,07:06 pm
06-09-1954,Mo Cnj Li,06:00 am
06-11-1954,Mo Cnj Sc,06:31 pm
06-14-1954,Mo Cnj Sa,06:38 am
06-16-1954,Mo Cnj Ca,05:06 pm
06-19-1954,Mo Cnj Aq,01:26 am
06-21-1954,Mo Cnj Pi,07:37 am
06-23-1954,Mo Cnj Ar,11:44 am
06-25-1954,Mo Cnj Ta,02:09 pm
06-27-1954,Mo Cnj Ge,03:42 pm
06-29-1954,Mo Cnj Ca,05:36 pm

July 1954
07-01-1954,Mo Cnj Le,09:17 pm
07-04-1954,Mo Cnj Vi,03:57 am
07-06-1954,Mo Cnj Li,01:54 pm
07-09-1954,Mo Cnj Sc,02:04 am
07-11-1954,Mo Cnj Sa,02:19 pm
07-14-1954,Mo Cnj Ca,00:40 am
07-16-1954,Mo Cnj Aq,08:19 am
07-18-1954,Mo Cnj Pi,01:33 pm
07-20-1954,Mo Cnj Ar,05:07 pm
07-22-1954,Mo Cnj Ta,07:53 pm
07-24-1954,Mo Cnj Ge,10:31 pm
07-27-1954,Mo Cnj Ca,01:42 am
07-29-1954,Mo Cnj Le,06:11 am
07-31-1954,Mo Cnj Vi,12:50 pm

August 1954
08-02-1954,Mo Cnj Li,10:14 pm
08-05-1954,Mo Cnj Sc,10:03 am
08-07-1954,Mo Cnj Sa,10:32 pm
08-10-1954,Mo Cnj Ca,09:20 am
08-12-1954,Mo Cnj Aq,04:54 pm
08-14-1954,Mo Cnj Pi,09:17 pm
08-16-1954,Mo Cnj Ar,11:38 pm
08-19-1954,Mo Cnj Ta,01:27 am
08-21-1954,Mo Cnj Ge,03:57 am
08-23-1954,Mo Cnj Ca,07:50 am
08-25-1954,Mo Cnj Le,01:22 pm
08-27-1954,Mo Cnj Vi,08:44 pm
08-30-1954,Mo Cnj Li,06:12 am

September 1954

09-01-1954,Mo Cnj Sc,05:48 pm
09-04-1954,Mo Cnj Sa,06:32 am
09-06-1954,Mo Cnj Ca,06:10 pm
09-09-1954,Mo Cnj Aq,02:31 am
09-11-1954,Mo Cnj Pi,06:56 am
09-13-1954,Mo Cnj Ar,08:23 am
09-15-1954,Mo Cnj Ta,08:45 am
09-17-1954,Mo Cnj Ge,09:55 am
09-19-1954,Mo Cnj Ca,01:13 pm
09-21-1954,Mo Cnj Le,07:04 pm
09-24-1954,Mo Cnj Vi,03:10 am
09-26-1954,Mo Cnj Li,01:11 pm
09-29-1954,Mo Cnj Sc,00:52 am

October 1954

10-01-1954,Mo Cnj Sa,01:42 pm
10-04-1954,Mo Cnj Ca,02:05 am
10-06-1954,Mo Cnj Aq,11:46 am
10-08-1954,Mo Cnj Pi,05:17 pm
10-10-1954,Mo Cnj Ar,06:58 pm
10-12-1954,Mo Cnj Ta,06:32 pm
10-14-1954,Mo Cnj Ge,06:10 pm
10-16-1954,Mo Cnj Ca,07:49 pm
10-19-1954,Mo Cnj Le,00:41 am
10-21-1954,Mo Cnj Vi,08:45 am
10-23-1954,Mo Cnj Li,07:13 pm
10-26-1954,Mo Cnj Sc,07:11 am
10-28-1954,Mo Cnj Sa,07:59 pm
10-31-1954,Mo Cnj Ca,08:37 am

November 1954

11-02-1954,Mo Cnj Aq,07:22 pm
11-05-1954,Mo Cnj Pi,02:34 am
11-07-1954,Mo Cnj Ar,05:42 am
11-09-1954,Mo Cnj Ta,05:49 am
11-11-1954,Mo Cnj Ge,04:51 am
11-13-1954,Mo Cnj Ca,04:59 am
11-15-1954,Mo Cnj Le,08:03 am
11-17-1954,Mo Cnj Vi,02:53 pm
11-20-1954,Mo Cnj Li,01:03 am
11-22-1954,Mo Cnj Sc,01:14 pm
11-25-1954,Mo Cnj Sa,02:02 am
11-27-1954,Mo Cnj Ca,02:24 pm
11-30-1954,Mo Cnj Aq,01:19 am

December 1954

12-02-1954,Mo Cnj Pi,09:38 am
12-04-1954,Mo Cnj Ar,02:35 pm
12-06-1954,Mo Cnj Ta,04:23 pm
12-08-1954,Mo Cnj Ge,04:17 pm
12-10-1954,Mo Cnj Ca,04:07 pm
12-12-1954,Mo Cnj Le,05:49 pm
12-14-1954,Mo Cnj Vi,10:54 pm
12-17-1954,Mo Cnj Li,07:52 pm
12-19-1954,Mo Cnj Sc,07:43 pm
12-22-1954,Mo Cnj Sa,08:35 am
12-24-1954,Mo Cnj Ca,08:40 pm
12-27-1954,Mo Cnj Aq,07:01 am
12-29-1954,Mo Cnj Pi,03:10 pm
12-31-1954,Mo Cnj Ar,08:57 pm

January 1955

01-03-1955,Mo Cnj Ta,00:25 am
01-05-1955,Mo Cnj Ge,02:05 am
01-07-1955,Mo Cnj Ca,03:01 am
01-09-1955,Mo Cnj Le,04:41 am
01-11-1955,Mo Cnj Vi,08:43 am
01-13-1955,Mo Cnj Li,04:15 pm
01-16-1955,Mo Cnj Sc,03:14 am
01-18-1955,Mo Cnj Sa,04:01 pm
01-21-1955,Mo Cnj Ca,04:09 am
01-23-1955,Mo Cnj Aq,01:59 pm
01-25-1955,Mo Cnj Pi,09:12 pm
01-28-1955,Mo Cnj Ar,02:20 am
01-30-1955,Mo Cnj Ta,06:07 am

February 1955

02-01-1955,Mo Cnj Ge,09:03 am
02-03-1955,Mo Cnj Ca,11:36 am
02-05-1955,Mo Cnj Le,02:28 pm
02-07-1955,Mo Cnj Vi,06:43 pm
02-10-1955,Mo Cnj Li,01:33 am
02-12-1955,Mo Cnj Sc,11:39 am
02-15-1955,Mo Cnj Sa,00:08 am
02-17-1955,Mo Cnj Ca,12:35 pm
02-19-1955,Mo Cnj Aq,10:34 pm
02-22-1955,Mo Cnj Pi,05:10 am
02-24-1955,Mo Cnj Ar,09:06 am
02-26-1955,Mo Cnj Ta,11:46 am
02-28-1955,Mo Cnj Ge,02:24 pm

March 1955

03-02-1955,Mo Cnj Ca,05:40 pm
03-04-1955,Mo Cnj Le,09:49 pm
03-07-1955,Mo Cnj Vi,03:09 am
03-09-1955,Mo Cnj Li,10:20 am
03-11-1955,Mo Cnj Sc,08:05 pm
03-14-1955,Mo Cnj Sa,08:14 am
03-16-1955,Mo Cnj Ca,09:02 pm
03-19-1955,Mo Cnj Aq,07:47 am
03-21-1955,Mo Cnj Pi,02:45 pm
03-23-1955,Mo Cnj Ar,06:09 pm
03-25-1955,Mo Cnj Ta,07:31 pm
03-27-1955,Mo Cnj Ge,08:42 pm
03-29-1955,Mo Cnj Ca,11:05 pm

April 1955

04-01-1955,Mo Cnj Le,03:21 am
04-03-1955,Mo Cnj Vi,09:32 am
04-05-1955,Mo Cnj Li,05:34 pm
04-08-1955,Mo Cnj Sc,03:39 am
04-10-1955,Mo Cnj Sa,03:42 am
04-13-1955,Mo Cnj Ca,04:41 am
04-15-1955,Mo Cnj Aq,04:20 pm
04-18-1955,Mo Cnj Pi,00:28 am
04-20-1955,Mo Cnj Ar,04:30 am
04-22-1955,Mo Cnj Ta,05:30 am
04-24-1955,Mo Cnj Ge,05:24 am
04-26-1955,Mo Cnj Ca,06:09 am
04-28-1955,Mo Cnj Le,09:09 am
04-30-1955,Mo Cnj Vi,02:58 pm

May 1955

05-02-1955,Mo Cnj Li,11:26 pm
05-05-1955,Mo Cnj Sc,10:04 am
05-07-1955,Mo Cnj Sa,10:19 pm
05-10-1955,Mo Cnj Ca,11:19 am
05-12-1955,Mo Cnj Aq,11:29 pm
05-15-1955,Mo Cnj Pi,08:53 am
05-17-1955,Mo Cnj Ar,02:21 pm
05-19-1955,Mo Cnj Ta,04:12 pm
05-21-1955,Mo Cnj Ge,03:57 pm
05-23-1955,Mo Cnj Ca,03:33 pm
05-25-1955,Mo Cnj Le,04:53 pm
05-27-1955,Mo Cnj Vi,09:16 pm
05-30-1955,Mo Cnj Li,05:08 am

June 1955

06-01-1955,Mo Cnj Sc,03:54 pm
06-04-1955,Mo Cnj Sa,04:24 am
06-06-1955,Mo Cnj Ca,05:21 pm
06-09-1955,Mo Cnj Aq,05:30 am
06-11-1955,Mo Cnj Pi,03:33 pm
06-13-1955,Mo Cnj Ar,10:25 pm
06-16-1955,Mo Cnj Ta,01:51 am
06-18-1955,Mo Cnj Ge,02:37 am
06-20-1955,Mo Cnj Ca,02:15 am
06-22-1955,Mo Cnj Le,02:36 am
06-24-1955,Mo Cnj Vi,05:26 am
06-26-1955,Mo Cnj Li,11:55 am
06-28-1955,Mo Cnj Sc,10:05 pm

July 1955

07-01-1955,Mo Cnj Sa,10:35 am
07-03-1955,Mo Cnj Ca,11:30 pm
07-06-1955,Mo Cnj Aq,11:19 am
07-08-1955,Mo Cnj Pi,09:09 pm
07-11-1955,Mo Cnj Ar,04:33 am
07-13-1955,Mo Cnj Ta,09:20 am
07-15-1955,Mo Cnj Ge,11:43 am
07-17-1955,Mo Cnj Ca,12:30 pm
07-19-1955,Mo Cnj Le,01:03 pm
07-21-1955,Mo Cnj Vi,03:06 pm
07-23-1955,Mo Cnj Li,08:16 pm
07-26-1955,Mo Cnj Sc,05:19 am
07-28-1955,Mo Cnj Sa,05:25 pm
07-31-1955,Mo Cnj Ca,06:19 am

August 1955

08-02-1955,Mo Cnj Aq,05:52 pm
08-05-1955,Mo Cnj Pi,03:04 am
08-07-1955,Mo Cnj Ar,09:59 am
08-09-1955,Mo Cnj Ta,03:03 pm
08-11-1955,Mo Cnj Ge,06:33 pm
08-13-1955,Mo Cnj Ca,08:51 pm
08-15-1955,Mo Cnj Le,10:34 pm
08-18-1955,Mo Cnj Vi,00:58 am
08-20-1955,Mo Cnj Li,05:34 am
08-22-1955,Mo Cnj Sc,01:38 pm
08-25-1955,Mo Cnj Sa,01:04 am
08-27-1955,Mo Cnj Ca,01:57 pm
08-30-1955,Mo Cnj Aq,01:35 am

September 1955
09-01-1955,Mo Cnj Pi,10:23 am
09-03-1955,Mo Cnj Ar,04:24 pm
09-05-1955,Mo Cnj Ta,08:37 pm
09-07-1955,Mo Cnj Ge,11:59 pm
09-10-1955,Mo Cnj Ca,03:01 am
09-12-1955,Mo Cnj Le,06:03 am
09-14-1955,Mo Cnj Vi,09:34 am
09-16-1955,Mo Cnj Li,02:36 pm
09-18-1955,Mo Cnj Sc,10:19 pm
09-21-1955,Mo Cnj Sa,09:11 am
09-23-1955,Mo Cnj Ca,10:01 pm
09-26-1955,Mo Cnj Aq,10:07 am
09-28-1955,Mo Cnj Pi,07:13 pm

October 1955
10-01-1955,Mo Cnj Ar,00:47 am
10-03-1955,Mo Cnj Ta,03:52 am
10-05-1955,Mo Cnj Ge,06:00 am
10-07-1955,Mo Cnj Ca,08:23 am
10-09-1955,Mo Cnj Le,11:42 am
10-11-1955,Mo Cnj Vi,04:11 pm
10-13-1955,Mo Cnj Li,10:13 pm
10-16-1955,Mo Cnj Sc,06:23 am
10-18-1955,Mo Cnj Sa,05:08 pm
10-21-1955,Mo Cnj Ca,05:52 am
10-23-1955,Mo Cnj Aq,06:33 pm
10-26-1955,Mo Cnj Pi,04:38 am
10-28-1955,Mo Cnj Ar,10:47 am
10-30-1955,Mo Cnj Ta,01:30 pm

November 1955
11-01-1955,Mo Cnj Ge,02:23 pm
11-03-1955,Mo Cnj Ca,03:11 pm
11-05-1955,Mo Cnj Le,05:20 pm
11-07-1955,Mo Cnj Vi,09:36 pm
11-10-1955,Mo Cnj Li,04:15 am
11-12-1955,Mo Cnj Sc,01:12 pm
11-15-1955,Mo Cnj Sa,00:17 am
11-17-1955,Mo Cnj Ca,01:00 pm
11-20-1955,Mo Cnj Aq,01:59 am
11-22-1955,Mo Cnj Pi,01:11 pm
11-24-1955,Mo Cnj Ar,08:48 pm
11-27-1955,Mo Cnj Ta,00:27 am
11-29-1955,Mo Cnj Ge,01:11 am

December 1955
12-01-1955,Mo Cnj Ca,00:46 am
12-03-1955,Mo Cnj Le,01:07 am
12-05-1955,Mo Cnj Vi,03:50 am
12-07-1955,Mo Cnj Li,09:49 am
12-09-1955,Mo Cnj Sc,07:00 pm
12-12-1955,Mo Cnj Sa,06:34 am
12-14-1955,Mo Cnj Ca,07:24 pm
12-17-1955,Mo Cnj Aq,08:20 am
12-19-1955,Mo Cnj Pi,08:02 pm
12-22-1955,Mo Cnj Ar,05:05 am
12-24-1955,Mo Cnj Ta,10:33 am
12-26-1955,Mo Cnj Ge,12:33 pm
12-28-1955,Mo Cnj Ca,12:18 pm
12-30-1955,Mo Cnj Le,11:37 am

January 1956
01-01-1956,Mo Cnj Vi,12:31 pm
01-03-1956,Mo Cnj Li,04:45 pm
01-06-1956,Mo Cnj Sc,01:01 am
01-08-1956,Mo Cnj Sa,12:33 pm
01-11-1956,Mo Cnj Ca,01:34 am
01-13-1956,Mo Cnj Aq,02:20 pm
01-16-1956,Mo Cnj Pi,01:47 am
01-18-1956,Mo Cnj Ar,11:17 am
01-20-1956,Mo Cnj Ta,06:11 pm
01-22-1956,Mo Cnj Ge,10:06 pm
01-24-1956,Mo Cnj Ca,11:20 pm
01-26-1956,Mo Cnj Le,11:07 pm
01-28-1956,Mo Cnj Vi,11:18 pm
01-31-1956,Mo Cnj Li,01:56 am

February 1956
02-02-1956,Mo Cnj Sc,08:33 am
02-04-1956,Mo Cnj Sa,07:13 pm
02-07-1956,Mo Cnj Ca,08:08 am
02-09-1956,Mo Cnj Aq,08:52 am
02-12-1956,Mo Cnj Pi,07:52 am
02-14-1956,Mo Cnj Ar,04:49 pm
02-16-1956,Mo Cnj Ta,11:49 pm
02-19-1956,Mo Cnj Ge,04:51 am
02-21-1956,Mo Cnj Ca,07:51 am
02-23-1956,Mo Cnj Le,09:11 am
02-25-1956,Mo Cnj Vi,10:05 am
02-27-1956,Mo Cnj Li,12:20 pm
02-29-1956,Mo Cnj Sc,05:45 pm

March 1956

03-03-1956,Mo Cnj Sa,03:09 am
03-05-1956,Mo Cnj Ca,03:33 pm
03-08-1956,Mo Cnj Aq,04:20 am
03-10-1956,Mo Cnj Pi,03:12 pm
03-12-1956,Mo Cnj Ar,11:27 pm
03-15-1956,Mo Cnj Ta,05:33 am
03-17-1956,Mo Cnj Ge,10:12 am
03-19-1956,Mo Cnj Ca,01:48 pm
03-21-1956,Mo Cnj Le,04:31 pm
03-23-1956,Mo Cnj Vi,06:53 pm
03-25-1956,Mo Cnj Li,10:00 pm
03-28-1956,Mo Cnj Sc,03:19 am
03-30-1956,Mo Cnj Sa,11:56 am

April 1956

04-01-1956,Mo Cnj Ca,11:38 pm
04-04-1956,Mo Cnj Aq,12:25 pm
04-06-1956,Mo Cnj Pi,11:38 pm
04-09-1956,Mo Cnj Ar,07:47 am
04-11-1956,Mo Cnj Ta,01:03 pm
04-13-1956,Mo Cnj Ge,04:31 pm
04-15-1956,Mo Cnj Ca,07:15 pm
04-17-1956,Mo Cnj Le,10:00 pm
04-20-1956,Mo Cnj Vi,01:17 am
04-22-1956,Mo Cnj Li,05:37 am
04-24-1956,Mo Cnj Sc,11:45 am
04-26-1956,Mo Cnj Sa,08:26 pm
04-29-1956,Mo Cnj Ca,07:45 am

May 1956

05-01-1956,Mo Cnj Aq,08:28 pm
05-04-1956,Mo Cnj Pi,08:16 am
05-06-1956,Mo Cnj Ar,05:05 pm
05-08-1956,Mo Cnj Ta,10:24 pm
05-11-1956,Mo Cnj Ge,01:01 am
05-13-1956,Mo Cnj Ca,02:21 am
05-15-1956,Mo Cnj Le,03:52 am
05-17-1956,Mo Cnj Vi,06:40 am
05-19-1956,Mo Cnj Li,11:26 am
05-21-1956,Mo Cnj Sc,06:27 pm
05-24-1956,Mo Cnj Sa,03:47 am
05-26-1956,Mo Cnj Ca,03:11 pm
05-29-1956,Mo Cnj Aq,03:52 am
05-31-1956,Mo Cnj Pi,04:09 pm

June 1956

06-03-1956,Mo Cnj Ar,02:05 am
06-05-1956,Mo Cnj Ta,08:22 am
06-07-1956,Mo Cnj Ge,11:10 am
06-09-1956,Mo Cnj Ca,11:43 am
06-11-1956,Mo Cnj Le,11:46 am
06-13-1956,Mo Cnj Vi,01:04 pm
06-15-1956,Mo Cnj Li,04:59 pm
06-18-1956,Mo Cnj Sc,00:03 am
06-20-1956,Mo Cnj Sa,09:55 am
06-22-1956,Mo Cnj Ca,09:43 pm
06-25-1956,Mo Cnj Aq,10:25 am
06-27-1956,Mo Cnj Pi,10:54 pm
06-30-1956,Mo Cnj Ar,09:43 am

July 1956

07-02-1956,Mo Cnj Ta,05:26 pm
07-04-1956,Mo Cnj Ge,09:27 pm
07-06-1956,Mo Cnj Ca,10:20 pm
07-08-1956,Mo Cnj Le,09:43 pm
07-10-1956,Mo Cnj Vi,09:35 pm
07-12-1956,Mo Cnj Li,11:54 pm
07-15-1956,Mo Cnj Sc,05:56 am
07-17-1956,Mo Cnj Sa,03:38 pm
07-20-1956,Mo Cnj Ca,03:41 am
07-22-1956,Mo Cnj Aq,04:29 pm
07-25-1956,Mo Cnj Pi,04:51 am
07-27-1956,Mo Cnj Ar,03:54 pm
07-30-1956,Mo Cnj Ta,00:41 am

August 1956

08-01-1956,Mo Cnj Ge,06:17 am
08-03-1956,Mo Cnj Ca,08:32 am
08-05-1956,Mo Cnj Le,08:27 am
08-07-1956,Mo Cnj Vi,07:49 am
08-09-1956,Mo Cnj Li,08:50 am
08-11-1956,Mo Cnj Sc,01:20 pm
08-13-1956,Mo Cnj Sa,10:00 pm
08-16-1956,Mo Cnj Ca,09:48 am
08-18-1956,Mo Cnj Aq,10:38 pm
08-21-1956,Mo Cnj Pi,10:48 am
08-23-1956,Mo Cnj Ar,09:30 pm
08-26-1956,Mo Cnj Ta,06:24 am
08-28-1956,Mo Cnj Ge,12:59 pm
08-30-1956,Mo Cnj Ca,04:51 pm

September 1956

09-01-1956,Mo Cnj Le,06:14 pm
09-03-1956,Mo Cnj Vi,06:20 pm
09-05-1956,Mo Cnj Li,07:05 pm
09-07-1956,Mo Cnj Sc,10:27 pm
09-10-1956,Mo Cnj Sa,05:47 am
09-12-1956,Mo Cnj Ca,04:46 pm
09-15-1956,Mo Cnj Aq,05:28 am
09-17-1956,Mo Cnj Pi,05:34 pm
09-20-1956,Mo Cnj Ar,03:47 am
09-22-1956,Mo Cnj Ta,12:01 pm
09-24-1956,Mo Cnj Ge,06:25 pm
09-26-1956,Mo Cnj Ca,11:00 pm
09-29-1956,Mo Cnj Le,01:49 am

October 1956

10-01-1956,Mo Cnj Vi,03:25 am
10-03-1956,Mo Cnj Li,05:02 am
10-05-1956,Mo Cnj Sc,08:20 am
10-07-1956,Mo Cnj Sa,02:47 pm
10-10-1956,Mo Cnj Ca,00:48 am
10-12-1956,Mo Cnj Aq,01:09 pm
10-15-1956,Mo Cnj Pi,01:25 am
10-17-1956,Mo Cnj Ar,11:35 am
10-19-1956,Mo Cnj Ta,07:07 pm
10-22-1956,Mo Cnj Ge,00:29 am
10-24-1956,Mo Cnj Ca,04:24 am
10-26-1956,Mo Cnj Le,07:28 am
10-28-1956,Mo Cnj Vi,10:10 am
10-30-1956,Mo Cnj Li,01:10 pm

November 1956

11-01-1956,Mo Cnj Sc,05:25 pm
11-03-1956,Mo Cnj Sa,11:56 pm
11-06-1956,Mo Cnj Ca,09:24 am
11-08-1956,Mo Cnj Aq,09:19 pm
11-11-1956,Mo Cnj Pi,09:51 am
11-13-1956,Mo Cnj Ar,08:37 pm
11-16-1956,Mo Cnj Ta,04:13 am
11-18-1956,Mo Cnj Ge,08:46 am
11-20-1956,Mo Cnj Ca,11:18 am
11-22-1956,Mo Cnj Le,01:11 pm
11-24-1956,Mo Cnj Vi,03:32 pm
11-26-1956,Mo Cnj Li,07:11 pm
11-29-1956,Mo Cnj Sc,00:34 am

December 1956

12-01-1956,Mo Cnj Sa,07:59 am
12-03-1956,Mo Cnj Ca,05:36 pm
12-06-1956,Mo Cnj Aq,05:17 am
12-08-1956,Mo Cnj Pi,05:57 pm
12-11-1956,Mo Cnj Ar,05:38 am
12-13-1956,Mo Cnj Ta,02:16 pm
12-15-1956,Mo Cnj Ge,07:07 pm
12-17-1956,Mo Cnj Ca,08:52 pm
12-19-1956,Mo Cnj Le,09:11 pm
12-21-1956,Mo Cnj Vi,09:56 pm
12-24-1956,Mo Cnj Li,00:39 am
12-26-1956,Mo Cnj Sc,06:09 am
12-28-1956,Mo Cnj Sa,02:20 pm

January 1957

01-02-1957,Mo Cnj Aq,12:25 pm
01-05-1957,Mo Cnj Pi,01:05 am
01-07-1957,Mo Cnj Ar,01:23 pm
01-09-1957,Mo Cnj Ta,11:27 pm
01-12-1957,Mo Cnj Ge,05:44 am
01-14-1957,Mo Cnj Ca,08:06 am
01-16-1957,Mo Cnj Le,07:50 am
01-18-1957,Mo Cnj Vi,07:04 am
01-20-1957,Mo Cnj Li,07:55 am
01-22-1957,Mo Cnj Sc,12:03 pm
01-24-1957,Mo Cnj Sa,07:53 am
01-27-1957,Mo Cnj Ca,06:33 am
01-29-1957,Mo Cnj Aq,06:43 pm

February 1957

02-01-1957,Mo Cnj Pi,07:21 am
02-03-1957,Mo Cnj Ar,07:42 pm
02-06-1957,Mo Cnj Ta,06:37 am
02-08-1957,Mo Cnj Ge,02:35 pm
02-10-1957,Mo Cnj Ca,06:39 pm
02-12-1957,Mo Cnj Le,07:19 pm
02-14-1957,Mo Cnj Vi,06:17 pm
02-16-1957,Mo Cnj Li,05:50 pm
02-18-1957,Mo Cnj Sc,08:06 pm
02-21-1957,Mo Cnj Sa,02:24 am
02-23-1957,Mo Cnj Ca,12:27 pm
02-26-1957,Mo Cnj Aq,00:43 am
02-28-1957,Mo Cnj Pi,01:25 pm

March 1957

03-03-1957,Mo Cnj Ar,01:31 am
03-05-1957,Mo Cnj Ta,12:21 pm

03-07-1957,Mo Cnj Ge,09:04 pm
03-10-1957,Mo Cnj Ca,02:46 am
03-12-1957,Mo Cnj Le,05:12 am
03-14-1957,Mo Cnj Vi,05:20 am
03-16-1957,Mo Cnj Li,04:59 am
03-18-1957,Mo Cnj Sc,06:15 am
03-20-1957,Mo Cnj Sa,10:54 am
03-22-1957,Mo Cnj Ca,07:34 pm
03-25-1957,Mo Cnj Aq,07:17 am
03-27-1957,Mo Cnj Pi,08:00 pm
03-30-1957,Mo Cnj Ar,07:55 am

April 1957
04-01-1957,Mo Cnj Ta,06:12 pm
04-04-1957,Mo Cnj Ge,02:31 am
04-06-1957,Mo Cnj Ca,08:38 am
04-08-1957,Mo Cnj Le,12:25 pm
04-10-1957,Mo Cnj Vi,02:13 pm
04-12-1957,Mo Cnj Li,03:09 pm
04-14-1957,Mo Cnj Sc,04:45 pm
04-16-1957,Mo Cnj Sa,08:43 pm
04-19-1957,Mo Cnj Ca,04:08 am
04-21-1957,Mo Cnj Aq,02:54 pm
04-24-1957,Mo Cnj Pi,03:23 am
04-26-1957,Mo Cnj Ar,03:22 pm
04-29-1957,Mo Cnj Ta,01:18 am

May 1957
05-01-1957,Mo Cnj Ge,08:47 am
05-03-1957,Mo Cnj Ca,02:09 pm
05-05-1957,Mo Cnj Le,05:54 pm
05-07-1957,Mo Cnj Vi,08:37 pm
05-09-1957,Mo Cnj Li,10:57 pm
05-12-1957,Mo Cnj Sc,01:48 am
05-14-1957,Mo Cnj Sa,06:14 am
05-16-1957,Mo Cnj Ca,01:14 pm
05-18-1957,Mo Cnj Aq,11:13 pm
05-21-1957,Mo Cnj Pi,11:21 am
05-23-1957,Mo Cnj Ar,11:34 pm
05-26-1957,Mo Cnj Ta,09:43 am
05-28-1957,Mo Cnj Ge,04:47 pm
05-30-1957,Mo Cnj Ca,09:06 pm

June 1957
06-01-1957,Mo Cnj Le,11:45 pm
06-04-1957,Mo Cnj Vi,01:59 am
06-06-1957,Mo Cnj Li,04:46 am

06-08-1957,Mo Cnj Sc,08:41 am
06-10-1957,Mo Cnj Sa,02:10 pm
06-12-1957,Mo Cnj Ca,09:37 pm
06-15-1957,Mo Cnj Aq,07:24 am
06-17-1957,Mo Cnj Pi,07:15 pm
06-20-1957,Mo Cnj Ar,07:46 am
06-22-1957,Mo Cnj Ta,06:38 pm
06-25-1957,Mo Cnj Ge,02:07 am
06-27-1957,Mo Cnj Ca,06:01 am
06-29-1957,Mo Cnj Le,07:31 am

July 1957
07-01-1957,Mo Cnj Vi,08:24 am
07-03-1957,Mo Cnj Li,10:17 am
07-05-1957,Mo Cnj Sc,02:11 pm
07-07-1957,Mo Cnj Sa,08:21 pm
07-10-1957,Mo Cnj Ca,04:35 am
07-12-1957,Mo Cnj Aq,02:43 pm
07-15-1957,Mo Cnj Pi,02:32 am
07-17-1957,Mo Cnj Ar,03:14 pm
07-20-1957,Mo Cnj Ta,02:58 am
07-22-1957,Mo Cnj Ge,11:34 am
07-24-1957,Mo Cnj Ca,04:06 pm
07-26-1957,Mo Cnj Le,05:17 pm
07-28-1957,Mo Cnj Vi,05:00 pm
07-30-1957,Mo Cnj Li,05:20 pm

August 1957
08-01-1957,Mo Cnj Sc,08:01 pm
08-04-1957,Mo Cnj Sa,01:47 am
08-06-1957,Mo Cnj Ca,10:23 am
08-08-1957,Mo Cnj Aq,09:01 pm
08-11-1957,Mo Cnj Pi,09:02 am
08-13-1957,Mo Cnj Ar,09:46 pm
08-16-1957,Mo Cnj Ta,10:01 am
08-18-1957,Mo Cnj Ge,07:52 pm
08-21-1957,Mo Cnj Ca,01:49 am
08-23-1957,Mo Cnj Le,03:52 am
08-25-1957,Mo Cnj Vi,03:26 am
08-27-1957,Mo Cnj Li,02:41 am
08-29-1957,Mo Cnj Sc,03:45 am
08-31-1957,Mo Cnj Sa,08:07 am

September 1957
09-02-1957,Mo Cnj Ca,04:05 pm
09-05-1957,Mo Cnj Aq,02:50 am
09-07-1957,Mo Cnj Pi,03:04 pm

09-10-1957,Mo Cnj Ar,03:45 am
09-12-1957,Mo Cnj Ta,03:58 pm
09-15-1957,Mo Cnj Ge,02:27 am
09-17-1957,Mo Cnj Ca,09:50 am
09-19-1957,Mo Cnj Le,01:31 pm
09-21-1957,Mo Cnj Vi,02:11 pm
09-23-1957,Mo Cnj Li,01:32 pm
09-25-1957,Mo Cnj Sc,01:40 pm
09-27-1957,Mo Cnj Sa,04:27 pm
09-29-1957,Mo Cnj Ca,11:00 pm

October 1957
10-02-1957,Mo Cnj Aq,09:05 am
10-04-1957,Mo Cnj Pi,09:18 pm
10-07-1957,Mo Cnj Ar,09:57 am
10-09-1957,Mo Cnj Ta,09:48 pm
10-12-1957,Mo Cnj Ge,08:01 am
10-14-1957,Mo Cnj Ca,03:54 pm
10-16-1957,Mo Cnj Le,08:59 pm
10-18-1957,Mo Cnj Vi,11:24 pm
10-21-1957,Mo Cnj Li,00:03 am
10-23-1957,Mo Cnj Sc,00:31 am
10-25-1957,Mo Cnj Sa,02:34 am
10-27-1957,Mo Cnj Ca,07:42 am
10-29-1957,Mo Cnj Aq,04:33 pm

November 1957
11-01-1957,Mo Cnj Pi,04:19 am
11-03-1957,Mo Cnj Ar,05:00 pm
11-06-1957,Mo Cnj Ta,04:38 am
11-08-1957,Mo Cnj Ge,02:09 pm
11-10-1957,Mo Cnj Ca,09:24 pm
11-13-1957,Mo Cnj Le,02:36 am
11-15-1957,Mo Cnj Vi,06:08 am
11-17-1957,Mo Cnj Li,08:26 am
11-19-1957,Mo Cnj Sc,10:18 am
11-21-1957,Mo Cnj Sa,12:52 pm
11-23-1957,Mo Cnj Ca,05:30 pm
11-26-1957,Mo Cnj Aq,01:16 am
11-28-1957,Mo Cnj Pi,12:16 pm

December 1957
12-01-1957,Mo Cnj Ar,00:56 am
12-03-1957,Mo Cnj Ta,12:48 pm
12-05-1957,Mo Cnj Ge,10:01 pm
12-08-1957,Mo Cnj Ca,04:16 am
12-10-1957,Mo Cnj Le,08:24 am

12-12-1957,Mo Cnj Vi,11:29 am
12-14-1957,Mo Cnj Li,02:23 pm
12-16-1957,Mo Cnj Sc,05:36 pm
12-18-1957,Mo Cnj Sa,09:31 pm
12-21-1957,Mo Cnj Ca,02:47 am
12-23-1957,Mo Cnj Aq,10:18 am
12-25-1957,Mo Cnj Pi,08:41 pm
12-28-1957,Mo Cnj Ar,09:13 am

January 1958
01-02-1958,Mo Cnj Ge,07:22 am
01-04-1958,Mo Cnj Ca,01:22 pm
01-06-1958,Mo Cnj Le,04:22 pm
01-08-1958,Mo Cnj Vi,05:59 pm
01-10-1958,Mo Cnj Li,07:52 pm
01-12-1958,Mo Cnj Sc,11:02 pm
01-15-1958,Mo Cnj Sa,03:49 am
01-17-1958,Mo Cnj Ca,10:13 am
01-19-1958,Mo Cnj Aq,06:22 pm
01-22-1958,Mo Cnj Pi,04:42 am
01-24-1958,Mo Cnj Ar,05:04 pm
01-27-1958,Mo Cnj Ta,05:57 am

February 1958
02-03-1958,Mo Cnj Le,02:38 am
02-05-1958,Mo Cnj Vi,03:11 am
02-07-1958,Mo Cnj Li,03:23 am
02-09-1958,Mo Cnj Sc,05:03 am
02-11-1958,Mo Cnj Sa,09:11 am
02-13-1958,Mo Cnj Ca,03:56 pm
02-16-1958,Mo Cnj Aq,00:52 am
02-18-1958,Mo Cnj Pi,11:40 am
02-21-1958,Mo Cnj Ar,00:02 am
02-23-1958,Mo Cnj Ta,01:05 pm
02-26-1958,Mo Cnj Ge,00:52 am
02-28-1958,Mo Cnj Ca,09:17 am

March 1958
03-02-1958,Mo Cnj Le,01:27 pm
03-04-1958,Mo Cnj Vi,02:15 pm
03-06-1958,Mo Cnj Li,01:35 pm
03-08-1958,Mo Cnj Sc,01:35 pm
03-10-1958,Mo Cnj Sa,03:57 pm
03-12-1958,Mo Cnj Ca,09:37 pm
03-15-1958,Mo Cnj Aq,06:29 am
03-17-1958,Mo Cnj Pi,05:42 pm
03-20-1958,Mo Cnj Ar,06:17 am

03-22-1958,Mo Cnj Ta,07:15 pm
03-25-1958,Mo Cnj Ge,07:19 am
03-27-1958,Mo Cnj Ca,04:53 pm
03-29-1958,Mo Cnj Le,10:46 pm

April 1958
04-01-1958,Mo Cnj Vi,01:01 am
04-03-1958,Mo Cnj Li,00:54 am
04-05-1958,Mo Cnj Sc,00:17 am
04-07-1958,Mo Cnj Sa,01:07 am
04-09-1958,Mo Cnj Ca,05:01 am
04-11-1958,Mo Cnj Aq,12:42 pm
04-13-1958,Mo Cnj Pi,11:39 pm
04-16-1958,Mo Cnj Ar,12:23 pm
04-19-1958,Mo Cnj Ta,01:16 am
04-21-1958,Mo Cnj Ge,01:03 pm
04-23-1958,Mo Cnj Ca,10:47 pm
04-26-1958,Mo Cnj Le,05:44 am
04-28-1958,Mo Cnj Vi,09:41 am
04-30-1958,Mo Cnj Li,11:07 am

May 1958
05-02-1958,Mo Cnj Sc,11:14 am
05-04-1958,Mo Cnj Sa,11:43 am
05-06-1958,Mo Cnj Ca,02:21 pm
05-08-1958,Mo Cnj Aq,08:29 pm
05-11-1958,Mo Cnj Pi,06:27 am
05-13-1958,Mo Cnj Ar,06:58 pm
05-16-1958,Mo Cnj Ta,07:50 am
05-18-1958,Mo Cnj Ge,07:15 pm
05-21-1958,Mo Cnj Ca,04:24 am
05-23-1958,Mo Cnj Le,11:15 am
05-25-1958,Mo Cnj Vi,04:00 pm
05-27-1958,Mo Cnj Li,06:55 pm
05-29-1958,Mo Cnj Sc,08:33 pm
05-31-1958,Mo Cnj Sa,09:53 pm

June 1958
06-03-1958,Mo Cnj Ca,00:22 am
06-05-1958,Mo Cnj Aq,05:33 am
06-07-1958,Mo Cnj Pi,02:24 pm
06-10-1958,Mo Cnj Ar,02:21 am
06-12-1958,Mo Cnj Ta,03:13 pm
06-15-1958,Mo Cnj Ge,02:32 am
06-17-1958,Mo Cnj Ca,11:04 am
06-19-1958,Mo Cnj Le,05:04 pm
06-21-1958,Mo Cnj Vi,09:22 pm

06-24-1958,Mo Cnj Li,00:42 am
06-26-1958,Mo Cnj Sc,03:30 am
06-28-1958,Mo Cnj Sa,06:12 am
06-30-1958,Mo Cnj Ca,09:33 am

July 1958
07-02-1958,Mo Cnj Aq,02:45 pm
07-04-1958,Mo Cnj Pi,10:57 pm
07-07-1958,Mo Cnj Ar,10:18 am
07-09-1958,Mo Cnj Ta,11:09 pm
07-12-1958,Mo Cnj Ge,10:47 am
07-14-1958,Mo Cnj Ca,07:15 pm
07-17-1958,Mo Cnj Le,00:31 am
07-19-1958,Mo Cnj Vi,03:42 am
07-21-1958,Mo Cnj Li,06:12 am
07-23-1958,Mo Cnj Sc,08:58 am
07-25-1958,Mo Cnj Sa,12:26 pm
07-27-1958,Mo Cnj Ca,04:54 pm
07-29-1958,Mo Cnj Aq,10:53 pm

August 1958
08-01-1958,Mo Cnj Pi,07:12 am
08-03-1958,Mo Cnj Ar,06:14 pm
08-06-1958,Mo Cnj Ta,07:04 am
08-08-1958,Mo Cnj Ge,07:16 pm
08-11-1958,Mo Cnj Ca,04:25 am
08-13-1958,Mo Cnj Le,09:44 am
08-15-1958,Mo Cnj Vi,12:07 pm
08-17-1958,Mo Cnj Li,01:17 pm
08-19-1958,Mo Cnj Sc,02:50 pm
08-21-1958,Mo Cnj Sa,05:49 pm
08-23-1958,Mo Cnj Ca,10:39 pm
08-26-1958,Mo Cnj Aq,05:28 am
08-28-1958,Mo Cnj Pi,02:25 pm
08-31-1958,Mo Cnj Ar,01:35 am

September 1958
09-02-1958,Mo Cnj Ta,02:24 pm
09-05-1958,Mo Cnj Ge,03:07 am
09-07-1958,Mo Cnj Ca,01:23 pm
09-09-1958,Mo Cnj Le,07:42 pm
09-11-1958,Mo Cnj Vi,10:20 pm
09-13-1958,Mo Cnj Li,10:45 pm
09-15-1958,Mo Cnj Sc,10:50 pm
09-18-1958,Mo Cnj Sa,00:16 am
09-20-1958,Mo Cnj Ca,04:13 am
09-22-1958,Mo Cnj Aq,11:03 am

09-24-1958,Mo Cnj Pi,08:33 pm
09-27-1958,Mo Cnj Ar,08:07 am
09-29-1958,Mo Cnj Ta,08:58 pm

October 1958
10-02-1958,Mo Cnj Ge,09:51 am
10-04-1958,Mo Cnj Ca,09:01 pm
10-07-1958,Mo Cnj Le,04:51 am
10-09-1958,Mo Cnj Vi,08:50 am
10-11-1958,Mo Cnj Li,09:44 am
10-13-1958,Mo Cnj Sc,09:11 am
10-15-1958,Mo Cnj Sa,09:09 am
10-17-1958,Mo Cnj Ca,11:22 am
10-19-1958,Mo Cnj Aq,05:04 pm
10-22-1958,Mo Cnj Pi,02:20 am
10-24-1958,Mo Cnj Ar,02:11 pm
10-27-1958,Mo Cnj Ta,03:08 am
10-29-1958,Mo Cnj Ge,03:50 pm

November 1958
11-01-1958,Mo Cnj Ca,03:09 am
11-03-1958,Mo Cnj Le,12:03 pm
11-05-1958,Mo Cnj Vi,05:46 pm
11-07-1958,Mo Cnj Li,08:16 pm
11-09-1958,Mo Cnj Sc,08:30 pm
11-11-1958,Mo Cnj Sa,08:03 pm
11-13-1958,Mo Cnj Ca,08:55 pm
11-16-1958,Mo Cnj Aq,00:53 am
11-18-1958,Mo Cnj Pi,08:57 am
11-20-1958,Mo Cnj Ar,08:29 pm
11-23-1958,Mo Cnj Ta,09:31 am
11-25-1958,Mo Cnj Ge,10:01 pm
11-28-1958,Mo Cnj Ca,08:51 am
11-30-1958,Mo Cnj Le,05:41 pm

December 1958
12-03-1958,Mo Cnj Vi,00:18 am
12-05-1958,Mo Cnj Li,04:31 am
12-07-1958,Mo Cnj Sc,06:29 am
12-09-1958,Mo Cnj Sa,07:02 am
12-11-1958,Mo Cnj Ca,07:47 am
12-13-1958,Mo Cnj Aq,10:38 am
12-15-1958,Mo Cnj Pi,05:12 pm
12-18-1958,Mo Cnj Ar,03:46 am
12-20-1958,Mo Cnj Ta,04:37 pm
12-23-1958,Mo Cnj Ge,05:09 am
12-25-1958,Mo Cnj Ca,03:33 pm

12-27-1958,Mo Cnj Le,11:33 pm
12-30-1958,Mo Cnj Vi,05:41 am

January 1959
01-01-1959,Mo Cnj Li,10:22 am
01-03-1959,Mo Cnj Sc,01:43 pm
01-05-1959,Mo Cnj Sa,03:56 pm
01-07-1959,Mo Cnj Ca,05:50 pm
01-09-1959,Mo Cnj Aq,08:52 pm
01-12-1959,Mo Cnj Pi,02:40 am
01-14-1959,Mo Cnj Ar,12:09 pm
01-17-1959,Mo Cnj Ta,00:33 am
01-19-1959,Mo Cnj Ge,01:16 pm
01-21-1959,Mo Cnj Ca,11:47 pm
01-24-1959,Mo Cnj Le,07:14 am
01-26-1959,Mo Cnj Vi,12:14 pm
01-28-1959,Mo Cnj Li,03:55 pm
01-30-1959,Mo Cnj Sc,07:06 pm

February 1959
02-01-1959,Mo Cnj Sa,10:11 pm
02-04-1959,Mo Cnj Ca,01:29 am
02-06-1959,Mo Cnj Aq,05:40 am
02-08-1959,Mo Cnj Pi,11:50 am
02-10-1959,Mo Cnj Ar,08:55 pm
02-13-1959,Mo Cnj Ta,08:48 am
02-15-1959,Mo Cnj Ge,09:40 pm
02-18-1959,Mo Cnj Ca,08:51 am
02-20-1959,Mo Cnj Le,04:39 pm
02-22-1959,Mo Cnj Vi,09:06 pm
02-24-1959,Mo Cnj Li,11:29 pm
02-27-1959,Mo Cnj Sc,01:15 am

March 1959
03-01-1959,Mo Cnj Sa,03:33 am
03-03-1959,Mo Cnj Ca,07:05 am
03-05-1959,Mo Cnj Aq,12:16 pm
03-07-1959,Mo Cnj Pi,07:26 pm
03-10-1959,Mo Cnj Ar,04:54 am
03-12-1959,Mo Cnj Ta,04:37 pm
03-15-1959,Mo Cnj Ge,05:31 am
03-17-1959,Mo Cnj Ca,05:28 pm
03-20-1959,Mo Cnj Le,02:23 am
03-22-1959,Mo Cnj Vi,07:28 am
03-24-1959,Mo Cnj Li,09:27 am
03-26-1959,Mo Cnj Sc,09:54 am

03-28-1959,Mo Cnj Sa,10:32 am
03-30-1959,Mo Cnj Ca,12:49 pm

06-27-1959,Mo Cnj Ar,06:28 am
06-29-1959,Mo Cnj Ta,06:11 pm

April 1959
04-01-1959,Mo Cnj Aq,05:42 pm
04-04-1959,Mo Cnj Pi,01:24 am
04-06-1959,Mo Cnj Ar,11:33 am
04-08-1959,Mo Cnj Ta,11:32 pm
04-11-1959,Mo Cnj Ge,12:25 pm
04-14-1959,Mo Cnj Ca,00:48 am
04-16-1959,Mo Cnj Le,10:55 am
04-18-1959,Mo Cnj Vi,05:28 pm
04-20-1959,Mo Cnj Li,08:19 pm
04-22-1959,Mo Cnj Sc,08:34 pm
04-24-1959,Mo Cnj Sa,08:00 pm
04-26-1959,Mo Cnj Ca,08:33 pm
04-28-1959,Mo Cnj Aq,11:56 pm

July 1959
07-02-1959,Mo Cnj Ge,07:06 am
07-04-1959,Mo Cnj Ca,07:04 pm
07-07-1959,Mo Cnj Le,05:09 am
07-09-1959,Mo Cnj Vi,01:16 pm
07-11-1959,Mo Cnj Li,07:27 pm
07-13-1959,Mo Cnj Sc,11:33 pm
07-16-1959,Mo Cnj Sa,01:42 am
07-18-1959,Mo Cnj Ca,02:42 am
07-20-1959,Mo Cnj Aq,04:05 am
07-22-1959,Mo Cnj Pi,07:41 am
07-24-1959,Mo Cnj Ar,02:54 pm
07-27-1959,Mo Cnj Ta,01:44 am
07-29-1959,Mo Cnj Ge,02:24 pm

May 1959
05-01-1959,Mo Cnj Pi,06:59 am
05-03-1959,Mo Cnj Ar,05:19 pm
05-06-1959,Mo Cnj Ta,05:39 am
05-08-1959,Mo Cnj Ge,06:34 pm
05-11-1959,Mo Cnj Ca,06:57 am
05-13-1959,Mo Cnj Le,05:41 pm
05-16-1959,Mo Cnj Vi,01:38 am
05-18-1959,Mo Cnj Li,06:07 am
05-20-1959,Mo Cnj Sc,07:25 am
05-22-1959,Mo Cnj Sa,06:51 am
05-24-1959,Mo Cnj Ca,06:24 am
05-26-1959,Mo Cnj Aq,08:10 am
05-28-1959,Mo Cnj Pi,01:42 pm
05-30-1959,Mo Cnj Ar,11:18 pm

August 1959
08-01-1959,Mo Cnj Ca,02:24 am
08-03-1959,Mo Cnj Le,12:10 pm
08-05-1959,Mo Cnj Vi,07:30 pm
08-08-1959,Mo Cnj Li,00:56 am
08-10-1959,Mo Cnj Sc,05:00 am
08-12-1959,Mo Cnj Sa,07:58 am
08-14-1959,Mo Cnj Ca,10:19 am
08-16-1959,Mo Cnj Aq,12:54 pm
08-18-1959,Mo Cnj Pi,05:00 pm
08-20-1959,Mo Cnj Ar,11:52 pm
08-23-1959,Mo Cnj Ta,09:59 am
08-25-1959,Mo Cnj Ge,10:19 pm
08-28-1959,Mo Cnj Ca,10:34 am
08-30-1959,Mo Cnj Le,08:33 pm

June 1959
06-02-1959,Mo Cnj Ta,11:37 am
06-05-1959,Mo Cnj Ge,00:35 am
06-07-1959,Mo Cnj Ca,12:44 pm
06-09-1959,Mo Cnj Le,11:20 pm
06-12-1959,Mo Cnj Vi,07:51 am
06-14-1959,Mo Cnj Li,01:43 pm
06-16-1959,Mo Cnj Sc,04:39 pm
06-18-1959,Mo Cnj Sa,05:15 pm
06-20-1959,Mo Cnj Ca,05:01 pm
06-22-1959,Mo Cnj Aq,06:00 pm
06-24-1959,Mo Cnj Pi,10:09 pm

September 1959
09-02-1959,Mo Cnj Vi,03:31 am
09-04-1959,Mo Cnj Li,07:57 am
09-06-1959,Mo Cnj Sc,10:53 am
09-08-1959,Mo Cnj Sa,01:21 pm
09-10-1959,Mo Cnj Ca,04:05 pm
09-12-1959,Mo Cnj Aq,07:44 pm
09-15-1959,Mo Cnj Pi,00:55 am
09-17-1959,Mo Cnj Ar,08:17 am
09-19-1959,Mo Cnj Ta,06:13 pm
09-22-1959,Mo Cnj Ge,06:16 am
09-24-1959,Mo Cnj Ca,06:49 pm

09-27-1959,Mo Cnj Le,05:37 am
09-29-1959,Mo Cnj Vi,01:04 pm

October 1959
10-01-1959,Mo Cnj Li,05:09 pm
10-03-1959,Mo Cnj Sc,06:55 pm
10-05-1959,Mo Cnj Sa,07:55 pm
10-07-1959,Mo Cnj Ca,09:39 pm
10-10-1959,Mo Cnj Aq,01:13 am
10-12-1959,Mo Cnj Pi,07:06 am
10-14-1959,Mo Cnj Ar,03:20 pm
10-17-1959,Mo Cnj Ta,01:40 am
10-19-1959,Mo Cnj Ge,01:40 pm
10-22-1959,Mo Cnj Ca,02:23 am
10-24-1959,Mo Cnj Le,02:04 pm
10-26-1959,Mo Cnj Vi,10:49 pm
10-29-1959,Mo Cnj Li,03:42 am
10-31-1959,Mo Cnj Sc,05:15 am

November 1959
11-02-1959,Mo Cnj Sa,05:02 am
11-04-1959,Mo Cnj Ca,05:05 am
11-06-1959,Mo Cnj Aq,07:14 am
11-08-1959,Mo Cnj Pi,12:35 pm
11-10-1959,Mo Cnj Ar,09:10 pm
11-13-1959,Mo Cnj Ta,08:04 am
11-15-1959,Mo Cnj Ge,08:17 pm
11-18-1959,Mo Cnj Ca,08:57 am
11-20-1959,Mo Cnj Le,09:05 pm
11-23-1959,Mo Cnj Vi,07:09 am
11-25-1959,Mo Cnj Li,01:42 pm
11-27-1959,Mo Cnj Sc,04:22 pm
11-29-1959,Mo Cnj Sa,04:12 pm

December 1959
12-01-1959,Mo Cnj Ca,03:11 pm
12-03-1959,Mo Cnj Aq,03:35 pm
12-05-1959,Mo Cnj Pi,07:16 pm
12-08-1959,Mo Cnj Ar,03:00 am
12-10-1959,Mo Cnj Ta,01:57 pm
12-13-1959,Mo Cnj Ge,02:25 am
12-15-1959,Mo Cnj Ca,03:01 pm
12-18-1959,Mo Cnj Le,02:58 am
12-20-1959,Mo Cnj Vi,01:30 pm
12-22-1959,Mo Cnj Li,09:29 pm
12-25-1959,Mo Cnj Sc,02:01 am
12-27-1959,Mo Cnj Sa,03:16 am

12-29-1959,Mo Cnj Ca,02:38 am
12-31-1959,Mo Cnj Aq,02:15 am

January 1960
01-02-1960,Mo Cnj Pi,04:19 am
01-04-1960,Mo Cnj Ar,10:22 am
01-06-1960,Mo Cnj Ta,08:23 pm
01-09-1960,Mo Cnj Ge,08:45 am
01-11-1960,Mo Cnj Ca,09:23 pm
01-14-1960,Mo Cnj Le,08:59 am
01-16-1960,Mo Cnj Vi,07:03 pm
01-19-1960,Mo Cnj Li,03:14 am
01-21-1960,Mo Cnj Sc,09:00 am
01-23-1960,Mo Cnj Sa,12:03 pm
01-25-1960,Mo Cnj Ca,01:00 pm
01-27-1960,Mo Cnj Aq,01:19 pm
01-29-1960,Mo Cnj Pi,02:57 pm
01-31-1960,Mo Cnj Ar,07:39 pm

February 1960
02-03-1960,Mo Cnj Ta,04:16 am
02-05-1960,Mo Cnj Ge,03:58 pm
02-08-1960,Mo Cnj Ca,04:37 am
02-10-1960,Mo Cnj Le,04:08 pm
02-13-1960,Mo Cnj Vi,01:35 am
02-15-1960,Mo Cnj Li,08:56 am
02-17-1960,Mo Cnj Sc,02:24 pm
02-19-1960,Mo Cnj Sa,06:12 pm
02-21-1960,Mo Cnj Ca,08:40 pm
02-23-1960,Mo Cnj Aq,10:33 pm
02-26-1960,Mo Cnj Pi,01:04 am
02-28-1960,Mo Cnj Ar,05:37 am

March 1960
03-01-1960,Mo,Cnj Ta,01:18 pm
03-04-1960,Mo Cnj Ge,00:08 am
03-06-1960,Mo Cnj Ca,12:37 pm
03-09-1960,Mo Cnj Le,00:25 am
03-11-1960,Mo Cnj Vi,09:48 am
03-13-1960,Mo Cnj Li,04:20 pm
03-15-1960,Mo Cnj Sc,08:37 pm
03-17-1960,Mo Cnj Sa,11:38 pm
03-20-1960,Mo Cnj Ca,02:14 am
03-22-1960,Mo Cnj Aq,05:10 am
03-24-1960,Mo Cnj Pi,09:02 am
03-26-1960,Mo Cnj Ar,02:30 pm

03-28-1960,Mo Cnj Ta,10:13 pm
03-31-1960,Mo Cnj Ge,08:32 am

April 1960

04-02-1960,Mo Cnj Ca,08:47 pm
04-05-1960,Mo Cnj Le,09:02 am
04-07-1960,Mo Cnj Vi,07:02 pm
04-10-1960,Mo Cnj Li,01:36 am
04-12-1960,Mo Cnj Sc,05:01 am
04-14-1960,Mo Cnj Sa,06:37 am
04-16-1960,Mo Cnj Ca,08:01 am
04-18-1960,Mo Cnj Aq,10:32 am
04-20-1960,Mo Cnj Pi,02:56 pm
04-22-1960,Mo Cnj Ar,09:23 pm
04-25-1960,Mo Cnj Ta,05:51 am
04-27-1960,Mo Cnj Ge,04:17 pm
04-30-1960,Mo Cnj Ca,04:23 am

May 1960

05-02-1960,Mo Cnj Le,04:59 pm
05-05-1960,Mo Cnj Vi,03:59 am
05-07-1960,Mo Cnj Li,11:30 am
05-09-1960,Mo Cnj Sc,03:07 pm
05-11-1960,Mo Cnj Sa,03:55 pm
05-13-1960,Mo Cnj Ca,03:51 pm
05-15-1960,Mo Cnj Aq,04:52 pm
05-17-1960,Mo Cnj Pi,08:24 pm
05-20-1960,Mo Cnj Ar,02:56 am
05-22-1960,Mo Cnj Ta,12:00 pm
05-24-1960,Mo Cnj Ge,10:55 pm
05-27-1960,Mo Cnj Ca,11:06 am
05-29-1960,Mo Cnj Le,11:50 pm

June 1960

06-01-1960,Mo Cnj Vi,11:38 am
06-03-1960,Mo Cnj Li,08:31 pm
06-06-1960,Mo Cnj Sc,01:20 am
06-08-1960,Mo Cnj Sa,02:31 am
06-10-1960,Mo Cnj Ca,01:48 am
06-12-1960,Mo Cnj Aq,01:24 am
06-14-1960,Mo Cnj Pi,03:18 am
06-16-1960,Mo Cnj Ar,08:43 am
06-18-1960,Mo Cnj Ta,05:33 pm
06-21-1960,Mo Cnj Ge,04:46 am
06-23-1960,Mo Cnj Ca,05:09 pm
06-26-1960,Mo Cnj Le,05:51 am
06-28-1960,Mo Cnj Vi,05:53 pm

July 1960

07-01-1960,Mo Cnj Li,03:47 am
07-03-1960,Mo Cnj Sc,10:09 am
07-05-1960,Mo Cnj Sa,12:43 pm
07-07-1960,Mo Cnj Ca,12:35 pm
07-09-1960,Mo Cnj Aq,11:44 am
07-11-1960,Mo Cnj Pi,12:19 pm
07-13-1960,Mo Cnj Ar,04:07 pm
07-15-1960,Mo Cnj Ta,11:48 pm
07-18-1960,Mo Cnj Ge,10:40 am
07-20-1960,Mo Cnj Ca,11:09 pm
07-23-1960,Mo Cnj Le,11:46 am
07-25-1960,Mo Cnj Vi,11:32 am
07-28-1960,Mo Cnj Li,09:34 am
07-30-1960,Mo Cnj Sc,04:55 pm

August 1960

08-01-1960,Mo Cnj Sa,09:04 pm
08-03-1960,Mo Cnj Ca,10:26 pm
08-05-1960,Mo Cnj Aq,10:21 pm
08-07-1960,Mo Cnj Pi,10:42 pm
08-10-1960,Mo Cnj Ar,01:21 am
08-12-1960,Mo Cnj Ta,07:36 am
08-14-1960,Mo Cnj Ge,05:30 pm
08-17-1960,Mo Cnj Ca,05:44 am
08-19-1960,Mo Cnj Le,06:18 pm
08-22-1960,Mo Cnj Vi,05:42 am
08-24-1960,Mo Cnj Li,03:10 pm
08-26-1960,Mo Cnj Sc,10:24 pm
08-29-1960,Mo Cnj Sa,03:19 am
08-31-1960,Mo Cnj Ca,06:09 am

September 1960

09-02-1960,Mo Cnj Aq,07:35 am
09-04-1960,Mo Cnj Pi,08:51 am
09-06-1960,Mo Cnj Ar,11:26 am
09-08-1960,Mo Cnj Ta,04:45 pm
09-11-1960,Mo Cnj Ge,01:32 am
09-13-1960,Mo Cnj Ca,01:11 pm
09-16-1960,Mo Cnj Le,01:47 am
09-18-1960,Mo Cnj Vi,01:07 pm
09-20-1960,Mo Cnj Li,09:58 pm
09-23-1960,Mo Cnj Sc,04:18 am
09-25-1960,Mo Cnj Sa,08:42 am
09-27-1960,Mo Cnj Ca,11:54 am
09-29-1960,Mo Cnj Aq,02:33 pm

October 1960

10-01-1960,Mo Cnj Pi,05:15 pm
10-03-1960,Mo Cnj Ar,08:47 pm
10-06-1960,Mo Cnj Ta,02:10 am
10-08-1960,Mo Cnj Ge,10:17 am
10-10-1960,Mo Cnj Ca,09:18 pm
10-13-1960,Mo Cnj Le,09:55 am
10-15-1960,Mo Cnj Vi,09:40 pm
10-18-1960,Mo Cnj Li,06:32 am
10-20-1960,Mo Cnj Sc,12:06 pm
10-22-1960,Mo Cnj Sa,03:16 pm
10-24-1960,Mo Cnj Ca,05:29 pm
10-26-1960,Mo Cnj Aq,07:58 pm
10-28-1960,Mo Cnj Pi,11:27 pm
10-31-1960,Mo Cnj Ar,04:12 am

November 1960

11-02-1960,Mo Cnj Ta,10:28 am
11-04-1960,Mo Cnj Ge,06:44 pm
11-07-1960,Mo Cnj Ca,05:26 am
11-09-1960,Mo Cnj Le,05:59 pm
11-12-1960,Mo Cnj Vi,06:24 am
11-14-1960,Mo Cnj Li,04:08 pm
11-16-1960,Mo Cnj Sc,09:54 pm
11-19-1960,Mo Cnj Sa,00:17 am
11-21-1960,Mo Cnj Ca,01:03 am
11-23-1960,Mo Cnj Aq,02:05 am
11-25-1960,Mo Cnj Pi,04:50 am
11-27-1960,Mo Cnj Ar,09:51 am
11-29-1960,Mo Cnj Ta,04:59 pm

December 1960

12-02-1960,Mo Cnj Ge,02:00 am
12-04-1960,Mo Cnj Ca,12:52 pm
12-07-1960,Mo Cnj Le,01:21 am
12-09-1960,Mo Cnj Vi,02:14 pm
12-12-1960,Mo Cnj Li,01:11 am
12-14-1960,Mo Cnj Sc,08:14 am
12-16-1960,Mo Cnj Sa,11:07 am
12-18-1960,Mo Cnj Ca,11:16 am
12-20-1960,Mo Cnj Aq,10:49 am
12-22-1960,Mo Cnj Pi,11:47 am
12-24-1960,Mo Cnj Ar,03:34 pm
12-26-1960,Mo Cnj Ta,10:30 pm
12-29-1960,Mo Cnj Ge,08:02 am
12-31-1960,Mo Cnj Ca,07:22 pm

January 1961

01-03-1961,Mo Cnj Le,07:54 am
01-05-1961,Mo Cnj Vi,08:49 pm
01-08-1961,Mo Cnj Li,08:31 am
01-10-1961,Mo Cnj Sc,05:09 pm
01-12-1961,Mo Cnj Sa,09:41 pm
01-14-1961,Mo Cnj Ca,10:41 pm
01-16-1961,Mo Cnj Aq,09:56 pm
01-18-1961,Mo Cnj Pi,09:32 pm
01-20-1961,Mo Cnj Ar,11:27 pm
01-23-1961,Mo Cnj Ta,04:52 am
01-25-1961,Mo Cnj Ge,01:51 pm
01-28-1961,Mo Cnj Ca,01:23 am
01-30-1961,Mo Cnj Le,02:05 pm

February 1961

02-02-1961,Mo Cnj Vi,02:48 am
02-04-1961,Mo Cnj Li,02:27 pm
02-06-1961,Mo Cnj Sc,11:51 pm
02-09-1961,Mo Cnj Sa,06:01 am
02-11-1961,Mo Cnj Ca,08:51 am
02-13-1961,Mo Cnj Aq,09:15 am
02-15-1961,Mo Cnj Pi,08:53 am
02-17-1961,Mo Cnj Ar,09:41 am
02-19-1961,Mo Cnj Ta,01:22 pm
02-21-1961,Mo Cnj Ge,08:52 pm
02-24-1961,Mo Cnj Ca,07:49 am
02-26-1961,Mo Cnj Le,08:34 pm

March 1961

03-01-1961,Mo Cnj Vi,09:12 am
03-03-1961,Mo Cnj Li,08:21 pm
03-06-1961,Mo Cnj Sc,05:24 am
03-08-1961,Mo Cnj Sa,12:04 pm
03-10-1961,Mo Cnj Ca,04:19 pm
03-12-1961,Mo Cnj Aq,06:30 pm
03-14-1961,Mo Cnj Pi,07:27 pm
03-16-1961,Mo Cnj Ar,08:33 pm
03-18-1961,Mo Cnj Ta,11:26 pm
03-21-1961,Mo Cnj Ge,05:32 am
03-23-1961,Mo Cnj Ca,03:22 pm
03-26-1961,Mo Cnj Le,03:48 am
03-28-1961,Mo Cnj Vi,04:30 pm
03-31-1961,Mo Cnj Li,03:22 am

April 1961

04-02-1961,Mo Cnj Sc,11:37 am
04-04-1961,Mo Cnj Sa,05:35 pm

04-06-1961,Mo Cnj Ca,09:53 pm
04-09-1961,Mo Cnj Aq,01:03 am
04-11-1961,Mo Cnj Pi,03:32 am
04-13-1961,Mo Cnj Ar,05:56 am
04-15-1961,Mo Cnj Ta,09:17 am
04-17-1961,Mo Cnj Ge,02:55 pm
04-19-1961,Mo Cnj Ca,11:50 pm
04-22-1961,Mo Cnj Le,11:44 am
04-25-1961,Mo Cnj Vi,00:32 am
04-27-1961,Mo Cnj Li,11:35 am
04-29-1961,Mo Cnj Sc,07:28 pm

May 1961
05-02-1961,Mo Cnj Sa,00:25 am
05-04-1961,Mo Cnj Ca,03:40 am
05-06-1961,Mo Cnj Aq,06:24 am
05-08-1961,Mo Cnj Pi,09:23 am
05-10-1961,Mo Cnj Ar,12:56 pm
05-12-1961,Mo Cnj Ta,05:25 pm
05-14-1961,Mo Cnj Ge,11:35 pm
05-17-1961,Mo Cnj Ca,08:17 am
05-19-1961,Mo Cnj Le,07:46 pm
05-22-1961,Mo Cnj Vi,08:39 am
05-24-1961,Mo Cnj Li,08:18 pm
05-27-1961,Mo Cnj Sc,04:35 am
05-29-1961,Mo Cnj Sa,09:11 am
05-31-1961,Mo Cnj Ca,11:20 am

June 1961
06-02-1961,Mo Cnj Aq,12:45 pm
06-04-1961,Mo Cnj Pi,02:51 pm
06-06-1961,Mo Cnj Ar,06:24 pm
06-08-1961,Mo Cnj Ta,11:38 pm
06-11-1961,Mo Cnj Ge,06:41 am
06-13-1961,Mo Cnj Ca,03:50 pm
06-16-1961,Mo Cnj Le,03:16 am
06-18-1961,Mo Cnj Vi,04:12 pm
06-21-1961,Mo Cnj Li,04:32 am
06-23-1961,Mo Cnj Sc,01:51 pm
06-25-1961,Mo Cnj Sa,07:06 pm
06-27-1961,Mo Cnj Ca,09:00 pm
06-29-1961,Mo Cnj Aq,09:18 pm

July 1961
07-01-1961,Mo Cnj Pi,09:53 pm
07-04-1961,Mo Cnj Ar,00:13 am
07-06-1961,Mo Cnj Ta,05:02 am

07-08-1961,Mo Cnj Ge,12:28 pm
07-10-1961,Mo Cnj Ca,10:13 pm
07-13-1961,Mo Cnj Le,09:56 am
07-15-1961,Mo Cnj Vi,10:54 pm
07-18-1961,Mo Cnj Li,11:38 am
07-20-1961,Mo Cnj Sc,10:05 pm
07-23-1961,Mo Cnj Sa,04:43 am
07-25-1961,Mo Cnj Ca,07:29 am
07-27-1961,Mo Cnj Aq,07:42 am
07-29-1961,Mo Cnj Pi,07:14 am
07-31-1961,Mo Cnj Ar,07:56 am

August 1961
08-02-1961,Mo Cnj Ta,11:19 am
08-04-1961,Mo Cnj Ge,06:04 pm
08-07-1961,Mo Cnj Ca,03:56 am
08-09-1961,Mo Cnj Le,03:59 pm
08-12-1961,Mo Cnj Vi,05:00 am
08-14-1961,Mo Cnj Li,05:44 pm
08-17-1961,Mo Cnj Sc,04:45 am
08-19-1961,Mo Cnj Sa,12:45 pm
08-21-1961,Mo Cnj Ca,05:08 pm
08-23-1961,Mo Cnj Aq,06:26 pm
08-25-1961,Mo Cnj Pi,06:03 pm
08-27-1961,Mo Cnj Ar,05:49 pm
08-29-1961,Mo Cnj Ta,07:37 pm

September 1961
09-01-1961,Mo Cnj Ge,00:52 am
09-03-1961,Mo Cnj Ca,10:00 am
09-05-1961,Mo Cnj Le,10:01 am
09-08-1961,Mo Cnj Vi,11:06 am
09-10-1961,Mo Cnj Li,11:34 pm
09-13-1961,Mo Cnj Sc,10:24 am
09-15-1961,Mo Cnj Sa,06:55 pm
09-18-1961,Mo Cnj Ca,00:42 am
09-20-1961,Mo Cnj Aq,03:43 am
09-22-1961,Mo Cnj Pi,04:36 am
09-24-1961,Mo Cnj Ar,04:40 am
09-26-1961,Mo Cnj Ta,05:42 am
09-28-1961,Mo Cnj Ge,09:32 am
09-30-1961,Mo Cnj Ca,05:20 pm

October 1961
10-03-1961,Mo Cnj Le,04:44 am
10-05-1961,Mo Cnj Vi,05:46 pm
10-08-1961,Mo Cnj Li,06:04 am

10-10-1961,Mo Cnj Sc,04:19 pm
10-13-1961,Mo Cnj Sa,00:21 am
10-15-1961,Mo Cnj Ca,06:24 am
10-17-1961,Mo Cnj Aq,10:37 am
10-19-1961,Mo Cnj Pi,01:10 pm
10-21-1961,Mo Cnj Ar,02:36 pm
10-23-1961,Mo Cnj Ta,04:07 pm
10-25-1961,Mo Cnj Ge,07:25 pm
10-28-1961,Mo Cnj Ca,02:04 am
10-30-1961,Mo Cnj Le,12:30 pm

November 1961
11-02-1961,Mo Cnj Vi,01:18 am
11-04-1961,Mo Cnj Li,01:42 pm
11-06-1961,Mo Cnj Sc,11:40 pm
11-09-1961,Mo Cnj Sa,06:51 am
11-11-1961,Mo Cnj Ca,12:00 pm
11-13-1961,Mo Cnj Aq,04:00 pm
11-15-1961,Mo Cnj Pi,07:19 pm
11-17-1961,Mo Cnj Ar,10:11 pm
11-20-1961,Mo Cnj Ta,01:04 am
11-22-1961,Mo Cnj Ge,05:00 am
11-24-1961,Mo Cnj Ca,11:21 am
11-26-1961,Mo Cnj Le,09:01 pm
11-29-1961,Mo Cnj Vi,09:25 am

December 1961
12-01-1961,Mo Cnj Li,10:08 pm
12-04-1961,Mo Cnj Sc,08:30 am
12-06-1961,Mo Cnj Sa,03:25 pm
12-08-1961,Mo Cnj Ca,07:31 pm
12-10-1961,Mo Cnj Aq,10:12 pm
12-13-1961,Mo Cnj Pi,00:42 am
12-15-1961,Mo Cnj Ar,03:45 am
12-17-1961,Mo Cnj Ta,07:39 am
12-19-1961,Mo Cnj Ge,12:48 pm
12-21-1961,Mo Cnj Ca,07:50 pm
12-24-1961,Mo Cnj Le,05:26 am
12-26-1961,Mo Cnj Vi,05:30 pm
12-29-1961,Mo Cnj Li,06:27 am
12-31-1961,Mo Cnj Sc,05:43 pm

January 1962
01-03-1962,Mo Cnj Sa,01:24 am
01-05-1962,Mo Cnj Ca,05:25 am
01-07-1962,Mo Cnj Aq,07:01 am
01-09-1962,Mo Cnj Pi,07:54 am

01-11-1962,Mo Cnj Ar,09:34 am
01-13-1962,Mo Cnj Ta,01:01 pm
01-15-1962,Mo Cnj Ge,06:42 pm
01-18-1962,Mo Cnj Ca,02:40 am
01-20-1962,Mo Cnj Le,12:50 pm
01-23-1962,Mo Cnj Vi,00:54 am
01-25-1962,Mo Cnj Li,01:53 pm
01-28-1962,Mo Cnj Sc,01:55 am
01-30-1962,Mo Cnj Sa,11:00 am

February 1962
02-01-1962,Mo Cnj Ca,04:10 pm
02-03-1962,Mo Cnj Aq,05:57 pm
02-05-1962,Mo Cnj Pi,05:53 pm
02-07-1962,Mo Cnj Ar,05:51 pm
02-09-1962,Mo Cnj Ta,07:35 pm
02-12-1962,Mo Cnj Ge,00:18 am
02-14-1962,Mo Cnj Ca,08:20 am
02-16-1962,Mo Cnj Le,07:04 pm
02-19-1962,Mo Cnj Vi,07:27 am
02-21-1962,Mo Cnj Li,08:22 pm
02-24-1962,Mo Cnj Sc,08:37 am
02-26-1962,Mo Cnj Sa,06:46 pm

March 1962
03-01-1962,Mo Cnj Ca,01:38 am
03-03-1962,Mo Cnj Aq,04:52 am
03-05-1962,Mo Cnj Pi,05:17 am
03-07-1962,Mo Cnj Ar,04:32 am
03-09-1962,Mo Cnj Ta,04:41 am
03-11-1962,Mo Cnj Ge,07:36 am
03-13-1962,Mo Cnj Ca,02:26 pm
03-16-1962,Mo Cnj Le,00:57 am
03-18-1962,Mo Cnj Vi,01:33 pm
03-21-1962,Mo Cnj Li,02:28 am
03-23-1962,Mo Cnj Sc,02:29 pm
03-26-1962,Mo Cnj Sa,00:49 am
03-28-1962,Mo Cnj Ca,08:46 am
03-30-1962,Mo Cnj Aq,01:44 pm

April 1962
04-01-1962,Mo Cnj Pi,03:43 pm
04-03-1962,Mo Cnj Ar,03:42 pm
04-05-1962,Mo Cnj Ta,03:26 pm
04-07-1962,Mo Cnj Ge,05:00 pm
04-09-1962,Mo Cnj Ca,10:13 pm
04-12-1962,Mo Cnj Le,07:36 am

04-14-1962,Mo Cnj Vi,07:57 pm
04-17-1962,Mo Cnj Li,08:54 am
04-19-1962,Mo Cnj Sc,08:37 pm
04-22-1962,Mo Cnj Sa,06:27 am
04-24-1962,Mo Cnj Ca,02:21 pm
04-26-1962,Mo Cnj Aq,08:09 pm
04-28-1962,Mo Cnj Pi,11:41 pm

May 1962
05-01-1962,Mo Cnj Ar,01:13 am
05-03-1962,Mo Cnj Ta,01:50 am
05-05-1962,Mo Cnj Ge,03:17 am
05-07-1962,Mo Cnj Ca,07:28 am
05-09-1962,Mo Cnj Le,03:35 pm
05-12-1962,Mo Cnj Vi,03:11 am
05-14-1962,Mo Cnj Li,04:03 pm
05-17-1962,Mo Cnj Sc,03:44 am
05-19-1962,Mo Cnj Sa,01:03 pm
05-21-1962,Mo Cnj Ca,08:09 pm
05-24-1962,Mo Cnj Aq,01:31 am
05-26-1962,Mo Cnj Pi,05:30 am
05-28-1962,Mo Cnj Ar,08:15 am
05-30-1962,Mo Cnj Ta,10:17 am

June 1962
06-01-1962,Mo Cnj Ge,12:40 pm
06-03-1962,Mo Cnj Ca,04:57 pm
06-06-1962,Mo Cnj Le,00:23 am
06-08-1962,Mo Cnj Vi,11:13 am
06-10-1962,Mo Cnj Li,11:52 pm
06-13-1962,Mo Cnj Sc,11:46 am
06-15-1962,Mo Cnj Sa,09:04 pm
06-18-1962,Mo Cnj Ca,03:30 am
06-20-1962,Mo Cnj Aq,07:49 am
06-22-1962,Mo Cnj Pi,10:59 am
06-24-1962,Mo Cnj Ar,01:43 pm
06-26-1962,Mo Cnj Ta,04:34 pm
06-28-1962,Mo Cnj Ge,08:10 pm

July 1962
07-01-1962,Mo Cnj Ca,01:19 am
07-03-1962,Mo Cnj Le,08:56 am
07-05-1962,Mo Cnj Vi,07:23 pm
07-08-1962,Mo Cnj Li,07:48 am
07-10-1962,Mo Cnj Sc,08:06 pm
07-13-1962,Mo Cnj Sa,06:01 am
07-15-1962,Mo Cnj Ca,12:32 pm

07-17-1962,Mo Cnj Aq,04:07 pm
07-19-1962,Mo Cnj Pi,06:00 pm
07-21-1962,Mo Cnj Ar,07:34 pm
07-23-1962,Mo Cnj Ta,09:57 pm
07-26-1962,Mo Cnj Ge,01:57 am
07-28-1962,Mo Cnj Ca,08:01 am
07-30-1962,Mo Cnj Le,04:21 pm

August 1962
08-02-1962,Mo Cnj Vi,02:58 am
08-04-1962,Mo Cnj Li,03:18 pm
08-07-1962,Mo Cnj Sc,03:56 am
08-09-1962,Mo Cnj Sa,02:48 pm
08-11-1962,Mo Cnj Ca,10:18 pm
08-14-1962,Mo Cnj Aq,02:08 am
08-16-1962,Mo Cnj Pi,03:17 am
08-18-1962,Mo Cnj Ar,03:26 am
08-20-1962,Mo Cnj Ta,04:21 am
08-22-1962,Mo Cnj Ge,07:28 am
08-24-1962,Mo Cnj Ca,01:34 pm
08-26-1962,Mo Cnj Le,10:30 pm
08-29-1962,Mo Cnj Vi,09:36 am
08-31-1962,Mo Cnj Li,10:01 pm

September 1962
09-03-1962,Mo Cnj Sc,10:46 am
09-05-1962,Mo Cnj Sa,10:26 pm
09-08-1962,Mo Cnj Ca,07:20 am
09-10-1962,Mo Cnj Aq,12:27 pm
09-12-1962,Mo Cnj Pi,02:02 pm
09-14-1962,Mo Cnj Ar,01:33 pm
09-16-1962,Mo Cnj Ta,01:01 pm
09-18-1962,Mo Cnj Ge,02:29 pm
09-20-1962,Mo Cnj Ca,07:26 pm
09-23-1962,Mo Cnj Le,04:07 am
09-25-1962,Mo Cnj Vi,03:31 pm
09-28-1962,Mo Cnj Li,04:08 am
09-30-1962,Mo Cnj Sc,04:49 pm

October 1962
10-03-1962,Mo Cnj Sa,04:41 am
10-05-1962,Mo Cnj Ca,02:36 pm
10-07-1962,Mo Cnj Aq,09:22 pm
10-10-1962,Mo Cnj Pi,00:29 am
10-12-1962,Mo Cnj Ar,00:41 am
10-13-1962,Mo Cnj Ta,11:43 pm
10-15-1962,Mo Cnj Ge,11:50 pm

10-18-1962,Mo Cnj Ca,03:05 am
10-20-1962,Mo Cnj Le,10:31 am
10-22-1962,Mo Cnj Vi,09:32 pm
10-25-1962,Mo Cnj Li,10:14 am
10-27-1962,Mo Cnj Sc,10:49 pm
10-30-1962,Mo Cnj Sa,10:20 am

November 1962
11-01-1962,Mo Cnj Ca,08:18 pm
11-04-1962,Mo Cnj Aq,04:02 am
11-06-1962,Mo Cnj Pi,08:52 am
11-08-1962,Mo Cnj Ar,10:45 am
11-10-1962,Mo Cnj Ta,10:45 am
11-12-1962,Mo Cnj Ge,10:44 am
11-14-1962,Mo Cnj Ca,12:49 pm
11-16-1962,Mo Cnj Le,06:41 pm
11-19-1962,Mo Cnj Vi,04:34 am
11-21-1962,Mo Cnj Li,04:58 pm
11-24-1962,Mo Cnj Sc,05:34 am
11-26-1962,Mo Cnj Sa,04:43 pm
11-29-1962,Mo Cnj Ca,02:00 am

December 1962
12-01-1962,Mo Cnj Aq,09:26 am
12-03-1962,Mo Cnj Pi,02:54 pm
12-05-1962,Mo Cnj Ar,06:17 pm
12-07-1962,Mo Cnj Ta,08:00 pm
12-09-1962,Mo Cnj Ge,09:08 pm
12-11-1962,Mo Cnj Ca,11:22 pm
12-14-1962,Mo Cnj Le,04:21 am
12-16-1962,Mo Cnj Vi,01:00 pm
12-19-1962,Mo Cnj Li,00:41 am
12-21-1962,Mo Cnj Sc,01:18 pm
12-24-1962,Mo Cnj Sa,00:33 am
12-26-1962,Mo Cnj Ca,09:19 am
12-28-1962,Mo Cnj Aq,03:43 pm
12-30-1962,Mo Cnj Pi,08:21 pm

January 1963
01-01-1963,Mo Cnj Ar,11:49 pm
01-04-1963,Mo Cnj Ta,02:34 am
01-06-1963,Mo Cnj Ge,05:15 am
01-08-1963,Mo Cnj Ca,08:42 am
01-10-1963,Mo Cnj Le,02:01 pm
01-12-1963,Mo Cnj Vi,10:07 pm
01-15-1963,Mo Cnj Li,09:05 am
01-17-1963,Mo Cnj Sc,09:36 pm

01-20-1963,Mo Cnj Sa,09:21 am
01-22-1963,Mo Cnj Ca,06:24 pm
01-25-1963,Mo Cnj Aq,00:15 am
01-27-1963,Mo Cnj Pi,03:36 am
01-29-1963,Mo Cnj Ar,05:45 am
01-31-1963,Mo Cnj Ta,07:55 am

February 1963
02-02-1963,Mo Cnj Ge,11:03 am
02-04-1963,Mo Cnj Ca,03:40 pm
02-06-1963,Mo Cnj Le,10:06 pm
02-09-1963,Mo Cnj Vi,06:36 am
02-11-1963,Mo Cnj Li,05:18 pm
02-14-1963,Mo Cnj Sc,05:39 am
02-16-1963,Mo Cnj Sa,05:58 pm
02-19-1963,Mo Cnj Ca,04:01 am
02-21-1963,Mo Cnj Aq,10:24 am
02-23-1963,Mo Cnj Pi,01:18 pm
02-25-1963,Mo Cnj Ar,02:05 pm
02-27-1963,Mo Cnj Ta,02:39 pm

March 1963
03-01-1963,Mo Cnj Ge,04:39 pm
03-03-1963,Mo Cnj Ca,09:08 pm
03-06-1963,Mo Cnj Le,04:15 am
03-08-1963,Mo Cnj Vi,01:34 pm
03-11-1963,Mo Cnj Li,00:36 am
03-13-1963,Mo Cnj Sc,12:52 pm
03-16-1963,Mo Cnj Sa,01:28 am
03-18-1963,Mo Cnj Ca,12:35 pm
03-20-1963,Mo Cnj Aq,08:21 pm
03-23-1963,Mo Cnj Pi,00:05 am
03-25-1963,Mo Cnj Ar,00:38 am
03-26-1963,Mo Cnj Ta,11:57 pm
03-29-1963,Mo Cnj Ge,00:13 am
03-31-1963,Mo Cnj Ca,03:14 am

April 1963
04-02-1963,Mo Cnj Le,09:46 am
04-04-1963,Mo Cnj Vi,07:21 pm
04-07-1963,Mo Cnj Li,06:50 am
04-09-1963,Mo Cnj Sc,07:14 pm
04-12-1963,Mo Cnj Sa,07:48 am
04-14-1963,Mo Cnj Ca,07:27 pm
04-17-1963,Mo Cnj Aq,04:34 am
04-19-1963,Mo Cnj Pi,09:54 am
04-21-1963,Mo Cnj Ar,11:30 am

04-23-1963,Mo Cnj Ta,10:51 am
04-25-1963,Mo Cnj Ge,10:07 am
04-27-1963,Mo Cnj Ca,11:28 am
04-29-1963,Mo Cnj Le,04:26 pm

May 1963
05-02-1963,Mo Cnj Vi,01:14 am
05-04-1963,Mo Cnj Li,12:43 pm
05-07-1963,Mo Cnj Sc,01:16 am
05-09-1963,Mo Cnj Sa,01:42 pm
05-12-1963,Mo Cnj Ca,01:14 am
05-14-1963,Mo Cnj Aq,10:52 am
05-16-1963,Mo Cnj Pi,05:33 pm
05-18-1963,Mo Cnj Ar,08:48 pm
05-20-1963,Mo Cnj Ta,09:22 pm
05-22-1963,Mo Cnj Ge,08:54 pm
05-24-1963,Mo Cnj Ca,09:29 pm
05-27-1963,Mo Cnj Le,00:59 am
05-29-1963,Mo Cnj Vi,08:22 am
05-31-1963,Mo Cnj Li,07:09 pm

June 1963
06-03-1963,Mo Cnj Sc,07:39 am
06-05-1963,Mo Cnj Sa,08:01 pm
06-08-1963,Mo Cnj Ca,07:07 am
06-10-1963,Mo Cnj Aq,04:23 pm
06-12-1963,Mo Cnj Pi,11:21 pm
06-15-1963,Mo Cnj Ar,03:47 am
06-17-1963,Mo Cnj Ta,05:55 am
06-19-1963,Mo Cnj Ge,06:44 am
06-21-1963,Mo Cnj Ca,07:46 am
06-23-1963,Mo Cnj Le,10:44 am
06-25-1963,Mo Cnj Vi,04:56 pm
06-28-1963,Mo Cnj Li,02:41 am
06-30-1963,Mo Cnj Sc,02:48 pm

July 1963
07-03-1963,Mo Cnj Sa,03:12 am
07-05-1963,Mo Cnj Ca,02:04 pm
07-07-1963,Mo Cnj Aq,10:37 pm
07-10-1963,Mo Cnj Pi,04:53 am
07-12-1963,Mo Cnj Ar,09:16 am
07-14-1963,Mo Cnj Ta,12:15 pm
07-16-1963,Mo Cnj Ge,02:27 pm
07-18-1963,Mo Cnj Ca,04:45 pm
07-20-1963,Mo Cnj Le,08:15 pm
07-23-1963,Mo Cnj Vi,02:07 am

07-25-1963,Mo Cnj Li,11:03 am
07-27-1963,Mo Cnj Sc,10:39 pm
07-30-1963,Mo Cnj Sa,11:09 am

August 1963
08-01-1963,Mo Cnj Ca,10:13 pm
08-04-1963,Mo Cnj Aq,06:26 am
08-06-1963,Mo Cnj Pi,11:46 am
08-08-1963,Mo Cnj Ar,03:06 am
08-10-1963,Mo Cnj Ta,05:38 am
08-12-1963,Mo Cnj Ge,08:16 pm
08-14-1963,Mo Cnj Ca,11:40 pm
08-17-1963,Mo Cnj Le,04:17 am
08-19-1963,Mo Cnj Vi,10:41 am
08-21-1963,Mo Cnj Li,07:26 pm
08-24-1963,Mo Cnj Sc,06:39 am
08-26-1963,Mo Cnj Sa,07:15 pm
08-29-1963,Mo Cnj Ca,06:57 am
08-31-1963,Mo Cnj Aq,03:37 pm

September 1963
09-02-1963,Mo Cnj Pi,08:37 pm
09-04-1963,Mo Cnj Ar,10:52 pm
09-07-1963,Mo Cnj Ta,00:03 am
09-09-1963,Mo Cnj Ge,01:46 am
09-11-1963,Mo Cnj Ca,05:08 am
09-13-1963,Mo Cnj Le,10:30 am
09-15-1963,Mo Cnj Vi,05:48 pm
09-18-1963,Mo Cnj Li,03:00 am
09-20-1963,Mo Cnj Sc,02:11 pm
09-23-1963,Mo Cnj Sa,02:50 am
09-25-1963,Mo Cnj Ca,03:15 pm
09-28-1963,Mo Cnj Aq,01:03 am
09-30-1963,Mo Cnj Pi,06:47 am

October 1963
10-02-1963,Mo Cnj Ar,08:49 am
10-04-1963,Mo Cnj Ta,08:51 am
10-06-1963,Mo Cnj Ge,08:59 am
10-08-1963,Mo Cnj Ca,11:01 am
10-10-1963,Mo Cnj Le,03:54 pm
10-12-1963,Mo Cnj Vi,11:34 pm
10-15-1963,Mo Cnj Li,09:24 am
10-17-1963,Mo Cnj Sc,08:52 pm
10-20-1963,Mo Cnj Sa,09:32 am
10-22-1963,Mo Cnj Ca,10:21 pm
10-25-1963,Mo Cnj Aq,09:21 am

10-27-1963,Mo Cnj Pi,04:37 pm
10-29-1963,Mo Cnj Ar,07:41 pm
10-31-1963,Mo Cnj Ta,07:43 pm

November 1963
11-02-1963,Mo Cnj Ge,06:49 pm
11-04-1963,Mo Cnj Ca,07:08 pm
11-06-1963,Mo Cnj Le,10:24 pm
11-09-1963,Mo Cnj Vi,05:14 am
11-11-1963,Mo Cnj Li,03:08 pm
11-14-1963,Mo Cnj Sc,02:57 am
11-16-1963,Mo Cnj Sa,03:40 pm
11-19-1963,Mo Cnj Ca,04:23 am
11-21-1963,Mo Cnj Aq,03:52 pm
11-24-1963,Mo Cnj Pi,00:33 am
11-26-1963,Mo Cnj Ar,05:25 am
11-28-1963,Mo Cnj Ta,06:49 am
11-30-1963,Mo Cnj Ge,06:15 am

December 1963
12-02-1963,Mo Cnj Ca,05:45 am
12-04-1963,Mo Cnj Le,07:20 am
12-06-1963,Mo Cnj Vi,12:27 pm
12-08-1963,Mo Cnj Li,09:22 pm
12-11-1963,Mo Cnj Sc,09:05 am
12-13-1963,Mo Cnj Sa,09:54 pm
12-16-1963,Mo Cnj Ca,10:22 am
12-18-1963,Mo Cnj Aq,09:29 pm
12-21-1963,Mo Cnj Pi,06:29 am
12-23-1963,Mo Cnj Ar,12:41 pm
12-25-1963,Mo Cnj Ta,03:57 pm
12-27-1963,Mo Cnj Ge,04:58 pm
12-29-1963,Mo Cnj Ca,05:07 pm
12-31-1963,Mo Cnj Le,06:10 pm

January 1964
01-02-1964,Mo Cnj Vi,09:48 pm
01-05-1964,Mo Cnj Li,05:11 am
01-07-1964,Mo Cnj Sc,04:04 pm
01-10-1964,Mo Cnj Sa,04:49 am
01-12-1964,Mo Cnj Ca,05:14 am
01-15-1964,Mo Cnj Aq,03:48 am
01-17-1964,Mo Cnj Pi,12:04 pm
01-19-1964,Mo Cnj Ar,06:11 pm
01-21-1964,Mo Cnj Ta,10:24 pm
01-24-1964,Mo Cnj Ge,01:05 am
01-26-1964,Mo Cnj Ca,02:52 am

01-28-1964,Mo Cnj Le,04:46 am
01-30-1964,Mo Cnj Vi,08:09 am

February 1964
02-01-1964,Mo Cnj Li,02:25 pm
02-04-1964,Mo Cnj Sc,00:13 am
02-06-1964,Mo Cnj Sa,12:35 pm
02-09-1964,Mo Cnj Ca,01:11 am
02-11-1964,Mo Cnj Aq,11:40 am
02-13-1964,Mo Cnj Pi,07:09 pm
02-16-1964,Mo Cnj Ar,00:11 am
02-18-1964,Mo Cnj Ta,03:46 am
02-20-1964,Mo Cnj Ge,06:49 am
02-22-1964,Mo Cnj Ca,09:50 am
02-24-1964,Mo Cnj Le,01:12 pm
02-26-1964,Mo Cnj Vi,05:30 pm
02-28-1964,Mo Cnj Li,11:46 pm

March 1964
03-02-1964,Mo Cnj Sc,08:54 am
03-04-1964,Mo Cnj Sa,08:47 pm
03-07-1964,Mo Cnj Ca,09:36 am
03-09-1964,Mo Cnj Aq,08:36 pm
03-12-1964,Mo Cnj Pi,04:06 am
03-14-1964,Mo Cnj Ar,08:16 am
03-16-1964,Mo Cnj Ta,10:31 am
03-18-1964,Mo Cnj Ge,12:26 pm
03-20-1964,Mo Cnj Ca,03:12 pm
03-22-1964,Mo Cnj Le,07:15 pm
03-25-1964,Mo Cnj Vi,00:42 am
03-27-1964,Mo Cnj Li,07:48 am
03-29-1964,Mo Cnj Sc,05:04 pm

April 1964
04-01-1964,Mo Cnj Sa,04:42 am
04-03-1964,Mo Cnj Ca,05:37 pm
04-06-1964,Mo Cnj Aq,05:25 am
04-08-1964,Mo Cnj Pi,01:47 pm
04-10-1964,Mo Cnj Ar,06:09 pm
04-12-1964,Mo Cnj Ta,07:37 pm
04-14-1964,Mo Cnj Ge,08:06 pm
04-16-1964,Mo Cnj Ca,09:24 pm
04-19-1964,Mo Cnj Le,00:40 am
04-21-1964,Mo Cnj Vi,06:18 am
04-23-1964,Mo Cnj Li,02:09 pm
04-26-1964,Mo Cnj Sc,00:02 am
04-28-1964,Mo Cnj Sa,11:47 am

May 1964

05-01-1964,Mo Cnj Ca,00:43 am
05-03-1964,Mo Cnj Aq,01:07 pm
05-05-1964,Mo Cnj Pi,10:43 pm
05-08-1964,Mo Cnj Ar,04:16 am
05-10-1964,Mo Cnj Ta,06:09 am
05-12-1964,Mo Cnj Ge,06:02 am
05-14-1964,Mo Cnj Ca,05:54 am
05-16-1964,Mo Cnj Le,07:32 am
05-18-1964,Mo Cnj Vi,12:03 pm
05-20-1964,Mo Cnj Li,07:42 pm
05-23-1964,Mo Cnj Sc,05:59 am
05-25-1964,Mo Cnj Sa,06:03 pm
05-28-1964,Mo Cnj Ca,07:00 am
05-30-1964,Mo Cnj Aq,07:32 pm

June 1964

06-02-1964,Mo Cnj Pi,06:01 am
06-04-1964,Mo Cnj Ar,01:03 pm
06-06-1964,Mo Cnj Ta,04:20 pm
06-08-1964,Mo Cnj Ge,04:51 pm
06-10-1964,Mo Cnj Ca,04:17 pm
06-12-1964,Mo Cnj Le,04:36 pm
06-14-1964,Mo Cnj Vi,07:28 pm
06-17-1964,Mo Cnj Li,01:54 am
06-19-1964,Mo Cnj Sc,11:49 am
06-22-1964,Mo Cnj Sa,00:03 am
06-24-1964,Mo Cnj Ca,01:02 pm
06-27-1964,Mo Cnj Aq,01:22 am
06-29-1964,Mo Cnj Pi,11:57 am

July 1964

07-01-1964,Mo Cnj Ar,07:53 pm
07-04-1964,Mo Cnj Ta,00:43 am
07-06-1964,Mo Cnj Ge,02:44 am
07-08-1964,Mo Cnj Ca,02:57 am
07-10-1964,Mo Cnj Le,03:01 am
07-12-1964,Mo Cnj Vi,04:44 am
07-14-1964,Mo Cnj Li,09:41 am
07-16-1964,Mo Cnj Sc,06:32 pm
07-19-1964,Mo Cnj Sa,06:28 am
07-21-1964,Mo Cnj Ca,07:27 pm
07-24-1964,Mo Cnj Aq,07:31 am
07-26-1964,Mo Cnj Pi,05:36 pm
07-29-1964,Mo Cnj Ar,01:26 am
07-31-1964,Mo Cnj Ta,07:01 am

August 1964

08-02-1964,Mo Cnj Ge,10:28 am
08-04-1964,Mo Cnj Ca,12:13 pm
08-06-1964,Mo Cnj Le,01:11 pm
08-08-1964,Mo Cnj Vi,02:50 pm
08-10-1964,Mo Cnj Li,06:52 pm
08-13-1964,Mo Cnj Sc,02:32 am
08-15-1964,Mo Cnj Sa,01:45 pm
08-18-1964,Mo Cnj Ca,02:39 am
08-20-1964,Mo Cnj Aq,02:40 pm
08-23-1964,Mo Cnj Pi,00:14 am
08-25-1964,Mo Cnj Ar,07:15 am
08-27-1964,Mo Cnj Ta,12:24 pm
08-29-1964,Mo Cnj Ge,04:16 pm
08-31-1964,Mo Cnj Ca,07:13 pm

September 1964

09-02-1964,Mo Cnj Le,09:37 pm
09-05-1964,Mo Cnj Vi,00:13 am
09-07-1964,Mo Cnj Li,04:20 am
09-09-1964,Mo Cnj Sc,11:21 am
09-11-1964,Mo Cnj Sa,09:48 pm
09-14-1964,Mo Cnj Ca,10:31 am
09-16-1964,Mo Cnj Aq,10:48 pm
09-19-1964,Mo Cnj Pi,08:22 am
09-21-1964,Mo Cnj Ar,02:44 pm
09-23-1964,Mo Cnj Ta,06:46 pm
09-25-1964,Mo Cnj Ge,09:46 pm
09-28-1964,Mo Cnj Ca,00:40 am
09-30-1964,Mo Cnj Le,03:53 am

October 1964

10-02-1964,Mo Cnj Vi,07:43 am
10-04-1964,Mo Cnj Li,12:45 pm
10-06-1964,Mo Cnj Sc,07:57 pm
10-09-1964,Mo Cnj Sa,06:03 am
10-11-1964,Mo Cnj Ca,06:32 pm
10-14-1964,Mo Cnj Aq,07:15 am
10-16-1964,Mo Cnj Pi,05:33 pm
10-19-1964,Mo Cnj Ar,00:05 am
10-21-1964,Mo Cnj Ta,03:25 am
10-23-1964,Mo Cnj Ge,05:04 am
10-25-1964,Mo Cnj Ca,06:38 am
10-27-1964,Mo Cnj Le,09:15 am
10-29-1964,Mo Cnj Vi,01:26 pm
10-31-1964,Mo Cnj Li,07:25 pm

November 1964

11-03-1964,Mo Cnj Sc,03:25 am
11-05-1964,Mo Cnj Sa,01:43 pm
11-08-1964,Mo Cnj Ca,02:06 am
11-10-1964,Mo Cnj Aq,03:08 pm
11-13-1964,Mo Cnj Pi,02:29 am
11-15-1964,Mo Cnj Ar,10:11 am
11-17-1964,Mo Cnj Ta,01:58 pm
11-19-1964,Mo Cnj Ge,02:59 pm
11-21-1964,Mo Cnj Ca,03:05 pm
11-23-1964,Mo Cnj Le,03:59 pm
11-25-1964,Mo Cnj Vi,07:03 pm
11-28-1964,Mo Cnj Li,00:54 am
11-30-1964,Mo Cnj Sc,09:31 am

December 1964

12-02-1964,Mo Cnj Sa,08:24 pm
12-05-1964,Mo Cnj Ca,08:54 am
12-07-1964,Mo Cnj Aq,09:58 pm
12-10-1964,Mo Cnj Pi,10:00 am
12-12-1964,Mo Cnj Ar,07:13 pm
12-15-1964,Mo Cnj Ta,00:33 am
12-17-1964,Mo Cnj Ge,02:22 am
12-19-1964,Mo Cnj Ca,02:03 am
12-21-1964,Mo Cnj Le,01:31 am
12-23-1964,Mo Cnj Vi,02:41 am
12-25-1964,Mo Cnj Li,07:04 am
12-27-1964,Mo Cnj Sc,03:12 pm
12-30-1964,Mo Cnj Sa,02:21 am

January 1965

01-01-1965,Mo Cnj Ca,03:07 pm
01-04-1965,Mo Cnj Aq,04:05 am
01-06-1965,Mo Cnj Pi,04:07 pm
01-09-1965,Mo Cnj Ar,02:08 am
01-11-1965,Mo Cnj Ta,09:11 am
01-13-1965,Mo Cnj Ge,12:48 pm
01-15-1965,Mo Cnj Ca,01:35 pm
01-17-1965,Mo Cnj Le,12:58 pm
01-19-1965,Mo Cnj Vi,12:55 pm
01-21-1965,Mo Cnj Li,03:28 pm
01-23-1965,Mo Cnj Sc,10:02 pm
01-26-1965,Mo Cnj Sa,08:33 am
01-28-1965,Mo Cnj Ca,09:22 pm
01-31-1965,Mo Cnj Aq,10:18 am

February 1965

02-02-1965,Mo Cnj Pi,09:56 pm
02-05-1965,Mo Cnj Ar,07:43 am
02-07-1965,Mo Cnj Ta,03:24 pm
02-09-1965,Mo Cnj Ge,08:36 pm
02-11-1965,Mo Cnj Ca,11:14 pm
02-13-1965,Mo Cnj Le,11:55 pm
02-16-1965,Mo Cnj Vi,00:06 am
02-18-1965,Mo Cnj Li,01:46 am
02-20-1965,Mo Cnj Sc,06:46 am
02-22-1965,Mo Cnj Sa,03:58 pm
02-25-1965,Mo Cnj Ca,04:17 am
02-27-1965,Mo Cnj Aq,05:14 pm

March 1965

03-02-1965,Mo Cnj Pi,04:38 am
03-04-1965,Mo Cnj Ar,01:45 pm
03-06-1965,Mo Cnj Ta,08:50 pm
03-09-1965,Mo Cnj Ge,02:15 am
03-11-1965,Mo Cnj Ca,06:04 am
03-13-1965,Mo Cnj Le,08:24 am
03-15-1965,Mo Cnj Vi,09:56 am
03-17-1965,Mo Cnj Li,12:05 pm
03-19-1965,Mo Cnj Sc,04:32 pm
03-22-1965,Mo Cnj Sa,00:37 am
03-24-1965,Mo Cnj Ca,12:07 pm
03-27-1965,Mo Cnj Aq,00:59 am
03-29-1965,Mo Cnj Pi,12:32 pm
03-31-1965,Mo Cnj Ar,09:19 pm

April 1965

04-03-1965,Mo Cnj Ta,03:29 am
04-05-1965,Mo Cnj Ge,07:56 am
04-07-1965,Mo Cnj Ca,11:25 am
04-09-1965,Mo Cnj Le,02:24 pm
04-11-1965,Mo Cnj Vi,05:15 pm
04-13-1965,Mo Cnj Li,08:39 pm
04-16-1965,Mo Cnj Sc,01:42 am
04-18-1965,Mo Cnj Sa,09:31 am
04-20-1965,Mo Cnj Ca,08:24 am
04-23-1965,Mo Cnj Aq,09:05 am
04-25-1965,Mo Cnj Pi,09:03 pm
04-28-1965,Mo Cnj Ar,06:13 am
04-30-1965,Mo Cnj Ta,12:04 pm

May 1965

05-02-1965,Mo Cnj Ge,03:27 pm
05-04-1965,Mo Cnj Ca,05:39 pm

05-06-1965,Mo Cnj Le,07:50 pm
05-08-1965,Mo Cnj Vi,10:47 pm
05-11-1965,Mo Cnj Li,03:04 am
05-13-1965,Mo Cnj Sc,09:10 am
05-15-1965,Mo Cnj Sa,05:32 pm
05-18-1965,Mo Cnj Ca,04:21 am
05-20-1965,Mo Cnj Aq,04:51 pm
05-23-1965,Mo Cnj Pi,05:15 am
05-25-1965,Mo Cnj Ar,03:19 pm
05-27-1965,Mo Cnj Ta,09:49 pm
05-30-1965,Mo Cnj Ge,00:59 am

June 1965
06-01-1965,Mo Cnj Ca,02:05 am
06-03-1965,Mo Cnj Le,02:47 am
06-05-1965,Mo Cnj Vi,04:33 am
06-07-1965,Mo Cnj Li,08:30 am
06-09-1965,Mo Cnj Sc,03:05 pm
06-12-1965,Mo Cnj Sa,00:11 am
06-14-1965,Mo Cnj Ca,11:21 am
06-16-1965,Mo Cnj Aq,11:52 am
06-19-1965,Mo Cnj Pi,12:29 pm
06-21-1965,Mo Cnj Ar,11:29 pm
06-24-1965,Mo Cnj Ta,07:16 am
06-26-1965,Mo Cnj Ge,11:18 am
06-28-1965,Mo Cnj Ca,12:21 pm
06-30-1965,Mo Cnj Le,12:00 pm

July 1965
07-02-1965,Mo Cnj Vi,12:12 pm
07-04-1965,Mo Cnj Li,02:44 pm
07-06-1965,Mo Cnj Sc,08:39 pm
07-09-1965,Mo Cnj Sa,05:54 am
07-11-1965,Mo Cnj Ca,05:29 pm
07-14-1965,Mo Cnj Aq,06:08 am
07-16-1965,Mo Cnj Pi,06:45 pm
07-19-1965,Mo Cnj Ar,06:13 am
07-21-1965,Mo Cnj Ta,03:14 pm
07-23-1965,Mo Cnj Ge,08:49 pm
07-25-1965,Mo Cnj Ca,10:54 pm
07-27-1965,Mo Cnj Le,10:38 pm
07-29-1965,Mo Cnj Vi,09:55 pm
07-31-1965,Mo Cnj Li,10:54 pm

August 1965
08-03-1965,Mo Cnj Sc,03:21 am
08-05-1965,Mo Cnj Sa,11:49 am

08-07-1965,Mo Cnj Ca,11:22 pm
08-10-1965,Mo Cnj Aq,12:09 pm
08-13-1965,Mo Cnj Pi,00:38 am
08-15-1965,Mo Cnj Ar,11:57 am
08-17-1965,Mo Cnj Ta,09:28 pm
08-20-1965,Mo Cnj Ge,04:21 am
08-22-1965,Mo Cnj Ca,08:05 am
08-24-1965,Mo Cnj Le,09:01 am
08-26-1965,Mo Cnj Vi,08:36 am
08-28-1965,Mo Cnj Li,08:52 am
08-30-1965,Mo Cnj Sc,11:54 am

September 1965
09-01-1965,Mo Cnj Sa,07:00 pm
09-04-1965,Mo Cnj Ca,05:52 am
09-06-1965,Mo Cnj Aq,06:34 pm
09-09-1965,Mo Cnj Pi,06:57 am
09-11-1965,Mo Cnj Ar,05:51 pm
09-14-1965,Mo Cnj Ta,02:57 am
09-16-1965,Mo Cnj Ge,10:07 am
09-18-1965,Mo Cnj Ca,03:01 pm
09-20-1965,Mo Cnj Le,05:35 pm
09-22-1965,Mo Cnj Vi,06:30 pm
09-24-1965,Mo Cnj Li,07:16 pm
09-26-1965,Mo Cnj Sc,09:47 pm
09-29-1965,Mo Cnj Sa,03:43 am

October 1965
10-01-1965,Mo Cnj Ca,01:30 pm
10-04-1965,Mo Cnj Aq,01:49 am
10-06-1965,Mo Cnj Pi,02:15 pm
10-09-1965,Mo Cnj Ar,00:54 am
10-11-1965,Mo Cnj Ta,09:17 am
10-13-1965,Mo Cnj Ge,03:40 pm
10-15-1965,Mo Cnj Ca,08:27 pm
10-17-1965,Mo Cnj Le,11:51 pm
10-20-1965,Mo Cnj Vi,02:13 am
10-22-1965,Mo Cnj Li,04:22 am
10-24-1965,Mo Cnj Sc,07:32 am
10-26-1965,Mo Cnj Sa,01:10 pm
10-28-1965,Mo Cnj Ca,10:06 pm
10-31-1965,Mo Cnj Aq,09:50 am

November 1965
11-02-1965,Mo Cnj Pi,10:23 pm
11-05-1965,Mo Cnj Ar,09:22 am
11-07-1965,Mo Cnj Ta,05:30 pm

11-09-1965,Mo Cnj Ge,10:54 pm
11-12-1965,Mo Cnj Ca,02:30 am
11-14-1965,Mo Cnj Le,05:14 am
11-16-1965,Mo Cnj Vi,07:55 am
11-18-1965,Mo Cnj Li,11:11 am
11-20-1965,Mo Cnj Sc,03:38 pm
11-22-1965,Mo Cnj Sa,09:57 pm
11-25-1965,Mo Cnj Ca,06:46 am
11-27-1965,Mo Cnj Aq,06:03 pm
11-30-1965,Mo Cnj Pi,06:40 am

December 1965
12-02-1965,Mo Cnj Ar,06:23 pm
12-05-1965,Mo Cnj Ta,03:12 am
12-07-1965,Mo Cnj Ge,08:28 am
12-09-1965,Mo Cnj Ca,10:58 am
12-11-1965,Mo Cnj Le,12:09 pm
12-13-1965,Mo Cnj Vi,01:36 pm
12-15-1965,Mo Cnj Li,04:34 pm
12-17-1965,Mo Cnj Sc,09:40 pm
12-20-1965,Mo Cnj Sa,05:01 am
12-22-1965,Mo Cnj Ca,02:27 pm
12-25-1965,Mo Cnj Aq,01:44 am
12-27-1965,Mo Cnj Pi,02:18 pm
12-30-1965,Mo Cnj Ar,02:40 am

January 1966
01-01-1966,Mo Cnj Ta,12:47 pm
01-03-1966,Mo Cnj Ge,07:07 pm
01-05-1966,Mo Cnj Ca,09:41 pm
01-07-1966,Mo Cnj Le,09:50 pm
01-09-1966,Mo Cnj Vi,09:35 pm
01-11-1966,Mo Cnj Li,10:53 pm
01-14-1966,Mo Cnj Sc,03:08 am
01-16-1966,Mo Cnj Sa,10:40 am
01-18-1966,Mo Cnj Ca,08:45 pm
01-21-1966,Mo Cnj Aq,08:27 am
01-23-1966,Mo Cnj Pi,08:59 pm
01-26-1966,Mo Cnj Ar,09:34 am
01-28-1966,Mo Cnj Ta,08:43 pm
01-31-1966,Mo Cnj Ge,04:44 am

February 1966
02-02-1966,Mo Cnj Ca,08:41 am
02-04-1966,Mo Cnj Le,09:14 am
02-06-1966,Mo Cnj Vi,08:11 am
02-08-1966,Mo Cnj Li,07:50 am

02-10-1966,Mo Cnj Sc,10:15 am
02-12-1966,Mo Cnj Sa,04:34 pm
02-15-1966,Mo Cnj Ca,02:27 am
02-17-1966,Mo Cnj Aq,02:27 pm
02-20-1966,Mo Cnj Pi,03:06 am
02-22-1966,Mo Cnj Ar,03:30 pm
02-25-1966,Mo Cnj Ta,02:53 am
02-27-1966,Mo Cnj Ge,12:03 pm

March 1966
03-01-1966,Mo Cnj Ca,05:48 pm
03-03-1966,Mo Cnj Le,07:57 pm
03-05-1966,Mo Cnj Vi,07:37 pm
03-07-1966,Mo Cnj Li,06:49 pm
03-09-1966,Mo Cnj Sc,07:48 pm
03-12-1966,Mo Cnj Sa,00:19 am
03-14-1966,Mo Cnj Ca,08:56 am
03-16-1966,Mo Cnj Aq,08:35 pm
03-19-1966,Mo Cnj Pi,09:19 am
03-21-1966,Mo Cnj Ar,09:33 am
03-24-1966,Mo Cnj Ta,08:32 am
03-26-1966,Mo Cnj Ge,05:42 pm
03-29-1966,Mo Cnj Ca,00:24 am
03-31-1966,Mo Cnj Le,04:13 am

April 1966
04-02-1966,Mo Cnj Vi,05:32 am
04-04-1966,Mo Cnj Li,05:40 am
04-06-1966,Mo Cnj Sc,06:31 am
04-08-1966,Mo Cnj Sa,09:54 am
04-10-1966,Mo Cnj Ca,05:02 pm
04-13-1966,Mo Cnj Aq,03:42 am
04-15-1966,Mo Cnj Pi,04:13 pm
04-18-1966,Mo Cnj Ar,04:27 am
04-20-1966,Mo Cnj Ta,03:01 am
04-22-1966,Mo Cnj Ge,11:28 pm
04-25-1966,Mo Cnj Ca,05:49 am
04-27-1966,Mo Cnj Le,10:10 am
04-29-1966,Mo Cnj Vi,12:50 pm

May 1966
05-01-1966,Mo Cnj Li,02:32 pm
05-03-1966,Mo Cnj Sc,04:24 pm
05-05-1966,Mo Cnj Sa,07:52 pm
05-08-1966,Mo Cnj Ca,02:12 am
05-10-1966,Mo Cnj Aq,11:51 am
05-12-1966,Mo Cnj Pi,11:55 pm

05-15-1966,Mo Cnj Ar,12:16 pm
05-17-1966,Mo Cnj Ta,10:50 pm
05-20-1966,Mo Cnj Ge,06:41 am
05-22-1966,Mo Cnj Ca,12:01 pm
05-24-1966,Mo Cnj Le,03:37 pm
05-26-1966,Mo Cnj Vi,06:22 pm
05-28-1966,Mo Cnj Li,09:00 pm
05-31-1966,Mo Cnj Sc,00:11 am

June 1966
06-02-1966,Mo Cnj Sa,04:38 am
06-04-1966,Mo Cnj Ca,11:10 am
06-06-1966,Mo Cnj Aq,08:21 pm
06-09-1966,Mo Cnj Pi,07:57 am
06-11-1966,Mo Cnj Ar,08:27 pm
06-14-1966,Mo Cnj Ta,07:30 am
06-16-1966,Mo Cnj Ge,03:26 pm
06-18-1966,Mo Cnj Ca,08:05 pm
06-20-1966,Mo Cnj Le,10:29 pm
06-23-1966,Mo Cnj Vi,00:08 am
06-25-1966,Mo Cnj Li,02:23 am
06-27-1966,Mo Cnj Sc,06:04 am
06-29-1966,Mo Cnj Sa,11:31 am

July 1966
07-01-1966,Mo Cnj Ca,06:52 pm
07-04-1966,Mo Cnj Aq,04:15 am
07-06-1966,Mo Cnj Pi,03:40 pm
07-09-1966,Mo Cnj Ar,04:16 am
07-11-1966,Mo Cnj Ta,04:04 pm
07-14-1966,Mo Cnj Ge,00:51 am
07-16-1966,Mo Cnj Ca,05:44 am
07-18-1966,Mo Cnj Le,07:28 am
07-20-1966,Mo Cnj Vi,07:47 am
07-22-1966,Mo Cnj Li,08:38 am
07-24-1966,Mo Cnj Sc,11:32 am
07-26-1966,Mo Cnj Sa,05:05 pm
07-29-1966,Mo Cnj Ca,01:05 am
07-31-1966,Mo Cnj Aq,11:02 am

August 1966
08-02-1966,Mo Cnj Pi,10:36 pm
08-05-1966,Mo Cnj Ar,11:14 am
08-07-1966,Mo Cnj Ta,11:37 pm
08-10-1966,Mo Cnj Ge,09:38 am
08-12-1966,Mo Cnj Ca,03:42 pm
08-14-1966,Mo Cnj Le,05:50 pm

08-16-1966,Mo Cnj Vi,05:35 pm
08-18-1966,Mo Cnj Li,05:06 pm
08-20-1966,Mo Cnj Sc,06:24 pm
08-22-1966,Mo Cnj Sa,10:51 pm
08-25-1966,Mo Cnj Ca,06:37 am
08-27-1966,Mo Cnj Aq,04:56 pm
08-30-1966,Mo Cnj Pi,04:48 am

September 1966
09-01-1966,Mo Cnj Ar,05:27 pm
09-04-1966,Mo Cnj Ta,05:59 am
09-06-1966,Mo Cnj Ge,04:53 pm
09-09-1966,Mo Cnj Ca,00:27 am
09-11-1966,Mo Cnj Le,04:02 am
09-13-1966,Mo Cnj Vi,04:26 am
09-15-1966,Mo Cnj Li,03:33 am
09-17-1966,Mo Cnj Sc,03:34 am
09-19-1966,Mo Cnj Sa,06:21 am
09-21-1966,Mo Cnj Ca,12:53 pm
09-23-1966,Mo Cnj Aq,10:48 pm
09-26-1966,Mo Cnj Pi,10:49 am
09-28-1966,Mo Cnj Ar,11:30 pm

October 1966
10-01-1966,Mo Cnj Ta,11:48 am
10-03-1966,Mo Cnj Ge,10:44 pm
10-06-1966,Mo Cnj Ca,07:13 am
10-08-1966,Mo Cnj Le,12:25 pm
10-10-1966,Mo Cnj Vi,02:27 pm
10-12-1966,Mo Cnj Li,02:29 pm
10-14-1966,Mo Cnj Sc,02:21 pm
10-16-1966,Mo Cnj Sa,03:59 pm
10-18-1966,Mo Cnj Ca,08:56 pm
10-21-1966,Mo Cnj Aq,05:41 am
10-23-1966,Mo Cnj Pi,05:21 pm
10-26-1966,Mo Cnj Ar,06:04 am
10-28-1966,Mo Cnj Ta,06:06 pm
10-31-1966,Mo Cnj Ge,04:28 am

November 1966
11-02-1966,Mo Cnj Ca,12:43 pm
11-04-1966,Mo Cnj Le,06:36 pm
11-06-1966,Mo Cnj Vi,10:10 pm
11-08-1966,Mo Cnj Li,11:54 pm
11-11-1966,Mo Cnj Sc,00:53 am
11-13-1966,Mo Cnj Sa,02:36 am
11-15-1966,Mo Cnj Ca,06:37 am

11-17-1966,Mo Cnj Aq,02:04 pm
11-20-1966,Mo Cnj Pi,00:54 am
11-22-1966,Mo Cnj Ar,01:31 pm
11-25-1966,Mo Cnj Ta,01:37 am
11-27-1966,Mo Cnj Ge,11:31 am
11-29-1966,Mo Cnj Ca,06:49 pm

December 1966
12-02-1966,Mo Cnj Le,00:02 am
12-04-1966,Mo Cnj Vi,03:48 am
12-06-1966,Mo Cnj Li,06:43 am
12-08-1966,Mo Cnj Sc,09:18 am
12-10-1966,Mo Cnj Sa,12:14 pm
12-12-1966,Mo Cnj Ca,04:31 pm
12-14-1966,Mo Cnj Aq,11:20 pm
12-17-1966,Mo Cnj Pi,09:18 am
12-19-1966,Mo Cnj Ar,09:39 pm
12-22-1966,Mo Cnj Ta,10:07 am
12-24-1966,Mo Cnj Ge,08:14 pm
12-27-1966,Mo Cnj Ca,02:58 am
12-29-1966,Mo Cnj Le,06:58 am
12-31-1966,Mo Cnj Vi,09:34 am

January 1967
01-02-1967,Mo Cnj Li,12:04 pm
01-04-1967,Mo Cnj Sc,03:17 pm
01-06-1967,Mo Cnj Sa,07:29 pm
01-09-1967,Mo Cnj Ca,00:54 am
01-11-1967,Mo Cnj Aq,08:06 am
01-13-1967,Mo Cnj Pi,05:45 pm
01-16-1967,Mo Cnj Ar,05:48 am
01-18-1967,Mo Cnj Ta,06:40 pm
01-21-1967,Mo Cnj Ge,05:39 am
01-23-1967,Mo Cnj Ca,12:52 pm
01-25-1967,Mo Cnj Le,04:21 pm
01-27-1967,Mo Cnj Vi,05:37 pm
01-29-1967,Mo Cnj Li,06:33 pm
01-31-1967,Mo Cnj Sc,08:44 pm

February 1967
02-03-1967,Mo Cnj Sa,00:56 am
02-05-1967,Mo Cnj Ca,07:10 am
02-07-1967,Mo Cnj Aq,03:17 pm
02-10-1967,Mo Cnj Pi,01:19 am
02-12-1967,Mo Cnj Ar,01:17 pm
02-15-1967,Mo Cnj Ta,02:19 am
02-17-1967,Mo Cnj Ge,02:16 pm

02-19-1967,Mo Cnj Ca,10:49 pm
02-22-1967,Mo Cnj Le,03:05 am
02-24-1967,Mo Cnj Vi,04:04 am
02-26-1967,Mo Cnj Li,03:44 am
02-28-1967,Mo Cnj Sc,04:09 am

March 1967
03-02-1967,Mo Cnj Sa,06:53 am
03-04-1967,Mo Cnj Ca,12:35 pm
03-06-1967,Mo Cnj Aq,09:04 pm
03-09-1967,Mo Cnj Pi,07:42 am
03-11-1967,Mo Cnj Ar,07:54 pm
03-14-1967,Mo Cnj Ta,08:55 am
03-16-1967,Mo Cnj Ge,09:19 am
03-19-1967,Mo Cnj Ca,07:10 am
03-21-1967,Mo Cnj Le,01:04 pm
03-23-1967,Mo Cnj Vi,03:08 pm
03-25-1967,Mo Cnj Li,02:50 pm
03-27-1967,Mo Cnj Sc,02:11 pm
03-29-1967,Mo Cnj Sa,03:09 pm
03-31-1967,Mo Cnj Ca,07:11 pm

April 1967
04-03-1967,Mo Cnj Aq,02:50 am
04-05-1967,Mo Cnj Pi,01:30 pm
04-08-1967,Mo Cnj Ar,01:57 am
04-10-1967,Mo Cnj Ta,02:56 am
04-13-1967,Mo Cnj Ge,03:15 am
04-15-1967,Mo Cnj Ca,01:37 pm
04-17-1967,Mo Cnj Le,08:54 pm
04-20-1967,Mo Cnj Vi,00:43 am
04-22-1967,Mo Cnj Li,01:42 am
04-24-1967,Mo Cnj Sc,01:19 am
04-26-1967,Mo Cnj Sa,01:28 am
04-28-1967,Mo Cnj Ca,03:55 am
04-30-1967,Mo Cnj Aq,09:58 am

May 1967
05-02-1967,Mo Cnj Pi,07:48 pm
05-05-1967,Mo Cnj Ar,08:10 am
05-07-1967,Mo Cnj Ta,09:09 pm
05-10-1967,Mo Cnj Ge,09:08 am
05-12-1967,Mo Cnj Ca,07:11 pm
05-15-1967,Mo Cnj Le,02:49 am
05-17-1967,Mo Cnj Vi,07:53 am
05-19-1967,Mo Cnj Li,10:32 am
05-21-1967,Mo Cnj Sc,11:30 am

05-23-1967,Mo Cnj Sa,12:06 pm
05-25-1967,Mo Cnj Ca,01:58 pm
05-27-1967,Mo Cnj Aq,06:44 pm
05-30-1967,Mo Cnj Pi,03:18 am

June 1967
06-01-1967,Mo Cnj Ar,03:07 pm
06-04-1967,Mo Cnj Ta,04:04 am
06-06-1967,Mo Cnj Ge,03:53 pm
06-09-1967,Mo Cnj Ca,01:18 am
06-11-1967,Mo Cnj Le,08:20 am
06-13-1967,Mo Cnj Vi,01:24 pm
06-15-1967,Mo Cnj Li,04:59 pm
06-17-1967,Mo Cnj Sc,07:25 pm
06-19-1967,Mo Cnj Sa,09:20 pm
06-21-1967,Mo Cnj Ca,11:46 pm
06-24-1967,Mo Cnj Aq,04:11 am
06-26-1967,Mo Cnj Pi,11:49 am
06-28-1967,Mo Cnj Ar,10:53 pm

July 1967
07-01-1967,Mo Cnj Ta,11:43 am
07-03-1967,Mo Cnj Ge,11:40 pm
07-06-1967,Mo Cnj Ca,08:48 am
07-08-1967,Mo Cnj Le,02:59 pm
07-10-1967,Mo Cnj Vi,07:08 pm
07-12-1967,Mo Cnj Li,10:20 pm
07-15-1967,Mo Cnj Sc,01:17 am
07-17-1967,Mo Cnj Sa,04:22 am
07-19-1967,Mo Cnj Ca,07:59 am
07-21-1967,Mo Cnj Aq,01:00 pm
07-23-1967,Mo Cnj Pi,08:29 pm
07-26-1967,Mo Cnj Ar,07:01 am
07-28-1967,Mo Cnj Ta,07:41 pm
07-31-1967,Mo Cnj Ge,08:01 am

August 1967
08-02-1967,Mo Cnj Ca,05:32 pm
08-04-1967,Mo Cnj Le,11:26 pm
08-07-1967,Mo Cnj Vi,02:36 am
08-09-1967,Mo Cnj Li,04:34 am
08-11-1967,Mo Cnj Sc,06:44 am
08-13-1967,Mo Cnj Sa,09:53 am
08-15-1967,Mo Cnj Ca,02:19 pm
08-17-1967,Mo Cnj Aq,08:18 pm
08-20-1967,Mo Cnj Pi,04:19 am
08-22-1967,Mo Cnj Ar,02:48 pm

08-25-1967,Mo Cnj Ta,03:22 am
08-27-1967,Mo Cnj Ge,04:08 pm
08-30-1967,Mo Cnj Ca,02:34 am

September 1967
09-01-1967,Mo Cnj Le,09:08 am
09-03-1967,Mo Cnj Vi,12:07 pm
09-05-1967,Mo Cnj Li,01:03 pm
09-07-1967,Mo Cnj Sc,01:44 pm
09-09-1967,Mo Cnj Sa,03:40 pm
09-11-1967,Mo Cnj Ca,07:43 pm
09-14-1967,Mo Cnj Aq,02:09 am
09-16-1967,Mo Cnj Pi,10:53 am
09-18-1967,Mo Cnj Ar,09:46 pm
09-21-1967,Mo Cnj Ta,10:20 am
09-23-1967,Mo Cnj Ge,11:21 pm
09-26-1967,Mo Cnj Ca,10:45 am
09-28-1967,Mo Cnj Le,06:42 pm
09-30-1967,Mo Cnj Vi,10:39 pm

October 1967
10-02-1967,Mo Cnj Li,11:35 pm
10-04-1967,Mo Cnj Sc,11:15 pm
10-06-1967,Mo Cnj Sa,11:32 pm
10-09-1967,Mo Cnj Ca,02:04 am
10-11-1967,Mo Cnj Aq,07:45 am
10-13-1967,Mo Cnj Pi,04:38 pm
10-16-1967,Mo Cnj Ar,03:58 am
10-18-1967,Mo Cnj Ta,04:41 pm
10-21-1967,Mo Cnj Ge,05:38 am
10-23-1967,Mo Cnj Ca,05:28 pm
10-26-1967,Mo Cnj Le,02:41 am
10-28-1967,Mo Cnj Vi,08:20 am
10-30-1967,Mo Cnj Li,10:32 am

November 1967
11-01-1967,Mo Cnj Sc,10:27 am
11-03-1967,Mo Cnj Sa,09:51 am
11-05-1967,Mo Cnj Ca,10:44 am
11-07-1967,Mo Cnj Aq,02:45 pm
11-09-1967,Mo Cnj Pi,10:43 pm
11-12-1967,Mo Cnj Ar,09:59 am
11-14-1967,Mo Cnj Ta,10:53 am
11-17-1967,Mo Cnj Ge,11:41 am
11-19-1967,Mo Cnj Ca,11:14 pm
11-22-1967,Mo Cnj Le,08:48 am
11-24-1967,Mo Cnj Vi,03:46 pm

11-26-1967,Mo Cnj Li,07:48 pm
11-28-1967,Mo Cnj Sc,09:13 pm
11-30-1967,Mo Cnj Sa,09:10 pm

December 1967
12-02-1967,Mo Cnj Ca,09:25 pm
12-04-1967,Mo Cnj Aq,11:57 pm
12-07-1967,Mo Cnj Pi,06:20 am
12-09-1967,Mo Cnj Ar,04:44 pm
12-12-1967,Mo Cnj Ta,05:33 am
12-14-1967,Mo Cnj Ge,06:19 pm
12-17-1967,Mo Cnj Ca,05:23 am
12-19-1967,Mo Cnj Le,02:21 pm
12-21-1967,Mo Cnj Vi,09:21 pm
12-24-1967,Mo Cnj Li,02:27 am
12-26-1967,Mo Cnj Sc,05:36 am
12-28-1967,Mo Cnj Sa,07:10 am
12-30-1967,Mo Cnj Ca,08:12 am

January 1968
01-01-1968,Mo Cnj Aq,10:24 am
01-03-1968,Mo Cnj Pi,03:36 pm
01-06-1968,Mo Cnj Ar,00:46 am
01-08-1968,Mo Cnj Ta,01:03 pm
01-11-1968,Mo Cnj Ge,01:54 am
01-13-1968,Mo Cnj Ca,12:54 pm
01-15-1968,Mo Cnj Le,09:09 pm
01-18-1968,Mo Cnj Vi,03:11 am
01-20-1968,Mo Cnj Li,07:48 am
01-22-1968,Mo Cnj Sc,11:28 am
01-24-1968,Mo Cnj Sa,02:24 pm
01-26-1968,Mo Cnj Ca,04:58 pm
01-28-1968,Mo Cnj Aq,08:07 pm
01-31-1968,Mo Cnj Pi,01:16 am

February 1968
02-02-1968,Mo Cnj Ar,09:40 am
02-04-1968,Mo Cnj Ta,09:15 pm
02-07-1968,Mo Cnj Ge,10:09 am
02-09-1968,Mo Cnj Ca,09:34 pm
02-12-1968,Mo Cnj Le,05:50 am
02-14-1968,Mo Cnj Vi,11:03 am
02-16-1968,Mo Cnj Li,02:22 pm
02-18-1968,Mo Cnj Sc,05:00 pm
02-20-1968,Mo Cnj Sa,07:48 pm
02-22-1968,Mo Cnj Ca,11:12 pm
02-25-1968,Mo Cnj Aq,03:37 am

02-27-1968,Mo Cnj Pi,09:42 am
02-29-1968,Mo Cnj Ar,06:14 pm

March 1968
03-03-1968,Mo Cnj Ta,05:28 am
03-05-1968,Mo Cnj Ge,06:17 pm
03-08-1968,Mo Cnj Ca,06:22 am
03-10-1968,Mo Cnj Le,03:28 pm
03-12-1968,Mo Cnj Vi,08:52 pm
03-14-1968,Mo Cnj Li,11:23 pm
03-17-1968,Mo Cnj Sc,00:33 am
03-19-1968,Mo Cnj Sa,01:54 am
03-21-1968,Mo Cnj Ca,04:35 am
03-23-1968,Mo Cnj Aq,09:16 am
03-25-1968,Mo Cnj Pi,04:15 pm
03-28-1968,Mo Cnj Ar,01:32 am
03-30-1968,Mo Cnj Ta,12:56 pm

April 1968
04-02-1968,Mo Cnj Ge,01:41 am
04-04-1968,Mo Cnj Ca,02:13 pm
04-07-1968,Mo Cnj Le,00:29 am
04-09-1968,Mo Cnj Vi,07:04 am
04-11-1968,Mo Cnj Li,10:01 am
04-13-1968,Mo Cnj Sc,10:32 am
04-15-1968,Mo Cnj Sa,10:23 am
04-17-1968,Mo Cnj Ca,11:23 am
04-19-1968,Mo Cnj Aq,02:57 pm
04-21-1968,Mo Cnj Pi,09:46 pm
04-24-1968,Mo Cnj Ar,07:33 am
04-26-1968,Mo Cnj Ta,07:23 am
04-29-1968,Mo Cnj Ge,08:12 am

May 1968
05-01-1968,Mo Cnj Ca,08:50 pm
05-04-1968,Mo Cnj Le,07:54 am
05-06-1968,Mo Cnj Vi,03:58 pm
05-08-1968,Mo Cnj Li,08:21 pm
05-10-1968,Mo Cnj Sc,09:30 pm
05-12-1968,Mo Cnj Sa,08:54 pm
05-14-1968,Mo Cnj Ca,08:31 pm
05-16-1968,Mo Cnj Aq,10:23 pm
05-19-1968,Mo Cnj Pi,03:54 am
05-21-1968,Mo Cnj Ar,01:15 pm
05-24-1968,Mo Cnj Ta,01:16 am
05-26-1968,Mo Cnj Ge,02:12 pm

05-29-1968,Mo Cnj Ca,02:43 am
05-31-1968,Mo Cnj Le,01:53 pm

June 1968
06-02-1968,Mo Cnj Vi,10:52 pm
06-05-1968,Mo Cnj Li,04:50 am
06-07-1968,Mo Cnj Sc,07:31 am
06-09-1968,Mo Cnj Sa,07:43 am
06-11-1968,Mo Cnj Ca,07:06 am
06-13-1968,Mo Cnj Aq,07:47 am
06-15-1968,Mo Cnj Pi,11:43 am
06-17-1968,Mo Cnj Ar,07:50 pm
06-20-1968,Mo Cnj Ta,07:25 am
06-22-1968,Mo Cnj Ge,08:22 pm
06-25-1968,Mo Cnj Ca,08:43 am
06-27-1968,Mo Cnj Le,07:31 pm
06-30-1968,Mo Cnj Vi,04:27 am

July 1968
07-02-1968,Mo Cnj Li,11:11 am
07-04-1968,Mo Cnj Sc,03:21 pm
07-06-1968,Mo Cnj Sa,05:05 pm
07-08-1968,Mo Cnj Ca,05:24 pm
07-10-1968,Mo Cnj Aq,06:04 pm
07-12-1968,Mo Cnj Pi,09:03 pm
07-15-1968,Mo Cnj Ar,03:52 am
07-17-1968,Mo Cnj Ta,02:30 pm
07-20-1968,Mo Cnj Ge,03:13 am
07-22-1968,Mo Cnj Ca,03:32 pm
07-25-1968,Mo Cnj Le,01:56 am
07-27-1968,Mo Cnj Vi,10:11 am
07-29-1968,Mo Cnj Li,04:33 pm
07-31-1968,Mo Cnj Sc,09:12 pm

August 1968
08-03-1968,Mo Cnj Sa,00:11 am
08-05-1968,Mo Cnj Ca,01:58 am
08-07-1968,Mo Cnj Aq,03:38 am
08-09-1968,Mo Cnj Pi,06:46 am
08-11-1968,Mo Cnj Ar,12:53 pm
08-13-1968,Mo Cnj Ta,10:37 pm
08-16-1968,Mo Cnj Ge,10:52 am
08-18-1968,Mo Cnj Ca,11:16 pm
08-21-1968,Mo Cnj Le,09:41 am
08-23-1968,Mo Cnj Vi,05:21 pm
08-25-1968,Mo Cnj Li,10:45 pm

08-28-1968,Mo Cnj Sc,02:38 am
08-30-1968,Mo Cnj Sa,05:41 am

September 1968
09-01-1968,Mo Cnj Ca,08:22 am
09-03-1968,Mo Cnj Aq,11:20 am
09-05-1968,Mo Cnj Pi,03:28 pm
09-07-1968,Mo Cnj Ar,09:50 pm
09-10-1968,Mo Cnj Ta,07:07 am
09-12-1968,Mo Cnj Ge,06:55 pm
09-15-1968,Mo Cnj Ca,07:29 am
09-17-1968,Mo Cnj Le,06:26 pm
09-20-1968,Mo Cnj Vi,02:16 am
09-22-1968,Mo Cnj Li,07:00 am
09-24-1968,Mo Cnj Sc,09:39 am
09-26-1968,Mo Cnj Sa,11:31 am
09-28-1968,Mo Cnj Ca,01:45 pm
09-30-1968,Mo Cnj Aq,05:12 pm

October 1968
10-02-1968,Mo Cnj Pi,10:22 pm
10-05-1968,Mo Cnj Ar,05:36 am
10-07-1968,Mo Cnj Ta,03:07 pm
10-10-1968,Mo Cnj Ge,02:44 am
10-12-1968,Mo Cnj Ca,03:23 pm
10-15-1968,Mo Cnj Le,03:08 am
10-17-1968,Mo Cnj Vi,11:59 am
10-19-1968,Mo Cnj Li,05:05 pm
10-21-1968,Mo Cnj Sc,07:06 pm
10-23-1968,Mo Cnj Sa,07:33 pm
10-25-1968,Mo Cnj Ca,08:14 pm
10-27-1968,Mo Cnj Aq,10:44 pm
10-30-1968,Mo Cnj Pi,03:55 am

November 1968
11-01-1968,Mo Cnj Ar,11:51 am
11-03-1968,Mo Cnj Ta,10:01 pm
11-06-1968,Mo Cnj Ge,09:48 am
11-08-1968,Mo Cnj Ca,10:27 pm
11-11-1968,Mo Cnj Le,10:45 am
11-13-1968,Mo Cnj Vi,08:55 pm
11-16-1968,Mo Cnj Li,03:27 am
11-18-1968,Mo Cnj Sc,06:07 am
11-20-1968,Mo Cnj Sa,06:05 am
11-22-1968,Mo Cnj Ca,05:20 am
11-24-1968,Mo Cnj Aq,06:02 am

11-26-1968,Mo Cnj Pi,09:53 am
11-28-1968,Mo Cnj Ar,05:26 pm

December 1968
12-01-1968,Mo Cnj Ta,03:58 am
12-03-1968,Mo Cnj Ge,04:06 pm
12-06-1968,Mo Cnj Ca,04:44 am
12-08-1968,Mo Cnj Le,05:03 pm
12-11-1968,Mo Cnj Vi,04:00 am
12-13-1968,Mo Cnj Li,12:09 pm
12-15-1968,Mo Cnj Sc,04:32 pm
12-17-1968,Mo Cnj Sa,05:28 pm
12-19-1968,Mo Cnj Ca,04:33 pm
12-21-1968,Mo Cnj Aq,04:00 pm
12-23-1968,Mo Cnj Pi,06:01 pm
12-26-1968,Mo Cnj Ar,00:02 am
12-28-1968,Mo Cnj Ta,09:57 am
12-30-1968,Mo Cnj Ge,10:12 pm

January 1969
01-02-1969,Mo Cnj Ca,10:54 am
01-04-1969,Mo Cnj Le,10:55 pm
01-07-1969,Mo Cnj Vi,09:43 am
01-09-1969,Mo Cnj Li,06:33 pm
01-12-1969,Mo Cnj Sc,00:32 am
01-14-1969,Mo Cnj Sa,03:19 am
01-16-1969,Mo Cnj Ca,03:39 am
01-18-1969,Mo Cnj Aq,03:17 am
01-20-1969,Mo Cnj Pi,04:21 am
01-22-1969,Mo Cnj Ar,08:44 am
01-24-1969,Mo Cnj Ta,05:14 pm
01-27-1969,Mo Cnj Ge,04:54 am
01-29-1969,Mo Cnj Ca,05:37 pm

February 1969
02-01-1969,Mo Cnj Le,05:29 am
02-03-1969,Mo Cnj Vi,03:41 am
02-06-1969,Mo Cnj Li,00:00 am
02-08-1969,Mo Cnj Sc,06:18 am
02-10-1969,Mo Cnj Sa,10:23 am
02-12-1969,Mo Cnj Ca,12:29 pm
02-14-1969,Mo Cnj Aq,01:31 pm
02-16-1969,Mo Cnj Pi,03:04 pm
02-18-1969,Mo Cnj Ar,06:49 pm
02-21-1969,Mo Cnj Ta,02:02 am
02-23-1969,Mo Cnj Ge,12:41 pm

02-26-1969,Mo Cnj Ca,01:11 am
02-28-1969,Mo Cnj Le,01:12 pm

March 1969
03-02-1969,Mo Cnj Vi,11:07 pm
03-05-1969,Mo Cnj Li,06:34 am
03-07-1969,Mo Cnj Sc,11:57 am
03-09-1969,Mo Cnj Sa,03:48 pm
03-11-1969,Mo Cnj Ca,06:41 pm
03-13-1969,Mo Cnj Aq,09:10 pm
03-16-1969,Mo Cnj Pi,00:04 am
03-18-1969,Mo Cnj Ar,04:27 am
03-20-1969,Mo Cnj Ta,11:21 am
03-22-1969,Mo Cnj Ge,09:12 pm
03-25-1969,Mo Cnj Ca,09:19 am
03-27-1969,Mo Cnj Le,09:37 pm
03-30-1969,Mo Cnj Vi,07:54 am

April 1969
04-01-1969,Mo Cnj Li,03:04 pm
04-03-1969,Mo Cnj Sc,07:23 pm
04-05-1969,Mo Cnj Sa,09:58 pm
04-08-1969,Mo Cnj Ca,00:05 am
04-10-1969,Mo Cnj Aq,02:46 am
04-12-1969,Mo Cnj Pi,06:41 am
04-14-1969,Mo Cnj Ar,12:13 pm
04-16-1969,Mo Cnj Ta,07:43 pm
04-19-1969,Mo Cnj Ge,05:29 am
04-21-1969,Mo Cnj Ca,05:18 pm
04-24-1969,Mo Cnj Le,05:52 am
04-26-1969,Mo Cnj Vi,04:57 pm
04-29-1969,Mo Cnj Li,00:44 am

May 1969
05-01-1969,Mo Cnj Sc,04:50 am
05-03-1969,Mo Cnj Sa,06:19 am
05-05-1969,Mo Cnj Ca,06:57 am
05-07-1969,Mo Cnj Aq,08:28 am
05-09-1969,Mo Cnj Pi,12:04 pm
05-11-1969,Mo Cnj Ar,06:09 pm
05-14-1969,Mo Cnj Ta,02:29 am
05-16-1969,Mo Cnj Ge,12:42 pm
05-19-1969,Mo Cnj Ca,00:31 am
05-21-1969,Mo Cnj Le,01:13 pm
05-24-1969,Mo Cnj Vi,01:07 am
05-26-1969,Mo Cnj Li,10:08 am

05-28-1969,Mo Cnj Sc,03:05 pm
05-30-1969,Mo Cnj Sa,04:30 pm

June 1969
06-01-1969,Mo Cnj Ca,04:07 pm
06-03-1969,Mo Cnj Aq,04:04 pm
06-05-1969,Mo Cnj Pi,06:14 pm
06-07-1969,Mo Cnj Ar,11:37 pm
06-10-1969,Mo Cnj Ta,08:07 am
06-12-1969,Mo Cnj Ge,06:49 pm
06-15-1969,Mo Cnj Ca,06:53 am
06-17-1969,Mo Cnj Le,07:35 pm
06-20-1969,Mo Cnj Vi,07:53 am
06-22-1969,Mo Cnj Li,06:03 pm
06-25-1969,Mo Cnj Sc,00:31 am
06-27-1969,Mo Cnj Sa,03:00 am
06-29-1969,Mo Cnj Ca,02:45 am

July 1969
07-01-1969,Mo Cnj Aq,01:50 am
07-03-1969,Mo Cnj Pi,02:27 am
07-05-1969,Mo Cnj Ar,06:17 am
07-07-1969,Mo Cnj Ta,01:54 pm
07-10-1969,Mo Cnj Ge,00:32 am
07-12-1969,Mo Cnj Ca,12:47 pm
07-15-1969,Mo Cnj Le,01:29 am
07-17-1969,Mo Cnj Vi,01:42 pm
07-20-1969,Mo Cnj Li,00:20 am
07-22-1969,Mo Cnj Sc,08:04 am
07-24-1969,Mo Cnj Sa,12:11 pm
07-26-1969,Mo Cnj Ca,01:10 pm
07-28-1969,Mo Cnj Aq,12:35 pm
07-30-1969,Mo Cnj Pi,12:31 pm

August 1969
08-01-1969,Mo Cnj Ar,02:55 pm
08-03-1969,Mo Cnj Ta,09:02 pm
08-06-1969,Mo Cnj Ge,06:49 am
08-08-1969,Mo Cnj Ca,06:57 pm
08-11-1969,Mo Cnj Le,07:38 am
08-13-1969,Mo Cnj Vi,07:33 pm
08-16-1969,Mo Cnj Li,05:52 am
08-18-1969,Mo Cnj Sc,01:55 pm
08-20-1969,Mo Cnj Sa,07:13 pm
08-22-1969,Mo Cnj Ca,09:49 pm
08-24-1969,Mo Cnj Aq,10:36 pm
08-26-1969,Mo Cnj Pi,11:03 pm

08-29-1969,Mo Cnj Ar,00:57 am
08-31-1969,Mo Cnj Ta,05:50 am

September 1969
09-02-1969,Mo Cnj Ge,02:24 pm
09-05-1969,Mo Cnj Ca,01:57 am
09-07-1969,Mo Cnj Le,02:37 pm
09-10-1969,Mo Cnj Vi,02:21 am
09-12-1969,Mo Cnj Li,12:02 pm
09-14-1969,Mo Cnj Sc,07:25 pm
09-17-1969,Mo Cnj Sa,00:42 am
09-19-1969,Mo Cnj Ca,04:14 am
09-21-1969,Mo Cnj Aq,06:31 am
09-23-1969,Mo Cnj Pi,08:22 am
09-25-1969,Mo Cnj Ar,10:56 am
09-27-1969,Mo Cnj Ta,03:29 pm
09-29-1969,Mo Cnj Ge,11:06 pm

October 1969
10-02-1969,Mo Cnj Ca,09:53 am
10-04-1969,Mo Cnj Le,10:26 pm
10-07-1969,Mo Cnj Vi,10:22 am
10-09-1969,Mo Cnj Li,07:49 pm
10-12-1969,Mo Cnj Sc,02:19 am
10-14-1969,Mo Cnj Sa,06:33 am
10-16-1969,Mo Cnj Ca,09:35 am
10-18-1969,Mo Cnj Aq,12:21 pm
10-20-1969,Mo Cnj Pi,03:26 pm
10-22-1969,Mo Cnj Ar,07:18 pm
10-25-1969,Mo Cnj Ta,00:33 am
10-27-1969,Mo Cnj Ge,08:01 am
10-29-1969,Mo Cnj Ca,06:13 pm

November 1969
11-01-1969,Mo Cnj Le,06:35 am
11-03-1969,Mo Cnj Vi,07:00 pm
11-06-1969,Mo Cnj Li,04:59 am
11-08-1969,Mo Cnj Sc,11:18 am
11-10-1969,Mo Cnj Sa,02:30 pm
11-12-1969,Mo Cnj Ca,04:09 pm
11-14-1969,Mo Cnj Aq,05:53 pm
11-16-1969,Mo Cnj Pi,08:53 pm
11-19-1969,Mo Cnj Ar,01:33 am
11-21-1969,Mo Cnj Ta,07:53 am
11-23-1969,Mo Cnj Ge,03:59 pm
11-26-1969,Mo Cnj Ca,02:10 am
11-28-1969,Mo Cnj Le,02:22 pm

December 1969
12-01-1969,Mo Cnj Vi,03:14 am
12-03-1969,Mo Cnj Li,02:17 pm
12-05-1969,Mo Cnj Sc,09:31 pm
12-08-1969,Mo Cnj Sa,00:43 am
12-10-1969,Mo Cnj Ca,01:21 am
12-12-1969,Mo Cnj Aq,01:28 am
12-14-1969,Mo Cnj Pi,02:57 am
12-16-1969,Mo Cnj Ar,06:56 am
12-18-1969,Mo Cnj Ta,01:35 pm
12-20-1969,Mo Cnj Ge,10:28 pm
12-23-1969,Mo Cnj Ca,09:08 am
12-25-1969,Mo Cnj Le,09:21 am
12-28-1969,Mo Cnj Vi,10:21 am
12-30-1969,Mo Cnj Li,10:19 pm

January 1970
01-02-1970,Mo Cnj Sc,07:04 am
01-04-1970,Mo Cnj Sa,11:34 am
01-06-1970,Mo Cnj Ca,12:30 pm
01-08-1970,Mo Cnj Aq,11:48 am
01-10-1970,Mo Cnj Pi,11:37 am
01-12-1970,Mo Cnj Ar,01:48 pm
01-14-1970,Mo Cnj Ta,07:20 pm
01-17-1970,Mo Cnj Ge,04:07 am
01-19-1970,Mo Cnj Ca,03:14 pm
01-22-1970,Mo Cnj Le,03:41 am
01-24-1970,Mo Cnj Vi,04:34 pm
01-27-1970,Mo Cnj Li,04:43 am
01-29-1970,Mo Cnj Sc,02:35 pm
01-31-1970,Mo Cnj Sa,08:50 pm

February 1970
02-02-1970,Mo Cnj Ca,11:22 pm
02-04-1970,Mo Cnj Aq,11:19 pm
02-06-1970,Mo Cnj Pi,10:37 pm
02-08-1970,Mo Cnj Ar,11:17 pm
02-11-1970,Mo Cnj Ta,02:59 am
02-13-1970,Mo Cnj Ge,10:29 am
02-15-1970,Mo Cnj Ca,09:18 pm
02-18-1970,Mo Cnj Le,09:54 am
02-20-1970,Mo Cnj Vi,10:42 pm
02-23-1970,Mo Cnj Li,10:30 am
02-25-1970,Mo Cnj Sc,08:23 pm
02-28-1970,Mo Cnj Sa,03:38 am

March 1970
03-02-1970,Mo Cnj Ca,07:54 am
03-04-1970,Mo Cnj Aq,09:35 am
03-06-1970,Mo Cnj Pi,09:49 am
03-08-1970,Mo Cnj Ar,10:17 am
03-10-1970,Mo Cnj Ta,12:44 pm
03-12-1970,Mo Cnj Ge,06:37 pm
03-15-1970,Mo Cnj Ca,04:19 am
03-17-1970,Mo Cnj Le,04:40 pm
03-20-1970,Mo Cnj Vi,05:30 am
03-22-1970,Mo Cnj Li,04:57 pm
03-25-1970,Mo Cnj Sc,02:10 am
03-27-1970,Mo Cnj Sa,09:07 am
03-29-1970,Mo Cnj Ca,02:00 pm
03-31-1970,Mo Cnj Aq,05:09 pm

April 1970
04-02-1970,Mo Cnj Pi,07:02 pm
04-04-1970,Mo Cnj Ar,08:33 pm
04-06-1970,Mo Cnj Ta,11:03 pm
04-09-1970,Mo Cnj Ge,04:02 am
04-11-1970,Mo Cnj Ca,12:33 pm
04-14-1970,Mo Cnj Le,00:16 am
04-16-1970,Mo Cnj Vi,01:07 pm
04-19-1970,Mo Cnj Li,00:35 am
04-21-1970,Mo Cnj Sc,09:16 am
04-23-1970,Mo Cnj Sa,03:15 pm
04-25-1970,Mo Cnj Ca,07:27 pm
04-27-1970,Mo Cnj Aq,10:44 pm
04-30-1970,Mo Cnj Pi,01:38 am

May 1970
05-02-1970,Mo Cnj Ar,04:33 am
05-04-1970,Mo Cnj Ta,08:05 am
05-06-1970,Mo Cnj Ge,01:17 pm
05-08-1970,Mo Cnj Ca,09:17 pm
05-11-1970,Mo Cnj Le,08:22 am
05-13-1970,Mo Cnj Vi,09:11 pm
05-16-1970,Mo Cnj Li,09:03 am
05-18-1970,Mo Cnj Sc,05:50 pm
05-20-1970,Mo Cnj Sa,11:12 pm
05-23-1970,Mo Cnj Ca,02:14 am
05-25-1970,Mo Cnj Aq,04:26 am
05-27-1970,Mo Cnj Pi,06:59 am
05-29-1970,Mo Cnj Ar,10:27 am
05-31-1970,Mo Cnj Ta,03:03 pm

June 1970

06-02-1970,Mo Cnj Ge,09:10 pm
06-05-1970,Mo Cnj Ca,05:26 am
06-07-1970,Mo Cnj Le,04:17 pm
06-10-1970,Mo Cnj Vi,05:03 am
06-12-1970,Mo Cnj Li,05:29 pm
06-15-1970,Mo Cnj Sc,03:02 am
06-17-1970,Mo Cnj Sa,08:39 am
06-19-1970,Mo Cnj Ca,11:05 am
06-21-1970,Mo Cnj Aq,12:01 pm
06-23-1970,Mo Cnj Pi,01:12 pm
06-25-1970,Mo Cnj Ar,03:52 pm
06-27-1970,Mo Cnj Ta,08:35 pm
06-30-1970,Mo Cnj Ge,03:25 am

July 1970

07-02-1970,Mo Cnj Ca,12:22 pm
07-04-1970,Mo Cnj Le,11:27 pm
07-07-1970,Mo Cnj Vi,12:12 pm
07-10-1970,Mo Cnj Li,01:03 am
07-12-1970,Mo Cnj Sc,11:41 am
07-14-1970,Mo Cnj Sa,06:26 pm
07-16-1970,Mo Cnj Ca,09:19 pm
07-18-1970,Mo Cnj Aq,09:45 pm
07-20-1970,Mo Cnj Pi,09:37 pm
07-22-1970,Mo Cnj Ar,10:43 pm
07-25-1970,Mo Cnj Ta,02:19 am
07-27-1970,Mo Cnj Ge,08:54 am
07-29-1970,Mo Cnj Ca,06:15 pm

August 1970

08-01-1970,Mo Cnj Le,05:44 am
08-03-1970,Mo Cnj Vi,06:34 pm
08-06-1970,Mo Cnj Li,07:32 am
08-08-1970,Mo Cnj Sc,06:56 pm
08-11-1970,Mo Cnj Sa,03:07 am
08-13-1970,Mo Cnj Ca,07:25 am
08-15-1970,Mo Cnj Aq,08:32 am
08-17-1970,Mo Cnj Pi,08:02 am
08-19-1970,Mo Cnj Ar,07:51 am
08-21-1970,Mo Cnj Ta,09:47 am
08-23-1970,Mo Cnj Ge,03:04 pm
08-25-1970,Mo Cnj Ca,11:58 pm
08-28-1970,Mo Cnj Le,11:38 am
08-31-1970,Mo Cnj Vi,00:36 am

September 1970

09-02-1970,Mo Cnj Li,01:26 pm
09-05-1970,Mo Cnj Sc,00:55 am
09-07-1970,Mo Cnj Sa,09:59 am
09-09-1970,Mo Cnj Ca,03:52 pm
09-11-1970,Mo Cnj Aq,06:34 pm
09-13-1970,Mo Cnj Pi,06:58 pm
09-15-1970,Mo Cnj Ar,06:35 pm
09-17-1970,Mo Cnj Ta,07:21 pm
09-19-1970,Mo Cnj Ge,11:02 pm
09-22-1970,Mo Cnj Ca,06:41 am
09-24-1970,Mo Cnj Le,05:54 am
09-27-1970,Mo Cnj Vi,06:54 am
09-29-1970,Mo Cnj Li,07:34 pm

October 1970

10-02-1970,Mo Cnj Sc,06:36 am
10-04-1970,Mo Cnj Sa,03:32 pm
10-06-1970,Mo Cnj Ca,10:11 pm
10-09-1970,Mo Cnj Aq,02:26 am
10-11-1970,Mo Cnj Pi,04:30 am
10-13-1970,Mo Cnj Ar,05:12 am
10-15-1970,Mo Cnj Ta,06:00 am
10-17-1970,Mo Cnj Ge,08:43 am
10-19-1970,Mo Cnj Ca,02:59 pm
10-22-1970,Mo Cnj Le,01:13 am
10-24-1970,Mo Cnj Vi,01:58 pm
10-27-1970,Mo Cnj Li,02:38 am
10-29-1970,Mo Cnj Sc,01:16 pm
10-31-1970,Mo Cnj Sa,09:24 pm

November 1970

11-03-1970,Mo Cnj Ca,03:33 am
11-05-1970,Mo Cnj Aq,08:11 am
11-07-1970,Mo Cnj Pi,11:33 am
11-09-1970,Mo Cnj Ar,01:52 pm
11-11-1970,Mo Cnj Ta,03:51 pm
11-13-1970,Mo Cnj Ge,06:49 pm
11-16-1970,Mo Cnj Ca,00:24 am
11-18-1970,Mo Cnj Le,09:37 am
11-20-1970,Mo Cnj Vi,09:50 pm
11-23-1970,Mo Cnj Li,10:39 am
11-25-1970,Mo Cnj Sc,09:25 pm
11-28-1970,Mo Cnj Sa,05:02 am
11-30-1970,Mo Cnj Ca,10:05 am

December 1970
12-02-1970,Mo Cnj Aq,01:45 pm
12-04-1970,Mo Cnj Pi,04:56 pm
12-06-1970,Mo Cnj Ar,08:04 pm
12-08-1970,Mo Cnj Ta,11:25 pm
12-11-1970,Mo Cnj Ge,03:34 am
12-13-1970,Mo Cnj Ca,09:33 am
12-15-1970,Mo Cnj Le,06:22 pm
12-18-1970,Mo Cnj Vi,06:05 am
12-20-1970,Mo Cnj Li,07:01 pm
12-23-1970,Mo Cnj Sc,06:27 am
12-25-1970,Mo Cnj Sa,02:28 pm
12-27-1970,Mo Cnj Ca,07:02 pm
12-29-1970,Mo Cnj Aq,09:24 pm

January 1971
01-01-1971,Mo Cnj Pi,04:08 am
01-03-1971,Mo Cnj Ar,06:27 am
01-05-1971,Mo Cnj Ta,10:01 am
01-07-1971,Mo Cnj Ge,03:09 pm
01-09-1971,Mo Cnj Ca,10:09 pm
01-12-1971,Mo Cnj Le,07:24 am
01-14-1971,Mo Cnj Vi,06:57 pm
01-17-1971,Mo Cnj Li,07:53 am
01-19-1971,Mo Cnj Sc,08:04 pm
01-22-1971,Mo Cnj Sa,05:16 am
01-24-1971,Mo Cnj Ca,10:33 am
01-26-1971,Mo Cnj Aq,12:37 pm
01-28-1971,Mo Cnj Pi,01:02 pm
01-30-1971,Mo Cnj Ar,01:36 pm

February 1971
02-01-1971,Mo Cnj Ta,03:49 pm
02-03-1971,Mo Cnj Ge,08:34 pm
02-06-1971,Mo Cnj Ca,04:07 am
02-08-1971,Mo Cnj Le,02:06 pm
02-11-1971,Mo Cnj Vi,01:58 am
02-13-1971,Mo Cnj Li,02:51 pm
02-16-1971,Mo Cnj Sc,03:22 am
02-18-1971,Mo Cnj Sa,01:46 pm
02-20-1971,Mo Cnj Ca,08:38 pm
02-22-1971,Mo Cnj Aq,11:43 pm
02-25-1971,Mo Cnj Pi,00:05 am
02-26-1971,Mo Cnj Ar,11:30 pm
02-28-1971,Mo Cnj Ta,11:54 pm

March 1971
03-03-1971,Mo Cnj Ge,03:01 am
03-05-1971,Mo Cnj Ca,09:48 am
03-07-1971,Mo Cnj Le,07:56 pm
03-10-1971,Mo Cnj Vi,08:11 am
03-12-1971,Mo Cnj Li,09:07 pm
03-15-1971,Mo Cnj Sc,09:32 am
03-17-1971,Mo Cnj Sa,08:24 pm
03-20-1971,Mo Cnj Ca,04:37 am
03-22-1971,Mo Cnj Aq,09:29 am
03-24-1971,Mo Cnj Pi,11:08 am
03-26-1971,Mo Cnj Ar,10:46 am
03-28-1971,Mo Cnj Ta,10:16 am
03-30-1971,Mo Cnj Ge,11:44 am

April 1971
04-01-1971,Mo Cnj Ca,04:51 pm
04-04-1971,Mo Cnj Le,02:06 am
04-06-1971,Mo Cnj Vi,02:17 pm
04-09-1971,Mo Cnj Li,03:17 am
04-11-1971,Mo Cnj Sc,03:28 pm
04-14-1971,Mo Cnj Sa,02:03 am
04-16-1971,Mo Cnj Ca,10:38 am
04-18-1971,Mo Cnj Aq,04:46 pm
04-20-1971,Mo Cnj Pi,08:08 pm
04-22-1971,Mo Cnj Ar,09:09 pm
04-24-1971,Mo Cnj Ta,09:07 pm
04-26-1971,Mo Cnj Ge,09:59 pm
04-29-1971,Mo Cnj Ca,01:44 am

May 1971
05-01-1971,Mo Cnj Le,09:35 am
05-03-1971,Mo Cnj Vi,09:03 pm
05-06-1971,Mo Cnj Li,09:59 am
05-08-1971,Mo Cnj Sc,10:03 am
05-11-1971,Mo Cnj Sa,08:08 am
05-13-1971,Mo Cnj Ca,04:09 pm
05-15-1971,Mo Cnj Aq,10:20 pm
05-18-1971,Mo Cnj Pi,02:40 am
05-20-1971,Mo Cnj Ar,05:12 am
05-22-1971,Mo Cnj Ta,06:32 am
05-24-1971,Mo Cnj Ge,08:02 am
05-26-1971,Mo Cnj Ca,11:26 am
05-28-1971,Mo Cnj Le,06:16 pm
05-31-1971,Mo Cnj Vi,04:48 am

June 1971
06-02-1971,Mo Cnj Li,05:27 pm
06-05-1971,Mo Cnj Sc,05:36 am
06-07-1971,Mo Cnj Sa,03:29 pm
06-09-1971,Mo Cnj Ca,10:46 pm
06-12-1971,Mo Cnj Aq,04:04 am
06-14-1971,Mo Cnj Pi,08:02 am
06-16-1971,Mo Cnj Ar,11:06 am
06-18-1971,Mo Cnj Ta,01:39 pm
06-20-1971,Mo Cnj Ge,04:24 pm
06-22-1971,Mo Cnj Ca,08:30 pm
06-25-1971,Mo Cnj Le,03:12 am
06-27-1971,Mo Cnj Vi,01:06 pm
06-30-1971,Mo Cnj Li,01:23 am

July 1971
07-02-1971,Mo Cnj Sc,01:47 pm
07-04-1971,Mo Cnj Sa,12:00 pm
07-07-1971,Mo Cnj Ca,07:04 am
07-09-1971,Mo Cnj Aq,11:27 am
07-11-1971,Mo Cnj Pi,02:15 pm
07-13-1971,Mo Cnj Ar,04:32 pm
07-15-1971,Mo Cnj Ta,07:10 pm
07-17-1971,Mo Cnj Ge,10:47 pm
07-20-1971,Mo Cnj Ca,03:57 am
07-22-1971,Mo Cnj Le,11:17 am
07-24-1971,Mo Cnj Vi,09:10 pm
07-27-1971,Mo Cnj Li,09:13 am
07-29-1971,Mo Cnj Sc,09:51 pm

August 1971
08-01-1971,Mo Cnj Sa,08:50 am
08-03-1971,Mo Cnj Ca,04:32 pm
08-05-1971,Mo Cnj Aq,08:47 pm
08-07-1971,Mo Cnj Pi,10:34 pm
08-09-1971,Mo Cnj Ar,11:27 pm
08-12-1971,Mo Cnj Ta,00:56 am
08-14-1971,Mo Cnj Ge,04:11 am
08-16-1971,Mo Cnj Ca,09:50 am
08-18-1971,Mo Cnj Le,05:58 pm
08-21-1971,Mo Cnj Vi,04:19 am
08-23-1971,Mo Cnj Li,04:23 pm
08-26-1971,Mo Cnj Sc,05:09 am
08-28-1971,Mo Cnj Sa,04:57 pm
08-31-1971,Mo Cnj Ca,01:54 am

September 1971
09-02-1971,Mo Cnj Aq,07:04 am
09-04-1971,Mo Cnj Pi,08:51 am
09-06-1971,Mo Cnj Ar,08:44 am
09-08-1971,Mo Cnj Ta,08:38 am
09-10-1971,Mo Cnj Ge,10:26 am
09-12-1971,Mo Cnj Ca,03:22 pm
09-14-1971,Mo Cnj Le,11:38 pm
09-17-1971,Mo Cnj Vi,10:29 am
09-19-1971,Mo Cnj Li,10:47 pm
09-22-1971,Mo Cnj Sc,11:33 am
09-24-1971,Mo Cnj Sa,11:43 pm
09-27-1971,Mo Cnj Ca,09:53 am
09-29-1971,Mo Cnj Aq,04:39 pm

October 1971
10-01-1971,Mo Cnj Pi,07:37 pm
10-03-1971,Mo Cnj Ar,07:41 pm
10-05-1971,Mo Cnj Ta,06:43 pm
10-07-1971,Mo Cnj Ge,06:54 pm
10-09-1971,Mo Cnj Ca,10:11 pm
10-12-1971,Mo Cnj Le,05:31 am
10-14-1971,Mo Cnj Vi,04:16 pm
10-17-1971,Mo Cnj Li,04:47 am
10-19-1971,Mo Cnj Sc,05:31 pm
10-22-1971,Mo Cnj Sa,05:32 am
10-24-1971,Mo Cnj Ca,04:06 pm
10-27-1971,Mo Cnj Aq,00:12 am
10-29-1971,Mo Cnj Pi,04:57 am
10-31-1971,Mo Cnj Ar,06:27 am

November 1971
11-02-1971,Mo Cnj Ta,05:56 am
11-04-1971,Mo Cnj Ge,05:27 am
11-06-1971,Mo Cnj Ca,07:15 am
11-08-1971,Mo Cnj Le,12:57 pm
11-10-1971,Mo Cnj Vi,10:44 pm
11-13-1971,Mo Cnj Li,11:06 am
11-15-1971,Mo Cnj Sc,11:50 pm
11-18-1971,Mo Cnj Sa,11:31 am
11-20-1971,Mo Cnj Ca,09:37 pm
11-23-1971,Mo Cnj Aq,05:53 am
11-25-1971,Mo Cnj Pi,11:48 am
11-27-1971,Mo Cnj Ar,03:04 pm
11-29-1971,Mo Cnj Ta,04:08 pm

December 1971

12-01-1971,Mo Cnj Ge,04:25 pm
12-03-1971,Mo Cnj Ca,05:51 pm
12-05-1971,Mo Cnj Le,10:17 pm
12-08-1971,Mo Cnj Vi,06:41 am
12-10-1971,Mo Cnj Li,06:20 pm
12-13-1971,Mo Cnj Sc,07:02 am
12-15-1971,Mo Cnj Sa,06:38 pm
12-18-1971,Mo Cnj Ca,04:08 am
12-20-1971,Mo Cnj Aq,11:33 am
12-22-1971,Mo Cnj Pi,05:10 pm
12-24-1971,Mo Cnj Ar,09:09 pm
12-26-1971,Mo Cnj Ta,11:45 pm
12-29-1971,Mo Cnj Ge,01:39 am
12-31-1971,Mo Cnj Ca,04:02 am

January 1972

01-02-1972,Mo Cnj Le,08:23 am
01-04-1972,Mo Cnj Vi,03:51 pm
01-07-1972,Mo Cnj Li,02:34 am
01-09-1972,Mo Cnj Sc,03:04 pm
01-12-1972,Mo Cnj Sa,02:57 am
01-14-1972,Mo Cnj Ca,12:26 pm
01-16-1972,Mo Cnj Aq,07:04 pm
01-18-1972,Mo Cnj Pi,11:28 pm
01-21-1972,Mo Cnj Ar,02:36 am
01-23-1972,Mo Cnj Ta,05:18 am
01-25-1972,Mo Cnj Ge,08:15 am
01-27-1972,Mo Cnj Ca,12:02 pm
01-29-1972,Mo Cnj Le,05:22 pm

February 1972

02-01-1972,Mo Cnj Vi,00:56 am
02-03-1972,Mo Cnj Li,11:07 am
02-05-1972,Mo Cnj Sc,11:18 pm
02-08-1972,Mo Cnj Sa,11:38 am
02-10-1972,Mo Cnj Ca,09:50 pm
02-13-1972,Mo Cnj Aq,04:37 am
02-15-1972,Mo Cnj Pi,08:12 am
02-17-1972,Mo Cnj Ar,09:51 am
02-19-1972,Mo Cnj Ta,11:12 am
02-21-1972,Mo Cnj Ge,01:36 pm
02-23-1972,Mo Cnj Ca,05:53 pm
02-26-1972,Mo Cnj Le,00:15 am
02-28-1972,Mo Cnj Vi,08:39 am

March 1972

03-01-1972,Mo Cnj Li,07:00 pm
03-04-1972,Mo Cnj Sc,07:00 am
03-06-1972,Mo Cnj Sa,07:37 pm
03-09-1972,Mo Cnj Ca,06:50 am
03-11-1972,Mo Cnj Aq,02:43 pm
03-13-1972,Mo Cnj Pi,06:40 pm
03-15-1972,Mo Cnj Ar,07:38 pm
03-17-1972,Mo Cnj Ta,07:28 pm
03-19-1972,Mo Cnj Ge,08:13 pm
03-21-1972,Mo Cnj Ca,11:26 pm
03-24-1972,Mo Cnj Le,05:46 am
03-26-1972,Mo Cnj Vi,02:48 pm
03-29-1972,Mo Cnj Li,01:42 am
03-31-1972,Mo Cnj Sc,01:49 pm

April 1972

04-03-1972,Mo Cnj Sa,02:28 am
04-05-1972,Mo Cnj Ca,02:21 pm
04-07-1972,Mo Cnj Aq,11:38 pm
04-10-1972,Mo Cnj Pi,04:58 am
04-12-1972,Mo Cnj Ar,06:32 am
04-14-1972,Mo Cnj Ta,05:55 am
04-16-1972,Mo Cnj Ge,05:17 am
04-18-1972,Mo Cnj Ca,06:46 am
04-20-1972,Mo Cnj Le,11:47 am
04-22-1972,Mo Cnj Vi,08:25 pm
04-25-1972,Mo Cnj Li,07:35 am
04-27-1972,Mo Cnj Sc,07:57 pm
04-30-1972,Mo Cnj Sa,08:31 am

May 1972

05-02-1972,Mo Cnj Ca,08:29 pm
05-05-1972,Mo Cnj Aq,06:35 am
05-07-1972,Mo Cnj Pi,01:28 pm
05-09-1972,Mo Cnj Ar,04:35 pm
05-11-1972,Mo Cnj Ta,04:48 pm
05-13-1972,Mo Cnj Ge,03:58 pm
05-15-1972,Mo Cnj Ca,04:17 pm
05-17-1972,Mo Cnj Le,07:39 pm
05-20-1972,Mo Cnj Vi,02:57 am
05-22-1972,Mo Cnj Li,01:37 pm
05-25-1972,Mo Cnj Sc,02:01 am
05-27-1972,Mo Cnj Sa,02:33 pm
05-30-1972,Mo Cnj Ca,02:13 am

June 1972
06-01-1972,Mo Cnj Aq,12:15 pm
06-03-1972,Mo Cnj Pi,07:52 pm
06-06-1972,Mo Cnj Ar,00:28 am
06-08-1972,Mo Cnj Ta,02:15 am
06-10-1972,Mo Cnj Ge,02:25 am
06-12-1972,Mo Cnj Ca,02:45 am
06-14-1972,Mo Cnj Le,05:10 am
06-16-1972,Mo Cnj Vi,11:04 am
06-18-1972,Mo Cnj Li,08:39 pm
06-21-1972,Mo Cnj Sc,08:43 am
06-23-1972,Mo Cnj Sa,09:14 pm
06-26-1972,Mo Cnj Ca,08:36 am
06-28-1972,Mo Cnj Aq,06:03 pm

July 1972
07-01-1972,Mo Cnj Pi,01:19 am
07-03-1972,Mo Cnj Ar,06:23 am
07-05-1972,Mo Cnj Ta,09:26 am
07-07-1972,Mo Cnj Ge,11:05 am
07-09-1972,Mo Cnj Ca,12:30 pm
07-11-1972,Mo Cnj Le,03:05 pm
07-13-1972,Mo Cnj Vi,08:16 pm
07-16-1972,Mo Cnj Li,04:49 am
07-18-1972,Mo Cnj Sc,04:15 pm
07-21-1972,Mo Cnj Sa,04:47 am
07-23-1972,Mo Cnj Ca,04:11 pm
07-26-1972,Mo Cnj Aq,01:08 am
07-28-1972,Mo Cnj Pi,07:30 am
07-30-1972,Mo Cnj Ar,11:51 am

August 1972
08-01-1972,Mo Cnj Ta,02:58 pm
08-03-1972,Mo Cnj Ge,05:33 pm
08-05-1972,Mo Cnj Ca,08:18 pm
08-07-1972,Mo Cnj Le,11:56 pm
08-10-1972,Mo Cnj Vi,05:23 am
08-12-1972,Mo Cnj Li,01:28 pm
08-15-1972,Mo Cnj Sc,00:20 am
08-17-1972,Mo Cnj Sa,12:50 pm
08-20-1972,Mo Cnj Ca,00:39 am
08-22-1972,Mo Cnj Aq,09:44 am
08-24-1972,Mo Cnj Pi,03:29 am
08-26-1972,Mo Cnj Ar,06:40 am
08-28-1972,Mo Cnj Ta,08:43 am
08-30-1972,Mo Cnj Ge,10:56 pm

September 1972
09-02-1972,Mo Cnj Ca,02:11 am
09-04-1972,Mo Cnj Le,06:54 am
09-06-1972,Mo Cnj Vi,01:16 pm
09-08-1972,Mo Cnj Li,09:37 pm
09-11-1972,Mo Cnj Sc,08:16 am
09-13-1972,Mo Cnj Sa,08:43 pm
09-16-1972,Mo Cnj Ca,09:08 am
09-18-1972,Mo Cnj Aq,07:04 pm
09-21-1972,Mo Cnj Pi,01:09 am
09-23-1972,Mo Cnj Ar,03:44 am
09-25-1972,Mo Cnj Ta,04:28 am
09-27-1972,Mo Cnj Ge,05:15 am
09-29-1972,Mo Cnj Ca,07:39 am

October 1972
10-01-1972,Mo Cnj Le,12:26 pm
10-03-1972,Mo Cnj Vi,07:31 pm
10-06-1972,Mo Cnj Li,04:35 am
10-08-1972,Mo Cnj Sc,03:27 pm
10-11-1972,Mo Cnj Sa,03:52 am
10-13-1972,Mo Cnj Ca,04:44 pm
10-16-1972,Mo Cnj Aq,03:51 am
10-18-1972,Mo Cnj Pi,11:13 am
10-20-1972,Mo Cnj Ar,02:23 pm
10-22-1972,Mo Cnj Ta,02:38 pm
10-24-1972,Mo Cnj Ge,02:03 pm
10-26-1972,Mo Cnj Ca,02:45 pm
10-28-1972,Mo Cnj Le,06:15 pm
10-31-1972,Mo Cnj Vi,01:00 am

November 1972
11-02-1972,Mo Cnj Li,10:27 am
11-04-1972,Mo Cnj Sc,09:46 pm
11-07-1972,Mo Cnj Sa,10:16 am
11-09-1972,Mo Cnj Ca,11:11 pm
11-12-1972,Mo Cnj Aq,11:03 am
11-14-1972,Mo Cnj Pi,07:57 pm
11-17-1972,Mo Cnj Ar,00:45 am
11-19-1972,Mo Cnj Ta,01:54 am
11-21-1972,Mo Cnj Ge,01:06 am
11-23-1972,Mo Cnj Ca,00:31 am
11-25-1972,Mo Cnj Le,02:12 am
11-27-1972,Mo Cnj Vi,07:24 am
11-29-1972,Mo Cnj Li,04:15 pm

December 1972
12-02-1972,Mo Cnj Sc,03:42 am
12-04-1972,Mo Cnj Sa,04:23 pm
12-07-1972,Mo Cnj Ca,05:07 am
12-09-1972,Mo Cnj Aq,04:54 pm
12-12-1972,Mo Cnj Pi,02:33 am
12-14-1972,Mo Cnj Ar,09:00 am
12-16-1972,Mo Cnj Ta,11:59 am
12-18-1972,Mo Cnj Ge,12:24 pm
12-20-1972,Mo Cnj Ca,11:57 am
12-22-1972,Mo Cnj Le,12:34 pm
12-24-1972,Mo Cnj Vi,04:03 pm
12-26-1972,Mo Cnj Li,11:22 pm
12-29-1972,Mo Cnj Sc,10:11 am
12-31-1972,Mo Cnj Sa,10:52 pm

January 1973
01-03-1973,Mo Cnj Ca,11:31 am
01-05-1973,Mo Cnj Aq,10:48 pm
01-08-1973,Mo Cnj Pi,08:03 am
01-10-1973,Mo Cnj Ar,02:58 pm
01-12-1973,Mo Cnj Ta,07:24 pm
01-14-1973,Mo Cnj Ge,09:41 pm
01-16-1973,Mo Cnj Ca,10:39 pm
01-18-1973,Mo Cnj Le,11:40 pm
01-21-1973,Mo Cnj Vi,02:24 am
01-23-1973,Mo Cnj Li,08:17 am
01-25-1973,Mo Cnj Sc,05:53 pm
01-28-1973,Mo Cnj Sa,06:11 am
01-30-1973,Mo Cnj Ca,06:54 pm

February 1973
02-02-1973,Mo Cnj Aq,05:55 am
02-04-1973,Mo Cnj Pi,02:22 pm
02-06-1973,Mo Cnj Ar,08:29 pm
02-09-1973,Mo Cnj Ta,00:54 am
02-11-1973,Mo Cnj Ge,04:10 am
02-13-1973,Mo Cnj Ca,06:45 am
02-15-1973,Mo Cnj Le,09:13 am
02-17-1973,Mo Cnj Vi,12:32 pm
02-19-1973,Mo Cnj Li,05:59 pm
02-22-1973,Mo Cnj Sc,02:35 am
02-24-1973,Mo Cnj Sa,02:15 pm
02-27-1973,Mo Cnj Ca,03:04 am

March 1973
03-01-1973,Mo Cnj Aq,02:22 pm
03-03-1973,Mo Cnj Pi,10:31 pm

03-06-1973,Mo Cnj Ar,03:37 am
03-08-1973,Mo Cnj Ta,06:51 am
03-10-1973,Mo Cnj Ge,09:32 am
03-12-1973,Mo Cnj Ca,12:30 pm
03-14-1973,Mo Cnj Le,04:08 pm
03-16-1973,Mo Cnj Vi,08:43 pm
03-19-1973,Mo Cnj Li,02:48 am
03-21-1973,Mo Cnj Sc,11:15 am
03-23-1973,Mo Cnj Sa,10:26 pm
03-26-1973,Mo Cnj Ca,11:16 am
03-28-1973,Mo Cnj Aq,11:13 pm
03-31-1973,Mo Cnj Pi,07:55 am

April 1973
04-02-1973,Mo Cnj Ar,12:49 pm
04-04-1973,Mo Cnj Ta,02:59 pm
04-06-1973,Mo Cnj Ge,04:12 pm
04-08-1973,Mo Cnj Ca,06:05 pm
04-10-1973,Mo Cnj Le,09:31 pm
04-13-1973,Mo Cnj Vi,02:47 am
04-15-1973,Mo Cnj Li,09:50 am
04-17-1973,Mo Cnj Sc,06:51 pm
04-20-1973,Mo Cnj Sa,06:02 am
04-22-1973,Mo Cnj Ca,06:50 pm
04-25-1973,Mo Cnj Aq,07:22 am
04-27-1973,Mo Cnj Pi,05:10 pm
04-29-1973,Mo Cnj Ar,10:54 pm

May 1973
05-02-1973,Mo Cnj Ta,01:02 am
05-04-1973,Mo Cnj Ge,01:16 am
05-06-1973,Mo Cnj Ca,01:35 am
05-08-1973,Mo Cnj Le,03:36 am
05-10-1973,Mo Cnj Vi,08:13 am
05-12-1973,Mo Cnj Li,03:31 pm
05-15-1973,Mo Cnj Sc,01:10 am
05-17-1973,Mo Cnj Sa,12:42 pm
05-20-1973,Mo Cnj Ca,01:31 am
05-22-1973,Mo Cnj Aq,02:18 pm
05-25-1973,Mo Cnj Pi,01:06 am
05-27-1973,Mo Cnj Ar,08:15 am
05-29-1973,Mo Cnj Ta,11:28 am
05-31-1973,Mo Cnj Ge,11:53 am

June 1973
06-02-1973,Mo Cnj Ca,11:21 am
06-04-1973,Mo Cnj Le,11:49 am

06-06-1973,Mo Cnj Vi,02:52 pm
06-08-1973,Mo Cnj Li,09:17 pm
06-11-1973,Mo Cnj Sc,06:53 am
06-13-1973,Mo Cnj Sa,06:44 pm
06-16-1973,Mo Cnj Ca,07:37 am
06-18-1973,Mo Cnj Aq,08:19 pm
06-21-1973,Mo Cnj Pi,07:29 am
06-23-1973,Mo Cnj Ar,03:48 pm
06-25-1973,Mo Cnj Ta,08:37 pm
06-27-1973,Mo Cnj Ge,10:18 pm
06-29-1973,Mo Cnj Ca,10:09 pm

July 1973
07-01-1973,Mo Cnj Le,09:56 pm
07-03-1973,Mo Cnj Vi,11:32 pm
07-06-1973,Mo Cnj Li,04:24 am
07-08-1973,Mo Cnj Sc,01:06 pm
07-11-1973,Mo Cnj Sa,00:48 am
07-13-1973,Mo Cnj Ca,01:45 pm
07-16-1973,Mo Cnj Aq,02:15 am
07-18-1973,Mo Cnj Pi,01:07 pm
07-20-1973,Mo Cnj Ar,09:44 pm
07-23-1973,Mo Cnj Ta,03:41 am
07-25-1973,Mo Cnj Ge,06:59 am
07-27-1973,Mo Cnj Ca,08:11 am
07-29-1973,Mo Cnj Le,08:30 am
07-31-1973,Mo Cnj Vi,09:35 am

August 1973
08-02-1973,Mo Cnj Li,01:12 pm
08-04-1973,Mo Cnj Sc,08:36 pm
08-07-1973,Mo Cnj Sa,07:37 am
08-09-1973,Mo Cnj Ca,08:30 pm
08-12-1973,Mo Cnj Aq,08:53 am
08-14-1973,Mo Cnj Pi,07:15 pm
08-17-1973,Mo Cnj Ar,03:16 am
08-19-1973,Mo Cnj Ta,09:15 am
08-21-1973,Mo Cnj Ge,01:27 pm
08-23-1973,Mo Cnj Ca,04:08 pm
08-25-1973,Mo Cnj Le,05:49 pm
08-27-1973,Mo Cnj Vi,07:33 pm
08-29-1973,Mo Cnj Li,10:52 pm

September 1973
09-01-1973,Mo Cnj Sc,05:18 am
09-03-1973,Mo Cnj Sa,03:25 pm
09-06-1973,Mo Cnj Ca,04:01 am

09-08-1973,Mo Cnj Aq,04:31 pm
09-11-1973,Mo Cnj Pi,02:41 am
09-13-1973,Mo Cnj Ar,09:56 am
09-15-1973,Mo Cnj Ta,02:59 pm
09-17-1973,Mo Cnj Ge,06:48 pm
09-19-1973,Mo Cnj Ca,10:01 pm
09-22-1973,Mo Cnj Le,00:56 am
09-24-1973,Mo Cnj Vi,03:58 am
09-26-1973,Mo Cnj Li,08:01 am
09-28-1973,Mo Cnj Sc,02:19 pm
09-30-1973,Mo Cnj Sa,11:48 pm

October 1973
10-03-1973,Mo Cnj Ca,12:03 pm
10-06-1973,Mo Cnj Aq,00:49 am
10-08-1973,Mo Cnj Pi,11:24 am
10-10-1973,Mo Cnj Ar,06:29 pm
10-12-1973,Mo Cnj Ta,10:36 pm
10-15-1973,Mo Cnj Ge,01:09 am
10-17-1973,Mo Cnj Ca,03:29 am
10-19-1973,Mo Cnj Le,06:25 am
10-21-1973,Mo Cnj Vi,10:19 am
10-23-1973,Mo Cnj Li,03:29 pm
10-25-1973,Mo Cnj Sc,10:29 pm
10-28-1973,Mo Cnj Sa,07:58 am
10-30-1973,Mo Cnj Ca,07:58 pm

November 1973
11-02-1973,Mo Cnj Aq,08:58 am
11-04-1973,Mo Cnj Pi,08:26 pm
11-07-1973,Mo Cnj Ar,04:19 am
11-09-1973,Mo Cnj Ta,08:26 am
11-11-1973,Mo Cnj Ge,10:00 am
11-13-1973,Mo Cnj Ca,10:47 am
11-15-1973,Mo Cnj Le,12:21 pm
11-17-1973,Mo Cnj Vi,03:42 pm
11-19-1973,Mo Cnj Li,09:16 pm
11-22-1973,Mo Cnj Sc,05:07 am
11-24-1973,Mo Cnj Sa,03:11 pm
11-27-1973,Mo Cnj Ca,03:13 am
11-29-1973,Mo Cnj Aq,04:17 pm

December 1973
12-02-1973,Mo Cnj Pi,04:32 am
12-04-1973,Mo Cnj Ar,01:51 pm
12-06-1973,Mo Cnj Ta,07:09 pm
12-08-1973,Mo Cnj Ge,08:59 pm

12-10-1973,Mo Cnj Ca,08:53 pm
12-12-1973,Mo Cnj Le,08:45 pm
12-14-1973,Mo Cnj Vi,10:21 pm
12-17-1973,Mo Cnj Li,02:54 am
12-19-1973,Mo Cnj Sc,10:44 am
12-21-1973,Mo Cnj Sa,09:20 pm
12-24-1973,Mo Cnj Ca,09:41 am
12-26-1973,Mo Cnj Aq,10:43 pm
12-29-1973,Mo Cnj Pi,11:10 am
12-31-1973,Mo Cnj Ar,09:35 pm

January 1974
01-03-1974,Mo Cnj Ta,04:39 am
01-05-1974,Mo Cnj Ge,08:01 am
01-07-1974,Mo Cnj Ca,08:29 am
01-09-1974,Mo Cnj Le,07:42 am
01-11-1974,Mo Cnj Vi,07:42 am
01-13-1974,Mo Cnj Li,10:21 am
01-15-1974,Mo Cnj Sc,04:54 pm
01-18-1974,Mo Cnj Sa,03:12 am
01-20-1974,Mo Cnj Ca,03:48 pm
01-23-1974,Mo Cnj Aq,04:51 am
01-25-1974,Mo Cnj Pi,05:01 pm
01-28-1974,Mo Cnj Ar,03:33 am
01-30-1974,Mo Cnj Ta,11:42 am

February 1974
02-01-1974,Mo Cnj Ge,04:54 pm
02-03-1974,Mo Cnj Ca,07:06 pm
02-05-1974,Mo Cnj Le,07:11 pm
02-07-1974,Mo Cnj Vi,06:52 pm
02-09-1974,Mo Cnj Li,08:10 pm
02-12-1974,Mo Cnj Sc,00:58 am
02-14-1974,Mo Cnj Sa,10:02 am
02-16-1974,Mo Cnj Ca,10:17 pm
02-19-1974,Mo Cnj Aq,11:22 am
02-21-1974,Mo Cnj Pi,11:16 pm
02-24-1974,Mo Cnj Ar,09:13 am
02-26-1974,Mo Cnj Ta,05:11 pm
02-28-1974,Mo Cnj Ge,11:10 pm

March 1974
03-03-1974,Mo Cnj Ca,03:00 am
03-05-1974,Mo Cnj Le,04:49 am
03-07-1974,Mo Cnj Vi,05:34 am
03-09-1974,Mo Cnj Li,06:52 am
03-11-1974,Mo Cnj Sc,10:41 am

03-13-1974,Mo Cnj Sa,06:21 pm
03-16-1974,Mo Cnj Ca,05:42 am
03-18-1974,Mo Cnj Aq,06:39 pm
03-21-1974,Mo Cnj Pi,06:33 am
03-23-1974,Mo Cnj Ar,04:03 pm
03-25-1974,Mo Cnj Ta,11:10 pm
03-28-1974,Mo Cnj Ge,04:33 am
03-30-1974,Mo Cnj Ca,08:40 am

April 1974
04-01-1974,Mo Cnj Le,11:41 am
04-03-1974,Mo Cnj Vi,01:57 pm
04-05-1974,Mo Cnj Li,04:24 pm
04-07-1974,Mo Cnj Sc,08:26 pm
04-10-1974,Mo Cnj Sa,03:28 am
04-12-1974,Mo Cnj Ca,01:56 pm
04-15-1974,Mo Cnj Aq,02:34 am
04-17-1974,Mo Cnj Pi,02:44 pm
04-20-1974,Mo Cnj Ar,00:20 am
04-22-1974,Mo Cnj Ta,06:54 am
04-24-1974,Mo Cnj Ge,11:12 am
04-26-1974,Mo Cnj Ca,02:18 pm
04-28-1974,Mo Cnj Le,05:04 pm
04-30-1974,Mo Cnj Vi,08:01 pm

May 1974
05-02-1974,Mo Cnj Li,11:39 pm
05-05-1974,Mo Cnj Sc,04:43 am
05-07-1974,Mo Cnj Sa,12:05 pm
05-09-1974,Mo Cnj Ca,10:15 pm
05-12-1974,Mo Cnj Aq,10:34 am
05-14-1974,Mo Cnj Pi,11:04 pm
05-17-1974,Mo Cnj Ar,09:20 am
05-19-1974,Mo Cnj Ta,04:11 pm
05-21-1974,Mo Cnj Ge,07:55 pm
05-23-1974,Mo Cnj Ca,09:46 pm
05-25-1974,Mo Cnj Le,11:12 pm
05-28-1974,Mo Cnj Vi,01:26 am
05-30-1974,Mo Cnj Li,05:16 am

June 1974
06-01-1974,Mo Cnj Sc,11:10 am
06-03-1974,Mo Cnj Sa,07:22 pm
06-06-1974,Mo Cnj Ca,05:49 am
06-08-1974,Mo Cnj Aq,06:03 pm
06-11-1974,Mo Cnj Pi,06:44 am
06-13-1974,Mo Cnj Ar,05:53 pm

06-16-1974,Mo Cnj Ta,01:47 am
06-18-1974,Mo Cnj Ge,05:59 am
06-20-1974,Mo Cnj Ca,07:21 am
06-22-1974,Mo Cnj Le,07:30 am
06-24-1974,Mo Cnj Vi,08:11 am
06-26-1974,Mo Cnj Li,10:57 am
06-28-1974,Mo Cnj Sc,04:40 pm

July 1974
07-01-1974,Mo Cnj Sa,01:21 am
07-03-1974,Mo Cnj Ca,12:20 pm
07-06-1974,Mo Cnj Aq,00:42 am
07-08-1974,Mo Cnj Pi,01:26 pm
07-11-1974,Mo Cnj Ar,01:11 am
07-13-1974,Mo Cnj Ta,10:21 am
07-15-1974,Mo Cnj Ge,03:54 pm
07-17-1974,Mo Cnj Ca,05:56 pm
07-19-1974,Mo Cnj Le,05:43 pm
07-21-1974,Mo Cnj Vi,05:10 pm
07-23-1974,Mo Cnj Li,06:19 pm
07-25-1974,Mo Cnj Sc,10:46 pm
07-28-1974,Mo Cnj Sa,07:00 am
07-30-1974,Mo Cnj Ca,06:11 pm

August 1974
08-02-1974,Mo Cnj Aq,06:46 am
08-04-1974,Mo Cnj Pi,07:26 pm
08-07-1974,Mo Cnj Ar,07:15 am
08-09-1974,Mo Cnj Ta,05:13 pm
08-12-1974,Mo Cnj Ge,00:15 am
08-14-1974,Mo Cnj Ca,03:49 am
08-16-1974,Mo Cnj Le,04:27 am
08-18-1974,Mo Cnj Vi,03:43 am
08-20-1974,Mo Cnj Li,03:45 am
08-22-1974,Mo Cnj Sc,06:37 am
08-24-1974,Mo Cnj Sa,01:34 pm
08-27-1974,Mo Cnj Ca,00:15 am
08-29-1974,Mo Cnj Aq,12:52 pm

September 1974
09-01-1974,Mo Cnj Pi,01:29 am
09-03-1974,Mo Cnj Ar,12:58 pm
09-05-1974,Mo Cnj Ta,10:51 pm
09-08-1974,Mo Cnj Ge,06:37 am
09-10-1974,Mo Cnj Ca,11:40 am
09-12-1974,Mo Cnj Le,01:55 pm
09-14-1974,Mo Cnj Vi,02:12 pm

09-16-1974,Mo Cnj Li,02:17 pm
09-18-1974,Mo Cnj Sc,04:14 pm
09-20-1974,Mo Cnj Sa,09:46 pm
09-23-1974,Mo Cnj Ca,07:22 am
09-25-1974,Mo Cnj Aq,07:38 pm
09-28-1974,Mo Cnj Pi,08:15 am
09-30-1974,Mo Cnj Ar,07:26 pm

October 1974
10-03-1974,Mo Cnj Ta,04:40 am
10-05-1974,Mo Cnj Ge,12:01 pm
10-07-1974,Mo Cnj Ca,05:31 pm
10-09-1974,Mo Cnj Le,09:03 pm
10-11-1974,Mo Cnj Vi,10:56 pm
10-14-1974,Mo Cnj Li,00:11 am
10-16-1974,Mo Cnj Sc,02:23 am
10-18-1974,Mo Cnj Sa,07:15 am
10-20-1974,Mo Cnj Ca,03:44 pm
10-23-1974,Mo Cnj Aq,03:21 am
10-25-1974,Mo Cnj Pi,03:58 pm
10-28-1974,Mo Cnj Ar,03:14 am
10-30-1974,Mo Cnj Ta,12:00 pm

November 1974
11-01-1974,Mo Cnj Ge,06:23 pm
11-03-1974,Mo Cnj Ca,11:01 pm
11-06-1974,Mo Cnj Le,02:30 am
11-08-1974,Mo Cnj Vi,05:18 am
11-10-1974,Mo Cnj Li,07:59 am
11-12-1974,Mo Cnj Sc,11:24 am
11-14-1974,Mo Cnj Sa,04:39 pm
11-17-1974,Mo Cnj Ca,00:43 am
11-19-1974,Mo Cnj Aq,11:40 am
11-22-1974,Mo Cnj Pi,00:12 am
11-24-1974,Mo Cnj Ar,11:59 am
11-26-1974,Mo Cnj Ta,09:05 pm
11-29-1974,Mo Cnj Ge,02:58 am

December 1974
12-01-1974,Mo Cnj Ca,06:22 am
12-03-1974,Mo Cnj Le,08:32 am
12-05-1974,Mo Cnj Vi,10:40 am
12-07-1974,Mo Cnj Li,01:43 pm
12-09-1974,Mo Cnj Sc,06:14 pm
12-12-1974,Mo Cnj Sa,00:35 am
12-14-1974,Mo Cnj Ca,09:04 am
12-16-1974,Mo Cnj Aq,07:48 pm

12-19-1974,Mo Cnj Pi,08:12 am
12-21-1974,Mo Cnj Ar,08:35 pm
12-24-1974,Mo Cnj Ta,06:45 am
12-26-1974,Mo Cnj Ge,01:16 pm
12-28-1974,Mo Cnj Ca,04:16 pm
12-30-1974,Mo Cnj Le,05:06 pm

January 1975
01-01-1975,Mo Cnj Vi,05:34 pm
01-03-1975,Mo Cnj Li,07:22 pm
01-05-1975,Mo Cnj Sc,11:39 pm
01-08-1975,Mo Cnj Sa,06:39 am
01-10-1975,Mo Cnj Ca,03:58 pm
01-13-1975,Mo Cnj Aq,03:03 am
01-15-1975,Mo Cnj Pi,03:23 pm
01-18-1975,Mo Cnj Ar,04:04 am
01-20-1975,Mo Cnj Ta,03:22 pm
01-22-1975,Mo Cnj Ge,11:24 am
01-25-1975,Mo Cnj Ca,03:21 am
01-27-1975,Mo Cnj Le,04:01 am
01-29-1975,Mo Cnj Vi,03:15 am
01-31-1975,Mo Cnj Li,03:14 am

February 1975
02-02-1975,Mo Cnj Sc,05:53 am
02-04-1975,Mo Cnj Sa,12:10 pm
02-06-1975,Mo Cnj Ca,09:42 pm
02-09-1975,Mo Cnj Aq,09:17 am
02-11-1975,Mo Cnj Pi,09:46 pm
02-14-1975,Mo Cnj Ar,10:23 am
02-16-1975,Mo Cnj Ta,10:10 pm
02-19-1975,Mo Cnj Ge,07:36 am
02-21-1975,Mo Cnj Ca,01:19 pm
02-23-1975,Mo Cnj Le,03:13 pm
02-25-1975,Mo Cnj Vi,02:37 pm
02-27-1975,Mo Cnj Li,01:38 pm

March 1975
03-01-1975,Mo Cnj Sc,02:34 pm
03-03-1975,Mo Cnj Sa,07:06 pm
03-06-1975,Mo Cnj Ca,03:40 am
03-08-1975,Mo Cnj Aq,03:10 am
03-11-1975,Mo Cnj Pi,03:50 am
03-13-1975,Mo Cnj Ar,04:19 pm
03-16-1975,Mo Cnj Ta,03:53 am
03-18-1975,Mo Cnj Ge,01:43 pm
03-20-1975,Mo Cnj Ca,08:49 pm

03-23-1975,Mo Cnj Le,00:31 am
03-25-1975,Mo Cnj Vi,01:21 am
03-27-1975,Mo Cnj Li,00:51 am
03-29-1975,Mo Cnj Sc,01:08 am
03-31-1975,Mo Cnj Sa,04:10 am

April 1975
04-02-1975,Mo Cnj Ca,11:09 am
04-04-1975,Mo Cnj Aq,09:46 pm
04-07-1975,Mo Cnj Pi,10:18 am
04-09-1975,Mo Cnj Ar,10:44 pm
04-12-1975,Mo Cnj Ta,09:54 am
04-14-1975,Mo Cnj Ge,07:14 pm
04-17-1975,Mo Cnj Ca,02:27 am
04-19-1975,Mo Cnj Le,07:15 am
04-21-1975,Mo Cnj Vi,09:43 am
04-23-1975,Mo Cnj Li,10:42 am
04-25-1975,Mo Cnj Sc,11:40 am
04-27-1975,Mo Cnj Sa,02:21 pm
04-29-1975,Mo Cnj Ca,08:09 pm

May 1975
05-02-1975,Mo Cnj Aq,05:34 am
05-04-1975,Mo Cnj Pi,05:34 pm
05-07-1975,Mo Cnj Ar,06:02 am
05-09-1975,Mo Cnj Ta,05:03 pm
05-12-1975,Mo Cnj Ge,01:45 am
05-14-1975,Mo Cnj Ca,08:08 am
05-16-1975,Mo Cnj Le,12:39 pm
05-18-1975,Mo Cnj Vi,03:46 pm
05-20-1975,Mo Cnj Li,06:06 pm
05-22-1975,Mo Cnj Sc,08:26 pm
05-24-1975,Mo Cnj Sa,11:52 pm
05-27-1975,Mo Cnj Ca,05:31 am
05-29-1975,Mo Cnj Aq,02:09 pm

June 1975
06-01-1975,Mo Cnj Pi,01:32 am
06-03-1975,Mo Cnj Ar,02:01 am
06-06-1975,Mo Cnj Ta,01:19 am
06-08-1975,Mo Cnj Ge,09:50 am
06-10-1975,Mo Cnj Ca,03:22 pm
06-12-1975,Mo Cnj Le,06:46 pm
06-14-1975,Mo Cnj Vi,09:11 pm
06-16-1975,Mo Cnj Li,11:41 pm
06-19-1975,Mo Cnj Sc,02:59 am
06-21-1975,Mo Cnj Sa,07:34 am

06-23-1975,Mo Cnj Ca,01:56 pm
06-25-1975,Mo Cnj Aq,10:33 pm
06-28-1975,Mo Cnj Pi,09:33 am
06-30-1975,Mo Cnj Ar,10:03 pm

July 1975
07-03-1975,Mo Cnj Ta,09:55 am
07-05-1975,Mo Cnj Ge,06:59 pm
07-08-1975,Mo Cnj Ca,00:24 am
07-10-1975,Mo Cnj Le,02:51 am
07-12-1975,Mo Cnj Vi,03:56 am
07-14-1975,Mo Cnj Li,05:21 am
07-16-1975,Mo Cnj Sc,08:23 am
07-18-1975,Mo Cnj Sa,01:32 pm
07-20-1975,Mo Cnj Ca,08:46 pm
07-23-1975,Mo Cnj Aq,05:56 am
07-25-1975,Mo Cnj Pi,04:59 pm
07-28-1975,Mo Cnj Ar,05:28 am
07-30-1975,Mo Cnj Ta,05:54 pm

August 1975
08-02-1975,Mo Cnj Ge,04:02 am
08-04-1975,Mo Cnj Ca,10:17 am
08-06-1975,Mo Cnj Le,12:44 pm
08-08-1975,Mo Cnj Vi,12:53 pm
08-10-1975,Mo Cnj Li,12:51 pm
08-12-1975,Mo Cnj Sc,02:30 pm
08-14-1975,Mo Cnj Sa,07:00 pm
08-17-1975,Mo Cnj Ca,02:26 am
08-19-1975,Mo Cnj Aq,12:10 pm
08-21-1975,Mo Cnj Pi,11:33 pm
08-24-1975,Mo Cnj Ar,12:03 pm
08-27-1975,Mo Cnj Ta,00:45 am
08-29-1975,Mo Cnj Ge,11:53 am
08-31-1975,Mo Cnj Ca,07:35 pm

September 1975
09-02-1975,Mo Cnj Le,11:08 pm
09-04-1975,Mo Cnj Vi,11:30 pm
09-06-1975,Mo Cnj Li,10:38 pm
09-08-1975,Mo Cnj Sc,10:46 pm
09-11-1975,Mo Cnj Sa,01:41 am
09-13-1975,Mo Cnj Ca,08:12 am
09-15-1975,Mo Cnj Aq,05:51 pm
09-18-1975,Mo Cnj Pi,05:32 am
09-20-1975,Mo Cnj Ar,06:07 pm
09-23-1975,Mo Cnj Ta,06:43 am

09-25-1975,Mo Cnj Ge,06:13 pm
09-28-1975,Mo Cnj Ca,03:07 am
09-30-1975,Mo Cnj Le,08:21 am

October 1975
10-02-1975,Mo Cnj Vi,10:04 am
10-04-1975,Mo Cnj Li,09:39 am
10-06-1975,Mo Cnj Sc,09:09 am
10-08-1975,Mo Cnj Sa,10:36 am
10-10-1975,Mo Cnj Ca,03:29 pm
10-13-1975,Mo Cnj Aq,00:10 am
10-15-1975,Mo Cnj Pi,11:40 am
10-18-1975,Mo Cnj Ar,00:20 am
10-20-1975,Mo Cnj Ta,12:43 pm
10-22-1975,Mo Cnj Ge,11:52 pm
10-25-1975,Mo Cnj Ca,08:58 am
10-27-1975,Mo Cnj Le,03:21 pm
10-29-1975,Mo Cnj Vi,06:47 pm
10-31-1975,Mo Cnj Li,07:55 pm

November 1975
11-02-1975,Mo Cnj Sc,08:08 pm
11-04-1975,Mo Cnj Sa,09:10 pm
11-07-1975,Mo Cnj Ca,00:45 am
11-09-1975,Mo Cnj Aq,07:59 am
11-11-1975,Mo Cnj Pi,06:42 pm
11-14-1975,Mo Cnj Ar,07:18 am
11-16-1975,Mo Cnj Ta,07:39 pm
11-19-1975,Mo Cnj Ge,06:15 am
11-21-1975,Mo Cnj Ca,02:37 pm
11-23-1975,Mo Cnj Le,08:48 pm
11-26-1975,Mo Cnj Vi,01:05 am
11-28-1975,Mo Cnj Li,03:48 am
11-30-1975,Mo Cnj Sc,05:37 am

December 1975
12-02-1975,Mo Cnj Sa,07:33 am
12-04-1975,Mo Cnj Ca,10:59 am
12-06-1975,Mo Cnj Aq,05:13 pm
12-09-1975,Mo Cnj Pi,02:52 am
12-11-1975,Mo Cnj Ar,03:07 pm
12-14-1975,Mo Cnj Ta,03:40 am
12-16-1975,Mo Cnj Ge,02:13 pm
12-18-1975,Mo Cnj Ca,09:49 pm
12-21-1975,Mo Cnj Le,02:53 am
12-23-1975,Mo Cnj Vi,06:28 am
12-25-1975,Mo Cnj Li,09:27 am

12-27-1975,Mo Cnj Sc,12:28 pm
12-29-1975,Mo Cnj Sa,03:53 pm
12-31-1975,Mo Cnj Ca,08:17 pm

January 1976
01-03-1976,Mo Cnj Aq,02:34 am
01-05-1976,Mo Cnj Pi,11:36 am
01-07-1976,Mo Cnj Ar,11:21 pm
01-10-1976,Mo Cnj Ta,12:10 pm
01-12-1976,Mo Cnj Ge,11:19 pm
01-15-1976,Mo Cnj Ca,07:01 am
01-17-1976,Mo Cnj Le,11:15 am
01-19-1976,Mo Cnj Vi,01:25 pm
01-21-1976,Mo Cnj Li,03:11 pm
01-23-1976,Mo Cnj Sc,05:49 pm
01-25-1976,Mo Cnj Sa,09:52 pm
01-28-1976,Mo Cnj Ca,03:25 am
01-30-1976,Mo Cnj Aq,10:34 am

February 1976
02-01-1976,Mo Cnj Pi,07:47 pm
02-04-1976,Mo Cnj Ar,07:17 am
02-06-1976,Mo Cnj Ta,08:13 pm
02-09-1976,Mo Cnj Ge,08:16 am
02-11-1976,Mo Cnj Ca,04:59 pm
02-13-1976,Mo Cnj Le,09:33 pm
02-15-1976,Mo Cnj Vi,11:00 pm
02-17-1976,Mo Cnj Li,11:15 pm
02-20-1976,Mo Cnj Sc,00:14 am
02-22-1976,Mo Cnj Sa,03:19 am
02-24-1976,Mo Cnj Ca,08:54 am
02-26-1976,Mo Cnj Aq,04:48 pm
02-29-1976,Mo Cnj Pi,02:42 am

March 1976
03-02-1976,Mo Cnj Ar,02:22 pm
03-05-1976,Mo Cnj Ta,03:18 am
03-07-1976,Mo Cnj Ge,03:56 pm
03-10-1976,Mo Cnj Ca,02:00 am
03-12-1976,Mo Cnj Le,07:56 am
03-14-1976,Mo Cnj Vi,09:59 am
03-16-1976,Mo Cnj Li,09:45 am
03-18-1976,Mo Cnj Sc,09:18 am
03-20-1976,Mo Cnj Sa,10:34 am
03-22-1976,Mo Cnj Ca,02:48 pm
03-24-1976,Mo Cnj Aq,10:20 pm

03-27-1976,Mo Cnj Pi,08:34 am
03-29-1976,Mo Cnj Ar,08:38 pm

April 1976
04-01-1976,Mo Cnj Ta,09:35 am
04-03-1976,Mo Cnj Ge,10:16 pm
04-06-1976,Mo Cnj Ca,09:07 am
04-08-1976,Mo Cnj Le,04:37 pm
04-10-1976,Mo Cnj Vi,08:16 pm
04-12-1976,Mo Cnj Li,08:54 pm
04-14-1976,Mo Cnj Sc,08:14 pm
04-16-1976,Mo Cnj Sa,08:15 pm
04-18-1976,Mo Cnj Ca,10:44 pm
04-21-1976,Mo Cnj Aq,04:48 am
04-23-1976,Mo Cnj Pi,02:29 pm
04-26-1976,Mo Cnj Ar,02:38 am
04-28-1976,Mo Cnj Ta,03:38 pm

May 1976
05-01-1976,Mo Cnj Ge,04:06 am
05-03-1976,Mo Cnj Ca,02:54 pm
05-05-1976,Mo Cnj Le,11:09 pm
05-08-1976,Mo Cnj Vi,04:21 am
05-10-1976,Mo Cnj Li,06:39 am
05-12-1976,Mo Cnj Sc,07:03 am
05-14-1976,Mo Cnj Sa,07:05 am
05-16-1976,Mo Cnj Ca,08:32 am
05-18-1976,Mo Cnj Aq,01:03 pm
05-20-1976,Mo Cnj Pi,09:27 pm
05-23-1976,Mo Cnj Ar,09:08 am
05-25-1976,Mo Cnj Ta,10:07 pm
05-28-1976,Mo Cnj Ge,10:22 am
05-30-1976,Mo Cnj Ca,08:39 pm

June 1976
06-02-1976,Mo Cnj Le,04:38 am
06-04-1976,Mo Cnj Vi,10:21 am
06-06-1976,Mo Cnj Li,02:00 pm
06-08-1976,Mo Cnj Sc,03:59 pm
06-10-1976,Mo Cnj Sa,05:07 pm
06-12-1976,Mo Cnj Ca,06:46 pm
06-14-1976,Mo Cnj Aq,10:31 pm
06-17-1976,Mo Cnj Pi,05:44 am
06-19-1976,Mo Cnj Ar,04:32 pm
06-22-1976,Mo Cnj Ta,05:21 am
06-24-1976,Mo Cnj Ge,05:37 pm

06-27-1976,Mo Cnj Ca,03:30 am
06-29-1976,Mo Cnj Le,10:40 am

July 1976
07-01-1976,Mo Cnj Vi,03:47 pm
07-03-1976,Mo Cnj Li,07:35 pm
07-05-1976,Mo Cnj Sc,10:34 pm
07-08-1976,Mo Cnj Sa,01:06 am
07-10-1976,Mo Cnj Ca,03:50 am
07-12-1976,Mo Cnj Aq,07:53 am
07-14-1976,Mo Cnj Pi,02:36 pm
07-17-1976,Mo Cnj Ar,00:40 am
07-19-1976,Mo Cnj Ta,01:11 pm
07-22-1976,Mo Cnj Ge,01:41 am
07-24-1976,Mo Cnj Ca,11:40 am
07-26-1976,Mo Cnj Le,06:20 pm
07-28-1976,Mo Cnj Vi,10:24 pm
07-31-1976,Mo Cnj Li,01:14 am

August 1976
08-02-1976,Mo Cnj Sc,03:56 am
08-04-1976,Mo Cnj Sa,07:03 am
08-06-1976,Mo Cnj Ca,10:54 am
08-08-1976,Mo Cnj Aq,03:57 pm
08-10-1976,Mo Cnj Pi,11:01 pm
08-13-1976,Mo Cnj Ar,08:50 am
08-15-1976,Mo Cnj Ta,09:06 pm
08-18-1976,Mo Cnj Ge,09:55 am
08-20-1976,Mo Cnj Ca,08:35 pm
08-23-1976,Mo Cnj Le,03:31 am
08-25-1976,Mo Cnj Vi,07:04 am
08-27-1976,Mo Cnj Li,08:42 am
08-29-1976,Mo Cnj Sc,10:05 am
08-31-1976,Mo Cnj Sa,12:28 pm

September 1976
09-02-1976,Mo Cnj Ca,04:29 pm
09-04-1976,Mo Cnj Aq,10:20 pm
09-07-1976,Mo Cnj Pi,06:12 am
09-09-1976,Mo Cnj Ar,04:19 pm
09-12-1976,Mo Cnj Ta,04:31 am
09-14-1976,Mo Cnj Ge,05:33 pm
09-17-1976,Mo Cnj Ca,05:07 am
09-19-1976,Mo Cnj Le,01:11 am
09-21-1976,Mo Cnj Vi,05:16 pm
09-23-1976,Mo Cnj Li,06:28 pm
09-25-1976,Mo Cnj Sc,06:34 pm

09-27-1976,Mo Cnj Sa,07:22 pm
09-29-1976,Mo Cnj Ca,10:14 pm

October 1976
10-02-1976,Mo Cnj Aq,03:50 am
10-04-1976,Mo Cnj Pi,12:11 pm
10-06-1976,Mo Cnj Ar,10:50 pm
10-09-1976,Mo Cnj Ta,11:11 am
10-12-1976,Mo Cnj Ge,00:14 am
10-14-1976,Mo Cnj Ca,12:24 pm
10-16-1976,Mo Cnj Le,09:50 pm
10-19-1976,Mo Cnj Vi,03:25 am
10-21-1976,Mo Cnj Li,05:27 am
10-23-1976,Mo Cnj Sc,05:18 am
10-25-1976,Mo Cnj Sa,04:49 am
10-27-1976,Mo Cnj Ca,05:56 am
10-29-1976,Mo Cnj Aq,10:06 am
10-31-1976,Mo Cnj Pi,05:54 pm

November 1976
11-03-1976,Mo Cnj Ar,04:46 am
11-05-1976,Mo Cnj Ta,05:23 pm
11-08-1976,Mo Cnj Ge,06:21 am
11-10-1976,Mo Cnj Ca,06:28 pm
11-13-1976,Mo Cnj Le,04:37 am
11-15-1976,Mo Cnj Vi,11:47 am
11-17-1976,Mo Cnj Li,03:35 pm
11-19-1976,Mo Cnj Sc,04:32 pm
11-21-1976,Mo Cnj Sa,04:04 pm
11-23-1976,Mo Cnj Ca,04:04 pm
11-25-1976,Mo Cnj Aq,06:30 pm
11-28-1976,Mo Cnj Pi,00:47 am
11-30-1976,Mo Cnj Ar,11:01 am

December 1976
12-02-1976,Mo Cnj Ta,11:42 pm
12-05-1976,Mo Cnj Ge,12:39 pm
12-08-1976,Mo Cnj Ca,00:22 am
12-10-1976,Mo Cnj Le,10:13 am
12-12-1976,Mo Cnj Vi,05:56 pm
12-14-1976,Mo Cnj Li,11:14 pm
12-17-1976,Mo Cnj Sc,02:02 am
12-19-1976,Mo Cnj Sa,02:54 am
12-21-1976,Mo Cnj Ca,03:12 am
12-23-1976,Mo Cnj Aq,04:48 am
12-25-1976,Mo Cnj Pi,09:36 am

12-27-1976,Mo Cnj Ar,06:32 pm
12-30-1976,Mo Cnj Ta,06:44 am

January 1977
01-01-1977,Mo Cnj Ge,07:44 pm
01-04-1977,Mo Cnj Ca,07:13 am
01-06-1977,Mo Cnj Le,04:21 pm
01-08-1977,Mo Cnj Vi,11:23 pm
01-11-1977,Mo Cnj Li,04:48 am
01-13-1977,Mo Cnj Sc,08:44 am
01-15-1977,Mo Cnj Sa,11:18 am
01-17-1977,Mo Cnj Ca,01:02 pm
01-19-1977,Mo Cnj Aq,03:12 pm
01-21-1977,Mo Cnj Pi,07:31 pm
01-24-1977,Mo Cnj Ar,03:20 am
01-26-1977,Mo Cnj Ta,02:42 pm
01-29-1977,Mo Cnj Ge,03:38 am
01-31-1977,Mo Cnj Ca,03:20 pm

February 1977
02-03-1977,Mo Cnj Le,00:12 am
02-05-1977,Mo Cnj Vi,06:17 am
02-07-1977,Mo Cnj Li,10:36 am
02-09-1977,Mo Cnj Sc,02:04 pm
02-11-1977,Mo Cnj Sa,05:11 pm
02-13-1977,Mo Cnj Ca,08:14 pm
02-15-1977,Mo Cnj Aq,11:46 pm
02-18-1977,Mo Cnj Pi,04:46 am
02-20-1977,Mo Cnj Ar,12:23 pm
02-22-1977,Mo Cnj Ta,11:07 pm
02-25-1977,Mo Cnj Ge,11:50 am
02-28-1977,Mo Cnj Ca,00:02 am

March 1977
03-02-1977,Mo Cnj Le,09:25 am
03-04-1977,Mo Cnj Vi,03:19 pm
03-06-1977,Mo Cnj Li,06:35 pm
03-08-1977,Mo Cnj Sc,08:37 pm
03-10-1977,Mo Cnj Sa,10:43 pm
03-13-1977,Mo Cnj Ca,01:40 am
03-15-1977,Mo Cnj Aq,06:00 am
03-17-1977,Mo Cnj Pi,12:06 pm
03-19-1977,Mo Cnj Ar,08:23 pm
03-22-1977,Mo Cnj Ta,07:05 am
03-24-1977,Mo Cnj Ge,07:39 pm
03-27-1977,Mo Cnj Ca,08:17 am
03-29-1977,Mo Cnj Le,06:41 pm

April 1977
04-01-1977,Mo Cnj Vi,01:26 am
04-03-1977,Mo Cnj Li,04:40 am
04-05-1977,Mo Cnj Sc,05:40 am
04-07-1977,Mo Cnj Sa,06:09 am
04-09-1977,Mo Cnj Ca,07:41 am
04-11-1977,Mo Cnj Aq,11:24 am
04-13-1977,Mo Cnj Pi,05:49 pm
04-16-1977,Mo Cnj Ar,02:52 am
04-18-1977,Mo Cnj Ta,02:03 pm
04-21-1977,Mo Cnj Ge,02:38 am
04-23-1977,Mo Cnj Ca,03:26 pm
04-26-1977,Mo Cnj Le,02:44 am
04-28-1977,Mo Cnj Vi,10:53 am
04-30-1977,Mo Cnj Li,03:13 pm

May 1977
05-02-1977,Mo Cnj Sc,04:24 pm
05-04-1977,Mo Cnj Sa,03:59 pm
05-06-1977,Mo Cnj Ca,03:54 pm
05-08-1977,Mo Cnj Aq,06:00 pm
05-10-1977,Mo Cnj Pi,11:29 pm
05-13-1977,Mo Cnj Ar,08:30 am
05-15-1977,Mo Cnj Ta,08:05 pm
05-18-1977,Mo Cnj Ge,08:51 am
05-20-1977,Mo Cnj Ca,09:36 pm
05-23-1977,Mo Cnj Le,09:14 am
05-25-1977,Mo Cnj Vi,06:31 pm
05-28-1977,Mo Cnj Li,00:28 am
05-30-1977,Mo Cnj Sc,02:57 am

June 1977
06-01-1977,Mo Cnj Sa,02:54 am
06-03-1977,Mo Cnj Ca,02:07 am
06-05-1977,Mo Cnj Aq,02:44 am
06-07-1977,Mo Cnj Pi,06:36 am
06-09-1977,Mo Cnj Ar,02:35 pm
06-12-1977,Mo Cnj Ta,01:58 am
06-14-1977,Mo Cnj Ge,02:51 pm
06-17-1977,Mo Cnj Ca,03:29 am
06-19-1977,Mo Cnj Le,02:54 pm
06-22-1977,Mo Cnj Vi,00:29 am
06-24-1977,Mo Cnj Li,07:35 am
06-26-1977,Mo Cnj Sc,11:42 am
06-28-1977,Mo Cnj Sa,01:02 pm
06-30-1977,Mo Cnj Ca,12:49 pm

July 1977

07-02-1977,Mo Cnj Aq,12:57 pm
07-04-1977,Mo Cnj Pi,03:32 pm
07-06-1977,Mo Cnj Ar,10:04 pm
07-09-1977,Mo Cnj Ta,08:33 am
07-11-1977,Mo Cnj Ge,09:15 pm
07-14-1977,Mo Cnj Ca,09:50 am
07-16-1977,Mo Cnj Le,08:51 pm
07-19-1977,Mo Cnj Vi,05:59 am
07-21-1977,Mo Cnj Li,01:10 pm
07-23-1977,Mo Cnj Sc,06:14 pm
07-25-1977,Mo Cnj Sa,09:05 pm
07-27-1977,Mo Cnj Ca,10:15 pm
07-29-1977,Mo Cnj Aq,11:05 pm

August 1977

08-01-1977,Mo Cnj Pi,01:24 am
08-03-1977,Mo Cnj Ar,06:54 am
08-05-1977,Mo Cnj Ta,04:18 pm
08-08-1977,Mo Cnj Ge,04:29 am
08-10-1977,Mo Cnj Ca,05:04 pm
08-13-1977,Mo Cnj Le,03:57 am
08-15-1977,Mo Cnj Vi,12:27 pm
08-17-1977,Mo Cnj Li,06:50 pm
08-19-1977,Mo Cnj Sc,11:36 pm
08-22-1977,Mo Cnj Sa,03:03 am
08-24-1977,Mo Cnj Ca,05:31 am
08-26-1977,Mo Cnj Aq,07:41 am
08-28-1977,Mo Cnj Pi,10:47 am
08-30-1977,Mo Cnj Ar,04:12 pm

September 1977

09-02-1977,Mo Cnj Ta,00:52 am
09-04-1977,Mo Cnj Ge,12:27 pm
09-07-1977,Mo Cnj Ca,01:04 am
09-09-1977,Mo Cnj Le,12:15 pm
09-11-1977,Mo Cnj Vi,08:35 pm
09-14-1977,Mo Cnj Li,02:08 am
09-16-1977,Mo Cnj Sc,05:46 am
09-18-1977,Mo Cnj Sa,08:28 am
09-20-1977,Mo Cnj Ca,11:04 am
09-22-1977,Mo Cnj Aq,02:12 am
09-24-1977,Mo Cnj Pi,06:30 pm
09-27-1977,Mo Cnj Ar,00:41 am
09-29-1977,Mo Cnj Ta,09:22 am

October 1977

10-01-1977,Mo Cnj Ge,08:34 pm
10-04-1977,Mo Cnj Ca,09:10 am
10-06-1977,Mo Cnj Le,08:58 pm
10-09-1977,Mo Cnj Vi,05:59 am
10-11-1977,Mo Cnj Li,11:29 am
10-13-1977,Mo Cnj Sc,02:11 pm
10-15-1977,Mo Cnj Sa,03:27 pm
10-17-1977,Mo Cnj Ca,04:51 pm
10-19-1977,Mo Cnj Aq,07:36 pm
10-22-1977,Mo Cnj Pi,00:27 am
10-24-1977,Mo Cnj Ar,07:35 am
10-26-1977,Mo Cnj Ta,04:54 pm
10-29-1977,Mo Cnj Ge,04:09 am
10-31-1977,Mo Cnj Ca,04:40 pm

November 1977

11-03-1977,Mo Cnj Le,05:03 am
11-05-1977,Mo Cnj Vi,03:17 pm
11-07-1977,Mo Cnj Li,09:51 pm
11-10-1977,Mo Cnj Sc,00:42 am
11-12-1977,Mo Cnj Sa,01:04 am
11-14-1977,Mo Cnj Ca,00:51 am
11-16-1977,Mo Cnj Aq,02:01 am
11-18-1977,Mo Cnj Pi,05:59 am
11-20-1977,Mo Cnj Ar,01:14 pm
11-22-1977,Mo Cnj Ta,11:10 pm
11-25-1977,Mo Cnj Ge,10:49 am
11-27-1977,Mo Cnj Ca,11:20 pm
11-30-1977,Mo Cnj Le,11:53 am

December 1977

12-02-1977,Mo Cnj Vi,11:06 pm
12-05-1977,Mo Cnj Li,07:18 am
12-07-1977,Mo Cnj Sc,11:34 am
12-09-1977,Mo Cnj Sa,12:22 pm
12-11-1977,Mo Cnj Ca,11:27 am
12-13-1977,Mo Cnj Aq,11:00 am
12-15-1977,Mo Cnj Pi,01:09 pm
12-17-1977,Mo Cnj Ar,07:11 pm
12-20-1977,Mo Cnj Ta,04:54 am
12-22-1977,Mo Cnj Ge,04:51 pm
12-25-1977,Mo Cnj Ca,05:30 am
12-27-1977,Mo Cnj Le,05:52 pm
12-30-1977,Mo Cnj Vi,05:14 am

January 1978

01-01-1978,Mo Cnj Li,02:32 pm
01-03-1978,Mo Cnj Sc,08:36 pm
01-05-1978,Mo Cnj Sa,11:04 pm
01-07-1978,Mo Cnj Ca,10:55 pm
01-09-1978,Mo Cnj Aq,10:05 pm
01-11-1978,Mo Cnj Pi,10:50 pm
01-14-1978,Mo Cnj Ar,03:05 am
01-16-1978,Mo Cnj Ta,11:30 am
01-18-1978,Mo Cnj Ge,11:07 pm
01-21-1978,Mo Cnj Ca,11:51 am
01-24-1978,Mo Cnj Le,00:03 am
01-26-1978,Mo Cnj Vi,10:57 am
01-28-1978,Mo Cnj Li,08:08 pm
01-31-1978,Mo Cnj Sc,03:04 am

February 1978

02-02-1978,Mo Cnj Sa,07:14 am
02-04-1978,Mo Cnj Ca,08:50 am
02-06-1978,Mo Cnj Aq,09:04 am
02-08-1978,Mo Cnj Pi,09:48 am
02-10-1978,Mo Cnj Ar,12:57 pm
02-12-1978,Mo Cnj Ta,07:51 pm
02-15-1978,Mo Cnj Ge,06:25 am
02-17-1978,Mo Cnj Ca,06:57 pm
02-20-1978,Mo Cnj Le,07:10 am
02-22-1978,Mo Cnj Vi,05:40 pm
02-25-1978,Mo Cnj Li,02:03 am
02-27-1978,Mo Cnj Sc,08:28 am

March 1978

03-01-1978,Mo Cnj Sa,01:02 pm
03-03-1978,Mo Cnj Ca,03:58 pm
03-05-1978,Mo Cnj Aq,05:51 pm
03-07-1978,Mo Cnj Pi,07:46 pm
03-09-1978,Mo Cnj Ar,11:09 pm
03-12-1978,Mo Cnj Ta,05:19 am
03-14-1978,Mo Cnj Ge,02:49 pm
03-17-1978,Mo Cnj Ca,02:49 am
03-19-1978,Mo Cnj Le,03:12 pm
03-22-1978,Mo Cnj Vi,01:49 am
03-24-1978,Mo Cnj Li,09:41 am
03-26-1978,Mo Cnj Sc,03:01 pm
03-28-1978,Mo Cnj Sa,06:38 pm
03-30-1978,Mo Cnj Ca,09:24 pm

April 1978

04-02-1978,Mo Cnj Aq,00:06 am
04-04-1978,Mo Cnj Pi,03:21 am
04-06-1978,Mo Cnj Ar,07:52 am
04-08-1978,Mo Cnj Ta,02:22 pm
04-10-1978,Mo Cnj Ge,11:28 pm
04-13-1978,Mo Cnj Ca,10:59 am
04-15-1978,Mo Cnj Le,11:31 pm
04-18-1978,Mo Cnj Vi,10:44 am
04-20-1978,Mo Cnj Li,06:53 pm
04-22-1978,Mo Cnj Sc,11:40 pm
04-25-1978,Mo Cnj Sa,02:01 am
04-27-1978,Mo Cnj Ca,03:28 am
04-29-1978,Mo Cnj Aq,05:29 am

May 1978

05-01-1978,Mo Cnj Pi,09:00 am
05-03-1978,Mo Cnj Ar,02:27 pm
05-05-1978,Mo Cnj Ta,09:52 pm
05-08-1978,Mo Cnj Ge,07:18 am
05-10-1978,Mo Cnj Ca,06:42 pm
05-13-1978,Mo Cnj Le,07:17 am
05-15-1978,Mo Cnj Vi,07:16 pm
05-18-1978,Mo Cnj Li,04:25 am
05-20-1978,Mo Cnj Sc,09:40 am
05-22-1978,Mo Cnj Sa,11:32 am
05-24-1978,Mo Cnj Ca,11:42 am
05-26-1978,Mo Cnj Aq,12:10 pm
05-28-1978,Mo Cnj Pi,02:37 pm
05-30-1978,Mo Cnj Ar,07:52 pm

June 1978

06-02-1978,Mo Cnj Ta,03:50 am
06-04-1978,Mo Cnj Ge,01:54 pm
06-07-1978,Mo Cnj Ca,01:31 am
06-09-1978,Mo Cnj Le,02:08 pm
06-12-1978,Mo Cnj Vi,02:36 am
06-14-1978,Mo Cnj Li,12:56 pm
06-16-1978,Mo Cnj Sc,07:29 pm
06-18-1978,Mo Cnj Sa,10:01 pm
06-20-1978,Mo Cnj Ca,09:52 pm
06-22-1978,Mo Cnj Aq,09:08 pm
06-24-1978,Mo Cnj Pi,09:57 pm
06-27-1978,Mo Cnj Ar,01:53 am
06-29-1978,Mo Cnj Ta,09:22 am

July 1978

07-01-1978,Mo Cnj Ge,07:38 pm
07-04-1978,Mo Cnj Ca,07:34 am
07-06-1978,Mo Cnj Le,08:14 pm
07-09-1978,Mo Cnj Vi,08:45 am
07-11-1978,Mo Cnj Li,07:48 pm
07-14-1978,Mo Cnj Sc,03:47 am
07-16-1978,Mo Cnj Sa,07:50 am
07-18-1978,Mo Cnj Ca,08:33 am
07-20-1978,Mo Cnj Aq,07:42 am
07-22-1978,Mo Cnj Pi,07:27 am
07-24-1978,Mo Cnj Ar,09:47 am
07-26-1978,Mo Cnj Ta,03:51 pm
07-29-1978,Mo Cnj Ge,01:31 am
07-31-1978,Mo Cnj Ca,01:29 pm

August 1978

08-03-1978,Mo Cnj Le,02:10 am
08-05-1978,Mo Cnj Vi,02:29 pm
08-08-1978,Mo Cnj Li,01:30 am
08-10-1978,Mo Cnj Sc,10:11 am
08-12-1978,Mo Cnj Sa,03:43 pm
08-14-1978,Mo Cnj Ca,06:03 pm
08-16-1978,Mo Cnj Aq,06:16 pm
08-18-1978,Mo Cnj Pi,06:05 pm
08-20-1978,Mo Cnj Ar,07:30 pm
08-23-1978,Mo Cnj Ta,00:06 am
08-25-1978,Mo Cnj Ge,08:31 am
08-27-1978,Mo Cnj Ca,07:59 pm
08-30-1978,Mo Cnj Le,08:40 am

September 1978

09-01-1978,Mo Cnj Vi,08:46 pm
09-04-1978,Mo Cnj Li,07:16 am
09-06-1978,Mo Cnj Sc,03:39 pm
09-08-1978,Mo Cnj Sa,09:40 pm
09-11-1978,Mo Cnj Ca,01:20 am
09-13-1978,Mo Cnj Aq,03:09 am
09-15-1978,Mo Cnj Pi,04:10 am
09-17-1978,Mo Cnj Ar,05:50 am
09-19-1978,Mo Cnj Ta,09:43 am
09-21-1978,Mo Cnj Ge,04:56 pm
09-24-1978,Mo Cnj Ca,03:31 am
09-26-1978,Mo Cnj Le,04:02 pm
09-29-1978,Mo Cnj Vi,04:12 am

October 1978

10-01-1978,Mo Cnj Li,02:18 pm
10-03-1978,Mo Cnj Sc,09:49 pm
10-06-1978,Mo Cnj Sa,03:07 am
10-08-1978,Mo Cnj Ca,06:53 am
10-10-1978,Mo Cnj Aq,09:43 am
10-12-1978,Mo Cnj Pi,12:13 pm
10-14-1978,Mo Cnj Ar,03:06 pm
10-16-1978,Mo Cnj Ta,07:22 pm
10-19-1978,Mo Cnj Ge,02:06 am
10-21-1978,Mo Cnj Ca,11:53 am
10-24-1978,Mo Cnj Le,00:05 am
10-26-1978,Mo Cnj Vi,12:33 pm
10-28-1978,Mo Cnj Li,10:52 pm
10-31-1978,Mo Cnj Sc,05:53 am

November 1978

11-02-1978,Mo Cnj Sa,10:03 am
11-04-1978,Mo Cnj Ca,12:41 pm
11-06-1978,Mo Cnj Aq,03:04 pm
11-08-1978,Mo Cnj Pi,06:06 pm
11-10-1978,Mo Cnj Ar,10:12 pm
11-13-1978,Mo Cnj Ta,03:36 am
11-15-1978,Mo Cnj Ge,10:45 am
11-17-1978,Mo Cnj Ca,08:17 pm
11-20-1978,Mo Cnj Le,08:10 am
11-22-1978,Mo Cnj Vi,08:58 pm
11-25-1978,Mo Cnj Li,08:07 am
11-27-1978,Mo Cnj Sc,03:39 pm
11-29-1978,Mo Cnj Sa,07:23 pm

December 1978

12-01-1978,Mo Cnj Ca,08:44 pm
12-03-1978,Mo Cnj Aq,09:36 pm
12-05-1978,Mo Cnj Pi,11:37 pm
12-08-1978,Mo Cnj Ar,03:40 am
12-10-1978,Mo Cnj Ta,09:51 am
12-12-1978,Mo Cnj Ge,05:55 pm
12-15-1978,Mo Cnj Ca,03:50 am
12-17-1978,Mo Cnj Le,03:38 pm
12-20-1978,Mo Cnj Vi,04:34 am
12-22-1978,Mo Cnj Li,04:40 pm
12-25-1978,Mo Cnj Sc,01:32 am
12-27-1978,Mo Cnj Sa,06:08 am
12-29-1978,Mo Cnj Ca,07:16 am
12-31-1978,Mo Cnj Aq,06:54 am

January 1979

01-02-1979,Mo Cnj Pi,07:09 am
01-04-1979,Mo Cnj Ar,09:42 am
01-06-1979,Mo Cnj Ta,03:18 pm
01-08-1979,Mo Cnj Ge,11:43 pm
01-11-1979,Mo Cnj Ca,10:14 am
01-13-1979,Mo Cnj Le,10:16 pm
01-16-1979,Mo Cnj Vi,11:10 am
01-18-1979,Mo Cnj Li,11:41 pm
01-21-1979,Mo Cnj Sc,09:51 am
01-23-1979,Mo Cnj Sa,04:09 pm
01-25-1979,Mo Cnj Ca,06:28 pm
01-27-1979,Mo Cnj Aq,06:13 pm
01-29-1979,Mo Cnj Pi,05:26 pm
01-31-1979,Mo Cnj Ar,06:11 pm

February 1979

02-02-1979,Mo Cnj Ta,10:03 pm
02-05-1979,Mo Cnj Ge,05:33 am
02-07-1979,Mo Cnj Ca,04:06 pm
02-10-1979,Mo Cnj Le,04:26 am
02-12-1979,Mo Cnj Vi,05:18 pm
02-15-1979,Mo Cnj Li,05:38 am
02-17-1979,Mo Cnj Sc,04:13 pm
02-19-1979,Mo Cnj Sa,11:52 pm
02-22-1979,Mo Cnj Ca,04:01 am
02-24-1979,Mo Cnj Aq,05:12 am
02-26-1979,Mo Cnj Pi,04:52 am
02-28-1979,Mo Cnj Ar,04:54 am

March 1979

03-02-1979,Mo Cnj Ta,07:09 am
03-04-1979,Mo Cnj Ge,12:58 pm
03-06-1979,Mo Cnj Ca,10:35 pm
03-09-1979,Mo Cnj Le,10:48 am
03-11-1979,Mo Cnj Vi,11:43 pm
03-14-1979,Mo Cnj Li,11:42 am
03-16-1979,Mo Cnj Sc,09:50 pm
03-19-1979,Mo Cnj Sa,05:38 am
03-21-1979,Mo Cnj Ca,10:56 am
03-23-1979,Mo Cnj Aq,01:52 pm
03-25-1979,Mo Cnj Pi,03:05 pm
03-27-1979,Mo Cnj Ar,03:48 pm
03-29-1979,Mo Cnj Ta,05:37 pm
03-31-1979,Mo Cnj Ge,10:09 pm

April 1979

04-03-1979,Mo Cnj Ca,06:24 am
04-05-1979,Mo Cnj Le,05:59 pm
04-08-1979,Mo Cnj Vi,06:52 am
04-10-1979,Mo Cnj Li,06:45 pm
04-13-1979,Mo Cnj Sc,04:16 am
04-15-1979,Mo Cnj Sa,11:18 am
04-17-1979,Mo Cnj Ca,04:23 pm
04-19-1979,Mo Cnj Aq,08:02 pm
04-21-1979,Mo Cnj Pi,10:42 pm
04-24-1979,Mo Cnj Ar,00:52 am
04-26-1979,Mo Cnj Ta,03:28 am
04-28-1979,Mo Cnj Ge,07:49 am
04-30-1979,Mo Cnj Ca,03:12 pm

May 1979

05-03-1979,Mo Cnj Le,01:57 am
05-05-1979,Mo Cnj Vi,02:41 pm
05-08-1979,Mo Cnj Li,02:47 am
05-10-1979,Mo Cnj Sc,12:10 pm
05-12-1979,Mo Cnj Sa,06:25 pm
05-14-1979,Mo Cnj Ca,10:26 pm
05-17-1979,Mo Cnj Aq,01:26 am
05-19-1979,Mo Cnj Pi,04:19 am
05-21-1979,Mo Cnj Ar,07:31 am
05-23-1979,Mo Cnj Ta,11:21 am
05-25-1979,Mo Cnj Ge,04:28 pm
05-27-1979,Mo Cnj Ca,11:51 pm
05-30-1979,Mo Cnj Le,10:08 am

June 1979

06-01-1979,Mo Cnj Vi,10:41 pm
06-04-1979,Mo Cnj Li,11:12 am
06-06-1979,Mo Cnj Sc,09:06 pm
06-09-1979,Mo Cnj Sa,03:15 am
06-11-1979,Mo Cnj Ca,06:24 am
06-13-1979,Mo Cnj Aq,08:07 am
06-15-1979,Mo Cnj Pi,09:57 am
06-17-1979,Mo Cnj Ar,12:53 pm
06-19-1979,Mo Cnj Ta,05:18 pm
06-21-1979,Mo Cnj Ge,11:22 pm
06-24-1979,Mo Cnj Ca,07:24 am
06-26-1979,Mo Cnj Le,05:47 pm
06-29-1979,Mo Cnj Vi,06:14 am

July 1979

07-01-1979,Mo Cnj Li,07:09 pm
07-04-1979,Mo Cnj Sc,05:58 am

07-06-1979,Mo Cnj Sa,12:57 pm
07-08-1979,Mo Cnj Ca,04:08 pm
07-10-1979,Mo Cnj Aq,04:59 pm
07-12-1979,Mo Cnj Pi,05:23 pm
07-14-1979,Mo Cnj Ar,06:57 pm
07-16-1979,Mo Cnj Ta,10:43 pm
07-19-1979,Mo Cnj Ge,05:00 am
07-21-1979,Mo Cnj Ca,01:41 pm
07-24-1979,Mo Cnj Le,00:31 am
07-26-1979,Mo Cnj Vi,01:02 pm
07-29-1979,Mo Cnj Li,02:07 am
07-31-1979,Mo Cnj Sc,01:47 pm

August 1979
08-02-1979,Mo Cnj Sa,10:06 pm
08-05-1979,Mo Cnj Ca,02:23 am
08-07-1979,Mo Cnj Aq,03:28 am
08-09-1979,Mo Cnj Pi,03:06 am
08-11-1979,Mo Cnj Ar,03:10 am
08-13-1979,Mo Cnj Ta,05:22 am
08-15-1979,Mo Cnj Ge,10:42 am
08-17-1979,Mo Cnj Ca,07:18 pm
08-20-1979,Mo Cnj Le,06:29 am
08-22-1979,Mo Cnj Vi,07:12 pm
08-25-1979,Mo Cnj Li,08:14 am
08-27-1979,Mo Cnj Sc,08:12 pm
08-30-1979,Mo Cnj Sa,05:39 am

September 1979
09-01-1979,Mo Cnj Ca,11:34 am
09-03-1979,Mo Cnj Aq,01:59 pm
09-05-1979,Mo Cnj Pi,02:03 pm
09-07-1979,Mo Cnj Ar,01:29 pm
09-09-1979,Mo Cnj Ta,02:13 pm
09-11-1979,Mo Cnj Ge,05:55 pm
09-14-1979,Mo Cnj Ca,01:28 am
09-16-1979,Mo Cnj Le,12:26 pm
09-19-1979,Mo Cnj Vi,01:16 am
09-21-1979,Mo Cnj Li,02:11 pm
09-24-1979,Mo Cnj Sc,01:54 am
09-26-1979,Mo Cnj Sa,11:36 am
09-28-1979,Mo Cnj Ca,06:40 pm
09-30-1979,Mo Cnj Aq,10:50 pm

October 1979
10-03-1979,Mo Cnj Pi,00:24 am
10-05-1979,Mo Cnj Ar,00:29 am

10-07-1979,Mo Cnj Ta,00:45 am
10-09-1979,Mo Cnj Ge,03:07 am
10-11-1979,Mo Cnj Ca,09:09 am
10-13-1979,Mo Cnj Le,07:12 pm
10-16-1979,Mo Cnj Vi,07:51 am
10-18-1979,Mo Cnj Li,08:45 pm
10-21-1979,Mo Cnj Sc,08:03 am
10-23-1979,Mo Cnj Sa,05:10 pm
10-26-1979,Mo Cnj Ca,00:12 am
10-28-1979,Mo Cnj Aq,05:17 am
10-30-1979,Mo Cnj Pi,08:29 am

November 1979
11-01-1979,Mo Cnj Ar,10:09 am
11-03-1979,Mo Cnj Ta,11:16 am
11-05-1979,Mo Cnj Ge,01:26 pm
11-07-1979,Mo Cnj Ca,06:24 pm
11-10-1979,Mo Cnj Le,03:15 am
11-12-1979,Mo Cnj Vi,03:21 pm
11-15-1979,Mo Cnj Li,04:17 am
11-17-1979,Mo Cnj Sc,03:30 pm
11-19-1979,Mo Cnj Sa,11:57 pm
11-22-1979,Mo Cnj Ca,06:02 am
11-24-1979,Mo Cnj Aq,10:37 am
11-26-1979,Mo Cnj Pi,02:17 pm
11-28-1979,Mo Cnj Ar,05:17 pm
11-30-1979,Mo Cnj Ta,07:55 pm

December 1979
12-02-1979,Mo Cnj Ge,11:02 pm
12-05-1979,Mo Cnj Ca,04:02 am
12-07-1979,Mo Cnj Le,12:10 pm
12-09-1979,Mo Cnj Vi,11:34 pm
12-12-1979,Mo Cnj Li,12:30 pm
12-15-1979,Mo Cnj Sc,00:09 am
12-17-1979,Mo Cnj Sa,08:37 am
12-19-1979,Mo Cnj Ca,01:55 pm
12-21-1979,Mo Cnj Aq,05:13 pm
12-23-1979,Mo Cnj Pi,07:50 pm
12-25-1979,Mo Cnj Ar,10:40 pm
12-28-1979,Mo Cnj Ta,02:08 am
12-30-1979,Mo Cnj Ge,06:33 am

January 1980
01-01-1980,Mo Cnj Ca,12:30 pm
01-03-1980,Mo Cnj Le,08:48 pm
01-06-1980,Mo Cnj Vi,07:49 am

01-08-1980,Mo Cnj Li,08:38 pm
01-11-1980,Mo Cnj Sc,08:56 am
01-13-1980,Mo Cnj Sa,06:17 pm
01-15-1980,Mo Cnj Ca,11:51 pm
01-18-1980,Mo Cnj Aq,02:25 am
01-20-1980,Mo Cnj Pi,03:34 am
01-22-1980,Mo Cnj Ar,04:52 am
01-24-1980,Mo Cnj Ta,07:32 am
01-26-1980,Mo Cnj Ge,12:12 pm
01-28-1980,Mo Cnj Ca,07:03 pm
01-31-1980,Mo Cnj Le,04:09 am

February 1980
02-02-1980,Mo Cnj Vi,03:21 pm
02-05-1980,Mo Cnj Li,04:04 am
02-07-1980,Mo Cnj Sc,04:46 pm
02-10-1980,Mo Cnj Sa,03:20 am
02-12-1980,Mo Cnj Ca,10:13 am
02-14-1980,Mo Cnj Aq,01:21 pm
02-16-1980,Mo Cnj Pi,01:55 pm
02-18-1980,Mo Cnj Ar,01:43 pm
02-20-1980,Mo Cnj Ta,02:36 pm
02-22-1980,Mo Cnj Ge,05:59 pm
02-25-1980,Mo Cnj Ca,00:35 am
02-27-1980,Mo Cnj Le,10:10 am
02-29-1980,Mo Cnj Vi,09:53 pm

March 1980
03-03-1980,Mo Cnj Li,10:40 am
03-05-1980,Mo Cnj Sc,11:23 pm
03-08-1980,Mo Cnj Sa,10:39 am
03-10-1980,Mo Cnj Ca,07:03 pm
03-12-1980,Mo Cnj Aq,11:46 pm
03-15-1980,Mo Cnj Pi,01:11 am
03-17-1980,Mo Cnj Ar,00:41 am
03-19-1980,Mo Cnj Ta,00:13 am
03-21-1980,Mo Cnj Ge,01:47 am
03-23-1980,Mo Cnj Ca,06:56 am
03-25-1980,Mo Cnj Le,03:59 am
03-28-1980,Mo Cnj Vi,03:53 am
03-30-1980,Mo Cnj Li,04:50 pm

April 1980
04-02-1980,Mo Cnj Sc,05:22 am
04-04-1980,Mo Cnj Sa,04:35 am
04-07-1980,Mo Cnj Ca,01:43 am
04-09-1980,Mo Cnj Aq,08:00 am

04-11-1980,Mo Cnj Pi,11:07 am
04-13-1980,Mo Cnj Ar,11:40 am
04-15-1980,Mo Cnj Ta,11:11 am
04-17-1980,Mo Cnj Ge,11:41 am
04-19-1980,Mo Cnj Ca,03:12 pm
04-21-1980,Mo Cnj Le,10:53 pm
04-24-1980,Mo Cnj Vi,10:13 am
04-26-1980,Mo Cnj Li,11:10 pm
04-29-1980,Mo Cnj Sc,11:36 am

May 1980
05-01-1980,Mo Cnj Sa,10:22 pm
05-04-1980,Mo Cnj Ca,07:14 am
05-06-1980,Mo Cnj Aq,02:04 pm
05-08-1980,Mo Cnj Pi,06:34 pm
05-10-1980,Mo Cnj Ar,08:45 pm
05-12-1980,Mo Cnj Ta,09:25 pm
05-14-1980,Mo Cnj Ge,10:08 pm
05-17-1980,Mo Cnj Ca,00:53 am
05-19-1980,Mo Cnj Le,07:15 am
05-21-1980,Mo Cnj Vi,05:33 pm
05-24-1980,Mo Cnj Li,06:12 am
05-26-1980,Mo Cnj Sc,06:37 pm
05-29-1980,Mo Cnj Sa,05:05 am
05-31-1980,Mo Cnj Ca,01:15 pm

June 1980
06-02-1980,Mo Cnj Aq,07:30 pm
06-05-1980,Mo Cnj Pi,00:10 am
06-07-1980,Mo Cnj Ar,03:24 am
06-09-1980,Mo Cnj Ta,05:31 am
06-11-1980,Mo Cnj Ge,07:23 am
06-13-1980,Mo Cnj Ca,10:30 am
06-15-1980,Mo Cnj Le,04:22 pm
06-18-1980,Mo Cnj Vi,01:47 am
06-20-1980,Mo Cnj Li,01:55 pm
06-23-1980,Mo Cnj Sc,02:27 am
06-25-1980,Mo Cnj Sa,01:02 pm
06-27-1980,Mo Cnj Ca,08:47 pm
06-30-1980,Mo Cnj Aq,02:05 am

July 1980
07-02-1980,Mo Cnj Pi,05:49 am
07-04-1980,Mo Cnj Ar,08:47 am
07-06-1980,Mo Cnj Ta,11:31 am
07-08-1980,Mo Cnj Ge,02:34 pm
07-10-1980,Mo Cnj Ca,06:45 pm

07-13-1980,Mo Cnj Le,01:03 am
07-15-1980,Mo Cnj Vi,10:11 am
07-17-1980,Mo Cnj Li,09:55 pm
07-20-1980,Mo Cnj Sc,10:34 am
07-22-1980,Mo Cnj Sa,09:43 pm
07-25-1980,Mo Cnj Ca,05:46 am
07-27-1980,Mo Cnj Aq,10:36 am
07-29-1980,Mo Cnj Pi,01:11 pm
07-31-1980,Mo Cnj Ar,02:54 pm

August 1980
08-02-1980,Mo Cnj Ta,04:55 pm
08-04-1980,Mo Cnj Ge,08:10 pm
08-07-1980,Mo Cnj Ca,01:12 am
08-09-1980,Mo Cnj Le,08:23 am
08-11-1980,Mo Cnj Vi,05:55 pm
08-14-1980,Mo Cnj Li,05:33 am
08-16-1980,Mo Cnj Sc,06:16 pm
08-19-1980,Mo Cnj Sa,06:09 am
08-21-1980,Mo Cnj Ca,03:12 pm
08-23-1980,Mo Cnj Aq,08:33 pm
08-25-1980,Mo Cnj Pi,10:44 pm
08-27-1980,Mo Cnj Ar,11:11 pm
08-29-1980,Mo Cnj Ta,11:41 pm

September 1980
09-01-1980,Mo Cnj Ge,01:50 am
09-03-1980,Mo Cnj Ca,06:40 am
09-05-1980,Mo Cnj Le,02:23 pm
09-08-1980,Mo Cnj Vi,00:32 am
09-10-1980,Mo Cnj Li,12:23 pm
09-13-1980,Mo Cnj Sc,01:07 am
09-15-1980,Mo Cnj Sa,01:28 am
09-17-1980,Mo Cnj Ca,11:45 am
09-20-1980,Mo Cnj Aq,06:31 am
09-22-1980,Mo Cnj Pi,09:27 am
09-24-1980,Mo Cnj Ar,09:38 am
09-26-1980,Mo Cnj Ta,08:54 am
09-28-1980,Mo Cnj Ge,09:21 am
09-30-1980,Mo Cnj Ca,12:47 pm

October 1980
10-02-1980,Mo Cnj Le,07:58 pm
10-05-1980,Mo Cnj Vi,06:20 am
10-07-1980,Mo Cnj Li,06:31 pm
10-10-1980,Mo Cnj Sc,07:15 am
10-12-1980,Mo Cnj Sa,07:37 pm

10-15-1980,Mo Cnj Ca,06:37 am
10-17-1980,Mo Cnj Aq,02:54 pm
10-19-1980,Mo Cnj Pi,07:32 pm
10-21-1980,Mo Cnj Ar,08:44 pm
10-23-1980,Mo Cnj Ta,07:56 pm
10-25-1980,Mo Cnj Ge,07:18 pm
10-27-1980,Mo Cnj Ca,09:01 pm
10-30-1980,Mo Cnj Le,02:39 am

November 1980
11-01-1980,Mo Cnj Vi,12:19 pm
11-04-1980,Mo Cnj Li,00:31 am
11-06-1980,Mo Cnj Sc,01:19 pm
11-09-1980,Mo Cnj Sa,01:26 am
11-11-1980,Mo Cnj Ca,12:16 pm
11-13-1980,Mo Cnj Aq,09:11 pm
11-16-1980,Mo Cnj Pi,03:22 am
11-18-1980,Mo Cnj Ar,06:22 am
11-20-1980,Mo Cnj Ta,06:51 am
11-22-1980,Mo Cnj Ge,06:28 am
11-24-1980,Mo Cnj Ca,07:19 am
11-26-1980,Mo Cnj Le,11:23 am
11-28-1980,Mo Cnj Vi,07:37 pm

December 1980
12-01-1980,Mo Cnj Li,07:13 am
12-03-1980,Mo Cnj Sc,08:01 pm
12-06-1980,Mo Cnj Sa,07:58 am
12-08-1980,Mo Cnj Ca,06:13 pm
12-11-1980,Mo Cnj Aq,02:37 am
12-13-1980,Mo Cnj Pi,09:04 am
12-15-1980,Mo Cnj Ar,01:22 pm
12-17-1980,Mo Cnj Ta,03:36 pm
12-19-1980,Mo Cnj Ge,04:40 pm
12-21-1980,Mo Cnj Ca,06:03 pm
12-23-1980,Mo Cnj Le,09:34 pm
12-26-1980,Mo Cnj Vi,04:33 am
12-28-1980,Mo Cnj Li,03:05 pm
12-31-1980,Mo Cnj Sc,03:37 am

January 1981
01-02-1981,Mo Cnj Sa,03:43 pm
01-05-1981,Mo Cnj Ca,01:42 am
01-07-1981,Mo Cnj Aq,09:13 am
01-09-1981,Mo Cnj Pi,02:42 pm
01-11-1981,Mo Cnj Ar,06:44 pm
01-13-1981,Mo Cnj Ta,09:45 pm

01-16-1981,Mo Cnj Ge,00:17 am
01-18-1981,Mo Cnj Ca,03:08 am
01-20-1981,Mo Cnj Le,07:21 am
01-22-1981,Mo Cnj Vi,02:03 pm
01-24-1981,Mo Cnj Li,11:46 pm
01-27-1981,Mo Cnj Sc,11:50 am
01-30-1981,Mo Cnj Sa,00:12 am

February 1981
02-01-1981,Mo Cnj Ca,10:37 am
02-03-1981,Mo Cnj Aq,05:55 pm
02-05-1981,Mo Cnj Pi,10:21 pm
02-08-1981,Mo Cnj Ar,01:02 am
02-10-1981,Mo Cnj Ta,03:11 am
02-12-1981,Mo Cnj Ge,05:52 am
02-14-1981,Mo Cnj Ca,09:44 am
02-16-1981,Mo Cnj Le,03:11 pm
02-18-1981,Mo Cnj Vi,10:35 pm
02-21-1981,Mo Cnj Li,08:13 am
02-23-1981,Mo Cnj Sc,07:55 pm
02-26-1981,Mo Cnj Sa,08:29 am
02-28-1981,Mo Cnj Ca,07:46 pm

March 1981
03-03-1981,Mo Cnj Aq,03:51 am
03-05-1981,Mo Cnj Pi,08:13 am
03-07-1981,Mo Cnj Ar,09:49 am
03-09-1981,Mo Cnj Ta,10:23 am
03-11-1981,Mo Cnj Ge,11:43 am
03-13-1981,Mo Cnj Ca,03:06 pm
03-15-1981,Mo Cnj Le,09:03 pm
03-18-1981,Mo Cnj Vi,05:20 am
03-20-1981,Mo Cnj Li,03:31 pm
03-23-1981,Mo Cnj Sc,03:14 am
03-25-1981,Mo Cnj Sa,03:51 pm
03-28-1981,Mo Cnj Ca,03:53 am
03-30-1981,Mo Cnj Aq,01:16 pm

April 1981
04-01-1981,Mo Cnj Pi,06:42 pm
04-03-1981,Mo Cnj Ar,08:26 pm
04-05-1981,Mo Cnj Ta,08:05 pm
04-07-1981,Mo Cnj Ge,07:48 pm
04-09-1981,Mo Cnj Ca,09:34 pm
04-12-1981,Mo Cnj Le,02:37 am
04-14-1981,Mo Cnj Vi,10:56 am
04-16-1981,Mo Cnj Li,09:38 pm

04-19-1981,Mo Cnj Sc,09:40 am
04-21-1981,Mo Cnj Sa,10:16 pm
04-24-1981,Mo Cnj Ca,10:32 am
04-26-1981,Mo Cnj Aq,08:58 pm
04-29-1981,Mo Cnj Pi,03:57 am

May 1981
05-01-1981,Mo Cnj Ar,06:58 am
05-03-1981,Mo Cnj Ta,07:00 am
05-05-1981,Mo Cnj Ge,06:01 am
05-07-1981,Mo Cnj Ca,06:18 am
05-09-1981,Mo Cnj Le,09:40 am
05-11-1981,Mo Cnj Vi,04:56 pm
05-14-1981,Mo Cnj Li,03:25 am
05-16-1981,Mo Cnj Sc,03:39 pm
05-19-1981,Mo Cnj Sa,04:15 am
05-21-1981,Mo Cnj Ca,04:21 pm
05-24-1981,Mo Cnj Aq,03:01 am
05-26-1981,Mo Cnj Pi,11:06 am
05-28-1981,Mo Cnj Ar,03:44 pm
05-30-1981,Mo Cnj Ta,05:11 pm

June 1981
06-01-1981,Mo Cnj Ge,04:49 pm
06-03-1981,Mo Cnj Ca,04:39 pm
06-05-1981,Mo Cnj Le,06:43 pm
06-08-1981,Mo Cnj Vi,00:27 am
06-10-1981,Mo Cnj Li,09:56 am
06-12-1981,Mo Cnj Sc,09:55 pm
06-15-1981,Mo Cnj Sa,10:32 am
06-17-1981,Mo Cnj Ca,10:21 pm
06-20-1981,Mo Cnj Aq,08:36 am
06-22-1981,Mo Cnj Pi,04:44 pm
06-24-1981,Mo Cnj Ar,10:19 pm
06-27-1981,Mo Cnj Ta,01:17 am
06-29-1981,Mo Cnj Ge,02:22 am

July 1981
07-01-1981,Mo Cnj Ca,02:58 am
07-03-1981,Mo Cnj Le,04:48 am
07-05-1981,Mo Cnj Vi,09:27 am
07-07-1981,Mo Cnj Li,05:43 pm
07-10-1981,Mo Cnj Sc,05:02 am
07-12-1981,Mo Cnj Sa,05:35 pm
07-15-1981,Mo Cnj Ca,05:19 am
07-17-1981,Mo Cnj Aq,03:02 am
07-19-1981,Mo Cnj Pi,10:26 pm

07-22-1981,Mo Cnj Ar,03:44 am
07-24-1981,Mo Cnj Ta,07:19 am
07-26-1981,Mo Cnj Ge,09:43 am
07-28-1981,Mo Cnj Ca,11:42 am
07-30-1981,Mo Cnj Le,02:21 pm

August 1981
08-01-1981,Mo Cnj Vi,06:55 pm
08-04-1981,Mo Cnj Li,02:24 am
08-06-1981,Mo Cnj Sc,12:58 pm
08-09-1981,Mo Cnj Sa,01:23 am
08-11-1981,Mo Cnj Ca,01:21 am
08-13-1981,Mo Cnj Aq,10:57 am
08-16-1981,Mo Cnj Pi,05:35 am
08-18-1981,Mo Cnj Ar,09:50 am
08-20-1981,Mo Cnj Ta,12:44 pm
08-22-1981,Mo Cnj Ge,03:19 pm
08-24-1981,Mo Cnj Ca,06:17 pm
08-26-1981,Mo Cnj Le,10:10 pm
08-29-1981,Mo Cnj Vi,03:32 am
08-31-1981,Mo Cnj Li,11:03 am

September 1981
09-02-1981,Mo Cnj Sc,09:11 pm
09-05-1981,Mo Cnj Sa,09:24 am
09-07-1981,Mo Cnj Ca,09:49 pm
09-10-1981,Mo Cnj Aq,08:00 am
09-12-1981,Mo Cnj Pi,02:35 pm
09-14-1981,Mo Cnj Ar,05:56 pm
09-16-1981,Mo Cnj Ta,07:30 pm
09-18-1981,Mo Cnj Ge,08:59 pm
09-20-1981,Mo Cnj Ca,11:40 pm
09-23-1981,Mo Cnj Le,04:08 am
09-25-1981,Mo Cnj Vi,10:29 am
09-27-1981,Mo Cnj Li,06:41 pm
09-30-1981,Mo Cnj Sc,04:54 am

October 1981
10-02-1981,Mo Cnj Sa,05:00 pm
10-05-1981,Mo Cnj Ca,05:50 am
10-07-1981,Mo Cnj Aq,05:01 pm
10-10-1981,Mo Cnj Pi,00:33 am
10-12-1981,Mo Cnj Ar,04:01 am
10-14-1981,Mo Cnj Ta,04:43 am
10-16-1981,Mo Cnj Ge,04:41 am
10-18-1981,Mo Cnj Ca,05:53 am
10-20-1981,Mo Cnj Le,09:35 am

10-22-1981,Mo Cnj Vi,04:06 pm
10-25-1981,Mo Cnj Li,00:57 am
10-27-1981,Mo Cnj Sc,11:39 am
10-29-1981,Mo Cnj Sa,11:49 pm

November 1981
11-01-1981,Mo Cnj Ca,12:46 pm
11-04-1981,Mo Cnj Aq,00:51 am
11-06-1981,Mo Cnj Pi,09:52 am
11-08-1981,Mo Cnj Ar,02:39 pm
11-10-1981,Mo Cnj Ta,03:45 pm
11-12-1981,Mo Cnj Ge,03:00 pm
11-14-1981,Mo Cnj Ca,02:37 pm
11-16-1981,Mo Cnj Le,04:33 pm
11-18-1981,Mo Cnj Vi,09:54 pm
11-21-1981,Mo Cnj Li,06:34 am
11-23-1981,Mo Cnj Sc,05:37 pm
11-26-1981,Mo Cnj Sa,06:00 am
11-28-1981,Mo Cnj Ca,06:52 pm

December 1981
12-01-1981,Mo Cnj Aq,07:09 am
12-03-1981,Mo Cnj Pi,05:16 pm
12-05-1981,Mo Cnj Ar,11:49 pm
12-08-1981,Mo Cnj Ta,02:32 am
12-10-1981,Mo Cnj Ge,02:31 am
12-12-1981,Mo Cnj Ca,01:41 am
12-14-1981,Mo Cnj Le,02:09 am
12-16-1981,Mo Cnj Vi,05:38 am
12-18-1981,Mo Cnj Li,12:58 pm
12-20-1981,Mo Cnj Sc,11:39 pm
12-23-1981,Mo Cnj Sa,12:11 pm
12-26-1981,Mo Cnj Ca,01:00 am
12-28-1981,Mo Cnj Aq,12:54 pm
12-30-1981,Mo Cnj Pi,11:02 pm

January 1982
01-02-1982,Mo Cnj Ar,06:34 am
01-04-1982,Mo Cnj Ta,11:03 am
01-06-1982,Mo Cnj Ge,12:49 pm
01-08-1982,Mo Cnj Ca,01:01 pm
01-10-1982,Mo Cnj Le,01:21 pm
01-12-1982,Mo Cnj Vi,03:37 pm
01-14-1982,Mo Cnj Li,09:17 pm
01-17-1982,Mo Cnj Sc,06:46 am
01-19-1982,Mo Cnj Sa,07:01 pm
01-22-1982,Mo Cnj Ca,07:52 am

01-24-1982,Mo Cnj Aq,07:26 pm
01-27-1982,Mo Cnj Pi,04:50 am
01-29-1982,Mo Cnj Ar,11:59 am
01-31-1982,Mo Cnj Ta,05:04 pm

February 1982

02-02-1982,Mo Cnj Ge,08:20 pm
02-04-1982,Mo Cnj Ca,10:18 pm
02-06-1982,Mo Cnj Le,11:50 pm
02-09-1982,Mo Cnj Vi,02:15 am
02-11-1982,Mo Cnj Li,07:02 am
02-13-1982,Mo Cnj Sc,03:16 pm
02-16-1982,Mo Cnj Sa,02:46 am
02-18-1982,Mo Cnj Ca,03:37 pm
02-21-1982,Mo Cnj Aq,03:16 am
02-23-1982,Mo Cnj Pi,12:09 pm
02-25-1982,Mo Cnj Ar,06:17 pm
02-27-1982,Mo Cnj Ta,10:32 pm

March 1982

03-02-1982,Mo Cnj Ge,01:50 am
03-04-1982,Mo Cnj Ca,04:49 am
03-06-1982,Mo Cnj Le,07:51 am
03-08-1982,Mo Cnj Vi,11:28 am
03-10-1982,Mo Cnj Li,04:35 pm
03-13-1982,Mo Cnj Sc,00:18 am
03-15-1982,Mo Cnj Sa,11:04 am
03-17-1982,Mo Cnj Ca,11:47 pm
03-20-1982,Mo Cnj Aq,11:53 am
03-22-1982,Mo Cnj Pi,09:01 pm
03-25-1982,Mo Cnj Ar,02:37 am
03-27-1982,Mo Cnj Ta,05:40 am
03-29-1982,Mo Cnj Ge,07:44 am
03-31-1982,Mo Cnj Ca,10:10 am

April 1982

04-02-1982,Mo Cnj Le,01:37 pm
04-04-1982,Mo Cnj Vi,06:19 pm
04-07-1982,Mo Cnj Li,00:27 am
04-09-1982,Mo Cnj Sc,08:33 am
04-11-1982,Mo Cnj Sa,07:07 pm
04-14-1982,Mo Cnj Ca,07:42 am
04-16-1982,Mo Cnj Aq,08:18 pm
04-19-1982,Mo Cnj Pi,06:20 am
04-21-1982,Mo Cnj Ar,12:24 pm
04-23-1982,Mo Cnj Ta,03:00 pm
04-25-1982,Mo Cnj Ge,03:49 pm

04-27-1982,Mo Cnj Ca,04:44 pm
04-29-1982,Mo Cnj Le,07:10 pm

May 1982

05-01-1982,Mo Cnj Vi,11:45 pm
05-04-1982,Mo Cnj Li,06:33 am
05-06-1982,Mo Cnj Sc,03:24 pm
05-09-1982,Mo Cnj Sa,02:17 am
05-11-1982,Mo Cnj Ca,02:50 pm
05-14-1982,Mo Cnj Aq,03:45 am
05-16-1982,Mo Cnj Pi,02:47 pm
05-18-1982,Mo Cnj Ar,10:05 pm
05-21-1982,Mo Cnj Ta,01:23 am
05-23-1982,Mo Cnj Ge,01:55 am
05-25-1982,Mo Cnj Ca,01:39 am
05-27-1982,Mo Cnj Le,02:27 am
05-29-1982,Mo Cnj Vi,05:43 am
05-31-1982,Mo Cnj Li,12:02 pm

June 1982

06-02-1982,Mo Cnj Sc,09:12 pm
06-05-1982,Mo Cnj Sa,08:32 am
06-07-1982,Mo Cnj Ca,09:13 pm
06-10-1982,Mo Cnj Aq,10:09 am
06-12-1982,Mo Cnj Pi,09:45 pm
06-15-1982,Mo Cnj Ar,06:21 am
06-17-1982,Mo Cnj Ta,11:07 am
06-19-1982,Mo Cnj Ge,12:34 pm
06-21-1982,Mo Cnj Ca,12:13 pm
06-23-1982,Mo Cnj Le,11:57 am
06-25-1982,Mo Cnj Vi,01:36 pm
06-27-1982,Mo Cnj Li,06:31 pm
06-30-1982,Mo Cnj Sc,03:02 am

July 1982

07-02-1982,Mo Cnj Sa,02:26 pm
07-05-1982,Mo Cnj Ca,03:16 am
07-07-1982,Mo Cnj Aq,04:03 pm
07-10-1982,Mo Cnj Pi,03:35 am
07-12-1982,Mo Cnj Ar,12:49 pm
07-14-1982,Mo Cnj Ta,07:00 pm
07-16-1982,Mo Cnj Ge,10:03 pm
07-18-1982,Mo Cnj Ca,10:46 pm
07-20-1982,Mo Cnj Le,10:36 pm
07-22-1982,Mo Cnj Vi,11:21 pm
07-25-1982,Mo Cnj Li,02:46 am

07-27-1982,Mo Cnj Sc,09:59 am
07-29-1982,Mo Cnj Sa,08:48 pm

August 1982
08-01-1982,Mo Cnj Ca,09:37 am
08-03-1982,Mo Cnj Aq,10:17 pm
08-06-1982,Mo Cnj Pi,09:23 am
08-08-1982,Mo Cnj Ar,06:21 pm
08-11-1982,Mo Cnj Ta,01:00 am
08-13-1982,Mo Cnj Ge,05:23 am
08-15-1982,Mo Cnj Ca,07:41 am
08-17-1982,Mo Cnj Le,08:41 am
08-19-1982,Mo Cnj Vi,09:40 am
08-21-1982,Mo Cnj Li,12:22 pm
08-23-1982,Mo Cnj Sc,06:21 pm
08-26-1982,Mo Cnj Sa,04:11 am
08-28-1982,Mo Cnj Ca,04:42 pm
08-31-1982,Mo Cnj Aq,05:24 am

September 1982
09-02-1982,Mo Cnj Pi,04:11 pm
09-05-1982,Mo Cnj Ar,00:24 am
09-07-1982,Mo Cnj Ta,06:28 am
09-09-1982,Mo Cnj Ge,10:58 am
09-11-1982,Mo Cnj Ca,02:19 pm
09-13-1982,Mo Cnj Le,04:47 pm
09-15-1982,Mo Cnj Vi,06:58 pm
09-17-1982,Mo Cnj Li,10:03 pm
09-20-1982,Mo Cnj Sc,03:33 am
09-22-1982,Mo Cnj Sa,12:30 pm
09-25-1982,Mo Cnj Ca,00:32 am
09-27-1982,Mo Cnj Aq,01:22 pm
09-30-1982,Mo Cnj Pi,00:19 am

October 1982
10-02-1982,Mo Cnj Ar,08:07 am
10-04-1982,Mo Cnj Ta,01:09 pm
10-06-1982,Mo Cnj Ge,04:39 pm
10-08-1982,Mo Cnj Ca,07:40 pm
10-10-1982,Mo Cnj Le,10:44 pm
10-13-1982,Mo Cnj Vi,02:09 am
10-15-1982,Mo Cnj Li,06:23 am
10-17-1982,Mo Cnj Sc,12:21 pm
10-19-1982,Mo Cnj Sa,09:03 pm
10-22-1982,Mo Cnj Ca,08:39 am
10-24-1982,Mo Cnj Aq,09:37 pm
10-27-1982,Mo Cnj Pi,09:13 am

10-29-1982,Mo Cnj Ar,05:26 pm
10-31-1982,Mo Cnj Ta,10:04 pm

November 1982
11-03-1982,Mo Cnj Ge,00:23 am
11-05-1982,Mo Cnj Ca,01:59 am
11-07-1982,Mo Cnj Le,04:10 am
11-09-1982,Mo Cnj Vi,07:40 am
11-11-1982,Mo Cnj Li,12:46 pm
11-13-1982,Mo Cnj Sc,07:43 pm
11-16-1982,Mo Cnj Sa,04:52 am
11-18-1982,Mo Cnj Ca,04:22 pm
11-21-1982,Mo Cnj Aq,05:21 am
11-23-1982,Mo Cnj Pi,05:43 pm
11-26-1982,Mo Cnj Ar,03:07 am
11-28-1982,Mo Cnj Ta,08:32 am
11-30-1982,Mo Cnj Ge,10:36 am

December 1982
12-02-1982,Mo Cnj Ca,10:58 am
12-04-1982,Mo Cnj Le,11:27 am
12-06-1982,Mo Cnj Vi,01:33 pm
12-08-1982,Mo Cnj Li,06:11 pm
12-11-1982,Mo Cnj Sc,01:35 am
12-13-1982,Mo Cnj Sa,11:27 am
12-15-1982,Mo Cnj Ca,11:16 am
12-18-1982,Mo Cnj Aq,12:12 pm
12-21-1982,Mo Cnj Pi,00:56 am
12-23-1982,Mo Cnj Ar,11:34 am
12-25-1982,Mo Cnj Ta,06:37 pm
12-27-1982,Mo Cnj Ge,09:49 pm
12-29-1982,Mo Cnj Ca,10:13 pm
12-31-1982,Mo Cnj Le,09:34 pm

January 1983
01-02-1983,Mo Cnj Vi,09:50 pm
01-05-1983,Mo Cnj Li,00:45 am
01-07-1983,Mo Cnj Sc,07:17 am
01-09-1983,Mo Cnj Sa,05:14 pm
01-12-1983,Mo Cnj Ca,05:26 am
01-14-1983,Mo Cnj Aq,06:26 pm
01-17-1983,Mo Cnj Pi,07:03 am
01-19-1983,Mo Cnj Ar,06:08 pm
01-22-1983,Mo Cnj Ta,02:37 am
01-24-1983,Mo Cnj Ge,07:41 am
01-26-1983,Mo Cnj Ca,09:29 am

01-28-1983,Mo Cnj Le,09:11 am
01-30-1983,Mo Cnj Vi,08:35 am

February 1983
02-01-1983,Mo Cnj Li,09:47 am
02-03-1983,Mo Cnj Sc,02:32 pm
02-05-1983,Mo Cnj Sa,11:29 pm
02-08-1983,Mo Cnj Ca,11:34 am
02-11-1983,Mo Cnj Aq,00:41 am
02-13-1983,Mo Cnj Pi,01:03 pm
02-15-1983,Mo Cnj Ar,11:47 pm
02-18-1983,Mo Cnj Ta,08:31 am
02-20-1983,Mo Cnj Ge,02:53 pm
02-22-1983,Mo Cnj Ca,06:32 pm
02-24-1983,Mo Cnj Le,07:47 pm
02-26-1983,Mo Cnj Vi,07:49 pm
02-28-1983,Mo Cnj Li,08:30 pm

March 1983
03-02-1983,Mo Cnj Sc,11:51 pm
03-05-1983,Mo Cnj Sa,07:15 am
03-07-1983,Mo Cnj Ca,06:30 pm
03-10-1983,Mo Cnj Aq,07:31 am
03-12-1983,Mo Cnj Pi,07:48 pm
03-15-1983,Mo Cnj Ar,06:01 am
03-17-1983,Mo Cnj Ta,02:05 pm
03-19-1983,Mo Cnj Ge,08:20 pm
03-22-1983,Mo Cnj Ca,00:53 am
03-24-1983,Mo Cnj Le,03:43 am
03-26-1983,Mo Cnj Vi,05:18 am
03-28-1983,Mo Cnj Li,06:49 am
03-30-1983,Mo Cnj Sc,09:58 am

April 1983
04-01-1983,Mo Cnj Sa,04:21 pm
04-04-1983,Mo Cnj Ca,02:31 am
04-06-1983,Mo Cnj Aq,03:07 pm
04-09-1983,Mo Cnj Pi,03:31 am
04-11-1983,Mo Cnj Ar,01:37 pm
04-13-1983,Mo Cnj Ta,08:59 pm
04-16-1983,Mo Cnj Ge,02:15 am
04-18-1983,Mo Cnj Ca,06:14 am
04-20-1983,Mo Cnj Le,09:27 am
04-22-1983,Mo Cnj Vi,12:12 pm
04-24-1983,Mo Cnj Li,03:05 pm
04-26-1983,Mo Cnj Sc,07:06 pm
04-29-1983,Mo Cnj Sa,01:29 am

May 1983
05-01-1983,Mo Cnj Ca,11:02 am
05-03-1983,Mo Cnj Aq,11:09 pm
05-06-1983,Mo Cnj Pi,11:44 am
05-08-1983,Mo Cnj Ar,10:16 pm
05-11-1983,Mo Cnj Ta,05:36 am
05-13-1983,Mo Cnj Ge,10:04 am
05-15-1983,Mo Cnj Ca,12:49 pm
05-17-1983,Mo Cnj Le,03:02 pm
05-19-1983,Mo Cnj Vi,05:38 pm
05-21-1983,Mo Cnj Li,09:12 pm
05-24-1983,Mo Cnj Sc,02:18 am
05-26-1983,Mo Cnj Sa,09:28 am
05-28-1983,Mo Cnj Ca,07:07 pm
05-31-1983,Mo Cnj Aq,07:00 am

June 1983
06-02-1983,Mo Cnj Pi,07:42 pm
06-05-1983,Mo Cnj Ar,07:00 am
06-07-1983,Mo Cnj Ta,03:06 pm
06-09-1983,Mo Cnj Ge,07:38 pm
06-11-1983,Mo Cnj Ca,09:33 pm
06-13-1983,Mo Cnj Le,10:22 pm
06-15-1983,Mo Cnj Vi,11:38 pm
06-18-1983,Mo Cnj Li,02:37 am
06-20-1983,Mo Cnj Sc,08:00 am
06-22-1983,Mo Cnj Sa,03:55 pm
06-25-1983,Mo Cnj Ca,02:08 am
06-27-1983,Mo Cnj Aq,02:07 pm
06-30-1983,Mo Cnj Pi,02:52 am

July 1983
07-02-1983,Mo Cnj Ar,02:49 pm
07-05-1983,Mo Cnj Ta,00:06 am
07-07-1983,Mo Cnj Ge,05:42 am
07-09-1983,Mo Cnj Ca,07:51 am
07-11-1983,Mo Cnj Le,07:54 am
07-13-1983,Mo Cnj Vi,07:43 am
07-15-1983,Mo Cnj Li,09:10 am
07-17-1983,Mo Cnj Sc,01:38 pm
07-19-1983,Mo Cnj Sa,09:32 pm
07-22-1983,Mo Cnj Ca,08:12 am
07-24-1983,Mo Cnj Aq,08:27 pm
07-27-1983,Mo Cnj Pi,09:12 am
07-29-1983,Mo Cnj Ar,09:21 pm

August 1983

08-01-1983,Mo Cnj Ta,07:37 am
08-03-1983,Mo Cnj Ge,02:43 pm
08-05-1983,Mo Cnj Ca,06:09 pm
08-07-1983,Mo Cnj Le,06:37 pm
08-09-1983,Mo Cnj Vi,05:49 pm
08-11-1983,Mo Cnj Li,05:52 pm
08-13-1983,Mo Cnj Sc,08:44 pm
08-16-1983,Mo Cnj Sa,03:35 am
08-18-1983,Mo Cnj Ca,02:00 pm
08-21-1983,Mo Cnj Aq,02:26 am
08-23-1983,Mo Cnj Pi,03:10 pm
08-26-1983,Mo Cnj Ar,03:08 am
08-28-1983,Mo Cnj Ta,01:38 pm
08-30-1983,Mo Cnj Ge,09:49 pm

September 1983

09-02-1983,Mo Cnj Ca,02:53 am
09-04-1983,Mo Cnj Le,04:48 am
09-06-1983,Mo Cnj Vi,04:37 am
09-08-1983,Mo Cnj Li,04:14 am
09-10-1983,Mo Cnj Sc,05:50 am
09-12-1983,Mo Cnj Sa,11:09 am
09-14-1983,Mo Cnj Ca,08:34 pm
09-17-1983,Mo Cnj Aq,08:46 am
09-19-1983,Mo Cnj Pi,09:30 pm
09-22-1983,Mo Cnj Ar,09:10 am
09-24-1983,Mo Cnj Ta,07:13 pm
09-27-1983,Mo Cnj Ge,03:25 am
09-29-1983,Mo Cnj Ca,09:25 am

October 1983

10-01-1983,Mo Cnj Le,12:55 pm
10-03-1983,Mo Cnj Vi,02:16 pm
10-05-1983,Mo Cnj Li,02:42 pm
10-07-1983,Mo Cnj Sc,04:06 pm
10-09-1983,Mo Cnj Sa,08:21 pm
10-12-1983,Mo Cnj Ca,04:31 am
10-14-1983,Mo Cnj Aq,04:00 pm
10-17-1983,Mo Cnj Pi,04:41 am
10-19-1983,Mo Cnj Ar,04:19 pm
10-22-1983,Mo Cnj Ta,01:48 am
10-24-1983,Mo Cnj Ge,09:11 am
10-26-1983,Mo Cnj Ca,02:48 pm
10-28-1983,Mo Cnj Le,06:51 pm
10-30-1983,Mo Cnj Vi,09:33 pm

November 1983

11-01-1983,Mo Cnj Li,11:31 pm
11-04-1983,Mo Cnj Sc,01:53 am
11-06-1983,Mo Cnj Sa,06:09 am
11-08-1983,Mo Cnj Ca,01:32 pm
11-11-1983,Mo Cnj Aq,00:11 am
11-13-1983,Mo Cnj Pi,12:41 pm
11-16-1983,Mo Cnj Ar,00:37 am
11-18-1983,Mo Cnj Ta,10:07 am
11-20-1983,Mo Cnj Ge,04:46 pm
11-22-1983,Mo Cnj Ca,09:11 pm
11-25-1983,Mo Cnj Le,00:20 am
11-27-1983,Mo Cnj Vi,03:02 am
11-29-1983,Mo Cnj Li,05:57 am

December 1983

12-01-1983,Mo Cnj Sc,09:41 am
12-03-1983,Mo Cnj Sa,02:56 pm
12-05-1983,Mo Cnj Ca,10:29 pm
12-08-1983,Mo Cnj Aq,08:40 am
12-10-1983,Mo Cnj Pi,08:54 pm
12-13-1983,Mo Cnj Ar,09:18 am
12-15-1983,Mo Cnj Ta,07:33 pm
12-18-1983,Mo Cnj Ge,02:24 am
12-20-1983,Mo Cnj Ca,06:02 am
12-22-1983,Mo Cnj Le,07:44 am
12-24-1983,Mo Cnj Vi,09:02 am
12-26-1983,Mo Cnj Li,11:19 am
12-28-1983,Mo Cnj Sc,03:27 pm

January 1984

01-02-1984,Mo Cnj Ca,06:08 am
01-04-1984,Mo Cnj Aq,04:31 pm
01-07-1984,Mo Cnj Pi,04:35 am
01-09-1984,Mo Cnj Ar,05:15 pm
01-12-1984,Mo Cnj Ta,04:36 am
01-14-1984,Mo Cnj Ge,12:40 pm
01-16-1984,Mo Cnj Ca,04:48 pm
01-18-1984,Mo Cnj Le,05:50 pm
01-20-1984,Mo Cnj Vi,05:36 pm
01-22-1984,Mo Cnj Li,06:08 pm
01-24-1984,Mo Cnj Sc,09:05 pm
01-27-1984,Mo Cnj Sa,03:13 am
01-29-1984,Mo Cnj Ca,12:13 pm
01-31-1984,Mo Cnj Aq,11:11 pm

February 1984
02-03-1984,Mo Cnj Pi,11:22 am
02-06-1984,Mo Cnj Ar,00:04 am
02-08-1984,Mo Cnj Ta,12:05 pm
02-10-1984,Mo Cnj Ge,09:40 pm
02-13-1984,Mo Cnj Ca,03:21 am
02-15-1984,Mo Cnj Le,05:10 am
02-17-1984,Mo Cnj Vi,04:32 am
02-19-1984,Mo Cnj Li,03:40 am
02-21-1984,Mo Cnj Sc,04:45 am
02-23-1984,Mo Cnj Sa,09:23 am
02-25-1984,Mo Cnj Ca,05:50 pm
02-28-1984,Mo Cnj Aq,05:02 am

March 1984
03-01-1984,Mo Cnj Pi,05:29 pm
03-04-1984,Mo Cnj Ar,06:07 am
03-06-1984,Mo Cnj Ta,06:09 pm
03-09-1984,Mo Cnj Ge,04:30 am
03-11-1984,Mo Cnj Ca,11:49 am
03-13-1984,Mo Cnj Le,03:22 pm
03-15-1984,Mo Cnj Vi,03:47 pm
03-17-1984,Mo Cnj Li,02:52 pm
03-19-1984,Mo Cnj Sc,02:49 pm
03-21-1984,Mo Cnj Sa,05:41 pm
03-24-1984,Mo Cnj Ca,00:36 am
03-26-1984,Mo Cnj Aq,11:09 am
03-28-1984,Mo Cnj Pi,11:38 pm
03-31-1984,Mo Cnj Ar,12:15 pm

April 1984
04-02-1984,Mo Cnj Ta,11:56 pm
04-05-1984,Mo Cnj Ge,10:05 am
04-07-1984,Mo Cnj Ca,06:00 pm
04-09-1984,Mo Cnj Le,11:02 pm
04-12-1984,Mo Cnj Vi,01:11 am
04-14-1984,Mo Cnj Li,01:29 am
04-16-1984,Mo Cnj Sc,01:41 am
04-18-1984,Mo Cnj Sa,03:44 am
04-20-1984,Mo Cnj Ca,09:11 am
04-22-1984,Mo Cnj Aq,06:28 pm
04-25-1984,Mo Cnj Pi,06:27 am
04-27-1984,Mo Cnj Ar,07:03 pm
04-30-1984,Mo Cnj Ta,06:31 am

May 1984
05-02-1984,Mo Cnj Ge,04:02 pm
05-04-1984,Mo Cnj Ca,11:26 pm

05-07-1984,Mo Cnj Le,04:43 am
05-09-1984,Mo Cnj Vi,08:02 am
05-11-1984,Mo Cnj Li,09:54 am
05-13-1984,Mo Cnj Sc,11:23 am
05-15-1984,Mo Cnj Sa,01:51 pm
05-17-1984,Mo Cnj Ca,06:44 pm
05-20-1984,Mo Cnj Aq,02:56 am
05-22-1984,Mo Cnj Pi,02:09 pm
05-25-1984,Mo Cnj Ar,02:40 am
05-27-1984,Mo Cnj Ta,02:13 pm
05-29-1984,Mo Cnj Ge,11:23 pm

June 1984
06-01-1984,Mo Cnj Ca,05:54 am
06-03-1984,Mo Cnj Le,10:19 am
06-05-1984,Mo Cnj Vi,01:28 pm
06-07-1984,Mo Cnj Li,04:04 pm
06-09-1984,Mo Cnj Sc,06:49 pm
06-11-1984,Mo Cnj Sa,10:27 pm
06-14-1984,Mo Cnj Ca,03:49 am
06-16-1984,Mo Cnj Aq,11:41 am
06-18-1984,Mo Cnj Pi,10:18 pm
06-21-1984,Mo Cnj Ar,10:40 am
06-23-1984,Mo Cnj Ta,10:38 pm
06-26-1984,Mo Cnj Ge,08:04 am
06-28-1984,Mo Cnj Ca,02:10 pm
06-30-1984,Mo Cnj Le,05:31 pm

July 1984
07-02-1984,Mo Cnj Vi,07:28 pm
07-04-1984,Mo Cnj Li,09:27 pm
07-07-1984,Mo Cnj Sc,00:29 am
07-09-1984,Mo Cnj Sa,05:03 am
07-11-1984,Mo Cnj Ca,11:23 am
07-13-1984,Mo Cnj Aq,07:41 pm
07-16-1984,Mo Cnj Pi,06:10 am
07-18-1984,Mo Cnj Ar,06:26 pm
07-21-1984,Mo Cnj Ta,06:53 am
07-23-1984,Mo Cnj Ge,05:11 pm
07-25-1984,Mo Cnj Ca,11:45 pm
07-28-1984,Mo Cnj Le,02:42 am
07-30-1984,Mo Cnj Vi,03:30 am

August 1984
08-01-1984,Mo Cnj Li,04:03 am
08-03-1984,Mo Cnj Sc,06:04 am
08-05-1984,Mo Cnj Sa,10:29 am

08-07-1984,Mo Cnj Ca,05:24 pm
08-10-1984,Mo Cnj Aq,02:25 am
08-12-1984,Mo Cnj Pi,01:13 pm
08-15-1984,Mo Cnj Ar,01:29 am
08-17-1984,Mo Cnj Ta,02:14 pm
08-20-1984,Mo Cnj Ge,01:32 am
08-22-1984,Mo Cnj Ca,09:21 am
08-24-1984,Mo Cnj Le,01:00 pm
08-26-1984,Mo Cnj Vi,01:32 pm
08-28-1984,Mo Cnj Li,12:57 pm
08-30-1984,Mo Cnj Sc,01:23 pm

September 1984
09-01-1984,Mo Cnj Sa,04:30 pm
09-03-1984,Mo Cnj Ca,10:55 pm
09-06-1984,Mo Cnj Aq,08:12 am
09-08-1984,Mo Cnj Pi,07:25 pm
09-11-1984,Mo Cnj Ar,07:47 am
09-13-1984,Mo Cnj Ta,08:33 pm
09-16-1984,Mo Cnj Ge,08:26 am
09-18-1984,Mo Cnj Ca,05:36 pm
09-20-1984,Mo Cnj Le,10:49 pm
09-23-1984,Mo Cnj Vi,00:19 am
09-24-1984,Mo Cnj Li,11:41 pm
09-26-1984,Mo Cnj Sc,11:04 pm
09-29-1984,Mo Cnj Sa,00:32 am

October 1984
10-01-1984,Mo Cnj Ca,05:29 am
10-03-1984,Mo Cnj Aq,02:04 pm
10-06-1984,Mo Cnj Pi,01:20 am
10-08-1984,Mo Cnj Ar,01:51 pm
10-11-1984,Mo Cnj Ta,02:28 am
10-13-1984,Mo Cnj Ge,02:14 pm
10-16-1984,Mo Cnj Ca,00:00 am
10-18-1984,Mo Cnj Le,06:41 am
10-20-1984,Mo Cnj Vi,09:56 am
10-22-1984,Mo Cnj Li,10:32 am
10-24-1984,Mo Cnj Sc,10:08 am
10-26-1984,Mo Cnj Sa,10:44 am
10-28-1984,Mo Cnj Ca,02:05 pm
10-30-1984,Mo Cnj Aq,09:14 pm

November 1984
11-02-1984,Mo Cnj Pi,07:50 am
11-04-1984,Mo Cnj Ar,08:20 pm
11-07-1984,Mo Cnj Ta,08:53 am

11-09-1984,Mo Cnj Ge,08:11 pm
11-12-1984,Mo Cnj Ca,05:32 am
11-14-1984,Mo Cnj Le,12:34 pm
11-16-1984,Mo Cnj Vi,05:08 pm
11-18-1984,Mo Cnj Li,07:30 pm
11-20-1984,Mo Cnj Sc,08:31 pm
11-22-1984,Mo Cnj Sa,09:34 pm
11-25-1984,Mo Cnj Ca,00:17 am
11-27-1984,Mo Cnj Aq,06:06 am
11-29-1984,Mo Cnj Pi,03:33 pm

December 1984
12-02-1984,Mo Cnj Ar,03:42 am
12-04-1984,Mo Cnj Ta,04:21 pm
12-07-1984,Mo Cnj Ge,03:25 am
12-09-1984,Mo Cnj Ca,11:57 am
12-11-1984,Mo Cnj Le,06:09 pm
12-13-1984,Mo Cnj Vi,10:36 pm
12-16-1984,Mo Cnj Li,01:52 am
12-18-1984,Mo Cnj Sc,04:27 am
12-20-1984,Mo Cnj Sa,06:58 am
12-22-1984,Mo Cnj Ca,10:21 am
12-24-1984,Mo Cnj Aq,03:47 pm
12-27-1984,Mo Cnj Pi,00:19 am
12-29-1984,Mo Cnj Ar,11:50 am

January 1985
01-01-1985,Mo Cnj Ta,00:37 am
01-03-1985,Mo Cnj Ge,12:01 pm
01-05-1985,Mo Cnj Ca,08:18 pm
01-08-1985,Mo Cnj Le,01:28 am
01-10-1985,Mo Cnj Vi,04:40 am
01-12-1985,Mo Cnj Li,07:13 am
01-14-1985,Mo Cnj Sc,10:07 am
01-16-1985,Mo Cnj Sa,01:48 pm
01-18-1985,Mo Cnj Ca,06:29 pm
01-21-1985,Mo Cnj Aq,00:39 am
01-23-1985,Mo Cnj Pi,09:03 am
01-25-1985,Mo Cnj Ar,08:06 pm
01-28-1985,Mo Cnj Ta,08:54 am
01-30-1985,Mo Cnj Ge,09:01 pm

February 1985
02-02-1985,Mo Cnj Ca,05:59 am
02-04-1985,Mo Cnj Le,11:02 am
02-06-1985,Mo Cnj Vi,01:09 pm
02-08-1985,Mo Cnj Li,02:11 pm

02-10-1985,Mo Cnj Sc,03:49 pm
02-12-1985,Mo Cnj Sa,07:09 pm
02-15-1985,Mo Cnj Ca,00:28 am
02-17-1985,Mo Cnj Aq,07:37 am
02-19-1985,Mo Cnj Pi,04:38 pm
02-22-1985,Mo Cnj Ar,03:43 am
02-24-1985,Mo Cnj Ta,04:27 pm
02-27-1985,Mo Cnj Ge,05:11 am

March 1985
03-01-1985,Mo Cnj Ca,03:24 pm
03-03-1985,Mo Cnj Le,09:29 pm
03-05-1985,Mo Cnj Vi,11:43 pm
03-07-1985,Mo Cnj Li,11:48 pm
03-09-1985,Mo Cnj Sc,11:48 pm
03-12-1985,Mo Cnj Sa,01:30 am
03-14-1985,Mo Cnj Ca,05:55 am
03-16-1985,Mo Cnj Aq,01:11 pm
03-18-1985,Mo Cnj Pi,10:50 pm
03-21-1985,Mo Cnj Ar,10:20 am
03-23-1985,Mo Cnj Ta,11:06 pm
03-26-1985,Mo Cnj Ge,12:02 pm
03-28-1985,Mo Cnj Ca,11:14 pm
03-31-1985,Mo Cnj Le,06:52 am

April 1985
04-02-1985,Mo Cnj Vi,10:26 am
04-04-1985,Mo Cnj Li,10:54 am
04-06-1985,Mo Cnj Sc,10:11 am
04-08-1985,Mo Cnj Sa,10:18 am
04-10-1985,Mo Cnj Ca,12:57 pm
04-12-1985,Mo Cnj Aq,07:04 pm
04-15-1985,Mo Cnj Pi,04:31 am
04-17-1985,Mo Cnj Ar,04:18 pm
04-20-1985,Mo Cnj Ta,05:13 am
04-22-1985,Mo Cnj Ge,06:01 pm
04-25-1985,Mo Cnj Ca,05:27 am
04-27-1985,Mo Cnj Le,02:11 pm
04-29-1985,Mo Cnj Vi,07:25 pm

May 1985
05-01-1985,Mo Cnj Li,09:22 pm
05-03-1985,Mo Cnj Sc,09:17 pm
05-05-1985,Mo Cnj Sa,08:56 pm
05-07-1985,Mo Cnj Ca,10:11 pm
05-10-1985,Mo Cnj Aq,02:38 am
05-12-1985,Mo Cnj Pi,10:56 pm

05-14-1985,Mo Cnj Ar,10:26 pm
05-17-1985,Mo Cnj Ta,11:24 am
05-20-1985,Mo Cnj Ge,00:02 am
05-22-1985,Mo Cnj Ca,11:05 am
05-24-1985,Mo Cnj Le,07:54 pm
05-27-1985,Mo Cnj Vi,02:06 am
05-29-1985,Mo Cnj Li,05:40 am
05-31-1985,Mo Cnj Sc,07:07 am

June 1985
06-02-1985,Mo Cnj Sa,07:33 am
06-04-1985,Mo Cnj Ca,08:34 am
06-06-1985,Mo Cnj Aq,11:52 am
06-08-1985,Mo Cnj Pi,06:47 pm
06-11-1985,Mo Cnj Ar,05:25 am
06-13-1985,Mo Cnj Ta,06:12 pm
06-16-1985,Mo Cnj Ge,06:46 am
06-18-1985,Mo Cnj Ca,05:22 pm
06-21-1985,Mo Cnj Le,01:32 am
06-23-1985,Mo Cnj Vi,07:33 am
06-25-1985,Mo Cnj Li,11:48 am
06-27-1985,Mo Cnj Sc,02:38 pm
06-29-1985,Mo Cnj Sa,04:31 pm

July 1985
07-01-1985,Mo Cnj Ca,06:23 pm
07-03-1985,Mo Cnj Aq,09:36 pm
07-06-1985,Mo Cnj Pi,03:41 am
07-08-1985,Mo Cnj Ar,01:21 pm
07-11-1985,Mo Cnj Ta,01:44 am
07-13-1985,Mo Cnj Ge,02:23 pm
07-16-1985,Mo Cnj Ca,00:54 am
07-18-1985,Mo Cnj Le,08:25 am
07-20-1985,Mo Cnj Vi,01:30 pm
07-22-1985,Mo Cnj Li,05:11 pm
07-24-1985,Mo Cnj Sc,08:17 pm
07-26-1985,Mo Cnj Sa,11:13 pm
07-29-1985,Mo Cnj Ca,02:22 am
07-31-1985,Mo Cnj Aq,06:26 am

August 1985
08-02-1985,Mo Cnj Pi,12:34 pm
08-04-1985,Mo Cnj Ar,09:43 pm
08-07-1985,Mo Cnj Ta,09:41 am
08-09-1985,Mo Cnj Ge,10:32 pm
08-12-1985,Mo Cnj Ca,09:29 am
08-14-1985,Mo Cnj Le,04:58 pm

08-16-1985,Mo Cnj Vi,09:16 pm
08-18-1985,Mo Cnj Li,11:44 pm
08-21-1985,Mo Cnj Sc,01:52 am
08-23-1985,Mo Cnj Sa,04:36 am
08-25-1985,Mo Cnj Ca,08:24 am
08-27-1985,Mo Cnj Aq,01:31 pm
08-29-1985,Mo Cnj Pi,08:25 pm

September 1985
09-01-1985,Mo Cnj Ar,05:42 am
09-03-1985,Mo Cnj Ta,05:28 pm
09-06-1985,Mo Cnj Ge,06:28 am
09-08-1985,Mo Cnj Ca,06:11 pm
09-11-1985,Mo Cnj Le,02:28 am
09-13-1985,Mo Cnj Vi,06:53 am
09-15-1985,Mo Cnj Li,08:34 am
09-17-1985,Mo Cnj Sc,09:17 am
09-19-1985,Mo Cnj Sa,10:40 am
09-21-1985,Mo Cnj Ca,01:49 pm
09-23-1985,Mo Cnj Aq,07:12 pm
09-26-1985,Mo Cnj Pi,02:51 am
09-28-1985,Mo Cnj Ar,12:43 pm

October 1985
10-01-1985,Mo Cnj Ta,00:36 am
10-03-1985,Mo Cnj Ge,01:37 pm
10-06-1985,Mo Cnj Ca,02:00 am
10-08-1985,Mo Cnj Le,11:34 am
10-10-1985,Mo Cnj Vi,05:10 pm
10-12-1985,Mo Cnj Li,07:12 pm
10-14-1985,Mo Cnj Sc,07:13 pm
10-16-1985,Mo Cnj Sa,07:05 pm
10-18-1985,Mo Cnj Ca,08:35 pm
10-21-1985,Mo Cnj Aq,00:55 am
10-23-1985,Mo Cnj Pi,08:28 am
10-25-1985,Mo Cnj Ar,06:48 pm
10-28-1985,Mo Cnj Ta,07:00 am
10-30-1985,Mo Cnj Ge,07:59 pm

November 1985
11-02-1985,Mo Cnj Ca,08:31 am
11-04-1985,Mo Cnj Le,07:04 pm
11-07-1985,Mo Cnj Vi,02:18 am
11-09-1985,Mo Cnj Li,05:52 am
11-11-1985,Mo Cnj Sc,06:31 am
11-13-1985,Mo Cnj Sa,05:53 am
11-15-1985,Mo Cnj Ca,05:54 am

11-17-1985,Mo Cnj Aq,08:26 am
11-19-1985,Mo Cnj Pi,02:43 pm
11-22-1985,Mo Cnj Ar,00:43 am
11-24-1985,Mo Cnj Ta,01:07 pm
11-27-1985,Mo Cnj Ge,02:08 am
11-29-1985,Mo Cnj Ca,02:23 pm

December 1985
12-02-1985,Mo Cnj Le,01:00 am
12-04-1985,Mo Cnj Vi,09:15 am
12-06-1985,Mo Cnj Li,02:34 pm
12-08-1985,Mo Cnj Sc,04:57 pm
12-10-1985,Mo Cnj Sa,05:14 pm
12-12-1985,Mo Cnj Ca,05:00 pm
12-14-1985,Mo Cnj Aq,06:15 pm
12-16-1985,Mo Cnj Pi,10:50 pm
12-19-1985,Mo Cnj Ar,07:36 am
12-21-1985,Mo Cnj Ta,07:40 pm
12-24-1985,Mo Cnj Ge,08:45 am
12-26-1985,Mo Cnj Ca,08:45 pm
12-29-1985,Mo Cnj Le,06:45 am
12-31-1985,Mo Cnj Vi,02:44 pm

January 1986
01-02-1986,Mo Cnj Li,08:46 pm
01-05-1986,Mo Cnj Sc,00:45 am
01-07-1986,Mo Cnj Sa,02:47 am
01-09-1986,Mo Cnj Ca,03:42 am
01-11-1986,Mo Cnj Aq,05:01 am
01-13-1986,Mo Cnj Pi,08:39 am
01-15-1986,Mo Cnj Ar,04:03 pm
01-18-1986,Mo Cnj Ta,03:14 am
01-20-1986,Mo Cnj Ge,04:13 pm
01-23-1986,Mo Cnj Ca,04:16 am
01-25-1986,Mo Cnj Le,01:48 pm
01-27-1986,Mo Cnj Vi,08:52 pm
01-30-1986,Mo Cnj Li,02:10 am

February 1986
02-01-1986,Mo Cnj Sc,06:19 am
02-03-1986,Mo Cnj Sa,09:32 am
02-05-1986,Mo Cnj Ca,12:02 pm
02-07-1986,Mo Cnj Aq,02:35 pm
02-09-1986,Mo Cnj Pi,06:33 pm
02-12-1986,Mo Cnj Ar,01:21 am
02-14-1986,Mo Cnj Ta,11:39 am
02-17-1986,Mo Cnj Ge,00:18 am

02-19-1986,Mo Cnj Ca,12:40 pm
02-21-1986,Mo Cnj Le,10:25 pm
02-24-1986,Mo Cnj Vi,04:58 am
02-26-1986,Mo Cnj Li,09:07 am
02-28-1986,Mo Cnj Sc,12:06 pm

March 1986
03-02-1986,Mo Cnj Sa,02:52 pm
03-04-1986,Mo Cnj Ca,05:56 pm
03-06-1986,Mo Cnj Aq,09:43 pm
03-09-1986,Mo Cnj Pi,02:49 am
03-11-1986,Mo Cnj Ar,10:04 am
03-13-1986,Mo Cnj Ta,08:05 pm
03-16-1986,Mo Cnj Ge,08:23 am
03-18-1986,Mo Cnj Ca,09:05 pm
03-21-1986,Mo Cnj Le,07:39 am
03-23-1986,Mo Cnj Vi,02:40 pm
03-25-1986,Mo Cnj Li,06:23 pm
03-27-1986,Mo Cnj Sc,08:06 pm
03-29-1986,Mo Cnj Sa,09:21 pm
03-31-1986,Mo Cnj Ca,11:26 pm

April 1986
04-03-1986,Mo Cnj Aq,03:12 am
04-05-1986,Mo Cnj Pi,09:04 am
04-07-1986,Mo Cnj Ar,05:12 pm
04-10-1986,Mo Cnj Ta,03:36 am
04-12-1986,Mo Cnj Ge,03:51 pm
04-15-1986,Mo Cnj Ca,04:42 am
04-17-1986,Mo Cnj Le,04:10 pm
04-20-1986,Mo Cnj Vi,00:24 am
04-22-1986,Mo Cnj Li,04:51 am
04-24-1986,Mo Cnj Sc,06:16 am
04-26-1986,Mo Cnj Sa,06:17 am
04-28-1986,Mo Cnj Ca,06:42 am
04-30-1986,Mo Cnj Aq,09:06 am

May 1986
05-02-1986,Mo Cnj Pi,02:30 pm
05-04-1986,Mo Cnj Ar,11:01 pm
05-07-1986,Mo Cnj Ta,09:59 am
05-09-1986,Mo Cnj Ge,10:26 pm
05-12-1986,Mo Cnj Ca,11:18 am
05-14-1986,Mo Cnj Le,11:16 pm
05-17-1986,Mo Cnj Vi,08:46 am
05-19-1986,Mo Cnj Li,02:42 pm
05-21-1986,Mo Cnj Sc,05:03 pm

05-23-1986,Mo Cnj Sa,04:57 pm
05-25-1986,Mo Cnj Ca,04:15 pm
05-27-1986,Mo Cnj Aq,05:00 pm
05-29-1986,Mo Cnj Pi,08:54 pm

June 1986
06-01-1986,Mo Cnj Ar,04:43 am
06-03-1986,Mo Cnj Ta,03:46 pm
06-06-1986,Mo Cnj Ge,04:27 am
06-08-1986,Mo Cnj Ca,05:17 pm
06-11-1986,Mo Cnj Le,05:12 am
06-13-1986,Mo Cnj Vi,03:19 pm
06-15-1986,Mo Cnj Li,10:38 pm
06-18-1986,Mo Cnj Sc,02:36 am
06-20-1986,Mo Cnj Sa,03:36 am
06-22-1986,Mo Cnj Ca,03:00 am
06-24-1986,Mo Cnj Aq,02:50 am
06-26-1986,Mo Cnj Pi,05:13 am
06-28-1986,Mo Cnj Ar,11:35 am
06-30-1986,Mo Cnj Ta,09:55 pm

July 1986
07-03-1986,Mo Cnj Ge,10:33 am
07-05-1986,Mo Cnj Ca,11:20 pm
07-08-1986,Mo Cnj Le,10:56 am
07-10-1986,Mo Cnj Vi,08:50 pm
07-13-1986,Mo Cnj Li,04:40 am
07-15-1986,Mo Cnj Sc,09:58 am
07-17-1986,Mo Cnj Sa,12:35 pm
07-19-1986,Mo Cnj Ca,01:10 pm
07-21-1986,Mo Cnj Aq,01:18 pm
07-23-1986,Mo Cnj Pi,02:59 pm
07-25-1986,Mo Cnj Ar,08:03 pm
07-28-1986,Mo Cnj Ta,05:12 am
07-30-1986,Mo Cnj Ge,05:20 pm

August 1986
08-02-1986,Mo Cnj Ca,06:04 am
08-04-1986,Mo Cnj Le,05:26 pm
08-07-1986,Mo Cnj Vi,02:45 am
08-09-1986,Mo Cnj Li,10:05 am
08-11-1986,Mo Cnj Sc,03:36 pm
08-13-1986,Mo Cnj Sa,07:18 pm
08-15-1986,Mo Cnj Ca,09:23 pm
08-17-1986,Mo Cnj Aq,10:45 pm
08-20-1986,Mo Cnj Pi,00:53 am
08-22-1986,Mo Cnj Ar,05:28 am

08-24-1986,Mo Cnj Ta,01:37 pm
08-27-1986,Mo Cnj Ge,01:00 am
08-29-1986,Mo Cnj Ca,01:40 pm

September 1986
09-01-1986,Mo Cnj Le,01:09 am
09-03-1986,Mo Cnj Vi,10:06 am
09-05-1986,Mo Cnj Li,04:34 pm
09-07-1986,Mo Cnj Sc,09:13 pm
09-10-1986,Mo Cnj Sa,00:41 am
09-12-1986,Mo Cnj Ca,03:29 am
09-14-1986,Mo Cnj Aq,06:08 am
09-16-1986,Mo Cnj Pi,09:27 am
09-18-1986,Mo Cnj Ar,02:34 pm
09-20-1986,Mo Cnj Ta,10:26 pm
09-23-1986,Mo Cnj Ge,09:14 am
09-25-1986,Mo Cnj Ca,09:45 am
09-28-1986,Mo Cnj Le,09:40 am
09-30-1986,Mo Cnj Vi,06:58 pm

October 1986
10-03-1986,Mo Cnj Li,01:04 am
10-05-1986,Mo Cnj Sc,04:36 am
10-07-1986,Mo Cnj Sa,06:48 am
10-09-1986,Mo Cnj Ca,08:53 am
10-11-1986,Mo Cnj Aq,11:45 am
10-13-1986,Mo Cnj Pi,04:03 pm
10-15-1986,Mo Cnj Ar,10:13 pm
10-18-1986,Mo Cnj Ta,06:35 am
10-20-1986,Mo Cnj Ge,05:16 pm
10-23-1986,Mo Cnj Ca,05:38 am
10-25-1986,Mo Cnj Le,06:03 pm
10-28-1986,Mo Cnj Vi,04:21 am
10-30-1986,Mo Cnj Li,11:05 am

November 1986
11-01-1986,Mo Cnj Sc,02:20 pm
11-03-1986,Mo Cnj Sa,03:19 pm
11-05-1986,Mo Cnj Ca,03:49 pm
11-07-1986,Mo Cnj Aq,05:29 pm
11-09-1986,Mo Cnj Pi,09:30 pm
11-12-1986,Mo Cnj Ar,04:15 am
11-14-1986,Mo Cnj Ta,01:25 pm
11-17-1986,Mo Cnj Ge,00:27 am
11-19-1986,Mo Cnj Ca,12:47 pm
11-22-1986,Mo Cnj Le,01:26 am
11-24-1986,Mo Cnj Vi,12:46 pm

11-26-1986,Mo Cnj Li,08:59 pm
11-29-1986,Mo Cnj Sc,01:13 am

December 1986
12-01-1986,Mo Cnj Sa,02:08 am
12-03-1986,Mo Cnj Ca,01:29 am
12-05-1986,Mo Cnj Aq,01:24 am
12-07-1986,Mo Cnj Pi,03:49 am
12-09-1986,Mo Cnj Ar,09:50 am
12-11-1986,Mo Cnj Ta,07:11 pm
12-14-1986,Mo Cnj Ge,06:42 am
12-16-1986,Mo Cnj Ca,07:09 pm
12-19-1986,Mo Cnj Le,07:44 am
12-21-1986,Mo Cnj Vi,07:30 pm
12-24-1986,Mo Cnj Li,05:05 am
12-26-1986,Mo Cnj Sc,11:07 am
12-28-1986,Mo Cnj Sa,01:20 pm
12-30-1986,Mo Cnj Ca,12:55 pm

January 1987
01-01-1987,Mo Cnj Aq,11:54 am
01-03-1987,Mo Cnj Pi,12:37 pm
01-05-1987,Mo Cnj Ar,04:51 pm
01-08-1987,Mo Cnj Ta,01:13 am
01-10-1987,Mo Cnj Ge,12:39 pm
01-13-1987,Mo Cnj Ca,01:18 am
01-15-1987,Mo Cnj Le,01:45 am
01-18-1987,Mo Cnj Vi,01:15 am
01-20-1987,Mo Cnj Li,11:10 am
01-22-1987,Mo Cnj Sc,06:31 pm
01-24-1987,Mo Cnj Sa,10:36 pm
01-26-1987,Mo Cnj Ca,11:43 pm
01-28-1987,Mo Cnj Aq,11:17 pm
01-30-1987,Mo Cnj Pi,11:25 pm

February 1987
02-02-1987,Mo Cnj Ar,02:09 am
02-04-1987,Mo Cnj Ta,08:53 am
02-06-1987,Mo Cnj Ge,07:23 pm
02-09-1987,Mo Cnj Ca,07:55 am
02-11-1987,Mo Cnj Le,08:22 pm
02-14-1987,Mo Cnj Vi,07:27 am
02-16-1987,Mo Cnj Li,04:45 pm
02-19-1987,Mo Cnj Sc,00:05 am
02-21-1987,Mo Cnj Sa,05:10 am
02-23-1987,Mo Cnj Ca,07:57 am

02-25-1987,Mo Cnj Aq,09:08 am
02-27-1987,Mo Cnj Pi,10:07 am

March 1987
03-01-1987,Mo Cnj Ar,12:37 pm
03-03-1987,Mo Cnj Ta,06:12 am
03-06-1987,Mo Cnj Ge,03:27 am
03-08-1987,Mo Cnj Ca,03:25 pm
03-11-1987,Mo Cnj Le,03:55 am
03-13-1987,Mo Cnj Vi,02:56 pm
03-15-1987,Mo Cnj Li,11:35 pm
03-18-1987,Mo Cnj Sc,05:57 am
03-20-1987,Mo Cnj Sa,10:32 am
03-22-1987,Mo Cnj Ca,01:48 pm
03-24-1987,Mo Cnj Aq,04:18 pm
03-26-1987,Mo Cnj Pi,06:46 pm
03-28-1987,Mo Cnj Ar,10:13 pm
03-31-1987,Mo Cnj Ta,03:47 am

April 1987
04-02-1987,Mo Cnj Ge,12:17 pm
04-04-1987,Mo Cnj Ca,11:34 pm
04-07-1987,Mo Cnj Le,12:04 pm
04-09-1987,Mo Cnj Vi,11:28 pm
04-12-1987,Mo Cnj Li,08:05 am
04-14-1987,Mo Cnj Sc,01:40 pm
04-16-1987,Mo Cnj Sa,05:01 pm
04-18-1987,Mo Cnj Ca,07:21 pm
04-20-1987,Mo Cnj Aq,09:46 pm
04-23-1987,Mo Cnj Pi,01:02 am
04-25-1987,Mo Cnj Ar,05:41 am
04-27-1987,Mo Cnj Ta,12:07 pm
04-29-1987,Mo Cnj Ge,08:43 pm

May 1987
05-02-1987,Mo Cnj Ca,07:39 am
05-04-1987,Mo Cnj Le,08:07 pm
05-07-1987,Mo Cnj Vi,08:07 am
05-09-1987,Mo Cnj Li,05:29 pm
05-11-1987,Mo Cnj Sc,11:10 pm
05-14-1987,Mo Cnj Sa,01:41 am
05-16-1987,Mo Cnj Ca,02:37 am
05-18-1987,Mo Cnj Aq,03:43 am
05-20-1987,Mo Cnj Pi,06:25 am
05-22-1987,Mo Cnj Ar,11:23 am
05-24-1987,Mo Cnj Ta,06:39 pm

05-27-1987,Mo Cnj Ge,03:55 am
05-29-1987,Mo Cnj Ca,02:59 pm

June 1987
06-01-1987,Mo Cnj Le,03:25 am
06-03-1987,Mo Cnj Vi,03:57 pm
06-06-1987,Mo Cnj Li,02:25 am
06-08-1987,Mo Cnj Sc,09:07 am
06-10-1987,Mo Cnj Sa,11:54 am
06-12-1987,Mo Cnj Ca,12:05 pm
06-14-1987,Mo Cnj Aq,11:45 am
06-16-1987,Mo Cnj Pi,12:55 pm
06-18-1987,Mo Cnj Ar,04:56 pm
06-21-1987,Mo Cnj Ta,00:09 am
06-23-1987,Mo Cnj Ge,09:54 am
06-25-1987,Mo Cnj Ca,09:22 pm
06-28-1987,Mo Cnj Le,09:53 am
06-30-1987,Mo Cnj Vi,10:35 pm

July 1987
07-03-1987,Mo Cnj Li,09:55 am
07-05-1987,Mo Cnj Sc,06:04 pm
07-07-1987,Mo Cnj Sa,10:05 pm
07-09-1987,Mo Cnj Ca,10:44 pm
07-11-1987,Mo Cnj Aq,09:49 pm
07-13-1987,Mo Cnj Pi,09:36 pm
07-16-1987,Mo Cnj Ar,00:00 am
07-18-1987,Mo Cnj Ta,06:05 am
07-20-1987,Mo Cnj Ge,03:33 pm
07-23-1987,Mo Cnj Ca,03:14 am
07-25-1987,Mo Cnj Le,03:50 pm
07-28-1987,Mo Cnj Vi,04:26 am
07-30-1987,Mo Cnj Li,04:00 pm

August 1987
08-02-1987,Mo Cnj Sc,01:09 am
08-04-1987,Mo Cnj Sa,06:47 am
08-06-1987,Mo Cnj Ca,08:51 am
08-08-1987,Mo Cnj Aq,08:37 am
08-10-1987,Mo Cnj Pi,08:01 am
08-12-1987,Mo Cnj Ar,09:10 am
08-14-1987,Mo Cnj Ta,01:39 pm
08-16-1987,Mo Cnj Ge,10:00 pm
08-19-1987,Mo Cnj Ca,09:20 am
08-21-1987,Mo Cnj Le,09:58 am
08-24-1987,Mo Cnj Vi,10:23 am
08-26-1987,Mo Cnj Li,09:36 pm

08-29-1987,Mo Cnj Sc,06:49 am
08-31-1987,Mo Cnj Sa,01:24 pm

September 1987
09-02-1987,Mo Cnj Ca,05:04 pm
09-04-1987,Mo Cnj Aq,06:22 pm
09-06-1987,Mo Cnj Pi,06:37 pm
09-08-1987,Mo Cnj Ar,07:35 pm
09-10-1987,Mo Cnj Ta,10:58 pm
09-13-1987,Mo Cnj Ge,05:55 am
09-15-1987,Mo Cnj Ca,04:22 pm
09-18-1987,Mo Cnj Le,04:50 am
09-20-1987,Mo Cnj Vi,05:13 pm
09-23-1987,Mo Cnj Li,03:58 am
09-25-1987,Mo Cnj Sc,12:30 pm
09-27-1987,Mo Cnj Sa,06:49 pm
09-29-1987,Mo Cnj Ca,11:09 pm

October 1987
10-02-1987,Mo Cnj Aq,01:52 am
10-04-1987,Mo Cnj Pi,03:40 am
10-06-1987,Mo Cnj Ar,05:35 am
10-08-1987,Mo Cnj Ta,08:58 am
10-10-1987,Mo Cnj Ge,03:04 pm
10-13-1987,Mo Cnj Ca,00:31 am
10-15-1987,Mo Cnj Le,12:34 pm
10-18-1987,Mo Cnj Vi,01:06 am
10-20-1987,Mo Cnj Li,11:50 am
10-22-1987,Mo Cnj Sc,07:42 pm
10-25-1987,Mo Cnj Sa,00:58 am
10-27-1987,Mo Cnj Ca,04:34 am
10-29-1987,Mo Cnj Aq,07:27 am
10-31-1987,Mo Cnj Pi,10:20 am

November 1987
11-02-1987,Mo Cnj Ar,01:40 pm
11-04-1987,Mo Cnj Ta,06:02 pm
11-07-1987,Mo Cnj Ge,00:16 am
11-09-1987,Mo Cnj Ca,09:10 am
11-11-1987,Mo Cnj Le,08:45 pm
11-14-1987,Mo Cnj Vi,09:30 am
11-16-1987,Mo Cnj Li,08:49 pm
11-19-1987,Mo Cnj Sc,04:48 am
11-21-1987,Mo Cnj Sa,09:17 am
11-23-1987,Mo Cnj Ca,11:32 am
11-25-1987,Mo Cnj Aq,01:13 pm

11-27-1987,Mo Cnj Pi,03:40 pm
11-29-1987,Mo Cnj Ar,07:36 pm

December 1987
12-02-1987,Mo Cnj Ta,01:06 am
12-04-1987,Mo Cnj Ge,08:14 am
12-06-1987,Mo Cnj Ca,05:21 pm
12-09-1987,Mo Cnj Le,04:41 am
12-11-1987,Mo Cnj Vi,05:31 pm
12-14-1987,Mo Cnj Li,05:41 am
12-16-1987,Mo Cnj Sc,02:42 pm
12-18-1987,Mo Cnj Sa,07:33 pm
12-20-1987,Mo Cnj Ca,09:08 pm
12-22-1987,Mo Cnj Aq,09:20 pm
12-24-1987,Mo Cnj Pi,10:10 pm
12-27-1987,Mo Cnj Ar,01:06 am
12-29-1987,Mo Cnj Ta,06:37 am
12-31-1987,Mo Cnj Ge,02:29 pm

January 1988
01-03-1988,Mo Cnj Ca,00:17 am
01-05-1988,Mo Cnj Le,11:48 am
01-08-1988,Mo Cnj Vi,00:35 am
01-10-1988,Mo Cnj Li,01:17 pm
01-12-1988,Mo Cnj Sc,11:39 pm
01-15-1988,Mo Cnj Sa,05:58 am
01-17-1988,Mo Cnj Ca,08:16 am
01-19-1988,Mo Cnj Aq,08:02 am
01-21-1988,Mo Cnj Pi,07:27 am
01-23-1988,Mo Cnj Ar,08:32 am
01-25-1988,Mo Cnj Ta,12:37 pm
01-27-1988,Mo Cnj Ge,08:03 pm
01-30-1988,Mo Cnj Ca,06:12 am

February 1988
02-01-1988,Mo Cnj Le,06:06 pm
02-04-1988,Mo Cnj Vi,06:54 am
02-06-1988,Mo Cnj Li,07:36 pm
02-09-1988,Mo Cnj Sc,06:42 am
02-11-1988,Mo Cnj Sa,02:36 pm
02-13-1988,Mo Cnj Ca,06:37 pm
02-15-1988,Mo Cnj Aq,07:26 pm
02-17-1988,Mo Cnj Pi,06:45 pm
02-19-1988,Mo Cnj Ar,06:35 pm
02-21-1988,Mo Cnj Ta,08:51 pm
02-24-1988,Mo Cnj Ge,02:42 am

02-26-1988,Mo Cnj Ca,12:12 pm
02-29-1988,Mo Cnj Le,00:12 am

March 1988
03-02-1988,Mo Cnj Vi,01:06 pm
03-05-1988,Mo Cnj Li,01:33 am
03-07-1988,Mo Cnj Sc,12:28 pm
03-09-1988,Mo Cnj Sa,08:59 pm
03-12-1988,Mo Cnj Ca,02:32 am
03-14-1988,Mo Cnj Aq,05:08 am
03-16-1988,Mo Cnj Pi,05:42 am
03-18-1988,Mo Cnj Ar,05:45 am
03-20-1988,Mo Cnj Ta,07:05 am
03-22-1988,Mo Cnj Ge,11:21 am
03-24-1988,Mo Cnj Ca,07:27 pm
03-27-1988,Mo Cnj Le,06:54 am
03-29-1988,Mo Cnj Vi,07:49 pm

April 1988
04-01-1988,Mo Cnj Li,08:06 am
04-03-1988,Mo Cnj Sc,06:27 pm
04-06-1988,Mo Cnj Sa,02:29 am
04-08-1988,Mo Cnj Ca,08:20 am
04-10-1988,Mo Cnj Aq,12:10 pm
04-12-1988,Mo Cnj Pi,02:24 pm
04-14-1988,Mo Cnj Ar,03:47 pm
04-16-1988,Mo Cnj Ta,05:32 pm
04-18-1988,Mo Cnj Ge,09:10 pm
04-21-1988,Mo Cnj Ca,04:05 am
04-23-1988,Mo Cnj Le,02:35 pm
04-26-1988,Mo Cnj Vi,03:17 am
04-28-1988,Mo Cnj Li,03:38 pm

May 1988
05-01-1988,Mo Cnj Sc,01:39 am
05-03-1988,Mo Cnj Sa,08:52 am
05-05-1988,Mo Cnj Ca,01:54 pm
05-07-1988,Mo Cnj Aq,05:37 pm
05-09-1988,Mo Cnj Pi,08:39 pm
05-11-1988,Mo Cnj Ar,11:24 pm
05-14-1988,Mo Cnj Ta,02:23 am
05-16-1988,Mo Cnj Ge,06:32 am
05-18-1988,Mo Cnj Ca,01:06 pm
05-20-1988,Mo Cnj Le,10:52 pm
05-23-1988,Mo Cnj Vi,11:13 am
05-25-1988,Mo Cnj Li,11:49 pm

05-28-1988,Mo Cnj Sc,10:06 am
05-30-1988,Mo Cnj Sa,04:57 pm

June 1988
06-01-1988,Mo Cnj Ca,08:59 pm
06-03-1988,Mo Cnj Aq,11:34 pm
06-06-1988,Mo Cnj Pi,02:01 am
06-08-1988,Mo Cnj Ar,05:05 am
06-10-1988,Mo Cnj Ta,09:03 am
06-12-1988,Mo Cnj Ge,02:15 pm
06-14-1988,Mo Cnj Ca,09:19 pm
06-17-1988,Mo Cnj Le,06:57 am
06-19-1988,Mo Cnj Vi,07:03 pm
06-22-1988,Mo Cnj Li,07:57 am
06-24-1988,Mo Cnj Sc,06:59 pm
06-27-1988,Mo Cnj Sa,02:18 am
06-29-1988,Mo Cnj Ca,06:01 am

July 1988
07-01-1988,Mo Cnj Aq,07:30 am
07-03-1988,Mo Cnj Pi,08:34 am
07-05-1988,Mo Cnj Ar,10:38 am
07-07-1988,Mo Cnj Ta,02:27 pm
07-09-1988,Mo Cnj Ge,08:16 pm
07-12-1988,Mo Cnj Ca,04:08 am
07-14-1988,Mo Cnj Le,02:11 pm
07-17-1988,Mo Cnj Vi,02:17 am
07-19-1988,Mo Cnj Li,03:22 pm
07-22-1988,Mo Cnj Sc,03:14 am
07-24-1988,Mo Cnj Sa,11:43 am
07-26-1988,Mo Cnj Ca,04:08 pm
07-28-1988,Mo Cnj Aq,05:26 pm
07-30-1988,Mo Cnj Pi,05:23 pm

August 1988
08-01-1988,Mo Cnj Ar,05:53 pm
08-03-1988,Mo Cnj Ta,08:24 pm
08-06-1988,Mo Cnj Ge,01:43 am
08-08-1988,Mo Cnj Ca,09:52 am
08-10-1988,Mo Cnj Le,08:27 pm
08-13-1988,Mo Cnj Vi,08:46 am
08-15-1988,Mo Cnj Li,09:52 pm
08-18-1988,Mo Cnj Sc,10:12 am
08-20-1988,Mo Cnj Sa,07:55 pm
08-23-1988,Mo Cnj Ca,01:49 am
08-25-1988,Mo Cnj Aq,04:05 am
08-27-1988,Mo Cnj Pi,04:01 am

08-29-1988,Mo Cnj Ar,03:29 am
08-31-1988,Mo Cnj Ta,04:22 am

September 1988
09-02-1988,Mo Cnj Ge,08:12 am
09-04-1988,Mo Cnj Ca,03:38 pm
09-07-1988,Mo Cnj Le,02:15 am
09-09-1988,Mo Cnj Vi,02:49 pm
09-12-1988,Mo Cnj Li,03:52 am
09-14-1988,Mo Cnj Sc,04:07 pm
09-17-1988,Mo Cnj Sa,02:25 am
09-19-1988,Mo Cnj Ca,09:45 am
09-21-1988,Mo Cnj Aq,01:43 pm
09-23-1988,Mo Cnj Pi,02:51 pm
09-25-1988,Mo Cnj Ar,02:30 pm
09-27-1988,Mo Cnj Ta,02:29 pm
09-29-1988,Mo Cnj Ge,04:44 pm

October 1988
10-01-1988,Mo Cnj Ca,10:40 pm
10-04-1988,Mo Cnj Le,08:32 am
10-06-1988,Mo Cnj Vi,09:02 pm
10-09-1988,Mo Cnj Li,10:04 am
10-11-1988,Mo Cnj Sc,09:58 pm
10-14-1988,Mo Cnj Sa,07:58 am
10-16-1988,Mo Cnj Ca,03:45 pm
10-18-1988,Mo Cnj Aq,09:05 pm
10-20-1988,Mo Cnj Pi,11:59 pm
10-23-1988,Mo Cnj Ar,01:00 am
10-25-1988,Mo Cnj Ta,01:23 am
10-27-1988,Mo Cnj Ge,02:56 am
10-29-1988,Mo Cnj Ca,07:29 am
10-31-1988,Mo Cnj Le,04:04 pm

November 1988
11-03-1988,Mo Cnj Vi,04:01 am
11-05-1988,Mo Cnj Li,05:04 pm
11-08-1988,Mo Cnj Sc,04:46 am
11-10-1988,Mo Cnj Sa,02:06 pm
11-12-1988,Mo Cnj Ca,09:13 pm
11-15-1988,Mo Cnj Aq,02:37 am
11-17-1988,Mo Cnj Pi,06:35 am
11-19-1988,Mo Cnj Ar,09:13 am
11-21-1988,Mo Cnj Ta,11:03 am
11-23-1988,Mo Cnj Ge,01:12 pm
11-25-1988,Mo Cnj Ca,05:20 pm

11-28-1988,Mo Cnj Le,00:52 am
11-30-1988,Mo Cnj Vi,12:00 pm

December 1988
12-03-1988,Mo Cnj Li,00:56 am
12-05-1988,Mo Cnj Sc,12:52 pm
12-07-1988,Mo Cnj Sa,09:56 pm
12-10-1988,Mo Cnj Ca,04:07 am
12-12-1988,Mo Cnj Aq,08:26 am
12-14-1988,Mo Cnj Pi,11:53 am
12-16-1988,Mo Cnj Ar,03:03 pm
12-18-1988,Mo Cnj Ta,06:11 pm
12-20-1988,Mo Cnj Ge,09:43 pm
12-23-1988,Mo Cnj Ca,02:35 am
12-25-1988,Mo Cnj Le,09:58 am
12-27-1988,Mo Cnj Vi,08:28 pm
12-30-1988,Mo Cnj Li,09:10 am

January 1989
01-01-1989,Mo Cnj Sc,09:35 pm
01-04-1989,Mo Cnj Sa,07:12 am
01-06-1989,Mo Cnj Ca,01:14 pm
01-08-1989,Mo Cnj Aq,04:31 pm
01-10-1989,Mo Cnj Pi,06:31 pm
01-12-1989,Mo Cnj Ar,08:36 pm
01-14-1989,Mo Cnj Ta,11:36 pm
01-17-1989,Mo Cnj Ge,03:57 am
01-19-1989,Mo Cnj Ca,09:58 am
01-21-1989,Mo Cnj Le,06:03 pm
01-24-1989,Mo Cnj Vi,04:33 am
01-26-1989,Mo Cnj Li,05:02 pm
01-29-1989,Mo Cnj Sc,05:49 am
01-31-1989,Mo Cnj Sa,04:30 pm

February 1989
02-02-1989,Mo Cnj Ca,11:30 pm
02-05-1989,Mo Cnj Aq,02:51 am
02-07-1989,Mo Cnj Pi,03:52 am
02-09-1989,Mo Cnj Ar,04:18 am
02-11-1989,Mo Cnj Ta,05:45 am
02-13-1989,Mo Cnj Ge,09:23 am
02-15-1989,Mo Cnj Ca,03:41 pm
02-18-1989,Mo Cnj Le,00:33 am
02-20-1989,Mo Cnj Vi,11:35 am
02-23-1989,Mo Cnj Li,00:05 am
02-25-1989,Mo Cnj Sc,12:57 pm
02-28-1989,Mo Cnj Sa,00:29 am

March 1989
03-02-1989,Mo Cnj Ca,08:58 am
03-04-1989,Mo Cnj Aq,01:37 pm
03-06-1989,Mo Cnj Pi,03:00 pm
03-08-1989,Mo Cnj Ar,02:37 pm
03-10-1989,Mo Cnj Ta,02:26 pm
03-12-1989,Mo Cnj Ge,04:17 pm
03-14-1989,Mo Cnj Ca,09:28 pm
03-17-1989,Mo Cnj Le,06:13 am
03-19-1989,Mo Cnj Vi,05:40 pm
03-22-1989,Mo Cnj Li,06:24 am
03-24-1989,Mo Cnj Sc,07:11 pm
03-27-1989,Mo Cnj Sa,06:54 am
03-29-1989,Mo Cnj Ca,04:26 pm
03-31-1989,Mo Cnj Aq,10:46 pm

April 1989
04-03-1989,Mo Cnj Pi,01:38 am
04-05-1989,Mo Cnj Ar,01:52 am
04-07-1989,Mo Cnj Ta,01:08 am
04-09-1989,Mo Cnj Ge,01:31 am
04-11-1989,Mo Cnj Ca,04:58 am
04-13-1989,Mo Cnj Le,12:31 pm
04-15-1989,Mo Cnj Vi,11:39 pm
04-18-1989,Mo Cnj Li,12:32 pm
04-21-1989,Mo Cnj Sc,01:14 am
04-23-1989,Mo Cnj Sa,12:39 pm
04-25-1989,Mo Cnj Ca,10:16 pm
04-28-1989,Mo Cnj Aq,05:34 am
04-30-1989,Mo Cnj Pi,10:04 am

May 1989
05-02-1989,Mo Cnj Ar,11:51 am
05-04-1989,Mo Cnj Ta,11:55 am
05-06-1989,Mo Cnj Ge,12:03 pm
05-08-1989,Mo Cnj Ca,02:20 pm
05-10-1989,Mo Cnj Le,08:23 pm
05-13-1989,Mo Cnj Vi,06:31 am
05-15-1989,Mo Cnj Li,07:08 pm
05-18-1989,Mo Cnj Sc,07:49 am
05-20-1989,Mo Cnj Sa,06:53 pm
05-23-1989,Mo Cnj Ca,03:55 am
05-25-1989,Mo Cnj Aq,11:01 am
05-27-1989,Mo Cnj Pi,04:13 pm
05-29-1989,Mo Cnj Ar,07:26 pm
05-31-1989,Mo Cnj Ta,09:00 pm

June 1989
06-02-1989,Mo Cnj Ge,10:03 pm
06-05-1989,Mo Cnj Ca,00:18 am
06-07-1989,Mo Cnj Le,05:29 am
06-09-1989,Mo Cnj Vi,02:30 pm
06-12-1989,Mo Cnj Li,02:32 am
06-14-1989,Mo Cnj Sc,03:12 pm
06-17-1989,Mo Cnj Sa,02:13 am
06-19-1989,Mo Cnj Ca,10:42 am
06-21-1989,Mo Cnj Aq,04:57 pm
06-23-1989,Mo Cnj Pi,09:36 pm
06-26-1989,Mo Cnj Ar,01:07 am
06-28-1989,Mo Cnj Ta,03:46 am
06-30-1989,Mo Cnj Ge,06:09 am

July 1989
07-02-1989,Mo Cnj Ca,09:20 am
07-04-1989,Mo Cnj Le,02:38 pm
07-06-1989,Mo Cnj Vi,11:05 pm
07-09-1989,Mo Cnj Li,10:31 am
07-11-1989,Mo Cnj Sc,11:09 pm
07-14-1989,Mo Cnj Sa,10:31 am
07-16-1989,Mo Cnj Ca,07:01 pm
07-19-1989,Mo Cnj Aq,00:36 am
07-21-1989,Mo Cnj Pi,04:07 am
07-23-1989,Mo Cnj Ar,06:41 am
07-25-1989,Mo Cnj Ta,09:11 am
07-27-1989,Mo Cnj Ge,12:16 pm
07-29-1989,Mo Cnj Ca,04:32 pm
07-31-1989,Mo Cnj Le,10:41 pm

August 1989
08-03-1989,Mo Cnj Vi,07:19 am
08-05-1989,Mo Cnj Li,06:28 pm
08-08-1989,Mo Cnj Sc,07:05 am
08-10-1989,Mo Cnj Sa,07:03 pm
08-13-1989,Mo Cnj Ca,04:17 am
08-15-1989,Mo Cnj Aq,10:00 am
08-17-1989,Mo Cnj Pi,12:46 pm
08-19-1989,Mo Cnj Ar,02:00 pm
08-21-1989,Mo Cnj Ta,03:11 pm
08-23-1989,Mo Cnj Ge,05:39 pm
08-25-1989,Mo Cnj Ca,10:13 pm
08-28-1989,Mo Cnj Le,05:11 am
08-30-1989,Mo Cnj Vi,02:29 pm

September 1989

09-02-1989,Mo Cnj Li,01:48 am
09-04-1989,Mo Cnj Sc,02:24 pm
09-07-1989,Mo Cnj Sa,02:52 am
09-09-1989,Mo Cnj Ca,01:14 pm
09-11-1989,Mo Cnj Aq,08:02 pm
09-13-1989,Mo Cnj Pi,11:08 pm
09-15-1989,Mo Cnj Ar,11:39 pm
09-17-1989,Mo Cnj Ta,11:23 pm
09-20-1989,Mo Cnj Ge,00:16 am
09-22-1989,Mo Cnj Ca,03:50 am
09-24-1989,Mo Cnj Le,10:44 am
09-26-1989,Mo Cnj Vi,08:33 pm
09-29-1989,Mo Cnj Li,08:16 am

October 1989

10-01-1989,Mo Cnj Sc,08:54 pm
10-04-1989,Mo Cnj Sa,09:30 am
10-06-1989,Mo Cnj Ca,08:46 pm
10-09-1989,Mo Cnj Aq,05:07 am
10-11-1989,Mo Cnj Pi,09:38 am
10-13-1989,Mo Cnj Ar,10:41 am
10-15-1989,Mo Cnj Ta,09:53 am
10-17-1989,Mo Cnj Ge,09:20 am
10-19-1989,Mo Cnj Ca,11:10 am
10-21-1989,Mo Cnj Le,04:48 pm
10-24-1989,Mo Cnj Vi,02:16 am
10-26-1989,Mo Cnj Li,02:12 pm
10-29-1989,Mo Cnj Sc,02:57 am
10-31-1989,Mo Cnj Sa,03:23 pm

November 1989

11-03-1989,Mo Cnj Ca,02:46 am
11-05-1989,Mo Cnj Aq,12:09 pm
11-07-1989,Mo Cnj Pi,06:25 pm
11-09-1989,Mo Cnj Ar,09:08 pm
11-11-1989,Mo Cnj Ta,09:10 pm
11-13-1989,Mo Cnj Ge,08:20 pm
11-15-1989,Mo Cnj Ca,08:52 pm
11-18-1989,Mo Cnj Le,00:46 am
11-20-1989,Mo Cnj Vi,08:55 am
11-22-1989,Mo Cnj Li,08:25 pm
11-25-1989,Mo Cnj Sc,09:13 am
11-27-1989,Mo Cnj Sa,09:30 pm
11-30-1989,Mo Cnj Ca,08:26 am

December 1989

12-02-1989,Mo Cnj Aq,05:42 pm
12-05-1989,Mo Cnj Pi,00:48 am
12-07-1989,Mo Cnj Ar,05:12 am
12-09-1989,Mo Cnj Ta,07:00 am
12-11-1989,Mo Cnj Ge,07:16 am
12-13-1989,Mo Cnj Ca,07:50 am
12-15-1989,Mo Cnj Le,10:42 am
12-17-1989,Mo Cnj Vi,05:19 pm
12-20-1989,Mo Cnj Li,03:45 am
12-22-1989,Mo Cnj Sc,04:18 pm
12-25-1989,Mo Cnj Sa,04:37 am
12-27-1989,Mo Cnj Ca,03:11 pm
12-29-1989,Mo Cnj Aq,11:39 pm

January 1990

01-01-1990,Mo Cnj Pi,06:11 am
01-03-1990,Mo Cnj Ar,10:57 am
01-05-1990,Mo Cnj Ta,02:04 pm
01-07-1990,Mo Cnj Ge,04:02 pm
01-09-1990,Mo Cnj Ca,05:52 pm
01-11-1990,Mo Cnj Le,09:02 pm
01-14-1990,Mo Cnj Vi,02:57 am
01-16-1990,Mo Cnj Li,12:18 pm
01-19-1990,Mo Cnj Sc,00:16 am
01-21-1990,Mo Cnj Sa,12:44 pm
01-23-1990,Mo Cnj Ca,11:28 pm
01-26-1990,Mo Cnj Aq,07:26 am
01-28-1990,Mo Cnj Pi,12:51 pm
01-30-1990,Mo Cnj Ar,04:34 pm

February 1990

02-01-1990,Mo Cnj Ta,07:27 pm
02-03-1990,Mo Cnj Ge,10:12 pm
02-06-1990,Mo Cnj Ca,01:27 am
02-08-1990,Mo Cnj Le,05:52 am
02-10-1990,Mo Cnj Vi,12:13 pm
02-12-1990,Mo Cnj Li,09:10 pm
02-15-1990,Mo Cnj Sc,08:35 am
02-17-1990,Mo Cnj Sa,09:08 pm
02-20-1990,Mo Cnj Ca,08:30 am
02-22-1990,Mo Cnj Aq,04:52 pm
02-24-1990,Mo Cnj Pi,09:50 pm
02-27-1990,Mo Cnj Ar,00:16 am

March 1990

03-01-1990,Mo Cnj Ta,01:43 am
03-03-1990,Mo Cnj Ge,03:38 am

03-05-1990,Mo Cnj Ca,07:03 am
03-07-1990,Mo Cnj Le,12:25 pm
03-09-1990,Mo Cnj Vi,07:48 pm
03-12-1990,Mo Cnj Li,05:10 am
03-14-1990,Mo Cnj Sc,04:26 pm
03-17-1990,Mo Cnj Sa,04:56 am
03-19-1990,Mo Cnj Ca,05:01 pm
03-22-1990,Mo Cnj Aq,02:31 am
03-24-1990,Mo Cnj Pi,08:09 am
03-26-1990,Mo Cnj Ar,10:16 am
03-28-1990,Mo Cnj Ta,10:27 am
03-30-1990,Mo Cnj Ge,10:43 am

April 1990
04-01-1990,Mo Cnj Ca,12:50 pm
04-03-1990,Mo Cnj Le,05:51 pm
04-06-1990,Mo Cnj Vi,01:42 am
04-08-1990,Mo Cnj Li,11:45 am
04-10-1990,Mo Cnj Sc,11:18 pm
04-13-1990,Mo Cnj Sa,11:48 am
04-16-1990,Mo Cnj Ca,00:15 am
04-18-1990,Mo Cnj Aq,10:53 am
04-20-1990,Mo Cnj Pi,05:57 pm
04-22-1990,Mo Cnj Ar,08:59 pm
04-24-1990,Mo Cnj Ta,09:04 pm
04-26-1990,Mo Cnj Ge,08:13 pm
04-28-1990,Mo Cnj Ca,08:40 pm

May 1990
05-01-1990,Mo Cnj Le,00:09 am
05-03-1990,Mo Cnj Vi,07:18 am
05-05-1990,Mo Cnj Li,05:28 pm
05-08-1990,Mo Cnj Sc,05:22 am
05-10-1990,Mo Cnj Sa,05:56 pm
05-13-1990,Mo Cnj Ca,06:22 am
05-15-1990,Mo Cnj Aq,05:31 pm
05-18-1990,Mo Cnj Pi,01:55 am
05-20-1990,Mo Cnj Ar,06:32 am
05-22-1990,Mo Cnj Ta,07:43 am
05-24-1990,Mo Cnj Ge,07:00 am
05-26-1990,Mo Cnj Ca,06:34 am
05-28-1990,Mo Cnj Le,08:29 am
05-30-1990,Mo Cnj Vi,02:08 pm

June 1990
06-01-1990,Mo Cnj Li,11:31 pm
06-04-1990,Mo Cnj Sc,11:22 am

06-07-1990,Mo Cnj Sa,00:00 am
06-09-1990,Mo Cnj Ca,12:12 pm
06-11-1990,Mo Cnj Aq,11:10 pm
06-14-1990,Mo Cnj Pi,08:00 am
06-16-1990,Mo Cnj Ar,01:55 pm
06-18-1990,Mo Cnj Ta,04:43 pm
06-20-1990,Mo Cnj Ge,05:14 pm
06-22-1990,Mo Cnj Ca,05:09 pm
06-24-1990,Mo Cnj Le,06:25 pm
06-26-1990,Mo Cnj Vi,10:42 pm
06-29-1990,Mo Cnj Li,06:47 am

July 1990
07-01-1990,Mo Cnj Sc,06:02 pm
07-04-1990,Mo Cnj Sa,06:36 am
07-06-1990,Mo Cnj Ca,06:40 pm
07-09-1990,Mo Cnj Aq,05:07 am
07-11-1990,Mo Cnj Pi,01:29 pm
07-13-1990,Mo Cnj Ar,07:36 pm
07-15-1990,Mo Cnj Ta,11:29 pm
07-18-1990,Mo Cnj Ge,01:32 am
07-20-1990,Mo Cnj Ca,02:44 am
07-22-1990,Mo Cnj Le,04:29 am
07-24-1990,Mo Cnj Vi,08:18 am
07-26-1990,Mo Cnj Li,03:19 pm
07-29-1990,Mo Cnj Sc,01:39 am
07-31-1990,Mo Cnj Sa,02:00 pm

August 1990
08-03-1990,Mo Cnj Ca,02:09 am
08-05-1990,Mo Cnj Aq,12:19 pm
08-07-1990,Mo Cnj Pi,07:54 pm
08-10-1990,Mo Cnj Ar,01:13 am
08-12-1990,Mo Cnj Ta,04:55 am
08-14-1990,Mo Cnj Ge,07:42 am
08-16-1990,Mo Cnj Ca,10:13 am
08-18-1990,Mo Cnj Le,01:12 pm
08-20-1990,Mo Cnj Vi,05:33 pm
08-23-1990,Mo Cnj Li,00:17 am
08-25-1990,Mo Cnj Sc,09:56 am
08-27-1990,Mo Cnj Sa,09:57 pm
08-30-1990,Mo Cnj Ca,10:23 am

September 1990
09-01-1990,Mo Cnj Aq,08:51 pm
09-04-1990,Mo Cnj Pi,04:06 am
09-06-1990,Mo Cnj Ar,08:23 am

09-08-1990,Mo Cnj Ta,10:56 am
09-10-1990,Mo Cnj Ge,01:05 pm
09-12-1990,Mo Cnj Ca,03:53 pm
09-14-1990,Mo Cnj Le,07:52 pm
09-17-1990,Mo Cnj Vi,01:18 am
09-19-1990,Mo Cnj Li,08:34 am
09-21-1990,Mo Cnj Sc,06:06 pm
09-24-1990,Mo Cnj Sa,05:52 am
09-26-1990,Mo Cnj Ca,06:37 pm
09-29-1990,Mo Cnj Aq,05:54 am

October 1990
10-01-1990,Mo Cnj Pi,01:43 pm
10-03-1990,Mo Cnj Ar,05:42 pm
10-05-1990,Mo Cnj Ta,07:06 pm
10-07-1990,Mo Cnj Ge,07:47 pm
10-09-1990,Mo Cnj Ca,09:29 pm
10-12-1990,Mo Cnj Le,01:16 am
10-14-1990,Mo Cnj Vi,07:20 am
10-16-1990,Mo Cnj Li,03:26 pm
10-19-1990,Mo Cnj Sc,01:24 am
10-21-1990,Mo Cnj Sa,01:10 pm
10-24-1990,Mo Cnj Ca,02:03 am
10-26-1990,Mo Cnj Aq,02:14 pm
10-28-1990,Mo Cnj Pi,11:22 pm
10-31-1990,Mo Cnj Ar,04:15 am

November 1990
11-02-1990,Mo Cnj Ta,05:32 am
11-04-1990,Mo Cnj Ge,05:06 am
11-06-1990,Mo Cnj Ca,05:07 am
11-08-1990,Mo Cnj Le,07:24 am
11-10-1990,Mo Cnj Vi,12:48 pm
11-12-1990,Mo Cnj Li,09:09 pm
11-15-1990,Mo Cnj Sc,07:40 am
11-17-1990,Mo Cnj Sa,07:40 pm
11-20-1990,Mo Cnj Ca,08:32 am
11-22-1990,Mo Cnj Aq,09:07 pm
11-25-1990,Mo Cnj Pi,07:32 am
11-27-1990,Mo Cnj Ar,02:06 pm
11-29-1990,Mo Cnj Ta,04:37 pm

December 1990
12-01-1990,Mo Cnj Ge,04:23 pm
12-03-1990,Mo Cnj Ca,03:28 pm
12-05-1990,Mo Cnj Le,04:00 pm
12-07-1990,Mo Cnj Vi,07:39 pm

12-10-1990,Mo Cnj Li,03:01 am
12-12-1990,Mo Cnj Sc,01:28 pm
12-15-1990,Mo Cnj Sa,01:44 am
12-17-1990,Mo Cnj Ca,02:35 pm
12-20-1990,Mo Cnj Aq,02:59 am
12-22-1990,Mo Cnj Pi,01:48 pm
12-24-1990,Mo Cnj Ar,09:45 pm
12-27-1990,Mo Cnj Ta,02:09 am
12-29-1990,Mo Cnj Ge,03:26 am
12-31-1990,Mo Cnj Ca,03:03 am

January 1991
01-02-1991,Mo Cnj Le,02:55 am
01-04-1991,Mo Cnj Vi,04:57 am
01-06-1991,Mo Cnj Li,10:33 am
01-08-1991,Mo Cnj Sc,07:59 pm
01-11-1991,Mo Cnj Sa,08:06 am
01-13-1991,Mo Cnj Ca,09:00 pm
01-16-1991,Mo Cnj Aq,09:05 am
01-18-1991,Mo Cnj Pi,07:24 pm
01-21-1991,Mo Cnj Ar,03:28 am
01-23-1991,Mo Cnj Ta,09:01 am
01-25-1991,Mo Cnj Ge,12:07 pm
01-27-1991,Mo Cnj Ca,01:24 pm
01-29-1991,Mo Cnj Le,02:04 pm
01-31-1991,Mo Cnj Vi,03:44 pm

February 1991
02-02-1991,Mo Cnj Li,08:02 pm
02-05-1991,Mo Cnj Sc,04:01 am
02-07-1991,Mo Cnj Sa,03:23 pm
02-10-1991,Mo Cnj Ca,04:16 am
02-12-1991,Mo Cnj Aq,04:17 pm
02-15-1991,Mo Cnj Pi,02:00 am
02-17-1991,Mo Cnj Ar,09:12 am
02-19-1991,Mo Cnj Ta,02:25 pm
02-21-1991,Mo Cnj Ge,06:11 pm
02-23-1991,Mo Cnj Ca,08:57 pm
02-25-1991,Mo Cnj Le,11:13 pm
02-28-1991,Mo Cnj Vi,01:50 am

March 1991
03-02-1991,Mo Cnj Li,06:03 am
03-04-1991,Mo Cnj Sc,01:08 pm
03-06-1991,Mo Cnj Sa,11:36 pm
03-09-1991,Mo Cnj Ca,12:15 pm
03-12-1991,Mo Cnj Aq,00:31 am

03-14-1991,Mo Cnj Pi,10:11 am
03-16-1991,Mo Cnj Ar,04:38 pm
03-18-1991,Mo Cnj Ta,08:41 pm
03-20-1991,Mo Cnj Ge,11:37 pm
03-23-1991,Mo Cnj Ca,02:27 am
03-25-1991,Mo Cnj Le,05:44 am
03-27-1991,Mo Cnj Vi,09:41 am
03-29-1991,Mo Cnj Li,02:50 pm
03-31-1991,Mo Cnj Sc,10:02 pm

April 1991
04-03-1991,Mo Cnj Sa,08:00 am
04-05-1991,Mo Cnj Ca,08:20 pm
04-08-1991,Mo Cnj Aq,09:00 am
04-10-1991,Mo Cnj Pi,07:17 pm
04-13-1991,Mo Cnj Ar,01:50 am
04-15-1991,Mo Cnj Ta,05:06 am
04-17-1991,Mo Cnj Ge,06:41 am
04-19-1991,Mo Cnj Ca,08:18 am
04-21-1991,Mo Cnj Le,11:05 am
04-23-1991,Mo Cnj Vi,03:30 pm
04-25-1991,Mo Cnj Li,09:37 pm
04-28-1991,Mo Cnj Sc,05:35 am
04-30-1991,Mo Cnj Sa,03:42 pm

May 1991
05-03-1991,Mo Cnj Ca,03:55 am
05-05-1991,Mo Cnj Aq,04:51 pm
05-08-1991,Mo Cnj Pi,04:04 am
05-10-1991,Mo Cnj Ar,11:35 am
05-12-1991,Mo Cnj Ta,03:08 pm
05-14-1991,Mo Cnj Ge,04:03 pm
05-16-1991,Mo Cnj Ca,04:15 pm
05-18-1991,Mo Cnj Le,05:31 pm
05-20-1991,Mo Cnj Vi,09:01 pm
05-23-1991,Mo Cnj Li,03:08 am
05-25-1991,Mo Cnj Sc,11:42 am
05-27-1991,Mo Cnj Sa,10:21 pm
05-30-1991,Mo Cnj Ca,10:40 am

June 1991
06-01-1991,Mo Cnj Aq,11:42 pm
06-04-1991,Mo Cnj Pi,11:37 am
06-06-1991,Mo Cnj Ar,08:26 pm
06-09-1991,Mo Cnj Ta,01:13 am
06-11-1991,Mo Cnj Ge,02:37 am
06-13-1991,Mo Cnj Ca,02:17 am

06-15-1991,Mo Cnj Le,02:11 am
06-17-1991,Mo Cnj Vi,04:03 am
06-19-1991,Mo Cnj Li,09:01 am
06-21-1991,Mo Cnj Sc,05:18 pm
06-24-1991,Mo Cnj Sa,04:16 am
06-26-1991,Mo Cnj Ca,04:50 pm
06-29-1991,Mo Cnj Aq,05:48 am

July 1991
07-01-1991,Mo Cnj Pi,05:52 pm
07-04-1991,Mo Cnj Ar,03:34 am
07-06-1991,Mo Cnj Ta,09:53 am
07-08-1991,Mo Cnj Ge,12:42 pm
07-10-1991,Mo Cnj Ca,01:03 pm
07-12-1991,Mo Cnj Le,12:35 pm
07-14-1991,Mo Cnj Vi,01:11 pm
07-16-1991,Mo Cnj Li,04:34 pm
07-18-1991,Mo Cnj Sc,11:41 pm
07-21-1991,Mo Cnj Sa,10:17 am
07-23-1991,Mo Cnj Ca,10:56 pm
07-26-1991,Mo Cnj Aq,11:50 am
07-28-1991,Mo Cnj Pi,11:35 pm
07-31-1991,Mo Cnj Ar,09:20 am

August 1991
08-02-1991,Mo Cnj Ta,04:32 pm
08-04-1991,Mo Cnj Ge,08:54 pm
08-06-1991,Mo Cnj Ca,10:47 pm
08-08-1991,Mo Cnj Le,11:09 pm
08-10-1991,Mo Cnj Vi,11:35 pm
08-13-1991,Mo Cnj Li,01:52 am
08-15-1991,Mo Cnj Sc,07:34 am
08-17-1991,Mo Cnj Sa,05:11 pm
08-20-1991,Mo Cnj Ca,05:35 am
08-22-1991,Mo Cnj Aq,06:27 pm
08-25-1991,Mo Cnj Pi,05:51 am
08-27-1991,Mo Cnj Ar,03:01 pm
08-29-1991,Mo Cnj Ta,10:00 pm

September 1991
09-01-1991,Mo Cnj Ge,03:02 am
09-03-1991,Mo Cnj Ca,06:20 am
09-05-1991,Mo Cnj Le,08:14 am
09-07-1991,Mo Cnj Vi,09:36 am
09-09-1991,Mo Cnj Li,11:52 am
09-11-1991,Mo Cnj Sc,04:43 pm
09-14-1991,Mo Cnj Sa,01:15 am

09-16-1991,Mo Cnj Ca,01:03 pm
09-19-1991,Mo Cnj Aq,01:57 am
09-21-1991,Mo Cnj Pi,01:20 pm
09-23-1991,Mo Cnj Ar,09:55 am
09-26-1991,Mo Cnj Ta,03:59 am
09-28-1991,Mo Cnj Ge,08:26 am
09-30-1991,Mo Cnj Ca,11:59 am

October 1991
10-02-1991,Mo Cnj Le,02:59 pm
10-04-1991,Mo Cnj Vi,05:45 pm
10-06-1991,Mo Cnj Li,09:01 pm
10-09-1991,Mo Cnj Sc,02:00 am
10-11-1991,Mo Cnj Sa,09:58 am
10-13-1991,Mo Cnj Ca,09:10 pm
10-16-1991,Mo Cnj Aq,10:04 am
10-18-1991,Mo Cnj Pi,09:53 pm
10-21-1991,Mo Cnj Ar,06:34 am
10-23-1991,Mo Cnj Ta,11:56 am
10-25-1991,Mo Cnj Ge,03:09 pm
10-27-1991,Mo Cnj Ca,05:37 pm
10-29-1991,Mo Cnj Le,08:21 pm
10-31-1991,Mo Cnj Vi,11:47 pm

November 1991
11-03-1991,Mo Cnj Li,04:12 am
11-05-1991,Mo Cnj Sc,10:08 am
11-07-1991,Mo Cnj Sa,06:21 pm
11-10-1991,Mo Cnj Ca,05:16 am
11-12-1991,Mo Cnj Aq,06:07 pm
11-15-1991,Mo Cnj Pi,06:34 am
11-17-1991,Mo Cnj Ar,04:08 pm
11-19-1991,Mo Cnj Ta,09:50 pm
11-22-1991,Mo Cnj Ge,00:23 am
11-24-1991,Mo Cnj Ca,01:25 am
11-26-1991,Mo Cnj Le,02:37 am
11-28-1991,Mo Cnj Vi,05:12 am
11-30-1991,Mo Cnj Li,09:47 am

December 1991
12-02-1991,Mo Cnj Sc,04:33 pm
12-05-1991,Mo Cnj Sa,01:33 am
12-07-1991,Mo Cnj Ca,12:42 pm
12-10-1991,Mo Cnj Aq,01:27 am
12-12-1991,Mo Cnj Pi,02:20 pm
12-15-1991,Mo Cnj Ar,01:07 am
12-17-1991,Mo Cnj Ta,08:10 am

12-19-1991,Mo Cnj Ge,11:22 am
12-21-1991,Mo Cnj Ca,11:55 am
12-23-1991,Mo Cnj Le,11:39 am
12-25-1991,Mo Cnj Vi,12:24 pm
12-27-1991,Mo Cnj Li,03:38 pm
12-29-1991,Mo Cnj Sc,10:04 pm

January 1992
01-01-1992,Mo Cnj Sa,07:31 am
01-03-1992,Mo Cnj Ca,07:10 pm
01-06-1992,Mo Cnj Aq,07:59 am
01-08-1992,Mo Cnj Pi,08:52 pm
01-11-1992,Mo Cnj Ar,08:22 am
01-13-1992,Mo Cnj Ta,05:00 pm
01-15-1992,Mo Cnj Ge,09:55 pm
01-17-1992,Mo Cnj Ca,11:26 pm
01-19-1992,Mo Cnj Le,10:57 pm
01-21-1992,Mo Cnj Vi,10:23 pm
01-23-1992,Mo Cnj Li,11:43 pm
01-26-1992,Mo Cnj Sc,04:33 am
01-28-1992,Mo Cnj Sa,01:20 pm
01-31-1992,Mo Cnj Ca,01:08 am

February 1992
02-02-1992,Mo Cnj Aq,02:09 pm
02-05-1992,Mo Cnj Pi,02:51 am
02-07-1992,Mo Cnj Ar,02:15 pm
02-09-1992,Mo Cnj Ta,11:36 pm
02-12-1992,Mo Cnj Ge,06:09 am
02-14-1992,Mo Cnj Ca,09:32 am
02-16-1992,Mo Cnj Le,10:16 am
02-18-1992,Mo Cnj Vi,09:47 am
02-20-1992,Mo Cnj Li,10:05 am
02-22-1992,Mo Cnj Sc,01:11 pm
02-24-1992,Mo Cnj Sa,08:26 pm
02-27-1992,Mo Cnj Ca,07:33 am
02-29-1992,Mo Cnj Aq,08:34 pm

March 1992
03-03-1992,Mo Cnj Pi,09:11 am
03-05-1992,Mo Cnj Ar,08:07 pm
03-08-1992,Mo Cnj Ta,05:06 am
03-10-1992,Mo Cnj Ge,12:04 pm
03-12-1992,Mo Cnj Ca,04:50 pm
03-14-1992,Mo Cnj Le,07:21 pm
03-16-1992,Mo Cnj Vi,08:14 pm
03-18-1992,Mo Cnj Li,08:55 pm

03-20-1992,Mo Cnj Sc,11:20 pm
03-23-1992,Mo Cnj Sa,05:13 am
03-25-1992,Mo Cnj Ca,03:09 pm
03-28-1992,Mo Cnj Aq,03:45 am
03-30-1992,Mo Cnj Pi,04:24 pm

April 1992
04-02-1992,Mo Cnj Ar,03:05 am
04-04-1992,Mo Cnj Ta,11:19 am
04-06-1992,Mo Cnj Ge,05:33 pm
04-08-1992,Mo Cnj Ca,10:19 pm
04-11-1992,Mo Cnj Le,01:46 am
04-13-1992,Mo Cnj Vi,04:09 am
04-15-1992,Mo Cnj Li,06:11 am
04-17-1992,Mo Cnj Sc,09:10 am
04-19-1992,Mo Cnj Sa,02:41 pm
04-21-1992,Mo Cnj Ca,11:41 pm
04-24-1992,Mo Cnj Aq,11:39 am
04-27-1992,Mo Cnj Pi,00:20 am
04-29-1992,Mo Cnj Ar,11:14 am

May 1992
05-01-1992,Mo Cnj Ta,07:10 pm
05-04-1992,Mo Cnj Ge,00:28 am
05-06-1992,Mo Cnj Ca,04:10 am
05-08-1992,Mo Cnj Le,07:07 am
05-10-1992,Mo Cnj Vi,09:56 am
05-12-1992,Mo Cnj Li,01:06 pm
05-14-1992,Mo Cnj Sc,05:16 pm
05-16-1992,Mo Cnj Sa,11:23 pm
05-19-1992,Mo Cnj Ca,08:13 am
05-21-1992,Mo Cnj Aq,07:44 pm
05-24-1992,Mo Cnj Pi,08:25 am
05-26-1992,Mo Cnj Ar,07:52 pm
05-29-1992,Mo Cnj Ta,04:16 am
05-31-1992,Mo Cnj Ge,09:19 am

June 1992
06-02-1992,Mo Cnj Ca,11:58 am
06-04-1992,Mo Cnj Le,01:35 pm
06-06-1992,Mo Cnj Vi,03:28 pm
06-08-1992,Mo Cnj Li,06:34 pm
06-10-1992,Mo Cnj Sc,11:27 pm
06-13-1992,Mo Cnj Sa,06:29 am
06-15-1992,Mo Cnj Ca,03:50 pm
06-18-1992,Mo Cnj Aq,03:19 am
06-20-1992,Mo Cnj Pi,03:59 pm

06-23-1992,Mo Cnj Ar,04:03 am
06-25-1992,Mo Cnj Ta,01:29 pm
06-27-1992,Mo Cnj Ge,07:14 pm
06-29-1992,Mo Cnj Ca,09:43 pm

July 1992
07-01-1992,Mo Cnj Le,10:16 pm
07-03-1992,Mo Cnj Vi,10:38 pm
07-06-1992,Mo Cnj Li,00:28 am
07-08-1992,Mo Cnj Sc,04:54 am
07-10-1992,Mo Cnj Sa,12:17 pm
07-12-1992,Mo Cnj Ca,10:15 pm
07-15-1992,Mo Cnj Aq,10:03 am
07-17-1992,Mo Cnj Pi,10:44 pm
07-20-1992,Mo Cnj Ar,11:08 am
07-22-1992,Mo Cnj Ta,09:37 pm
07-25-1992,Mo Cnj Ge,04:45 am
07-27-1992,Mo Cnj Ca,08:09 am
07-29-1992,Mo Cnj Le,08:40 am
07-31-1992,Mo Cnj Vi,08:01 am

August 1992
08-02-1992,Mo Cnj Li,08:17 am
08-04-1992,Mo Cnj Sc,11:16 am
08-06-1992,Mo Cnj Sa,05:57 pm
08-09-1992,Mo Cnj Ca,04:00 am
08-11-1992,Mo Cnj Aq,04:07 pm
08-14-1992,Mo Cnj Pi,04:52 am
08-16-1992,Mo Cnj Ar,05:12 am
08-19-1992,Mo Cnj Ta,04:10 am
08-21-1992,Mo Cnj Ge,12:37 pm
08-23-1992,Mo Cnj Ca,05:37 pm
08-25-1992,Mo Cnj Le,07:15 pm
08-27-1992,Mo Cnj Vi,06:46 pm
08-29-1992,Mo Cnj Li,06:10 pm
08-31-1992,Mo Cnj Sc,07:38 pm

September 1992
09-03-1992,Mo Cnj Sa,00:50 am
09-05-1992,Mo Cnj Ca,10:07 am
09-07-1992,Mo Cnj Aq,10:09 pm
09-10-1992,Mo Cnj Pi,10:57 am
09-12-1992,Mo Cnj Ar,11:02 am
09-15-1992,Mo Cnj Ta,09:47 am
09-17-1992,Mo Cnj Ge,06:40 pm
09-20-1992,Mo Cnj Ca,00:59 am
09-22-1992,Mo Cnj Le,04:19 am

09-24-1992,Mo Cnj Vi,05:08 am
09-26-1992,Mo Cnj Li,04:56 am
09-28-1992,Mo Cnj Sc,05:44 am
09-30-1992,Mo Cnj Sa,09:34 am

October 1992
10-02-1992,Mo Cnj Ca,05:30 pm
10-05-1992,Mo Cnj Aq,04:53 am
10-07-1992,Mo Cnj Pi,05:38 pm
10-10-1992,Mo Cnj Ar,05:36 am
10-12-1992,Mo Cnj Ta,03:48 pm
10-15-1992,Mo Cnj Ge,00:08 am
10-17-1992,Mo Cnj Ca,06:36 am
10-19-1992,Mo Cnj Le,11:02 am
10-21-1992,Mo Cnj Vi,01:28 pm
10-23-1992,Mo Cnj Li,02:40 pm
10-25-1992,Mo Cnj Sc,04:05 pm
10-27-1992,Mo Cnj Sa,07:29 pm
10-30-1992,Mo Cnj Ca,02:18 am

November 1992
11-01-1992,Mo Cnj Aq,12:43 pm
11-04-1992,Mo Cnj Pi,01:12 am
11-06-1992,Mo Cnj Ar,01:19 pm
11-08-1992,Mo Cnj Ta,11:19 pm
11-11-1992,Mo Cnj Ge,06:50 am
11-13-1992,Mo Cnj Ca,12:20 pm
11-15-1992,Mo Cnj Le,04:24 pm
11-17-1992,Mo Cnj Vi,07:29 pm
11-19-1992,Mo Cnj Li,10:03 pm
11-22-1992,Mo Cnj Sc,00:52 am
11-24-1992,Mo Cnj Sa,05:01 am
11-26-1992,Mo Cnj Ca,11:38 am
11-28-1992,Mo Cnj Aq,09:19 pm

December 1992
12-01-1992,Mo Cnj Pi,09:23 am
12-03-1992,Mo Cnj Ar,09:49 pm
12-06-1992,Mo Cnj Ta,08:17 am
12-08-1992,Mo Cnj Ge,03:38 pm
12-10-1992,Mo Cnj Ca,08:06 pm
12-12-1992,Mo Cnj Le,10:48 pm
12-15-1992,Mo Cnj Vi,00:56 am
12-17-1992,Mo Cnj Li,03:33 am
12-19-1992,Mo Cnj Sc,07:19 am
12-21-1992,Mo Cnj Sa,12:42 pm
12-23-1992,Mo Cnj Ca,08:04 pm

12-26-1992,Mo Cnj Aq,05:43 am
12-28-1992,Mo Cnj Pi,05:29 pm
12-31-1992,Mo Cnj Ar,06:08 am

January 1993
01-02-1993,Mo Cnj Ta,05:31 pm
01-05-1993,Mo Cnj Ge,01:43 am
01-07-1993,Mo Cnj Ca,06:11 am
01-09-1993,Mo Cnj Le,07:49 am
01-11-1993,Mo Cnj Vi,08:20 am
01-13-1993,Mo Cnj Li,09:30 am
01-15-1993,Mo Cnj Sc,12:42 pm
01-17-1993,Mo Cnj Sa,06:31 pm
01-20-1993,Mo Cnj Ca,02:47 am
01-22-1993,Mo Cnj Aq,01:01 pm
01-25-1993,Mo Cnj Pi,00:48 am
01-27-1993,Mo Cnj Ar,01:28 am
01-30-1993,Mo Cnj Ta,01:37 am

February 1993
02-01-1993,Mo Cnj Ge,11:15 am
02-03-1993,Mo Cnj Ca,04:57 pm
02-05-1993,Mo Cnj Le,06:51 pm
02-07-1993,Mo Cnj Vi,06:29 pm
02-09-1993,Mo Cnj Li,05:59 pm
02-11-1993,Mo Cnj Sc,07:24 pm
02-14-1993,Mo Cnj Sa,00:08 am
02-16-1993,Mo Cnj Ca,08:21 am
02-18-1993,Mo Cnj Aq,07:06 pm
02-21-1993,Mo Cnj Pi,07:12 am
02-23-1993,Mo Cnj Ar,07:50 pm
02-26-1993,Mo Cnj Ta,08:11 am
02-28-1993,Mo Cnj Ge,06:52 pm

March 1993
03-03-1993,Mo Cnj Ca,02:17 am
03-05-1993,Mo Cnj Le,05:41 am
03-07-1993,Mo Cnj Vi,05:53 am
03-09-1993,Mo Cnj Li,04:47 am
03-11-1993,Mo Cnj Sc,04:40 am
03-13-1993,Mo Cnj Sa,07:34 am
03-15-1993,Mo Cnj Ca,02:28 pm
03-18-1993,Mo Cnj Aq,00:52 am
03-20-1993,Mo Cnj Pi,01:11 pm
03-23-1993,Mo Cnj Ar,01:51 am
03-25-1993,Mo Cnj Ta,01:59 pm

03-28-1993,Mo Cnj Ge,00:48 am
03-30-1993,Mo Cnj Ca,09:15 am

April 1993
04-01-1993,Mo Cnj Le,02:22 pm
04-03-1993,Mo Cnj Vi,04:11 pm
04-05-1993,Mo Cnj Li,03:55 pm
04-07-1993,Mo Cnj Sc,03:32 pm
04-09-1993,Mo Cnj Sa,05:10 pm
04-11-1993,Mo Cnj Ca,10:24 pm
04-14-1993,Mo Cnj Aq,07:36 am
04-16-1993,Mo Cnj Pi,07:33 pm
04-19-1993,Mo Cnj Ar,08:15 am
04-21-1993,Mo Cnj Ta,08:08 pm
04-24-1993,Mo Cnj Ge,06:28 am
04-26-1993,Mo Cnj Ca,02:46 pm
04-28-1993,Mo Cnj Le,08:40 pm

May 1993
05-01-1993,Mo Cnj Vi,00:00 am
05-03-1993,Mo Cnj Li,01:20 am
05-05-1993,Mo Cnj Sc,01:57 am
05-07-1993,Mo Cnj Sa,03:35 am
05-09-1993,Mo Cnj Ca,07:51 am
05-11-1993,Mo Cnj Aq,03:44 pm
05-14-1993,Mo Cnj Pi,02:51 am
05-16-1993,Mo Cnj Ar,03:25 pm
05-19-1993,Mo Cnj Ta,03:17 am
05-21-1993,Mo Cnj Ge,01:08 pm
05-23-1993,Mo Cnj Ca,08:39 pm
05-26-1993,Mo Cnj Le,02:03 am
05-28-1993,Mo Cnj Vi,05:46 am
05-30-1993,Mo Cnj Li,08:18 am

June 1993
06-05-1993,Mo Cnj Ca,05:27 pm
06-08-1993,Mo Cnj Aq,00:40 am
06-10-1993,Mo Cnj Pi,10:57 am
06-12-1993,Mo Cnj Ar,11:14 pm
06-15-1993,Mo Cnj Ta,11:20 am
06-17-1993,Mo Cnj Ge,09:12 pm
06-20-1993,Mo Cnj Ca,04:05 am
06-22-1993,Mo Cnj Le,08:26 am
06-24-1993,Mo Cnj Vi,11:18 am
06-26-1993,Mo Cnj Li,01:46 pm
06-28-1993,Mo Cnj Sc,04:38 pm
06-30-1993,Mo Cnj Sa,08:29 pm

July 1993
07-03-1993,Mo Cnj Ca,01:49 am
07-05-1993,Mo Cnj Aq,09:15 am
07-07-1993,Mo Cnj Pi,07:10 pm
07-10-1993,Mo Cnj Ar,07:11 am
07-12-1993,Mo Cnj Ta,07:37 pm
07-15-1993,Mo Cnj Ge,06:06 am
07-17-1993,Mo Cnj Ca,01:08 pm
07-19-1993,Mo Cnj Le,04:48 pm
07-21-1993,Mo Cnj Vi,06:24 pm
07-23-1993,Mo Cnj Li,07:40 pm
07-25-1993,Mo Cnj Sc,10:01 pm
07-28-1993,Mo Cnj Sa,02:13 am
07-30-1993,Mo Cnj Ca,08:27 am

August 1993
08-01-1993,Mo Cnj Aq,04:36 pm
08-04-1993,Mo Cnj Pi,02:43 am
08-06-1993,Mo Cnj Ar,02:39 pm
08-09-1993,Mo Cnj Ta,03:23 am
08-11-1993,Mo Cnj Ge,02:47 pm
08-13-1993,Mo Cnj Ca,10:47 pm
08-16-1993,Mo Cnj Le,02:44 am
08-18-1993,Mo Cnj Vi,03:41 am
08-20-1993,Mo Cnj Li,03:36 am
08-22-1993,Mo Cnj Sc,04:28 am
08-24-1993,Mo Cnj Sa,07:45 am
08-26-1993,Mo Cnj Ca,01:58 pm
08-28-1993,Mo Cnj Aq,10:41 pm
08-31-1993,Mo Cnj Pi,09:18 am

September 1993
09-02-1993,Mo Cnj Ar,09:21 pm
09-05-1993,Mo Cnj Ta,10:10 am
09-07-1993,Mo Cnj Ge,10:17 pm
09-10-1993,Mo Cnj Ca,07:37 am
09-12-1993,Mo Cnj Le,12:52 pm
09-14-1993,Mo Cnj Vi,02:20 pm
09-16-1993,Mo Cnj Li,01:44 pm
09-18-1993,Mo Cnj Sc,01:14 pm
09-20-1993,Mo Cnj Sa,02:53 pm
09-22-1993,Mo Cnj Ca,07:54 pm
09-25-1993,Mo Cnj Aq,04:19 am
09-27-1993,Mo Cnj Pi,03:13 pm
09-30-1993,Mo Cnj Ar,03:29 am

October 1993
10-02-1993,Mo Cnj Ta,04:14 pm
10-05-1993,Mo Cnj Ge,04:27 am
10-07-1993,Mo Cnj Ca,02:43 pm
10-09-1993,Mo Cnj Le,09:34 pm
10-12-1993,Mo Cnj Vi,00:36 am
10-14-1993,Mo Cnj Li,00:47 am
10-16-1993,Mo Cnj Sc,00:01 am
10-18-1993,Mo Cnj Sa,00:23 am
10-20-1993,Mo Cnj Ca,03:42 am
10-22-1993,Mo Cnj Aq,10:50 am
10-24-1993,Mo Cnj Pi,09:18 pm
10-27-1993,Mo Cnj Ar,09:40 am
10-29-1993,Mo Cnj Ta,10:20 pm

November 1993
11-01-1993,Mo Cnj Ge,10:13 am
11-03-1993,Mo Cnj Ca,08:25 pm
11-06-1993,Mo Cnj Le,04:06 am
11-08-1993,Mo Cnj Vi,08:47 am
11-10-1993,Mo Cnj Li,10:43 am
11-12-1993,Mo Cnj Sc,11:00 am
11-14-1993,Mo Cnj Sa,11:21 am
11-16-1993,Mo Cnj Ca,01:35 pm
11-18-1993,Mo Cnj Aq,07:08 pm
11-21-1993,Mo Cnj Pi,04:28 am
11-23-1993,Mo Cnj Ar,04:30 pm
11-26-1993,Mo Cnj Ta,05:14 am
11-28-1993,Mo Cnj Ge,04:48 pm

December 1993
12-01-1993,Mo Cnj Ca,02:17 am
12-03-1993,Mo Cnj Le,09:33 am
12-05-1993,Mo Cnj Vi,02:44 pm
12-07-1993,Mo Cnj Li,06:04 pm
12-09-1993,Mo Cnj Sc,08:05 pm
12-11-1993,Mo Cnj Sa,09:40 pm
12-14-1993,Mo Cnj Ca,00:06 am
12-16-1993,Mo Cnj Aq,04:51 am
12-18-1993,Mo Cnj Pi,12:59 pm
12-21-1993,Mo Cnj Ar,00:19 am
12-23-1993,Mo Cnj Ta,01:04 pm
12-26-1993,Mo Cnj Ge,00:46 am
12-28-1993,Mo Cnj Ca,09:47 am
12-30-1993,Mo Cnj Le,04:00 pm

January 1994
01-01-1994,Mo Cnj Vi,08:15 pm
01-03-1994,Mo Cnj Li,11:31 pm
01-06-1994,Mo Cnj Sc,02:29 am
01-08-1994,Mo Cnj Sa,05:34 am
01-10-1994,Mo Cnj Ca,09:16 am
01-12-1994,Mo Cnj Aq,02:25 pm
01-14-1994,Mo Cnj Pi,10:04 pm
01-17-1994,Mo Cnj Ar,08:42 am
01-19-1994,Mo Cnj Ta,09:23 pm
01-22-1994,Mo Cnj Ge,09:35 am
01-24-1994,Mo Cnj Ca,06:56 pm
01-27-1994,Mo Cnj Le,00:39 am
01-29-1994,Mo Cnj Vi,03:39 am
01-31-1994,Mo Cnj Li,05:34 am

February 1994
02-02-1994,Mo Cnj Sc,07:49 am
02-04-1994,Mo Cnj Sa,11:14 am
02-06-1994,Mo Cnj Ca,04:02 pm
02-08-1994,Mo Cnj Aq,10:17 pm
02-11-1994,Mo Cnj Pi,06:23 am
02-13-1994,Mo Cnj Ar,04:50 pm
02-16-1994,Mo Cnj Ta,05:21 am
02-18-1994,Mo Cnj Ge,06:06 pm
02-21-1994,Mo Cnj Ca,04:28 am
02-23-1994,Mo Cnj Le,10:48 am
02-25-1994,Mo Cnj Vi,01:27 pm
02-27-1994,Mo Cnj Li,02:06 pm

March 1994
03-01-1994,Mo Cnj Sc,02:43 pm
03-03-1994,Mo Cnj Sa,04:54 pm
03-05-1994,Mo Cnj Ca,09:25 pm
03-08-1994,Mo Cnj Aq,04:16 am
03-10-1994,Mo Cnj Pi,01:10 pm
03-12-1994,Mo Cnj Ar,11:59 pm
03-15-1994,Mo Cnj Ta,12:28 pm
03-18-1994,Mo Cnj Ge,01:29 am
03-20-1994,Mo Cnj Ca,12:54 pm
03-22-1994,Mo Cnj Le,08:39 pm
03-25-1994,Mo Cnj Vi,00:14 am
03-27-1994,Mo Cnj Li,00:47 am
03-29-1994,Mo Cnj Sc,00:15 am
03-31-1994,Mo Cnj Sa,00:42 am

April 1994
04-02-1994,Mo Cnj Ca,03:38 am
04-04-1994,Mo Cnj Aq,09:46 am
04-06-1994,Mo Cnj Pi,06:51 pm
04-09-1994,Mo Cnj Ar,06:09 am
04-11-1994,Mo Cnj Ta,06:47 pm
04-14-1994,Mo Cnj Ge,07:48 am
04-16-1994,Mo Cnj Ca,07:41 pm
04-19-1994,Mo Cnj Le,04:45 am
04-21-1994,Mo Cnj Vi,09:59 am
04-23-1994,Mo Cnj Li,11:41 am
04-25-1994,Mo Cnj Sc,11:19 am
04-27-1994,Mo Cnj Sa,10:49 am
04-29-1994,Mo Cnj Ca,12:05 pm

May 1994
05-01-1994,Mo Cnj Aq,04:35 pm
05-04-1994,Mo Cnj Pi,00:47 am
05-06-1994,Mo Cnj Ar,12:01 pm
05-09-1994,Mo Cnj Ta,00:50 am
05-11-1994,Mo Cnj Ge,01:44 pm
05-14-1994,Mo Cnj Ca,01:28 am
05-16-1994,Mo Cnj Le,10:59 am
05-18-1994,Mo Cnj Vi,05:32 pm
05-20-1994,Mo Cnj Li,08:55 pm
05-22-1994,Mo Cnj Sc,09:51 pm
05-24-1994,Mo Cnj Sa,09:43 pm
05-26-1994,Mo Cnj Ca,10:17 pm
05-29-1994,Mo Cnj Aq,01:19 am
05-31-1994,Mo Cnj Pi,08:03 am

June 1994
06-02-1994,Mo Cnj Ar,06:31 pm
06-05-1994,Mo Cnj Ta,07:15 am
06-07-1994,Mo Cnj Ge,08:04 pm
06-10-1994,Mo Cnj Ca,07:23 am
06-12-1994,Mo Cnj Le,04:30 pm
06-14-1994,Mo Cnj Vi,11:17 pm
06-17-1994,Mo Cnj Li,03:48 am
06-19-1994,Mo Cnj Sc,06:20 am
06-21-1994,Mo Cnj Sa,07:32 am
06-23-1994,Mo Cnj Ca,08:37 am
06-25-1994,Mo Cnj Aq,11:10 am
06-27-1994,Mo Cnj Pi,04:45 pm
06-30-1994,Mo Cnj Ar,02:07 am

July 1994
07-02-1994,Mo Cnj Ta,02:24 pm
07-05-1994,Mo Cnj Ge,03:13 am
07-07-1994,Mo Cnj Ca,02:18 pm
07-09-1994,Mo Cnj Le,10:44 pm
07-12-1994,Mo Cnj Vi,04:48 am
07-14-1994,Mo Cnj Li,09:15 am
07-16-1994,Mo Cnj Sc,12:35 pm
07-18-1994,Mo Cnj Sa,03:10 pm
07-20-1994,Mo Cnj Ca,05:31 pm
07-22-1994,Mo Cnj Aq,08:39 pm
07-25-1994,Mo Cnj Pi,01:57 am
07-27-1994,Mo Cnj Ar,10:31 am
07-29-1994,Mo Cnj Ta,10:13 pm

August 1994
08-01-1994,Mo Cnj Ge,11:05 am
08-03-1994,Mo Cnj Ca,10:22 pm
08-06-1994,Mo Cnj Le,06:31 am
08-08-1994,Mo Cnj Vi,11:42 am
08-10-1994,Mo Cnj Li,03:07 pm
08-12-1994,Mo Cnj Sc,05:56 pm
08-14-1994,Mo Cnj Sa,08:54 pm
08-17-1994,Mo Cnj Ca,00:19 am
08-19-1994,Mo Cnj Aq,04:34 am
08-21-1994,Mo Cnj Pi,10:28 am
08-23-1994,Mo Cnj Ar,06:55 pm
08-26-1994,Mo Cnj Ta,06:13 am
08-28-1994,Mo Cnj Ge,07:07 pm
08-31-1994,Mo Cnj Ca,07:00 am

September 1994
09-02-1994,Mo Cnj Le,03:37 pm
09-04-1994,Mo Cnj Vi,08:34 pm
09-06-1994,Mo Cnj Li,10:57 pm
09-09-1994,Mo Cnj Sc,00:26 am
09-11-1994,Mo Cnj Sa,02:26 am
09-13-1994,Mo Cnj Ca,05:45 am
09-15-1994,Mo Cnj Aq,10:43 am
09-17-1994,Mo Cnj Pi,05:31 pm
09-20-1994,Mo Cnj Ar,02:29 am
09-22-1994,Mo Cnj Ta,01:47 pm
09-25-1994,Mo Cnj Ge,02:42 am
09-27-1994,Mo Cnj Ca,03:12 pm
09-30-1994,Mo Cnj Le,00:56 am

October 1994

10-02-1994,Mo Cnj Vi,06:40 am
10-04-1994,Mo Cnj Li,08:57 am
10-06-1994,Mo Cnj Sc,09:22 am
10-08-1994,Mo Cnj Sa,09:47 am
10-10-1994,Mo Cnj Ca,11:44 am
10-12-1994,Mo Cnj Aq,04:09 pm
10-14-1994,Mo Cnj Pi,11:18 pm
10-17-1994,Mo Cnj Ar,08:56 am
10-19-1994,Mo Cnj Ta,08:35 pm
10-22-1994,Mo Cnj Ge,09:28 am
10-24-1994,Mo Cnj Ca,10:16 pm
10-27-1994,Mo Cnj Le,09:05 am
10-29-1994,Mo Cnj Vi,04:22 pm
10-31-1994,Mo Cnj Li,07:46 pm

November 1994

11-02-1994,Mo Cnj Sc,08:19 pm
11-04-1994,Mo Cnj Sa,07:46 pm
11-06-1994,Mo Cnj Ca,08:01 pm
11-08-1994,Mo Cnj Aq,10:48 pm
11-11-1994,Mo Cnj Pi,05:04 am
11-13-1994,Mo Cnj Ar,02:44 pm
11-16-1994,Mo Cnj Ta,02:45 am
11-18-1994,Mo Cnj Ge,03:42 pm
11-21-1994,Mo Cnj Ca,04:21 am
11-23-1994,Mo Cnj Le,03:33 pm
11-26-1994,Mo Cnj Vi,00:09 am
11-28-1994,Mo Cnj Li,05:22 am
11-30-1994,Mo Cnj Sc,07:22 am

December 1994

12-02-1994,Mo Cnj Sa,07:13 am
12-04-1994,Mo Cnj Ca,06:43 am
12-06-1994,Mo Cnj Aq,07:52 am
12-08-1994,Mo Cnj Pi,12:25 pm
12-10-1994,Mo Cnj Ar,09:04 pm
12-13-1994,Mo Cnj Ta,08:56 am
12-15-1994,Mo Cnj Ge,10:00 pm
12-18-1994,Mo Cnj Ca,10:25 am
12-20-1994,Mo Cnj Le,09:13 pm
12-23-1994,Mo Cnj Vi,06:01 am
12-25-1994,Mo Cnj Li,12:28 pm
12-27-1994,Mo Cnj Sc,04:18 pm
12-29-1994,Mo Cnj Sa,05:46 pm
12-31-1994,Mo Cnj Ca,05:58 pm

January 1995

01-02-1995,Mo Cnj Aq,06:39 pm
01-04-1995,Mo Cnj Pi,09:49 pm
01-07-1995,Mo Cnj Ar,04:57 am
01-09-1995,Mo Cnj Ta,03:58 pm
01-12-1995,Mo Cnj Ge,04:57 am
01-14-1995,Mo Cnj Ca,05:20 pm
01-17-1995,Mo Cnj Le,03:37 am
01-19-1995,Mo Cnj Vi,11:40 am
01-21-1995,Mo Cnj Li,05:54 pm
01-23-1995,Mo Cnj Sc,10:33 pm
01-26-1995,Mo Cnj Sa,01:37 am
01-28-1995,Mo Cnj Ca,03:27 am
01-30-1995,Mo Cnj Aq,05:03 am

February 1995

02-01-1995,Mo Cnj Pi,08:05 am
02-03-1995,Mo Cnj Ar,02:12 pm
02-06-1995,Mo Cnj Ta,00:09 am
02-08-1995,Mo Cnj Ge,12:44 pm
02-11-1995,Mo Cnj Ca,01:17 am
02-13-1995,Mo Cnj Le,11:32 am
02-15-1995,Mo Cnj Vi,06:52 pm
02-18-1995,Mo Cnj Li,00:01 am
02-20-1995,Mo Cnj Sc,03:55 am
02-22-1995,Mo Cnj Sa,07:13 am
02-24-1995,Mo Cnj Ca,10:11 am
02-26-1995,Mo Cnj Aq,01:14 pm
02-28-1995,Mo Cnj Pi,05:16 pm

March 1995

03-02-1995,Mo Cnj Ar,11:30 pm
03-05-1995,Mo Cnj Ta,08:51 am
03-07-1995,Mo Cnj Ge,08:56 pm
03-10-1995,Mo Cnj Ca,09:41 am
03-12-1995,Mo Cnj Le,08:29 pm
03-15-1995,Mo Cnj Vi,03:55 am
03-17-1995,Mo Cnj Li,08:18 am
03-19-1995,Mo Cnj Sc,10:52 am
03-21-1995,Mo Cnj Sa,12:57 pm
03-23-1995,Mo Cnj Ca,03:31 pm
03-25-1995,Mo Cnj Aq,07:10 pm
03-28-1995,Mo Cnj Pi,00:18 am
03-30-1995,Mo Cnj Ar,07:26 am

April 1995

04-01-1995,Mo Cnj Ta,04:59 pm
04-04-1995,Mo Cnj Ge,04:50 am

04-06-1995,Mo Cnj Ca,05:41 pm
04-09-1995,Mo Cnj Le,05:16 am
04-11-1995,Mo Cnj Vi,01:39 pm
04-13-1995,Mo Cnj Li,06:20 pm
04-15-1995,Mo Cnj Sc,08:13 pm
04-17-1995,Mo Cnj Sa,08:52 pm
04-19-1995,Mo Cnj Ca,09:54 pm
04-22-1995,Mo Cnj Aq,00:39 am
04-24-1995,Mo Cnj Pi,05:51 am
04-26-1995,Mo Cnj Ar,01:42 pm
04-28-1995,Mo Cnj Ta,11:53 pm

May 1995
05-01-1995,Mo Cnj Ge,11:53 am
05-04-1995,Mo Cnj Ca,00:45 am
05-06-1995,Mo Cnj Le,12:55 pm
05-08-1995,Mo Cnj Vi,10:33 pm
05-11-1995,Mo Cnj Li,04:30 am
05-13-1995,Mo Cnj Sc,06:54 am
05-15-1995,Mo Cnj Sa,06:59 am
05-17-1995,Mo Cnj Ca,06:36 am
05-19-1995,Mo Cnj Aq,07:40 am
05-21-1995,Mo Cnj Pi,11:41 am
05-23-1995,Mo Cnj Ar,07:13 pm
05-26-1995,Mo Cnj Ta,05:47 am
05-28-1995,Mo Cnj Ge,06:07 pm
05-31-1995,Mo Cnj Ca,06:59 am

June 1995
06-02-1995,Mo Cnj Le,07:17 pm
06-05-1995,Mo Cnj Vi,05:47 am
06-07-1995,Mo Cnj Li,01:14 pm
06-09-1995,Mo Cnj Sc,05:04 pm
06-11-1995,Mo Cnj Sa,05:50 pm
06-13-1995,Mo Cnj Ca,05:05 pm
06-15-1995,Mo Cnj Aq,04:52 pm
06-17-1995,Mo Cnj Pi,07:13 pm
06-20-1995,Mo Cnj Ar,01:29 am
06-22-1995,Mo Cnj Ta,11:35 am
06-25-1995,Mo Cnj Ge,00:02 am
06-27-1995,Mo Cnj Ca,12:57 pm
06-30-1995,Mo Cnj Le,01:02 am

July 1995
07-02-1995,Mo Cnj Vi,11:36 am
07-04-1995,Mo Cnj Li,07:56 am
07-07-1995,Mo Cnj Sc,01:19 am

07-09-1995,Mo Cnj Sa,03:38 am
07-11-1995,Mo Cnj Ca,03:43 am
07-13-1995,Mo Cnj Aq,03:21 am
07-15-1995,Mo Cnj Pi,04:37 am
07-17-1995,Mo Cnj Ar,09:23 am
07-19-1995,Mo Cnj Ta,06:21 pm
07-22-1995,Mo Cnj Ge,06:24 am
07-24-1995,Mo Cnj Ca,07:17 pm
07-27-1995,Mo Cnj Le,07:08 am
07-29-1995,Mo Cnj Vi,05:13 pm

August 1995
08-01-1995,Mo Cnj Li,01:24 am
08-03-1995,Mo Cnj Sc,07:29 am
08-05-1995,Mo Cnj Sa,11:14 am
08-07-1995,Mo Cnj Ca,12:52 pm
08-09-1995,Mo Cnj Aq,01:28 pm
08-11-1995,Mo Cnj Pi,02:47 pm
08-13-1995,Mo Cnj Ar,06:41 pm
08-16-1995,Mo Cnj Ta,02:26 am
08-18-1995,Mo Cnj Ge,01:41 pm
08-21-1995,Mo Cnj Ca,02:24 am
08-23-1995,Mo Cnj Le,02:13 pm
08-25-1995,Mo Cnj Vi,11:51 pm
08-28-1995,Mo Cnj Li,07:15 am
08-30-1995,Mo Cnj Sc,12:51 pm

September 1995
09-01-1995,Mo Cnj Sa,04:57 pm
09-03-1995,Mo Cnj Ca,07:45 pm
09-05-1995,Mo Cnj Aq,09:48 pm
09-08-1995,Mo Cnj Pi,00:09 am
09-10-1995,Mo Cnj Ar,04:15 am
09-12-1995,Mo Cnj Ta,11:22 am
09-14-1995,Mo Cnj Ge,09:48 pm
09-17-1995,Mo Cnj Ca,10:16 am
09-19-1995,Mo Cnj Le,10:20 pm
09-22-1995,Mo Cnj Vi,08:01 am
09-24-1995,Mo Cnj Li,02:50 pm
09-26-1995,Mo Cnj Sc,07:21 pm
09-28-1995,Mo Cnj Sa,10:31 pm

October 1995
10-01-1995,Mo Cnj Ca,01:11 am
10-03-1995,Mo Cnj Aq,04:00 am
10-05-1995,Mo Cnj Pi,07:36 am
10-07-1995,Mo Cnj Ar,12:42 pm

10-09-1995,Mo Cnj Ta,08:05 pm
10-12-1995,Mo Cnj Ge,06:10 am
10-14-1995,Mo Cnj Ca,06:20 pm
10-17-1995,Mo Cnj Le,06:47 am
10-19-1995,Mo Cnj Vi,05:12 pm
10-22-1995,Mo Cnj Li,00:16 am
10-24-1995,Mo Cnj Sc,04:07 am
10-26-1995,Mo Cnj Sa,05:57 am
10-28-1995,Mo Cnj Ca,07:15 am
10-30-1995,Mo Cnj Aq,09:24 am

November 1995
11-01-1995,Mo Cnj Pi,01:18 pm
11-03-1995,Mo Cnj Ar,07:21 pm
11-06-1995,Mo Cnj Ta,03:35 am
11-08-1995,Mo Cnj Ge,01:55 pm
11-11-1995,Mo Cnj Ca,01:57 am
11-13-1995,Mo Cnj Le,02:38 pm
11-16-1995,Mo Cnj Vi,02:03 am
11-18-1995,Mo Cnj Li,10:19 am
11-20-1995,Mo Cnj Sc,02:41 pm
11-22-1995,Mo Cnj Sa,03:57 pm
11-24-1995,Mo Cnj Ca,03:48 pm
11-26-1995,Mo Cnj Aq,04:15 pm
11-28-1995,Mo Cnj Pi,06:59 pm

December 1995
12-01-1995,Mo Cnj Ar,00:51 am
12-03-1995,Mo Cnj Ta,09:40 am
12-05-1995,Mo Cnj Ge,08:35 pm
12-08-1995,Mo Cnj Ca,08:45 am
12-10-1995,Mo Cnj Le,09:25 am
12-13-1995,Mo Cnj Vi,09:27 am
12-15-1995,Mo Cnj Li,07:09 pm
12-18-1995,Mo Cnj Sc,01:07 am
12-20-1995,Mo Cnj Sa,03:13 am
12-22-1995,Mo Cnj Ca,02:46 am
12-24-1995,Mo Cnj Aq,01:52 am
12-26-1995,Mo Cnj Pi,02:45 am
12-28-1995,Mo Cnj Ar,07:06 am
12-30-1995,Mo Cnj Ta,03:22 pm

January 1996
01-02-1996,Mo Cnj Ge,02:30 am
01-04-1996,Mo Cnj Ca,02:56 pm
01-07-1996,Mo Cnj Le,03:31 am
01-09-1996,Mo Cnj Vi,03:30 pm

01-12-1996,Mo Cnj Li,01:55 am
01-14-1996,Mo Cnj Sc,09:30 am
01-16-1996,Mo Cnj Sa,01:25 pm
01-18-1996,Mo Cnj Ca,02:07 pm
01-20-1996,Mo Cnj Aq,01:15 pm
01-22-1996,Mo Cnj Pi,01:02 pm
01-24-1996,Mo Cnj Ar,03:37 pm
01-26-1996,Mo Cnj Ta,10:17 pm
01-29-1996,Mo Cnj Ge,08:43 am
01-31-1996,Mo Cnj Ca,09:11 pm

February 1996
02-03-1996,Mo Cnj Le,09:46 am
02-05-1996,Mo Cnj Vi,09:22 pm
02-08-1996,Mo Cnj Li,07:30 am
02-10-1996,Mo Cnj Sc,03:36 pm
02-12-1996,Mo Cnj Sa,08:59 pm
02-14-1996,Mo Cnj Ca,11:30 pm
02-17-1996,Mo Cnj Aq,00:00 am
02-19-1996,Mo Cnj Pi,00:10 am
02-21-1996,Mo Cnj Ar,01:59 am
02-23-1996,Mo Cnj Ta,07:08 am
02-25-1996,Mo Cnj Ge,04:14 pm
02-28-1996,Mo Cnj Ca,04:10 am

March 1996
03-01-1996,Mo Cnj Le,04:47 pm
03-04-1996,Mo Cnj Vi,04:13 am
03-06-1996,Mo Cnj Li,01:41 pm
03-08-1996,Mo Cnj Sc,09:06 pm
03-11-1996,Mo Cnj Sa,02:33 am
03-13-1996,Mo Cnj Ca,06:08 am
03-15-1996,Mo Cnj Aq,08:15 am
03-17-1996,Mo Cnj Pi,09:51 am
03-19-1996,Mo Cnj Ar,12:15 pm
03-21-1996,Mo Cnj Ta,04:59 pm
03-24-1996,Mo Cnj Ge,01:00 am
03-26-1996,Mo Cnj Ca,12:06 pm
03-29-1996,Mo Cnj Le,00:38 am
03-31-1996,Mo Cnj Vi,12:15 pm

April 1996
04-02-1996,Mo Cnj Li,09:27 pm
04-05-1996,Mo Cnj Sc,03:57 am
04-07-1996,Mo Cnj Sa,08:22 am
04-09-1996,Mo Cnj Ca,11:30 am
04-11-1996,Mo Cnj Aq,02:09 pm

04-13-1996,Mo Cnj Pi,05:00 pm
04-15-1996,Mo Cnj Ar,08:43 pm
04-18-1996,Mo Cnj Ta,02:06 am
04-20-1996,Mo Cnj Ge,09:55 am
04-22-1996,Mo Cnj Ca,08:26 pm
04-25-1996,Mo Cnj Le,08:45 am
04-27-1996,Mo Cnj Vi,08:49 pm
04-30-1996,Mo Cnj Li,06:27 am

May 1996
05-02-1996,Mo Cnj Sc,12:43 pm
05-04-1996,Mo Cnj Sa,04:05 pm
05-06-1996,Mo Cnj Ca,05:54 pm
05-08-1996,Mo Cnj Aq,07:39 pm
05-10-1996,Mo Cnj Pi,10:29 pm
05-13-1996,Mo Cnj Ar,03:01 am
05-15-1996,Mo Cnj Ta,09:25 am
05-17-1996,Mo Cnj Ge,05:49 pm
05-20-1996,Mo Cnj Ca,04:17 am
05-22-1996,Mo Cnj Le,04:28 pm
05-25-1996,Mo Cnj Vi,04:59 pm
05-27-1996,Mo Cnj Li,03:33 pm
05-29-1996,Mo Cnj Sc,10:30 pm

June 1996
06-01-1996,Mo Cnj Sa,01:43 am
06-03-1996,Mo Cnj Ca,02:29 am
06-05-1996,Mo Cnj Aq,02:45 am
06-07-1996,Mo Cnj Pi,04:20 am
06-09-1996,Mo Cnj Ar,08:24 am
06-11-1996,Mo Cnj Ta,03:11 pm
06-14-1996,Mo Cnj Ge,00:16 am
06-16-1996,Mo Cnj Ca,11:08 am
06-18-1996,Mo Cnj Le,11:22 pm
06-21-1996,Mo Cnj Vi,12:07 pm
06-23-1996,Mo Cnj Li,11:38 pm
06-26-1996,Mo Cnj Sc,07:54 am
06-28-1996,Mo Cnj Sa,12:02 pm
06-30-1996,Mo Cnj Ca,12:48 pm

July 1996
07-02-1996,Mo Cnj Aq,12:06 pm
07-04-1996,Mo Cnj Pi,12:07 pm
07-06-1996,Mo Cnj Ar,02:42 pm
07-08-1996,Mo Cnj Ta,08:43 pm
07-11-1996,Mo Cnj Ge,05:52 am
07-13-1996,Mo Cnj Ca,05:08 pm

07-16-1996,Mo Cnj Le,05:31 am
07-18-1996,Mo Cnj Vi,06:17 pm
07-21-1996,Mo Cnj Li,06:14 am
07-23-1996,Mo Cnj Sc,03:44 pm
07-25-1996,Mo Cnj Sa,09:24 pm
07-27-1996,Mo Cnj Ca,11:18 pm
07-29-1996,Mo Cnj Aq,10:48 pm
07-31-1996,Mo Cnj Pi,10:01 pm

August 1996
08-02-1996,Mo Cnj Ar,11:05 pm
08-05-1996,Mo Cnj Ta,03:33 am
08-07-1996,Mo Cnj Ge,11:49 am
08-09-1996,Mo Cnj Ca,10:58 pm
08-12-1996,Mo Cnj Le,11:30 am
08-15-1996,Mo Cnj Vi,00:08 am
08-17-1996,Mo Cnj Li,11:56 am
08-19-1996,Mo Cnj Sc,09:51 pm
08-22-1996,Mo Cnj Sa,04:49 am
08-24-1996,Mo Cnj Ca,08:22 am
08-26-1996,Mo Cnj Aq,09:10 am
08-28-1996,Mo Cnj Pi,08:49 am
08-30-1996,Mo Cnj Ar,09:15 am

September 1996
09-01-1996,Mo Cnj Ta,12:20 pm
09-03-1996,Mo Cnj Ge,07:09 pm
09-06-1996,Mo Cnj Ca,05:30 am
09-08-1996,Mo Cnj Le,05:55 pm
09-11-1996,Mo Cnj Vi,06:29 am
09-13-1996,Mo Cnj Li,05:52 pm
09-16-1996,Mo Cnj Sc,03:20 am
09-18-1996,Mo Cnj Sa,10:31 am
09-20-1996,Mo Cnj Ca,03:12 pm
09-22-1996,Mo Cnj Aq,05:39 pm
09-24-1996,Mo Cnj Pi,06:43 pm
09-26-1996,Mo Cnj Ar,07:46 pm
09-28-1996,Mo Cnj Ta,10:24 pm

October 1996
10-01-1996,Mo Cnj Ge,04:02 am
10-03-1996,Mo Cnj Ca,01:15 pm
10-06-1996,Mo Cnj Le,01:12 am
10-08-1996,Mo Cnj Vi,01:49 pm
10-11-1996,Mo Cnj Li,01:00 am
10-13-1996,Mo Cnj Sc,09:46 am
10-15-1996,Mo Cnj Sa,04:07 pm

10-17-1996,Mo Cnj Ca,08:38 pm
10-19-1996,Mo Cnj Aq,11:52 pm
10-22-1996,Mo Cnj Pi,02:23 am
10-24-1996,Mo Cnj Ar,04:51 am
10-26-1996,Mo Cnj Ta,08:12 am
10-28-1996,Mo Cnj Ge,01:35 pm
10-30-1996,Mo Cnj Ca,09:57 pm

November 1996
11-02-1996,Mo Cnj Le,09:16 am
11-04-1996,Mo Cnj Vi,09:57 pm
11-07-1996,Mo Cnj Li,09:29 am
11-09-1996,Mo Cnj Sc,06:02 pm
11-11-1996,Mo Cnj Sa,11:27 pm
11-14-1996,Mo Cnj Ca,02:44 am
11-16-1996,Mo Cnj Aq,05:15 am
11-18-1996,Mo Cnj Pi,08:01 am
11-20-1996,Mo Cnj Ar,11:34 am
11-22-1996,Mo Cnj Ta,04:12 pm
11-24-1996,Mo Cnj Ge,10:20 pm
11-27-1996,Mo Cnj Ca,06:37 am
11-29-1996,Mo Cnj Le,05:30 pm

December 1996
12-02-1996,Mo Cnj Vi,06:11 am
12-04-1996,Mo Cnj Li,06:24 pm
12-07-1996,Mo Cnj Sc,03:39 am
12-09-1996,Mo Cnj Sa,08:59 am
12-11-1996,Mo Cnj Ca,11:15 am
12-13-1996,Mo Cnj Aq,12:14 pm
12-15-1996,Mo Cnj Pi,01:44 pm
12-17-1996,Mo Cnj Ar,04:55 pm
12-19-1996,Mo Cnj Ta,10:09 pm
12-22-1996,Mo Cnj Ge,05:17 am
12-24-1996,Mo Cnj Ca,02:14 pm
12-27-1996,Mo Cnj Le,01:09 am
12-29-1996,Mo Cnj Vi,01:46 pm

January 1997
01-01-1997,Mo Cnj Li,02:33 am
01-03-1997,Mo Cnj Sc,01:02 pm
01-05-1997,Mo Cnj Sa,07:28 pm
01-07-1997,Mo Cnj Ca,09:55 pm
01-09-1997,Mo Cnj Aq,10:00 pm
01-11-1997,Mo Cnj Pi,09:51 pm
01-13-1997,Mo Cnj Ar,11:21 am
01-16-1997,Mo Cnj Ta,03:40 am

01-18-1997,Mo Cnj Ge,10:54 am
01-20-1997,Mo Cnj Ca,08:29 pm
01-23-1997,Mo Cnj Le,07:51 am
01-25-1997,Mo Cnj Vi,08:27 pm
01-28-1997,Mo Cnj Li,09:22 am
01-30-1997,Mo Cnj Sc,08:48 pm

February 1997
02-02-1997,Mo Cnj Sa,04:51 am
02-04-1997,Mo Cnj Ca,08:45 am
02-06-1997,Mo Cnj Aq,09:21 am
02-08-1997,Mo Cnj Pi,08:34 am
02-10-1997,Mo Cnj Ar,08:30 am
02-12-1997,Mo Cnj Ta,10:57 am
02-14-1997,Mo Cnj Ge,04:54 pm
02-17-1997,Mo Cnj Ca,02:13 am
02-19-1997,Mo Cnj Le,01:53 pm
02-22-1997,Mo Cnj Vi,02:38 am
02-24-1997,Mo Cnj Li,03:23 pm
02-27-1997,Mo Cnj Sc,02:57 am

March 1997
03-01-1997,Mo Cnj Sa,12:01 pm
03-03-1997,Mo Cnj Ca,05:39 pm
03-05-1997,Mo Cnj Aq,07:55 pm
03-07-1997,Mo Cnj Pi,07:58 pm
03-09-1997,Mo Cnj Ar,07:33 pm
03-11-1997,Mo Cnj Ta,08:38 pm
03-14-1997,Mo Cnj Ge,00:49 am
03-16-1997,Mo Cnj Ca,08:51 am
03-18-1997,Mo Cnj Le,08:08 pm
03-21-1997,Mo Cnj Vi,08:59 am
03-23-1997,Mo Cnj Li,09:35 pm
03-26-1997,Mo Cnj Sc,08:42 am
03-28-1997,Mo Cnj Sa,05:40 pm
03-31-1997,Mo Cnj Ca,00:08 am

April 1997
04-02-1997,Mo Cnj Aq,04:00 am
04-04-1997,Mo Cnj Pi,05:43 am
04-06-1997,Mo Cnj Ar,06:20 am
04-08-1997,Mo Cnj Ta,07:21 am
04-10-1997,Mo Cnj Ge,10:28 am
04-12-1997,Mo Cnj Ca,05:03 pm
04-15-1997,Mo Cnj Le,03:22 am
04-17-1997,Mo Cnj Vi,04:01 pm
04-20-1997,Mo Cnj Li,04:37 am

04-22-1997,Mo Cnj Sc,03:20 pm
04-24-1997,Mo Cnj Sa,11:33 pm
04-27-1997,Mo Cnj Ca,05:33 am
04-29-1997,Mo Cnj Aq,09:51 am

May 1997
05-01-1997,Mo Cnj Pi,12:50 pm
05-03-1997,Mo Cnj Ar,02:59 pm
05-05-1997,Mo Cnj Ta,05:05 pm
05-07-1997,Mo Cnj Ge,08:21 pm
05-10-1997,Mo Cnj Ca,02:13 am
05-12-1997,Mo Cnj Le,11:33 am
05-14-1997,Mo Cnj Vi,11:45 am
05-17-1997,Mo Cnj Li,12:28 pm
05-19-1997,Mo Cnj Sc,11:12 pm
05-22-1997,Mo Cnj Sa,06:51 am
05-24-1997,Mo Cnj Ca,11:51 am
05-26-1997,Mo Cnj Aq,03:20 pm
05-28-1997,Mo Cnj Pi,06:18 pm
05-30-1997,Mo Cnj Ar,09:18 pm

June 1997
06-02-1997,Mo Cnj Ta,00:39 am
06-04-1997,Mo Cnj Ge,04:55 am
06-06-1997,Mo Cnj Ca,11:03 am
06-08-1997,Mo Cnj Le,07:59 pm
06-11-1997,Mo Cnj Vi,07:44 am
06-13-1997,Mo Cnj Li,08:36 pm
06-16-1997,Mo Cnj Sc,07:51 am
06-18-1997,Mo Cnj Sa,03:39 pm
06-20-1997,Mo Cnj Ca,08:03 pm
06-22-1997,Mo Cnj Aq,10:21 pm
06-25-1997,Mo Cnj Pi,00:09 am
06-27-1997,Mo Cnj Ar,02:39 am
06-29-1997,Mo Cnj Ta,06:24 am

July 1997
07-01-1997,Mo Cnj Ge,11:36 am
07-03-1997,Mo Cnj Ca,06:33 pm
07-06-1997,Mo Cnj Le,03:45 am
07-08-1997,Mo Cnj Vi,03:22 pm
07-11-1997,Mo Cnj Li,04:21 am
07-13-1997,Mo Cnj Sc,04:21 pm
07-16-1997,Mo Cnj Sa,01:03 am
07-18-1997,Mo Cnj Ca,05:46 am
07-20-1997,Mo Cnj Aq,07:30 am
07-22-1997,Mo Cnj Pi,08:00 am

07-24-1997,Mo Cnj Ar,09:04 am
07-26-1997,Mo Cnj Ta,11:54 am
07-28-1997,Mo Cnj Ge,05:05 pm
07-31-1997,Mo Cnj Ca,00:38 am

August 1997
08-02-1997,Mo Cnj Le,10:27 am
08-04-1997,Mo Cnj Vi,10:15 pm
08-07-1997,Mo Cnj Li,11:17 am
08-09-1997,Mo Cnj Sc,11:50 pm
08-12-1997,Mo Cnj Sa,09:46 am
08-14-1997,Mo Cnj Ca,03:43 pm
08-16-1997,Mo Cnj Aq,05:59 pm
08-18-1997,Mo Cnj Pi,06:02 pm
08-20-1997,Mo Cnj Ar,05:45 pm
08-22-1997,Mo Cnj Ta,06:58 pm
08-24-1997,Mo Cnj Ge,10:56 pm
08-27-1997,Mo Cnj Ca,06:11 am
08-29-1997,Mo Cnj Le,04:19 pm

September 1997
09-01-1997,Mo Cnj Vi,04:27 am
09-03-1997,Mo Cnj Li,05:30 pm
09-06-1997,Mo Cnj Sc,06:10 am
09-08-1997,Mo Cnj Sa,04:55 pm
09-11-1997,Mo Cnj Ca,00:24 am
09-13-1997,Mo Cnj Aq,04:10 am
09-15-1997,Mo Cnj Pi,05:00 am
09-17-1997,Mo Cnj Ar,04:25 am
09-19-1997,Mo Cnj Ta,04:21 am
09-21-1997,Mo Cnj Ge,06:39 am
09-23-1997,Mo Cnj Ca,12:33 pm
09-25-1997,Mo Cnj Le,10:13 pm
09-28-1997,Mo Cnj Vi,10:28 am
09-30-1997,Mo Cnj Li,11:33 pm

October 1997
10-03-1997,Mo Cnj Sc,11:58 am
10-05-1997,Mo Cnj Sa,10:43 pm
10-08-1997,Mo Cnj Ca,07:04 am
10-10-1997,Mo Cnj Aq,12:29 pm
10-12-1997,Mo Cnj Pi,03:00 pm
10-14-1997,Mo Cnj Ar,03:25 pm
10-16-1997,Mo Cnj Ta,03:16 pm
10-18-1997,Mo Cnj Ge,04:27 pm
10-20-1997,Mo Cnj Ca,08:46 pm
10-23-1997,Mo Cnj Le,05:11 am

10-25-1997,Mo Cnj Vi,05:00 pm
10-28-1997,Mo Cnj Li,06:06 am
10-30-1997,Mo Cnj Sc,06:16 pm

November 1997
11-02-1997,Mo Cnj Sa,04:27 am
11-04-1997,Mo Cnj Ca,12:31 pm
11-06-1997,Mo Cnj Aq,06:34 pm
11-08-1997,Mo Cnj Pi,10:35 pm
11-11-1997,Mo Cnj Ar,00:44 am
11-13-1997,Mo Cnj Ta,01:46 am
11-15-1997,Mo Cnj Ge,03:06 am
11-17-1997,Mo Cnj Ca,06:33 am
11-19-1997,Mo Cnj Le,01:39 pm
11-22-1997,Mo Cnj Vi,00:33 am
11-24-1997,Mo Cnj Li,01:29 pm
11-27-1997,Mo Cnj Sc,01:43 am
11-29-1997,Mo Cnj Sa,11:29 am

December 1997
12-01-1997,Mo Cnj Ca,06:39 pm
12-03-1997,Mo Cnj Aq,11:58 pm
12-06-1997,Mo Cnj Pi,04:08 am
12-08-1997,Mo Cnj Ar,07:25 am
12-10-1997,Mo Cnj Ta,10:01 am
12-12-1997,Mo Cnj Ge,12:36 pm
12-14-1997,Mo Cnj Ca,04:25 pm
12-16-1997,Mo Cnj Le,10:58 pm
12-19-1997,Mo Cnj Vi,09:00 am
12-21-1997,Mo Cnj Li,09:35 pm
12-24-1997,Mo Cnj Sc,10:08 am
12-26-1997,Mo Cnj Sa,08:08 pm
12-29-1997,Mo Cnj Ca,02:49 am
12-31-1997,Mo Cnj Aq,06:59 am

January 1998
01-02-1998,Mo Cnj Pi,09:57 am
01-04-1998,Mo Cnj Ar,12:44 pm
01-06-1998,Mo Cnj Ta,03:53 pm
01-08-1998,Mo Cnj Ge,07:42 pm
01-11-1998,Mo Cnj Ca,00:43 am
01-13-1998,Mo Cnj Le,07:45 am
01-15-1998,Mo Cnj Vi,05:31 pm
01-18-1998,Mo Cnj Li,05:45 am
01-20-1998,Mo Cnj Sc,06:35 pm
01-23-1998,Mo Cnj Sa,05:26 am
01-25-1998,Mo Cnj Ca,12:40 pm

01-27-1998,Mo Cnj Aq,04:28 pm
01-29-1998,Mo Cnj Pi,06:09 pm
01-31-1998,Mo Cnj Ar,07:21 pm

February 1998
02-02-1998,Mo Cnj Ta,09:25 pm
02-05-1998,Mo Cnj Ge,01:09 am
02-07-1998,Mo Cnj Ca,06:58 am
02-09-1998,Mo Cnj Le,02:57 pm
02-12-1998,Mo Cnj Vi,01:10 am
02-14-1998,Mo Cnj Li,01:18 pm
02-17-1998,Mo Cnj Sc,02:14 am
02-19-1998,Mo Cnj Sa,01:57 pm
02-21-1998,Mo Cnj Ca,10:30 pm
02-24-1998,Mo Cnj Aq,03:10 am
02-26-1998,Mo Cnj Pi,04:42 am
02-28-1998,Mo Cnj Ar,04:42 am

March 1998
03-02-1998,Mo Cnj Ta,05:01 am
03-04-1998,Mo Cnj Ge,07:15 am
03-06-1998,Mo Cnj Ca,12:27 pm
03-08-1998,Mo Cnj Le,08:47 pm
03-11-1998,Mo Cnj Vi,07:36 am
03-13-1998,Mo Cnj Li,07:59 pm
03-16-1998,Mo Cnj Sc,08:51 am
03-18-1998,Mo Cnj Sa,08:56 pm
03-21-1998,Mo Cnj Ca,06:43 am
03-23-1998,Mo Cnj Aq,01:02 pm
03-25-1998,Mo Cnj Pi,03:43 pm
03-27-1998,Mo Cnj Ar,03:49 pm
03-29-1998,Mo Cnj Ta,03:07 pm
03-31-1998,Mo Cnj Ge,03:38 pm

April 1998
04-02-1998,Mo Cnj Ca,07:10 pm
04-05-1998,Mo Cnj Le,02:37 am
04-07-1998,Mo Cnj Vi,01:26 pm
04-10-1998,Mo Cnj Li,02:05 am
04-12-1998,Mo Cnj Sc,02:56 pm
04-15-1998,Mo Cnj Sa,02:52 am
04-17-1998,Mo Cnj Ca,01:05 pm
04-19-1998,Mo Cnj Aq,08:42 pm
04-22-1998,Mo Cnj Pi,01:07 am
04-24-1998,Mo Cnj Ar,02:32 am
04-26-1998,Mo Cnj Ta,02:10 am

04-28-1998,Mo Cnj Ge,01:56 am
04-30-1998,Mo Cnj Ca,03:57 am

May 1998
05-02-1998,Mo Cnj Le,09:50 am
05-04-1998,Mo Cnj Vi,07:47 pm
05-07-1998,Mo Cnj Li,08:19 am
05-09-1998,Mo Cnj Sc,09:10 pm
05-12-1998,Mo Cnj Sa,08:48 am
05-14-1998,Mo Cnj Ca,06:40 pm
05-17-1998,Mo Cnj Aq,02:31 am
05-19-1998,Mo Cnj Pi,08:04 am
05-21-1998,Mo Cnj Ar,11:06 am
05-23-1998,Mo Cnj Ta,12:07 pm
05-25-1998,Mo Cnj Ge,12:25 pm
05-27-1998,Mo Cnj Ca,01:58 pm
05-29-1998,Mo Cnj Le,06:38 pm

June 1998
06-01-1998,Mo Cnj Vi,03:21 am
06-03-1998,Mo Cnj Li,03:17 pm
06-06-1998,Mo Cnj Sc,04:06 am
06-08-1998,Mo Cnj Sa,03:35 pm
06-11-1998,Mo Cnj Ca,00:51 am
06-13-1998,Mo Cnj Aq,08:04 am
06-15-1998,Mo Cnj Pi,01:32 pm
06-17-1998,Mo Cnj Ar,05:23 pm
06-19-1998,Mo Cnj Ta,07:47 pm
06-21-1998,Mo Cnj Ge,09:26 pm
06-23-1998,Mo Cnj Ca,11:39 pm
06-26-1998,Mo Cnj Le,04:04 am
06-28-1998,Mo Cnj Vi,11:55 am
06-30-1998,Mo Cnj Li,11:06 pm

July 1998
07-03-1998,Mo Cnj Sc,11:46 am
07-05-1998,Mo Cnj Sa,11:25 pm
07-08-1998,Mo Cnj Ca,08:28 am
07-10-1998,Mo Cnj Aq,02:52 pm
07-12-1998,Mo Cnj Pi,07:22 pm
07-14-1998,Mo Cnj Ar,10:45 pm
07-17-1998,Mo Cnj Ta,01:34 am
07-19-1998,Mo Cnj Ge,04:18 am
07-21-1998,Mo Cnj Ca,07:43 am
07-23-1998,Mo Cnj Le,12:49 pm
07-25-1998,Mo Cnj Vi,08:35 pm

07-28-1998,Mo Cnj Li,07:15 am
07-30-1998,Mo Cnj Sc,07:45 pm

August 1998
08-02-1998,Mo Cnj Sa,07:48 am
08-04-1998,Mo Cnj Ca,05:18 pm
08-06-1998,Mo Cnj Aq,11:31 pm
08-09-1998,Mo Cnj Pi,03:04 am
08-11-1998,Mo Cnj Ar,05:11 am
08-13-1998,Mo Cnj Ta,07:05 am
08-15-1998,Mo Cnj Ge,09:47 am
08-17-1998,Mo Cnj Ca,01:56 pm
08-19-1998,Mo Cnj Le,08:01 pm
08-22-1998,Mo Cnj Vi,04:22 am
08-24-1998,Mo Cnj Li,03:02 am
08-27-1998,Mo Cnj Sc,03:25 am
08-29-1998,Mo Cnj Sa,03:55 pm

September 1998
09-01-1998,Mo Cnj Ca,02:23 am
09-03-1998,Mo Cnj Aq,09:21 am
09-05-1998,Mo Cnj Pi,12:48 pm
09-07-1998,Mo Cnj Ar,01:53 pm
09-09-1998,Mo Cnj Ta,02:17 pm
09-11-1998,Mo Cnj Ge,03:41 pm
09-13-1998,Mo Cnj Ca,07:20 pm
09-16-1998,Mo Cnj Le,01:48 am
09-18-1998,Mo Cnj Vi,10:52 am
09-20-1998,Mo Cnj Li,09:57 pm
09-23-1998,Mo Cnj Sc,10:22 am
09-25-1998,Mo Cnj Sa,11:05 pm
09-28-1998,Mo Cnj Ca,10:31 am
09-30-1998,Mo Cnj Aq,06:54 pm

October 1998
10-02-1998,Mo Cnj Pi,11:24 pm
10-05-1998,Mo Cnj Ar,00:33 am
10-06-1998,Mo Cnj Ta,11:58 pm
10-08-1998,Mo Cnj Ge,11:44 pm
10-11-1998,Mo Cnj Ca,01:48 am
10-13-1998,Mo Cnj Le,07:25 am
10-15-1998,Mo Cnj Vi,04:32 pm
10-18-1998,Mo Cnj Li,04:03 am
10-20-1998,Mo Cnj Sc,04:37 pm
10-23-1998,Mo Cnj Sa,05:17 am
10-25-1998,Mo Cnj Ca,05:06 pm

10-28-1998,Mo Cnj Aq,02:45 am
10-30-1998,Mo Cnj Pi,08:59 am

November 1998
11-01-1998,Mo Cnj Ar,11:27 am
11-03-1998,Mo Cnj Ta,11:12 am
11-05-1998,Mo Cnj Ge,10:11 am
11-07-1998,Mo Cnj Ca,10:39 am
11-09-1998,Mo Cnj Le,02:33 pm
11-11-1998,Mo Cnj Vi,10:38 pm
11-14-1998,Mo Cnj Li,09:59 am
11-16-1998,Mo Cnj Sc,10:42 pm
11-19-1998,Mo Cnj Sa,11:13 am
11-21-1998,Mo Cnj Ca,10:46 pm
11-24-1998,Mo Cnj Aq,08:43 am
11-26-1998,Mo Cnj Pi,04:14 pm
11-28-1998,Mo Cnj Ar,08:34 pm
11-30-1998,Mo Cnj Ta,09:53 pm

December 1998
12-02-1998,Mo Cnj Ge,09:30 pm
12-04-1998,Mo Cnj Ca,09:28 pm
12-06-1998,Mo Cnj Le,11:56 pm
12-09-1998,Mo Cnj Vi,06:22 am
12-11-1998,Mo Cnj Li,04:44 pm
12-14-1998,Mo Cnj Sc,05:17 am
12-16-1998,Mo Cnj Sa,05:48 pm
12-19-1998,Mo Cnj Ca,04:55 am
12-21-1998,Mo Cnj Aq,02:17 pm
12-23-1998,Mo Cnj Pi,09:45 pm
12-26-1998,Mo Cnj Ar,03:04 am
12-28-1998,Mo Cnj Ta,06:05 am
12-30-1998,Mo Cnj Ge,07:23 am

January 1999
01-01-1999,Mo Cnj Ca,08:16 am
01-03-1999,Mo Cnj Le,10:32 am
01-05-1999,Mo Cnj Vi,03:50 pm
01-08-1999,Mo Cnj Li,00:53 am
01-10-1999,Mo Cnj Sc,12:49 pm
01-13-1999,Mo Cnj Sa,01:23 am
01-15-1999,Mo Cnj Ca,12:29 pm
01-17-1999,Mo Cnj Aq,09:12 pm
01-20-1999,Mo Cnj Pi,03:41 am
01-22-1999,Mo Cnj Ar,08:26 am
01-24-1999,Mo Cnj Ta,11:53 am
01-26-1999,Mo Cnj Ge,02:30 pm

01-28-1999,Mo Cnj Ca,04:57 pm
01-30-1999,Mo Cnj Le,08:16 pm

February 1999
02-02-1999,Mo Cnj Vi,01:37 am
02-04-1999,Mo Cnj Li,09:56 am
02-06-1999,Mo Cnj Sc,09:06 pm
02-09-1999,Mo Cnj Sa,09:39 am
02-11-1999,Mo Cnj Ca,09:11 pm
02-14-1999,Mo Cnj Aq,05:58 am
02-16-1999,Mo Cnj Pi,11:41 am
02-18-1999,Mo Cnj Ar,03:07 pm
02-20-1999,Mo Cnj Ta,05:29 pm
02-22-1999,Mo Cnj Ge,07:54 pm
02-24-1999,Mo Cnj Ca,11:09 pm
02-27-1999,Mo Cnj Le,03:44 am

March 1999
03-01-1999,Mo Cnj Vi,10:05 am
03-03-1999,Mo Cnj Li,06:35 pm
03-06-1999,Mo Cnj Sc,05:23 am
03-08-1999,Mo Cnj Sa,05:47 pm
03-11-1999,Mo Cnj Ca,05:54 am
03-13-1999,Mo Cnj Aq,03:32 pm
03-15-1999,Mo Cnj Pi,09:31 pm
03-18-1999,Mo Cnj Ar,00:13 am
03-20-1999,Mo Cnj Ta,01:09 am
03-22-1999,Mo Cnj Ge,02:05 am
03-24-1999,Mo Cnj Ca,04:34 am
03-26-1999,Mo Cnj Le,09:23 am
03-28-1999,Mo Cnj Vi,04:35 pm
03-31-1999,Mo Cnj Li,01:50 am

April 1999
04-02-1999,Mo Cnj Sc,12:50 pm
04-05-1999,Mo Cnj Sa,01:08 am
04-07-1999,Mo Cnj Ca,01:39 pm
04-10-1999,Mo Cnj Aq,00:24 am
04-12-1999,Mo Cnj Pi,07:35 am
04-14-1999,Mo Cnj Ar,10:46 am
04-16-1999,Mo Cnj Ta,11:08 am
04-18-1999,Mo Cnj Ge,10:40 am
04-20-1999,Mo Cnj Ca,11:28 am
04-22-1999,Mo Cnj Le,03:07 pm
04-24-1999,Mo Cnj Vi,10:05 pm
04-27-1999,Mo Cnj Li,07:47 am
04-29-1999,Mo Cnj Sc,07:13 pm

May 1999

05-02-1999,Mo Cnj Sa,07:36 am
05-04-1999,Mo Cnj Ca,08:12 pm
05-07-1999,Mo Cnj Aq,07:40 am
05-09-1999,Mo Cnj Pi,04:16 pm
05-11-1999,Mo Cnj Ar,08:54 pm
05-13-1999,Mo Cnj Ta,09:57 pm
05-15-1999,Mo Cnj Ge,09:08 pm
05-17-1999,Mo Cnj Ca,08:40 pm
05-19-1999,Mo Cnj Le,10:38 pm
05-22-1999,Mo Cnj Vi,04:16 am
05-24-1999,Mo Cnj Li,01:29 pm
05-27-1999,Mo Cnj Sc,01:05 am
05-29-1999,Mo Cnj Sa,01:37 pm

June 1999

06-01-1999,Mo Cnj Ca,02:06 am
06-03-1999,Mo Cnj Aq,01:37 pm
06-05-1999,Mo Cnj Pi,11:01 pm
06-08-1999,Mo Cnj Ar,05:09 am
06-10-1999,Mo Cnj Ta,07:44 am
06-12-1999,Mo Cnj Ge,07:49 am
06-14-1999,Mo Cnj Ca,07:14 am
06-16-1999,Mo Cnj Le,08:07 am
06-18-1999,Mo Cnj Vi,12:12 pm
06-20-1999,Mo Cnj Li,08:10 pm
06-23-1999,Mo Cnj Sc,07:18 am
06-25-1999,Mo Cnj Sa,07:52 pm
06-28-1999,Mo Cnj Ca,08:12 am
06-30-1999,Mo Cnj Aq,07:20 pm

July 1999

07-03-1999,Mo Cnj Pi,04:35 am
07-05-1999,Mo Cnj Ar,11:22 am
07-07-1999,Mo Cnj Ta,03:22 pm
07-09-1999,Mo Cnj Ge,05:00 pm
07-11-1999,Mo Cnj Ca,05:27 pm
07-13-1999,Mo Cnj Le,06:25 pm
07-15-1999,Mo Cnj Vi,09:39 pm
07-18-1999,Mo Cnj Li,04:20 am
07-20-1999,Mo Cnj Sc,02:31 pm
07-23-1999,Mo Cnj Sa,02:49 am
07-25-1999,Mo Cnj Ca,03:09 pm
07-28-1999,Mo Cnj Aq,01:55 am
07-30-1999,Mo Cnj Pi,10:28 am

August 1999

08-01-1999,Mo Cnj Ar,04:47 pm
08-03-1999,Mo Cnj Ta,09:09 pm
08-05-1999,Mo Cnj Ge,11:57 pm
08-08-1999,Mo Cnj Ca,01:53 am
08-10-1999,Mo Cnj Le,03:56 am
08-12-1999,Mo Cnj Vi,07:22 am
08-14-1999,Mo Cnj Li,01:25 pm
08-16-1999,Mo Cnj Sc,10:41 pm
08-19-1999,Mo Cnj Sa,10:32 am
08-21-1999,Mo Cnj Ca,11:00 pm
08-24-1999,Mo Cnj Aq,09:49 am
08-26-1999,Mo Cnj Pi,05:50 pm
08-28-1999,Mo Cnj Ar,11:09 pm
08-31-1999,Mo Cnj Ta,02:41 am

September 1999

09-02-1999,Mo Cnj Ge,05:25 am
09-04-1999,Mo Cnj Ca,08:10 am
09-06-1999,Mo Cnj Le,11:30 am
09-08-1999,Mo Cnj Vi,03:57 pm
09-10-1999,Mo Cnj Li,10:17 pm
09-13-1999,Mo Cnj Sc,07:09 am
09-15-1999,Mo Cnj Sa,06:35 pm
09-18-1999,Mo Cnj Ca,07:13 am
09-20-1999,Mo Cnj Aq,06:38 pm
09-23-1999,Mo Cnj Pi,02:51 am
09-25-1999,Mo Cnj Ar,07:34 am
09-27-1999,Mo Cnj Ta,09:51 am
09-29-1999,Mo Cnj Ge,11:22 am

October 1999

10-01-1999,Mo Cnj Ca,01:32 pm
10-03-1999,Mo Cnj Le,05:14 pm
10-05-1999,Mo Cnj Vi,10:40 pm
10-08-1999,Mo Cnj Li,05:52 am
10-10-1999,Mo Cnj Sc,03:02 pm
10-13-1999,Mo Cnj Sa,02:18 am
10-15-1999,Mo Cnj Ca,03:03 pm
10-18-1999,Mo Cnj Aq,03:17 am
10-20-1999,Mo Cnj Pi,12:33 pm
10-22-1999,Mo Cnj Ar,05:42 pm
10-24-1999,Mo Cnj Ta,07:26 pm
10-26-1999,Mo Cnj Ge,07:34 pm
10-28-1999,Mo Cnj Ca,08:10 pm
10-30-1999,Mo Cnj Le,10:47 pm

November 1999

11-02-1999,Mo Cnj Vi,04:07 am
11-04-1999,Mo Cnj Li,11:57 am
11-06-1999,Mo Cnj Sc,09:46 pm
11-09-1999,Mo Cnj Sa,09:15 am
11-11-1999,Mo Cnj Ca,10:00 pm
11-14-1999,Mo Cnj Aq,10:46 am
11-16-1999,Mo Cnj Pi,09:21 pm
11-19-1999,Mo Cnj Ar,03:58 am
11-21-1999,Mo Cnj Ta,06:27 am
11-23-1999,Mo Cnj Ge,06:14 am
11-25-1999,Mo Cnj Ca,05:29 am
11-27-1999,Mo Cnj Le,06:18 am
11-29-1999,Mo Cnj Vi,10:11 am

December 1999

12-01-1999,Mo Cnj Li,05:30 pm
12-04-1999,Mo Cnj Sc,03:36 am
12-06-1999,Mo Cnj Sa,03:28 pm
12-09-1999,Mo Cnj Ca,04:14 am
12-11-1999,Mo Cnj Aq,04:59 pm
12-14-1999,Mo Cnj Pi,04:18 am
12-16-1999,Mo Cnj Ar,12:30 pm
12-18-1999,Mo Cnj Ta,04:45 pm
12-20-1999,Mo Cnj Ge,05:39 pm
12-22-1999,Mo Cnj Ca,04:52 pm
12-24-1999,Mo Cnj Le,04:32 pm
12-26-1999,Mo Cnj Vi,06:34 pm
12-29-1999,Mo Cnj Li,00:15 am
12-31-1999,Mo Cnj Sc,09:37 am

January 2000

01-02-2000,Mo Cnj Sa,09:33 pm
01-05-2000,Mo Cnj Ca,10:24 am
01-07-2000,Mo Cnj Aq,10:53 pm
01-10-2000,Mo Cnj Pi,09:59 am
01-12-2000,Mo Cnj Ar,06:48 pm
01-15-2000,Mo Cnj Ta,00:38 am
01-17-2000,Mo Cnj Ge,03:25 am
01-19-2000,Mo Cnj Ca,04:01 am
01-21-2000,Mo Cnj Le,03:59 am
01-23-2000,Mo Cnj Vi,05:08 am
01-25-2000,Mo Cnj Li,09:10 am
01-27-2000,Mo Cnj Sc,05:02 pm
01-30-2000,Mo Cnj Sa,04:18 am

February 2000

02-01-2000,Mo Cnj Ca,05:10 pm
02-04-2000,Mo Cnj Aq,05:31 am
02-06-2000,Mo Cnj Pi,04:02 pm
02-09-2000,Mo Cnj Ar,00:18 am
02-11-2000,Mo Cnj Ta,06:21 am
02-13-2000,Mo Cnj Ge,10:23 am
02-15-2000,Mo Cnj Ca,12:46 pm
02-17-2000,Mo Cnj Le,02:12 pm
02-19-2000,Mo Cnj Vi,03:54 pm
02-21-2000,Mo Cnj Li,07:21 pm
02-24-2000,Mo Cnj Sc,01:58 am
02-26-2000,Mo Cnj Sa,12:10 pm
02-29-2000,Mo Cnj Ca,00:45 am

March 2000

03-02-2000,Mo Cnj Aq,01:14 pm
03-04-2000,Mo Cnj Pi,11:30 pm
03-07-2000,Mo Cnj Ar,06:55 am
03-09-2000,Mo Cnj Ta,12:02 pm
03-11-2000,Mo Cnj Ge,03:46 pm
03-13-2000,Mo Cnj Ca,06:52 pm
03-15-2000,Mo Cnj Le,09:43 pm
03-18-2000,Mo Cnj Vi,00:49 am
03-20-2000,Mo Cnj Li,04:57 am
03-22-2000,Mo Cnj Sc,11:17 am
03-24-2000,Mo Cnj Sa,08:43 pm
03-27-2000,Mo Cnj Ca,08:51 am
03-29-2000,Mo Cnj Aq,09:35 pm

April 2000

04-01-2000,Mo Cnj Pi,08:13 am
04-03-2000,Mo Cnj Ar,03:22 pm
04-05-2000,Mo Cnj Ta,07:29 pm
04-07-2000,Mo Cnj Ge,09:58 pm
04-10-2000,Mo Cnj Ca,00:16 am
04-12-2000,Mo Cnj Le,03:16 am
04-14-2000,Mo Cnj Vi,07:19 am
04-16-2000,Mo Cnj Li,12:36 pm
04-18-2000,Mo Cnj Sc,07:36 pm
04-21-2000,Mo Cnj Sa,04:58 am
04-23-2000,Mo Cnj Ca,04:48 pm
04-26-2000,Mo Cnj Aq,05:43 am
04-28-2000,Mo Cnj Pi,05:06 pm

May 2000

05-01-2000,Mo Cnj Ar,00:55 am
05-03-2000,Mo Cnj Ta,04:54 am

05-05-2000,Mo Cnj Ge,06:23 am
05-07-2000,Mo Cnj Ca,07:14 am
05-09-2000,Mo Cnj Le,09:01 am
05-11-2000,Mo Cnj Vi,12:41 pm
05-13-2000,Mo Cnj Li,06:28 pm
05-16-2000,Mo Cnj Sc,02:17 am
05-18-2000,Mo Cnj Sa,12:10 pm
05-21-2000,Mo Cnj Ca,00:01 am
05-23-2000,Mo Cnj Aq,01:00 pm
05-26-2000,Mo Cnj Pi,01:07 am
05-28-2000,Mo Cnj Ar,10:08 am
05-30-2000,Mo Cnj Ta,03:02 pm

June 2000
06-01-2000,Mo Cnj Ge,04:35 pm
06-03-2000,Mo Cnj Ca,04:30 pm
06-05-2000,Mo Cnj Le,04:46 pm
06-07-2000,Mo Cnj Vi,06:58 pm
06-09-2000,Mo Cnj Li,11:59 pm
06-12-2000,Mo Cnj Sc,07:56 am
06-14-2000,Mo Cnj Sa,06:18 pm
06-17-2000,Mo Cnj Ca,06:26 am
06-19-2000,Mo Cnj Aq,07:26 pm
06-22-2000,Mo Cnj Pi,07:51 am
06-24-2000,Mo Cnj Ar,05:56 pm
06-27-2000,Mo Cnj Ta,00:19 am
06-29-2000,Mo Cnj Ge,03:00 am

July 2000
07-01-2000,Mo Cnj Ca,03:10 am
07-03-2000,Mo Cnj Le,02:38 am
07-05-2000,Mo Cnj Vi,03:19 am
07-07-2000,Mo Cnj Li,06:47 am
07-09-2000,Mo Cnj Sc,01:48 pm
07-12-2000,Mo Cnj Sa,00:06 am
07-14-2000,Mo Cnj Ca,12:27 pm
07-17-2000,Mo Cnj Aq,01:27 am
07-19-2000,Mo Cnj Pi,01:44 pm
07-22-2000,Mo Cnj Ar,00:10 am
07-24-2000,Mo Cnj Ta,07:44 am
07-26-2000,Mo Cnj Ge,12:02 pm
07-28-2000,Mo Cnj Ca,01:30 pm
07-30-2000,Mo Cnj Le,01:24 pm

August 2000
08-01-2000,Mo Cnj Vi,01:27 pm
08-03-2000,Mo Cnj Li,03:31 pm

08-05-2000,Mo Cnj Sc,09:04 pm
08-08-2000,Mo Cnj Sa,06:30 am
08-10-2000,Mo Cnj Ca,06:44 pm
08-13-2000,Mo Cnj Aq,07:43 am
08-15-2000,Mo Cnj Pi,07:42 pm
08-18-2000,Mo Cnj Ar,05:44 am
08-20-2000,Mo Cnj Ta,01:31 pm
08-22-2000,Mo Cnj Ge,06:55 pm
08-24-2000,Mo Cnj Ca,09:59 pm
08-26-2000,Mo Cnj Le,11:17 pm
08-28-2000,Mo Cnj Vi,11:55 pm
08-31-2000,Mo Cnj Li,01:33 am

September 2000
09-02-2000,Mo Cnj Sc,05:55 am
09-04-2000,Mo Cnj Sa,02:09 pm
09-07-2000,Mo Cnj Ca,01:48 am
09-09-2000,Mo Cnj Aq,02:45 pm
09-12-2000,Mo Cnj Pi,02:34 am
09-14-2000,Mo Cnj Ar,12:00 pm
09-16-2000,Mo Cnj Ta,07:05 pm
09-19-2000,Mo Cnj Ge,00:22 am
09-21-2000,Mo Cnj Ca,04:16 am
09-23-2000,Mo Cnj Le,07:00 am
09-25-2000,Mo Cnj Vi,09:02 am
09-27-2000,Mo Cnj Li,11:22 am
09-29-2000,Mo Cnj Sc,03:30 pm

October 2000
10-01-2000,Mo Cnj Sa,10:51 pm
10-04-2000,Mo Cnj Ca,09:43 am
10-06-2000,Mo Cnj Aq,10:33 pm
10-09-2000,Mo Cnj Pi,10:36 am
10-11-2000,Mo Cnj Ar,07:51 pm
10-14-2000,Mo Cnj Ta,02:06 am
10-16-2000,Mo Cnj Ge,06:19 am
10-18-2000,Mo Cnj Ca,09:37 am
10-20-2000,Mo Cnj Le,12:43 pm
10-22-2000,Mo Cnj Vi,03:53 pm
10-24-2000,Mo Cnj Li,07:31 pm
10-27-2000,Mo Cnj Sc,00:24 am
10-29-2000,Mo Cnj Sa,07:41 am
10-31-2000,Mo Cnj Ca,06:02 pm

November 2000
11-03-2000,Mo Cnj Aq,06:40 am
11-05-2000,Mo Cnj Pi,07:12 pm

11-08-2000,Mo Cnj Ar,05:02 am
11-10-2000,Mo Cnj Ta,11:12 am
11-12-2000,Mo Cnj Ge,02:28 pm
11-14-2000,Mo Cnj Ca,04:21 pm
11-16-2000,Mo Cnj Le,06:19 pm
11-18-2000,Mo Cnj Vi,09:16 pm
11-21-2000,Mo Cnj Li,01:35 am
11-23-2000,Mo Cnj Sc,07:33 am
11-25-2000,Mo Cnj Sa,03:33 pm
11-28-2000,Mo Cnj Ca,01:57 am
11-30-2000,Mo Cnj Aq,02:26 pm

December 2000
12-03-2000,Mo Cnj Pi,03:23 am
12-05-2000,Mo Cnj Ar,02:18 pm
12-07-2000,Mo Cnj Ta,09:28 pm
12-10-2000,Mo Cnj Ge,00:51 am
12-12-2000,Mo Cnj Ca,01:49 am
12-14-2000,Mo Cnj Le,02:09 am
12-16-2000,Mo Cnj Vi,03:30 am
12-18-2000,Mo Cnj Li,07:01 am
12-20-2000,Mo Cnj Sc,01:12 pm
12-22-2000,Mo Cnj Sa,09:57 pm
12-25-2000,Mo Cnj Ca,08:54 am
12-27-2000,Mo Cnj Aq,09:26 pm
12-30-2000,Mo Cnj Pi,10:28 am

January 2001
01-01-2001,Mo Cnj Ar,10:15 pm
01-04-2001,Mo Cnj Ta,06:57 am
01-06-2001,Mo Cnj Ge,11:44 am
01-08-2001,Mo Cnj Ca,01:09 pm
01-10-2001,Mo Cnj Le,12:44 pm
01-12-2001,Mo Cnj Vi,12:26 pm
01-14-2001,Mo Cnj Li,02:05 pm
01-16-2001,Mo Cnj Sc,07:03 pm
01-19-2001,Mo Cnj Sa,03:36 am
01-21-2001,Mo Cnj Ca,02:57 pm
01-24-2001,Mo Cnj Aq,03:44 am
01-26-2001,Mo Cnj Pi,04:39 pm
01-29-2001,Mo Cnj Ar,04:35 am
01-31-2001,Mo Cnj Ta,02:21 pm

February 2001
02-02-2001,Mo Cnj Ge,08:56 pm
02-05-2001,Mo Cnj Ca,00:00 am
02-07-2001,Mo Cnj Le,00:21 am
02-08-2001,Mo Cnj Vi,11:35 pm

02-10-2001,Mo Cnj Li,11:46 pm
02-13-2001,Mo Cnj Sc,02:52 am
02-15-2001,Mo Cnj Sa,10:03 am
02-17-2001,Mo Cnj Ca,09:00 pm
02-20-2001,Mo Cnj Aq,09:54 am
02-22-2001,Mo Cnj Pi,10:45 pm
02-25-2001,Mo Cnj Ar,10:20 am
02-27-2001,Mo Cnj Ta,08:05 pm

March 2001
03-02-2001,Mo Cnj Ge,03:36 am
03-04-2001,Mo Cnj Ca,08:25 am
03-06-2001,Mo Cnj Le,10:31 am
03-08-2001,Mo Cnj Vi,10:45 am
03-10-2001,Mo Cnj Li,10:48 am
03-12-2001,Mo Cnj Sc,12:43 pm
03-14-2001,Mo Cnj Sa,06:17 pm
03-17-2001,Mo Cnj Ca,04:02 am
03-19-2001,Mo Cnj Aq,04:36 pm
03-22-2001,Mo Cnj Pi,05:28 am
03-24-2001,Mo Cnj Ar,04:44 pm
03-27-2001,Mo Cnj Ta,01:51 am
03-29-2001,Mo Cnj Ge,09:02 am
03-31-2001,Mo Cnj Ca,02:24 pm

April 2001
04-02-2001,Mo Cnj Le,05:55 pm
04-04-2001,Mo Cnj Vi,07:47 pm
04-06-2001,Mo Cnj Li,08:57 pm
04-08-2001,Mo Cnj Sc,11:02 pm
04-11-2001,Mo Cnj Sa,03:47 am
04-13-2001,Mo Cnj Ca,12:21 pm
04-16-2001,Mo Cnj Aq,00:11 am
04-18-2001,Mo Cnj Pi,01:01 pm
04-21-2001,Mo Cnj Ar,00:18 am
04-23-2001,Mo Cnj Ta,08:57 am
04-25-2001,Mo Cnj Ge,03:12 pm
04-27-2001,Mo Cnj Ca,07:50 pm
04-29-2001,Mo Cnj Le,11:25 pm

May 2001
05-02-2001,Mo Cnj Vi,02:16 am
05-04-2001,Mo Cnj Li,04:50 am
05-06-2001,Mo Cnj Sc,08:01 am
05-08-2001,Mo Cnj Sa,01:05 pm
05-10-2001,Mo Cnj Ca,09:10 pm
05-13-2001,Mo Cnj Aq,08:20 am
05-15-2001,Mo Cnj Pi,09:02 pm

05-18-2001,Mo Cnj Ar,08:42 am
05-20-2001,Mo Cnj Ta,05:30 pm
05-22-2001,Mo Cnj Ge,11:12 pm
05-25-2001,Mo Cnj Ca,02:43 am
05-27-2001,Mo Cnj Le,05:12 am
05-29-2001,Mo Cnj Vi,07:38 am
05-31-2001,Mo Cnj Li,10:41 am

June 2001
06-02-2001,Mo Cnj Sc,02:56 pm
06-04-2001,Mo Cnj Sa,08:58 pm
06-07-2001,Mo Cnj Ca,05:24 am
06-09-2001,Mo Cnj Aq,04:20 pm
06-12-2001,Mo Cnj Pi,04:54 am
06-14-2001,Mo Cnj Ar,05:03 pm
06-17-2001,Mo Cnj Ta,02:39 am
06-19-2001,Mo Cnj Ge,08:42 am
06-21-2001,Mo Cnj Ca,11:41 am
06-23-2001,Mo Cnj Le,12:55 pm
06-25-2001,Mo Cnj Vi,01:58 pm
06-27-2001,Mo Cnj Li,04:11 pm
06-29-2001,Mo Cnj Sc,08:29 pm

July 2001
07-02-2001,Mo Cnj Sa,03:14 am
07-04-2001,Mo Cnj Ca,12:22 pm
07-06-2001,Mo Cnj Aq,11:33 pm
07-09-2001,Mo Cnj Pi,12:05 pm
07-12-2001,Mo Cnj Ar,00:35 am
07-14-2001,Mo Cnj Ta,11:13 am
07-16-2001,Mo Cnj Ge,06:26 pm
07-18-2001,Mo Cnj Ca,09:56 pm
07-20-2001,Mo Cnj Le,10:43 pm
07-22-2001,Mo Cnj Vi,10:29 pm
07-24-2001,Mo Cnj Li,11:08 pm
07-27-2001,Mo Cnj Sc,02:17 am
07-29-2001,Mo Cnj Sa,08:45 am
07-31-2001,Mo Cnj Ca,06:16 pm

August 2001
08-03-2001,Mo Cnj Aq,05:53 am
08-05-2001,Mo Cnj Pi,06:30 pm
08-08-2001,Mo Cnj Ar,07:05 am
08-10-2001,Mo Cnj Ta,06:23 pm
08-13-2001,Mo Cnj Ge,02:59 am
08-15-2001,Mo Cnj Ca,07:55 am
08-17-2001,Mo Cnj Le,09:26 am
08-19-2001,Mo Cnj Vi,08:53 am

08-21-2001,Mo Cnj Li,08:19 am
08-23-2001,Mo Cnj Sc,09:50 am
08-25-2001,Mo Cnj Sa,02:59 pm
08-28-2001,Mo Cnj Ca,00:02 am
08-30-2001,Mo Cnj Aq,11:47 am

September 2001
09-02-2001,Mo Cnj Pi,00:32 am
09-04-2001,Mo Cnj Ar,12:58 pm
09-07-2001,Mo Cnj Ta,00:18 am
09-09-2001,Mo Cnj Ge,09:41 am
09-11-2001,Mo Cnj Ca,04:10 pm
09-13-2001,Mo Cnj Le,07:16 pm
09-15-2001,Mo Cnj Vi,07:39 pm
09-17-2001,Mo Cnj Li,07:00 pm
09-19-2001,Mo Cnj Sc,07:27 pm
09-21-2001,Mo Cnj Sa,11:02 pm
09-24-2001,Mo Cnj Ca,06:49 am
09-26-2001,Mo Cnj Aq,06:05 pm
09-29-2001,Mo Cnj Pi,06:51 am

October 2001
10-01-2001,Mo Cnj Ar,07:08 pm
10-04-2001,Mo Cnj Ta,06:01 am
10-06-2001,Mo Cnj Ge,03:12 pm
10-08-2001,Mo Cnj Ca,10:19 pm
10-11-2001,Mo Cnj Le,02:54 am
10-13-2001,Mo Cnj Vi,04:58 am
10-15-2001,Mo Cnj Li,05:26 am
10-17-2001,Mo Cnj Sc,06:03 am
10-19-2001,Mo Cnj Sa,08:47 am
10-21-2001,Mo Cnj Ca,03:12 pm
10-24-2001,Mo Cnj Aq,01:27 am
10-26-2001,Mo Cnj Pi,01:56 pm
10-29-2001,Mo Cnj Ar,02:15 am
10-31-2001,Mo Cnj Ta,12:48 pm

November 2001
11-02-2001,Mo Cnj Ge,09:12 pm
11-05-2001,Mo Cnj Ca,03:44 am
11-07-2001,Mo Cnj Le,08:34 am
11-09-2001,Mo Cnj Vi,11:49 am
11-11-2001,Mo Cnj Li,01:53 pm
11-13-2001,Mo Cnj Sc,03:45 pm
11-15-2001,Mo Cnj Sa,06:52 pm
11-18-2001,Mo Cnj Ca,00:40 am
11-20-2001,Mo Cnj Aq,09:55 am
11-22-2001,Mo Cnj Pi,09:52 pm

11-25-2001,Mo Cnj Ar,10:21 am
11-27-2001,Mo Cnj Ta,09:06 pm
11-30-2001,Mo Cnj Ge,05:04 am

December 2001

12-02-2001,Mo Cnj Ca,10:30 am
12-04-2001,Mo Cnj Le,02:16 pm
12-06-2001,Mo Cnj Vi,05:12 pm
12-08-2001,Mo Cnj Li,07:57 pm
12-10-2001,Mo Cnj Sc,11:10 pm
12-13-2001,Mo Cnj Sa,03:30 am
12-15-2001,Mo Cnj Ca,09:48 am
12-17-2001,Mo Cnj Aq,06:43 pm
12-20-2001,Mo Cnj Pi,06:09 am
12-22-2001,Mo Cnj Ar,06:45 pm
12-25-2001,Mo Cnj Ta,06:13 am
12-27-2001,Mo Cnj Ge,02:39 pm
12-29-2001,Mo Cnj Ca,07:41 pm
12-31-2001,Mo Cnj Le,10:10 pm

January 2002

01-02-2002,Mo Cnj Vi,11:35 pm
01-05-2002,Mo Cnj Li,01:24 am
01-07-2002,Mo Cnj Sc,04:41 am
01-09-2002,Mo Cnj Sa,09:57 am
01-11-2002,Mo Cnj Ca,05:18 pm
01-14-2002,Mo Cnj Aq,02:41 am
01-16-2002,Mo Cnj Pi,02:00 pm
01-19-2002,Mo Cnj Ar,02:35 am
01-21-2002,Mo Cnj Ta,02:48 pm
01-24-2002,Mo Cnj Ge,00:28 am
01-26-2002,Mo Cnj Ca,06:18 am
01-28-2002,Mo Cnj Le,08:31 am
01-30-2002,Mo Cnj Vi,08:40 am

February 2002

02-01-2002,Mo Cnj Li,08:44 am
02-03-2002,Mo Cnj Sc,10:35 am
02-05-2002,Mo Cnj Sa,03:21 pm
02-07-2002,Mo Cnj Ca,11:09 pm
02-10-2002,Mo Cnj Aq,09:15 am
02-12-2002,Mo Cnj Pi,08:54 pm
02-15-2002,Mo Cnj Ar,09:26 am
02-17-2002,Mo Cnj Ta,09:58 pm
02-20-2002,Mo Cnj Ge,08:50 am
02-22-2002,Mo Cnj Ca,04:16 pm
02-24-2002,Mo Cnj Le,07:36 pm

02-26-2002,Mo Cnj Vi,07:47 pm
02-28-2002,Mo Cnj Li,06:47 pm

March 2002

03-02-2002,Mo Cnj Sc,06:52 pm
03-04-2002,Mo Cnj Sa,09:55 pm
03-07-2002,Mo Cnj Ca,04:49 am
03-09-2002,Mo Cnj Aq,02:57 pm
03-12-2002,Mo Cnj Pi,02:57 am
03-14-2002,Mo Cnj Ar,03:34 pm
03-17-2002,Mo Cnj Ta,04:01 am
03-19-2002,Mo Cnj Ge,03:19 pm
03-22-2002,Mo Cnj Ca,00:06 am
03-24-2002,Mo Cnj Le,05:13 am
03-26-2002,Mo Cnj Vi,06:44 am
03-28-2002,Mo Cnj Li,06:04 am
03-30-2002,Mo Cnj Sc,05:22 am

April 2002

04-01-2002,Mo Cnj Sa,06:49 am
04-03-2002,Mo Cnj Ca,11:59 am
04-05-2002,Mo Cnj Aq,09:07 pm
04-08-2002,Mo Cnj Pi,08:58 am
04-10-2002,Mo Cnj Ar,09:40 pm
04-13-2002,Mo Cnj Ta,09:55 am
04-15-2002,Mo Cnj Ge,08:56 pm
04-18-2002,Mo Cnj Ca,06:01 am
04-20-2002,Mo Cnj Le,12:21 pm
04-22-2002,Mo Cnj Vi,03:35 pm
04-24-2002,Mo Cnj Li,04:23 pm
04-26-2002,Mo Cnj Sc,04:16 pm
04-28-2002,Mo Cnj Sa,05:13 pm
04-30-2002,Mo Cnj Ca,09:03 pm

May 2002

05-03-2002,Mo Cnj Aq,04:43 am
05-05-2002,Mo Cnj Pi,03:46 pm
05-08-2002,Mo Cnj Ar,04:22 am
05-10-2002,Mo Cnj Ta,04:32 pm
05-13-2002,Mo Cnj Ge,03:05 am
05-15-2002,Mo Cnj Ca,11:34 am
05-17-2002,Mo Cnj Le,05:53 pm
05-19-2002,Mo Cnj Vi,10:01 pm
05-22-2002,Mo Cnj Li,00:19 am
05-24-2002,Mo Cnj Sc,01:38 am
05-26-2002,Mo Cnj Sa,03:20 am
05-28-2002,Mo Cnj Ca,06:54 am
05-30-2002,Mo Cnj Aq,01:35 pm

June 2002

06-01-2002,Mo Cnj Pi,11:37 pm
06-04-2002,Mo Cnj Ar,11:52 am
06-07-2002,Mo Cnj Ta,00:07 am
06-09-2002,Mo Cnj Ge,10:30 am
06-11-2002,Mo Cnj Ca,06:16 pm
06-13-2002,Mo Cnj Le,11:40 pm
06-16-2002,Mo Cnj Vi,03:24 am
06-18-2002,Mo Cnj Li,06:11 am
06-20-2002,Mo Cnj Sc,08:42 am
06-22-2002,Mo Cnj Sa,11:42 am
06-24-2002,Mo Cnj Ca,04:01 pm
06-26-2002,Mo Cnj Aq,10:36 pm
06-29-2002,Mo Cnj Pi,08:01 am

July 2002

07-01-2002,Mo Cnj Ar,07:50 pm
07-04-2002,Mo Cnj Ta,08:17 am
07-06-2002,Mo Cnj Ge,07:01 pm
07-09-2002,Mo Cnj Ca,02:37 am
07-11-2002,Mo Cnj Le,07:08 am
07-13-2002,Mo Cnj Vi,09:40 am
07-15-2002,Mo Cnj Li,11:39 am
07-17-2002,Mo Cnj Sc,02:13 pm
07-19-2002,Mo Cnj Sa,06:02 pm
07-21-2002,Mo Cnj Ca,11:26 pm
07-24-2002,Mo Cnj Aq,06:40 am
07-26-2002,Mo Cnj Pi,04:05 pm
07-29-2002,Mo Cnj Ar,03:39 am
07-31-2002,Mo Cnj Ta,04:17 pm

August 2002

08-03-2002,Mo Cnj Ge,03:46 am
08-05-2002,Mo Cnj Ca,12:01 pm
08-07-2002,Mo Cnj Le,04:27 pm
08-09-2002,Mo Cnj Vi,06:03 pm
08-11-2002,Mo Cnj Li,06:38 pm
08-13-2002,Mo Cnj Sc,08:01 pm
08-15-2002,Mo Cnj Sa,11:26 pm
08-18-2002,Mo Cnj Ca,05:16 am
08-20-2002,Mo Cnj Aq,01:17 pm
08-22-2002,Mo Cnj Pi,11:11 pm
08-25-2002,Mo Cnj Ar,10:47 am
08-27-2002,Mo Cnj Ta,11:31 pm
08-30-2002,Mo Cnj Ge,11:45 am

September 2002

09-01-2002,Mo Cnj Ca,09:14 pm
09-04-2002,Mo Cnj Le,02:37 am
09-06-2002,Mo Cnj Vi,04:17 am
09-08-2002,Mo Cnj Li,03:57 am
09-10-2002,Mo Cnj Sc,03:49 am
09-12-2002,Mo Cnj Sa,05:44 am
09-14-2002,Mo Cnj Ca,10:48 am
09-16-2002,Mo Cnj Aq,06:54 pm
09-19-2002,Mo Cnj Pi,05:18 am
09-21-2002,Mo Cnj Ar,05:11 pm
09-24-2002,Mo Cnj Ta,05:54 am
09-26-2002,Mo Cnj Ge,06:27 pm
09-29-2002,Mo Cnj Ca,05:02 am

October 2002

10-01-2002,Mo Cnj Le,11:59 am
10-03-2002,Mo Cnj Vi,02:52 pm
10-05-2002,Mo Cnj Li,02:52 pm
10-07-2002,Mo Cnj Sc,01:57 pm
10-09-2002,Mo Cnj Sa,02:20 pm
10-11-2002,Mo Cnj Ca,05:45 pm
10-14-2002,Mo Cnj Aq,00:51 am
10-16-2002,Mo Cnj Pi,11:07 am
10-18-2002,Mo Cnj Ar,11:14 pm
10-21-2002,Mo Cnj Ta,11:57 am
10-24-2002,Mo Cnj Ge,00:18 am
10-26-2002,Mo Cnj Ca,11:11 am
10-28-2002,Mo Cnj Le,07:20 pm
10-30-2002,Mo Cnj Vi,11:59 pm

November 2002

11-02-2002,Mo Cnj Li,01:28 am
11-04-2002,Mo Cnj Sc,01:10 am
11-06-2002,Mo Cnj Sa,01:01 am
11-08-2002,Mo Cnj Ca,02:59 am
11-10-2002,Mo Cnj Aq,08:27 am
11-12-2002,Mo Cnj Pi,05:42 pm
11-15-2002,Mo Cnj Ar,05:38 am
11-17-2002,Mo Cnj Ta,06:24 pm
11-20-2002,Mo Cnj Ge,06:25 am
11-22-2002,Mo Cnj Ca,04:48 pm
11-25-2002,Mo Cnj Le,01:00 am
11-27-2002,Mo Cnj Vi,06:41 am
11-29-2002,Mo Cnj Li,09:54 am

December 2002
12-01-2002,Mo Cnj Sc,11:15 am
12-03-2002,Mo Cnj Sa,11:58 am
12-05-2002,Mo Cnj Ca,01:39 pm
12-07-2002,Mo Cnj Aq,05:55 pm
12-10-2002,Mo Cnj Pi,01:46 am
12-12-2002,Mo Cnj Ar,12:58 pm
12-15-2002,Mo Cnj Ta,01:43 am
12-17-2002,Mo Cnj Ge,01:43 pm
12-19-2002,Mo Cnj Ca,11:30 pm
12-22-2002,Mo Cnj Le,06:48 am
12-24-2002,Mo Cnj Vi,12:05 pm
12-26-2002,Mo Cnj Li,03:54 pm
12-28-2002,Mo Cnj Sc,06:42 pm
12-30-2002,Mo Cnj Sa,09:02 pm

January 2003
01-01-2003,Mo Cnj Ca,11:43 pm
01-04-2003,Mo Cnj Aq,03:57 am
01-06-2003,Mo Cnj Pi,10:57 am
01-08-2003,Mo Cnj Ar,09:15 pm
01-11-2003,Mo Cnj Ta,09:47 am
01-13-2003,Mo Cnj Ge,10:07 pm
01-16-2003,Mo Cnj Ca,07:56 am
01-18-2003,Mo Cnj Le,02:29 pm
01-20-2003,Mo Cnj Vi,06:32 pm
01-22-2003,Mo Cnj Li,09:23 pm
01-25-2003,Mo Cnj Sc,00:09 am
01-27-2003,Mo Cnj Sa,03:26 am
01-29-2003,Mo Cnj Ca,07:30 am
01-31-2003,Mo Cnj Aq,12:44 pm

February 2003
02-02-2003,Mo Cnj Pi,07:54 pm
02-05-2003,Mo Cnj Ar,05:44 am
02-07-2003,Mo Cnj Ta,05:59 pm
02-10-2003,Mo Cnj Ge,06:46 am
02-12-2003,Mo Cnj Ca,05:20 pm
02-15-2003,Mo Cnj Le,00:05 am
02-17-2003,Mo Cnj Vi,03:23 am
02-19-2003,Mo Cnj Li,04:48 am
02-21-2003,Mo Cnj Sc,06:09 am
02-23-2003,Mo Cnj Sa,08:46 am
02-25-2003,Mo Cnj Ca,01:11 pm
02-27-2003,Mo Cnj Aq,07:24 pm

March 2003
03-02-2003,Mo Cnj Pi,03:26 am
03-04-2003,Mo Cnj Ar,01:30 pm
03-07-2003,Mo Cnj Ta,01:37 am
03-09-2003,Mo Cnj Ge,02:38 pm
03-12-2003,Mo Cnj Ca,02:12 am
03-14-2003,Mo Cnj Le,10:07 am
03-16-2003,Mo Cnj Vi,01:53 pm
03-18-2003,Mo Cnj Li,02:43 pm
03-20-2003,Mo Cnj Sc,02:38 pm
03-22-2003,Mo Cnj Sa,03:33 pm
03-24-2003,Mo Cnj Ca,06:48 pm
03-27-2003,Mo Cnj Aq,00:51 am
03-29-2003,Mo Cnj Pi,09:26 am
03-31-2003,Mo Cnj Ar,08:05 pm

April 2003
04-03-2003,Mo Cnj Ta,08:21 am
04-05-2003,Mo Cnj Ge,09:24 pm
04-08-2003,Mo Cnj Ca,09:36 am
04-10-2003,Mo Cnj Le,06:54 pm
04-13-2003,Mo Cnj Vi,00:07 am
04-15-2003,Mo Cnj Li,01:42 am
04-17-2003,Mo Cnj Sc,01:16 am
04-19-2003,Mo Cnj Sa,00:52 am
04-21-2003,Mo Cnj Ca,02:21 am
04-23-2003,Mo Cnj Aq,06:59 am
04-25-2003,Mo Cnj Pi,03:03 pm
04-28-2003,Mo Cnj Ar,01:55 am
04-30-2003,Mo Cnj Ta,02:26 pm

May 2003
05-03-2003,Mo Cnj Ge,03:27 am
05-05-2003,Mo Cnj Ca,03:42 pm
05-08-2003,Mo Cnj Le,01:46 am
05-10-2003,Mo Cnj Vi,08:31 am
05-12-2003,Mo Cnj Li,11:43 am
05-14-2003,Mo Cnj Sc,12:14 pm
05-16-2003,Mo Cnj Sa,11:43 am
05-18-2003,Mo Cnj Ca,12:04 pm
05-20-2003,Mo Cnj Aq,03:01 pm
05-22-2003,Mo Cnj Pi,09:41 pm
05-25-2003,Mo Cnj Ar,07:59 am
05-27-2003,Mo Cnj Ta,08:32 pm
05-30-2003,Mo Cnj Ge,09:31 am

June 2003
06-01-2003,Mo Cnj Ca,09:28 pm
06-04-2003,Mo Cnj Le,07:25 am
06-06-2003,Mo Cnj Vi,02:51 pm

06-08-2003,Mo Cnj Li,07:31 pm
06-10-2003,Mo Cnj Sc,09:39 pm
06-12-2003,Mo Cnj Sa,10:13 pm
06-14-2003,Mo Cnj Ca,10:38 pm
06-17-2003,Mo Cnj Aq,00:41 am
06-19-2003,Mo Cnj Pi,05:56 am
06-21-2003,Mo Cnj Ar,03:05 pm
06-24-2003,Mo Cnj Ta,03:15 am
06-26-2003,Mo Cnj Ge,04:13 pm
06-29-2003,Mo Cnj Ca,03:53 am

July 2003
07-01-2003,Mo Cnj Le,01:14 pm
07-03-2003,Mo Cnj Vi,08:17 pm
07-06-2003,Mo Cnj Li,01:21 am
07-08-2003,Mo Cnj Sc,04:44 am
07-10-2003,Mo Cnj Sa,06:48 am
07-12-2003,Mo Cnj Ca,08:21 am
07-14-2003,Mo Cnj Aq,10:38 am
07-16-2003,Mo Cnj Pi,03:13 pm
07-18-2003,Mo Cnj Ar,11:20 pm
07-21-2003,Mo Cnj Ta,10:48 am
07-23-2003,Mo Cnj Ge,11:43 pm
07-26-2003,Mo Cnj Ca,11:24 am
07-28-2003,Mo Cnj Le,08:17 pm
07-31-2003,Mo Cnj Vi,02:27 am

August 2003
08-02-2003,Mo Cnj Li,06:48 am
08-04-2003,Mo Cnj Sc,10:12 am
08-06-2003,Mo Cnj Sa,01:11 pm
08-08-2003,Mo Cnj Ca,04:02 pm
08-10-2003,Mo Cnj Aq,07:24 pm
08-13-2003,Mo Cnj Pi,00:19 am
08-15-2003,Mo Cnj Ar,08:01 am
08-17-2003,Mo Cnj Ta,06:53 pm
08-20-2003,Mo Cnj Ge,07:41 am
08-22-2003,Mo Cnj Ca,07:44 pm
08-25-2003,Mo Cnj Le,04:48 am
08-27-2003,Mo Cnj Vi,10:26 am
08-29-2003,Mo Cnj Li,01:41 pm
08-31-2003,Mo Cnj Sc,04:00 pm

September 2003
09-02-2003,Mo Cnj Sa,06:32 pm
09-04-2003,Mo Cnj Ca,09:52 pm
09-07-2003,Mo Cnj Aq,02:15 am

09-09-2003,Mo Cnj Pi,08:08 am
09-11-2003,Mo Cnj Ar,04:10 pm
09-14-2003,Mo Cnj Ta,02:50 am
09-16-2003,Mo Cnj Ge,03:32 pm
09-19-2003,Mo Cnj Ca,04:07 am
09-21-2003,Mo Cnj Le,02:02 pm
09-23-2003,Mo Cnj Vi,08:05 pm
09-25-2003,Mo Cnj Li,10:49 pm
09-27-2003,Mo Cnj Sc,11:52 pm
09-30-2003,Mo Cnj Sa,00:58 am

October 2003
10-02-2003,Mo Cnj Ca,03:22 am
10-04-2003,Mo Cnj Aq,07:46 am
10-06-2003,Mo Cnj Pi,02:21 pm
10-08-2003,Mo Cnj Ar,11:07 pm
10-11-2003,Mo Cnj Ta,10:05 am
10-13-2003,Mo Cnj Ge,10:44 pm
10-16-2003,Mo Cnj Ca,11:41 am
10-18-2003,Mo Cnj Le,10:42 pm
10-21-2003,Mo Cnj Vi,06:02 am
10-23-2003,Mo Cnj Li,09:28 am
10-25-2003,Mo Cnj Sc,10:09 am
10-27-2003,Mo Cnj Sa,09:55 am
10-29-2003,Mo Cnj Ca,10:37 am
10-31-2003,Mo Cnj Aq,01:41 pm

November 2003
11-02-2003,Mo Cnj Pi,07:52 pm
11-05-2003,Mo Cnj Ar,05:02 am
11-07-2003,Mo Cnj Ta,04:29 pm
11-10-2003,Mo Cnj Ge,05:15 am
11-12-2003,Mo Cnj Ca,06:11 pm
11-15-2003,Mo Cnj Le,05:49 am
11-17-2003,Mo Cnj Vi,02:37 pm
11-19-2003,Mo Cnj Li,07:42 pm
11-21-2003,Mo Cnj Sc,09:24 pm
11-23-2003,Mo Cnj Sa,09:03 pm
11-25-2003,Mo Cnj Ca,08:31 pm
11-27-2003,Mo Cnj Aq,09:48 pm
11-30-2003,Mo Cnj Pi,02:25 am

December 2003
12-02-2003,Mo Cnj Ar,10:56 am
12-04-2003,Mo Cnj Ta,10:30 pm
12-07-2003,Mo Cnj Ge,11:27 am
12-10-2003,Mo Cnj Ca,00:12 am

12-12-2003,Mo Cnj Le,11:41 am
12-14-2003,Mo Cnj Vi,09:07 pm
12-17-2003,Mo Cnj Li,03:47 am
12-19-2003,Mo Cnj Sc,07:20 am
12-21-2003,Mo Cnj Sa,08:16 am
12-23-2003,Mo Cnj Ca,07:55 am
12-25-2003,Mo Cnj Aq,08:13 am
12-27-2003,Mo Cnj Pi,11:10 am
12-29-2003,Mo Cnj Ar,06:09 pm

January 2004
01-01-2004,Mo Cnj Ta,05:02 am
01-03-2004,Mo Cnj Ge,05:59 pm
01-06-2004,Mo Cnj Ca,06:39 am
01-08-2004,Mo Cnj Le,05:38 pm
01-11-2004,Mo Cnj Vi,02:37 am
01-13-2004,Mo Cnj Li,09:38 am
01-15-2004,Mo Cnj Sc,02:33 pm
01-17-2004,Mo Cnj Sa,05:18 pm
01-19-2004,Mo Cnj Ca,06:25 pm
01-21-2004,Mo Cnj Aq,07:11 pm
01-23-2004,Mo Cnj Pi,09:29 pm
01-26-2004,Mo Cnj Ar,03:06 am
01-28-2004,Mo Cnj Ta,12:46 pm
01-31-2004,Mo Cnj Ge,01:18 am

February 2004
02-02-2004,Mo Cnj Ca,02:03 pm
02-05-2004,Mo Cnj Le,00:50 am
02-07-2004,Mo Cnj Vi,09:03 am
02-09-2004,Mo Cnj Li,03:13 pm
02-11-2004,Mo Cnj Sc,07:58 pm
02-13-2004,Mo Cnj Sa,11:36 pm
02-16-2004,Mo Cnj Ca,02:15 am
02-18-2004,Mo Cnj Aq,04:28 am
02-20-2004,Mo Cnj Pi,07:27 am
02-22-2004,Mo Cnj Ar,12:45 pm
02-24-2004,Mo Cnj Ta,09:30 pm
02-27-2004,Mo Cnj Ge,09:22 am
02-29-2004,Mo Cnj Ca,10:12 pm

March 2004
03-03-2004,Mo Cnj Le,09:18 am
03-05-2004,Mo Cnj Vi,05:18 pm
03-07-2004,Mo Cnj Li,10:31 pm
03-10-2004,Mo Cnj Sc,02:03 am
03-12-2004,Mo Cnj Sa,04:58 am

03-14-2004,Mo Cnj Ca,07:52 am
03-16-2004,Mo Cnj Aq,11:10 am
03-18-2004,Mo Cnj Pi,03:26 pm
03-20-2004,Mo Cnj Ar,09:29 pm
03-23-2004,Mo Cnj Ta,06:09 am
03-25-2004,Mo Cnj Ge,05:35 pm
03-28-2004,Mo Cnj Ca,06:24 am
03-30-2004,Mo Cnj Le,06:08 pm

April 2004
04-02-2004,Mo Cnj Vi,02:46 am
04-04-2004,Mo Cnj Li,07:53 am
04-06-2004,Mo Cnj Sc,10:24 am
04-08-2004,Mo Cnj Sa,11:50 am
04-10-2004,Mo Cnj Ca,01:33 pm
04-12-2004,Mo Cnj Aq,04:33 pm
04-14-2004,Mo Cnj Pi,09:24 pm
04-17-2004,Mo Cnj Ar,04:25 am
04-19-2004,Mo Cnj Ta,01:43 pm
04-22-2004,Mo Cnj Ge,01:11 am
04-24-2004,Mo Cnj Ca,01:57 pm
04-27-2004,Mo Cnj Le,02:15 am
04-29-2004,Mo Cnj Vi,12:00 pm

May 2004
05-01-2004,Mo Cnj Li,06:03 pm
05-03-2004,Mo Cnj Sc,08:39 pm
05-05-2004,Mo Cnj Sa,09:08 pm
05-07-2004,Mo Cnj Ca,09:17 pm
05-09-2004,Mo Cnj Aq,10:47 pm
05-12-2004,Mo Cnj Pi,02:53 am
05-14-2004,Mo Cnj Ar,10:03 am
05-16-2004,Mo Cnj Ta,07:58 pm
05-19-2004,Mo Cnj Ge,07:48 am
05-21-2004,Mo Cnj Ca,08:35 pm
05-24-2004,Mo Cnj Le,09:07 am
05-26-2004,Mo Cnj Vi,07:52 pm
05-29-2004,Mo Cnj Li,03:22 am
05-31-2004,Mo Cnj Sc,07:08 am

June 2004
06-02-2004,Mo Cnj Sa,07:52 am
06-04-2004,Mo Cnj Ca,07:13 am
06-06-2004,Mo Cnj Aq,07:10 am
06-08-2004,Mo Cnj Pi,09:39 am
06-10-2004,Mo Cnj Ar,03:50 pm
06-13-2004,Mo Cnj Ta,01:37 am

06-15-2004,Mo Cnj Ge,01:44 pm
06-18-2004,Mo Cnj Ca,02:37 am
06-20-2004,Mo Cnj Le,03:05 pm
06-23-2004,Mo Cnj Vi,02:10 am
06-25-2004,Mo Cnj Li,10:50 am
06-27-2004,Mo Cnj Sc,04:13 pm
06-29-2004,Mo Cnj Sa,06:16 pm

July 2004
07-01-2004,Mo Cnj Ca,06:02 pm
07-03-2004,Mo Cnj Aq,05:22 pm
07-05-2004,Mo Cnj Pi,06:27 pm
07-07-2004,Mo Cnj Ar,11:03 pm
07-10-2004,Mo Cnj Ta,07:50 am
07-12-2004,Mo Cnj Ge,07:44 pm
07-15-2004,Mo Cnj Ca,08:40 am
07-17-2004,Mo Cnj Le,08:56 pm
07-20-2004,Mo Cnj Vi,07:45 am
07-22-2004,Mo Cnj Li,04:39 pm
07-24-2004,Mo Cnj Sc,11:09 pm
07-27-2004,Mo Cnj Sa,02:48 am
07-29-2004,Mo Cnj Ca,03:58 am
07-31-2004,Mo Cnj Aq,03:54 am

August 2004
08-02-2004,Mo Cnj Pi,04:34 am
08-04-2004,Mo Cnj Ar,07:59 am
08-06-2004,Mo Cnj Ta,03:26 pm
08-09-2004,Mo Cnj Ge,02:33 am
08-11-2004,Mo Cnj Ca,03:21 pm
08-14-2004,Mo Cnj Le,03:30 am
08-16-2004,Mo Cnj Vi,01:50 pm
08-18-2004,Mo Cnj Li,10:10 pm
08-21-2004,Mo Cnj Sc,04:37 am
08-23-2004,Mo Cnj Sa,09:08 am
08-25-2004,Mo Cnj Ca,11:46 am
08-27-2004,Mo Cnj Aq,01:08 pm
08-29-2004,Mo Cnj Pi,02:33 pm
08-31-2004,Mo Cnj Ar,05:46 pm

September 2004
09-03-2004,Mo Cnj Ta,00:16 am
09-05-2004,Mo Cnj Ge,10:25 am
09-07-2004,Mo Cnj Ca,10:51 am
09-10-2004,Mo Cnj Le,11:06 am
09-12-2004,Mo Cnj Vi,09:17 pm
09-15-2004,Mo Cnj Li,04:54 am

09-17-2004,Mo Cnj Sc,10:25 am
09-19-2004,Mo Cnj Sa,02:30 pm
09-21-2004,Mo Cnj Ca,05:35 pm
09-23-2004,Mo Cnj Aq,08:10 pm
09-25-2004,Mo Cnj Pi,10:56 pm
09-28-2004,Mo Cnj Ar,02:58 am
09-30-2004,Mo Cnj Ta,09:25 am

October 2004
10-02-2004,Mo Cnj Ge,06:56 pm
10-05-2004,Mo Cnj Ca,06:54 am
10-07-2004,Mo Cnj Le,07:23 pm
10-10-2004,Mo Cnj Vi,06:00 am
10-12-2004,Mo Cnj Li,01:32 pm
10-14-2004,Mo Cnj Sc,06:10 pm
10-16-2004,Mo Cnj Sa,08:58 pm
10-18-2004,Mo Cnj Ca,11:07 pm
10-21-2004,Mo Cnj Aq,01:38 am
10-23-2004,Mo Cnj Pi,05:14 am
10-25-2004,Mo Cnj Ar,10:25 am
10-27-2004,Mo Cnj Ta,05:38 pm
10-30-2004,Mo Cnj Ge,03:11 am

November 2004
11-01-2004,Mo Cnj Ca,02:53 pm
11-04-2004,Mo Cnj Le,03:32 am
11-06-2004,Mo Cnj Vi,03:00 pm
11-08-2004,Mo Cnj Li,11:23 pm
11-11-2004,Mo Cnj Sc,04:06 am
11-13-2004,Mo Cnj Sa,05:57 am
11-15-2004,Mo Cnj Ca,06:34 am
11-17-2004,Mo Cnj Aq,07:39 am
11-19-2004,Mo Cnj Pi,10:38 am
11-21-2004,Mo Cnj Ar,04:11 pm
11-24-2004,Mo Cnj Ta,00:16 am
11-26-2004,Mo Cnj Ge,10:25 am
11-28-2004,Mo Cnj Ca,10:10 pm

December 2004
12-01-2004,Mo Cnj Le,10:50 am
12-03-2004,Mo Cnj Vi,11:01 pm
12-06-2004,Mo Cnj Li,08:47 am
12-08-2004,Mo Cnj Sc,02:44 pm
12-10-2004,Mo Cnj Sa,04:55 pm
12-12-2004,Mo Cnj Ca,04:42 pm
12-14-2004,Mo Cnj Aq,04:10 pm
12-16-2004,Mo Cnj Pi,05:24 pm

12-18-2004,Mo Cnj Ar,09:52 pm
12-21-2004,Mo Cnj Ta,05:52 am
12-23-2004,Mo Cnj Ge,04:32 pm
12-26-2004,Mo Cnj Ca,04:38 am
12-28-2004,Mo Cnj Le,05:15 pm
12-31-2004,Mo Cnj Vi,05:34 am

January 2005
01-02-2005,Mo Cnj Li,04:20 pm
01-05-2005,Mo Cnj Sc,00:00 am
01-07-2005,Mo Cnj Sa,03:45 am
01-09-2005,Mo Cnj Ca,04:11 am
01-11-2005,Mo Cnj Aq,03:07 am
01-13-2005,Mo Cnj Pi,02:51 am
01-15-2005,Mo Cnj Ar,05:27 am
01-17-2005,Mo Cnj Ta,12:07 pm
01-19-2005,Mo Cnj Ge,10:25 pm
01-22-2005,Mo Cnj Ca,10:43 am
01-24-2005,Mo Cnj Le,11:22 pm
01-27-2005,Mo Cnj Vi,11:25 am
01-29-2005,Mo Cnj Li,10:13 pm

February 2005
02-01-2005,Mo Cnj Sc,06:51 am
02-03-2005,Mo Cnj Sa,12:22 pm
02-05-2005,Mo Cnj Ca,02:32 pm
02-07-2005,Mo Cnj Aq,02:27 pm
02-09-2005,Mo Cnj Pi,02:00 pm
02-11-2005,Mo Cnj Ar,03:22 pm
02-13-2005,Mo Cnj Ta,08:19 pm
02-16-2005,Mo Cnj Ge,05:19 am
02-18-2005,Mo Cnj Ca,05:13 pm
02-21-2005,Mo Cnj Le,05:55 pm
02-23-2005,Mo Cnj Vi,05:44 pm
02-26-2005,Mo Cnj Li,03:59 am
02-28-2005,Mo Cnj Sc,12:21 pm

March 2005
03-02-2005,Mo Cnj Sa,06:30 pm
03-04-2005,Mo Cnj Ca,10:12 pm
03-06-2005,Mo Cnj Aq,11:50 pm
03-09-2005,Mo Cnj Pi,00:34 am
03-11-2005,Mo Cnj Ar,02:04 am
03-13-2005,Mo Cnj Ta,06:06 am
03-15-2005,Mo Cnj Ge,01:45 pm
03-18-2005,Mo Cnj Ca,00:44 am
03-20-2005,Mo Cnj Le,01:17 pm
03-23-2005,Mo Cnj Vi,01:10 am

03-25-2005,Mo Cnj Li,11:00 am
03-27-2005,Mo Cnj Sc,06:30 pm
03-29-2005,Mo Cnj Sa,11:57 pm

April 2005
04-01-2005,Mo Cnj Ca,03:49 am
04-03-2005,Mo Cnj Aq,06:32 am
04-05-2005,Mo Cnj Pi,08:46 am
04-07-2005,Mo Cnj Ar,11:29 am
04-09-2005,Mo Cnj Ta,03:50 pm
04-11-2005,Mo Cnj Ge,10:55 pm
04-14-2005,Mo Cnj Ca,09:03 am
04-16-2005,Mo Cnj Le,09:18 pm
04-19-2005,Mo Cnj Vi,09:28 am
04-21-2005,Mo Cnj Li,07:28 pm
04-24-2005,Mo Cnj Sc,02:26 am
04-26-2005,Mo Cnj Sa,06:47 am
04-28-2005,Mo Cnj Ca,09:33 am
04-30-2005,Mo Cnj Aq,11:54 am

May 2005
05-02-2005,Mo Cnj Pi,02:43 pm
05-04-2005,Mo Cnj Ar,06:36 pm
05-07-2005,Mo Cnj Ta,00:01 am
05-09-2005,Mo Cnj Ge,07:29 am
05-11-2005,Mo Cnj Ca,05:21 pm
05-14-2005,Mo Cnj Le,05:18 am
05-16-2005,Mo Cnj Vi,05:48 pm
05-19-2005,Mo Cnj Li,04:31 am
05-21-2005,Mo Cnj Sc,11:49 am
05-23-2005,Mo Cnj Sa,03:39 pm
05-25-2005,Mo Cnj Ca,05:11 pm
05-27-2005,Mo Cnj Aq,06:10 pm
05-29-2005,Mo Cnj Pi,08:09 pm

June 2005
06-01-2005,Mo Cnj Ar,00:08 am
06-03-2005,Mo Cnj Ta,06:20 am
06-05-2005,Mo Cnj Ge,02:36 pm
06-08-2005,Mo Cnj Ca,00:47 am
06-10-2005,Mo Cnj Le,12:40 pm
06-13-2005,Mo Cnj Vi,01:23 am
06-15-2005,Mo Cnj Li,12:59 pm
06-17-2005,Mo Cnj Sc,09:24 pm
06-20-2005,Mo Cnj Sa,01:45 am
06-22-2005,Mo Cnj Ca,02:52 am
06-24-2005,Mo Cnj Aq,02:37 am
06-26-2005,Mo Cnj Pi,03:04 am

06-28-2005,Mo Cnj Ar,05:52 am
06-30-2005,Mo Cnj Ta,11:46 am

July 2005
07-02-2005,Mo Cnj Ge,08:27 pm
07-05-2005,Mo Cnj Ca,07:08 am
07-07-2005,Mo Cnj Le,07:11 pm
07-10-2005,Mo Cnj Vi,07:57 am
07-12-2005,Mo Cnj Li,08:09 pm
07-15-2005,Mo Cnj Sc,05:51 am
07-17-2005,Mo Cnj Sa,11:35 am
07-19-2005,Mo Cnj Ca,01:27 pm
07-21-2005,Mo Cnj Aq,12:56 pm
07-23-2005,Mo Cnj Pi,12:13 pm
07-25-2005,Mo Cnj Ar,01:24 pm
07-27-2005,Mo Cnj Ta,05:55 pm
07-30-2005,Mo Cnj Ge,02:03 am

August 2005
08-01-2005,Mo Cnj Ca,12:53 pm
08-04-2005,Mo Cnj Le,01:10 am
08-06-2005,Mo Cnj Vi,01:54 pm
08-09-2005,Mo Cnj Li,02:09 am
08-11-2005,Mo Cnj Sc,12:35 pm
08-13-2005,Mo Cnj Sa,07:48 pm
08-15-2005,Mo Cnj Ca,11:14 pm
08-17-2005,Mo Cnj Aq,11:39 pm
08-19-2005,Mo Cnj Pi,10:53 pm
08-21-2005,Mo Cnj Ar,11:02 pm
08-24-2005,Mo Cnj Ta,01:58 am
08-26-2005,Mo Cnj Ge,08:43 am
08-28-2005,Mo Cnj Ca,06:57 pm
08-31-2005,Mo Cnj Le,07:15 am

September 2005
09-02-2005,Mo Cnj Vi,07:57 pm
09-05-2005,Mo Cnj Li,07:53 am
09-07-2005,Mo Cnj Sc,06:11 pm
09-10-2005,Mo Cnj Sa,02:04 am
09-12-2005,Mo Cnj Ca,06:57 am
09-14-2005,Mo Cnj Aq,09:03 am
09-16-2005,Mo Cnj Pi,09:25 am
09-18-2005,Mo Cnj Ar,09:43 am
09-20-2005,Mo Cnj Ta,11:48 am
09-22-2005,Mo Cnj Ge,05:07 pm
09-25-2005,Mo Cnj Ca,02:11 am
09-27-2005,Mo Cnj Le,02:03 pm
09-30-2005,Mo Cnj Vi,02:45 am

October 2005
10-02-2005,Mo Cnj Li,02:25 pm
10-05-2005,Mo Cnj Sc,00:04 am
10-07-2005,Mo Cnj Sa,07:28 am
10-09-2005,Mo Cnj Ca,12:44 pm
10-11-2005,Mo Cnj Aq,04:05 pm
10-13-2005,Mo Cnj Pi,06:06 pm
10-15-2005,Mo Cnj Ar,07:40 pm
10-17-2005,Mo Cnj Ta,10:05 pm
10-20-2005,Mo Cnj Ge,02:45 am
10-22-2005,Mo Cnj Ca,10:42 am
10-24-2005,Mo Cnj Le,09:49 pm
10-27-2005,Mo Cnj Vi,10:29 am
10-29-2005,Mo Cnj Li,10:15 pm

November 2005
11-01-2005,Mo Cnj Sc,07:29 am
11-03-2005,Mo Cnj Sa,01:55 pm
11-05-2005,Mo Cnj Ca,06:17 pm
11-07-2005,Mo Cnj Aq,09:31 pm
11-10-2005,Mo Cnj Pi,00:23 am
11-12-2005,Mo Cnj Ar,03:23 am
11-14-2005,Mo Cnj Ta,07:04 am
11-16-2005,Mo Cnj Ge,12:11 pm
11-18-2005,Mo Cnj Ca,07:43 pm
11-21-2005,Mo Cnj Le,06:10 am
11-23-2005,Mo Cnj Vi,06:42 pm
11-26-2005,Mo Cnj Li,06:58 am
11-28-2005,Mo Cnj Sc,04:33 pm
11-30-2005,Mo Cnj Sa,10:33 pm

December 2005
12-03-2005,Mo Cnj Ca,01:43 am
12-05-2005,Mo Cnj Aq,03:37 am
12-07-2005,Mo Cnj Pi,05:45 am
12-09-2005,Mo Cnj Ar,09:03 am
12-11-2005,Mo Cnj Ta,01:47 pm
12-13-2005,Mo Cnj Ge,08:00 pm
12-16-2005,Mo Cnj Ca,04:01 am
12-18-2005,Mo Cnj Le,02:18 pm
12-21-2005,Mo Cnj Vi,02:39 am
12-23-2005,Mo Cnj Li,03:27 pm
12-26-2005,Mo Cnj Sc,02:04 am
12-28-2005,Mo Cnj Sa,08:45 am
12-30-2005,Mo Cnj Ca,11:36 am

APPENDIX 2

Sun Signs

Sun Sign	Dates
Aries	March 21–April 19
Taurus	April 20–May 20
Gemini	May 21–June 21
Cancer	June 22–July 22
Leo	July 23–August 22
Virgo	August 23–September 22
Libra	September 23–October 22
Scorpio	October 23–November 21
Sagittarius	November 22–December 21
Capricorn	December 22–January 19
Aquarius	January 20–February 18
Pisces	February 19–March 20

APPENDIX 3

Signs of the North Node, 1945–2006

Locate the span of dates that includes your birth date. The sign of the North Node is at the end of that line. Your South Node would be in the opposite sign. If your North Node is in Libra, then your South Node is in Aries.

May 11, 1944–Dec 2, 1945 Cancer
Dec 3, 1945–August 1, 1947 Gemini
August 2, 1947–January 24, 1949 Taurus
January 25, 1949–July 25, 1950 Aries
July 26, 1950–March 27, 1952 Pisces
March 28, 1952–October 8, 1953 Aquarius
October 9, 1953–April 1, 1955 Capricorn
April 2, 1955–October 3, 1956 Sagittarius
October 4, 1956–June 15, 1958 Scorpio
June 16, 1958–December 14, 1959 Libra
December 15, 1959–June 9, 1961 Virgo
June 10, 1961–December 22, 1962 Leo
December 23, 1962–August 24, 1964 Cancer
August 25, 1964–February 18, 1966
    Gemini
February 19, 1966–August 18, 1967 Taurus
August 19, 1967–April 18, 1969 Aries
April 19, 1969–November 1, 1970 Pisces
November 2, 1970–April 26, 1972 Aquarius
April 27, 1972–October 26, 1973 Capricorn
October 27, 1973–July 9, 1975 Sagittarius
July 10, 1975–January 6, 1977 Scorpio

July 7, 1977–July 4, 1978 Libra
July 5, 1978–January 11, 1980 Virgo
January 12, 1980–September 23, 1981 Leo
September 24, 1981–March 15, 1983
    Cancer
March 16, 1983–September 10, 1984 Gemini
September 11, 1984–April 5, 1986 Taurus
April 6, 1986–December 1, 1987 Aries
December 2, 1987–May 21, 1989 Pisces
May 22, 1989–November 17, 1990
    Aquarius
November 18, 1990–August 1, 1992
    Capricorn
August 2, 1992–January 30, 1994 Sagittarius
February 1, 1994–July 30, 1995 Scorpio
July 31, 1995–January 24, 1997 Libra
January 25, 1997–October 19, 1998 Virgo
October 20, 1998–April 8, 2000 Leo
April 9, 2000–October 11, 2001 Cancer
October 12, 2001–April 12, 2003 Gemini
April 13, 2003–December 24, 2004 Taurus
December 25, 2004–June 20, 2006 Aries

APPENDIX 4
Charts

Chart 1: Jane Roberts

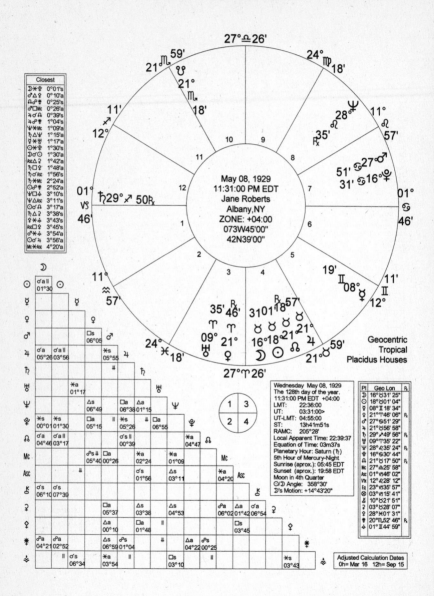

Closest
☽✶♇	0°01's
♂△♀	0°10'a
☊♂♀	0°25's
♂□Mc	0°26's
♃☍☊	0°39's
♃☍♇	1°04's
♆✶Mc	1°09'a
♄△♆	1°15'a
☿✶♅	1°17'a
☉✶☽	1°30's
☽♂☉	1°30'a
Asc△♀	1°42'a
♄□♀	1°48'a
♄♂Asc	1°56's
♄✶Mc	2°24'a
☉♂♆	2°52'a
♆□♃	3°10's
♆✶Asc	3°11's
☉♂☊	3°17'a
♄△♃	3°38's
♀✶♀	3°43's
Asc□♃	3°45's
♂✶♅	3°54'a
☉✶♃	3°56'a
Mc✶Asc	4°20'a

Inner chart data:

May 08, 1929
11:31:00 PM EDT
Jane Roberts
Albany, NY
ZONE: +04:00
073W45'00"
42N39'00"

Geocentric
Tropical
Placidus Houses

Wednesday May 08, 1929
The 128th day of the year.
11:31:00 PM EDT +04:00
LMT: 22:36:00
UT: 03:31:00>
UT-LMT: 04:55:00
ST: 13h41m51s
RAMC: 205°28'
Local Apparent Time: 22:39:37
Equation of Time: 03m37s
Planetary Hour: Saturn (♄)
5th Hour of Mercury-Night
Sunrise (aprox.): 05:45 EDT
Sunset (aprox.): 19:58 EDT
Moon in 4th Quarter
☉/☽ Angle: 358°30'
☽'s Motion: +14°43'20"

Pl	Geo Lon	R
☽	16°♉31' 25"	
☉	18°♉01' 04"	
☿	08°♊18' 34"	
♀	21°♈46' 06"	
♂	27°♐51' 29"	
♃	21°♉56' 58"	
♄	29°♐49' 56"	R
♅	09°♈35' 22"	
♆	28°♌35' 24"	R
♇	16°♋30' 44"	R
☊	21°♉17' 50"	R
Asc	01°♋46' 02"	
Vtx	12°♌28' 12"	
☒	23°♑35' 57"	
⊗	03°♈15' 41"	
⚸	10°♉21' 51"	
♃	03°♉28' 07"	
♀	28°♓01' 31"	
⚷	20°♏52' 46"	R
♆	01°♊44' 59"	

Adjusted Calculation Dates
0h= Mar 16   12h= Sep 15

Aspect grid (left/bottom):

	☉	☿	♀	♂	♃	♄	♅	♆	♇	☊	Mc	Asc	⚷	☊	♀	⚸	⚸
☉	☉																
☿	♂a II 01°30	☿															
♀			♀														
♂			□s 06°05	♂													
♃		♂a 05°26	♂a II 03°56	✶s 05°55	♃												
♄				♃		♄											
♅							♅										
♆		✶a 01°17						♆									
♇	✶s 00°01	✶s 01°30		△s 06°49	□a 05°15	□a 06°38	△a 01°15		♇								
☊	♂a 04°46	♂a 03°17			□a 05°15	✶a 05°26	II □a 06°55			☊							
Mc					♂s II 00°39						Mc						
					♂s♃ 05°40	□a 00°26	✶a 02°24	✶a 01°09			✶a 04°47						
Asc					♃		♂s 01°56	△s 03°11			Mc	✶a 04°20	Asc				
⚷	♂s 06°10	♂s 07°39											⚷				
☊					□a 05°37	△s 03°38	△s 04°53				♂a 06°02	△a 01°42	♂a 06°54	☊			
♀					△a 00°10	□a 01°48	II				□s 03°45				♀		
⚸	♂a 04°21	♂a 02°52			△s 06°59	♂s 01°00	♃				△a 04°22	♂s 00°25				⚸	
⚸				♂s 06°34	✶a 03°54	II		□s 03°10							✶s 03°43		⚸

Chart 2: Richard Demian

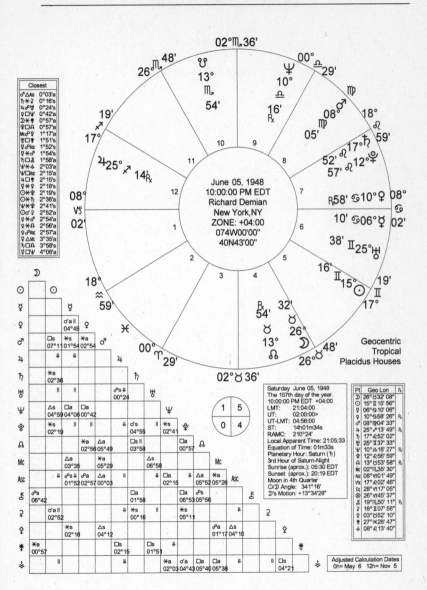

Geocentric
Tropical
Placidus Houses

June 05, 1948
10:00:00 PM EDT
Richard Demian
New York,NY
ZONE: +04:00
074W00'00"
40N43'00"

Saturday June 05, 1948
The 157th day of the year.
10:00:00 PM EDT +04:00
LMT: 21:04:00
UT: 02:00:00>
UT-LMT: 04:56:00
ST: 14h01m33s
RAMC: 210°24'
Local Apparent Time: 21:05:33
Equation of Time: 01m33s
Planetary Hour: Saturn (♄)
3rd Hour of Saturn-Night
Sunrise (aprox.): 05:30 EDT
Sunset (aprox.): 20:19 EDT
Moon in 4th Quarter
☉/☽ Angle: 341°16'
☽'s Motion: +13°34'28"

Adjusted Calculation Dates
0h= May 6 12h= Nov 5

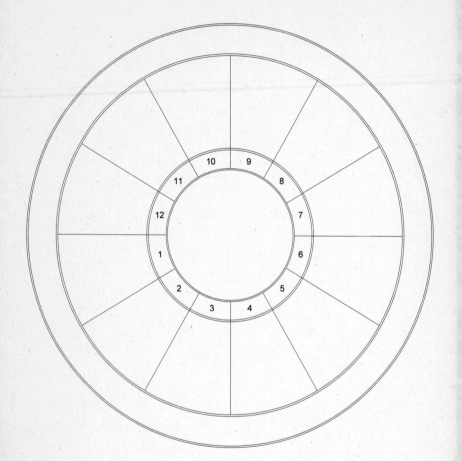

This wheel is intentionally blank!

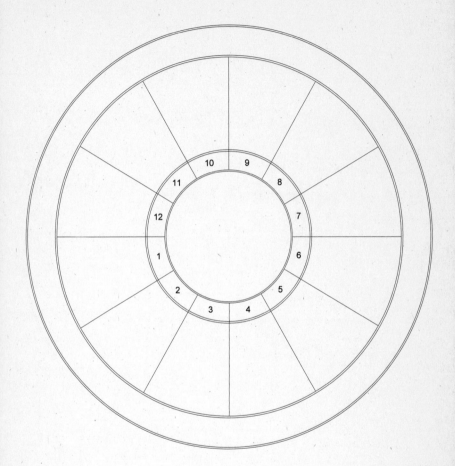

This wheel is intentionally blank!

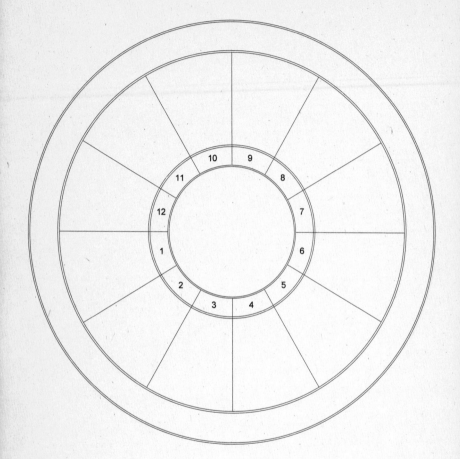

This wheel is intentionally blank!

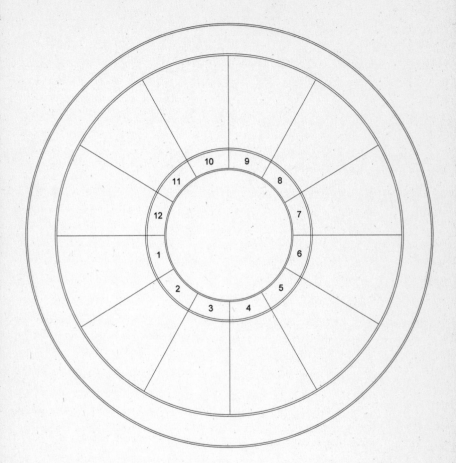

This wheel is intentionally blank!

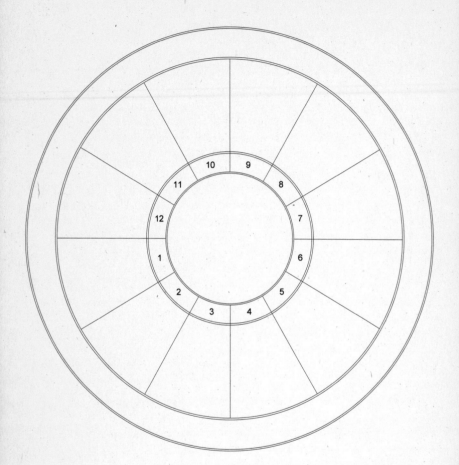

This wheel is intentionally blank!

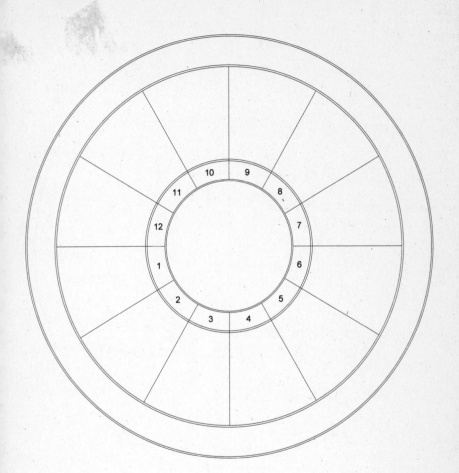

This wheel is intentionally blank!